ISSUES FOR DEBATE IN
AMERICAN PUBLIC POLICY

CQ Press, an imprint of SAGE, is the leading publisher of books, periodicals, and electronic products on American government and international affairs. CQ Press consistently ranks among the top commercial publishers in terms of quality, as evidenced by the numerous awards its products have won over the years. CQ Press owes its existence to Nelson Poynter, former publisher of the *St. Petersburg Times,* and his wife Henrietta, with whom he founded Congressional Quarterly in 1945. Poynter established CQ with the mission of promoting democracy through education and in 1975 founded the Modern Media Institute, renamed The Poynter Institute for Media Studies after his death. The Poynter Institute (*www.poynter.org*) is a nonprofit organization dedicated to training journalists and media leaders.

In 2008, CQ Press was acquired by SAGE, a leading international publisher of journals, books, and electronic media for academic, educational, and professional markets. Since 1965, SAGE has helped inform and educate a global community of scholars, practitioners, researchers, and students spanning a wide range of subject areas, including business, humanities, social sciences, and science, technology, and medicine. A privately owned corporation, SAGE has offices in Los Angeles, London, New Delhi, Singapore, and Melbourne, in addition to the Washington DC office of CQ Press.

ISSUES FOR DEBATE IN AMERICAN PUBLIC POLICY

17TH EDITION

⑤SAGE | CQPRESS

FOR INFORMATION:

CQ Press
An Imprint of SAGE Publications, Inc.
2455 Teller Road
Thousand Oaks, California 91320
E-mail: order@sagepub.com

SAGE Publications Ltd.
1 Oliver's Yard
55 City Road
London EC1Y 1SP
United Kingdom

SAGE Publications India Pvt. Ltd.
B 1/I 1 Mohan Cooperative Industrial Area
Mathura Road, New Delhi 110 044
India

SAGE Publications Asia-Pacific Pte. Ltd.
3 Church Street
#10-04 Samsung Hub
Singapore 049483

Printed in the United States of America

ISBN 978-1-5063-4715-8

Library of Congress Control Number: 2016937093

This book is printed on acid-free paper.

Acquisitions Editor: Michael Kerns
Editorial Assistant: Zachary Hoskins
Production Editor: Kelly DeRosa
Typesetter: C&M Digitals (P) Ltd.
Cover Designer: Michael Dubowe
Marketing Manager: Amy Whitaker

16 17 18 19 20 10 9 8 7 6 5 4 3 2 1

Contents

Annotated Contents

ENVIRONMENT

Air Pollution and Climate Change

Air pollution kills 3.3 million people a year world-wide, including 55,000 Americans, according to a recent study by an international group of scientists. Moreover, airborne pollutants, especially carbon dioxide (CO_2), are contributing to global climate change. In response, President Obama, frustrated by congressional inaction, has used his executive authority to institute a sweeping plan aimed at limiting CO_2 emissions from coal-fired power plants, curbing smog-causing ozone and encouraging the growth of renewable energy. Industry officials are challenging Obama's Clean Power Plan in court, arguing the regulations are too costly and that market forces are enough to bring about reductions in pollution. Environmental advocates dismiss those claims and say the administration should have gone further in tightening emission standards. Meanwhile, the United States and almost all the other nations on Earth began climate talks in Paris last year to seek consensus on ways to curb emissions to stave off further warming of the planet.

Pesticide Controversies

Pesticides shield crops from destructive insects, weeds and molds. They also are used in homes, factories, parks and backyards to control pests that spread infectious diseases. But some public health experts, along with environmental and health advocates, argue that pesticides also threaten human health and the environment. Pesticide residues in food have decreased over the past 20 years as the Environmental Protection Agency (EPA) has reduced permissible levels in many foods and canceled use of some older pesticides. But consumer advocates warn that some products remain unsafe. Studies indicate that pesticides are contributing to widespread declines of bees, butterflies and other creatures that pollinate plants, including many food crops. The declines can drive up costs for farmers and reduce harvests of some crops. The EPA has proposed tighter standards to protect farmworkers from pesticide exposure. However, critics say federal agencies also need to pay more attention to health risks associated with long-term exposure to very low levels of pesticides.

BUSINESS AND ECONOMY
Marijuana Industry

Sales of medical and recreational marijuana totaled nearly $3 billion in 2014, in what is one of the nation's fastest-growing industries. Experts say sales could reach $35 billion by 2020 if all 50 states and the District of Colombia legalize the drug. Currently, 23 states and the District of Colombia sanction medical marijuana, and four of those states and the District allow both medical and recreational use. Voters in more states are expected to legalize cannabis in 2016. Yet the industry faces big hurdles. Possession or sale of marijuana remains illegal under federal law, and while the Obama administration has opted not to enforce the law against users in states that have legalized pot, the next president could abandon that policy. What's more, banks fearful of violating the federal law are refusing to offer financial services to marijuana entrepreneurs, making it difficult for them to expand their businesses and meet soaring public demand. And while legal marijuana is generating millions in state taxes, critics say the social costs, such as marijuana-impaired driving, far outweigh the benefits.

Unions at a Crossroads

Labor unions have played a central role in recent national fights to raise the minimum wage, reduce income disparity and make work hours and rules more worker friendly. In addition, unions have sought to expand their message and membership ranks to nonunion groups and some white-collar sectors, such as adjunct college faculty and lawyers, and to offer union leadership positions to black women, one of their most loyal constituencies. The recent surge in union activity has prompted some observers to speculate that organized labor may be ripe for a revival. However, some academic experts and labor activists say the odds are stacked against that. They point to continued declines in union membership and unyielding opposition from many businesses and the Republican Party, as well as structural shifts in the workplace toward foreign outsourcing and temporary employees. Even some traditionally pro-union Democratic politicians have split with unions over the Trans-Pacific Partnership, a global trade treaty backed by President Obama that labor officials argue would lead to lost jobs and lower wages.

RIGHTS AND LIBERTIES
Free Speech on Campus

Several recent incidents in which college students have spewed racist or misogynistic language on campus have renewed debate about how much freedom of speech the U.S. constitution actually permits. Among the most notorious examples: the singing of a racist chant last year by several University of Oklahoma fraternity members. College presidents at Oklahoma and other campuses have swiftly disciplined students for speech deemed inappropriate, but civil liberties advocates say college officials are violating students' First Amendment rights to free speech. Meanwhile, critics say a small but growing movement to give students "trigger warnings" about curriculum material that might traumatize them indicates that colleges are becoming overly protective. American universities also have come under fire for accepting money from China and other autocratic governments to create overseas branches and international institutes on their home campuses. Defenders of such programs say they are vital for global understanding, but critics say they may compromise academic freedom.

Housing Discrimination

Almost 50 years after enactment of the Fair Housing Act, racial segregation in housing persists in the United States, in large cities and suburbs alike. Fair-housing advocacy groups blame the federal government for lax enforcement of the law and state and local housing agencies for limited efforts to disperse affordable housing into predominantly white neighborhoods. They also cite federal studies and court cases that show continuing discrimination against African-Americans, in particular by mortgage bankers, landlords and real estate brokers. The Supreme Court cheered fair-housing advocates with a decision last June endorsing broad application of the law against policies that have a "disparate impact" on minorities. The Department of Housing and Urban Development (HUD) followed with a rule aimed at requiring communities to do more to advance fair-housing policies, but local resistance may slow those efforts. Meanwhile, complaints of housing discrimination against individuals with disabilities now account for a majority of the cases HUD receives each year.

Religious Freedom

Religious liberty is enshrined in the First Amendment to the Constitution, but several high-profile legal cases recently have tested the limits of that freedom, deeply dividing the nation. The Supreme Court's 2015 decision granting same-sex couples the right to marry has led some Christians to refuse to serve gay couples. And the inclusion of a contraception benefit for women in the Affordable Care Act, known as Obamacare, has prompted some Christians to challenge the contraception mandate in court. They say their religious faith will not allow them to support or participate in marriages or birth control they believe violate God's will. But their critics say that by citing their religious faith as a reason to refuse to serve people or recognize their legal rights, they are imposing their religious views on others in violation of the Constitution. Meanwhile, other court battles over religious liberty have involved the right of members of minority religions in the United States, particularly Muslims, to practice their faith.

Transgender Rights

Throughout history, people with gender-identity issues were either ignored or abused. In fact, until recently, transgender individuals—those who don't identify emotionally and psychologically with the sex they were born with—were regarded as mentally ill and were widely spurned, even by gays and lesbians. The picture is beginning to change, however, with the Obama administration championing transgender rights, the Pentagon

signaling it will allow transgender soldiers and sailors to serve openly beginning next year and pop culture favorably portraying transgender celebrities. Nevertheless, transgender people continue to struggle with poor health care coverage, high rates of unemployment, violence—including murder—and suicide. Congress and most states have refused to mandate anti-discrimination protections for transgender individuals, in part because of a backlash over the issue of which public restrooms transgender people should use. While transgender individuals are experiencing growing public and political support, they have a long way to go before they can achieve full acceptance.

SOCIAL POLICY
Campus Sexual Assault

Charges of rape and other sexual assaults on college and university campuses—and how school officials investigate and adjudicate them—are receiving unprecedented attention. Young women who believe their schools mishandled their cases have formed advocacy groups, and they and others have filed complaints with the U.S. Department of Education, which is investigating 86 colleges and universities. The White House created a special task force on campus sexual assault, and Congress passed legislation in 2013 mandating training for school personnel and ongoing education for students on the issue. But as momentum builds to hold schools more accountable, civil libertarians say the pressure is leading schools to violate the rights of accused students. Meanwhile, the standard of evidence schools use when deciding sexual assault cases is under debate, along with whether schools' adoption of so-called affirmative consent for sexual encounters is too intrusive, and whether schools should turn over all investigations to police.

Reforming Juvenile Justice

Youth advocates are seizing on bipartisan interest in criminal justice reform and historically low crime rates to lobby states to lighten sentencing standards for juveniles. They also advocate more efforts to prepare troubled teenagers—even those convicted of the most violent crimes—to be productive members of society. In 2012 the U.S. Supreme Court ruled that mandatory life terms without parole for juveniles were unconstitutional, and this fall it will hear a case on whether to make that decision retroactive for adult prisoners who committed their crimes as juveniles. But prosecutors and victims' rights advocates say youths still must be held accountable for their crimes and judges should be able to refer repeat and violent offenders to adult court. Forming a backdrop to the debate is neuroscientific research on adolescent brain development that indicates juveniles' reasoning abilities and impulse control are limited well into their 20s. The research also suggests that they can change their behavior, raising questions about youths' culpability and likelihood of rehabilitation.

Racial Conflict

Race-centered conflicts in several U.S. cities have led to the strongest calls for policy reforms since the turbulent civil rights era of the 1960s. Propelled largely by videos of violent police confrontations with African-Americans, protesters have taken to the streets in Chicago, New York and other cities demanding changes in police tactics. Meanwhile, students—black and white—at several major universities have pressured school presidents to deal aggressively with racist incidents on campus. And activists in the emerging Black Lives Matter movement are charging that "institutional racism" persists in public institutions and laws a half century after legally sanctioned discrimination was banned. Critics of that view argue that moral failings in the black community—and not institutional racism—explain why many African-Americans lack parity with whites in such areas as wealth, employment, housing and educational attainment. But those who cite institutional racism say enormous socioeconomic gaps and entrenched housing and school segregation patterns stem from societal decisions that far outweigh individuals' life choices.

HEALTH

Prisoners and Mental Illness

Thousands of people with schizophrenia, severe depression, delusional disorders or other mental problems are locked up, often in solitary confinement. While some committed violent crimes and remain a threat to themselves or other inmates and prison staff,

many are incarcerated for minor offenses, simply because there is no place to send them for treatment. The number of mentally ill inmates has mushroomed in recent years as states have closed their psychiatric hospitals in favor of outpatient community mental health centers that typically are underfunded and overcrowded. In an attempt to reduce the influx of mentally ill inmates, some 300 specialized mental health courts have diverted them into court-monitored treatment instead of jail. Yet, many participants re-offend, and some experts say psychiatric treatment alone won't prevent criminal behavior. Meanwhile, courts in more than a half-dozen states have declared solitary confinement unconstitutional for those with mental illness. However, some corrections officials say solitary is necessary to separate dangerous prisoners.

Reforming Veterans' Health Care

The Department of Veterans Affairs is struggling to recover from revelations that some of its facilities forced military veterans to wait months for health care and that some VA officials kept bogus records to conceal the delays. VA Secretary Robert A. McDonald—a West Point graduate and former CEO of consumer-products giant Procter & Gamble—has vowed to streamline the vast department into a more effective organization better able to serve the 6.6 million patients who seek its medical services each year. But critics complain the former paratrooper has been too slow to fire those responsible for the scandals, and they worry that his lack of health care and government experience may prevent him from succeeding. Despite its recent problems, the VA has conducted Nobel Prize-level research and—especially over the last two decades—delivered high-quality care to most of its patients.

NATIONAL SECURITY
Immigrant Detention

In 2014, 425,000 undocumented immigrants—far more people than are held in federal prison—were held in the 250 detention centers run by U.S. Immigration and Customs Enforcement (ICE). Most of the detainees were awaiting deportation or a ruling on their eligibility to remain in the United States, including thousands of

Central American mothers and children seeking asylum from gang violence at home. While most detainees move through the system in days or weeks, some are held for months or even years waiting for backlogged immigration courts to settle their cases. Critics say the detention system leads to physical and mental abuse, the breakup of immigrant families and, in some cases, death by suicide or neglect. Most detainees pose no risk of flight or criminal behavior and should be free pending their hearings, immigrant supporters contend. But groups seeking tighter curbs on immigration say detention is necessary to protect public safety and to ensure that undocumented immigrants do not disappear into the general population before their cases are decided.

Intelligence Reform

New and evolving national security threats are raising questions about the U.S. intelligence community's effectiveness. A decade after the nation's 16 spy agencies were consolidated under the Office of the Director of National Intelligence, security experts are expressing concerns about interagency rivalries and questioning whether the intelligence community is prepared to deal with domestic and foreign threats, including cyberattacks and recruitment of young Westerners by the Islamic State (ISIS). Meanwhile, Congress has been wrangling over whether to allow the National Security Agency to continue collecting bulk cellphone data from Americans, a practice the spy agency says is necessary to safeguard the nation from terrorism but that civil libertarians say erodes one of the very principles of democracy it is intended to protect—citizens' right to privacy. At the same time, critics say international reactions to alleged CIA torture of terrorism suspects in the wars in Iraq and Afghanistan continue to undermine the intelligence community's effectiveness on the world stage.

Police Tactics

The killing in August 2014 of an unarmed, black 18-year-old by police in Ferguson, Mo., has intensified a long-simmering debate over how police do their jobs. The shooting of Michael Brown by white officer Darren Wilson has led to angry and sometimes violent protests, initially heightened when police in military-style gear and armored vehicles responded to the unrest. The tactics highlighted what some criticize as the "militarization" of America's police forces, fueled by a Pentagon program that supplies local police with surplus weapons and vehicles. Others say police overuse SWAT teams to serve warrants and enforce drug laws. The Ferguson shooting and other recent high-profile police killings of unarmed African-Americans also has ignited a national outcry against what many say is disproportionate police action against black males. Police respond that low-income communities of all races have the highest crime rates and that they need military-style equipment to defend themselves in a heavily armed society.

Preface

Are tougher air pollution regulations necessary to limit climate change? Can transgender people achieve equality? Is the U.S. system of detention for unauthorized immigrants too harsh? These questions—and many more—are at the heart of American public policy. How can instructors best engage students with these crucial issues? We feel that students need objective, yet provocative examinations of these issues to understand how they affect citizens today and will for years to come. This annual collection aims to promote in-depth discussion, facilitate further research and help readers formulate their own positions on crucial issues. Get your students talking both inside and outside the classroom about *Issues for Debate in American Public Policy.*

This seventeenth edition includes sixteen up-to-date reports by *CQ Researcher*, an award-winning weekly policy brief that brings complicated issues down to earth. Each report chronicles and analyzes executive, legislative, and judicial activities at all levels of government. This collection is divided into six diverse policy areas: environment; business and economy; rights and liberties; social policy; health; and national security—to cover a range of issues found in most American government and public policy courses.

CQ RESEARCHER

CQ Researcher was founded in 1923 as *Editorial Research Reports* and was sold primarily to newspapers as a research tool. The magazine was renamed and redesigned in 1991 as *CQ Researcher.* Today, students are its primary audience. While still used by hundreds of journalists and newspapers, many of which reprint portions of the reports, the *Researcher's* main subscribers are now high school, college and public libraries. In 2002, *Researcher* won the American Bar Association's coveted Silver Gavel award for magazine excellence for a series of nine reports on civil liberties and other legal issues.

Researcher writers—all highly experienced journalists—sometimes compare the experience of writing a Researcher report to drafting a college term paper. Indeed, there are many similarities. Each report is as long as many term papers—about 11,000 words—and is written by one person without any significant outside help. One of the key differences is that writers interview leading experts, scholars and government officials for each issue.

Like students, writers begin the creative process by choosing a topic. Working with the *Researcher's* editors, the writer identifies a controversial subject that has important public policy implications. After a topic is selected, the writer embarks on one to two weeks of intense research. Newspaper and magazine articles are clipped or downloaded, books are ordered and information is gathered from a wide variety of sources, including interest groups, universities and the government. Once the writers are well informed, they develop a detailed outline, and begin the interview process. Each report requires a minimum of ten to fifteen interviews with academics, officials, lobbyists and people working in the field. Only after all interviews are completed does the writing begin.

CHAPTER FORMAT

Each issue of *CQ Researcher*, and therefore each selection in this book, is structured in the same way. Each begins with an overview, which briefly summarizes the areas that will be explored in greater detail in the rest of the chapter. The next section chronicles important and current debates on the topic under discussion and is structured around a number of key questions, such as "Is legalized marijuana good for the U.S. economy?" and "Should university conduct codes ban offensive speech?" These questions are usually the subject of much debate among practitioners and scholars in the field. Hence, the answers presented are never conclusive but detail the range of opinion on the topic.

Next, the "Background" section provides a history of the issue being examined. This retrospective covers important legislative measures, executive actions and court decisions that illustrate how current policy has evolved. Then the "Current Situation" section examines contemporary policy issues, legislation under consideration and legal action being taken. Each selection concludes with an "Outlook" section, which addresses possible regulation, court rulings, and initiatives from Capitol Hill and the White House over the next five to ten years.

Each report contains features that augment the main text: two to three sidebars that examine issues related to the topic at hand, a pro versus con debate between two experts, a chronology of key dates and events and an annotated bibliography detailing major sources used by the writer.

ACKNOWLEDGMENTS

We wish to thank many people for helping to make this collection a reality. Thomas J. Billitteri, managing editor of *CQ Researcher*, gave us his enthusiastic support and cooperation as we developed this seventeenth edition. He and his talented editors and writers have amassed a first-class library of *Researcher* reports, and we are fortunate to have access to that rich cache. We also thankfully acknowledge the advice and feedback from current readers and are gratified by their satisfaction with the book.

Some readers may be learning about *CQ Researcher* for the first time. We expect that many readers will want regular access to this excellent weekly research tool. For subscription information or a no-obligation free trial of *Researcher*, please contact CQ Press at www.cqpress.com or toll-free at 1-866-4CQ-PRESS (1-866-427-7737).

We hope that you will be pleased by the seventeenth edition of *Issues for Debate in American Public Policy.* We welcome your feedback and suggestions for future editions. Please direct comments to Michael Kerns, Acquisitions Editor for Public Administration and Public Policy, CQ Press, an imprint of SAGE, 2600 Virginia Avenue, NW, Suite 600, Washington, DC 20037; or send e-mail to Michael.Kerns@sagepub.com.

—The Editors of CQ Press

Contributors

Jill U. Adams writes a health column for *The Washington Post* and reports on health, biomedical research and environmental issues for magazines such as *Audubon, Scientific American* and *Science*. She holds a Ph.D. in pharmacology from Emory University.

Sarah Glazer contributes regularly to *CQ Researcher*. Her articles on health, education and social-policy issues also have appeared in *The New York Times* and *The Washington Post*. Her recent *CQ Researcher* reports include "Treating Autism" and "Treating Schizophrenia." She graduated from the University of Chicago with a B.A. in American history.

Alan Greenblatt is a staff writer at *Governing* magazine. Previously he covered politics and government for NPR and *CQ Weekly*, where he won the National Press Club's Sandy Hume Award for political journalism. He graduated from San Francisco State University in 1986 and received a master's degree in English literature from the University of Virginia in 1988. His *CQ Researcher* reports include "Gentrification," "Future of the GOP," "Immigration Debate," "Media Bias" and "Downtown Revival."

Kenneth Jost has written 170 reports for *CQ Researcher* since 1991 on topics ranging from legal affairs and social policy to national security and international relations. He is the author of *The Supreme Court Yearbook* and *Supreme Court From A to Z* (both CQ Press). He is an honors graduate of Harvard College and Georgetown Law School, where he teaches media law as an adjunct professor. He also writes the blog *Jost on Justice* (http://joston justice.blogspot.com). His earlier reports include "Racial Diversity in Public Schools" (September 2007) and "School Desegregation" (April 2004).

Reed Karaim, a freelance writer in Tucson, Ariz., has written for *The Washington Post, U.S. News & World Report, Smithsonian, American Scholar, USA Weekend* and other publications. He is the author of the novel *If Men Were Angels*, which was selected for the Barnes & Noble Discover Great New Writers series. He is also the winner of the Robin Goldstein Award for Outstanding Regional Reporting and other journalism honors. Karaim is a graduate of North Dakota State University in Fargo.

Peter Katel is a *CQ Researcher* contributing writer who previously reported on Haiti and Latin America for *Time* and *Newsweek* and covered the Southwest for newspapers in New Mexico. He has received several journalism awards, including the Bartolomé Mitre Award for coverage of drug trafficking from the Inter-American Press Association. He holds an A.B. in university studies from the University of New Mexico. His recent reports include "U.S. Global Engagement" and "Central American Gangs."

Christina L. Lyons, a freelance journalist based in the Washington, D.C. area, writes primarily about U.S. government and politics. She is a contributing author for CQ Press reference books, including *CQ's Guide to Congress*, and is a contributing editor for Bloomberg BNA's *International Trade Daily*. A former editor for *Congressional Quarterly*, she also was co-author of CQ's *Politics in America 2010*. Lyons began her career as a newspaper reporter in Maryland and then covered environment and health care policy on Capitol Hill. She has a master's degree in political science from American University.

Barbara Mantel is a freelance writer in New York City. She was a 2012 Kiplinger Fellow and has won several journalism awards, including the National Press Club's Best Consumer Journalism Award and the Front Page Award from the Newswomen's Club of New York for her Nov. 1, 2009, *CQ Global Researcher* report "Terrorism and the Internet." She holds a B.A. in history and economics from the University of Virginia and an M.A. in economics from Northwestern University.

Chuck McCutcheon is a freelance writer in Washington, D.C. He has been a reporter and editor for *Congressional Quarterly* and Newhouse News Service and is co-author of the 2012 and 2014 editions of *The Almanac of American Politics* and *Dog Whistles, Walk-Backs and Washington Handshakes: Decoding the Jargon, Slang and Bluster of American Political Speech*. He also has written books on climate change and nuclear waste.

Tom Price is a Washington-based freelance journalist and a contributing writer for *CQ Researcher*. Previously, he was a correspondent in the Cox Newspapers Washington Bureau and chief politics writer for the *Dayton Daily News* and The (Dayton) *Journal Herald*. He is author or coauthor of five books including, with former U.S. Rep. Tony Hall (D-Ohio), *Changing the Face of Hunger: One Man's Story of How Liberals, Conservatives, Democrats, Republicans and People of Faith Are Joining Forces to Help the Hungry, the Poor and the Oppressed*.

Bill Wanlund is a freelance writer in the Washington, D.C. area. He is a former Foreign Services officer, with service in Europe, Asia, Africa and South America. He holds a journalism degree from The George Washington University and has written for *CQ Researcher* on abortion and intelligence reform.

Jennifer Weeks is a Massachusetts freelance writer who specializes in the environment, science, and health. She has written for *The Washington Post, Audubon, Popular Mechanics* and other magazines and previously was a policy analyst, congressional staffer and lobbyist. She has an A.B. degree from Williams College and master's degrees from the University of North Carolina and Harvard. Her recent *CQ Researcher* reports include "Regulating Toxic Chemicals" and "Protecting the Oceans."

Issues for Debate
in American
Public Policy

1

Air Pollution and Climate Change

Jill U. Adams

The smog-shrouded Los Angeles skyline sets the scene for tourists taking a selfie on May 31, 2015. More than 3 million people a year die as a result of air pollution, including 55,000 Americans. The United States and most of the world's other nations met in Paris in November 2015 to establish policies to curb polluting emissions that are dangerously warming the planet.

From *CQ Researcher*, November 13, 2015.

In the battle to clean up the nation's air, progress is as hazy as the Los Angeles skyline on a hot, smoggy day.

In the past 15 years, the city has cut ozone* — the main component of smog — by more than one-third and fine-particle pollution, or soot, by about half.[1]

For car-clogged California, which has some of the nation's worst air pollution, that is a significant step forward. Yet the Los Angeles region ranked No. 1 in a 2015 listing of U.S. cities with the worst air quality, including the most ozone pollution and the third most soot, according to the American Lung Association.[2]

The good news/bad news in Los Angeles reflects the complexity of the air pollution fight in the United States and worldwide.[3]

The days of pedestrians in U.S. cities being unable to see across a smoggy street are largely over, but air pollution remains the world's biggest environmental health risk, with some of the worst problems in developing nations such as China and India.[4]

Air pollution kills 3.3 million people a year, including 55,000 in the United States, mostly from strokes and heart attacks, according to a study by scientists from the United States, Europe and the Middle East, published in September.[5] Worldwide, air pollution is

---

* Ozone, a major component of smog, is created when hydrocarbons, nitrogen oxides and other pollutants emitted by cars, power plants and factories mix in the air on hot, sunny days.

implicated in nearly one in eight premature deaths from respiratory and cardiovascular diseases, as well as in many cancers, according to the World Health Organization.[6] And the International Agency for Research on Cancer said evidence shows a causal link between air pollution and lung cancer and a heightened risk of bladder cancer.[7]

Air pollution also poses other, potentially catastrophic, consequences for global climate change. It is inextricably bound up with global climate change because of pollutants in the atmosphere known as greenhouse gases. Produced largely by burning coal and oil, these gases, including carbon dioxide (CO_2), contribute to the greenhouse, or warming, effect in the Earth's atmosphere.

A widely cited figure suggested in 2009 by former NASA climate scientist James Hansen set a CO_2 level of 350 parts per million (ppm) as a threshold for Earth's safety. Any level above that will lead to dangerous warming not seen since the Pliocene era (5.3 million to 2.6 million years ago), Hansen warned. In May 2013, the level reached 400 ppm at a monitoring station in Hawaii for the first time, and this year it appears that 400 will be the new normal, the World Meteorological Organization announced in early November. The planet's temperature will rise at least 2 degrees by the end of the century, according to current projections, and an increase topping that could lead to a host of environmental crises, including flooding from rising sea levels and catastrophic weather events.[8]

On Nov. 30, the United States and 195 other countries will attend the 21st United Nations Climate Change Conference in Paris, or COP21. The conference will set global targets for reducing carbon emissions and mitigating climate change. Participating countries already have pledged to reduce their emissions, but experts say that is only a start. "Paris must be the floor, not the ceiling, for collective ambition," said United Nations Secretary-General Ban Ki-moon of South Korea.[9]

Domestic politics, including in the United States, may limit how far national leaders can go in addressing climate change. Frustrated by congressional inaction on the environment, convinced that climate change is at a crisis point and determined to set an example for other nations in the run-up to COP21, President Obama used his executive power in early August to issue regulations setting strict carbon-emission limits for states. Claiming authority under the 1970 Clean Air Act, he said his Clean Power Plan will cut carbon dioxide emissions from power plants and other industrial sources by 32 percent from 2005 levels by 2030.[10]

Obama's plan has raised a slew of objections from all sides: The power industry, manufacturers and conservatives condemn it as a jobs-killer, unneeded and in violation of the Clean Air Act, and they have sued to block its implementation. Environmentalists applaud the plan's goals but say it doesn't go far enough. The opposing views crystallize a fierce debate over what should be done about climate change, carbon dioxide emissions and air pollution.

Carbon emissions actually have been decreasing in the United States in recent years as the power grid increasingly is fed by sources other than coal and oil. [11] Natural gas supplies are plentiful and cheap, and the renewable energy sector — including wind and solar power — is growing rapidly. In addition, so-called clean-coal technologies promise to further curb carbon emissions once they are more widely deployed. These technologies, such as carbon capture, "clean" coal by capturing its emissions before they enter the atmosphere.[12]

The Clean Power Plan defines carbon dioxide as a pollutant under the Clean Air Act and sets limits on carbon emissions produced by electricity-generating power plants, the source of about 37 percent of U.S. carbon emissions, the most of any sector.[13] Transportation is second, contributing 31 percent, and industry third, at 15 percent.[14]

Proponents cite studies showing the Clean Power Plan will lead to 3,600 fewer premature deaths in the United States and 90,000 fewer childhood asthma attacks. The plan also will boost investment in renewable energy technologies, backers say. And it provides flexibility by phasing in the stricter standards and letting states decide how to meet their reductions — whether by using more clean energy, increasing efficiency or trading emission credits (plants whose emissions are below allowable levels can "sell" their credits for unused emissions to those plants unable to meet their targets).[15]

"It's a simple idea that will change the world: Cut carbon pollution today so our kids won't inherit climate chaos tomorrow," said Rhea Suh, president of the Natural Resources Defense Council, an environmental

Carbon Dioxide Levels Accelerating

Concentrations of carbon dioxide (CO_2) in Earth's atmosphere reached 400 parts per million (ppm) for the first time in 2013, but when CO_2 hit 400 ppm again this year, scientists said that level would be the new normal, and well over the 350 ppm that is considered the threshold for Earth's safety. CO_2 levels have risen 27 percent since 1958, when scientists first began measuring them.

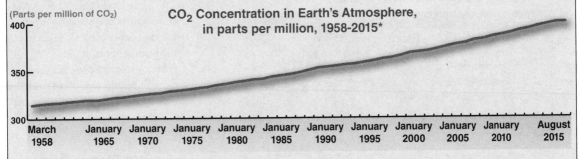

CO₂ Concentration in Earth's Atmosphere, in parts per million, 1958-2015*

(Parts per million of CO₂)

March 1958 — January 1965 — January 1970 — January 1975 — January 1980 — January 1985 — January 1990 — January 1995 — January 2000 — January 2005 — January 2010 — August 2015

March 1958 through August 2015, seasonally adjusted.

Source: C. D. Keeling et. al, "Exchanges of atmospheric CO_2 and 13 CO_2 with the terrestrial biosphere and oceans from 1978 to 2000," Scripps Institution of Oceanography, University of California San Diego, accessed Nov. 3, 2015, http://tinyurl.com/nalmrzlc; caption information from Philip Bump, "So Much for 350: The Atmosphere's Carbon Dioxide Tops 400," *The Wire*, April 29, 2013, http://tinyurl.com/oka5nkj

advocacy group. "That's what this historic plan will achieve. . . . Now we are going to fight with everything we've got to ensure the plan moves forward and provides the necessary momentum for unified global action."[16]

Opponents, including states that produce and burn coal and dozens of energy companies, say the Clean Power Plan is an economic vise, harming industries that provide a necessary product — electric power. Twenty-five states and several industry groups are suing to block the plan, arguing that Obama overstepped his executive power by illegally basing his plan on an obscure provision of the Clean Air Act and that the plan will drive up utility rates for homeowners and businesses and slash jobs in the power industry.[17]

Mike Dugan, president and CEO of the American Coalition for Clean Coal Electricity, rejects the Clean Power Plan in its finalized form, as published by the EPA. "Even in the face of damning analyses and scathing opposition from across the country, [the Environmental Protection Agency's] final carbon rule reveals what we've said for months — this agency is pursuing an illegal plan that will drive up electricity costs and put people out of

work," said Dugan. "This rule fails across the board, but most troubling is that it fails the millions of families and businesses who rely on affordable electricity to help them keep food on the table and the lights on."[18]

Opponents also say the new regulations are unneeded because carbon emissions are already falling. Natural gas is providing new incentives for utilities to switch from coal. Although it is a fossil fuel, natural gas produces fewer emissions than coal and oil when it burns.

Environmentalists say government regulations are necessary to further reduce carbon emissions. They also note that the gains in lower emissions thus far are not uniform. Recent data from the Energy Information Administration show that from 2000 to 2013 carbon emissions increased in 13 states — mostly in the Plains, where oil and gas drilling has been booming — with Nebraska recording the biggest rise.[19]

A second component of Obama's effort to improve air quality is a tougher ozone standard, announced by the EPA on Oct. 1. It will require states and counties to lower their ozone levels from 75 parts per billion (ppb) to 70 ppb in the next five to 22 years (the amount of time

Ozone Pollution Hits California Cities Hardest

Largely because of auto emissions, California contains a majority of the top 15 cities in the United States with the worst pollution from ozone, the main component of smog.

Top 15 Ozone-Polluted Cities, 2011-2013

Rank	City	State
1	Los Angeles-Long Beach	California
2	Visalia-Porterville-Hanford	California
3	Bakersfield	California
4	Fresno-Madera	California
5	Sacramento-Roseville	California
6	Houston-The Woodlands	Texas
7	Dallas-Fort Worth	Texas
8	Modesto-Merced	California
9	Las Vegas-Henderson	Nevada
10	Phoenix-Mesa-Scottsdale	Arizona
11	New York-Newark	New York-New Jersey
12	Tulsa-Muskogee-Bartlesville	Oklahoma
13	Denver-Aurora	Colorado
14	El Centro	California
15	Oklahoma City-Shawnee	Oklahoma

Source: "State of the Air 2015," American Lung Association, 2015, http://tinyurl.com/pl98d94

depends on the state and the severity of that state's ozone problem).

Ground-level ozone is a pollutant regulated by the Clean Air Act, primarily because of its harmful effects on human health. In contrast, the ozone layer in the upper atmosphere (the stratosphere) protects life on Earth by blocking much of the sun's ultraviolet light.

Under the Clean Air Act, ground-level ozone standards are supposed to be revisited every five years or so. Although the new standard was expected, the U.S. Chamber of Commerce, the National Association of Manufacturers (NAM) and other opponents said it will hurt the economy. "Manufacturers have been leading the way in lowering ozone levels; yet, the Obama administration forges on with a regulation that will stunt growth, production and job creation," said Jay Timmons, president and CEO of NAM.[20]

But environmental advocates such as the group Clear Air Watch and medical associations such as the American Lung Association (ALA) say the new standard doesn't go far enough. "Given the health threats from ozone, greater health protections are clearly needed," said Harold Wimmer, president and CEO of the ALA. "The level chosen of 70 parts per billion simply does not reflect what the science shows is necessary to truly protect public health."[21]

As controversy swirls around Obama's regulatory plans and the best way to improve air quality, here are some of the questions being debated:

Is President Obama's Clean Power Plan good policy?

When Obama announced his Clean Power Plan on Aug. 3, he said its primary purpose was to reduce the nation's greenhouse emissions. Lowering the amount of carbon dioxide that power-generating plants release into the atmosphere, he said, is one step in addressing climate change. Obama called the plan a moral obligation, a public health issue and a matter of national security.[22]

Environmental advocacy groups hailed the plan, whose emission limits will phase in over eight years beginning in 2022, as a "game-changer," a "great start" and "the most significant step in U.S. history toward reducing the pollution that causes climate change."[23] Critics had an opposite reaction: The Clean Power Plan, they said, will be costly to implement and represents government overreach at its worst. They contend Obama should have worked through Congress instead of issuing an executive order.

The limits in the plan "exceed the EPA's legal authority under the Clean Air Act," Republican Gov. Mike Pence of Indiana wrote Obama in a June 24 letter, when the plan was in proposal phase. Besides threatening jobs and the supply of energy, Pence continued, "your plan ignores the separation of powers enshrined in our nation's Constitution."[24]

Ann Weeks, senior counsel and legal director for the Clean Air Task Force, a Boston-based nonprofit that advocates for reductions in air pollution, says the rule aims for a maximum decrease in carbon dioxide while not being overly burdensome in terms of cost. "It's an ambitious standard that looks forward to what can be achieved over the regulatory period — eight years," she says. "The rule applies to existing sources and new sources. States are directed to make plans to accomplish this in a cost-effective way."

"The Clean Power Plan will sharply reduce carbon pollution and other dangerous air pollutants by shifting our electric power system toward cleaner energy sources at a steady but achievable pace," wrote David Doniger and Derek Murrow of the Natural Resources Defense Council. "Enforceable carbon pollution limits will kick in starting in 2022 and ramp up into full effect by 2030."[25]

Although she praises Obama for acting, Weeks says, "We could have done this years ago. We could have had more leadership. Canada has had these standards in place for a while."

Opponents say the Clean Power Plan will be too costly for industry to implement. Building a power-generating plant is expensive, and it takes decades for a company to recover the up-front investment, says Christi Tezak, managing director of research at ClearView Energy Partners, an independent research firm in Washington that analyzes U.S. energy policy. With the new rule, "we may be pulling offline a perfectly serviceable power plant before it's paid for," she says. "It's like wanting a shiny new car, but you haven't paid off your last car yet."

Closing older plants that have been paid off carries costs as well, says Arnold Reitze, a law professor at the University of Utah in Salt Lake City who has 50 years of air pollution litigation experience. Such plants produce "very inexpensive electricity" because they incur only fuel and operating costs, he says. "You can't build a new plant and sell electricity at prices like that."

Opponents also argue that the new regulations are unnecessary and unfairly penalize the coal industry. "We're fine with market forces," says Paul Bailey, senior vice president for federal affairs and policy at the American Coalition for Clean Coal Electricity. The falling price of natural gas has already tipped the balance

against coal. But with new regulations on power plant emissions, including the Clean Power Plan and a new rule on mercury and other toxic emissions, it's as if "EPA has their finger on the scale," Bailey says.

Giving the EPA such power is dangerous for another reason, Bailey and other foes of the Clean Power Plan say: Market forces, not the government, do the best job of picking winners and losers in the energy sector.

They point to Solyndra, the California-based maker of solar cells that went bankrupt in August 2011 despite receiving a $535 million loan guarantee from the Department of Energy only two years earlier. President Obama enthusiastically praised the company during a 2010 visit to Solyndra, touting it as a model of clean energy and a job creator, only for the company to fail. Industry and free-market advocates say the loan wasted taxpayer money and unfairly backed renewable energy over traditional energy sources. Solyndra, they say, offers dramatic evidence as to why the government should not intervene in the energy marketplace.[26]

Besides, Bailey says, targeting coal and the traditional energy sector will lead to higher electricity prices. "And when energy prices go up, it harms those at the low end of the economic spectrum," he says.

Environmentalists counter that Solyndra was an aberration, that the marketplace has its own shortcomings, and that government has played an important role in encouraging nascent industries. Although they concede that market forces are helping to lower carbon emissions, they say the market alone is not enough to achieve the reductions needed. "For us, the [Clean Power Plan] provides the opportunity to lock in" falling levels of carbon, emissions of which are down 15 percent from 10 years ago, says Nicholas Bianco, director of regulatory analysis and strategic partnerships for the Environmental Defense Fund, an environmental advocacy group. "Otherwise, there's no guarantee that these trends will continue."

Is the EPA's new ozone standard good policy?

When EPA Administrator Gina McCarthy announced in August that the national ozone standard would be tightened, she said, "While the days are gone when cities like Los Angeles were so smoggy that people had trouble seeing across the street, science tells us that ozone is still making people sick and we still have work to do."[27]

Getty Images/*The Washington Post*/Ricky Carioti

Protesters at the White House demand an end to coal mining by so-called mountaintop removal on Sept. 27, 2010. President Obama used his executive authority in August to institute a sweeping plan to limit CO2 emissions from coalfired power plants, curb smog-causing ozone and encourage the growth of renewable energy sources. Industry officials say Obama's Clean Power Plan requires industry changes that will be too costly and that market forces can achieve reductions in pollution.

The agency contends the health benefits of the tougher standard, effective Dec. 28, far outweigh the costs. The new standard will require municipalities to enforce pollution-limiting strategies, such as implementing pollution-control technologies on vehicles, factories and power plants, shutting down pollution-emitting plants and freezing new development, including transportation projects and new industrial facilities.

The EPA estimates that economic costs to businesses will run a total of $1.4 billion per year for modifying some plants and potentially shutting down others, but that $2.9 billion to $5.9 billion will be saved each year due to fewer missed days of work and school, emergency room visits and premature deaths.[28]

While proponents praised the EPA for tightening the standard, many wanted the agency to go further. Scientific advisory panels have recommended standards as demanding as 60 ppb, based on evidence that higher levels of ozone harm public health. "Disappointing is too mild a term," said Frank O'Donnell, president of the advocacy group Clean Air Watch. "The big polluters won this time, for the most part."[29]

Opponents were unhappy, too, but they recognized that things could have been worse. "Today, the Obama administration finalized a rule that is overly burdensome,

costly and misguided," said Timmons of the National Association of Manufacturers. "For months, the administration threatened to impose on manufacturers an even harsher rule, with even more devastating consequences. After an unprecedented level of outreach by manufacturers and other stakeholders, the worst-case scenario was avoided."[30]

Whether it's the ozone standard or carbon emission restrictions, Tezak of ClearView Energy Partners asks, "Are we doing something that's nice to have, or are we doing something that's smart?" If an old plant is to be taken offline at some point in the future, she says, perhaps it's wiser to work within that longer timeline and get to the same pollution reductions without people losing their investments.

"The new regulations simply change the rate of change," says Robert Hebner, director of the Center for Electromechanics at the University of Texas, Austin, which researches energy storage and power generation. Hebner, who experienced similar policy debates when he served at the Office of Management and Budget in 1990, sees the new ozone and carbon regulations as being on "the trailing edge," because the energy sector has been moving away from coal for some time. "They're replacing it with so-called clean coal, increasing the use of natural gas and renewables," he says. "And it's working."

Ozone levels have decreased by about a third from 1980 to 2014, according to EPA records. "Why the urgent need now, then, to impose such a draconian new regulatory scheme?" asked David Johnson, CEO of a family-owned clay products manufacturing company in Appalachian, Ohio.[31]

Ozone primarily affects the airways and the lungs. As people inhale the pollutant it can irritate the lining of the throat, causing inflammation; trigger coughing and shortness of breath; and decrease lung function. In susceptible individuals, ozone can spark serious asthma attacks, heart attacks and premature death. Children, the elderly and people with asthma or respiratory illnesses are particularly sensitive to ozone.[32]

A 2010 analysis of the medical literature by a scientific advisory panel convened by the EPA quantified the impact of different levels of ozone in terms of illness and premature deaths. The panel determined that tightening the standard from 75 ppb to 70 ppb would prevent about 2,200 heart attacks, 23,000 asthma attacks and 1,500 to 4,300 premature deaths per year. A change from 75 ppb to 60 ppb would dramatically improve those numbers even more — averting 5,300 heart attacks, 58,000 asthma attacks and 4,000 to 12,000 premature deaths.[33]

Clean Air Watch's O'Donnell said numbers like that are why he is disappointed in the new ozone standard: "EPA has taken a baby step, when what was really needed is a giant stride to protect people's health from dirty air," he said. "It is really a missed opportunity."[34]

Can renewable energy become a major contributor to the power industry?

Many experts say generating more electricity from renewable energy sources is a good idea because it would improve air quality and slow climate change. But they disagree over how soon that can happen.

Already solar and wind power are experiencing record growth, but their overall contributions to the energy sector remain small.

Solar energy has been growing spectacularly. In 2010, it provided 2,300 megawatts of electricity in the United States; compared with more than 12,000 in 2014, or enough to power about 1.2 million homes.* Even so, solar power accounts for only 1 percent of electricity generated in the United States.[35]

Wind energy's growth also has been robust, rising from 40,000 megawatts of capacity in 2010 to more than 65,000 in 2014 — about 4 percent of the electricity generated in the United States.[36]

The energy industry sees these trends continuing at least for the next four years, according to a survey conducted by the global energy consulting firm DNV GL. One in two respondents said they thought that by 2030 renewables would be generating 70 percent of the energy in markets that have actively adopted green technologies (primarily in Europe and North America).[37]

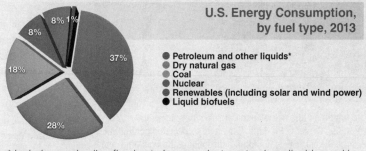

Fossil Fuels Supply Most U.S. Energy

Coal and petroleum — fossil fuels that emit large amounts of carbon dioxide when burned — produced more than half the energy consumed in the United States in 2013. Natural gas, a cleaner-burning fossil fuel, represented more than a fourth, while biofuels, nuclear power and renewables supplied less than a fifth.

U.S. Energy Consumption, by fuel type, 2013

- Petroleum and other liquids*
- Dry natural gas
- Coal
- Nuclear
- Renewables (including solar and wind power)
- Liquid biofuels

37% 28% 18% 8% 8% 1%

* Includes crude oil, refined petroleum products, natural gas liquids used in petroleum production and liquids derived from other hydrocarbon sources.

Source: "Annual Energy Outlook 2015," U.S. Energy Information Administration, April 2015, p. 15, http://tinyurl.com/o5bohzb

"We've seen an explosion in both solar and wind generation throughout the country — some 43 percent of all new electricity generated was from these cleaner fuel sources," said Suh of the Natural Resources Defense Council. "That's going to [rise] further under this new framework that the president has unveiled," she added, referring to the Clean Power Plan and its incentives for increasing renewable energy by offering emissions credits.[38]

Renewable technology is a big industry in some surprising places, such as Colorado, Illinois and North Carolina, Suh said. "It's not necessarily just the hotbeds of solar energy like Southern California or the Southwest. It's really an opportunity throughout the country that we're seeing in the development of clean energy technologies."[39]

Those tracking the investment market also see a coming boom. *Bloomberg New Energy Finance* predicts wind and solar will generate 18 percent of North America's electricity by 2030 — more than triple this year's 5 percent, driven by a desire to diversify energy sources, improving economics for green technologies and new policies, such

---

* One megawatt can power 1,000 homes.

Computer monitors at the PacifiCorp Transmissions Grid Operations Center in Portland, Ore., help technicians control the delivery of electricity to customers throughout the Western United States. The utility firm, a subsidiary of Warren Buffett's Berkshire Hathaway Energy, is a major user of wind turbines to produce clean energy.

as the Clean Power Plan. Rooftop solar panels will achieve a 10 percent share of the U.S. energy mix in the same time frame, according to Bloomberg.[40]

Other analyses are less optimistic. In a detailed look at the U.S. energy market, *Forbes* magazine found that a bump in natural gas prices — as occurred during a January 2014 polar vortex, when temperatures throughout much of the nation plunged and demand for heat spiked — forced oil-burning backup generators into service and triggered some gas-to-coal switching. The lesson, *Forbes* said: Local and short-term conditions can squeeze the system in ways that favor old, standby energy sources.[41]

The Clean Air Task Force's Weeks questions how big a boost the Clean Power Plan will actually give the clean-energy industry. Technical limitations remain, she says, "including the fact that we don't have an advanced [energy] storage system."

Energy analyst Tezak agrees the storage issue is critical. "The wind doesn't always blow and the sun doesn't always shine," she says. Yet public utilities have an obligation to provide power around the clock when solar or wind power is unavailable, she says.

Grid problems are cropping up in some places. "In Arizona, there's so much solar [energy]," Tezak says, that it's costing utilities revenue. Homeowners with rooftop

solar panels might owe nothing on their monthly bill. And yet those homeowners are getting a service — use of the electric grid on cloudy days. Utilities are scrambling to come up with new rate structures to charge for that benefit.

These problems aren't intractable, says energy expert Hebner. "But is it difficult? Yes. It needs money to get it done," he says, referring to improved storage and grid upgrades. He cites Florida as a place where old and new energy sources are beginning to play nicely together. "For instance, Florida Power & Light is making progress — they're combining natural gas and solar," he says. Other regions are integrating natural gas and wind power, where both those sources are competitive in price.

However, if natural gas prices continue to drop, the renewable energy sector's growth could slow, because its prices would be less competitive, analysts say.

Some states have set ambitious goals to reduce reliance on fossil fuels and increase renewables. California wants to cut fossil fuel use by a third by 2020. New York's energy plan says renewable sources, which currently provide about 11 percent of the state's energy, could meet up to 40 percent by 2030.

Environmental advocates say investments in renewable energy make economic sense. Although jobs may be lost in the fossil fuel sector, other jobs will be created in solar and wind, they say. Between January 2011 and June 2014, the renewable sector (solar, wind, biomass and geothermal) gained 1,800 jobs, with solar power leading the way, according to the Bureau of Labor Statistics (BLS). The number of solar jobs tripled during that period, although the wind sector still employs twice as many as solar, the BLS said.[42]

Government policies can help shift the balance toward renewables, many experts say. "Look at Germany, where there's enormous solar installations but virtually no sun," said Kevin Book, managing director of research at the energy research firm ClearView Energy Partners. "What's the thing that moved solar there? Well, it was government incentive programs."[43]

BACKGROUND
Early Air Pollution

As early as the 13th century, a national leader tried to curb air pollution by restricting the use of fossil fuels.

England's King Edward banned the burning of coal in London because of the smoke it created.[44] However, the ban was largely ineffective, although it may have reduced burning for a while.

By the 17th century, the ill effects of coal smoke were widely recognized, although Londoners' dependence on coal outweighed concerns about health. As energy policy expert Barbara Freese, who wrote a history of coal, noted, "Coal's pollution may have been killing them slowly, but a lack of heat would have killed them quickly."[45]

In the late 18th and early 19th centuries, coal helped fuel the Industrial Revolution in England. The newly invented steam engine, the building of mechanized factories and the growing use of locomotives — all powered by coal — helped transform society. "Thanks in large part to its coal — and its ability to turn that coal into motion as well as heat — Britain would remain the most powerful nation in the world until the end of the 19th century," Freese said.[46]

As the Industrial Revolution spread to other countries, including the fledgling United States, air pollution from soot and smog worsened. The United States had thick forests from which to harvest wood, but it didn't take long before Americans discovered rich coal deposits — including huge coal fields under the Appalachian Mountains and in Illinois and Missouri, states half the size of Europe itself.[47]

Industrialization and coal spurred urbanization in places such as Pittsburgh, which began growing as an industrial town in the late 1700s and became noted for its sooty gloom, even in daytime.[48] Early studies in Germany and the United States documented the existence of lung-related illnesses, including pneumonia, in smoky areas. And yet, "few people then could imagine a world not heavily dependent on coal," according to Freese. "In 1910 natural gas and oil still represented less than 10 percent of the nation's energy supplies, slightly less than wood."[49]

Carbon Dioxide Measured

In the late 1800s a few scientists began to examine the factors determining temperatures on Earth. French physicist Joseph Fourier postulated that the Earth's atmosphere acted like a greenhouse, allowing heat radiation from the sun to be trapped near the planet's surface. In 1862, Irish physicist John Tyndall wrote: "As a dam built across a river causes a local deepening of the stream, so our atmosphere, thrown as a barrier across the terrestrial infrared rays, produces a local heightening of the temperature at the Earth's surface."[50]

Tyndall wondered what components in the atmosphere caused the trapping. With laboratory experiments, he showed that nitrogen and oxygen, the atmosphere's most abundant gases, were transparent to heat rays. In contrast, carbon dioxide-containing coal gas — piped into the laboratory for heat — blocked heat radiation as a solid material might. Tyndall not only determined that carbon dioxide was responsible, but he also found that naturally occurring (and very low) concentrations of carbon dioxide were enough to trap heat radiation in surface air.[51]

The impact of the Ice Age — the opposite of global warming — also captured the imagination of scientists at the time. Geological evidence in North America and Europe showed that glaciers covered much of the two continents 20,000 years earlier. Faced with such evidence, scientists set about theorizing how the Earth's climate could change so dramatically.

In 1896, Swedish scientist Svante Arrhenius reasoned that several geologic and atmospheric events interacted to chill the Earth in a sustained way. Volcanic eruptions add carbon dioxide to the air and can cause warming, in turn leading to more moisture in the atmosphere and a greenhouse effect. What if the opposite happened? A particularly quiet volcanic stretch, Arrhenius suspected, could lead to a drop in carbon dioxide, which might mean cooler temperatures and less atmospheric water vapor, which would mean even less heat trapped near Earth's surface — a vicious cycle of cooling.[52]

Four decades later Englishman Guy Stewart Callendar documented rising temperatures in many different locations on Earth and expanded on Arrhenius' work to study the greenhouse effect of carbon dioxide in the atmosphere. In 1938, Callendar, an engineer by training, presented his data and a new theory to the Royal Meteorological Society in London: that humans were contributing to global warming by burning fossil fuels.[53]

Much of this early work was speculation. What evidence existed came from controlled laboratory experiments and did not include the many dozens of factors that influence the planet's temperature and climate — not the least of which was how much carbon dioxide the oceans can absorb.[54]

CHRONOLOGY

1700s-1930s *Industrialization ramps up and is implicated in climate change.*

1780s-90s Industrial Revolution spreads, replacing handicraft industries with polluting factories.

1862 Irish physicist John Tyndall describes how the Earth's atmosphere acts as a greenhouse, holding warmth close to the ground.

1896 Swedish scientist Svante Arrhenius the- orizes on the geophysical events that brought about the ice age, including reduced atmospheric carbon dioxide.

1938 English engineer Guy Stewart Callendar asserts that burning fossil fuels adds enough carbon dioxide to the atmosphere to affect global temperatures.

1950s-1960s *Geophysics advances include research into pollution, monitoring of the air and new environmental regulations.*

1957-58 International Geophysical Year brings researchers together to explore interdisciplinary questions about Earth science.

1958 Mauna Loa Observatory in Hawaii begins recording atmospheric carbon dioxide concentrations.

1960s Scientists blame coal-burning emissions for acidifying rain and harming fish populations and forests in the Northeast United States and Scandinavia.

1967 Air Quality Act establishes first emission standards in the United States.

1970s *New agencies and regulations address air pollution.*

1970 Nixon administration creates the National Oceanic and Atmospheric Administration and Environmental Protection Agency (EPA). . . . Congress passes Clean Air Act, bringing all previous clean air efforts under one federal statute.

1979 European and North American countries at the United Nations Convention on Long-Range Transboundary Air Pollution agree to cut fossil fuel emissions.

1990s *United States curbs some air pollution.*

1990 In its first report, the new International Panel on Climate Change says the world has been warming. . . . Congress amends Clean Air Act to control acid rain and prohibit leaded gasoline (to reduce lead emissions).

1995 A cap-and-trade scheme to reduce sulfur dioxide emissions, and thereby acid rain, goes into effect in the United States.

1997 Kyoto Protocol sets targets for industrialized nations to reduce greenhouse gas emissions, but Congress never ratifies it. . . . EPA lowers ozone standard to 80 parts per billion (ppb) for public health reasons.

2000-Present *Regulators seek further reductions in carbon emissions and ozone.*

2007 U.S. Supreme Court says EPA must regulate carbon emissions from cars.

2008 EPA lowers the ozone standard to 75 ppb, even though a scientific advisory panel wanted a lower standard — 60 ppb to 65 ppb.

2009 Legislation to create a cap-and- trade mechanism for carbon emissions passes the House but dies in the Senate.

2014 President Obama, citing authority under the Clean Air Act, announces the Clean Power Plan, which regulates carbon emissions from power plants. . . . EPA lowers ozone standard to 70 ppb.

2015 Twenty-five states and industry groups challenge Clean Power Plan. . . . Obama rejects Keystone XL oil pipeline to carry Canadian crude oil to the Gulf of Mexico. . . . World leaders to meet in Paris Nov. 30 for 21st U.N. Climate Change Conference (COP21).

By the 1950s, scientists began measuring carbon dioxide in the atmosphere and in ocean surface waters. Some government funding was secured in 1957-58, when researchers worked together during the International Geophysical Year — a yearlong effort to design ambitious interdisciplinary projects. One involved setting up an instrument atop the volcanic Mauna Loa peak in Hawaii, where Charles David Keeling, a young American scientist, could measure carbon dioxide concentrations in the atmosphere far away from human sources of the gas.[55] (The Mauna Loa observatory still monitors carbon dioxide levels.[56])

Clean Air Act

Several forces led to passage of the Clean Air Act in 1970, including decades of serious smog events that forced people to face the dangers of industrial pollution.

In 1948, a thick cloud of smog formed in Donora, Pa., an industrial town of 14,000, and lingered for five days. The pollution was implicated in the sickening of 6,000 people and the deaths of 20. In 1952, similarly, London's "Killer Fog" killed more than 3,000. [57] Serious smog problems also arose in Los Angeles, where auto pollution gets trapped by the mountain ranges surrounding the city.[58]

Early iterations of the Clean Air Act — both called the Air Pollution Control Act — were passed in 1955 and 1963; both provided funding for research and sought to promote public health and welfare. The 1965 act also funded efforts to curb air pollution from motor vehicles and industrial smokestacks. In 1967, an amendment called the Air Quality Act divided the nation into Air Quality Control Regions, in which states monitored air quality in their regions. The 1967 act also established national emission standards for industry, to be enforced by states.[59]

Pushed by Republican President Richard M. Nixon, the Clean Air Act of 1970 overhauled these previous efforts and pulled together federal anti-pollution programs. It included National Ambient Air Quality Standards for six pollutants: carbon monoxide (CO), nitrogen dioxide (NO_2), ozone (O3), sulfur dioxide (SO_2), particulate matter (particles 10 micrometers or less in size) and lead.[60] The act's New Source Performance Standards strictly regulated new sources of air pollution,

applicable to new facilities as well as expansions of old ones. With clear emissions limits established, the act allowed citizens to sue violators of the standards.[61]

The EPA, created by Nixon the same year, was charged with implementing the new law. The first Earth Day also took place in 1970, the brainchild of Sen. Gaylord Nelson, a Wisconsin Democrat.[62]

Congress revised and expanded the Clean Air Act in 1990, granting even broader authority to the EPA to implement and enforce regulations reducing air pollutant emissions.[63]

Acid Rain

The Clean Air Act also targeted acid rain. Concern over the environmental scourge began in the 1960s, when scientists puzzled over the disappearance of once-plentiful fish species in Swedish and upstate New York lakes. Large stands of trees also were dying in the same areas. Through dogged research, scientists learned that sulfur dioxide emissions from coal-burning power plants were leading to the acidification of rain, making it lethal to fish and trees. The problem crossed state and national borders: Wind-blown pollution from Germany and Britain was poisoning Scandinavia, and pollution from the industrial Midwest in the United States was harming the Northeast and Canada.[64]

Fossil fuels are the main contributor to acid rain, although natural sources such as volcanoes are also a cause. In the United States, coal-fired electric power plants account for about two-thirds of all sulfur dioxide.[65]

"As the evidence linking acid rain to coal poured in, the response of the electric and coal industries was to deny the link, to question the motives of those investigating the connection and always to call for more research," coal historian Freese noted. "In October 1980, the head of the National Coal Association dismissed acid rain as 'a campaign of misleading publicity which seems designed to gain public support for new legislative and regulatory measures.'"[66]

In 1979, governments from Europe and North America met at the United Nations Convention on Long-range Transboundary Air Pollution, where they agreed to cut fossil fuel emissions. The initial agreement funded monitoring efforts; a protocol added in 1985 called for a 30 percent decrease in sulfur dioxide emissions.[67] During the presidency of Republican Ronald Reagan, however,

Wearable Monitors Track Pollution

Scientists debate the reliability of personal sensing devices.

To better understand how cars and trucks contribute to air pollution, environmental scientist Mark Nieuwenhuijsen and his colleagues turned to some unusual helpers — 54 Barcelona schoolchildren ages 7 to 11.

The scientists, who work for the Centre for Research in Environmental Epidemiology, a public research institution in the Spanish city, placed small pollution sensors on the children's clothing, enabling them to collect data on black carbon — a form of soot — common in diesel fumes.[1]

The study is part of a trend in which researchers use wearable monitors to track air pollution in various locations, and at different times of day, so they can gain a more accurate picture of black carbon and other forms of pollution than fixed monitors provide. The scientists also want to better understand individuals' exposure to pollution: A major shortcoming of fixed pollution- monitoring stations, they say, is their inability to track pollution's effects on people in a variety of settings.

Relying only on fixed monitors means "researchers take data from a couple of monitors in a city and assume that everyone in the city has that level of exposure," says Nieuwenhuijsen. However, "the level of a pollutant at a background monitoring station might be quite different than near a major roadway."

A study by academic and government scientists from the United States and Canada found that air quality conditions in Detroit neighborhoods were not well represented by the nearby state of Michigan fixed station. The researchers fitted 65 non- smoking adults in the Detroit area with pollution-monitoring vests, which participants wore for five consecutive days. The participants' blood pressure, checked each evening, increased as the vest monitor showed increases in pollution. The fixed monitor, located two to 18 miles from where participants lived and worked, showed no such correlation between pollutant levels and blood pressure.[2]

In the Barcelona study, which monitored the children around the clock on two typical weekdays during 2012 and 2013, black carbon exposure was low when the children were at home, somewhat higher when they were in school and two to three times higher when they were traveling to and from school.[3]

Small sensors used in other studies can track a range of pollutants, including nitrogen oxides, carbon monoxide and ozone. But critics question their reliability, saying that cheap ones do not work well and that small devices can give inaccurate readings.

Top-of-the-line devices like the ones that Nieuwenhuijsen uses in his studies cost more than $8,000 each. Midrange devices cost about $1,000. But simple sensors can be

the federal government took no regulatory action against acid rain. "By the end of the Reagan administration [in January 1989], Congress had put forward and slapped down 70 different acid rain bills, and frustration ran so deep that Canada's prime minister bleakly joked about declaring war on the United States," wrote one observer of the period.[68]

Still, sulfur dioxide emissions were gradually dropping because of regulations already in the Clean Air Act. It wasn't until 1990 that Congress passed amendments to the act that included a goal to reduce sulfur dioxide emissions by half over the next 20 years.

The 1990 amendment, which had bipartisan support, included a creative market mechanism called cap-and-trade. While the new regulation required cutting all sulfur emissions in half, it allowed individual companies to determine how and where to make those cuts: If a power plant emitted less than its cap, it could sell its remaining allowance to another plant, which would use it to keep under its own cap.[69]

The Environmental Defense Fund helped come up with the idea and worked with the new administration of Republican President George H. W. Bush to create the legislation implementing cap-and-trade.[70]

built from scratch from online instructions for as little as $50 or bought assembled for about $250.

The low-cost sensors target the consumer market and are less reliable and accurate as the top-of-the-line ones, Nieuwenhuijsen says. Moreover, he says, small handheld or wearable sensors, even the pricey ones, tend to be sensitive to changes in temperature and humidity, which can affect results. Environmental researchers typically conduct quality checks to validate the monitors' data.

Ben Barratt, an air-quality scientist at King's College in London, said inaccurate information can invalidate data comparisons. "Monitoring air pollution levels is far more involved than the manu- facturers and suppliers of cheap sensors suggest," he said.[4]

But other scientists say the lower-cost versions have virtues, such as allowing researchers to deploy more monitors to track small variations in pollutant concentrations. "The fact that you can buy 50 low-cost sensors for the cost of one [top-of-the-line] sensor is a tremendously powerful thing," said Joshua Apte, an air quality engineer at the University of Texas, Austin.[5]

University of Pennsylvania researchers used multiple pocketsized monitors to detect black carbon in 17 locations outside homes, schools and parks in a Philadelphia neighborhood located between a major highway and a shipping port. Higher soot levels were recorded closer to the highway and during morning and evening rush hours, moreso than at other times of day or by weather factors.[6]

A number of devices are on the market; one is the Air Quality Egg, made by Ithaca, N.Y.-based Wicked Device, for consumers who want to detect pollution in their immediate environment and to send that information to a central database and a grassroots community online forum for sharing air pollution experiences and information.

Scientists are taking advantage of citizen scientists in Europe to better understand local variation in air pollution in cities such as Athens, London, Rome and Manchester, England. "This is a project that means anyone with the right phone can take part in a real life science experiment, that will produce real data and help us know more about our environment," said University of Manchester chemistry professor Carl Percival.[7]

— Jill U. Adams

[1]Mark J. Nieuwenhuijsen *et al.,* "Variability in and Agreement between Modeled and Personal Continuously Measured Black Carbon Levels Using Novel Smartphone and Sensor Technologies," *Environmental Science & Technology,* Jan. 26, 2015, pp. 2977–2982, http://tinyurl.com/prd37lp.

[2]Robert D. Brook et al., "Differences in Blood Pressure and Vascular Responses Associated with Ambient Fine Particulate Matter Exposures Measure at the Personal versus Community Level," *Occupational and Environmental Medicine,* March 2011, pp. 224–230, http://tinyurl.com/nuosltu.

[3]Nieuwenhuijsen *et al., op. cit.*

[4]Kat Austen, "Environmental science: Pollution patrol," *Nature News,* Jan. 8, 2015, pp. 136–138, http://tinyurl.com/ny2ufbk.

[5]*Ibid.*

[6]Michelle C. Kondo *et al.,* "Black carbon concentrations in a goods-movement neighborhood of Philadelphia, PA," *Environmental Monitoring and Assessment,* July 2014, pp. 4605–4618, http://tinyurl.com/nhpue48.

[7]Quoted in "Citizen science project to measure air pollution," Manchester University press release, Sept. 9, 2015, http://tinyurl.com/p6tfkvr.

The cap on acid-rain-producing emissions took effect in 1995 and had an immediate impact, reducing emissions by 3 million tons in the first year, according to the EPA. Eight years later, the EPA reported that costs to industry averaged $1 billion to $2 billion per year — a quarter of what the agency had predicted and only a tiny fraction of what utility executives had feared.[71] In addition, the health of Adirondack lakes in New York state rebounded, visibility in national parks improved and harms to human health decreased, according to the Environmental Defense Fund.[72]

Regulating Emissions

In 2007, in response to a suit brought by environmental organizations, the Supreme Court ruled that the EPA had authority to regulate carbon dioxide and other greenhouse gases as air pollutants under the Clean Air Act. In the wake of that decision, the EPA concluded that greenhouse emissions did indeed endanger public health and welfare, and in 2010 it issued a final rule on limiting the pollutants from motor vehicles.[73]

Meanwhile, the Democratic-controlled House of Representatives passed a bill to cap carbon emissions from all sources in 2009, modeled on the same cap-and-trade

Germany's Push for Renewables Generates Debate

Supporters see it as a model, critics a warning.

An ambitious plan by Germany to reduce air pollution by phasing out nuclear power and switching to renewable energy is garnering both high praise and bitter criticism.

To its advocates, the *energiewende* — or energy transition — has lowered carbon emissions, created jobs and strengthened Germany's economy. To its critics, the effort has sent domestic energy prices soaring and harmed both utilities and the economy.

Both sides agree *energiewende* is bold: Renewable energy from wind, solar and biomass is supplying more than 30 percent of Germany's electricity, up from 5 percent 15 years ago. Germany wants to increase renewable energy's share of the nation's power supply to about 45 percent by 2025, 60 percent by 2035 and 80 percent by 2050.[1] The nation also seeks to reduce its carbon emissions by 40 percent from 1990 levels by 2020, a far more aggressive goal than the European Union's target of 20 percent.[2]

In contrast, the Obama administration's Clean Power Plan focuses not on renewables but on reducing power plant carbon emissions by 32 percent from 2005 levels by 2030. The energy industry can meet that target by adopting so-called clean-coal technology or switching to natural gas, without necessarily boosting renewable-energy contributions, according to a White House statement.[3]

Germany began weaning itself from fossil fuels in 1999, when the Ecological Tax Reform Act increased taxes on oil and gas and placed a levy on electricity. Higher energy prices helped force the nation to become more energy-efficient and to seek alternative-energy solutions.[4]

In 2014, the German parliament passed comprehensive legislation to decrease carbon emissions, back renewable energy projects and wean the nation from nuclear power, an effort that some international energy experts praised as the world's most far-reaching green power initiative. Economic incentives included feed-in tariffs, which are guaranteed above-market prices for the energy produced by renewable suppliers.[5]

"The German example reveals that, while aligning politics, policies and governance structure for such a transition is a heavy lift requiring robust agenda-setting efforts, implementation occurs quickly and with overwhelming economic benefits once these pieces are in place," wrote Peter Sopher, a policy analyst with the Environmental Defense Fund, an environmental advocacy group in Washington. "Energiewende is creating jobs, raising GDP [gross domestic product] and attracting business."[6]

But some analysts call Germany's plan a costly mistake, saying the price of energy is too high and the country has a glut of unused power. "Germany's renewable energy producers enjoy a guaranteed minimum price for their energy. So they can successfully produce and sell it at a guaranteed price, regardless of what customers want," said Fred Roeder, a Berlin-based economic consultant who now works for the Washington, D.C.-based PR firm Young Voices. "Many farmers and municipalities are producing green energy no one actually needs but are entitled to sell it. In the end, consumers have to pay for it. These policies caused a doubling of energy prices for German consumers over 10 years."[7]

Critics also say the push for renewables has hurt German utilities. "A reckoning is at hand, and nowhere is that clearer than in Germany," wrote *New York Times* economics writer Justin Gillis. "Even as the country sets records nearly every month for renewable power production, the changes have devastated its utility companies, whose profits from power generation have collapsed."[8]

mechanism that had proved successful in reducing acid rain.[74] However, the legislation, popularly called the Waxman-Markey bill (for co-sponsors Rep. Henry Waxman, D-Calif., and Sen. Edward Markey, D-Mass.), died in the Senate.

Many observers blamed Republican opposition and industry lobbying for the bill's failure. But the severe recession — preceded by the 2008 Wall Street meltdown and the bursting of the housing bubble — also contributed to the Senate defeat.[75]

Indeed, by guaranteeing above-market prices for renewable energy, the feed-in tariffs have fostered growth in that sector at the expense of traditional utilities. Recognizing the problem, the government has proposed to roll back those incentives, putting green energy producers in more direct competition with coal-powered energy plants and rebalancing the economic playing field.[9]

Renewable energy in Germany comes from rooftop photovoltaic panels, which contribute 90 percent of the solar energy consumed.[10] In addition, producers are building offshore wind farms in the North and Baltic seas, where the winds blows more regularly than on land.[11] Eight offshore wind farms are in operation and still growing; the country's target is to produce 6,500 megawatts a year from wind by 2020.[12] Germany set a record for a single day's renewable energy use on July 25, when 78 percent of its electricity came from renewable sources.[13]

Despite such a milestone, many analysts predict that, even with its aggressive renewable energy plan, Germany will struggle to meet its carbon emissions goal because the number of cars and other vehicles is rising, and coal still accounts for about 44 percent of the nation's energy.[14]

Political will in Germany has helped the country forge this new path. No one expected to pull it off without a hitch, said Patrick Graichen, who leads a Berlin energy think tank. "The question is: How can we turn the energy transition into a success story?" he said.[15]

— *Jill U. Adams*

German Economy Minister and Vice Chancellor Sigmar Gabriel visits an offshore wind farm in the Baltic Ocean on Aug. 5, 2014, near Barhoeft, Germany.

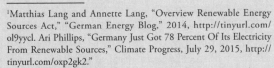

[1]Matthias Lang and Annette Lang, "Overview Renewable Energy Sources Act," "German Energy Blog," 2014, http://tinyurl.com/ol9yycl. Ari Phillips, "Germany Just Got 78 Percent Of Its Electricity From Renewable Sources," Climate Progress, July 29, 2015, http://tinyurl.com/oxp2gk2."

[2]Vera Eckert, "German CO2 emissions in 2014 down 4.1 pct in EU trade scheme," Reuters, May 22, 2015, http://tinyurl.com/ochpvjp.

[3]"Fact Sheet: President Obama to Announce Historic Carbon Pollution Standards for Power Plants," White House press release, Aug. 3, 2015, http://tinyurl.com/nzjl5qh.

[4]Ralph Buehler *et al.*, "How Germany Became Europe's Green Leader: A Look at Four Decades of Sustainable Policymaking," *The Solutions Journal*, October 2011, http://tinyurl.com/3b38t5s.

[5]Peter Dinkloh, "EEG 2.0 — A new legal framework for the German energy transition," *Clean Energy Wire*, Aug. 1, 2014, http://tinyurl.com/qgnu5wl.

[6]Peter Sopher, "Germany is revolutionizing how we use energy . . . and the U.S. could learn a thing or two," "Energy Exchange," Environmental Defense Fund, May 14, 2014, http://tinyurl.com/py6lgrp. Peter Sopher, "While critics debate energiewende, Germany is gaining a global advantage," "Energy Exchange," Environmental Defense Fund, Oct. 6, 2014, http://tinyurl.com/ptgrsee.

[7]Fred Roeder, "What the U.S. can learn from Germany's green energy debacle," *Forbes*, Nov. 7, 2013, http://tinyurl.com/pttrj3x.

[8]Justin Gillis, "Sun and Wind Alter Global Landscape, Leaving Utilities Behind," *The New York Times*, Sept. 13, 2014, http://tinyurl.com/pmld8ej.

[9]Dinkloh, *op. cit.*

[10]"Germany Breaks Solar Power Records Again," *Permaculture*, June 23, 2014, http://tinyurl.com/nlc3y94.

[11]Gillis, *op cit.*

[12]Jorg Luyken, "German offshore wind power breaks records," *The Local*, July 20, 2015, http://tinyurl.com/pre59nz.

[13]Phillips, *op. cit.*

[14]Robert Kunzig, "Germany Could Be a Model for How We'll Get Power in the Future," *National Geographic*, Oct. 15, 2015, http://tinyurl.com/pmldlcn.

[15]Gillis, *op. cit.*

Once the courts determined that carbon dioxide was a pollutant that could be regulated under the Clean Air Act, the EPA began considering how to regulate carbon emissions, which eventually led to Obama's Clean Power Plan.

However, despite efforts in the United States and abroad to mitigate climate change, global temperatures are still rising. The 10 hottest years on record have occurred since 1998; last year was the hottest and 2015 will likely surpass it.[76] The Greenland and Antarctic ice

Rep. Diana DeGette, D-Colo., questions a U.S. Volkswagen official on Oct. 8, 2015, during an Energy and Commerce subcommittee investigating admitted cheating by VW on emissions tests of its diesel-powered cars. In November, as an apology for its cheating, VW offered $1,000 in gift cards and vouchers to the owners of more than 400,000 diesel-powered VWs in the United States.

sheets are shrinking. Sea levels have risen by more than six inches in the last century. And evidence is building that climate change is behind an increasing number of extreme weather events.[77]

CURRENT SITUATION
Global Negotiations

Although President Obama faces domestic opposition to his Clean Power Plan, he is positioning the United States as a willing partner in global efforts to combat carbon emissions. On Nov. 6, he formally rejected the 1,179-mile Keystone XL pipeline, partly out of fears the pipeline, which would have carried carbon-heavy petroleum from the Canadian oil sands to the Gulf Coast, would have contributed to global warming by encouraging the extraction of more oil.[78] In June, he hosted Brazilian President Dilma Rousseff, and the two leaders agreed to increase the amount of electricity their countries generate from renewable sources to 20 percent by 2030, a doubling for Brazil and a tripling for the United States.[79]

When Chinese President Xi Jinping visited Washington in September, he and Obama agreed to tighten carbon emission targets, with the Chinese leadership saying it will use cap-and-trade to achieve reductions.[80] The meeting solidified pledges the two countries made last November. Experts hope the pledges by the two giant economies

will help participating nations reach agreement on emission reductions at the United Nations Conference on Climate Change in Paris at the end of this month.[81]

Aside from its impact on climate change, air pollution overall remains a serious global problem. It kills 3.3 million more people worldwide than HIV and malaria combined, according to an international team of researchers in one of the most detailed reports to date. Published in the journal *Nature*, the study said if current trends hold, the rate of air pollution deaths can be expected to double in only 35 years. China leads in air pollution-related deaths, with an estimated 1.4 million; India and Pakistan follow with 645,000 and 110,000 respectively. The United States is seventh with 55,000 deaths.[82]

Burning of coal, wood and animal dung for heat and cooking, incineration of trash and the use of diesel generators contribute to air pollution in developing countries. The *Nature* study estimated that more than 30 percent of deaths in China and 50 percent of those in India can be attributed to such residential and commercial activity. In contrast, auto and truck pollution was a bigger problem in the United States and Germany, accounting for about 20 percent of premature deaths.[83]

Besides its cap-and-trade program, China hints that it may take the drastic step of barring construction of more coal-fired plants.[84] India lags other nations in anti-pollution programs but is preparing to take the first step — measuring pollutant levels in the air of 10 cities, including Delhi, Agra and Bangalore.[85]

In Europe, vehicular pollution is fouling urban air, experts say, with illegal actions by Volkswagen contributing to the problem. The German-based automaker admitted cheating on government-mandated emissions tests by installing "shielding" software in diesel-powered cars. During the tests, the software switched on pollution controls that limit emissions of nitrogen oxides, but the controls were disabled by the software when owners drove their VWs on the road. Nitrogen oxides, ozone and particulate matter are often above legal limits in large European cities, such as Paris and London, where many cars run on diesel. Some experts say that if Volkswagen's clean diesel fleet had performed as advertised, urban pollution would be less severe.[86]

Canada represents an international bright spot.[87] It ranks among the least-polluted countries. Ontario and Quebec — the country's two largest and most populated provinces — have committed to a cap-and-trade program

AT ISSUE

Is the Clean Power Plan good policy?

YES

David Doniger
Director, Climate and Clean Air
Program, Natural Resources Defense Council

Written for *CQ Researcher*, November 2015

The Clean Power Plan is good policy because it is grounded in federal law, backed by Supreme Court rulings, protects public health and addresses the central, and growing, environmental challenge of our time — climate change.

Congress passed and President Richard M. Nixon signed the Clean Air Act in 1970, creating the nation's fundamental law to address air pollution. In 2007, the Supreme Court ruled that the Environmental Protection Agency (EPA) could limit greenhouse gases if those gases endangered the public's health or welfare. Then, in 2011, the high court ruled that the EPA had the authority to curb pollution from the nation's fleet of power plants under Section 111(d).

Under President Obama's direction, the EPA drafted the Clean Power Plan using that provision. It requires each state, with EPA assistance, to develop "standards of performance" for existing stationary sources such as power plants, and to draft a plan to reach those standards. The performance standards seek to limit emissions through the best system available, taking into account the costs of achieving that reduction.

Our country limits arsenic, lead, soot and other air pollutants, but not the dangerous carbon pollution driving climate change. The Clean Power Plan builds on those policies by setting the first limits on carbon pollution from power plants, the nation's biggest source of carbon emissions. The plan will sharply reduce carbon pollution and other dangerous air pollutants by shifting our electric power system toward cleaner energy sources at a steady but achievable pace, reaching a 32 percent reduction in carbon emissions by 2030.

The Clean Power Plan is also good policy because it is fair and flexible. States and power providers can design their most cost-effective pathway to reduce pollution, and without disrupting the reliability of the nation's energy supply. Reining in power plant pollution will speed America's transition away from fossil fuels, protect our health, help safeguard future generations from the worst effects of climate change and position the United States for global leadership on climate change — all valuable outcomes of sound policy.

The hallmark of good policy is whether it delivers substantial benefits, at reasonable cost, to the American people. The Clean Power Plan exceeds that test. We need it now because it's the most powerful step our country can take to reduce the threat of climate change before it's too late.

NO

JEFF HOLMSTEAD
Partner, Bracewell & Giuliani; Former Assistant
Administrator, Office of Air And Radiation,
Environmental Protection Agency

Written for *CQ Researcher*, November 2015

Regardless of how you feel about climate change, you should be troubled by the Clean Power Plan (CPP). Across the U.S. political spectrum, there has traditionally been a commitment to the rule of law — the notion that public officials, including the president, must act within the authority they have been given by duly elected legislatures and not by executive fiat. The CPP flies in the face of this tradition.

White House officials say they want climate change to be a "legacy issue" for the president. Historically, presidents have secured such a legacy by working with Congress to pass legislation. But when it comes to climate change, the administration has never done the hard work necessary to pass major legislation. To be sure, the president has called for climate change legislation, but the administration never actually developed a legislative proposal or made serious efforts to engage Congress or hammer out a compromise. This stands in stark contrast to the effort the first Bush administration made to secure passage of the 1990 Clean Air Act amendments — the last major piece of environmental legislation adopted in the United States.

Instead of working with Congress, the Obama administration claims to have discovered all the authority it needs to restructure the U.S. electricity system in a short, 45-year-old provision of the Clean Air Act. This obscure provision allows the EPA, under certain limited circumstances, to require states to set an emission standard for individual facilities within their borders based on the best system that can be used to control emissions at such a facility. But the administration makes the remarkable assertion that it gives the EPA authority to shut down coal-fired power plants throughout the country and require wind and solar plants be built to replace them.

The Supreme Court will almost certainly reject the administration's attempt to restructure the electricity system based on a few words in the Clean Air Act. In a recent case that partially invalidated another EPA regulation dealing with climate change, the court went out of its way to state: "When an agency claims to discover in a long-extant statute an unheralded power to regulate 'a significant portion of the American economy,' we typically greet its announcement with a measure of skepticism. We expect Congress to speak clearly if it wishes to assign to an agency decisions of vast 'economic and political significance.' " The Clean Power Plan clearly fails this test.

A man eats dinner at the Christ's Hands soup kitchen and food pantry in Harlan, Ky. Thousands of coal miners in Kentucky and throughout the Appalachian region have lost jobs in recent years as mines have shut down in the face of concern about pollution and safety and the rising use of renewable energy sources.

designed to help reduce carbon emissions by 15 percent to 20 percent below 1990 levels by 2020. Although other provinces have not signed on to cap-and-trade, many have set ambitious targets for carbon emission reductions. British Columbia aims to cut emissions to a third below 2007 levels by 2020, and Saskatchewan wants to reach 20 percent below 2006 levels by 2020.[88]

Canada also has the world's first large-scale carbon capture and storage power plant, a coal-burning power plant that captures carbon dioxide before it escapes the smokestack and pumps it underground, where it is stored. "It just went online," says the Clean Air Task Force's Weeks. According to the plant owners, the technology will cut carbon emissions from the plant by up to 90 percent and prevent 1 million tons of the greenhouse gas from entering the atmosphere each year — the equivalent of taking 250,000 cars off the road.[89]

Carbon-capture technology is expensive, however. A carbon-capture power plant in Texas had been scheduled to go online this year, but progress has stalled, in large part because of economics. The current low prices of oil and natural gas make the costly investment in clean-coal technology seem risky. And current economics favor power companies switching to cleaner-burning natural gas over investments in costly new technology.[90]

Court Fight

In the United States, further progress in cutting carbon emissions may hinge on the courts. Two and a half months after Obama announced the Clean Power Plan, the final rule was published in the *Federal Register*, which makes the regulation official. The same day, 25 states, including coal producers such as West Virginia and Ohio, and industry groups filed lawsuits challenging the rule.[91]

The power industry argues that the Clean Power Plan overreaches because the EPA wrote it to regulate the power sector as a whole rather than at the source — power plant by power plant.[92] "The EPA has gone way beyond its statutory authority," says Jeff Holmstead, who was an EPA lawyer during the George W. Bush administration and is now at the Washington-based law firm Bracewell & Giuliani and often represents energy companies. "All the companies I deal with are concerned about greenhouse gases. And pretty much all of them think that the Clean Power Plan is not a lawful way of doing this."

Much of the dispute focuses on Section 111(d) of the original Clean Air Act, which requires states to develop standards of performance for smokestack pollutants not covered elsewhere in the act. It's a catch-all clause, written to cover harmful pollutants identified after 1970. But, argues Holmstead, carbon dioxide is already covered elsewhere in the Clean Air Act. "EPA has the authority to regulate carbon dioxide, but they can't regulate it under two sections — 112 and 111," he says. (Section 212 covers hazardous air pollutants, including carbon species.)

An Environmental Defense Fund analysis disagreed, stating that "standards under Section 112 must not be 'interpreted, construed or applied to diminish or replace' more stringent requirements under Section 111 — a strong indication that Congress intended for Section 112 to work seamlessly with, not displace, Section 111(d)."[93]

Environmental advocates say the Clean Air Act provides strong legal footing for the Clean Power Plan. "The courts have been quite clear on this matter — carbon dioxide is a pollutant and EPA has the authority to regulate it," the Environmental Defense Fund's Bianco says.

A three-judge panel of the U.S. Court of Appeals for the District of Columbia will consider the lawsuits and issue a ruling. Because the decision by the panel can be appealed to the Supreme Court, the process could take years. In the meantime, some of the same states suing the Obama administration have started drafting plans to comply with the new regulations.[94]

Natural gas, meanwhile, is poised to assume an ever-larger proportion of U.S. power generation. Indeed, for two months in 2015, natural gas generated more electricity than coal, according to the U.S. Energy Information Administration. Many people in industry expect this to become routine. "You just can't go with new coal [plants] at this point in time," said Charles Patton, president of Appalachian Power, a utility that provides electricity for parts of West Virginia, Virginia and Tennessee. "It is just not economically feasible to do so."[95]

OUTLOOK

Obama Agenda

With the Clean Power Plan headed to court, stakeholders are as divided on their predictions as they are on whether the rule is good policy.

"We're very confident that it will survive review," says environmental advocate Doniger.

"It's very likely that it will be overturned, if not in the D.C. Circuit Court, then by the U.S. Supreme Court," says energy industry lawyer Holmstead.

The University of Utah's Reitze says, "It will probably survive. The questionable provisions that were in there were dropped, and the final rule has much stronger legal footing."

"For the next three years, we're going to be involved in lawsuits," says the Clean Air Task Force's Weeks. At the same time, she says, "the states will be moving forward with their plans, and we'll see more movement toward clean solutions." This may mean natural gas replacing coal at power plants, improved carbon capture and more renewables, Week says.

"Companies and industries are looking at solutions," Weeks says, no matter how they see the outcome of legal challenges to the Clean Power Plan. "It's like the stages of grief," she says, describing how companies react to new regulations. "First they say, 'We can't do it! It's too costly! Let's fight back!' With time, they come to grips with their new reality. And eventually they say, 'Wow, that wasn't so bad.' This is exactly what happened with sulfur emissions in the 1970s."

The Clean Power Plan may also become a campaign issue in the 2016 presidential race. Predictably, presidential candidates' opinions of the Clean Power Plan fall along party lines. Democrats support Obama's rule and its goals of mitigating climate change and spurring growth in renewable energy sources. Republicans lambast the rule as job-killing and harmful to families faced with higher electricity bills.

Doniger says voters' views are more nuanced than politicians indicate. "A wide range of polling in blue, purple and even red states consistently shows strong support — usually 60 to 70 percent — for EPA standards to limit dangerous carbon pollution from power plants and other industries," he wrote in his blog. "Support levels are strong — often majorities, even among Republicans — even when respondents are prompted with dire messages of economic impact."[96]

Political observers point out that swing states such as Ohio remain central to the 2016 presidential race, and yet it was one of the hardest-hit states in terms of the Clean Power Plan's goals: Ohio must cut carbon emissions by 37 percent from its 2012 levels. Ohio Gov. and Republican presidential candidate John Kasich calls the Clean Power Plan "an unemployment plan" for his state, which relies on coal for 67 percent of its energy.[97]

If a Republican is elected president, the new administration will likely try to do away with the rule. However, undoing a rule is not as simple as it sounds. "To actually repeal a rule that has already been finalized, EPA would have to go through a new rule-making process, which takes years," said environmental writer Ben Adler. "And it would be challenged in court, forcing the agency to demonstrate a 'rational basis' for its action."[98]

A Republican president could choose not to enforce the regulation, or he or she could approve state plans that do not meet their carbon-reduction targets. The Clean Power Plan says the EPA will create compliance plans for states that come up short, but a Republican administration is not likely to push that action along either.[99]

Much of this debate — how to cut emissions without harming the economy — is also playing out globally. After the Paris talks conclude, individual countries could be forced to deal with recalcitrant legislatures and constituencies and find ways to implement the pledges they made at the conference. Some climate experts warn the Paris pledges will fall short anyway. The main goal, according to scientists, is to prevent global temperatures from rising 2 degrees Celsius by the end of the century.

That's the amount that Earth can withstand and still stave off the most catastrophic consequences of climate change, they say.[100]

Failure could mean frequent extreme weather events such as the heat waves, stronger hurricanes and tsunamis already occurring. Marine ecosystems would be stressed to the point of collapse, according to the Intergovernmental Panel on Climate Change. Food and water security, infrastructure and human health will be threatened.[101]

"At 1 degree we are already experiencing damages," says Anders Levermann, a professor of climate science at the Potsdam Institute for Climate Impact Research in Germany. "Sea-level rise in the long term . . . is somewhere in the vicinity of 2 meters. That puts cities like New York, Calcutta and Shanghai in difficult positions, and they need to protect themselves."

NOTES

1. Tony Barboza, "L.A., Central Valley have worst air quality, American Lung Association says," *Los Angeles Times*, April 29, 2014, http://tinyurl.com/pye5eo6.

2. "State of the Air 2015," American Lung Association, 2015, http://tinyurl.com/pl98d94.

3. J. Lieleveld *et al*, "The contribution of outdoor air pollution sources to premature mortality on a global scale," *Nature*, Sept. 17, 2015, http://tinyurl.com/pvw9dm5.

4. Chris Buckley, "China Burns Much More Coal Than Reported, Complicating Climate Talks," *The New York Times*, Nov. 3, 2015, http://tinyurl.com/ocu7jef.

5. Lieleveld, *op. cit.*

6. Sushmi Dey, "Air pollution is world's top environmental health risk, WHO says," *The Economic Times*, June 2, 2015, http://tinyurl.com/nmmswcj.

7. Stacy Simon, "World Health Organization: Outdoor Air Pollution Causes Cancer," American Cancer Society, Oct. 17, 2013, http://tinyurl.com/oby8too.

8. Andrew C. Revkin, "Starting Later This Year, 400 and Up is Likely to Be the New Normal for CO2 Measurements," *The New York Times*, Oct. 22, 2015, http://tinyurl.com/p6mk9ng; Joby Warrick, "Greenhouse gases hit new milestone, fueling worries about climate change," *The Washington Post*, Nov. 8, 2015, http://tinyurl.com/otsq2dv.

9. Justin Gillis and Somini Sengupta, "Limited Progress Seen Even as More Nations Step Up on Climate," *The New York Times*, Sept. 28, 2015, http://tinyurl.com/q7vb89t.

10. "Fact Sheet: President Obama to Announce Historic Carbon Pollution Standards for Power Plants," press release, The White House, Aug. 3, 2015, http://tinyurl.com/nzjl5qh.

11. "Overview of Greenhouse Gases," Environmental Protection Agency, undated, http://tinyurl.com/nuuf3x4.

12. "'Clean Coal' Technologies, Carbon Capture & Sequestration," World Nuclear Association, August 2015, http://tinyurl.com/nnepfmv.

13. David Doniger, "The Clean Air Act and Climate Change: Where We've Been and Where We're Going," "Switchboard," Natural Resources Defense Council, Nov. 18, 2014, http://tinyurl.com/q3x6swq.

14. Environmental Protection Agency, *op. cit.*

15. "Fact Sheet: President Obama to Announce Historic Carbon Pollution Standards for Power Plants," *op. cit.*

16. "The Clean Power Plan: An Idea that will Change the World," press release, Natural Resources Defense Council, Aug. 3, 2015, http://tinyurl.com/nnhexby.

17. Valerie Volcovici and Lawrence Hurley, "States, business groups challenge Obama's carbon rules in court," Reuters, Oct. 23, 2015, http://tinyurl.com/ncjmadm.

18. "ACCCE Blasts Finalized EPA Carbon Emissions Rule," press release, American Coalition for Clean Coal Electricity, Aug. 3, 2015, http://tinyurl.com/oxdzfk7.

19. "Energy-Related Carbon Dioxide Emissions at the State Level, 2000-2013," Energy Information Administration, Oct. 26, 2015, http://tinyurl.com/cxtk7l6.

20. Mallory Micetich, "NAM Launches New Ozone Ads Highlighting Progress of Manufacturing and Bipartisan Opposition to Proposed Regulation," press release, National Association of Manufacturers, Sept. 25, 2015, http://tinyurl.com/nzxk86e.

21. "American Lung Association Responds to EPA Ozone Standard Update, Impact on Public Health,"

American Lung Association press release, Oct. 1, 2015, http://tinyurl.com/qc52gvt.

22. Colleen McCain Nelson and Amy Harder, "Obama Announces Rule to Cut Carbon Emissions from Power Plants," *The Wall Street Journal*, Aug. 3, 2015, http://tinyurl.com/phv8ckg.

23. David Doniger and Derek Murrow, "Understanding the EPA's Clean Power Plan," "Switchboard," Natural Resources Defense Council, Aug. 11, 2015, http://tinyurl.com/ompe9n4; Ann Weeks and Jay Duffy, "Let's Go EPA — Remain Strong on Power Plant Rules!" "Ahead of the Curve," Clean Air Task Force, June 15, 2015, http://tinyurl.com/on3ye8g; and "A new national Clean Power Plan," Environmental Defense Fund, undated, http://tinyurl.com/q5aj4oy.

24. "Indiana Gov. Michael R. Pence to President Obama," *Scribd*, June 24, 2015, http://tinyurl.com/oefbywo.

25. Doniger and Murrow, *op. cit.*

26. "Solyndra scandal timeline," *The Washington Post*, December 2011, http://tinyurl.com/l54e7jz.

27. Juliet Eilperin and Joby Warrick, "Obama administration tightens smog limits but satisfies few," *The Washington Post*, Oct. 1, 2015, http://tinyurl.com/nbzzujz.

28. Coral Davenport, "New Limit for Smog-Causing Emissions Isn't as Strict as Many Had Expected," *The New York Times*, Oct. 1, 2015, http://tinyurl.com/o4ru35s.

29. *Ibid.*

30. *Ibid.*

31. David W. Johnson, "Ozone standard will be crippling," *The Times and Democrat* (Orangeburg, S.C.), Sept. 29, 2015, http://tinyurl.com/ooodtbs.

32. Jill U. Adams, "A closer look: Setting a 'safer' ozone level," *Los Angeles Times*, Sept. 26, 2011, http://tinyurl.com/nz2r6dx.

33. "Fact Sheet: Supplement to the Regulatory Impact Analysis for Ozone," Environmental Protection Agency, Jan. 7, 2010, http://tinyurl.com/pgnfv83.

34. Frank O'Donnell, "Clean Air Watch Reaction to EPA Smog Decision," press release, Clean Air Watch, Oct. 1, 2015, http://tinyurl.com/nf8wgxr.

35. Daniel Cusick and Climate Wire, "Solar Power Grows 400 Percent in Only 4 Years," *Scientific American*, April 24, 2014, http://tinyurl.com/melak56.

36. "Wind Energy Facts at a Glance," American Wind Energy Association, undated, http://tinyurl.com/mg2ofvs. "Wind Energy Facts at a Glance," American Wind Energy Association, undated, http://tinyurl.com/mg2ofvs.

37. Etienne te Brake, "DNV GL Survey: 82 percent of global industry respondents say electricity system can be 70 percent renewable by 2050," DNV GL, March 18, 2015, http://tinyurl.com/orsagdx.

38. Quoted in "President Obama Announces New Limits on Power Plant Carbon Emissions," "The Diane Rehm Show," Aug. 4, 2015, http://tinyurl.com/prfydx8.

39. *Ibid.*

40. Tristan Edis, "Bloomberg sees a solar power takeover," *Business Spectator*, July 2, 2014, http://tinyurl.com/o2c43qz.

41. Christopher Helman, "Solar Power is Booming, But Will Never Replace Coal. Here's Why," *Forbes*, April 24, 2014, http://tinyurl.com/lgdxpl2.

42. Robert McManmon, "Power sector employment declines, except for renewable electricity generators," *Today in Energy*, Dec. 19, 2014, http://tinyurl.com/kc4ee9t.

43. "The Diane Rehm Show," *op. cit.*

44. David Urbinato, "London's Historic 'Pea-Soupers,'" *EPA Journal*, Summer 1994, http://tinyurl.com/on2cz37.

45. Barbara Freese, *Coal: A Human History* (2003), pp. 40-41.

46. *Ibid.*, pp. 43-69.

47. *Ibid.*, p. 105.

48. *Ibid.*, pp. 108-109.

49. *Ibid.*, pp. 153.

50. Spencer R. Weart, *The Discovery of Global Warming* (2008), pp. 2-4.

51. *Ibid.*

52. *Ibid.*, pp. 4-5, 53.

53. *Ibid.*, p. 2.

54. *Ibid.*, pp. 26-27.

55. *Ibid.*, pp. 33-35.

56. "The Keeling Curve," Scripps Institution of Oceanography, Nov. 3, 2015, http://tinyurl.com/lrvgj2z.

57. "Understanding the Clean Air Act," Environmental Protection Agency, "Plain English Guide to the Clean Air Act," Sept. 10, 2015, http://tinyurl.com/o57gt7y.

58. Sarah Gardner, "LA Smog: the battle against air pollution," "Marketplace," July 14, 2014, http://tinyurl.com/mfudhkl.

59. James R. Fleming and Bethany R. Knorr, "History of the Clean Air Act," American Meteorological Society, 1999, http://tinyurl.com/oonadp2.

60. "Clean Air Act Requirements and History," Environmental Protection Agency, http://tinyurl.com/o2me86d.

61. Fleming and Knorr, *op. cit.*

62. "Understanding the Clean Air Act," *op. cit.*

63. *Ibid.*

64. Freese, *op. cit.*, p. 169.

65. "What is Acid Rain?" Environmental Protection Agency, Dec. 4, 2012, http://tinyurl.com/ogt4ct7.

66. Freese, *op. cit.*, p. 170.

67. "The 1979 Geneva Convention on Long-range Transboundary Air Pollution," United Nations Economic Commission for Europe, undated, http://tinyurl.com/nnmd4hj; Rachel Rothschild, "Acid Wash," *Foreign Affairs*, Aug. 24, 2015, http://tinyurl.com/ods6myj.

68. Richard Coniff, "The Political History of Cap and Trade," *Smithsonian*, August 2009, http://tinyurl.com/prvwx42.

69. "Acid Rain: The power of markets to help the planet," Environmental Defense Fund, undated, http://tinyurl.com/o7p27bd.

70. Coniff, *op. cit.*

71. "Cap and Trade: Acid Rain Program Results," Environmental Protection Agency, undated, http://tinyurl.com/neunfa6; Coniff, *op. cit.*

72. "Acid Rain: The power of markets to help the planet," *op. cit.*

73. "Background and History of EPA Regulation of Greenhouse Gas Emissions Under the Clean Air Act," National Association of Clean Air Agencies, July 19, 2011, http://tinyurl.com/owo497l.

74. Chris Arnold, "GOP Demonizes Once Favored Cap-And-Trade Policy," NPR, June 3, 2014, http://tinyurl.com/py5sto9.

75. Daniel J. Weiss, "Anatomy of a Senate Climate Bill Death," Center for American Progress, Oct. 12, 2010, http://tinyurl.com/psrbpjz.

76. Justin Gillis, "2015 Likely to Be Hottest Year Ever Recorded," *The New York Times*, Oct. 21, 2015, http://tinyurl.com/po7949b.

77. "Climate change: How do we know?" NASA, undated, http://tinyurl.com/yhsnaz8.

78. Coral Davenport, "Citing Climate Change, Obama Rejects Construction of Keystone XL Oil Pipeline," *The New York Times*, Nov. 6, 2015, http://tinyurl.com/qaqkcbg.

79. Coral Davenport, "Global Climate Pact Gains Momentum as China, U.S. and Brazil Detail Plans," *The New York Times*, June 30, 2015, http://tinyurl.com/ofhonn3.

80. David Stanway, "China-US deal sets bar low ahead of Paris climate talks," Reuters, Sept. 28, 2015, http://tinyurl.com/naxtsal.

81. *Ibid.*

82. Lieleveld *et al.*, *op. cit.*

83. Michael Jerrett, "The death toll from air-pollution sources," *Nature*, Sept. 17, 2015, http://tinyurl.com/pz9pmz4.

84 Keith Johnson, "China's Leaner and Greener 5-year Plan," *Foreign Policy*, Oct. 30, 2015, http://tinyurl.com/q6zu7bn.

85. Andrew Freedman, "India, home to the world's most polluted city, launches air quality index," *Mashable*, April 6, 2015, http://tinyurl.com/pahf2os.

86. Matthew Dalton, "Volkswagen Scandal Puts Spotlight on Europe's Dirty Air," *The Wall Street Journal*, Oct. 13, 2015, http://tinyurl.com/p73cxdt; Tom Krisher, "AP News Guide: A look at the Volkswagen emissions scandal," *The Washington Post*, Nov. 5, 2015, http://tinyurl.com/pnkxpaz.

87. "Canada's air quality 3rd best in the world," CBC News, Sept. 26, 2011, http://tinyurl.com/qhmpewh.

88. Kazi Stastna, "How Canada's provinces are tackling greenhouse gas emissions," CBC News, April 14, 2015, http://tinyurl.com/mtu8u7g.

89. Suzanne Goldenberg, "Canada switches on world's first carbon capture power plant," *The Guardian*, Oct. 1, 2014, http://tinyurl.com/l9qtkd4.

90. Jordan Blum, "Low oil prices cloud futures of clean coal and carbon capture," *Houston Chronicle*, Oct. 2, 2015, http://tinyurl.com/p6dccz3.

91. Valerie Volcovici and Lawrence Hurley, "States, business groups challenge Obama's carbon rules in court," Reuters, Oct. 23, 2015, http://tinyurl.com/ncjmadm.

92. *Ibid.*

93. Tomas Carbonell, "Misguided Legal Attacks on Clear Power Plan Seek to Undermine Clean Air Act, Public Participation," "Climate 411," Environmental Defense Fund, Feb. 13, 2015, http://tinyurl.com/qhs7vwc.

94. Volcovici and Hurley, *op. cit.*; Coral Davenport, "Numerous States Prepare Lawsuits Against Obama's Climate Policy," *The New York Times*, Oct. 22, 2015, http://tinyurl.com/nu5xd8a.

95. Chris Mooney, "How super low natural gas prices are reshaping how we get our power," *The Washington Post*, Oct. 28, 2015, http://tinyurl.com/oaqv8tp.

96. Doniger, "The Clean Air Act and Climate Change," *op. cit.*

97. Philip A. Wallach, "Will the Clean Power Plan Swing the 2016 Presidential Election?" "FixGov" blog, Brookings Institution, Aug. 11, 2015, http://tinyurl.com/pfmokc3.

98. Ben Adler, "Here's how a Republican president could undermine the Clean Power Plan," *Grist*, Aug. 5, 2015, http://tinyurl.com/oe2cdpv.

99. *Ibid.*

100. Robin McKie, "World will pass crucial 2C global warming limit, experts warn," *The Guardian*, Oct. 10, 2015, http://tinyurl.com/p234y6x.

101. Roz Pidcock, "What happens if we overshoot the two degree target for limiting global warming?" *Carbon Brief*, Oct. 12, 2014, http://tinyurl.com/nw8c2vd.

BIBLIOGRAPHY

Selected Sources

Books

Freese, Barbara, *Coal: A Human History*, Perseus Publishing, 2003.
A former Minnesota assistant attorney general who helped enforce the state's air-pollution laws traces the use of coal over centuries, including during the Industrial Revolution.

Jacobson, Mark Z., *Air Pollution and Global Warming: History, Science, and Solutions*, Cambridge University Press, 2012.
A Stanford University professor of civil and environmental engineering integrates scientific study and policy approaches in a textbook addressing the modern problems of air pollution.

Lenart, Melanie, *Life in the Hothouse: How a Living Planet Survives Climate Change*, University of Arizona Press, 2010.
An environmental scientist and writer describes how the Earth responds to changes in climate.

McDaniel, Carl N., *Wisdom for a Livable Planet*, Trinity University Press, 2005.
A Rensselaer Polytechnic University biology professor profiles eight environmental activists who have worked to improve the environment.

Weart, Spencer R., *The Discovery of Global Warming*, Harvard University Press, 2008.
An historian trained in physics details the history of climate-change research.

Articles

Coniff, Richard, "The Political History of Cap and Trade," *Smithsonian Magazine*, August 2009, http://tinyurl.com/prvwx42.
A business journalist details how environmentalists and free-market conservatives created a mechanism for trading emissions credits.

Eilperin, Juliet, and Joby Warrick, "Obama administration tightens smog limits but satisfies few," *The Washington Post*, Oct. 1, 2015, http://tinyurl.com/nbzzujz.
Environmentalists say a stricter EPA ozone standard does not go far enough.

Jerrett, Michael, "The death toll from air-pollution sources," *Nature*, Sept. 17, 2015, http://tinyurl.com/pz9pmz4.
A University of California-Los Angeles environmental health sciences professor analyzes the latest study on worldwide deaths from air pollution.

McBride, James, "Modernizing the U.S. Energy Grid," Council on Foreign Relations, Aug. 3, 2015, http://tinyurl.com/phw5hwp.
A writer for a think tank provides background on how the nation's power grid works and what needs to change as wind and solar energy comes online.

Nelson, Colleen McCain, and Amy Harder, "Obama Announces Rule to Cut Carbon Emissions from Power Plants," *The Wall Street Journal*, Aug. 3, 2015, http://tinyurl.com/phv8ckg.
President Obama unveils the Clean Power Plan aimed at tightening carbon dioxide emissions.

Nuccitelli, Dana, "Is the fossil fuel industry, like the tobacco industry, guilty of racketeering?" *The Guardian*, Sept. 29, 2015, http://tinyurl.com/of9ubvh.
ExxonMobil scientists warned about the dangers of climate change years before the company began attacking climate research, *InsideClimate News* alleges.

Pearce, Fred, "Will the Paris Climate Talks Be Too Little and Too Late?" *Yale Environment 360*, Sept. 14, 2015, http://tinyurl.com/nche5uc.
An environmental consultant takes a broad look at the global political scene on climate change and reducing carbon emissions in advance of the 2015 United Nations Climate Change Conference in Paris.

Powell, Alvin, "Air Pollution's Invisible Toll," *Environment@Harvard*, June 9, 2014, http://tinyurl.com/ndh2ten.
A study documents the health effects of air pollution over two decades in six American cities.

Reports and Studies

"Advancing the Science of Climate Change," National Academy of Sciences, 2010, http://tinyurl.com/a3u2xu8.
The research group provides an in-depth look at the scientific evidence for climate change.

"Climate Change 2014: Synthesis Report Summary for Policymakers," Intergovernmental Panel on Climate Change, 2014, http://tinyurl.com/q4jnuxj.
The Intergovernmental Panel on Climate Change presents the latest in a series of reports on how humans are accelerating climate change.

"Issue Brief: What to Expect in Clean Power Plan Litigation," Natural Resources Defense Council, 2015, http://tinyurl.com/pdu3dbq.
The environmental advocacy group reports on the legal aspects of challenges to the Clean Power Plan.

"State of the Air 2015," American Lung Association, 2015, http://tinyurl.com/o9mvuen.
The health advocacy group presents its latest report on ozone and particle pollution in the United States.

For More Information

American Coalition for Clean Coal Electricity, 1152 15th St., N.W., Suite 400, Washington, DC 20005; 202-459-4800; www.americaspower.org. Partnership organization of the coal industry; advocates for the responsible use of coal.

Clean Air Task Force, 18 Tremont St., Suite 530, Boston, MA 02108; 617-292-0234; www.catf.us. Nonprofit environmental group that provides research and analysis aimed at finding solutions for climate change.

Energy Institute at the University of Texas, Flawn Academic Center, FAC 428, 2304 Whitis Ave., Stop C2400, Austin, TX 78712; 512-475-8447; http://energy.utexas.edu. Academic center that provides research and develops technology that aims to inform and improve energy policy.

Environmental Defense Fund, 257 Park Ave., South, New York, NY 10010; 800-684-3322; www.edf.org. Environmental advocacy organization that seeks ways to protect the environment.

Intergovernmental Panel on Climate Change, c/o World Meteorological Organization, 7bis Avenue de la Paix, C.P. 2300, CH 1211 Geneva 2, Switzerland; +41- 22-730-8208; www.ipcc.ch/index.htm. U.N body assessing global climate change.

National Association of Manufacturers, 733 10th St., N.W., Suite 700, Washington, DC 20001; 800-814-8468; www.nam.org. Trade association representing small and large American manufacturers.

Natural Resources Defense Council, 40 W. 20th St., New York, NY 10011; 212- 727-2700; www.nrdc.org. Nonprofit group that conducts public education on environmental issues, such as how to combat global climate change.

U.S. Environmental Protection Agency, 1200 Pennsylvania Ave., N.W., Washington, DC 20460; 202-272-0167; http://www3.epa.gov. Federal agency that develops and enforces regulations to support environmental legislation enacted by Congress. Also awards grants and publishes information related to environmental issues in the United States.

2

Pesticide Controversies

Jennifer Weeks

AP Photo/Kathy Willens

Beekeeper Kellen Henry inspects bees from a community garden hive in Brooklyn in October 2013. Pesticides are among several factors thought to have caused a serious bee die-off in the United States since 2006. Between April 2014 and April 2015, about 42 percent of the honeybees in managed colonies died. Insects — mainly bees — pollinate an estimated $16 billion worth of crops yearly.

From *CQ Researcher*,
June 5, 2015.

Every winter, as bald eagles gather around rivers and lakes to feed on fish, scientists and birdwatchers fan out across the United States to count the birds. This year's tally was high from New England to the Southwest, and many sites set records.[1]

The numbers confirmed a dramatic turnaround. A half-century ago, hunting, development and DDT — a highly toxic pesticide that had been widely used on crops, city parks and suburban backyards since the late 1940s — had winnowed the number of bald eagles almost to extinction.

In 1967 only an estimated 467 breeding pairs were scattered across the continental United States.[2] DDT killed many insect pests, but it also concentrated in aquatic plants and fish. When eagles ate the fish, DDT built up in their bodies and caused females to produce eggs with thin, weak shells. Many eggs broke in nests or failed to hatch.

After the U.S. Environmental Protection Agency (EPA) banned DDT in 1972, the bald eagle population slowly recovered.[3] By 2006, the lower 48 states had 9,789 breeding pairs. In 2007 the eagles were removed from the federal Endangered Species List.[4]

While bald eagles have rebounded, many scientists and health and environmental advocates argue that farmers, ranchers, homeowners and business operators remain far too reliant on other pesticides. Modern pesticides typically are more targeted at certain pests, less toxic than DDT and do not persist in the environment for long periods. But some widely used versions nonetheless threaten human health and wildlife, experts contend. A major concern is whether

Most Pesticides Used on Corn, Soybeans

Corn, soybeans, potatoes and cotton accounted for nearly 79 percent of pesticides applied to 21 selected U.S. crops in 2008, the latest year for which the U.S. Department of Agriculture has figures. The remainder was used on wheat, sorghum and 15 other crops, mostly fruits and vegetables.

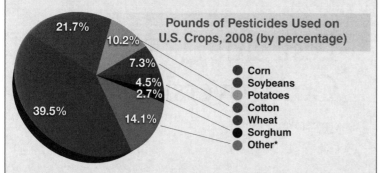

Pounds of Pesticides Used on U.S. Crops, 2008 (by percentage)

- Corn
- Soybeans
- Potatoes
- Cotton
- Wheat
- Sorghum
- Other*

21.7%
10.2%
7.3%
4.5%
2.7%
39.5%
14.1%

Includes oranges, peanuts, tomatoes, grapes, rice, apples, sugarcane, lettuce, pears, sweet corn, barley, peaches, grapefruit, pecans and lemons.

Source: Jorge Fernandez-Cornejo et al., "Pesticide Use in U.S. Agriculture: 21 Selected Crops, 1960-2008," Economic Research Service and U.S. Department of Agriculture, May 2014, p. 16, http://tinyurl.com/q66a4es

pesticides are killing bees and other insects that pollinate many U.S. food crops.

"Regulators need to take a very different approach to licensing and regulating pesticides," says Mark Winston, a biologist at Simon Fraser University in British Columbia, Canada, who is renowned for his expertise on bee health. "The goal should be to reduce their use in agriculture. We should think of pesticides like veterinary medicines that require a prescription to use."

Americans used about 1.1 billion pounds of pesticides in 2007, the most recent year for which data are available, including products targeted against insects (insecticides), weeds (herbicides), molds (fungicides) and other species such as rats and mice. About 77 percent of pesticides were used in agriculture, and the rest in homes and industrial and commercial facilities, such as factories and office buildings.[5]

Under the Federal Insecticide, Fungicide, and Rodenticide Act (FIFRA), pesticide manufacturers must register their products with the EPA and provide test data on each pesticide's toxicity. The EPA approves pesticides only for specific uses, such as controlling certain species of worms on tomatoes. Using pesticides in ways not approved and listed on their labels is illegal.

Companies that produce and apply pesticides say this system effectively protects workers, consumers and the environment. "Manufacturers spend tens of millions of dollars on studies to determine product safety," says Ray McAllister, senior director for regulatory policy at CropLife America, a trade association in Washington representing pesticide manufacturers. "And when a product is approved, testing doesn't end. We are always working to understand interactions with the environment and impacts on human health."

But health experts say exposure to pesticides can be hazardous, especially over time. A 2010 report from the President's Cancer Panel — a high-level federal advisory committee — warned: "The entire U.S. population is exposed on a daily basis to numerous agricultural chemicals, some of which also are used in residential and commercial landscaping. Many of these chemicals have known or suspected carcinogenic or endocrine-disrupting properties."[6] *

Studies of farmworkers who handle pesticides routinely have found evidence of health risks. The Agricultural Health Study by federal agencies has been examining effects on thousands of Iowa and North Carolina farmers and their wives since 1993. Recent findings show that exposure to various pesticides is associated with increased risk of developing Parkinson's disease, depression and lung cancer.[7] Pesticide exposure may also increase the risk of allergic asthma, diabetes, thyroid disease and colorectal and pancreatic cancer and melanoma.[8]

* Endocrine disruptors are chemicals that mimic or block the actions of hormones and disrupt the body's endocrine system — a network of glands that regulates growth and many other body functions.

Consumers are exposed to pesticide residues in food, especially fruits and vegetables. In the 1996 Food Quality Protection Act, Congress directed the EPA to set lower limits for pesticide residues in foods so that they pose a "reasonable certainty of no harm." The law was enacted after a National Research Council study concluded that prior limits were so high that they were allowing infants and children — who are especially vulnerable to toxic substances — to be exposed to unsafe doses of pesticides.[9]

"Exposures to the most toxic pesticides have been drastically reduced in the past 15 years," says Michael Hansen, a senior scientist with Consumers Union, a consumer-protection advocacy group. "Many of the most harmful products have been taken off the market." In his view, however, the EPA should make studying health risks from pesticides that are endocrine disrupting chemicals (EDCs) a higher priority. The problem, Hansen argues, is that the EPA sets standards for pesticide residues in food based on maximum safe doses, but EDCs may cause harm through very low-level exposures.

"Endocrine disruptors raise fundamental problems for traditional toxicology, and they have not been studied adequately," Hansen says.[10]

More than 100 pesticides already have been identified as endocrine disruptors.[11] Congress has charged the EPA with testing numerous chemicals for endocrine effects: all chemicals in pesticides (including both active and inert ingredients), and other substances that could be found in drinking water. In total, the agency estimates that these mandates could include some 10,000 chemicals, although not all are likely to be screened.[12] The EPA expects to finish screening 67 chemicals this year to see whether they have potential endocrine effects, and is shifting to faster, less expensive laboratory techniques for a second list of 107 chemicals.[13]

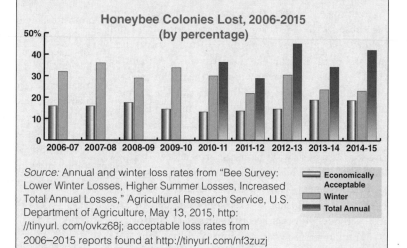

Honeybee Losses Higher than 'Acceptable'

About 42 percent of honeybees in managed (domesticated) colonies died between April 2014 and April 2015, more than double the 18.7 percent die-off rate that beekeepers say is economically acceptable. It was the second-highest annual loss since researchers began measuring such losses in 2010. Winter losses, which are expected each year, have been improving since peaking in 2007–08 at 36 percent. Scientists say pesticides are one of several factors causing bees to die at economically unacceptable rates since 2006.

Honeybee Colonies Lost, 2006-2015 (by percentage)

Source: Annual and winter loss rates from "Bee Survey: Lower Winter Losses, Higher Summer Losses, Increased Total Annual Losses," Agricultural Research Service, U.S. Department of Agriculture, May 13, 2015, http://tinyurl. com/ovkz68j; acceptable loss rates from 2006–2015 reports found at http://tinyurl.com/nf3zuzj

Earlier this year the International Agency for Research on Cancer (IARC), part of the United Nations' World Health Organization, declared that glyphosate — the active ingredient in the weed killer Roundup and many other broad-spectrum herbicides (products that kill many types of weeds) — probably causes cancer in humans. Monsanto, the company that originally patented glyphosate and markets Roundup, strongly disagreed.

Philip Miller, Monsanto's vice president for global regulatory affairs, called the IARC's finding "a dramatic departure from the conclusion reached by all regulatory agencies around the globe" and asserted that the IARC had excluded studies showing that glyphosate was not a health risk.[14]

The EPA is reviewing glyphosate's standing but does not currently believe it is carcinogenic.[15] Consumers Union and other advocacy groups have urged the EPA to "weigh heavily" IARC's decision. They noted that glyphosate use has risen in recent years as farmers have planted vast quantities of corn and soybeans genetically engineered to be "Roundup Ready," a registered trademark for seeds modified to make them resistant to glyphosate. Farmers who plant these varieties can spray the herbicides widely without harming crops.

"It is very likely that millions of Americans inhale glyphosate during the application season," the groups argued. "The chemical also likely contaminates rivers, lakes and reservoirs that serve as drinking water sources for millions of Americans."[16]

In the past EPA and other regulatory agencies, including those in the 28-nation European Union, did not believe that glyphosate residues in food threatened human health, and the U.S. Department of Agriculture (USDA) does not currently test for them. But in April the EPA, which reportedly will release a new assessment of risks from glyphosate soon, said it might advise the USDA to begin testing for the herbicide in food.[17]

Environmentalists, sustainable agriculture advocates and some scientists want more resources allocated to pest control methods that rely less on chemicals. Integrated pest management (IPM) is an alternative strategy that emphasizes monitoring for pests and using benign control methods, with chemical pesticides as a last resort.

"Human nature wants to control things, but IPM emphasizes economics, the environment and human health equally," says Stephen Young, director of the USDA's Northeastern IPM Center at Cornell University.

Although IPM has been researched since the late 1960s and the general concept is widely accepted, no authoritative definition of what it means to be "doing" IPM exists, so it is hard to quantify how broadly it is being used.

Another promising option is biopesticides — controls based on natural organisms such as plant and soil microbes, rather than synthetic chemicals. Biopesticides typically are less toxic than synthetic pesticides, affect only their target pests, break down quickly in the environment and are effective in very small quantities. Synthetic chemical pesticides have dominated the market for decades, but as more insects and weeds develop resistance to these products, interest in biopesticides is growing.

As industry officials, scientists, regulators and consumer advocates debate the public health and environmental effects of pesticides, here are some issues they are addressing:

Are pesticides killing off bees?

Many people may view both bees and plant pollen, which often triggers allergies, as nuisances. But without bees and other insects that fertilize plants by carrying pollen from one flower to another, people's diets would be much less interesting.

In the United States alone, insects pollinate an estimated $16 billion worth of crops every year. Honeybees do three-quarters of this work. Many key crops — including apples, broccoli, carrots and onions — depend almost totally on insect pollinators.[18]

Honeybees, monarch butterflies and other pollinators have been declining worldwide for several decades. In 2006, U.S. bee keepers began to report adult bees disappearing from hives, leaving queens and a few immature insects behind. This syndrome, which researchers could not explain, came to be known as colony collapse disorder (CCD).[19]

In a normal year about 10 percent of the bees in a colony might die during winter, but from 2006–2011 annual losses averaged about 33 percent. Some beekeepers lost 90 percent of their bees in a single year. Winter losses have eased since 2012, but beekeepers still lost a total of 42 percent of their colonies in 2014–2015.[20] Today the United States has about 2.5 million managed (domesticated) bee colonies, half the number in the 1940s.[21]

Beekeepers blamed CCD for about one-third of the 2006–2011 losses. Other stresses include pathogens and pests that prey on bees — especially varroa mites that suck honeybees' blood — and industrial beekeeping, in which beekeepers put hives on trucks and drive thousands of miles in a year, stopping to let bees pollinate local crops.

"Farmers have become dependent on bringing in managed honeybees to do the job that nature used to do for them," says Winston of Simon Fraser University. "But moving long-distance is very stressful for bees."

Climate change may also be a factor. Many studies have shown that flowers are blooming and pollinators are taking flight earlier in spring as temperatures warm.[22] But some researchers have found that these changes are not happening at the same speed, and warn that if bees emerge before or after flowers bloom, pollination may decline.[23]

Scientists say pesticides also are stressing bees. A study published in 2010 found 121 different pesticides in bees' wax honeycombs, including chemicals that beekeepers used to kill mites and other bee parasites, along with pesticides and herbicides used on field crops. Many of the pesticides were known to be toxic to bees, and some had been withdrawn from the market well before the study was carried out.[24]

"Both field pesticides and miticides [which kill mites] can affect bees' immune systems," says Winston. "We are seeing interactions between low levels of many pesticides and increasing disease problems, such as mites. These very subtle interactive effects are turning out to be catastrophic."

Large-scale intensive agriculture also is a factor, Winston says. "When farmers plant crops that are genetically modified to tolerate herbicides and then use heavy amounts of weed killer, they eliminate virtually all weeds, which are extremely important forage for honeybees and wild bees," he says. "Even though herbicides aren't directly toxic to bees, they have transformed the habitat in which bees forage. Their diet has become very limited."

In the past several years studies have identified a class of pesticides called neonicotinoids (so named because they are chemically similar to nicotine) as harmful to bees. Introduced in the early 1990s, neonicotinoids were thought to be less toxic to honeybees than earlier classes of insecticides. But an international scientific panel that reviewed more than 1,100 published papers concluded in 2014 that neonicotinoids were harming many beneficial species, including earthworms, bees, butterflies and freshwater snails.[25]

"There is an urgent need to reduce the use of these chemicals and to switch to sustainable methods of food production and pest control that do not further reduce global biodiversity," four scientists from the panel wrote.[26] By this time the European Union had temporarily banned the use of three neonicotinoids on flowering crops on which bees feed, though the pesticides can still be used in winter and in greenhouses.[27]

Neonicotinoids are widely used in the United States, and manufacturers say they are safe when used correctly. The pesticides "have relatively high toxicity to pollinators at specific levels of exposures, but use in the field by and large is well below those levels," says CropLife America's McAllister. "They mainly are used to treat seeds of major row crops, which then are inserted directly into the soil. That greatly reduces exposure for nontarget species. Overall, neonicotinoids have been beneficial for pollinators."

But some U.S. communities, including Portland, Ore., and Seattle, have banned neonicotinoid use on city property because of concern about their effects.[28] The U.S. Fish and Wildlife Service, which allows limited farming in wildlife refuges to create food and habitat for wildlife, announced in 2014 that it would phase out use of neonicotinoid-treated seeds in wildlife refuges across the United States.[29] And in April the EPA, which is reviewing the uses it has approved for neonicotinoids, notified manufacturers that it was unlikely to approve any new uses for the products until it finished studying their impact on bees.[30]

Environmentalists want the EPA to move faster. "We are losing pollinators," says Jennifer Sass, a senior scientist with the Natural Resources Defense Council (NRDC), a national environmental advocacy group. "There's no single cause, but pesticides are the thing we can address most easily that will have a big impact. We want EPA to expedite its review because there is so much data showing harm."

Although Winston says pesticides are having serious effects on bees, he does not believe banning neonicotinoids will solve the problem. "Neonicotinoids are no worse and probably better than the pesticides that farmers used in the past and will likely go back to if they are banned," he says. "We need to reduce chemical inputs and shift conventional agriculture in a more sustainable direction," through such means as crop rotation and buffer strips of weeds around crop fields for pollinators to feed on.

Do genetically modified crops reduce harm from pesticides?

Nearly all of the genetically modified (GM) seeds sold to U.S. farmers over the past two decades were engineered to help protect the plants against weeds and insects.[31] Today about half of U.S. cropland is planted with GM versions of three major commodity crops: corn, soybeans and cotton.[32]

These crops have been engineered in two ways. Roundup Ready and other herbicide-tolerant seeds have been modified to make them resistant to glyphosate.

A farmworker pours the widely used weed killer Roundup into a tank. Early this year a U.N. agency declared that glyphosate — the active ingredient in Roundup — probably causes cancer in humans. But Monsanto, the company that patented glyphosate and markets Roundup, strongly disagreed. The EPA is reviewing glyphosate's standing but does not currently believe it is carcinogenic.

Scientists have added genes to other crops that enable them to produce proteins manufactured naturally by a soil bacterium called *Bacillus thuringiensis* (Bt) that are effective at killing many insect pests.

Manufacturers say these crops benefit human health and the environment by reducing the need for pesticides. For example, Syngenta, a global agricultural chemical company based in Basel, Switzerland, states on its website that "the development of insect resistant GM cotton has greatly reduced the use of pesticides."[33] And Monsanto says using Roundup on Roundup Ready crops "has allowed farmers to conserve fuel, reduce tillage and decrease the overall use of herbicides."[34]

But recent studies show a mixed picture. In 2012 Washington State University research professor Charles Benbrook reviewed 16 years of USDA data and found that use of Bt crops in the United States from 1996–2011 had reduced insecticide use by 123 million pounds. However, he calculated that planting herbicide-resistant crops had increased herbicide use by 527 million pounds. Initially, wide use of Roundup killed off weeds and reduced the need for other herbicides. But this approach spurred rapid evolution and spread of glyphosate-resistant weeds, which required farmers to use more herbicide, Benbrook found.[35]

"Without major change, a crisis in weed management systems is likely, triggering possibly ominous economic, public health and environmental consequences," Benbrook wrote.[36]

According to CropLife America's McAllister, simply measuring herbicide use does not capture all of the benefits from GM crops. "You can add up pounds, but glyphosate has a very good safety profile with respect to nontarget organisms," he says. "Other herbicides might [be more toxic] but used in lesser quantities, so it balances out."

A 2014 review by USDA researchers found the same pattern as Benbrook's study: Planting Bt corn and cotton significantly reduced pesticide use per acre in the United States from 1996–2013, but herbicide use began to rebound after falling initially. But, they concluded, because glyphosate was "significantly less toxic and persistent than traditional herbicides," using herbicide-resistant crops still was a net benefit to the environment. For example, conservation tillage — leaving residues such as corn stalks and wheat stubble on fields before and after planting to reduce runoff and erosion — had greatly increased on fields planted with herbicide-tolerant crops.[37]

Manufacturers say they are addressing herbicide resistance. One strategy is to develop crops resistant to several herbicides that work in different ways. The EPA has approved a new Dow AgroSciences pesticide called Enlist Duo that combines glyphosate and a weed killer called 2,4-D for use in 15 states in the Midwest, Great Plains and South. Dow also has developed Enlist-tolerant corn and soybeans and is field-testing Enlist-tolerant cotton.[38]

Environmentalists oppose Enlist Duo, which they say will further harm pollinators and could threaten human health. In 2007 the EPA listed 2,4-D as a possible endocrine disruptor, and the IARC has classified it as possibly carcinogenic.[39] But the EPA has reviewed 2,4-D several times and concluded that not enough evidence exists to link it to cancer in humans.

Environmentalists are concerned about both human and wildlife impacts. The risk to pollinators is clear, they say. "Herbicide use is killing milkweed, which is the only plant that monarch butterflies lay eggs on," says the NRDC's Sass. "It's a critical food source for them, but farmers see it as just one more weed. Glyphosate and 2,4-D are killing it off."

Earlier this year the Obama administration initiated a plan to restore monarch butterfly populations, which have shrunk by 90 percent over the past 20 years.[40] Like honeybees, monarchs face many threats, including single-crop farming and milkweed destruction.

In May the White House announced it would plant wildflowers and other plants that serve as food for pollinators on 7 million acres across the Midwest — an area slightly larger than Maryland — by 2020.[41] And the EPA proposed a new rule that would halt spraying of nearly all pesticides, including neonicotinoids, while certain flowers are in bloom and commercial bee colonies are present pollinating crops. The rule "may not be ideal, but it's the best news in about 120 years," said May Berenbaum, an entomologist at the University of Illinois.[42]

Some scientists argue that pesticide and GM seed producers are perpetuating an endless cycle in which pests will adapt to whatever technological controls humans apply. "Nature's response is automatic — it simply and quickly adapts to new stresses in the environment," says Andrew Dyer, a plant biologist at the University of South Carolina at Aiken. "The agriculture and biotech industries think it's possible to eradicate pests, but we have never eliminated pests. This is not a race we win. There is no finish line."

Other experts say GM crops' most valuable effect is in developing countries, where farmers have fewer tools for protecting their crops and often use many toxic pesticides. A recent review of 147 studies on the impact of GM crops by two professors at Germany's University of Goettingen found that the crops reduced pesticide use and increased farm yields and profits more sharply in developing countries than in advanced countries.[43]

In parts of India farmers spray more than 60 different insecticides on eggplant, known as brinjal, during the growing season. Several years ago an Indian seed company developed four types of Bt brinjal, but protests from GM opponents prevented the engineered versions from winning government approval.

"It was madness to stop Bt brinjal," said Kulvinder Gill, an agricultural geneticist at Washington State University who is from India but was not involved with the project. "People should not even be eating this brinjal because it has so much insecticide on it. Anything to reduce that would be extremely beneficial."[44]

Is organic produce safer to eat than conventional produce?

Many Americans are concerned about possible health risks from pesticide residues in food.[45] Some consumers buy organically grown fruits and vegetables because they believe they are safer than conventional produce. But while experts broadly agree that organic produce contains lower levels of pesticide residues than conventional produce, they disagree about whether that makes organic fruits and vegetables safer.

The USDA regularly samples both domestically grown and imported foods for pesticide residues. In 2013 the agency tested more than 10,000 food samples, 85 percent of them fruits and vegetables. It found detectable pesticide residues in slightly less than 60 percent of the samples. Of those, 23 samples (less than 1 percent) contained pesticide residues that exceeded tolerance levels set by the EPA. The agency also found pesticides in 286 produce samples for which the EPA had not yet set tolerance levels.[46]

Health and environmental advocates argue that pesticide residues in some conventional fruits and vegetables are unsafe even if they are within EPA tolerance levels, because the EPA only sets limits for individual pesticides, not the cumulative quantity of pesticide residues a food can contain. And very little research has been done on how exposure to combinations of pesticides affects human health.

Last March Consumers Union published a report that used a "dietary risk index" to rank the risk of pesticide exposure from 52 fruits and vegetables. The index scores reflected the amount and frequency of residues on various foods, typical serving size for each food and toxicity of the pesticide.

The group found that many fruits and vegetables grown in the United States, Canada and Latin America had low risk scores. For certain high-risk products, however — including peaches, tangerines, nectarines, strawberries, green beans, bell peppers and carrots — it recommended always buying organic.[47] Consumers Union's top recommendation was to eat five or more servings a day of fruits and vegetables — even if they fall into its high-risk categories — but to choose organic produce whenever available and affordable.[48]

Many consumers believe organic produce is grown without pesticides. However, organic farmers routinely use pesticides made from naturally occurring substances, and they use a limited number of synthetic products that have been approved for organic use. The natural pesticides they use may be simple, naturally occurring chemicals, such as sulfur or copper, or substances produced by living organisms, such as neem oil, derived from seeds of the tropical neem tree and effective against many insects, mites and fungi.

In a 2010 pilot study the USDA found detectable pesticide residue levels in about 43 percent of 571 samples of organic produce. Twenty-one samples contained pesticide levels greater than 5 percent of the EPA's tolerance levels, a violation of the USDA's organic regulations.[49]

While acknowledging that organic produce may contain pesticide residues, health and environmental advocates say organic pesticides pose less risk to human health. "Critics have never really shown that too much of a natural pesticide like copper causes significant harm," says Hansen of Consumers Union. "The issues are frequency of use, residue levels and toxicity, and when you measure those, organic pesticides have orders of magnitude lower toxicities."

But industry representatives assert that organic pesticides are not automatically safer. "Some organic pesticides have significant toxicity concerns," says CropLife America's McAllister. "For example, elemental sulfur has serious inhalation concerns, and some copper compounds have toxicity concerns, but they are approved for organic use. Also, organic pesticides often have lower efficacy than conventional products, so they have to be used in larger quantities and applied more than once."

Some studies have focused on whether eating organic food reduces pesticide risks for certain vulnerable groups. One focus is young children, who are at higher risk from pesticides in their diet than adults because they consume higher doses relative to their body weight. Chensheng "Alex" Lu, an associate professor at the Harvard School of Public Health, has found that when young children switch from conventional to organic produce, detectable traces of pesticides in their urine disappear within days.[50]

"Yes, there is a beneficial effect [from] eating organic produce," said Lu. "We believe the most vulnerable populations . . . are infants and children, in part because [of] their small body weight. Also, they are still growing, so there are a lot of detoxifying mechanisms that we have as adults that they don't have."[51]

But some parents decide not to go organic after weighing the added cost of organic produce and the fact that most pesticide residues in conventional produce are hundreds of times lower than the EPA's exposure limits. Parents "should stop worrying so much about whether the apples we buy are organic or conventional — we should just start giving our kids more apples," writes Melinda Wenner Moyer, a science journalist and parenting advice columnist for the online magazine *Slate*, in an article reviewing findings from multiple studies on pesticide residues in produce.

"It is far, far better for your kids' long-term health to get them in the habit of eating whole fruits and vegetables, regardless of what type of farm they came from, than to give them pretty much anything else to eat, no matter how organic or all-natural it may be," she contends.[52]

BACKGROUND
Pests and Weeds

Before commercial pesticides were developed, insects and weeds took heavy tolls on food production. Pioneers who settled the Great Plains in the 19th century fought to save their crops from locusts and beetles. One massive grasshopper outbreak in 1874 produced a swarm of insects that reached from Canada to Texas.[53] Laura Ingalls Wilder, whose family homesteaded on the Plains in the 1870s, described a grasshopper storm that destroyed her family's wheat crop in her book *On the Banks of Plum Creek:*

"The cloud was hailing grasshoppers. The cloud was grasshoppers. Their bodies hid the sun and made darkness. Their thin, large wings gleamed and glittered. The rasping whirring of their wings filled the whole air and they hit the ground and the house with the noise of a hailstorm."[54]

Weeds reduced food yields by competing with crops for sunlight and soil nutrients. Farmers spent countless hours plowing and hoeing to turn over dirt and cut weeds off at the roots.

In the mid-1800s farmers began to find that some chemicals helped control insects, molds and fungi. Early remedies included powdered sulfur, which helped prevent mildew on grapes, and an arsenic compound called Paris green that killed Colorado potato beetles.[55] In the 1890s lead arsenate, developed to kill gypsy moth caterpillars in New England orchards and forests, was widely adopted for use against many pests.[56] Farmers who could not afford commercial pesticides used homemade concoctions or simply picked bugs off plants by hand.[57]

Pests also caused serious problems in cities. Cockroaches, rats and flies infested food supplies and spread disease. Vermin were rampant in poor neighborhoods, feeding on garbage tossed into the street. Outhouses and streets clogged with horse manure were breeding grounds for flies, which many public health advocates contended carried diseases.[58]

These concerns fostered the emergence of the pest-control industry in the early 1900s. Progressive-era housing codes began requiring landlords to get rid of bedbugs, flies and other infestations or hire exterminators. These companies marketed their services as "preventive medicine" for families, based on expert knowledge about pests, germs and pesticides.[59]

Super Weapon

In 1939 Swiss chemist Paul Muller made a discovery that launched the modern pesticide industry. He found that DDT, a compound first synthesized in 1873, was highly effective at killing many kinds of insects. It also was long-acting and cheaper than other options. Federal agencies tested DDT extensively over the next several years. They focused almost entirely on acute effects (immediate poisoning from large doses), with very little attention to chronic effects (harm from low-level exposure over time), which toxicologists were just learning to measure.[60]

The U.S. Army put DDT to use during the last several years of World War II (1941–45). Soldiers, refugees and prisoners of war in Italy were dusted with DDT mixed into a powder to kill lice, which spread typhus. In the South Pacific, where malaria caused five times more casualties than combat injuries, the Army sprayed DDT from airplanes and inside mess halls, barracks and latrines to kill mosquitos that carried the disease.[61]

After the war, the use of DDT and other synthetic pesticides quickly expanded. From 1947 through 1949, 13 Southeastern states and the U.S. Public Health Service carried out a national malaria-eradication program that included spraying DDT inside more than 4.6 million homes. By 1949 malaria, a serious public health problem before the war, had effectively been eliminated in the United States.[62]

Getty Images/CBS

Concern about pesticides exploded in 1962 with the publication of Silent Spring, by Rachel Carson, a former aquatic biologist and writer for the Fish and Wildlife Service. Carson's best-seller warned that continuing to apply DDT and other pesticides would cause widespread harm to humans and animals.

Production of DDT and other chemically similar pesticides, known as organochlorines, soared from 1945 through the 1950s. These pesticides stuck to surfaces and soil and built up in animals' and birds' fatty tissues. Researchers with the U.S. Fish and Wildlife Service warned that DDT was highly toxic to birds, and medical groups began studying the human health effects of pesticide exposure.

In 1954 the American Medical Association warned that insecticide vaporizers, which released pesticide fumes into indoor air, were unsafe. But officials at the U.S. Public Health Service and the Department of Agriculture maintained that DDT was safe.[63]

Pesticide safety controversies burst into the public consciousness in 1962 when Rachel Carson, a former aquatic biologist and writer for the Fish and Wildlife Service, published *Silent Spring*, a sweeping critique of pesticide overuse. Carson warned that continuing to apply DDT and other pesticides "almost universally to farms, gardens, forests, and homes" would cause them to build up in the bodies of animals and humans, and could trigger insect outbreaks if pests developed resistance to the products.[64] She also cited toxicity studies and actual events to show that wide use of pesticides could kill many kinds of animals, fish and birds.

CHRONOLOGY

1800s–1930s *Insects, fungi and weeds damage crops and spread diseases.*

1874 Swarms of locusts destroy crops from the Dakotas to Texas.

1939 Swiss chemist Paul Muller discovers that the synthetic compound DDT kills insects effectively. In 1948 he is awarded the Nobel Prize in Physiology or Medicine.

1940–1970 *Growing use of synthetic pesticides after World War II prompts Congress to enact regulations, but advocates call for stronger controls to protect human health and the environment.*

1947 Federal Insecticide, Fungicide and Rodenticide Act (FIFRA) requires manufacturers to test pesticides for safety and effectiveness.

1958 The Delaney clause, named for Rep. James J. Delaney, D-N.Y., bars the use in processed foods of chemicals known to cause cancer; it also puts the Food and Drug Administration (FDA) in charge of regulating pesticide residues in processed food.

1962 In her influential best-seller *Silent Spring*, American aquatic biologist and writer Rachel Carson warns of environmental and health threats from continuing to apply DDT and other pesticides.

1970 Environmental Protection Agency (EPA) is created and authorized to review and register pesticides for specified uses.

1970–1990s *Less toxic pesticides gradually replace earlier products, but concerns about pesticide residues in food rise.*

1972 EPA bans use of DDT and other chlorinated hydrocarbon pesticides on food produced in the United States. . . . Department of Agriculture funds the first major federal research on integrated pest management (IPM), a pest control strategy that emphasizes biological tools, with pesticides as a last option.

1973 Congress passes the Endangered Species Act, prohibiting actions that harm endangered or threatened species or their habitats. . . . EPA bans chlordane, a highly toxic pesticide, for use on food crops in 1978; all other uses are banned in 1988.

1984 Dow, Monsanto and other chemical companies settle class-action lawsuit by agreeing to create a $180 million fund to compensate Vietnam War veterans who contended they were harmed by exposure to Agent Orange, an herbicide used by the military to defoliate trees and vegetation.

1988 Michigan becomes first state to require use of IPM in schools.

1993 National Research Council report finds that pesticide residues in food pose significant health risks to infants and children.

1996 Congress passes Food Quality Protection Act, tightening standards for pesticide residues in foods and requiring the EPA to reassess tolerance standards within a decade.

2001–Present *Research indicates that pesticides play a role in bee die-offs and are promoting growth of herbicide-resistant weeds.*

2001 EPA bans indoor, residential use of chlorpyrifos, an insecticide containing phosphate that is linked to neurological and developmental problems.

2005 New York City law requires reduced use of toxic pesticides and increased use of IPM.

2013 Responding to concerns about their effects on pollination, European Union imposes a two-year ban on neonicotinoid pesticides.

2014 President Obama calls on the EPA to assess the effects of neonicotinoids and other pesticides on pollinators.

2015 World Health Organization agency concludes that the widely used herbicide glyphosate probably causes cancer in humans. . . . EPA announces it will not approve new uses for neonicotinoids until it has reviewed their safety.

Critics accused Carson of fear-mongering and ignoring the benefits of pesticide use, but her book became a best-seller. In 1964 U.S. government scientists reported that DDT, DDE, endrin and other pesticides were washing from farmlands in the Southeast into the Mississippi River and killing millions of fish.[65] In 1967 environmental groups began suing state agencies and petitioning the federal government to ban DDT. Its use in the United States fell from 80 million pounds in 1959 to about 12 million pounds in the early 1970s.[66]

New Risks

Rising concern over health risks from pesticides helped fuel an emerging environmental movement in the late 1960s and early '70s. In 1972 William Ruckelshaus, administrator of the newly established EPA, banned DDT. Over the next several years, the EPA also banned the organochlorine pesticides chlordane, dieldrin and aldrin, reacting to concerns about their effects on humans and wildlife.

In response, farmers and consumers began using more organophosphates, often referred to as the second generation of synthetic pesticides. These products broke down more easily in the environment than organochlorines, but many of them were even more toxic to humans and wildlife than DDT.[67] In fact, Carson had pointed out in *Silent Spring* that organophosphates were "among the most poisonous chemicals in the world."[68] Some early versions were adapted (although never used) by German researchers as chemical weapons during World War II.[69]

At the same time, insect resistance to pesticides was rising, forcing farmers to apply pesticides more frequently and heavily. "Through the 1940s, three pests caused problems for U.S. cotton farmers: boll weevils, cotton bollworms and tobacco budworms," says Dyer of the University of South Carolina. "When DDT came along, it controlled each of those to some degree. But five more minor pests emerged that weren't suppressed by DDT. Then the first three species developed resistance to DDT, so farmers had to deal with eight pests."

Corn followed a similar pattern. Growers had to manage three main types of insects in the 1950s but more than 40 by the late '70s.[70]

Manufacturers strove to develop less-hazardous controls. In the 1970s they introduced synthetic pyrethroids — chemicals modeled on natural pesticides found in some types of chrysanthemum flowers and significantly less toxic than organophosphates. And in the early 1980s researchers began patenting pesticides chemically similar to another natural insecticide: nicotine, found in tobacco leaves. They called these products neonicotinoids.

Highly toxic organophosphates were routinely used not only on the farm in the 1970s and '80s, but also in public housing and private homes and gardens, where roaches and other pests were becoming increasingly resistant to common pesticides. In 1980 the National Academy of Sciences warned that homeowners and commercial exterminators were relying on two organophosphates, chlorpyrifos and diazinon, which were "of marginal safety for use in households."[71]

To reduce exposure risks, exterminators shifted from spraying pesticides indoors to more targeted approaches such as "bait stations." These small, enclosed traps contained insecticides mixed in food that ants and roaches would eat and then carry back to their nests before they died, spreading the poisons to other insects.

Food-Safety Warnings

In 1993 a National Research Council report spotlighted risks to infants and young children from pesticide residues in food. Based on a four-year congressionally mandated study, it found that children were more vulnerable than adults because they ate a narrower range of foods and consumed more foods that contained pesticides (mainly fruits and vegetables) relative to their total body weight. It concluded that some children could be receiving doses of organophosphate pesticides greater than tolerance levels set by the EPA — in some cases, potentially high enough to produce "symptoms of acute organophosphate pesticide poisoning."[72]

In response Congress passed the Food Quality Protection Act of 1996, which required the EPA to set lower standards for pesticide residues for both raw and processed foods that would protect human health more effectively. It directed the EPA to factor in nondietary exposures, such as pesticide use in homes and gardens, and the higher vulnerability of infants and young children.

That same year, Monsanto began a new phase in pest control when it patented its first genetically engineered commodity crop: Roundup-resistant soybeans. Insect-resistant Bt versions of cotton and corn soon followed. Biotechnology companies said these products would help

Return of the Bedbug

The pest has rebounded, thanks to insecticide resistance and global travel.

Millions of Americans recall the rhyme "Good night, sleep tight, don't let the bedbugs bite." In the 1950s and for decades afterwards, it was merely a fanciful ditty. Bedbugs — tiny six-legged insects about the size of an apple seed — were largely eliminated in developed countries with the introduction of the pesticide DDT. Since the late 1990s, however, bedbugs have returned with a vengeance, infesting homes and hotels across the United States and Western Europe.

In a survey this year by the National Pest Management Association, 99.6 percent of the pest control professionals who responded said they had treated sites for bedbugs in the preceding year, compared with only 25 percent 15 years ago.[1]

Bedbugs are parasites that feed on human blood. Unlike other blood-sucking insects like ticks and mosquitos, bedbugs do not transmit disease, so they are not considered a top-level public health threat.[2] But they are a real nuisance, leaving victims covered with itchy red welts that cause allergic reactions in some people. In 2010, the U.S. Environmental Protection Agency (EPA) and the Centers for Disease Control and Prevention issued a joint statement calling bedbugs "a pest of significant public health importance," noting that many people with bedbug infestations suffer from insomnia and anxiety, and that getting rid of the insections can be expensive and time-consuming.[3]

Scientists believe bedbugs developed thousands of years ago along the Mediterranean coast, initially feeding on bats but then preying on humans. As civilization spread into Europe, Asia and eventually North America, bedbugs moved with it.

"In a way, we created the modern bed bug: It evolved to live on us and to follow us," writes journalist Brooke Borel. "We became an efficient vehicle to spread it around the world."[4]

By the mid-1800s, bedbugs were widespread in American cities. Many people wrongly believed that the pests were found only in unsanitary homes. In fact, bedbugs thrived in all kinds of settings, from mansions to tenements, although wealthy homeowners had more time and resources for thorough cleaning, vacuuming and disinfecting to get rid of them.

After World War II, when powdered household insecticides containing DDT became widely available, bedbugs became rare in the United States but remained common in developing countries. Although the EPA banned domestic use of DDT in 1972, it remained in use abroad. DDT resistance developed in bedbugs and other insects in places such as Africa and Central America, where the pesticide was widely used.

In the late 1990s pest control companies began reporting bedbug infestations in U.S. cities. Possible causes included deregulation of the airline industry in the 1980s and '90s, which increased the number of flight routes worldwide and drove down ticket prices. Global commerce also increased as companies moved manufacturing jobs to developing countries and shipped goods back to customers in wealthy nations. Bedbugs hitched rides overseas on luggage, clothing and furniture. And as the world's population became more urban, growing numbers of people lived in close quarters — conditions that favored the spread of bedbugs.[5]

In New York City, confirmed cases of bedbugs rose from 82 in 2004 to 4,808 in 2010 before falling back to 2,268 in 2013.[6] To address the problem, the city's Health Department strengthened requirements for property owners to notify tenants about infestations, inform them about ways to prevent and control bedbugs and provide regulators with affidavits from pest control companies that properties had been treated.[7]

farmers reduce pesticide use. But environmentalists warned that they could create new generations of pesticide- and herbicide-resistant plants and insects.

"It's all work this out as you go and hope to God it works," said Margaret Mellon, director of agriculture and biotechnology programs at the Union of Concerned Scientists, a national environmental advocacy group.[73]

On the urban front, a new concern emerged in the mid-1990s: increasing reports of bedbugs in U.S. and European cities. Heavy use of DDT had virtually eliminated bedbugs in developed countries in the 1950s, but they had never disappeared in the developing world. Experts could not identify any single cause for the re-emergence of bedbugs in developed countries

But bait traps, the standard technique for controlling ants and roaches, were ineffective against bedbugs, which were not attracted to the poisoned food in the traps because they feed on blood. That meant exterminators had to switch back to an older technique: spraying insecticides along baseboards and in other areas where bedbugs might be found. And scientists studying the resurgence of bedbugs soon made an ominous discovery: Some strains were resistant to pyrethroid insecticides, which were the only type that could legally be sprayed indoors. Pyrethroids affect insects' nervous systems in the same way DDT does, so DDT resistance may also have made some types of bedbugs resistant to pyrethroids.[8]

Now other cities are infested. Crews with Orkin, a national pest-control company, performed more bedbug treatments in Chicago in 2013 than in any other U.S. city; New York ranked 17th, down seven places from 2012. Chicago's City Council passed an ordinance that year requiring condominium managers to have formal plans for detecting and treating bedbugs. Other cities at the top of Orkin's list were, in order, Los Angeles; Columbus, Ohio; Detroit; Cincinnati; Cleveland/Akron/Canton; Dayton, Ohio; Washington; Denver; and Indianapolis.[9]

As cities tighten controls, many residents are apparently coming to accept that once again bedbugs are a feature of urban life. Early in New York's bedbug surge, "it was like alarms were going off. People were, 'AAGH! I've got bedbugs!' " said Brooklyn exterminator Bill Swan. "Now it's like, 'Eh, I've got a couple of bedbugs.' It seems like they're becoming a little more nonchalant, like an occasional roach or something."[10]

— *Jennifer Weeks*

Getty Images/Justin Sullivan

A bedbug-sniffing beagle seeks out the tiny, six-legged insects. Scientists blame the recent resurgence of bedbugs on international travel and the bugs' resistance to pesticides.

Feb. 13, 2015, pp. 145-168, and Jennifer Weeks, "Lyme Disease," *CQ Researcher*, Nov. 8, 2013, pp. 957-980.

[3] "Joint Statement on bed bug control in the United States from the U.S. Centers for Disease Control and Prevention (CDC) and the U.S. Environmental Protection Agency (EPA)," 2010, http://tinyurl.com/mzlzssn.

[4] Brooke Borel, *Infested: How the Bed Bug Infiltrated Our Bedrooms and Took Over the World* (2015), p. 9.

[5] *Ibid.*, pp. 63-64.

[6] *Ibid.*, p. xiii; Samantha Tata and Greg Mocker, "Bed bug cases in NYC drop to 4-year low," Pix11 News, June 3, 2014, http://tinyurl.com/lw4t5el. Dates are for the city's fiscal year, which begin in August and ends in July.

[7] "Enforcement Protocols for Bed Bug Complaints: What Property Owners Should Know," New York City Department of Health and Mental Hygiene, http://tinyurl.com/l3hzsu9.

[8] Borel, *op. cit.*, pp. 57-60.

[9] "Chicago Tops Bed Bug Cities List for Second Year in a Row," Orkin, undated, accessed May 20, 2015, http://tinyurl.com/kgw3qo5.

[10] "Brooklyn Exterminator Shares His Best Bed Bug Horror Stories," *Gothamist*, May 23, 2013, http://tinyurl.com/q6h2wwd.

[1] "Bed Bug Information," National Pest Management Association, 2015, http://tinyurl.com/777g9k8.

[2] For background on other diseases transmitted by animals and insects, see Marcia Clemmitt, "Emerging Infectious Diseases," *CQ Researcher*,

but said likely factors included rising international travel and the fact that many strains of bedbugs had developed resistance to multiple pesticides.[74]

Another worrisome trend appeared in 2006 when beekeepers in many states began reporting that up to 70 percent of their bees were dying off in a single season. Experts cited many possible causes, including

mite infestations, pesticide exposure and loss of habitat, which were reducing the availability of many wildflowers that were traditional food sources for bees.[75]

As for pesticides, suspicion focused on neonicotinoids — "systemic" chemicals that could move through plants' circulatory systems to their leaves and flowers, where bees came in contact with them. France had already

Integrated Pest Management Slowly Gains Ground

Technique using biological controls casts chemical pesticides as a last resort.

Experts who want to reduce pesticide use in the United States say a technique that relies heavily on preventive action and biological controls against pests offers a better approach than relying mainly on chemical pesticides.

Integrated pest management (IPM) uses many methods to keep pests in check, starting with monitoring them and taking action only when damage reaches a certain level. Then it emphasizes pre-emptive actions, such as eliminating food and breeding areas for pests, and using non-chemical approaches, such as benign insects that prey on pest species. Chemical pesticides are a last resort.

Federal agencies have funded IPM research and adoption since the early 1970s. The concept is slowly becoming more mainstream: Many farmers and pest control companies have begun using various IPM methods in settings ranging from cotton fields to urban schools. But IPM advocates say there is plenty of room for growth.

Health and environmental advocacy groups, sustainable-agriculture advocates and some academic researchers argue that IPM should be the primary pest-control strategy nationwide. But that goal has remained elusive.

"IPM has been practiced for decades and taught in colleges and universities, but it hasn't been adopted widely enough yet to prevent current pest problems," says Stephen Young, director of the Northeastern IPM Center at Cornell University. The center is one of four funded by the U.S. Department of Agriculture (USDA) to promote IPM.

"It's not fast, cheap or easy," Young says. "IPM takes knowledge and a desire to understand what's happening in the field, not just a focus on [crop] yield." And without training and detailed record-keeping, programs may fail.

For example, New Jersey law requires schools to use IPM, and New York state has a voluntary school IPM program. But during recent site visits, Environmental Protection Agency (EPA) officials found that some principals and custodians in large urban school districts did not know what IPM was or how to track whether pests were present. Many schools had failed to take basic steps such as sealing holes where pests could enter buildings. Inspectors saw clear evidence that some schools were infested with roaches and mice.

The EPA found few problems in suburban districts — perhaps because their schools had more staff and resources to train them about IPM.[1]

No two IPM programs are identical because they are designed to manage specific pests under specific conditions. But successful IPM programs take a four-step approach:

• Set a threshold for action — typically, when a pest population threatens human health or crop damage reaches a certain level. Not every single pest needs to be eliminated.

• Monitor and identify pests so strategies can focus on organisms actually doing harm.

• Take preventive action. Farms can rotate crops instead of planting the same crop repeatedly in a field, or plant pest-resistant strains. In homes or schools, prevention might include removing garbage that attracts vermin or sealing holes where pests enter buildings.

• Use controls, starting with biological methods such as introducing ladybugs to prey on aphids. Chemical pesticides should be used only if other methods do not work, and they should target only the pest.[2]

banned some uses of imidacloprid, a neonicotinoid, after French beekeepers reported that it was affecting bees' behavior.

Other researchers used DNA analysis to assess how viruses and fungi were affecting bees. "This is like [the TV show] "C.S.I." [Crime Scene Investigation] for agriculture," said W. Ian Lipkin, director of an infectious disease laboratory at Columbia University. "It is painstaking, gumshoe detective work."[76]

IPM is not an all-or-nothing strategy. Many farmers and pest-control companies use some of the techniques along with chemical pesticides. "IPM uses common-sense techniques to get rid of things that pests need to survive — most importantly, food, water and hiding places," says Bob Rosenberg, executive vice president of the National Pest Management Association. And where exterminators once sprayed insecticides directly onto carpets or baseboards, they now take a more targeted approach. "An applicator may place baits in cracks and crevices, or apply pesticides in a narrow band around [the exterior of] a house instead of using them indoors," Rosenberg says.

Because there is no single standard for what it means to practice IPM, the question of how widely farmers are adopting the technique has yet to be answered. "Until there is an agreed-upon definition for IPM, as there is for organic agriculture, we will never know actual numbers," says Young.

Indeed, available information on IPM adoption is both dated and inconclusive. In 1993, the USDA and EPA set a goal that 75 percent of U.S. cropland would use some level of IPM by 2000. The department and agency predicted this would reduce pesticide use. In 2000, USDA estimated that the goal had nearly been reached, with IPM applied on some 70 percent of farmed land.

But the Government Accountability Office (GAO) disagreed, noting that the Agriculture Department was counting all IPM practices, even though some — such as monitoring for pests — did not reduce pesticide use. The GAO contended that advanced IPM methods, such as bio-controls, were being used much more sparsely, and that total use of agricultural pesticides had increased between 1993 and 2000.[3]

Still, some assessments indicate that IPM techniques are increasingly common on U.S. farms. For example, according to the USDA's Western IPM Center, based at the University of California, Davis, "a large percentage of growers and on a majority of agricultural acreage" across the western United States are using many IPM techniques. In California, which has a $35 billion agricultural industry, the quantity of pesticides applied per $1,000 of output fell from nearly nine pounds in 1995 to less than four pounds in 2012. [4]

IPM has been required on all federal property since 1996. [5] Today 23 states have laws or regulations mandating IPM use in schools. [6] And many city governments require or recommend IPM for pest control in parks and public spaces.

In 2005 New York City began requiring city agencies to end the use of pesticides considered to potentially cause cancer or birth defects. Instead the city uses IPM techniques, such as replacing wire-mesh trash baskets that attract rats with solid steel cans; eliminating standing pools of water in parks that serve as breeding grounds for mosquitos; and switching to a bio-based herbicide in Central Park. [7]

"IPM is the only current, widely used approach that has a chance of reducing our chemical-based strategy," says Andrew Dyer, a professor of biology at the University of South Carolina, Aiken. "It's based on trial-and-error science, using appropriate tools at appropriate times, understanding the ecology of pest and crop species, and learning from mistakes."

— Jennifer Weeks

---

[1]Marcia Anderson, "Challenges to Implementing Integrated Pest Management in Schools: What We Have Learned From Field Visits," *Applied Environmental Education and Communication*, vol. 14, no. 1 (2015), pp. 3-13.

[2]"Integrated Past Management (IPM) Fact Sheet," U.S. Environmental Protection Agency, updated May 9, 2013, http://tinyurl.com/prcsw3v.

[3]"Agricultural Pesticides: Management Improvements Needed To Further Promote Integrated Pest Management," U.S. Government Accountability Office, August 2001, pp. 1-3, http://tinyurl.com/q8alkzn.

[4]James J. Farrar, Matthew E. Bauer and Steve Elliott, "Abstract: Adoption and Impacts of Integrated Pest Management in Agriculture in the Western United States," Western IPM Center, March 2015, http://tinyurl.com/nmxdaj7.

[5]"Integrated Pest Management," U.S. General Services Administration, http://tinyurl.com/opk6n8k.

[6]"Overview of State School Pest Management Requirements," National Pest Management Association, http://tinyurl.com/o7r3d4g.

[7]"An Update on Integrated Pest Management in New York City for 2013," NYC Health, Jan. 1, 2014, http://tinyurl.com/pvo3rks.

CURRENT SITUATION
Protecting Workers

The EPA is strengthening rules aimed at safeguarding farmworkers against pesticide poisoning.

No comprehensive database tracks farmworker exposure to pesticides, but in 2008 the EPA estimated that between 10,000 and 20,000 pesticide poisonings occurred annually among farmworkers.[77] And studies have shown that such incidents are underreported. Many farmworkers are especially unlikely to seek help because they speak little or no English or fear losing their jobs or being deported.

Current EPA standards, adopted in 1992, require employers to give workers advance notice when pesticides will be used, offer basic safety training and provide protective gear. They also must keep workers out of areas being treated and limit access after treatment for specific periods, depending on the pesticide and how it is applied.[78]

Now the agency is proposing to:

• Require training for workers yearly instead of every five years;
• Prevent children under age 16 from handling pesticides, except on family farms;
• Require no-entry buffer zones around pesticide-treated fields; and
• Require record-keeping for two years on pesticide use and worker training to help states regulate pesticide use and investigate violations.[79]

Environmental and health advocates say these changes are long overdue. "Right now there's really no structure for farmworker pesticide training, and it doesn't happen frequently enough," says Amy Liebman, director of environmental and occupational health for the Migrant Clinicians Network, a nonprofit based in Texas that supports health professionals who care for migrant workers. "There should be guidelines for what it covers. Farmworkers should be treated more like chemical factory workers, who get training about the specific chemicals they work with and often are monitored for exposure to them."

The Occupational Safety and Health Administration (OSHA), part of the Department of Labor, is the main agency that enforces farmworker safety regulations. However, since 1976 Congress has barred OSHA from inspecting farms that have 10 or fewer employees and have not had a temporary labor camp in the past 12 months.[80] The standards also do not apply to family farms that have no nonfamily employees.

But 25 states, Puerto Rico and the U.S. Virgin Islands have OSHA-approved state plans, which let those states enforce their own occupational safety and health programs with standards at least as strict as OSHA's.[81] "In some states, such as Washington and California, agencies can enforce safety regulations on farms without the limits that OSHA has to meet," says Liebman.

Manufacturers argue that current regulations are working and that the EPA's proposed changes would burden farmers without improving farmworker health. "Training could be improved, but we do not support increases in record-keeping, buffer zone requirements that are not based on scientific standards or requirements to post more warnings," says CropLife America's McAllister. "These changes do not add any value, but they do substantially increase compliance costs for producers."

The American Farm Bureau Federation, which represents farmers nationwide, also opposes the EPA's changes. In comments last year the organization called the proposed new rule "wholly unworkable, unfair to agricultural employers, costly, and of questionable benefit to the individuals it is supposed to protect."[82]

Liebman says more protections are needed at both the federal and state levels. "Thirty states require doctors to report suspected or confirmed cases of pesticide poisoning, but only about a dozen states have an active surveillance system that follows up on these reports," she says. "Many agricultural workers aren't eligible for worker's compensation. Overall, agriculture has fewer regulatory protections than other industries."

Even states with their own OSHA plans may fail to enforce standards. In May Darryl Ivy, a truck driver working on a spray crew in Oregon, gave time-stamped photos and hours of video clips to *The Oregonian* newspaper that showed a helicopter pilot repeatedly spraying toxic weed killers directly over co-workers on the ground, in violation of federal regulations. Ivy was never told that pilots were not supposed to spray workers, or that he should change his clothes if herbicides landed on them. The pilot told Ivy that the herbicide would not hurt him, but after less than three weeks on the job Ivy was coughing up blood.[83]

Oregon's Agriculture and Forestry departments give timber companies broad discretion to decide where and how to spray weed killer on forest lands. An agency spokesperson told *The Oregonian* a Forestry Department monitor had been onsite during the spray operations and had not seen any violations, but that the department was investigating Ivy's claim.

Ivy, diagnosed with acute chemical exposure and acute contact dermatitis (skin irritation), said, "I thought I was resilient. . . . But it's got me a little worried. I can't breathe right."[84]

Endocrine Disruptors

A debate in the European Union (EU) over regulating chemicals that are endocrine disruptors (EDs) is causing friction between the United States and Europe. The outcome could affect some pesticides widely used on U.S. crops and disrupt trans-Atlantic trade.

In 2011 the EU decided to forbid the use of pesticides that could act as EDs. It has proposed two approaches to define EDs. One would rely on "hazard identification" — scientific findings that a substance is or could be an ED.[85] This policy reflects the so-called precautionary principle, a central theme in EU chemical regulations that holds that if scientific evidence shows that something could cause serious harm, regulators should act even if the evidence is not conclusive.[86]

The other strategy would identify hazards and then conduct risk assessments — studies of who was likely to be exposed, how large the doses might be and whether they were likely to cause harm.[87] The EPA is using that approach to identify and test pesticides that may be EDs.

Commenting on the EU's proposal, the Obama administration argued that regulating pesticides based on the hazard approach could disrupt U.S. agricultural exports to Europe, worth some $5 billion annually. It also argued that regulating EDs without considering actual risk "weakens scientific credibility, creates confusion . . . and in the end produces an inferior product."[88] For example, it noted, coffee, garlic and apples all contain naturally occurring substances that can interfere with normal hormone actions. However, banning them would not benefit human health because people do not consume enough of those products to cause harm.[89]

But many U.S. health and environmental advocates say the EPA is taking too long to review pesticides and determine whether they are EDs. Although Congress directed the agency to carry out that review in the 1996 Food Quality Protection Act, it took the agency more than a decade to develop policies and procedures for the first screening step — determining whether chemicals are potential EDs. The agency currently is ordering tests on about 200 pesticides. By 2019 it plans to have analyzed those results and determined whether chemicals should be tested further to measure the amounts required to produce an effect.[90]

Many other agencies worldwide also are struggling to measure the health impacts of ED. According to the World Health Organization, only a small fraction of hundreds of chemicals known or suspected to be EDs have been analyzed using methods that can identify clear endocrine effects. And few studies have been done to explore links between ED exposure and endocrine diseases such as cancer, obesity and diabetes.[91]

"The benchmark standard in toxicology is still acute toxicity" (harm from high doses), says Florida State University history professor Frederick Rowe Davis. "There is a lot of uncertainty around other effects that emerge over long periods of time, including cancer and endocrine disruption. Toxicologists believed that there were thresholds [safe exposure levels] for many chemicals because they couldn't find a correspondence between very low-level exposures and particular outcomes. But as science evolves, they've found that there may not be threshold levels."

Mosquito Control

As global climate change raises temperatures, mosquitos are expanding northward. Some are carrying tropical diseases into the United States. Many state and local health departments spray to control mosquitos, but researchers are testing a new strategy in Florida that could protect public health without using chemical pesticides.

The threat is clear. Asian tiger mosquitos, which carry West Nile virus, dengue fever and other diseases, first appeared in Texas in 1985 and have spread as far as southern New York and Pennsylvania.[92] Last year, 2,122 cases of West Nile virus were reported in the continental United States, including 85 deaths.[93]

Moreover, malaria — carried by the Anopheles mosquito strain, which is already present in the United States — could return. According to some climate models, the mosquito parasite that causes malaria could spread from Central America into the Southern and Western United States by 2050.[94]

Urban mosquito control begins with preventive steps — most importantly, getting rid of standing water sources such as backyard pools and bird baths, where

Should neonicotinoid pesticides be banned?

YES — Tim Knapp
Mayor, Wilsonville, Ore.

Excerpted from testimony before the Committee on Agriculture and Natural Resources, Oregon House of Representatives, March 26, 2015

The city of Wilsonville supports the concepts of [House Bill] 2589 to protect pollinators from harmful chemicals containing nitro-group neonicotinoids.

The city of Wilsonville was the site in June 2013 of reportedly the largest pollinator bumblebee kill in the history of the United States, a distinction that our community does not relish — all due to the application of neonicotinoid pesticides. This powerful class of pesticides has been shown conclusively to harm pollinators throughout the lifecycle of the product, with detrimental effects continuing long after initial treatment since plants take up the pesticide into their tissues. . . .

Many local farming and nursery businesses are dependent upon pollinator health for propagation of key nut, fruit and vegetable crops. Pacific Natural Foods, a major national organic food processor with substantial employment and operations in Tualatin, [Ore.] and Wilsonville, is dependent on healthy populations of pollinators for successfully farming over 1,000 acres in the Willamette Valley.

The city supported the Oregon Department of Agriculture's adoption in February 2015 of [a regulation] that "prohibits the application of four neonicotinoid insecticides, regardless of application methods, on linden trees." The department found that four separate bumblebee kill incidents related to applications of dinotefuran or imidacloprid in 2013 and three separate bee kill incidents in 2014.

The city notes that each of these pollinator-killing incidents was brought about by the use of neonicotinoid insecticides by duly licensed pesticide applicators — technicians trained in correct pesticide application. One might observe . . ., "If the experts can't get it right, what would make us think that homeowners and others can do a better job?"

The department reports that pesticide applicators began using the insecticides thiamethoxam or clothianidin as replacements for dinotefuran or imidacloprid. The department found that thiamexotham and clothianidin are closely related to dinotefuran and imidacloprid (all are nitroguanidine neonicotinoid insecticides) and can be equally or possibly more hazardous to bumblebees.

Thus, after evaluating the toxicity and half-lives of thiamexotham and clothianidin and investigating potential alternatives, and discussing the findings with industry, the department concluded that a change in the rule is appropriate to safeguard pollinator health, which is crucial for the success of Oregon's long-term agricultural operations.

NO — Jeff Stone
Executive Director, Oregon Association of Nurseries

Excerpted from testimony before the Committee on Agriculture and Natural Resources, Oregon House of Representatives, March 26, 2015

The nursery industry needs pollinators and tools to battle pest and disease. As a proud part of U.S. agriculture, we certainly understand the importance of pollinators to the agricultural industry and our natural environment. We also recognize the importance of having effective pesticides with low environmental impact.

House Bill 2589 targets neonicotinoids (or neonics), a chemical class [that] when used properly, is vital to the success of our industry. They are important tools in defending trees, shrubs and plants against destructive invasive species like the Japanese beetle, hemlock woolly adelgid and Asian longhorned beetle, in dealing with invasive and often chemical-resistant whitefly species and in preventing the spread of these and other pests. . . .

Based on current science, the Environmental Protection Agency (EPA) continues to allow application of neonicotinoids with appropriate guidelines. These chemistries are among the safest available to combat many pests. We have encouraged Congress to direct the research community to pursue its work on this issue without bias and identify the appropriate steps to alleviate environmental and pest pressures on pollinator health.

The call in House Bill 2589 to ban neonicotinoids flies in the face of a cadre of reports that suggest their role in declining bee health is small. The [U.S. Department of Agriculture's] 2013 report on honeybee health put pesticides, in general, near the bottom of the list of factors impacting bee health. The report highlighted other issues like colony management, viruses, bacteria, poor nutrition, lack of genetic diversity and habitat loss as more impactful. The report continued to stress that "the single most detrimental pest of honeybees is the parasitic Varroa mite, first discovered in the U.S. in 1987." Recent reports from the Australian Government's Pesticides and Veterinary Medicines Authority . . . supported the conclusions of the USDA report.

While we can understand the concerns of beekeepers, and the public at large, and conflicting national studies relating to declining bee populations, unfortunately there is no simple answer. In fact, research on colony collapse disorder . . . has highlighted a complex interaction of factors that play a role in bee health. No singular cause of the problem has been found. While pesticides are often noted as one factor, they are not considered the primary one. . . .

House Bill 2589 is not a productive use of the state's time, and we all have work to do to protect pollinators in Oregon.

mosquitos lay their eggs. Water sources that cannot be eliminated, such as canals, can be treated with pesticides or covered with a thin layer of mineral oil to drown larvae.[95] To reduce the odds of residents getting bitten, public health agencies often advise them to wear long sleeves and long pants and use repellents in mosquito-prone areas.

Many U.S. cities and towns trap mosquitos and test samples regularly to see whether any carry West Nile or other tropical infectious diseases. Often when a test comes back positive or a case of West Nile is reported, cities will spray insecticides from backpack sprayers, trucks or airplanes. Spraying typically takes place at night, when mosquitos are active, and the active ingredients in common public health sprays usually last no more than 24 to 48 hours in the environment, so they are considered low-risk for people and wildlife.[96]

In the Florida Keys, where dengue fever reappeared in 2009, a British company is seeking federal permission to test a new weapon: genetically modified mosquitos. The engineered insects carry a specially designed gene that will cause their offspring to die soon after birth, thus reducing dengue transmission. The mosquitos are already being field-tested in trials in the Cayman Islands, Panama, Brazil and Malaysia.[97]

In the Keys, some residents oppose the tests, which they say are not necessary and could have unexpected consequences. But researchers say the problem is urgent.

"What we do know is that nearly half the world's population is already at risk for mosquito-borne disease," wrote Shannon LaDeau, an associate scientist at the Cary Institute of Ecosystem Studies in New York. "Field release trials of GM mosquitos will assess the potential for this technique to address this major global health threat. Potential risks are likely to be less damaging than the known impacts of pesticide use on amphibians and birds."[98]

OUTLOOK

Feeding the World

With global population projected to grow through the year 2100, and climate change stressing many regions, producing enough food for up to 11 billion people will be a major challenge.[99] Agriculture and biotech companies say pesticides will be needed to meet that goal.

"Pests and diseases will be with us as long as we need to eat," says CropLife America's McAllister. "That means pesticides will play an essential role in agriculture for the foreseeable future. If we want to use fewer pesticides and a smaller number of chemicals, those products will have to control a larger range of pests. That means they will have to be less selective and more toxic, and we'll need larger quantities."

Other experts contend that the structure of American agriculture needs to change. "Shifting conventional agriculture in a more sustainable direction would help bees and other pollinators survive," says Winston of Simon Fraser University. "Organic agriculture is considerably better than conventional large-scale monoculture [single-crop] farming for bees and other beneficial insects," he says. "But there is a middle ground that focuses on polyculture (planting mixed crops) and reduced pesticide use." Polyculture is a common practice in organic agriculture, although some large organic producers use monoculture.

Learning to manage pests sustainably will be more productive in the long run than relying on massive chemical applications to keep them under control, the University of South Carolina's Dyer contends. "Technology is part of the strategy, but it can't be the whole answer," he says. "DDT and DDE lost their effectiveness within five years. Farming needs to take advantage of ecosystem services that we've been killing off with chemicals, such as helpful insects and soil micro-organisms. We can't keep degrading soil quality and trying to increase production on our remaining farmland."

Pesticide companies are already moving in that direction. Today major producers such as Monsanto, DuPont and Bayer CropScience that have long focused on synthetic chemical products are buying smaller companies that produce biopesticides and developing their own bio-based products.

The EPA often requires less than a year to license biopesticides, compared to three years or more for conventional pesticides.[100] The agency approved more than 430 biologically active ingredients for use in agriculture in 2012, and Assistant Administrator Jim Jones predicted that they may overtake synthetic chemicals in agriculture at some point if their use continues to grow strongly.[101]

In Dyer's view, biological controls are the only practical long-term option, since pests will always evolve resistance to synthetic pesticides. "Chemical pesticides work by brute force," he says. "Using beneficial insect as biocontrols plays by the rules of evolutionary biology, instead of just looking for new chemical controls. No one has produced an herbicide with a new mode of action (way of killing weeds) in the last 20 years. Manufacturers are out of solutions."

NOTES

1. "Record Number of Eagles Recorded at Blackwater National Wildlife Refuge," U.S. Fish and Wildlife Service, Jan. 8, 2015, http://tinyurl.com/ok8eec2; Gary Garth, Bald Eagles No Longer Rarity in Kentucky," *Louisville Courier-Journal*, Jan. 10, 2015, http://tinyurl.com/nwbasou; Keith Rogers, "American Bald Eagles Spotted on Lake Mead, Mojave," *Las Vegas Review-Journal*, Jan. 10, 2015, http://tinyurl.com/o44jp7b; Iain Wilson, "N.H. Audubon Eagle Survey Tallies 90 Bald Eagles, Sets New Record," *The Concord Monitor*, Feb. 10, 2015, http://tinyurl.com/qff2dfx.

2. Bald eagles are more common in Alaska and were never threatened with extinction there.

3. "DDT Ban Takes Effect," U.S. Environmental Protection Agency, Dec. 31, 1972, http://tinyurl.com/k3l3jqg.

4. "Chart and Table of Bald Eagle Breeding Pairs in Lower 48 States," U.S. Fish and Wildlife Service, updated April 20, 2015, http://tinyurl.com/nvrhgyb.

5. Frederick M. Fishel, "Pesticide Use Trends in the United States: A 25-Year U.S. Summary," University of Florida Extension, revised April 2014, pp. 7–10, http://tinyurl.com/ov3dv9f. All quantities measure pounds of active ingredients — i.e., the chemicals in pesticides that actually kill or suppress pests.

6. "Reducing Environmental Cancer Risk: What We Can Do Now," President's Cancer Panel, 2010, p. iii, http://tinyurl.com/2dgxawc.

7. C. C. Lerro *et al.*, "Use of Acetochlor and Cancer Incidence in the Agricultural Health Study," *International Journal of Cancer*, Jan. 23, 2015, http://onlinelibrary.wiley.com/doi/10.1002/ijc.29416/full.

8. "About the Study," Agricultural Health Study, http://tinyurl.com/qdegc94; Rena R. Jones *et al.*, "Incidence of Solid Tumours Among Pesticide Applicators Exposed to the Organophosphate Insecticide Diazinon in the Agricultural Health Study: An Updated Analysis," *Occupational and Environmental Medicine*, April 23, 2015, http://oem.bmj.com/content/early/2015/04/23/oemed-2014–102728.abstract; Lerro *et al.*, *ibid.*; John D. Beard *et al.*, "Pesticide Exposure and Depression among Male Private Pesticide Applicators in the Agricultural Health Study," *Environmental Health Perspectives*, Vol. 122, No. 9, September 2014, http://ehp.niehs.nih.gov/1307450/.

9. National Research Council, *Pesticides in the Diets of Infants and Young Children* (1993), pp. 6–9, http://tinyurl.com/p32t2u3.

10. For background see Jennifer Weeks, "Regulating Toxic Chemicals," *CQ Researcher*, July 18, 2014, pp. 601–624.

11. Wissem Mnif *et al.*, "Effect of Endocrine Disruptor Pesticides: A Review," *International Journal of Environmental Research and Public Health*, Vol. 8, no. 6, June 2011, http://tinyurl.com/oedzv7j.

12. "Endocrine Disruptor Screening Program," U.S. Environmental Protection Agency, updated Nov. 25, 2014, http://tinyurl.com/28yrpjb.

13. "Overview of the 2009 Final List of Chemicals for Initial Tier I Screening," U.S. Environmental Protection Agency, updated Aug. 8, 2011, http://tinyurl.com/n9wapah, and "Overview of the Second List of Chemicals for Tier I Screening," http://tinyurl.com/nawybsl.

14. "Monsanto Disagrees with IARC Classification for Glyphosate," news release, Monsanto, March 20, 2015, http://tinyurl.com/pmzsusv. See also "IARC Monographs Volume 112: evaluation of five organophosphate insecticides and herbicides," International Agency for Research on Cancer and World Health Organization, March 20, 2015.

15. Andrew Pollack, "Weed Killer, Long Cleared, Is Doubted," *The New York Times*, March 27, 2015, http://tinyurl.com/qcltu8o.

16. "Public Interest Groups on WHO's Decision on Glyphosate," Environmental Working Group, March 26, 2015, http://tinyurl.com/ovr9py9.

17. Carey Gillam, "U.S. Regulators May Recommend Testing Food for Glyphosate Residues," Reuters, April 17, 2015, http://tinyurl.com/on4ryxf; Carey Gillam, "EPA Regulator Says Set to Release Key Herbicide Report, Lauds Biopesticides," Reuters, May 5, 2015, http://tinyurl.com/oaot44v.

18. Renee Johnson and M. Lynne Corn, "Bee Health: Background and Issues for Congress," Congressional Research Service, Nov. 3, 2014, p. 1, http://tinyurl.com/phmaju3.

19. "Honey Bee Health and Colony Collapse Disorder," Agricultural Research Service, U.S. Department of Agriculture, updated May 13, 2015, http://tinyurl.com/533udq.

20. Michael Wines, "A Sharp Spike in Honeybee Deaths Deepens a Worrisome Trend," *The New York Times*, May 13, 2015, http://tinyurl.com/mvoqbsx.

21. *Ibid.*; Chris Gonzales, "The Pollinator Puzzle," Integrated Pest Management Insights, May 13, 2015, pp. 2–3, http://tinyurl.com/p7tmxo3; "Honey Bee Health and Colony Collapse Disorder," *op. cit.*

22. For an overview see Richard Primack, Walden, *Warming: Climate Change Comes to Thoreau's Woods* (2014), pp. 39–55 and 133–150.

23. Gaku Kudo and Takashi Ida, "Early Onset of Spring Increases the Phenological Mismatch Between Plants and Pollinators," *Ecology*, Vol. 94 (2013), http://tinyurl.com/po9gafr; Damian Carrington, "Climate Change is Disrupting Flower pollination, Research shows," *The Guardian*, Nov. 6, 2014, http://tinyurl.com/ldma3xl.

24. Christopher A. Mullin *et al.*, "High Levels of Miticides and Agrochemicals in North American Apiaries: Implications for Honey Bee health," PLoS One, March 19, 2010, http://tinyurl.com/olcmzm7.

25. "Major Findings," Task Force on Systemic Pesticides, 2015, http://tinyurl.com/pa54wcq.

26. Maarten Bijleveld van Lexmond *et al.*, "Worldwide Integrated Assessment on Systemic Pesticides," Environmental Science and Pollution Research, Aug. 23, 2014, p. 3, http://tinyurl.com/qcbfbul.

27. Damian Carrington, "Bees and the European Neonicotinoids Pesticide Ban: Q&A," *The Guardian*, April 29, 2013, http://tinyurl.com/ng48qng.

28. Laura Zuckerman, "Portland Bans Insecticide to Protect Declining Honey Bees," Reuters, April 1, 2015, http://tinyurl.com/ocaalyw.

29. "Neonicotinoid Insecticides: Increasing Usage and Potential Threats," U.S. Fish and Wildlife Service, Aug. 14, 2014, http://tinyurl.com/p2qcdvh.

30. EPA letter to registrants of nitroguanidine neonicotinoid products, Environmental Protection Agency, April 2, 2015, http://tinyurl.com/ns3oc4x.

31. For background, see Jason McClure, "Genetically Modified Food," *CQ Researcher*, Aug. 31, 2012, pp. 717–740.

32. Jorge Fernandez-Conejo *et al.*, "Adoption of Genetically Engineered Crops by U.S. Farmers Has Increased Steadily for Over 15 Years," *Amber Waves*, U.S. Department of Agriculture, March 4, 2014, http://tinyurl.com/o82mjtm.

33. Biotechnology FAQ, "Do GM crops increase the use of pesticides?" Syngenta, undated, http://tinyurl.com/pha5dae.

34. "Agricultural Herbicides," Monsanto, undated, http://tinyurl.com/q9p4my7.

35. Charles M. Benbrook, "Impacts of Genetically Engineered Crops on Pesticide Use in the U.S. — The First Sixteen Years," *Environmental Sciences Europe*, Vol. 24, No. 24 (2012), http://tinyurl.com/av9h7fk.

36. *Ibid.*

37. Fernandez-Conejo *et al.*, *op. cit.*

38. For details see "Enlist Duo Herbicide," http://tinyurl.com/poebqag.

39. "2,4-D Technical Fact Sheet," National Pesticide Information Center, p. 5, http://tinyurl.com/kd3vfrd.

40. Suzanne Goldenburg, "U.S. launches Plan to Halt Decline of Monarch Butterfly," *The Guardian*, Feb. 9, 2015, http://tinyurl.com/kd84mwj.

41. Michael Wines, "U.S. Details New Efforts to Support Ailing Bees," *The New York Times*, May 19, 2015, http://tinyurl.com/olglsks.

42. Seth Borenstein, "EPA Plans Temporary Pesticide Restrictions While Bees Feed," The Associated Press, May 28, 2015, http://tinyurl.com/ocwhjxm.

43. Wilhelm Klumper and Matin Qaim, "A Meta-Analysis of the Impacts of Genetically Modified Crops," PLoS One, November 2014, http://tinyurl.com/nf4qxhh.

44. Amy Maxmen, "GMOs May Feed the World Using Fewer Pesticides," NOVANext, July 24, 2013, http://tinyurl.com/n78wo6x.

45. Hank Schultz, "Survey Reveals Consumers Want to Avoid Pesticides, But Are Unsure How Label Certifications Help Them Do That," Food Navigator, Oct. 29, 2013, http://tinyurl.com/nvw3cur; "Eat the Peach, Not the Pesticide," Consumer Reports, March 15, 2015, http://tinyurl.com/nbs95r7.

46. "Pesticide Data Program Annual Summary, Calendar Year 2013," U.S. Department of Agriculture, December 2014, pp. ix-x and appendix M, http://tinyurl.com/m7armdh.

47. "From Crop to Table: Pesticide Use in Produce," Consumer Reports Food and Sustainability Center, March 4, 2015, pp. 30–31, http://tinyurl.com/muayeho.

48. "Eat the Peach, Not the Pesticide," op. cit.

49. "2010–2011 Pilot Study: Pesticide Residue Testing of Organic Produce," U.S. Department of Agriculture, November 2012, p. 6, http://tinyurl.com/pagkhx6.

50. Chensheng Lu et al., "Organic diets significantly lower children's dietary exposure to organophosphorus pesticides," Environmental Health Perspectives, February 2006, pp. 260–263, http://tinyurl.com/pbuuz2a; Chensheng Lu et al., "Dietary intake and its contribution to longitudinal organophosphorus pesticide exposure in urban/suburban children," Environmental Health Perspectives, April 2008, http://tinyurl.com/qfjg9gp.

51. "Exposure to Pesticides in Produce with Dr. Alex Lu, Harvard," Environmental Working Group, April 19, 2013, http://tinyurl.com/oymrw7d.

52. Melinda Wenner Moyer, "Organic Shmorganic," Slate, Jan. 28, 2014, http://tinyurl.com/qaa46aa.

53. Paul J. Driscoll, "The Mysterious Disappearance of the Rocky Mountain Locust," The Bozeman Magpie, April 11, 2013, http://tinyurl.com/of2yt6h.

54. Laura Ingalls Wilder, On the Banks of Plum Creek (1971), pp. 194–95.

55. Nancy M. Trautmann et al., "Modern Agriculture: Its Effects on the Environment," Cornell University Cooperative Extension Program, 2012, http://tinyurl.com/7udd8xb.

56. Frederick Rowe Davis, Banned: A History of Pesticides and the Science of Toxicology (2014), p. 4.

57. For example, see "Killing Bugs One at a Time," Wessels Living History Farm, York, Nebraska, http://tinyurl.com/oyxoh7l.

58. Suellen Hoy, Chasing Dirt: The American Pursuit of Cleanliness (1995), pp. 104–106; Dawn Day Biehler, Pests in the City: Flies, Bedbugs, Cockroaches and Rats (2013), pp. 32–38.

59. Biehler, ibid., pp. 64–66.

60. Davis, op. cit., pp. 39, 69–70.

61. Preventive Medicine in World War II, Vol. VI: Communicable Diseases: Malaria, Office of Medical History, U.S. Army Medical Department, pp. 400–402, http://tinyurl.com/pxek3ma.

62. "Elimination of Malaria in the United States," U.S. Centers for Disease Control and Prevention, 2012, http://tinyurl.com/3afm79j.

63. William Souder, On a Farther Shore: The Life and Legacy of Rachel Carson (2012), pp. 254–263.

64. Ibid., pp. 350–352.

65. David Anderson, "Poisons Kill Fish in the Mississippi," The New York Times, March 22, 1964, http://tinyurl.com/pl8d8g3.

66. "DDT Regulatory History: A Brief Survey (to 1975)," U.S. Environmental Protection Agency, July 1975, http://tinyurl.com/qffo98t.

67. Davis, op. cit., p. 185.

68. Rachel Carson, Silent Spring (1962), p. 27, online at http://tinyurl.com/p2ssyxa.

69. Frances M. Dyro et al., "Organophosphates," Medscape, updated May 21, 2014, http://tinyurl.com/ktkyjul.

70. Andy Dyer, Chasing the Red Queen: The Evolutionary Race Between Agricultural Pests and Poisons (2014), pp. 108–109.

71. Quoted in Biehler, op. cit., p. 191.

72. Pesticides in the Diets of Infants and Young Children, op. cit., p. 7.

73. Barnaby J. Feder, "Out of the Lab, A Revolution on the Farm," *The New York Times*, March 3, 1996, http://tinyurl.com/pqbd3ks.

74. James Owen, "Bloodthirsty Bedbugs Stage Comeback in U.S., Europe," *National Geographic News*, May 13, 2004, http://tinyurl.com/7x9xl; Denise Mann, "Bedbugs: Why they're Back," *WebMD*, Dec. 6, 2011, http://tinyurl.com/oyxh7gt.

75. Alexei Barrionuevo, "Honeybees Vanish, Leaving Keepers in Peril," *The New York Times*, Feb. 27, 2007, *http://tinyurl.com/85zfoa*.

76. Alexei Barrionuevo, "Bees Vanish, and Scientists Race for Reasons," *The New York Times*, April 24, 2007, http://tinyurl.com/22fwvq.

77. Quoted in Louise Saw *et al.*, "Surveillance Data on Pesticide and Agricultural Chemical Releases and Associated Public Health Consequences in Selected U.S. States, 2003–2007," *Journal of Medical Toxicology*, Vol. 7, No. 2 (2011), http://tinyurl.com/nodwejy.

78. "Current Agricultural Worker Protection Standard," U.S. Environmental Protection Agency, updated May 15, 2014, http://tinyurl.com/nvho84j.

79. "Proposed Changes to the Farm Worker Protection Standard," U.S. Environmental Protection Agency, Feb. 20, 2014, http://tinyurl.com/p7p7yzb.

80. Peggy Kirk Hall, "OSHA Issues New Guidance on the Small Farm Exemption," *Ohio's Country Journal*, Aug. 5, 2014, http://tinyurl.com/pqy7zhx.

81. "State Plans," Occupational Safety and Health Administration, undated, http://tinyurl.com/olrw8fv.

82. "Comments on proposed revisions to Worker Protection Standard," American Farm Bureau Federation, April 25, 2014, p. 2, http://tinyurl.com/q2buzlz.

83. Rob Davis, "Whistleblower Videos Reveal Helicopter Spraying Workers with Weed Killers," *The Oregonian/OregonLive*, May 20, 2015, http://tinyurl.com/m2jvs53.

84. *Ibid.*

85. "Defining criteria for identifying endocrine disruptors in the context of the implementation of the Plant Protection Regulation and Biocidal Products Regulation," European Commission, June 2014, p. 6, http://tinyurl.com/nvkcppm.

86. For background, see Jennifer Weeks, "Regulating Toxic Chemicals," *CQ Researcher*, Jan. 23, 2009, pp. 49–72.

87. *Ibid.*

88. "European Commission's Public Consultation on Defining Criteria for Identifying Endocrine Disruptors (EDs) in the Context of the Implementation of the Plant Protection Product Regulation and Biocidal Products Regulation: Comments of the U.S. Government," European Commission, Jan. 16, 2015, pp. 13–14, http://tinyurl.com/plfy32r.

89. *Ibid.*, p. 4.

90. "U.S. Environmental Protection Agency Endocrine Disruptor Screening Comprehensive Management Plan," U.S. Environmental Protection Agency, Feb. 14, 2014, pp. 2–4, http://tinyurl.com/o6ll7mp.

91. "State of the Science of Endocrine Disrupting Chemicals — 2012," World Health Organization, 2013, pp. viii-ix, http://tinyurl.com/nzlpg2l.

92. Ilia Rochlin *et al.*, "Climate Change and Range Expansion of the Asian Tiger Mosquito (Aedes albopictus) in Northeastern USA: Implications for Public Health Practitioners," PLoSOne, Vol. 8, No. 4, April 2, 2013, http://tinyurl.com/nfxh8eh.

93. "Comprehensive Mosquito Surveillance and Control Plan," City of New York Department of Health and Mental Hygiene, 2015, p. 3, http://tinyurl.com/phgglvw.

94. "Climate Change and Vector-Borne Disease," University Corporation for Atmospheric Research, Center for Science Education, 2011, http://tinyurl.com/o8n5nkn.

95. "Controlling Mosquitos at the Larval Stage," U.S. Environmental Protection Agency, updated May 6, 2015, http://tinyurl.com/o2ymlpb.

96. Mike Merchant, "FAQs About Aerial Spraying for West Nile Virus Mosquitos," Texas A&M Agrilife Extension Program, Aug. 14, 2012, http://tinyurl.com/pamudh9.

97. Lizette Alvarez, "A Mosquito Solution (More Mosquitoes) Raises Heat in Florida Keys," *The New York Times*, Feb. 19, 2015, http://tinyurl.com/qywtxdp.

98. Shannon LaDeau, "Reducing Mosquitos Is Vital to Human Health," *The New York Times*, Feb. 23, 2015, http://tinyurl.com/lahmowo.

99. For background, see Tom Price, "Global Hunger," *CQ Researcher*, Aug. 8, 2014, pp. 673–696.

100. "What are Biopesticides?" U.S. Environmental Protection Agency, updated Feb. 6, 2015, http://tinyurl.com/odxhd8j.

101. "EPA Regulator Sees Bright Future for Biopesticides," *AgLine News*, May 6, 2015, http://tinyurl.com/onfbtbd.

BIBLIOGRAPHY
Selected Sources
Books

Biehler, Dawn Ray, *Pests in the City: Flies, Bedbugs, Cockroaches, and Rats*, University of Washington Press, 2013.
An assistant professor of geography and environmental studies at the University of Maryland-Baltimore shows how geography, social inequality and social policies have shaped pest control efforts in U.S. cities since 1900.

Borel, Brooke, *Infested: How the Bed Bug Infiltrated Our Bedrooms and Took Over the World*, University of Chicago Press, 2015.
A journalist explores the biology and history of bedbugs and explains why they have reappeared in the United States after seemingly disappearing in the 1950s.

Davis, Frederick Rowe, *Banned: A History of Pesticides and the Science of Toxicology*, Yale University Press, 2014.
A professor of history at Florida State University traces the parallel development of the pesticide industry and the science of toxicology and calls for new approaches to regulating pesticides.

Dyer, Andy, *Chasing the Red Queen: The Evolutionary Race Between Agricultural Pests and Poisons*, Island Press, 2014.
A biology professor at the University of South Carolina contends that. sustainable agriculture practices, such as crop rotation, are more effective than pesticides because insects and weeds inevitably become resistant to poisons.

Souder, William, *On a Farther Shore: The Life and Legacy of Rachel Carson*, Broadway Books, 2012.
Published on the 50th anniversary of the release of Carson's best-seller *Silent Spring*, this biography shows how Carson's early love for science and the natural world led her to write a sweeping warning against the overuse of synthetic pesticides.

Winston, Mark L., *Bee Time: Lessons From the Hive*, Harvard University Press, 2014.
Winston, a professor of biology at Simon Fraser University in British Columbia, examines bees' social structures and ecological roles and explains the role of pesticides in bee population declines.

Articles

McFerron, Whitney, "Bugs Invade Europe as Save-Bees Cry Spurs Pesticide Ban," *Bloomberg Business*, Jan. 7, 2015, http://tinyurl.com/mhdlqjo.
Since European Union regulators imposed a partial ban on three neonicotinoid (nicotine-like) pesticides in late 2013, harvests of rapeseed, an important oil crop, are falling due to pest infestations.

Pollack, Andrew, "Weed Killer, Long Cleared, Is Doubted," *The New York Times*, March 27, 2015, http://tinyurl.com/qcltu8o.
The U.S. Environmental Protection Agency determined in 1985 that Roundup, a widely used weed killer, might cause cancer, then reversed its opinion six years later. Now an agency of the World Health Organization says that glyphosate, the active ingredient in Roundup, "probably" causes cancer in humans.

Xia, Rosanna, "Santa Ana to be sprayed with insecticide amid big West Nile outbreak," *Los Angeles Times*, Sept. 7, 2014, http://tinyurl.com/nbtm777.
To combat the worst recorded outbreak of West Nile virus, in Orange County, Calif., officials used trucks equipped with foggers to spray parts of Santa Ana for mosquitos in 2014.

Zimmer, Carl, "In Bedbugs, Scientists See a Model of Evolution," *The New York Times*, Feb. 5, 2015, http://tinyurl.com/kkqadnu.
Bedbugs' ability to adapt has been key to their resurgence. Now many that feed on humans carry a gene that makes them resistant to pesticides.

Reports and Studies

"Agricultural Pesticide Use Near Public Schools in California," California Environmental Health Tracking Program, April 2014, http://tinyurl.com/n7al4ol.
Two California state agencies find that although pesticide use near most schools was negligible, high levels were detected near a small number of schools — and those schools were more likely to be attended by Hispanics than by whites.

"Food Safety: FDA and USDA Should Strengthen Pesticide Residue Monitoring Programs and Further Disclose Monitoring Limitations," Government Accountability Office, October 2014, http://tinyurl.com/o3h2cgg.
Congress' watchdog reviews data from two federal agencies and reports pesticide residue violations are low, but adds that neither agency tests for all commonly used pesticides.

"From Crop to Table: Pesticide Use in Produce," Consumer Reports Food and Sustainability Center, March 2015, http://tinyurl.com/muayeho.
The nation's largest consumer advocacy group surveys use of chemical pesticides in fruit and vegetable production in the United States and calculates pesticide residue levels in many common types of produce.

For More Information

Consumers Union, 101 Truman Ave., Yonkers, NY 10703; 914-378-2000; www.consumersunion.org. Public health and consumer-safety advocacy group.

CropLife America, 1156 15th St., N.W., Washington, DC 20005; 202-296-1585; www.croplifeamerica.org. Trade association representing companies that develop, manufacture and distribute pesticides for agriculture and pest management.

Migrant Clinicians Network, P.O. Box 164285, Austin, TX 78716; 512-327-2017; www.migrantclinician.org. Nonprofit that supports medical professionals who care for migrant workers and their families.

National Pest Management Association, 10460 North St., Fairfax, VA 22030; 800-678-6722; https://npmapestworld.org. Trade association representing the urban pest-management industry.

Natural Resources Defense Council, 40 W. 20th St., New York, NY 10011; 212-727-2700; www.nrdc.org. National environmental advocacy group that works on issues including protecting people and the environment from toxic chemicals.

Northeastern IPM Center, 340 Tower Rd., Cornell University, Ithaca, NY 14853; 607-255-5523; www.northeastipm.org. One of four regional centers funded by the U.S. Department of Agriculture to promote the development and adoption of integrated pest management practices.

3

Marijuana Industry

William Wanlund

Marijuana proponents call for legalization of pot during the annual Hash Bash rally at the University of Michigan in Ann Arbor on April 4, 2015. The marijuana industry could reach $20 billion a year in sales by 2020 — and $35 billion if all 50 states and Washington, D.C., legalize the drug.

From *CQ Researcher*, October 16, 2015.

From the outside, the Seattle Cannabis Co. is not much to look at — a squat, asphalt-gray building on a gritty street in Seattle's industrial SoDo (South of Downtown) district. Opaque windows thwart curious passersby, and a polite but no-nonsense doorman checks photo IDs to verify customers are over 21.

Inside, however, the store's spacious, brightly lit showroom gives customers a glitzy 21st-century welcome to the new world of legal recreational marijuana. Glittering display cases line the walls, showing off dozens of types of marijuana — Maui Wowie, Permafrost and Snoop's Dream among them. Upbeat, contemporary music murmurs quietly as customers and sales staff — "budtenders" — discuss the effects produced by the different strains of pot. On the walls, flat-screen televisions advertise the store's myriad products — including brownies and other edibles and concentrates that can be inhaled, eaten, drunk or rubbed onto the skin.

"Typically we get 100 to 150 customers a day," says Steven Ode, chief of operations. "Business is good. We're meeting payroll and paying our bills. We're in a good position for the future. The profits aren't there yet, but they will come. It just comes with the territory of breaking into a new industry."

It's a very new industry, indeed. Washington is one of four states plus the District of Columbia that have legalized the recreational use of marijuana. The nation's first legal retail stores selling marijuana for recreational use opened in Colorado on Jan. 1, 2014, followed by stores in Washington state on July 8 of that year. Recreational sales in

Medical Marijuana Legal in 23 States

Twenty-three states and the District of Columbia have legalized medical marijuana, but only Alaska, Colorado, Oregon and Washington state, plus the District, allow residents to possess, grow or consume recreational and medical marijuana. D.C. alone bars businesses from selling marijuana for recreational purposes.

Marijuana Laws by State (as of June 19, 2015)

Recreational and Medical Marijuana Legal

Medical Marijuana Legal

Source: "State Marijuana Laws Map," *Governing*, updated June 19, 2015, http://tinyurl.com/lv4r7f3

Oregon began this past Oct. 1. Alaska and Washington, D.C., also have legalized recreational marijuana, but sales have yet to begin. In addition, 23 states and the District have legalized marijuana for medicinal use.

Marijuana businesses operate in a hazy legal environment. Under the federal Controlled Substances Act, marijuana is classified along with cocaine and heroin as a Schedule I drug — the most dangerous — and is illegal to grow, possess or sell. The Department of Justice (DOJ) announced it will not challenge state pot laws unless they conflict with federal priorities — to prevent distribution to minors and keep marijuana-generated revenue from reaching criminals.

But the no-prosecution directive only prescribes current DOJ procedures under the Obama administration. Since marijuana is illegal under federal law, investors and entrepreneurs are wary of getting into the industry, and stores like Ode's find it difficult to get banking services such as checking accounts and credit card processing. "This is a cash-only business," Ode says.

Aiding and abetting production and distribution of marijuana remains a felony under federal law, wrote Julie Andersen Hill, an associate law professor at the University of Alabama. "By providing a loan and placing the proceeds in a checking account, the [banking] institution would be conspiring to distribute marijuana," Hill wrote. "Facilitating customers' credit card payments would be aiding and abetting the distribution of marijuana."[1]

Rep. Earl Blumenauer, an Oregon Democrat who is cosponsoring federal legislation to allow banks to provide services for legitimate marijuana-related enterprises, says he finds the possibility of federal charges "ludicrous."

He asks: "If you care about money laundering or tax evasion or criminal threat, what's the public policy that's advanced if legal marijuana businesses have to accumulate shopping bagsful of $20 bills to pay their state taxes? It's dangerous and it's ill-advised."[2]

But Calvina Fay, executive director of the anti-legalization Drug Free America Foundation, says she is "stunned that anyone in Congress would seriously consider" letting banks deal with marijuana enterprises. "Banks are federally regulated, and marijuana is still illegal at the federal level," she says. "Regardless of how anyone feels about marijuana, laws are laws, and we are supposed to be a country that respects the laws."

Taylor West, deputy director of the Denver-based National Cannabis Industry Association (NCIA), says banking restrictions are "not safe, and they create accounting issues. And, from the regulatory perspective, if you want to be able to keep track of what's happening with these businesses, then you don't want them operating entirely in cash. [The government doesn't] force any other industry to do that."

However, West says, "I've never heard of a situation in which a financial institution had actually been prosecuted for dealing with a state-legal marijuana business."

Federal tax policy is another major hurdle for the marijuana industry, West says. "The federal tax code says if you engage in trafficking of a controlled substance, you cannot deduct your normal business expenses," she says. "That means businesses that cultivate and sell marijuana legally under state law are paying taxes roughly on their gross revenue rather than their profit, unlike every other business in the United States."

Geneva Shaunette, general manager of Alpine Wellness, a medical and recreational marijuana dispensary in Telluride, Colo., says her company pays a "staggering" amount of taxes. "We're sending anywhere from $30,000 to $50,000 to the federal government every month" just in payroll and income taxes, she says. And because the company cannot open a bank account, she adds, "I spend a couple of hours every morning counting cash and setting it aside in piles to pay salaries, to pay rent, to pay electric bills."

Nevertheless, recreational marijuana sales are soaring. From July 8, 2014, to June 30, 2015, the first full year of legalization in Washington state, retail recreational marijuana sales statewide totaled almost $260 million.[3] Recreational sales in Colorado's first year (Jan. 1-Dec. 31, 2014) totaled $313 million.[4] *

The ArcView Group, a network of cannabis-industry investors that includes venture capitalists and entrepreneurs, estimated the industry's combined 2014 retail and wholesale sales (including medical marijuana) at $2.7 billion, a 74 percent increase over 2013, making marijuana the "fastest-growing industry in America," according to the group.[5]

However, the laws governing medical marijuana vary widely from state to state. Patients must register and obtain physician approval in all states. But while most jurisdictions allow marijuana use only for specific medical conditions such as glaucoma, Crohn's disease and

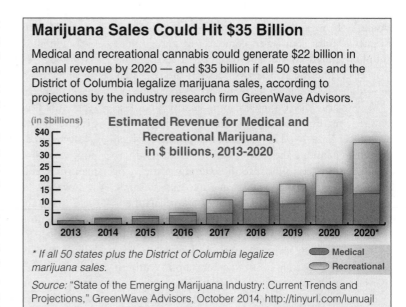

Marijuana Sales Could Hit $35 Billion

Medical and recreational cannabis could generate $22 billion in annual revenue by 2020 — and $35 billion if all 50 states and the District of Columbia legalize marijuana sales, according to projections by the industry research firm GreenWave Advisors.

(in $billions) **Estimated Revenue for Medical and Recreational Marijuana, in $ billions, 2013-2020**

* If all 50 states plus the District of Columbia legalize marijuana sales.

Source: "State of the Emerging Marijuana Industry: Current Trends and Projections," GreenWave Advisors, October 2014, http://tinyurl.com/lunuajl

some forms of cancer, in places such as California a recommending physician currently can decide whether marijuana would be a suitable therapy regardless of the condition.[6] Some states allow dispensaries to sell to eligible patients from other states; others do not. And some jurisdictions allow qualified patients to grow marijuana for their own medical use.[7]

California's medical marijuana industry, the nation's largest, has generally been regarded as the most loosely regulated, but changes are in store. Legislation signed by Democratic Gov. Jerry Brown in October 2015 establishes a state medical marijuana bureau to oversee transportation, distribution and sale of the drug. It also requires marijuana farmers to obtain state licenses and establishes procedures to oversee physicians who prescribe the drug. Brown said the new regulations, which go into effect in 2018, "will make sure patients have access to medical marijuana, while ensuring a robust tracking system."[8]

Oversight of the medical marijuana industry in many states is fairly loose compared to the strict regulations governing state-authorized recreational marijuana growers and distributors. Thus, some authorities suspect that medical marijuana cultivation facilities, or "grows," and dispensaries serve as cover for black-market activities. Loopholes in Colorado's medical marijuana regulations "allow people to grow way more than they could possibly

---

* Retail sales in Oregon began on Oct. 1, 2015; Alaska's are expected to begin in 2016. Although Washington, D.C., voters legalized recreational marijuana in 2014, Congress has blocked its implementation.

smoke" for medical use, says Sheriff Bill Masters of San Miguel County. "Smugglers come to [the grow], buy a couple hundred pounds and transport it to the black market in other states," he says. "It's not the regulated, recreational side of the industry that causes the problem."

A new drug that is growing in popularity, known as synthetic marijuana, could represent a challenge for the marijuana industry. The noncannabis product, which contains chemicals and dried plant material, produces psychoactive effects similar to those produced by marijuana but is more dangerous: It can cause death, seizures, psychotic episodes, heart attacks and strokes.[9] Synthetic marijuana killed 15 people in the first half of 2015 — three times as many as in same period in 2014, according to the Centers for Disease Control and Prevention. And phone calls to poison control centers about synthetic marijuana rose 229 percent during the same period.[10]

Synthetic marijuana is also cheaper than marijuana and is readily available online and in gas stations, drug paraphernalia shops or tobacco shops, raising questions about whether it could eat into the profits of those selling regular marijuana in states where it is legal. Marijuana retailers are prohibited from dealing in synthetic marijuana.

However, NCIA's West says so far synthetic marijuana has not had "any significant impact" on the legal market, nor has it caused an anti-cannabis public backlash.

Responding to growing interest in commercial marijuana, at least eight brick-and-mortar colleges and universities, including Harvard, Ohio State and Vanderbilt, are offering courses in various aspects of marijuana business and law.[11] Nonaccredited Oaksterdam University in Oakland, Calif., offers cannabis-related courses ranging from horticulture to culinary arts to business management. And several institutions, including THC University and the College of Cannabis, offer online courses.

As marijuana's economic impact grows, here are some of the questions being debated:

Is legalized marijuana good for the U.S. economy?

In February 2014, a month after Colorado became the first state to legalize recreational marijuana use, Democratic Gov. John Hickenlooper predicted first-year cannabis sales would generate $98 million in state sales, excise and other fees and taxes.[12]

It didn't happen. That year, marijuana netted Colorado just $52.6 million in tax revenue.[13] Some analysts thought the sales tax made prices for legal marijuana uncompetitive with what buyers could find on the black market. In January 2014, legal marijuana prices were reportedly two to three times higher than in the underground market.[14] The Marijuana Policy Group, a Denver-based advocacy firm that analyzes marijuana policies, estimated that only 60 percent of 2014 marijuana purchases in the state occurred in legal outlets.[15]

Revenues in the first seven months of 2015, however, were greater than all of last year. As of July 31, Colorado had taken in nearly $73.5 million in taxes and fees.[16] Although that represents only a fraction of Colorado's $25 billion 2015–16 budget, the revenues are earmarked for new school construction and drug treatment and prevention programs.[17] The consumer information website NerdWallet concluded that if marijuana were legal nationwide, states could collect about $3.1 billion a year in tax revenue.[18]

Kevin Sabet, president and CEO of Smart Approaches to Marijuana (SAM), an advocacy group opposed to legalization, says such revenue won't compensate for the social costs of legalization. The income "is going to be pennies compared to the cost," he says, such as car accidents resulting from marijuana-impaired driving and emergency room visits for children who eat cannabis-infused brownies and candy. "The industry is marketing these kinds of products and targeting kids," Sabet says.

The National Cannabis Industry Association's West replies, "Where is the evidence that businesses are targeting children? No street dealer is checking IDs or providing child-proof packaging or carefully labeling products," she says. "When we take cannabis out of the underground market and put it behind a legal, regulated counter, we create a safer, more responsible system."

Legalization supporters say a regulated cannabis industry also will boost employment. *Marijuana Business Daily*, an industry publication, estimates that between 46,000 and 60,000 people are in the legal cannabis industry, working for growers, retailers, testing labs and makers of infused (non-smoked) products such as edibles, beverages and ointments. Sales of ancillary products and services could increase the total by 50 percent, the newspaper said.[19] Ancillary businesses include

Rep. Earl Blumenauer, D-Ore., has co-sponsored legislation that would enable banks to provide services for legitimate marijuana-related enterprises. Because marijuana is illegal under federal law, investors and entrepreneurs are wary of getting into the industry, and many stores find it difficult to get banking services such as checking accounts and credit card processing.

lighting manufacturers, contractors who build grower warehouses, and those who install climate control systems and provide soil, additives and nutrients.

In addition, says West, dispensaries need "software for inventory tracking and point of sale, packaging and specialized services — accounting, attorneys, branding and market research and human resources — pretty much any service that a packaged-goods industry or a horticultural industry would need."

Legalization also can reduce law enforcement costs, supporters say. A 2005 study by Jeffrey Miron, then a visiting professor of economics at Harvard University, found that legalizing marijuana nationwide would save federal, state and local law enforcement agencies $7.7 billion a year. The savings would accrue, he said, because fewer police, prosecutorial, judicial and correctional resources would be needed.[20]

But David Evans, a lawyer in Pittstown, N.J., and special adviser to the Drug Free America Foundation, which opposes marijuana legalization, says the idea that "you're going to save all this prison and court time" is "a complete falsehood." People are not in prison "for having a couple of joints in their pocket," he says. "The people in prison for possession are major traffickers."

People arrested for marijuana have usually been arrested for something more serious, and had marijuana on their person, Evans says. "They'll plead guilty to the marijuana charge so their record shows they were found guilty of marijuana possession, when their sentence was really only the result of a plea bargain."

Rep. Blumenauer of Oregon says legal cannabis can greatly benefit the U.S. economy. "If we can have a rational marijuana policy, I think we will see in the next 10 years a shift of well over $100 billion in net savings just to government, to say nothing about opportunities for the private sector," he says. "We really don't know the full extent of what a legal marijuana industry would be because, by definition, most of this so far is in the shadows."

According to Alejandro Hope, director of security policy at the Mexican Competitive Institute, a Mexico City think tank, "Approximately 30 percent of [drug] cartels' export revenues come from marijuana. The market is definitely changing, but cartel adaptation will happen in years not months," Hope said. "In the long term, Mexican marijuana could be displaced by legal production in the United States."[21]

Nationwide, marijuana seizures decreased 21 percent in 2014 — from 2.4 million pounds in 2013 to 1.9 million pounds, based on U.S. Customs and Border Protection figures.[22]

Javier Osorio, a professor and criminal violence researcher at the John Jay College of Criminal Justice in New York City, said if marijuana were legalized nationwide, "between 16 and 20 percent of Mexican drug trafficking income could be affected."[23]

But Evans, the Drug Free America Foundation adviser, says legalization isn't hurting the cartels. "The Mexican cartels aren't making a lot of money on marijuana, because it's big, too bulky to transport, it's not that pricey and it's a lot harder to distribute," he says. "They're more interested in cocaine, heroin, stuff like that. Marijuana is grown all over the U.S., so why bother going to Mexico to get it and running the risk of bringing it across the border?"

Should medical and recreational marijuana be regulated differently?

In 1998, Washington — the first state to permit marijuana use for medical purposes — applied the gentlest of regulatory touches: Patients with certain conditions such as cancer, HIV/AIDS or multiple sclerosis could purchase marijuana with only a doctor's recommendation. Patients could grow up to 15 plants and possess up to 24 ounces of "usable" marijuana. Dispensaries and the potency and source of the drug were unregulated.

Seattle lawyer Hilary Bricken says legalization of medical marijuana stemmed from pressure from HIV/AIDS and cancer patients seeking cheaper, effective alternative treatment options. Some studies have found that marijuana improves food intake in HIV patients, relieves pain from damaged nerve endings and eases chemotherapy nausea, according to the American Cancer Society.[24]

"The sentiment behind the early medical marijuana laws was that the industry would be small, it would not be commercial, and it would not have an impact on the economy or the surrounding communities," Bricken says. But a few years ago, she says, commercialization "came on very strongly, supported by people who read the law, saw the loopholes and found a way to monetize it."

Rick Garza, director of the Washington State Liquor and Cannabis Board (LCB), which administers state marijuana laws, said the state's medical regulations were "looser than anywhere in the country," and the "vast majority" of those using medical marijuana were in fact recreational users.[25]

"No one even knows how many outlets are selling medical marijuana," says LCB spokesman Brian Smith. "These guys don't pay taxes, they're not registered anywhere, they can just pop up overnight, put a green cross on the door and sell marijuana."

This year Washington's Legislature brought medical marijuana under the state's more tightly controlled recreational marijuana regime, which requires "seed-to-sale" inventory tracking, in which each plant is assigned a unique 16-digit bar code that follows it and its byproducts from harvest to sale.[26] The new regulations, effective next July, will also tighten patient eligibility requirements, establish a state-run medical marijuana patient registry and reduce the amounts patients can possess. Dispensaries that existed under the previous laws are being closed. Medical marijuana will be available only at licensed retail shops endorsed by the LCB and subject to the same testing, packaging and labeling restrictions that apply to recreational cannabis.[27]

In effect, the new regulations merge the state's recreational and medical marijuana markets into a single retail industry. Democratic state Rep. Eileen Cody, a sponsor of the legislation, said the changes were intended to "make sure . . . we have a medical-marijuana system that fits with recreational, is safe and provides the safety mechanisms for our patients that recreational enjoys, [and] that everyone has access."

However, Republican state Rep. Ed Orcutt said he fears the new regulations limit the medical marijuana industry to the point that some patients "aren't going to be able to get the right form or the right variety for what they need."[28]

Deidre Finley, owner of MMJ Universe, a medical marijuana business in Black Diamond, Wash., said her business will close under the new regulations. "They're making the requirements on who can get a medical license so difficult. I won't qualify," she said. Finley worries that products needed by some patients may no longer be available at recreational stores.[29]

Medical patients will be exempt from the 10 percent retail sales tax paid by recreational customers, but they will have to pay the same 37 percent excise tax paid by recreational customers. Such taxes could substantially boost Washington's tax revenues. The state's Economic and Revenue Forecast Council (ERFC) predicts marijuana will generate $115.2 million in fiscal 2016, the first year under the new taxation structure, compared with $65 million in 2015, the first year of legal recreational sales. By fiscal 2017, ERFC foresees marijuana tax revenue reaching $256.2 million.[30]

But Lauren Vazquez, deputy director of communications for the pro-legalization Marijuana Policy Project, says the new taxing plan is unfair. "Drugs prescribed by a physician are not subject to taxes, and neither should medical marijuana," she says. "Many patients already have trouble paying for their medications, and some use medical marijuana specifically because it is less expensive than other treatments."

And she adds, "Because medical marijuana patients often must use more marijuana than nonpatients, the most sick would end up paying the most taxes."

Washington State Liquor and Cannabis Board spokesman Smith says the new plan is about fair commerce. "Legitimate businesses in the recreational industry asked, 'Why am I competing with somebody down the street who's playing by different rules?' Reining in the existing medical system and bringing it under regulation means everybody is following the same rules," he says.

The National Cannabis Industry Association's West worries, "What happens to these dispensaries that have been providing patients for years? They're being forced out of business without a chance to keep serving their patients."

Seattle attorney Bricken says medical and recreational sales can be handled in a single location. "Regulators asked, 'Instead of creating two separate and distinct systems, with separate and distinct rules, why not create a single hybrid model?' " she says. "You can have medical in a shop with people who are trained in giving advice about medical cannabis and its effects. We don't need to spend the money or the manpower to have a separate industry, and we can still have [product] accountability, traceability and quality assurance."

However, Jazmin Hupp, cofounder and CEO of Women Grow, a Denver organization that promotes the interests of women in the industry, says medical and recreational marijuana "are two distinct products for different purposes, and require different levels of expertise to meet those needs. As long as those systems are allowed to exist, [the industry will] do quite well."

For now, national pharmacy chains like CVS and Walgreens are eschewing the medical marijuana business because it presents too many obstacles to overcome, said David Yang, an analyst with the research firm IBISWorld. Marijuana's federal illegality is one stumbling block, said CVS spokeswoman Carolyn Castel, because it would violate the company's registration with the Drug Enforcement Administration (DEA).[31]

Is the marijuana industry's growth rate sustainable?

If legislative barriers continue to fall, and cannabis becomes legal for recreational and medical use nationwide, marijuana could be a $35 billion market by 2020, according to the industry research firm Green Wave Advisors, which tracks cannabis sales in the states where recreational marijuana is legal.[32] That is about the same

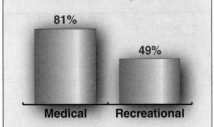

Large Majority Supports Medical Marijuana

Four in five American adults favor legalizing marijuana for medical purposes in their home states, while nearly half support legalization for recreational use.

Percentage of Americans Who Support Marijuana Legalization in Their State, 2015

81% Medical

49% Recreational

Source: "Increasing Percentages of Americans are Ready for Legal Marijuana," The Harris Poll, May 7, 2015, http://tinyurl.com/pm8gts9

level of retail sales for the worldwide vitamin and nutritional supplement industry.[33]

Green Wave founder and managing partner Matt Karnes says nationwide legalization will happen, though not necessarily in the next five years. "I can't handicap the timing, but it's coming," he says. "States have too much riding on it now — tax revenues, job creation, etc."

For now, Karnes does not recommend that the average investor sink money into the industry because it's too complicated. "Everything is state-specific," he says. For example, "you have to be a resident of Colorado to make an equity investment in that state; Washington is not as restrictive. It complicates investing."

Marijuana's uncertain legal status means the industry "is navigating uncharted legal waters," complicating the industry's future, says John Hudak, a fellow in governance studies at the Brookings Institution, a Washington, D.C., think tank. "They are dealing with a product that is legal in some states but still illegal federally.

"And even at the federal level, some parts of the government recognize the [legalization] experiments going on in the states as valid, and other parts still consider [them] illegal," he continues. So, depending on which agency a marijuana retailer or grower or investor is dealing with, they are either considered a criminal enterprise or . . . a state-legal operating entity. That contradiction makes life for the industry quite difficult."

Nevertheless, some investors believe in the durability of the industry. In April, Privateer Holdings, a Seattle-based private equity firm, announced it had raised $82 million to invest in marijuana companies worldwide.[34]

Founders Fund, a venture capital company started by PayPal co-founder Peter Thiel, is one of those companies. "This highlights a change that's going on in the market," said Leslie Bocskor, an investment banker and founding chairman of the Nevada Cannabis Industry

A medical marijuana user sniffs a sample at a cannabis farmer's market held by the West Coast Collective, a medicinal marijuana dispensary, in Los Angeles on July 4, 2014. The medical properties of cannabis have been known for thousands of years. The first-century Chinese surgeon Hua Tuo reportedly performed painless surgery using an anesthetic made from cannabis resin and wine.

Association. The cannabis industry "is now in a second wave, where we're seeing professionals who have had success in other industries come in."[35]

Others believe the industry will continue to show strength even if the rest of the economy is going sour. Derek Peterson, president and CEO of Terra Tech, an agricultural technology company in Irvine, Calif., said, "[In] times of economic collapse, [cannabis is] a product that's quasi-medical and quasi-recreational. It's going to withstand the market more so than a company dependent on high-end consumer goods."[36]

However, Shad Ewart, who teaches a course at Anne Arundel Community College in Maryland on entrepreneurial opportunities in the marijuana industry, foresees potential political troubles. "The big one is the 2016 presidential election," he says. "Some candidates have aggressively disagreed with state-level legalization and vow to shut the entire industry down if they are elected."

Bloomberg Intelligence, the research arm of the Bloomberg financial information company, has identified 55 publicly traded companies whose stock traded at 10 cents or more per share as of April 15 and "whose business is based largely or completely on legal marijuana." They include pharmaceutical companies, marijuana growers and technology firms, with combined market capitalization — the total value of outstanding shares — of $3 billion. "Many of these companies have experienced the pitfalls common to penny stocks: infrequent trading and wild swings in share price," Bloomberg wrote. "[They] aren't for the faint of heart."[37]

Seattle attorney Bricken is skeptical about marijuana stocks, citing "the volatility of the marketplace and the nature of the stocks being traded." Most of the companies whose stocks are being traded are in ancillary businesses, she says. "When you look at what these people are actually trading on, there's no real value. There's no history of doing business, there's no rap sheet [performance record] of the CEOs. . . . And when [investors] perform that screening, I think they'll find that most of the stocks are just not worth it."

Jon Gettman, who teaches criminal justice at Shenandoah University in Winchester, Va., and management at the Graduate School of the University of Maryland University College, supports marijuana legalization. He says "a free and open market" would sort out the questions about the economic health of the cannabis market.

"Risk . . . is part of the [economic] landscape, especially with new markets," Gettman says. "A lot of risk derives from uncertainty, particularly about market size and regulatory conditions. These, in turn, create uncertainty about price and, consequently, return on investment. On the other hand, such uncertainty . . . is mitigated by the gradual path the nation is taking to legalize marijuana by way of state-by-state reform initiatives."

Chris Walsh, managing editor of *Marijuana Business Daily*, says the industry's growth rate "is definitely sustainable, as long as we don't get some huge public backlash from major problems with either medical or recreational. If people start getting sick from marijuana, if [drug-related] crime goes up, if children are harmed, that could cause the industry to stumble.

"But it's probably impossible to put the genie back in the bottle," he continues. "You have states making tens of millions in tax dollars, and thousands of businesses and people employed. Trying to reel this industry in and go back in time probably wouldn't work."

BACKGROUND

Early Cannabis Use

The earliest record of cannabis use comes from China. Fibers from hemp cord — made from a variety of cannabis closely related to marijuana — were found in decorated pottery from 8000 B.C. unearthed in present-day Taiwan.[38] Unlike marijuana, hemp contains only 0.3 percent tetrahydrocannabinol (THC), the psychoactive chemical responsible for most of marijuana's psychoactive effects.

Cannabis seeds and oil were used as food in China around 6000 B.C. And cannabis' medical properties have been known for thousands of years. The first-century surgeon Hua Tuo reportedly performed painless surgery using an anesthetic made from cannabis resin and wine.[39]

The plant's psychoactive properties also were known. A Chinese medical pharmacopoeia from the first century B.C. noted that "to take too much [marijuana] makes people see demons and throw themselves about like maniacs. But if one takes it over a long period of time one can communicate with the spirits and one's own body becomes light." In India, a Hindu sacred text, the *Artharvaveda*, which dates to at least 1000 B.C., describes cannabis as an herb that can "release us from anxiety."[40]

Nomadic Scythians, from present-day Iran, made hemp garments and bathed in the vapor from heated hemp seeds, causing them to "howl like wolves," reported the Greek historian Herodotus.[41] The Scythians brought hemp to northern Europe: An urn found near Berlin, dating to around 500 B.C., contained cannabis residue.[42]

Hemp was cultivated in England beginning around A.D. 400; its fibers were used for rope. The Moors, who conquered Spain in 711, brought with them a technique for making paper from hemp. The first hemp paper mill was constructed near Valencia in 1150. In 1215, the Magna Carta, a landmark legal document establishing the rights of English royal subjects, was printed on hemp paper, as was the first Gutenberg Bible, the first major book printed in Western Europe with moveable metal type, in 1455.[43]

The medicinal qualities of cannabis gained recognition in Europe beginning in the 17th century. Robert Burton's *The Anatomy of Melancholy*, published in 1621, recommended using cannabis to counter depression. *The New English Dispensatory* of 1764 suggested applying hemp roots to the skin for inflammation.[44] In the late 19th century, British Queen Victoria's doctor prescribed marijuana tea to treat patients' menstrual cramps, though there is no evidence the queen herself was given the drug.[45]

In the early 17th century, the English turned to their North American colonies to help feed the growing demand for hemp. In 1619, the Virginia Company directed Jamestown colonists to cultivate 100 cannabis plants per household. The colonies soon developed their own hemp market for cloth and rope. In 1639, the General Court of Massachusetts required every household to plant hemp seed so "that we might in time have supply of linen cloth among ourselves."[46]

The United States Pharmacopeia, established in the 1820s to identify and standardize medical drugs, listed marijuana in 1850 as a treatment for conditions ranging from labor pains and nausea to rheumatism (the drug remained listed until 1942).[47] In 1860, the Ohio State Medical Society devoted a conference to the use of medical marijuana. In the conference report, which included observations by physicians who had prescribed or conducted experiments with marijuana, cannabis committee Chairman R. R. McMeens, M.D., called marijuana a "remarkable and renowned exotic."[48]

During the second half of the 19th century, marijuana was widely available in American pharmacies and general stores, as were products containing opium and cocaine. In the 1860s, the Gunjah Wallah Co. began producing candy from maple sugar and hashish (compressed cannabis resin). For more than 40 years it was sold over the counter, listed in Sears, Roebuck & Co. catalogs and advertised in newspapers as a "pleasureable (sic) and harmless stimulant" and a remedy for a variety of ailments.[49]

Regulating Marijuana

The Pure Food and Drug Act of 1906, passed in response to concerns over the safety and purity of food and medicines, was the first U.S. law regulating marijuana. It banned the interstate transportation of adulterated or mislabeled food and drugs, including cannabis, and established advertising accuracy standards. The law did not ban the sale or use of marijuana and other drugs, but the truth-in-labeling requirement resulted in many patent medicines with unproven claims being removed from the market.[50]

CHRONOLOGY

1840–1911 *Cannabis enters the American marketplace.*

1840 Cannabis-based medicines are sold in U.S. drug stores.

1850 United States Pharmacopeia lists marijuana as a remedy for labor pains, nausea and rheumatism.

1906 U.S. Pure Food and Drug Act regulates labeling of products containing cannabis, opiates and other ingredients.

1911 Massachusetts becomes first state to ban cannabis.

1930s–1940s *Marijuana and hemp are outlawed, but hemp gets a wartime reprieve.*

1930 Federal Bureau of Narcotics Commissioner Harry J. Anslinger links marijuana to violence.

1937 Marihuana Tax Act criminalizes untaxed possession of marijuana and effectively ends U.S. hemp cultivation.

1942 Cannabis is removed from the U.S. Pharmacopoeia, ending recognition of its medicinal use. . . . Government encourages hemp production.

1945 Federal ban on hemp cultivation is restored.

1950s–1960s *Federal government tightens restrictions on cannabis.*

1951 Boggs Act sets fines and mandatory sentences for marijuana.

1956 Narcotic Control Act further stiffens drug penalties.

1969 Supreme Court finds the 1937 Marihuana Tax Act violates Fifth Amendment protections against self-incrimination.

1970s–1980s *Federal government declares war on drugs while states begin to decriminalize marijuana.*

1970 Federal Comprehensive Drug Abuse Prevention and Control Act categorizes marijuana among the most dangerous illegal substances.

1973 Oregon decriminalizes marijuana possession; 10 more states follow by the end of the decade.

1976 President Gerald R. Ford bans federal funding for research into marijuana's medical benefits.

1978 New Mexico legalizes limited medical use of marijuana.

1986 Anti-Drug Abuse Act institutes mandatory sentences for drug crimes and raises federal penalties for marijuana possession.

1990s–Present *Legalization gathers steam.*

1996 Arizona and California voters approve medical use of marijuana; Arizona legislature nullifies the action in that state a year later.

1998 District of Columbia voters approve medical marijuana use. Congress blocks implementation.

2012 Voters in Colorado and Washington state approve recreational use of marijuana by adults.

2013 Justice Department announces it will not challenge state marijuana laws.

2014 Recreational marijuana sales begin in Colorado and Washington. . . . Voters in Alaska, Oregon and Washington, D.C., approve recreational use; Congress blocks implementation of the D.C. law. . . . Federal legislation authorizes industrial hemp production for research purposes. . . . Colorado officials face lawsuits challenging the state's recreational-use laws.

2015 Georgia becomes 23rd state to legalize medical marijuana. . . . Recreational sales begin in Oregon. . . . Ohioans vote on Nov. 3 on an amendment to the state constitution that would legalize both recreational and medical marijuana.

November 2016 Nevada to vote on whether to permit recreational marijuana. In 15 other states, legalization advocates are pushing ballot initiatives that would give voters a chance to make recreational marijuana legal.

The Mexican Revolution of 1910 caused large numbers of Mexicans to immigrate to the United States over the next decade, some bringing marijuana that they smoked recreationally. The use of "tea" quickly caught on in parts of American society, particularly among jazz musicians and other entertainers. Marijuana clubs known as "tea pads" appeared in several major cities; authorities generally tolerated them because marijuana was not illegal, and patrons were usually well behaved.[51]

But marijuana's association with immigrants generated a backlash in the United States, "tinged perhaps with anti-Mexican xenophobia," wrote Stephen Siff, an associate professor of journalism at Miami University in Ohio. In 1911, Massachusetts became the first state to ban cannabis. Then, between 1914 and 1925, Siff wrote, 26 states passed laws prohibiting the plant, which passed with little controversy.[52]

In the late 1920s newspapers owned by publisher William Randolph Hearst launched an anti-marijuana campaign, linking marijuana to acts of torture and murder, although the articles often lacked evidentiary details.[53]

In 1930, Harry J. Anslinger became the first commissioner of the U.S. Treasury Department's Federal Bureau of Narcotics. Initially, he was reluctant to take up the anti-marijuana cause, partly because the drug was legal under federal law and partly because he felt his bureau lacked the personnel for an effective effort.

However, Anslinger came to believe that marijuana was a "killer weed" and in 1933 "began a war against marijuana," according to researchers at the University of Delaware. "He used the popular press to prey upon the fears of the American public, including racial fear and division," they wrote. By 1937, due largely to Anslinger's campaign, 46 of the then 48 states had passed anti-marijuana laws, the researchers said.[54]

Anslinger also drafted the federal Marihuana (sic) Tax Act, enacted by Congress in 1937. The law effectively criminalized possession of marijuana and hemp, except for those who paid a $1 excise tax for authorized medical and industrial use. (The tax was not intended to raise revenue, but "to criminalize marijuana sales and usage," according to the Tax Foundation, a Washington, D.C., think tank.[55]) Violators were subject to a $2,000 fine and five years' imprisonment.[56]

In 1951, however, a Senate investigation concluded that, despite existing state and federal drug laws, "the traffic in narcotics still flourishes," due largely to a shortage of enforcement personnel and "the comparatively gentle treatment narcotics offenders have been receiving at the hands of the courts."[57] Accordingly, Congress passed the Narcotic Drugs Import and Export Act of 1951, known as the Boggs Act after its House sponsor, Rep. Thomas Hale Boggs Sr., a Louisiana Democrat. It established a mandatory prison sentence of two to five years and a $2,000 fine for a first drug offense. Five years later, deciding that even tougher measures were needed, Congress passed the Narcotic Control Act of 1956, which increased the mandatory sentence and raised the fine to up to $20,000.[58]

Path to Legalization

In 1969 the Supreme Court ruled that the 1937 Marihuana Tax Act was unconstitutional because it violated the Fifth Amendment protection against self-incrimination — since paying the tax required acknowledging possession of marijuana in states where it was illegal.[59] In 1970 President Richard M. Nixon signed the Comprehensive Drug Abuse and Prevention and Control Act, which became known as the Controlled Substances Act (CSA), named after Title II of the new law.[60]

The CSA removed or reduced most existing mandatory drug penalties. But — significantly for the yet-to-emerge legal marijuana industry — it also established five categories, or schedules, for drugs according to their potential for abuse, medical applications and safety. By classifying cannabis (including hemp) — along with heroin, LSD and others — as a Schedule I drug, the law deemed marijuana as having a "high potential for abuse" and "no currently accepted medical use." Thus, the drug became illegal to possess or sell.[61]

However, some states soon began to fashion their own approaches to marijuana. In 1973, Oregon became the first to "decriminalize" marijuana (removing or reducing penalties for its possession or use, although the drug remains illegal), followed by at least 11 states in the 1970s.[62]

In February 1978, New Mexico became the first state to legalize the medicinal use of marijuana, albeit in a limited way. After lopsided votes for approval in both houses of the Legislature, then-Gov. Jerry Apodaca signed the Controlled Substances Therapeutic Research Act. It

Cannabis College Cultivates Pot Professionals

Oaksterdam University educates entrepreneurs but has faced controversy.

Jeff Gaudette began cultivating cannabis in British Columbia at age 20, eventually becoming a licensed medical marijuana grower at 27. Now 37, he runs his own dispensary in Vernon, British Columbia, along with two growing-equipment stores and a medical marijuana consultancy.

"Medical marijuana is my passion," he says.

Despite his extensive experience, Gaudette traveled in April 2014 to Oakland, Calif., to attend four three-month cannabis horticulture and business courses at Oaksterdam University, which is not a conventional accredited university but a trade school that teaches students how to grow marijuana and work in the cannabis industry.

"There's nothing else like it in the world," he says. "You work with actual plants in your classroom to feel, touch, see, clip, trim, clone. A textbook is only so good."

Oaksterdam calls itself "America's first cannabis college."[1] Founder Richard Lee, a former dispensary owner and activist inspired by a visit to Amsterdam's community-based Cannabis College in the Netherlands, taught the school's first class on growing marijuana in 2007.[2] The school's name is a combination of Oakland and Amsterdam, where marijuana use is legal and widespread.[3] (California legalized medical marijuana in 1996.)

Oaksterdam's curriculum now includes accounting, business law, culinary arts and economics as they apply to cannabis, and its faculty includes lawyers, business owners, nutritionists and accountants. But its offerings remain controversial because of marijuana's federally illegal status, and the school suffered financial setbacks and staff cuts after federal agents raided it in 2012.[4]

Oaksterdam encourages students to pursue opportunities beyond the basics of growing and dispensing cannabis, such as lab testing of marijuana, producing medicinal oils and lotions from extracts and designing electrical systems and lighting for growing operations.

Many students arrive with business backgrounds and technical skills from other professions. "They have a phenomenal skill set that can be applied to the cannabis industry," says Executive Chancellor Dale Sky Jones.

To be admitted, students only have to possess a valid ID showing they are at least 18 years old and pay tuition, which ranges from $1,195 to $1,495 for a 14-week full-time semester or $495 to $995 for two- to four-day seminars offered in Oakland, Las Vegas, Washington, D.C., and elsewhere.[5] In both the semester and seminar programs, students can enroll for a "classic" track, which covers the politics, law and economics of cannabis, among other subjects, or a horticulture-intensive track, which covers both indoor and outdoor growing.[6] Nearly 25,000 people have completed coursework at Oaksterdam, according to Jones.

Oaksterdam's competitors include Humboldt Cannabis College in Northern California and Cannabis University and Clover Leaf University, both in Denver. Clover Leaf was accredited by the Colorado Department of Higher Education in 2013, becoming the nation's only accredited cannabis school.[7]

Oaksterdam says it may apply for California state accreditation in 2016, according to Aseem Sappal, provost and dean of the faculty. "Because we're in the cannabis industry, we would like to be accredited because it helps with perception," he says.

Top-ranked horticulture programs at accredited four-year colleges still do not teach students how to grow cannabis, even though recreational marijuana use is legal in four states and the District of Columbia, and medical marijuana is legal in 23 states and the District.[8]

Oaksterdam has faced federal scrutiny: In 2012, agents from the IRS, along with agents from the U.S. Marshals Service and Drug Enforcement Administration, raided the school. Authorities seized large amounts of marijuana, which remains illegal to sell under federal law, from a nearby medical marijuana dispensary operated by Lee, plus equipment and files from four other buildings, including the school, briefly shutting it down.[9]

The IRS did not give reasons for the Oaksterdam raid and never filed charges. The raid took place during a two-year period in which federal agencies closed more than 200 medical dispensaries in California.[10]

School officials said the raid and seizures left Oaksterdam "on life support." Lee stepped down shortly afterward, saying he had "done [his] duty" and wanted to separate his ongoing legal issues from the university's future. The school appointed Jones as his successor.[11]

Horticulture industry experts say that while trade schools like Oaksterdam address a market niche, the skills required to grow cannabis are not all that different from those needed to cultivate other crops. Graduates of four-year horticulture programs who apply for the limited number of marijuana-growing licenses issued by states to allow growers to legally cultivate cannabis may be more competitive candidates than those from cannabis trade schools, says Craig Regelbrugge, senior vice president of Industry Advocacy and Research at AmericanHort, a national trade association for horticulturists.

"The person who is going to succeed [will] be the one who knows how to succeed in the real world, not necessarily a person who has a niche academic experience," Regelbrugge says.

Law schools at Ohio State and Vanderbilt universities, among others, now offer cannabis-related courses.[12] Jones says she envisions opportunities to collaborate with colleges in the future.

"I see major universities having full colleges of cannabis," says Jones. "You have a clear fit within the horticulture programs. It would be treated just like any other crop."

— *Ethan McLeod*

Getty Images/Justin Sullivan

Oaksterdam University founder Richard Lee was inspired to start the Oakland, Calif., school after a visit to Amsterdam's community-based Cannabis College in the Netherlands.

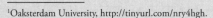

[1]Oaksterdam University, http://tinyurl.com/nry4hgh.

[2]Jason Motlagh, "Where Marijuana Gets You Higher Education," *Time*, March 28, 2011, http://content.time.com/time/nation/article/0,8599,2061398,00.html.

[3]Rona Marech, "Medical pot patients flock to 'Oaksterdam,' " *San Francisco Chronicle*, Aug. 10, 2003, http://tinyurl.com/pm58w3a.

[4]"Semester Programs," Oaksterdam University, http://tinyurl.com/ofgm94f.

[5]"Oaksterdam University Tuition and Fees," Oaksterdam University, http:// tinyurl.com/p9kfjd4.

[6]"Semester Programs," http://tinyurl.com/n9hvyow; "Horticulture Programs," http://tinyurl.com/ov34qrm.

[7]Jackie Salo, "Marijuana Legalization 2015: Is It Time For The Cannabis Industry To Grow Up And Go To College?" *International Business Times*, Aug. 16, 2015, http://tinyurl.com/pbvd2up; Homepage, http://tinyurl.com/pnhcyvs.

[8]"State Marijuana Laws Map," *Governing*, updated June 19, 2015, http://tinyurl. com/lv4r7f3.

[9]Lori Preuitt and Christie Smith, "Feds Raid Oakland's Oaksterdam," NBC Bay Area, April 2, 2012, http://tinyurl.com/7v5jztt; also see Madeleine Thomas, "After the raid: The financial fallout for Oaksterdam and Oakland's pot business," *OaklandNorth*, April 9, 2013, http://tinyurl.com/oq6xpny.

[10]Thomas, *op. cit.*; "Feds under Obama appear tougher on medical marijuana, disappointing voters," Fox News, April 27, 2012, http://tinyurl.com/d795c6z.

[11]Jesse McKinley, " '4/20' observance highlights friction between pot supporters, detractors," *The Seattle Times*, April 20, 2012, http://tinyurl.com/odxx3t4; Anne-Sophie Braendlin, "Dale Sky Jones to become new head of Oaksterdam University," *OaklandNorth*, April 17, 2012, http://tinyurl.com/obsskus.

[12]Collin Blinkley, "Legalized pot gets Ohio State class of its own," *The Columbus Dispatch*, March 10, 2015, http://tinyurl.com/qxs783y; "Course Information: Marijuana Law and Policy," Vanderbilt Law School, undated, http://tinyurl.com/qf9q98c.

Hemp Farmers Watching the Legal Skies

Crop promises profits, but police oppose legalization.

Like most farmers, Andrew Graves of Winchester, Ky., keeps a nervous eye on the weather. "We've sunk thousands of dollars per acre" into the crop, says Graves. "Suppose there's a freak August hailstorm? I've got my rear end in the wind out there."

That's because Graves, CEO of Atalo Holdings, an agribusiness company, cannot obtain federally subsidized crop insurance for his hemp plants, a variety of cannabis and a close relative of marijuana.

Smoking hemp does not produce a high — it contains less than 0.3 percent of the psychoactive chemical tetrahydrocannabinol (THC) compared to about 15 percent in marijuana. But because of hemp's kinship to cannabis, the Controlled Substances Act of 1970 banned hemp and marijuana cultivation without a DEA permit, so hemp is not covered under the federal crop insurance program.

Graves can grow hemp legally because Kentucky is one of 13 states that within the past year have legalized industrial hemp cultivation, authorized by the 2014 farm bill to conduct research on hemp's commercial potential.[1]

Atalo, which has a state hemp research permit, contracts with 30 farmers in Kentucky who this year will harvest 200 to 300 acres of hemp, producing about 1,000 pounds of seed per acre. The seeds will be processed into oil, hemp nuts and protein powder for commercial sale under the farm bill's commercial research provision.

The nonpartisan Congressional Research Service (CRS), which conducts policy studies for Congress, estimated that "the global market for hemp consists of more than 25,000 products," much of it produced in Europe, Canada and China, where cultivation is legal.

Hemp fibers are used in fabrics and textiles, paper, carpeting, home furnishings, auto parts and construction and insulation materials, among other products. Hurd — the hemp stalk's elastic, woody core — is used to make such goods as animal bedding and paper. Hemp seed and oilcake are used in a range of foods and beverages and can be a protein source, while oil from crushed hemp seed is an ingredient in body-care products and nutritional supplements, according to CRS.[2]

"The United States is the world's largest market for hemp products," says Eric Steenstra, executive director of the Hemp Industries Association (HIA). The group estimated the 2014 U.S. retail market for hemp products at $620 million, most of it imported. Under U.S. Customs and Border Protection regulations, hemp products such as cosmetics, clothing and food can be imported if they do not contain THC.[3]

Steenstra says the current restrictions on U.S. hemp production means "American farmers are being denied an opportunity to participate" in a market with "tremendous potential," while Canadian, European and Chinese farmers are free to grow and export the crop.

Pending federal legislation would change hemp's legal status and brighten its commercial outlook. The Industrial Hemp Farming Act of 2015 defines industrial hemp as containing no more than 0.3 percent of THC, excludes it from the definition of marijuana under the Controlled Substances Act and authorizes states to regulate its growing and processing.[4]

Sen. Ron Wyden, an Oregon Democrat who cosponsored the measure in the Senate, emphasized hemp's economic potential. "Allowing farmers throughout our nation to cultivate industrial hemp and benefit from its many uses will boost our economy and bring much-needed jobs to the agriculture industry," he said.[5]

But the Drug Enforcement Administration (DEA) has expressed concerns about industrial hemp's legalization.

---

permitted cancer patients whose chemotherapy caused nausea and vomiting to smoke marijuana or ingest tetra-hydrocannabinol (THC, the chemical responsible for most of marijuana's psychoactive effects) through a program administered by the state Health and Environment Department and conducted by the University of New Mexico.[63] The program required approval by the DEA, Food and Drug Administration and National Institute on Drug Abuse, and patients needed physician approval to participate.[64]

Despite apparent clinical success, the state Legislature halted funding for the program in 1986 due to opposition from federal drug agencies. (New Mexico relegalized medical marijuana in 2007.[65])

In 1991, San Francisco voters, with 80 percent in favor, approved Proposition P, which called on

"First," the DEA said in 2013, "it is impossible to distinguish a marijuana plant containing 0.3% or less of THC from a marijuana plant containing higher THC levels without scientific analysis . . . [and] there would be no way to establish probable cause to obtain a search warrant without first entering the [cultivation site] to collect samples. Second, even if all the marijuana plants contained 0.3 percent or less THC . . . it is very easy and inexpensive to convert low-grade marijuana into high-grade hashish oil."[6] The DEA said in 2014 that its policy on industrial hemp was "under review."

Hemp had a bumpy legal history over the past century. Its U.S. production was drastically curtailed by the 1937 Marihuana Tax Act, which classified both hemp and marijuana as narcotics. But hemp was suddenly back in demand when fighting in World War II's Pacific Theater cut off supplies from the Philippines of "Manila hemp," needed for naval cordage, fire hoses and parachute webbing.[7] The government subsidized hemp cultivation, boosting production from about 1 million pounds before the war to more than 150 million in 1943.

As the war wound down production declined, dropping to 3 million pounds by 1948, with no recorded production after the late 1950s, due largely to "increasing public anti-drug sentiment," according to CRS.[8]

But Graves, who says he is the "seventh generation of hemp farmers, same family growing on the same land," is optimistic. So far, Atalo's operations are limited to processing hemp seeds, but Graves hopes to expand into fiber processing once the company's revenue stream from the seeds allows the acquisition of the necessary equipment.

"We're having success, but it's hard to measure," Graves says. "I see unlimited possibility for [hemp] in the next 10 years; it all depends on how quickly we can ramp up and have our own seed available, how fast our seed technology can be put in place.

"But these are all good problems to have. It's a lot of fun."

— *William Wanlund*

Getty Images/*The Denver Post*/Brent Lewis

Hemp plants are grown in hoop houses by CBDrx, a grower in Pueblo, Colo. The nonpartisan Congressional Research Service estimates "the global market for hemp consists of more than 25,000 products."

[1] "State Industrial Hemp Statutes," National Association of State Legislatures, March 26, 2015, http://tinyurl.com/opt8xzy.

[2] Renée Johnson, "Hemp as an Agricultural Commodity," Congressional Research Service, Feb. 2, 2015, http://tinyurl.com/pa8nm6b.

[3] "Importing hemp products into the U.S.," U.S. Customs and Border Protection Q&A, http://tinyurl.com/qaa9b52.

[4] "Industrial Hemp Farming Act of 2015," U.S. Senate bill S.134, http://tiny url.com/os42dx2. Companion legislation, H.R. 525, was introduced in the House of Representatives.

[5] Press release, "Senators Introduce Bipartisan Bill to Roll Back Hemp Restrictions," Sen. Ron Wyden, Jan. 8, 2015, http://tinyurl.com/oz553oq.

[6] "Hemp Talking Points," U.S. Drug Enforcement Administration, June 2013, http://tinyurl.com/p2mdl2k.

[7] "Hemp for Victory" film, transcript, U.S. Department of Agriculture, 1942, http://tinyurl.com/nrru3de.

[8] Johnson, *op. cit.*

California state legislators to legalize marijuana use for medical purposes.[66] In 1994 and again in 1995, the Legislature approved such measures, but both times Republican Gov. Pete Wilson vetoed the legislation.

In 1996, however, supported by a $2.5 million promotional effort, California voters approved, with 56 percent of the vote, Proposition 215. The Compassionate Use Act, which was not subject to gubernatorial veto, protected from prosecution anyone who grew, used or possessed marijuana for a broad range of medical purposes along with the physicians who recommended it. The presidential administrations of Bill Clinton (1993–2001) and George W. Bush (2001–09) staunchly opposed Proposition 215, but it survived legal challenges.[67]

By this September, 23 states and Washington, D.C., had enacted laws permitting at least some use of medical cannabis.[68] In addition, 15 states allow the use of certain cannabis extracts, such as the non-psychoactive cannabidiol, or CBD, for qualified patients.[69]

Colorado, which legalized medical marijuana in 2000, became the first state also to permit its sale for recreational use: On Nov. 6, 2012, voters approved a constitutional amendment allowing those 21 or older to "consume or possess limited amounts of marijuana" and providing for cultivation, manufacturing, testing and retail sales.[70] Sales began Jan. 1, 2014.[71] Washington state, where voters approved recreational marijuana use in 2012, began retail sales July 8, 2014.[72]

Voters in Oregon, Alaska and Washington, D.C., legalized recreational marijuana in November 2014. (In D.C., residents may now grow and possess marijuana and consume it in private. However, Congress, which reviews the city's laws and has authority over its budget, has blocked recreational sale of the drug.[73])

CURRENT SITUATION

Legal Issues

Colorado, as the nation's leader in legalizing recreational use, is now a legal battleground between the cannabis industry and those who would halt, restrict or even reverse its growth. The future of the legal marijuana industry could hinge on the outcome of several suits challenging a state's right to enact a law that conflicts with federal law.

In a case pending before the U.S. Supreme Court, Nebraska and Oklahoma, which do not allow recreational marijuana use, have asked the justices to invalidate Colorado's legalization. Colorado marijuana crosses into Nebraska and Oklahoma, the lawsuit argues, straining their police and judicial resources and undermining their own marijuana-control efforts.[74]

"If our law gets killed, the black market will be back and the Sinaloans [a Mexican drug cartel] will be back in business," says Colorado Sheriff Masters. "I think the other states need to pass some reasonable legislation, and that way they'll torpedo this problem."

In a case filed in Colorado federal district court in March, six Colorado sheriffs are suing to strike down Colorado's marijuana statutes, saying the discrepancy between federal and state laws causes the sheriffs to violate their oath of office, which requires them to uphold both state and federal laws. Six plaintiffs from neighboring Kansas and Nebraska joined

the suit on the grounds that Colorado's marijuana laws placed extra stress on their law enforcement resources, causing them "direct and significant harm."[75]

But Masters says the right to possess and sell marijuana "is part of the Colorado constitution. I'm bound to uphold the constitution, and I have to protect those constitutional rights." The high court has not yet agreed to hear the case.

And the Safe Streets Alliance, a Washington, D.C.-based organization opposed to marijuana legalization, has filed two suits in Colorado federal district court claiming that Colorado's legalization violates the U.S. Constitution's "supremacy clause," which holds that federal law supersedes state law.[76] The court has not yet ruled on whether it will hear the cases.

The disparity between state and federal laws creates "a very awkward problem," says Stuart Taylor, a Washington, D.C-area journalist and author and a nonresident senior fellow at the Brookings Institution think tank. "The conflict between federal and state law means that any state that legalizes [marijuana] is in violation of federal law," Taylor says. "It looks like a form of lawlessness.

"The feds don't have nearly enough people in the DEA or related positions to enforce federal law rigorously everywhere all the time," he says. "If they take down the [state-] regulated marijuana businesses, it leaves the entire [illegal] market much harder to control and more likely to lead to all the problems that the federal law is designed to prevent — transport across state lines, distribution to minors, stuff with dangerous concentrations of THC — all the things the state regulations are designed to prevent."

Cannabis Business

Despite marijuana's legal uncertainties, the industry is beginning to attract big money. Kris Krane, a co-founder and managing partner of 4Front Advisors, a cannabis industry consulting firm in Phoenix, says startup costs vary from state to state but can be daunting.

In New York, which legalized medical marijuana in 2014 and awarded its first business licenses on July 31, 2015, "groups were spending on average a million and a half dollars or so just to get through the licensing process," says Krane. Getting the business up and running, he says, could cost "upwards of $25 or $30 million."

That's partly because in New York, a dispensary must grow and process the marijuana it sells. And each licensee — the state has granted five so far — must operate four dispensaries.[77] "There are only going to

AT ISSUE

Should federal laws be enforced where marijuana is legal?

YES
David G. Evans, Esq.
Special Advisor,
Drug Free America Foundation

Written for *CQ Researcher,* October 2015

NO
Paul Armentano
Deputy Director, NORML *(National Organization*
for the Reform of Marijuana Laws); Co-author,
Marijuana is Safer: So Why Are We Driving
People to Drink?

Written for *CQ Researcher,* October 2015

Federal law should be enforced. The marijuana industry wants to make big profits from selling marijuana, just like the large tobacco companies do from tobacco, so they argue that marijuana legalization is a "states' rights" issue. States should be allowed to set national drug policy, they argue.

However, the U.S. Supreme Court has repeatedly held that this is a federal issue because marijuana crosses state lines and thus is part of interstate commerce, which is governed by federal law. Because what is done in one state when it comes to marijuana spills over into other states, Congress must establish nationwide marijuana laws.

Marijuana is illegal under the federal Controlled Substances Act (CSA), which is Title II of the Comprehensive Drug Abuse Prevention and Control Act of 1970. The CSA categorizes marijuana as a Schedule I drug — among the most dangerous of illegal substances. Congress enacted the law in order to consolidate drug laws into a comprehensive statute and to strengthen law enforcement tools against illegal drug trafficking. Currently, Nebraska and Oklahoma are suing Colorado to enforce the CSA because marijuana from Colorado is coming into their states, and they do not want it.

States that have commercialized marijuana are having buyer's remorse. Thousands of young people are becoming addicted. For example, in Colorado impaired driving, youth marijuana use and addiction, adult marijuana use and marijuana-related emergency room admissions are all up substantially. This costs the state money.

But our country is not helpless. The marijuana commercialization epidemic is imposed on us by criminal acts that produce an abundant supply of inexpensive marijuana. Stopping these criminal acts by enforcing federal law will stop the epidemic.

Before President Obama was elected, our nation confronted drug use with effective public health measures emphasizing education, prevention and treatment as well as programs to reduce production and to interdict the drugs. It worked. Despite what the marijuana advocates claim, drug use went down. The Obama administration does not enforce the federal law. Drug use is now up, especially marijuana.

The Obama administration has allowed commercialized marijuana to spread drug use on an ever-widening scale, undermining prevention and treatment. Now the big marijuana industry flourishes and is spreading addiction throughout America.

Protect our children and enforce the law.

Never in modern history has greater public support existed for ending our nation's nearly century-long experiment with marijuana prohibition and replacing it with a taxed and regulated adult marketplace. Twenty-three states and Washington, D.C., now permit the medicinal use of cannabis. Four of these states, and Washington, D.C., also permit marijuana for recreational use by adults. Federal officials should not stand in the way of these policies.

The ongoing enforcement of cannabis prohibition financially burdens taxpayers, encroaches upon civil liberties, engenders disrespect for the law, impedes legitimate scientific research into the plant's therapeutic properties and disproportionately affects young people and communities of color.

Federal lawmakers should cease ceding control of the marijuana market to untaxed criminal enterprises and allow states to pursue alternative regulatory policies. A pragmatic regulatory framework that allows for the legal, licensed, commercial production and sale of cannabis to adults — coupled with a legal environment that fosters open, honest parent-child dialogue about cannabis' potential harms — best reduces the risks associated with the plant's use or abuse.

According to a recent Pew Research Center poll, 60 percent of Americans believe the government "should not enforce federal marijuana laws in states that allow use." Surveys from early primary states, including Iowa, New Hampshire and South Carolina, report even greater voter sentiment in favor of this position.

Neither science nor public opinion supports the federal government's contention that marijuana should be a Schedule I controlled substance — a classification that equates the plant's abuse potential to that of heroin and ignores its therapeutic utility.

Fortunately, America's federalist system does not mandate states to be beholden to this intellectually and morally bankrupt policy. The 10th Amendment to the Constitution provides that all "powers not delegated to the United States by the Constitution, nor prohibited by it to the States, are reserved to the States respectively, or to the people." Indeed, Supreme Court Justice Louis Brandeis (1916-1939) famously opined, "[A] state may, if its citizens choose, serve as a laboratory; and try novel social and economic experiments without risk to the rest of the country." Today, many states are doing just that.

Public sentiment and common sense are driving necessary and long overdue changes in state-level marijuana policies. America's longstanding federalist principles demand that we permit these policies to evolve free from federal interference.

be 20 stores in a state of 20 million people," Krane says. "The capacity . . . to meet demand has to be really large."

Although New York is "a bit of an outlier," Krane says, "it's hard to start an operation in any state for under a million dollars."

Some predict large companies, particularly in the tobacco industry, will enter the cannabis market. Researchers from the University of California, San Francisco, and Finland's University of Helsinki reviewed archived tobacco industry documents which revealed that since 1970 three multinational companies — Philip Morris, Brown & Williamson, and RJ Reynolds — have all considered manufacturing cigarettes containing cannabis. "The documents demonstrate the tobacco industry's willingness and preparedness to enter legalized marijuana markets, which the companies believed to have a large sales potential," the researchers said.[78]

Spokespersons for Altria Group, which manufactures Philip Morris cigarettes and other tobacco products, and Reynolds American (Camel, Pall Mall and other brands), say their companies are not planning to enter the commercial marijuana market. "Marijuana remains illegal under federal law, and Altria's companies have no plans to sell marijuana-based products," says Altria spokesman Jeff Caldwell.

But some legalization advocates are skeptical. "My concern is the Marlboro-ization or Budweiser-ization of marijuana," said Ethan Nadelmann, executive director of the pro-legalization Drug Policy Alliance. "That's not what I'm fighting for."[79]

Shenandoah University's Gettman says, "Certainly, the tobacco industry knows how to take a plant, turn it into cigarettes and sell it to people." But there are many differences between marijuana and tobacco, he says. For instance, modern cigarettes contain "all sorts of additives and flavors," while "I can go out in my backyard, grow a marijuana plant, dry the flowers and smoke that product, and be quite happy with it."

The ease of producing marijuana plants means the market will be very competitive, he says. "The idea of six or seven firms collectively controlling the entire industry — that's going to be hard to do."

Retailer Ode of the Seattle Cannabis Co. isn't bothered either way. "I don't anticipate that big tobacco moving in would have a huge advantage," he says. "But if they offered a good product at a good price, I'd love to have them in the store."

2016 Elections

The outcome of upcoming elections could determine whether the legal marijuana market continues its robust growth — or whether the market may already have peaked.

Ohioans vote Nov. 3 on an amendment to the state constitution that would legalize both recreational and medical marijuana. If it succeeds, it would mark the first time a state will have legalized recreational marijuana without first establishing a medical marijuana program.[80]

In 15 states legalization advocates are organizing petitions to put initiatives on next year's ballot on whether recreational use of marijuana should be legal. As of September, only Nevada had put the question on the 2016 ballot.[81] But legalization advocates are confident more states will vote on the issue in November 2016, and that at least five may choose to end prohibition. Journalist Philip Smith wrote that public opinion surveys in Arizona, California, Massachusetts, Michigan and Nevada show a majority of those polled favoring legalization, and in 2013 a survey in Maine had a pro-legalization plurality of 48 percent to 39 percent.[82]

Paul Armentano, deputy director of the pro-legalization National Organization for the Reform of Marijuana Laws (NORML), says if California votes to legalize recreational marijuana next year, "It would be regulating and legalizing the largest market in the country for cannabis production, use and sale."[83] In addition, he says, "California often sets a trend for the rest of the country and for national politics and voter sentiment in general," so passage of legalization or regulation in California "would be a harbinger of national changes in the fairly immediate future."

A March poll by the Public Policy Institute of California showed 55 percent of likely California voters support legalization, but Republican political consultant Rob Stutzman said, "I don't think it's a slam dunk to pass. There's a lot of opposition to it. There will be a lot of concern about unintended consequences."[84]

Bipartisan measures are pending in Congress that would affect the future of the industry. In the Senate, the CARERS Act, sponsored by Sen. Cory Booker, D-N.J., would downgrade marijuana from a Schedule I to a Schedule II drug, acknowledging that it has an accepted "medical use" or a "medical use with severe restrictions."[85]

It would end enforcement of federal marijuana laws in jurisdictions where it is legal and allow banks to provide services to legitimate marijuana-related businesses.[86] A companion bill, introduced by Reps. Steve Cohen, D-Tenn., and Don Young, R-Alaska, has bipartisan co-sponsorship in the House.

GovTrack.us, which follows legislation through Congress, has given the bills almost no chance of passage during this Congress. Michael Correia, director of government relations for the National Cannabis Industry Association, says members of Congress represent their own state interests, and if legalization is not happening in their state, it's harder for them to get involved. But as more states legalize recreational use of the drug, he says, it will get on the "radar screens" of more members of Congress.

However, congressional approval is not required to reschedule marijuana under the CSA. If the administration wanted to push for rescheduling, the attorney general, in conjunction with the DEA and the Department of Health and Human Services, could change the drug's schedule or even remove it from CSA scheduling altogether. However, the "notoriously cumbersome procedure" would require "months if not years of formal hearings," said Vanderbilt University law professor Robert Mikos, and it would not affect the laws in states where marijuana is still illegal.[87]

Nationwide, a Harris poll in May found that 81 percent of American adults favor legalizing medical marijuana in their home states, while 49 percent support legalizing it for recreational use.[88]

As for the 2016 presidential election, Rep. Blumenauer says, "I don't think there's any question" but that marijuana legalization will be a factor. "This is . . . being considered across the country, and when you get into the home stretch of the 2016 election, it's not going to be something that [candidates] will be able to ignore," he says. "They're either going to be for it or against it, or they're going to look like they're waffling."

But Sabet of Smart Approaches to Marijuana says legalizing marijuana "is "one of those issues candidates don't want to talk about. I think they're on the fence about where they want to go," but they are also aware of public opinion on the issue.

Hudak at Brookings said legalization will "absolutely" be an issue in 2016 because "states are very blatantly violating federal law, and it is an absolute presidential consideration about what to do about this. It's an issue that candidates won't be able to be silent about.

"But the question is not just about marijuana," Hudak continues. "It is about public policy experimentation; states' rights; small business; medical marijuana and health care; privacy; and access to medicine. A 2016 candidate's views on marijuana are part of a broader public policy worldview or set of values that really reveals who that candidate is."

OUTLOOK
De Facto Legalization?

When asked about the future of the marijuana industry, Walsh of *Marijuana Business Daily* throws up his hands. "Trying to figure out what the industry is going to look like in six months or so is very difficult," he says. "Five years is almost impossible, and 10 years is another generation."

Within five years, he says, the federal government could decide to let the states decide the issue on their own. "The feds will say, 'We're just going to leave it up to you guys' " in the states.

Walsh's prediction echoes that of many industry observers: that de facto legalization is on the way. It's not a question of if but when, they say, and it will resemble the end of alcohol prohibition. "The federal government did not legalize alcohol," NORML's Armentano says. "The feds simply got out of the way and left the states free to pursue alternatives to the prohibition of alcohol. The states developed distinct policies on how alcohol was consumed and sold, and to some degree those policies reflected the cultural mores specific to those states."

A similar patchwork of laws could emerge for the regulation of cannabis, he says, "a substance that is arguably far more politically charged than alcohol ever was."

But Alan Shinn, executive director of the Coalition for a Drug-Free Hawaii, said, "I don't think that legalization is inevitable. . . . There's other alternatives to legalization. We should really be taking a public health approach to this, especially with our youth."[89]

Sabet of Smart Approaches to Marijuana says he fears "the commercialization impact" of marijuana legalization. "I'm really concerned with what I call 'Big Tobacco 2.0.' We have to be very careful about whether we want to roll out the red carpet for another industry, one that makes big money off of the heavy user."

As the industry grows, observers say, the structure of the marijuana business will evolve. "You will see very large growers with very large brands — equivalent to the Budweisers or the Coors of the world," predicts Ewart of Anne Arundel Community College. "But you will also see the craft growers, like the craft brewers, out there producing unique strains with different tastes and different effects."

If the ban on interstate transportation is ended, it could also shake up the industry's structure, says Green Wave's Karnes. "There will be mass consolidation or extinction of the cultivators," he predicts. "The proven leaders among the cultivators will likely be taken over by tobacco companies or food and beverage conglomerates. On the retail side we'll likely see some branding occur, where some of the products will be distributed all over the country on a national level — and quite probably international as well — just like there are various types of alcohol available."

Rep. Blumenauer predicts that within the next two decades, marijuana "will be legal in most states." The federal government will have rescheduled or delisted marijuana, which will be taxed and regulated, he adds, and "there will be a very strong regime to protect our children. Within 20 years, marijuana is going to be an accepted part of our landscape."

NOTES

1. Julie Andersen Hill, "Banks, Marijuana, and Federalism," *Case Western Reserve Law Review*, Vol. 65, Issue 3, 2015, http://tinyurl.com/q2uwc4v.

2. "H.R.2076 — Marijuana Businesses Access to Banking Act of 2015," http://tinyurl.com/oz6atwz.

3. "Weekly Report," Washington State Liquor and Cannabis Board, Sept. 23, 2015, http://tinyurl.com/qjq4egx.

4. Christopher Ingraham, "Colorado's legal weed market: $700 million in sales last year, $1 billion by 2016," *The Washington Post*, Feb. 12, 2015, http://tinyurl.com/ojawekq.

5. Troy Dayton, "Letter from the Publisher," Executive Summary, The State of Legal Marijuana Markets," 3rd ed., ArcView Market Research, ArcView Group, 2015, http://tinyurl.com/mwcu5d4.

6. Bailey Rahn, "Qualifying Conditions for Medical Marijuana by State," *Leafly*, July 7, 2015, http://tinyurl.com/nlzsgat.

7. "State Medical Marijuana Laws," National Conference of State Legislatures, Sept. 14, 2015, http://tinyurl.com/nfoy2gr.

8. Jessica Calefati, "Brown OKs state rules for medical marijuana," *San Jose Mercury News*, Oct. 9, 2015, http://tinyurl.com/ofx4q4x.

9. Jessica Zimmer, "The Dangers of Synthetic Marijuana," *The Fix*, Sept. 24, 2014, http://tinyurl.com/naqdqrc. Also see "Drug Facts: K2/Spice ("Synthetic Marijuana"), National Institute on Drug Abuse, December 2012, http://tinyurl.com/nmptcg2.

10. Amy Kraft, "Big increase in deaths, poisonings from synthetic marijuana, CBS News, June 11, 2015, http://tinyurl.com/q9lfghy.

11. "Marijuana Courses Being Offered at Colleges Across the Country," Fox News, Feb. 16, 2015, http://tinyurl.com/ovbtwbv.

12. Kristen Wyatt, "Governor: Colorado pot market exceeds tax hopes," The Associated Press, *The Denver Post*, Feb. 19, 2014, http://tinyurl.com/mfu9y4r.

13. "Marijuana Taxes, Licenses, and Fees Transfers and Distribution," Colorado Department of Revenue, February 2015, http://tinyurl.com/nrp2qrk.

14. Jacob Sullum, "Yes, Legal Pot Does Cost More Than Black-Market Pot (For Now At Least)," *Forbes*, Jan. 6, 2014, http://tinyurl.com/k5bkp5u.

15. Robert W. Wood, "$21.5 Million In Marijuana Taxes Just Went Up In Smoke," *Forbes*, Sept. 2, 2014, http://tinyurl.com/oy4epnf.

16. Ricardo Baca, "Colorado pot sales spike in July, set recreational and medical records," *The Cannabist*, Sept. 11, 2015, http://tinyurl.com/p5sqqp2.

17. John Frank, "Gov. Hickenlooper signs 2015–16 Colorado budget," *The Denver Post*, April 25, 2015, http://tinyurl.com/pmcfzlo.

18. Divya Raghavan, "Cannabis Cash: How Much Money Could Your State Make From Marijuana Legalization?" *NerdWallet*, Aug. 27, 2015, http://tinyurl.com/nb3fnjb.

19. Excerpts, *Marijuana Business Daily Factbook 2015*, April 2015, http://tinyurl.com/q3ryjr2.

20. Jeffrey A. Miron, "The Budgetary Implications of Marijuana Prohibition," Marijuana Policy Project, June 2005, http://tinyurl.com/lvyk6nq.

21. Rafa Fernandez De Castro, "How Mexican drug cartels are reacting to marijuana legalization in the U.S.," *Fusion*, March 23, 2015, http://tinyurl.com/o75cekn.

22. "United States Border Patrol Sector Profile — Fiscal Year 2014," U.S. Border Patrol, undated, accessed Oct. 9, 2015, http://tinyurl.com/p9vlfu6; "United States Border Patrol Sector Profile — Fiscal 2013," http://tinyurl.com/nmphqny.

23. De Castro, *op. cit.*

24. "Marijuana and Cancer," American Cancer Society, undated, accessed Oct. 9, 2015, http://tinyurl.com/pvz8euw.

25. Anna Callaghan, "Why Washington state is extinguishing medical marijuana," *Mashable*, May 6, 2015, http://tinyurl.com/p2ceyvk.

26. "Traceability System," Washington State Liquor and Cannabis Board, 2015, http://tinyurl.com/p5d3tl9.

27. "Medical Marijuana — What's New?" Washington State Department of Health, undated, accessed, Oct. 9, 2015, http://tinyurl.com/o2ga4rm.

28. Rachel LaCorte, "House moves to reconcile medical, recreational pot industries," The Associated Press, *The Seattle Times*, April 10, 2015, http://tinyurl.com/pl5xlu3.

29. Summer Meza, "King County warns medical marijuana shops: Shut down or else," *Seattle Post-Intelligencer*, July 8, 2015, http://tinyurl.com/nzmue8m.

30. "ERFC Estimates, May 2015," Economic and Revenue Forecast Council, State of Washington, May 2015.

31. Shannon Pettypiece and Sonali Basak, "Pot Firms Gain as CVS, Walgreen Competition a Pipe Dream," *Bloomberg Business*, May 13, 2014, http://tinyurl.com/otvjpho.

32. Kathleen Burke, "Marijuana could be a $35 billion market by 2020," MarketWatch, July 15, 2015, http://tinyurl.com/nm9cg2d.

33. "Vitamin, Nutritional Supplement & Other Health-Related Product Manufacturing Industry Profile," First Research, July 27, 2015, http://tinyurl.com/pn8sodg.

34. "Privateer Holdings Closes $75 Million Funding Round," press release, Privateer Holdings, April 7, 2015, http://tinyurl.com/obq3w36.

35. Jonathan Shieber, "New Funding For Privateer Highlights Marijuana's Massive Market In The U.S.," TechCrunch.com, Jan. 8, 2015, http://tinyurl.com/nrleczj.

36. Kathleen Burke, "Amid the stock market volatility, turn to the stability of the marijuana market," MarketWatch, Aug. 30, 2015, http://tinyurl.com/qc256yl.

37. "For These 55 Marijuana Companies, Every Day is 4/20," *Bloomberg Business*, http://tinyurl.com/nkhtvbb.

38. "Cannabis in the Ancient World," Marijuana — The First Twelve Thousand Years, Schaffer Library of Drug Policy, http://tinyurl.com/d2rw6fu.

39. *Ibid.*

40. Richard Rudgley, "Cannabis," *The Encyclopedia of Psychoactive Substances* (1998), http://tinyurl.com/pezvdv5.

41. G. C. Macaulay (trans.), "The History of Herodotus, Vol. 1 (Chapter 4)," http://tinyurl.com/pcl9jjw.

42. Erowid, "Cannabis Timeline," The Vaults of Erowid, http://tinyurl.com/nks392k.

43. "12 Things You Didn't Know about Hemp," *The 420 Times*, Issue 35, http://tinyurl.com/nhkwtgw.

44. Lester Grinspoon, M.D., "Whither American Medical Marijuana," *RX Marijuana*, 2000, http://tinyurl.com/qhzdncs.

45. Kristina Aikens, "Victorian Women on Drugs, Part 1: Queen Victoria," *Points: The Blog of the Alcohol and Drugs Historical Society*, April 4, 2012, http://tinyurl.com/prkz6bu.

46. "Hemp Since The Beginning Of Time," *Global Hemp*, Jan. 1, 2001, http://tinyurl.com/cyrbgth.

47. "History of Marijuana — Early Marijuana Use," Narconon, http://tinyurl.com/2cr8qxo.

48. R. R. McMeens, M.D., "Report of the Ohio State Medical Committee on Cannabis Indica," June 12–14, 1860, http://tinyurl.com/q3mg4w2.

49. "Hasheesh Candy" advertisement, MarijuanaDoctors.com, http://tinyurl.com/nnjc62k.

50. Adrienne Lerner, "Pure Food and Drug Act of 1906," Gale Global Issues in Context, http://tinyurl.com/pme3bvv.

51. "History of Marijuana — Early Marijuana Use," *op. cit.*

52. Stephen Siff, "The Illegalization of Marijuana: A Brief History," *ORIGINS: Current Events in Historical Perspective*, Vol. 7, No. 8, May 2014, http://tinyurl.com/qa5f8sd.

53. Michael Mills, "A smear campaign: a history of the US' relationship with cannabis," *The New Economy*, March 27, 2015, http://tinyurl.com/poy5ag5. For an example, see Annie Laurie, "Mother sacrifices children, home, reputation for dope," *San Francisco Examiner*, Feb. 27, 1930, http://tinyurl.com/olrauqv.

54. Lana D. Harrison, Michael Backenheimer and James A. Inciardi, "History of drug legislation," Centrum voor Drugsonderzoek, Universiteit van Amsterdam, 1995, http://tinyurl.com/pckg4ws.

55. Joseph Henchman, "Colorado Debates Marijuana Tax; Would Be First Genuine Revenue-Raising Tax on Illegal Drug," Tax Foundation, Nov. 15, 2012, http://tinyurl.com/nvw3ve3.

56. "Marijuana Tax Act Law & Legal Definition," USLegal.com, undated, accessed Oct. 9, 2015, http://tinyurl.com/oljcatm.

57. "Kefauver Committee Final Report Aug. 31, 1951," U.S. Senate Special Committee to Investigate Organized Crime in Interstate Commerce, undated, accessed Oct. 9, 2015, http://tinyurl.com/nberfzt.

58. Rufus King, "The Drug Hang Up, America's Fifty-Year Folly," The Schaffer Library of Drug Policy, undated, accessed Oct. 9, 2015, http://tinyurl.com/pl3pksf.

59. *Leary v. United States*, U.S. Supreme Court, May 19, 1969, http://tinyurl.com/on4llue.

60. Harrison *et al.*, *op. cit.*

61. "Drug Schedules," Drug Enforcement Administration, http://tinyurl.com/pgfjqhw.

62. Emilee Mooney Scott, "Marijuana Decriminalization," Connecticut General Assembly Office of Legislative Research, May 5, 2010, http://tinyurl.com/ohk2c8m.

63. "Who are Lynn and Erin?" Minerva Canna Group Inc., undated, accessed Oct. 9, 2015, http://tinyurl.com/o6td3cz.

64. "The Lynn Pierson Therapeutic Research Program," New Mexico Health and Environment Department, March 1983, http://tinyurl.com/8y4x7zk.

65. "New Mexico Legalizes Medical Marijuana," ProCon.org, Aug. 31, 2007, http://tinyurl.com/qyry8rf.

66. "Proposition P," San Francisco ballot initiative, November 1991, http://tinyurl.com/o8klcrp.

67. Y. Lu, "Medical Marijuana Policy in the United States," Huntington's Outreach Program for Education, Stanford University, May 15, 2012, http://tinyurl.com/ovew6bj.

68. "State Medical Marijuana Laws," *op. cit.*; also see Aaron C. Davis, "Budget bill outlaws pot sales in D.C. for 2 years," *The Washington Post*, June 11, 2015, http://tinyurl.com/ozant9o.

69. "Medical Marijuana," National Organization for the Reform of Marijuana Laws, http://tinyurl.com/7wd2uam.

70. "Use and Regulation of Marijuana," proposed Amendment 64 to Colorado state Constitution, November 2012, http://tinyurl.com/na22gz2.

71. John Ingold, "World's first legal recreational marijuana sales begin in Colorado," *The Denver Post*, Jan. 1, 2014, http://tinyurl.com/kjt6pqn.

72. Kirk Johnson, "Sales of Recreational Marijuana Begin in Washington State," *The New York Times*, July 8, 2014, http://tinyurl.com/op455mt.

73. Brianna Gurciullo and Karen Mawdsley, "Marijuana law creates confusion but finds growing acceptance in District," *The Washington Post*, Aug. 9, 2015, http://tinyurl.com/p63dzgo.

74. "States of Nebraska and Oklahoma, Plaintiffs, vs. State of Colorado, Defendant," Motion to the U.S. Supreme Court, December 2014, http://tinyurl.com/plsaapz.

75. "Justin E. Smith et al., v. John W. Hickenlooper," U.S. District Court for the District of Colorado, March 5, 2015, http://tinyurl.com/qzo5wlb.

76. "Our Lawsuit to Block the Legalization of Marijuana," Safe Streets Alliance, undated, accessed Oct. 9, 2015, http://tinyurl.com/oh7xwpw.

77. Jesse McKinley, "New York State Awards 5 Medical Marijuana Licenses," *The New York Times*, July 31, 2015, http://tinyurl.com/otpnyn4.

78. Rachel Ann Barry, Heikki Hilamo and Stanton A. Glantz, "Waiting for the Opportune Moment: The Tobacco Industry and Marijuana Legalization," *The Milbank Quarterly*, Vol. 92, No. 2, 2014, pp. 207–242, http://tinyurl.com/kmsq4sz.

79. Tony Dokoupil, "Vice Wars: Tobacco, Alcohol and the Rise of Big Marijuana," NBC News, Nov. 29, 2014, http://tinyurl.com/lbcxsxu.

80. Aaron Smith, "Ohio to vote on marijuana legalization," CNN, Aug. 13, 2015, http://tinyurl.com/oyvcceb.

81. "Marijuana on the ballot," Ballotpedia.com, 2015, http://tinyurl.com/ooxv6aa.

82. Philip Smith, "An Overview Of The 2016 Marijuana Legalization Initiatives," *The Weed Blog*, July 31, 2015, http://tinyurl.com/ofwmod7.

83. "CA NORML Analysis Finds Marijuana Legalization Could Yield California $1.5-$2.5 Billion Per Year," CA NORML, undated, accessed Oct. 9, 2015, http://tinyurl.com/dcbghx.

84. Alison Vekshin, "Marijuana Legalization Across U.S. May Hinge on 2016 California Vote," Bloomberg, April 13, 2015, http://tinyurl.com/nz2b478.

85. "Title 21 United States Code, Controlled Substances Act, Subchapter I — Control and Enforcement," U.S. Department of Justice, Drug Enforcement Administration, http://tinyurl.com/3eqg7sk.

86. The Senate bill is S.683, "Compassionate Access, Research Expansion, and Respect States Act of 2015," U.S. Senate, undated, accessed Oct. 9, 2015, http://tinyurl.com/nhozocb.

87. Robert Mikos, "Can President Obama single-handedly legalize marijuana?" *Marijuana Law, Policy & Reform*, Jan. 21, 2014, http://tinyurl.com/p6glbcv.

88. "Increasing Percentages of Americans are Ready for Legal Marijuana," The Harris Poll, May 7, 2015, http://tinyurl.com/pm8gts9.

89. Brianna Gurciullo, Karen Mawdsley and Katie Campbell, "Pro-legalization groups prepare for marijuana measures in 2016," New England Center for Investigative Reporting, Aug. 16, 2015, http://tinyurl.com/qdtfmgg.

BIBLIOGRAPHY

Selected Sources

Books

Barcott, Bruce, *Weed the People: The Future of Legal Marijuana in America*, Time Books, 2015.

A nonfiction writer discusses marijuana's evolution from the shadows of criminality to a serious economic presence with a powerful impact on law and culture.

Clements, Kenneth W., and Xueyan Zhao, *Economics and Marijuana: Consumption, Pricing and Legalisation*, Cambridge University Press, 2014.

Two Australian economists analyze marijuana price and consumption patterns and apply the data to the legalization debate.

Fine, Doug, *Too High to Fail: Cannabis and the New Green Economic Revolution*, Gotham Books, 2012.

An investigative reporter describes legal marijuana's potential to transform the American economy.

Newton, David E., *Marijuana: A Reference Handbook*, ABC-CLIO, 2012.

A science and business writer sets out the economic, legal and social arguments surrounding marijuana legalization, placing them in an historical context.

Articles

Bomboy, Scott, "Interest picks up in legal marijuana as constitutional issue," National Constitution Center blog, April 16, 2015, http://tinyurl.com/p7xsaog.

The editor-in-chief of the National Constitution Center in Philadelphia, a museum established by Congress, examines the conflict between state laws that legalize marijuana and federal law that criminalizes it.

Geiger, Keri, Jesse Hamilton, and Elizabeth Dexheimer, "Does Anybody Want $3 Billion in Cash From Pot Sales? Big Banks Say No, Thanks," Bloomberg, May 12, 2015, http://tinyurl.com/ohsb6ox.

Journalists from a financial news service investigate the legal complications banks face in dealing with the marijuana industry.

Hudak, John, "Marijuana: The gateway to the 2016 presidential race," Brookings Institution, blog posting, March 4, 2015, http://tinyurl.com/mpwbcwg.

A fellow in governance studies at a Washington think tank argues that marijuana policy is an issue that political candidates can no longer ignore.

Hughes, Trevor, "Patchwork of pot rules hampers marijuana business expansion," *USA Today*, June 17, 2015, http://tinyurl.com/paggqzq.

State-by-state differences in the regulation of legal marijuana make it difficult for the industry to expand, the newspaper reports.

Nitti, Tony, "Ninth Circuit: Legal Or Not, Marijuana Facility Cannot Deduct Its Expenses," *Forbes*, **July 10, 2015, http://tinyurl.com/nghvf5m.**
The business magazine examines the federal tax situation faced by a legal cannabis enterprise.

Olson, Becky, "Chart of the Week: Marijuana Stock Volatility Underscores Uncertainty, Industry's Challenges," *Marijuana Business Daily*, **July 20, 2015, http://tinyurl.com/nvrzq39.**
A marijuana industry analyst discusses obstacles facing those who would invest in the industry.

Sides, Hampton, "High Science," *National Geographic*, **June 2015, http://tinyurl.com/khvdzjo.**
An historian and writer examines marijuana's chemistry, its effects on the body and the outlook for medicinal use of the drug.

Reports and Studies

Adler, Jonathan H., "Marijuana, Federal Power, and the States," *Case Western Reserve Law Review*, **Vol. 65, Issue 3, 2015, http://tinyurl.com/nprmbja.**

The director of the Center for Business Law & Regulation at Case Western Reserve University School of Law discusses options available to the federal government when its laws collide with those of the states.

Johnson, Renée, "Hemp as an Agricultural Commodity," **Congressional Research Service, Feb. 2, 2015, http://tinyurl.com/pa8nm6b.**
An agricultural specialist discusses the history and potential of hemp as an agricultural commodity in the context of federal legislation.

Light, Miles, *et al.*, **"Market Size and Demand for Marijuana in Colorado," The Marijuana Policy Group, March 25, 2014, http://tinyurl.com/pfu5mjz.**
A study by an independent research organization for the Colorado Department of Revenue provides consumption and economic estimates to help state policymakers design a regulatory framework for the fledgling industry.

Phillips, Richard, "Issues with Taxing Marijuana at the State Level," The Institute on Taxation and Economic Policy, May 2015, http://tinyurl.com/ov5vaem.
A senior tax policy analyst examines issues surrounding the design and implementation of taxes on marijuana at the state and local levels and explains how states can raise revenue while mitigating the negative effects of the drug's use.

For More Information

Hemp Industries Association, P.O. Box 575, Summerland, CA 93067; 707-874-3648; www.thehia.org/. Promotes development of a hemp industry.

Marijuana Policy Project, P.O. Box 77492, Washington, DC 20013; 202-462-5747; www.mpp.org/about/. Lobbies for marijuana decriminalization and legalization.

National Cannabis Industries Association, 1410 Grant St., B-301, Denver, CO 80203; 888-683-5650; www.thecannabisindustry.org/. Trade association for the legal cannabis industry.

NORML (National Organization for the Reform of Marijuana Laws), 1100 H St., N.W., Suite 830, Washington, DC 20005; 202-483-5500; http://norml.org/. Advocates for marijuana legalization.

Office of National Drug Control Policy, The White House, 1600 Pennsylvania Ave., N.W., Washington, DC 20500; 202-456-1111; www.whitehouse.gov/ondcp. Advises the president on drug-control issues and coordinates drug-control activities across the federal government.

Partnership for Drug-Free Kids (formerly Partnership for a Drug-Free America), 352 Park Ave. S., No. 901, New York, NY 10010; 212-922-1560; www.drugfree.org/. Seeks to reduce teen substance abuse and support families affected by addiction.

Smart Approaches to Marijuana, San Diego and Washington, D.C.; https://learn aboutsam.org/. Advocates for policies to reduce marijuana use.

Women Grow, Denver and Oakland, Calif.; http://womengrow.com/. Promotes greater acceptance of women in the marijuana industry.

4

Unions at a Crossroads

Chuck McCutcheon

Getty Images/Light Rocket/Pacific Press/Mark Apollo

Union hotel workers rally on April 15 in New York City for a $15-an-hour minimum wage. Union pressure has helped put wage-increase proposals on the ballot in several states and cities and prompted Walmart and McDonald's to increase workers' pay. Some observers say unions' renewed activity may point to a revival of organized labor's former influence.

Some 1,300 foot-stomping fast-food workers from around the country rallied in June at Detroit's Cobo Center auditorium to make two demands: a pay increase and the right to join a labor union. Wearing "We Are Worth More" T-shirts, they chanted, "We work, we sweat, put $15 on our check!"

"Two years ago, wage inequality was not even being mentioned," said Terrance Wise, a McDonald's and Burger King employee from Kansas City, Mo., and a leading figure in the "Fight for $15" movement organized by community groups and the 2 million-member Service Employees International Union (SEIU). "Now there's talk of how all workers need benefits and a raise, and the benefits of joining a union."[1]

The national debate over the minimum wage has cast a newly intensified spotlight on unions. For more than a century labor organizations have portrayed themselves as the champions of American workers, while critics have attacked them as dinosaurs from a bygone era, selfishly interfering with companies' ability to earn a profit.

As unions continue to play a central role in the minimum wage fight, along with such issues as pension benefits and international trade, they are seeking to expand their social and economic influence and attract new members. With its new high profile, some observers think organized labor may be ripe for a revival.

"There's more activity around the core issue of a voice in the workplace than there's been in decades," says Damon Silvers, policy director for the AFL-CIO, the 12.5-million-member union umbrella group.

From *CQ Researcher*,
August 7, 2015.

Most "Right-to-Work" States in South, Midwest

Twenty-five states have passed "right-to-work" laws, which guarantee that no person can be compelled, as a condition of employment, to join or pay dues to a union.

States with "Right-to-Work" Laws

Source: "Right-To-Work Resources," National Conference of State Legislatures, updated March 2015, http://tinyurl.com/pd578gn

But some labor scholars and union activists say the odds are stacked against a comeback: They point to a long decline in union membership and unyielding opposition from many businesses and the Republican Party, as well as shifts in the workplace toward foreign outsourcing and temporary employees, which have helped to erode union power.

Union membership stood last year at 14.6 million nonfarm private- and public-sector employees, or 11.1 percent of the nation's workforce. In 1983, the first year for which comparable figures are available, unions had 17.7 million members, or 20.1 percent of workers.[2]

"Today, the labor movement's decline is widely considered an irreversible reality — the inevitable outcome of globalization and automation, and the norm for a postindustrial economy, hardly worthy of comment," said Kim Phillips-Fein, an associate professor of history at New York University.[3]

Still, unions have succeeded in recent months at promoting their message and, in the case of the minimum wage, exerting pressure on policymakers and businesses to act in ways favorable to workers.

Labor was also at the center of a recent high-stakes fight against the Trans-Pacific Partnership trade agreement with 11 Asian-Pacific nations that President Obama has aggressively backed. Although the bill became law, unions managed to delay its passage in the Republican-controlled Congress by mobilizing their Democratic allies to argue that the pact would hurt employment.[4]

And pressed by the SEIU, the Los Angeles City Council voted in June to raise the minimum wage to $15 by 2020, joining voter approval of ballot measures for wage hikes in four states plus the cities of San Francisco and Oakland. At the same time, union lobbying helped promt nonunion corporate giants Wal-Mart and McDonald's to voluntarily increase the pay of some workers, and the Obama administration announced an overhaul of overtime rules, giving millions of workers a raise.[5]

"Unions have done a good job since the financial crisis in increasing their visibility," says Karl Petrick, an assistant professor of economics at Western New England University in Springfield, Mass., who studies labor. "We're seeing some of the old unions . . . becoming more visible talking about why something that's abstract to the average citizen is really, really important."

Experts say unions are trying to adjust to cultural and demographic trends and shed the seedy stereotype perpetuated by such infamous figures as Jimmy Hoffa, the International Brotherhood of Teamsters leader linked to organized crime before he vanished in 1975. Unions have reached out to minority groups, young people and white-collar workers, such as part-time adjunct faculty at many colleges and universities and lawyers and judges.[6]

At the same time, unions are trying to reach people in places where organized labor already has a presence. The American Federation of State, County and Municipal Employees (AFSCME), which represents 1.6 million government workers, said in July that it had signed up 140,000 more full members — who pay more in dues than "fair share" members — since the beginning of last year as part of a drive that President Lee Saunders said occurred after the union began intensifying efforts to unionize places it had tended to ignore.[7]

Unions have combined the issues of income inequality, low wages and poverty to tell a larger story about basic fairness in America, says Jake Rosenfeld, an associate professor of sociology at the University of Washington and author of the 2014 book *What Unions No Longer Do.*

"These are issues that are usually discussed in isolation, but by bringing them together it makes it absolutely clear to people, from the president on down, that you really aren't going to combat them without a revitalized labor movement," Rosenfeld says.

A Pew Research Center poll in April showed the public's opinion of labor has improved in recent years after remaining fairly constant over the past three decades. It found unions had a 48 percent favorable/39 percent unfavorable rating. Americans under age 30 had the highest favorable percentage (55 percent).[8]

But Rosenfeld and others inside and outside the labor movement say its revitalization is far from assured. As the economy has shifted away from manufacturing and toward a greater reliance on part-time and temporary workers, unions have suffered.

Carl Van Horn, a Rutgers University public policy professor and the founding director of the school's John J. Heldrich Center for Workforce Development, says many of the sectors in which unions have held sway are in decline.

"Some of the industries where [unions] once dominated have continued to migrate to other countries or just declined altogether, like manufacturing and durable goods," he says. "Construction is an area where they've had some success, but that's been diminished because of the post-recession economy."

Private-Sector Union Membership Declines

Membership in private-sector unions fell from about 17 percent of the non-farm workforce to less than 7 percent over the past three decades. The rate for public-sector unions held steadier during that period, with about a third of employees belonging to a government labor organization.

Percentage of Workers Age 16 or Older Who Are Union Members, 1983-2014

* Excludes agricultural and self-employed workers.

Source: "Table 3. Union affiliation of employed wage and salary workers by occupation and industry," U.S. Bureau of Labor Statistics, accessed July 28, 2015, http://tinyurl.com/owf3m6r

With the GOP in control of the U.S. House and Senate, unions have been unable to get any of their legislative priorities considered. Many Republicans and large companies accuse organized labor of such hidden agendas as disrupting businesses' practices by staging protests, trying to co-opt unwilling employees and demanding exemptions from laws so they can bolster their ranks.[9]

"Their ability to prosper is dependent on political support at the state legislatures and in the federal government," Van Horn says of unions, "and the smaller they become, the harder it is for them to maintain that support."

Despite its recent concessions on pay, Walmart — the nation's largest private employer — has aggressively fought unionization. It has flown anti-union teams to stores from its corporate headquarters in Bentonville, Ark., and once responded to a unionization move by meat department workers at a Texas store by announcing it would use prepackaged meat instead of relying on butchers.[10]

Even when Democrats controlled both chambers of Congress in 2009, unions failed to persuade lawmakers to pass one of labor's biggest priorities: the Employee Free Choice Act, which would require employers to recognize a union as soon as a majority of workers signed cards saying they wanted one.[11] Unions also have been unable to get Congress to raise the federal minimum wage.[12]

Public-sector unions, such as those representing teachers, firefighters and police officers, are far more prevalent than private-sector unions.[13] In 2014, the public sector had a unionization rate of 35.7 percent — more than five times the 6.6 percent level for nonfarm private-sector workers.[14]

Still, public-sector unions have clashed with Republican governors and even a few Democrats. Some have accused unions of being selfish for refusing to accept cuts in generous employee pension plans that have created state budget headaches.

Wisconsin Republican Gov. Scott Walker has vaulted to the top tier of 2016 GOP presidential contenders by stressing his successful showdowns with unions. His support of limiting collective bargaining * for state workers led to a 2012 recall election, which he won with ease. He was re-elected in 2014 and signed a bill in March making Wisconsin the nation's 25th "right-to-work" state, guaranteeing that no person can be compelled, as a condition of employment, to join or pay dues to a union.

The situation has led some observers to predict unions could flourish in areas with a supportive liberal base but decline in more moderate or conservative parts of the country.

"Here in Los Angeles, it's a very vibrant movement," says Victor Narro, project director for the UCLA Labor Center, which brings together students, labor leaders and activists to tackle workplace concerns. "But I've become pessimistic about what happens when you go outside of California."

As union officials, business leaders, academics and others debate the future of unions, here are some of the questions under discussion:

Do today's workers need unions?

To labor's supporters, unions aren't essential simply because of their historic role of helping workers earn a decent wage and protecting them from being fired unjustly. They argue that unions now serve as a crucial check on the influence of corporations and the wealthy and an antidote to what many Americans see as growing income disparity.

"Absent a substantial union movement, the American middle class will shrink," wrote Harold Meyerson, editor-at-large for the liberal magazine *The American*

Prospect and a *Washington Post* columnist. "Absent a substantial union movement, the concentration of wealth will increase. Absent a substantial union movement, the corporate domination of government will grow."

Even as American workers have become better educated since the late 1970s, "what they lack is power," he said. "The current [economic] recovery is different from previous recoveries, because few unions remain to press workers' demands."[15]

The AFL-CIO's Silvers agrees that unions can be a mechanism to address broader societal concerns about income. "Never in my lifetime has the objective need for workers' organizing and increased bargaining power been more obvious," he says. "It's not just long-term wage stagnation. It's a whole lot of people realizing that our society isn't functioning properly, and that our public policies reproduce radical inequality. Anybody who's involved in public life knows . . . that when the labor movement is weak, workers aren't able to secure their share of the wealth they produce, and the wealthy dominate the public-policy process."

Labor supporters say unions are needed for other reasons, too: Union contracts often set the wage scale for nonunion workers in a local area. Labor has been in the forefront of securing workplace safety and anti-discrimination measures that apply to all workers. And unions often provide a trained workforce for companies.

In Missouri, the workplace training issue arose in May as state lawmakers debated a right-to-work bill. It passed, but supporters could not muster a sufficient margin to override Democratic Gov. Jay Nixon's veto.[16]

"The No. 1 thing that Missouri is missing, that businesses are looking for, is workforce development," said Republican state Rep. John McCaherty, who opposed the right-to-work measure. "They were looking for trained individuals. You know what they're looking for training in? Construction. Machinists. Welders. Our unions are training people to do those jobs."[17]

Meanwhile, the 2007–09 recession has sparked greater interest in unionizing white-collar workers by the AFL-CIO, whose Department for Professional Employees is a coalition of 22 national unions representing more than 4 million highly skilled workers.[18]

The unionization efforts have yielded results in areas of the country that already enjoy union support. In Washington, D.C., a group of administrative law judges voted in 2014 to unionize after an organizing effort by the International Federation of Professional and Technical Engineers.[19] And in New York City, members of United Auto Workers Local 2320 went on strike in 2013 to protest benefit cuts. Nearly half of its members were lawyers who joined after becoming frustrated with how they were being treated.[20]

Another group being courted by unions is so-called "contingent faculty," such as college adjuncts and lecturers, who make up more than 70 percent of the faculty who teach college undergraduate courses, according to the American Association of University Professors.[21]

Besides low pay, most contingent faculty receive no benefits and have no job security. Colleges use adjuncts "like substitute teachers, but pay them less than the average high school teacher," said Alice Kitchen, an adjunct who teaches a social work course at the University of Missouri-Kansas City.[22]

But many in the business world and in Republican policy circles counter that unions are an unnecessary drag on companies and, in turn, the economy.

"They function like an albatross around a company's neck — making it less flexible, less able to react wisely to the demands of a changing marketplace," said Edwin Feulner, founder of the Heritage Foundation, a conservative think tank in Washington.[23]

Feulner and other critics say union contracts are too rigid regarding wages and job requirements. They also complain that unions demand preferential treatment. For example, critics say, during the minimum-wage debate in Los Angeles, although labor leaders favor a higher minimum wage, they wanted exemptions in unionized workplaces. The exemptions, said Diana Furchtgott-Roth, a senior fellow at the Manhattan Institute, a conservative think tank in New York City, "would allow them greater strength in organizing workplaces. Unions can tell fast food chains, hotels and hospitals that if they agree to union representation, their wage bill will be substantially lower."

"It's blatantly obvious these minimum-wage campaigns are cynical efforts for expanding union rolls," a U.S. Chamber of Commerce blog post said.[24]

Other critics say some union workers' salaries are inflated, making it difficult for companies to invest in other areas, leading them to pass on the cost to consumers. An oft-cited example came in 2013, when an outcry arose during a strike at New York's Carnegie Hall over the

In one of the highest-profile strikes in recent years, unionized teachers rally in Chicago on Sept. 13, 2012, during a walkout over contract terms that stopped classes for seven days. The strike ended with the teachers ratifying a three-year contract giving them annual raises but agreeing to a lengthier school day and permitting colleagues to be evaluated based, in part, on student test scores.

fact that some union stagehands earned more than $300,000 annually.[25]

James Sherk, a senior policy analyst in labor economics at Heritage, said unions unnecessarily constrict Web designers and information technology professionals: "These jobs depend on the creativity and skills of individual employees. Few workers today want a one-size-fits-all contract that ignores what they individually bring to the bargaining table. Union-negotiated, seniority-based promotions and raises feel like chains to workers who want to get ahead."[26]

Another challenge to unions is the increasing desire of employers — and growing popularity among some workers — of using independent contractors or freelancers, who don't receive benefits. Such workers made up about 30 percent of the workforce in 2006, the last time the federal government counted them, and that figure is expected to exceed 40 percent by 2020.[27]

Meanwhile, critics of public-sector unions say they have made government less responsive and innovative by protecting unproductive employees.

"With poor [job] prospects in the ultracompetitive private sector, government work is increasingly desirable for those with limited skills," said Daniel DiSalvo, a senior fellow at the Manhattan Institute's Center for State and Local Leadership and an assistant professor of political science at The City College of New York-CUNY.[28]

Do unions have substantial political clout?

Proponents of unions point to local and statewide successes on the minimum wage and unions' ability to delay passage of the Trans-Pacific Partnership trade agreement as evidence that labor remains a potent political force, especially in helping Democrats.

Although the trade bill became law, the AFL-CIO and other labor groups succeeded in blocking an initial attempt in June to allow an up-or-down vote. They mustered a broad coalition — which included organizations that the measure did not directly affect — in arguing that, contrary to Obama's assertions, the pact would hurt American workers.

"They did a good job getting out and defining [the trade agreement] early among Democratic House members, really peeling off an enormous number of folks who didn't have a long history or an understanding of the issue, prior to the White House engaging," said Simon Rosenberg, president and founder of the centrist advocacy group New Democrat Network and a supporter of the trade measure.[29]

After Rep. Kathleen Rice, D-N.Y., announced she would reverse her position and support the measure, the AFL-CIO spent more than $100,000 running advertisements accusing her of having "flip-flopped." Opponents of the deal also spent $84,000 on ads against Rep. Ami Bera, D-Calif., after he wrote an op-ed column supporting the agreement.[30]

Despite their disagreement with Obama on that issue, unions played a large role in electing him in 2008 and 2012. In 2008 alone, labor leaders said unions and their political action committees spent nearly $450 million during the presidential race while making millions of phone calls and knocking on millions of doors.[31]

An analysis by the political website *FiveThirtyEight* found that ballots cast by union members and members of households with a union worker boosted Obama's share of the vote by 1.7 percentage points in 2008.[32] (Obama won by 7 percentage points.)[33] Four years later, according to *FiveThirtyEight*, Obama's re-election win over Mitt Romney would have been reduced from nearly 4 percentage points to just over 1 percentage point without the support of union workers.[34]

In the 2016 campaign, Democratic presidential front-runner Hillary Rodham Clinton has reached out to labor groups, some of which backed Obama when she ran for president in 2008. She said in a July economic policy speech that the "decline of unions may be responsible for a third of the [income] inequality among men."[35]

The AFL-CIO's Working America initiative concentrates on recruiting pro-union candidates and advancing pro-labor causes at the state and local levels. It played an important role in fending off a Republican initiative aimed at curtailing collective bargaining for state employees in Ohio, as well as helping to raise the minimum wage in New Mexico and winning an earned-sick-day law for workers in Portland, Ore., said labor historian Nelson Lichtenstein, director of the University of California, Santa Barbara's Center for the Study of Work, Labor, and Democracy.[36]

But some labor experts say unions' political power has greatly diminished. Unions spent $235 million in the 2014 midterm elections, nearly all of it going to Democrats; overall, Democratic congressional candidates raised $736 million.[37] But the party suffered massive setbacks, losing its Senate majority.

One major problem is the legal requirement that if workers use a union to politick, they must first organize for economic, collective-bargaining purposes, said Benjamin Sachs, a professor of labor and industry at Harvard Law School and a former assistant general counsel for the SEIU.[38]

"This bundling of functions, an artifact of how unions formed historically, is a major problem for political organizing today," Sachs said. "This is true most obviously because managerial opposition to collective bargaining has become pervasive. . . . Because substantial numbers of American workers say they do not want to collectively bargain with their employers, traditional unions are not an attractive form of political organization for many."[39]

The influx of money into campaigns stemming from the Supreme Court's landmark *Citizens United v. Federal Election Commission* ruling in 2010 also has helped corporations blunt unions' influence, says John Delaney, a professor of business administration at the University of Pittsburgh who recently stepped down as dean of its business school.[40]

Citizens United eased restrictions on political spending by corporations and unions, with the former far outspending the latter. One of the biggest pro-business "super PACs" that formed in the wake of the law, the Freedom Partners Action Fund organized by billionaire industrialists Charles and David Koch, spent more than $23 million in the 2014 cycle, or 10 times more than the AFL-CIO's Workers' Voices super PAC.[41]

"Over time, the labor advantage in politics has declined because of all of the other money involved in the political sphere," Delaney says. "And some of the positions that labor has taken are so supportive of the labor movement — which is just a portion of the overall economy — that people see it as self-serving."

The spread of right-to-work laws is another reason unions are seen as having lost clout. Most of the 25 states with those laws are in the South and Midwest, with Wisconsin and Michigan having joined Indiana in passing them in recent years.[42]

Studies have shown right-to-work states have had lower levels of employment than other states, and that private-sector job growth in right-to-work states increased slightly during the previous decade and following the recent economic recession.

But the evidence that those laws actually spur job growth has been mixed, according to the fact-checking site *PolitiFact*. And while right-to-work states overall have had higher levels of income growth, the website found no consensus among five economists that it consulted on the significance of right-to-work status.[43]

"What seems clear is that the volume and tone of the debate over right-to-work laws far outstrips actual certainty about the impact," *The Christian Science Monitor* concluded.[44]

Are strikes an effective union tactic?

Strikes have long been a powerful weapon for unions. In the 20th century, large strikes against coal, automobile and

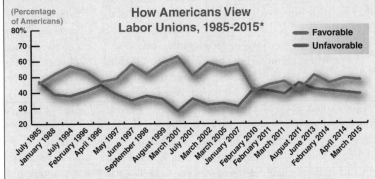

Americans Divided on Unions

Forty-eight percent of Americans view labor unions favorably and 39 percent unfavorably. Support for organized labor reached 63 percent in March 2001 and has fluctuated between 59 percent and 41 percent since then.

(Percentage of Americans)

How Americans View Labor Unions, 1985-2015*

━━ Favorable
━━ Unfavorable

* Excludes respondents who said they were unfamiliar with labor unions or did not know how to answer.

Source: "Mixed Views of Impact of Long-Term Decline in Union Membership," Pew Research Center, April 27, 2015, pp. 5, 12, http://tinyurl.com/qf2n6xp

steel companies, along with the U.S. Postal Service, all led to higher wages and improved working conditions.[45]

Last year, at the behest of the union-backed Organization for Respect at Wal-Mart (OUR Wal-Mart), workers at the retail giant in more than a dozen states continued a practice of walking off the job on the day after Thanksgiving, the busy start of the holiday retail season. Some began a 24-hour fast to protest wages that they complained were so low that they left many employees hungry.

Organizers say such tactics have had an effect: In April 2014, the retailer began a new policy benefiting pregnant workers by giving them less physically taxing work if they are having trouble performing their jobs, as well as making changes in scheduling that enable workers to get more shifts — and thus bigger paychecks.[46] And Walmart also has raised wages for some workers.

At Seattle-Tacoma International Airport, the SEIU and the Teamsters union recently fought Hertz's rule against prayer breaks for Muslims after the car-rental company suspended some Somali shuttle car drivers who had sought to pray on their shifts during Ramadan. The unions joined in organizing a multifaith pray-in at the company's airport counters, eventually winning substantial publicity and concessions.

"By inviting leaders of different faiths to rally at the Hertz counter, the union connected the dots between religious freedom and the secular union principles of anti-discrimination and due process," said labor organizer Jonathan Rosenblum, who served as director of the Hertz campaign.[47]

One of the highest-profile recent strikes occurred in Chicago, where unionized teachers in the nation's third-largest school system staged a walkout in 2012 that ended classes for seven school days. The teachers were protesting school-day lengths, performance evaluations and potential job losses. Much of the Chicago Teachers Union's anger was directed at Democratic Mayor Rahm Emanuel, a former House member and White House chief of staff who had cultivated support from labor for his party. The strike ended with the teachers ratifying a three-year contract giving them annual raises but calling for longer school days and permitting teacher evaluations, in part, based on student test scores.[48]

But large-scale strikes or lockouts — work stoppages involving more than 1,000 workers in which an employer tries to get workers to accept certain conditions by refusing to allow them to be on the job — have become rare. At their peak in 1952, 470 strikes or lockouts occurred. Last year, only 11 occurred — down from 15 in 2013 and tied for the second lowest total on record.

"Strikes are just incredibly risky [for unions] these days," said the University of Washington's Rosenfeld.[49]

He and others say companies have more options to withstand strikes, including relocating operations or producing goods and services from more locations with fewer employees. In addition, they say, the 2007–09 recession made it difficult to strike against companies that are in bankruptcy proceedings or other serious financial trouble.

"The notion that the only way you can impose your will on employers is by breaking them isn't working any more," the University of Pittsburgh's Delaney says.

Rutgers' Van Horn says the decline in unions' membership also has hurt their ability to strike.

"The more people that you have in a union, the more that strikes can be successful," he says. "They were successful [in the past] because a union with a grievance had support in its community with other workers who were willing not to cross picket lines. There was a herd instinct."

Some labor organizers, however, say strikes and other mass disruptions still can succeed. They cite this year's work slowdowns in 29 West Coast shipping terminals, which handle goods accounting for more than 12 percent of the U.S. economy. Workers seeking higher pay held up shipments. They received a new contract after Obama ordered Labor Secretary Tom Perez and Commerce Secretary Penny Pritzker to mediate the dispute.[50]

Those sympathetic to labor say the "Fight for $15" movement has also been highly effective. Historian Lichtenstein noted that the movement's periodic strikes and pickets have been directed not against individual fast-food franchises but against the entire industry.

"This has proven a brilliant stratagem: It unites rather than divides a workforce that in any event cycles from one low-paid service job to another; it keeps the attention of workers and the public focused upon the problems common to all employers in one huge industry," he said. "It points the way to the enactment of a set of seemingly traditional legislative reforms that can generate immediate payoffs on the state and municipal level, if not in the nation as a whole."[51]

BACKGROUND
Birth of Unions

The establishment of modern labor unions paralleled the surge of American industrial might in the late 19th and early 20th centuries.

Between 1870 and 1929, U.S. industrial output increased 14 times, creating a huge demand for immigrants with skills to sustain the swelling economy.[52]

By the 1880s, most Americans put in 14-hour days, six days a week, without sick pay or overtime. Children as young as 8 worked in coal mines, where they developed health problems associated with older people.[53]

Leaders of local craft unions, organized around particular skills and trades, in 1881 created the Federation of Organized Trades and Labor Unions, which five years later became the American Federation of Labor. Founder Samuel Gompers, an English-born cigar maker, became its first president in 1886 and held the post for nearly 40 years.

Gompers sought to restrict union membership to wage earners (excluding employers) and to group workers into "locals" based on their trade or craft. At the outset of his presidency he tried to focus on economic rather than political issues, but when political action became necessary, he urged labor to follow a course of "political nonpartisan-ship" that meant winning the endorsements of whichever political parties were in power.[54]

Union membership skyrocketed. In the building trades, it grew from 67,000 in 1897 to 391,600 in 1904, while in transportation membership jumped from 116,000 to 446,300. Stunning growth also came in coal mining: Aided by a 1902 strike that led to significant organizing efforts, membership rose from 447,000 to more than 2 million between 1897 and 1904.[55]

Strikes and Violence

But strikes also became associated with violence — sometimes instigated by company owners and sometimes by unions. An 1892 lockout and strike at Pennsylvania's Homestead Steel and a strike two years later at Illinois' Pullman railway car company sparked deadly riots that ended after the federal government and states sent in reinforcements to assist local police. In 1914, the "Ludlow Massacre" at the Colorado Fuel and Iron Co., which wealthy industrialist John D. Rockefeller Jr. owned, fol-lowed a strike by coal miners and coke oven workers. State militia fired machine guns at miners' tents; accord-ing to various reports, as many as 66 died. The dead included two women and 11 children who suffocated in a pit they had dug beneath their tent.[56]

By this time, the U.S. Department of Labor had been established, having been signed into law by a reluctant Republican President William Howard Taft in March 1913 just hours before Democrat Woodrow Wilson was sworn in to succeed him.[57] In 1917, Wilson became the first president to speak at an AFL convention, and Gompers saw an opportunity to increase the group's power and influence by taking a more directly political course during World War I, when he spoke out against socialist influ-ences in the United States.

The Great Depression eroded Americans' faith in business and led to another increase in worker demand for unions. But disputes persisted within the labor movement between those who believed that only skilled workers had the economic clout to deal with manage-ment and others who said that less-skilled workers should be organized based on the industry that employed them.

Teamsters union leader Jimmy Hoffa appears in the late 1950s before the Senate McClellan Committee, which was investigating corruption in labor unions under the aggressive direction of Chief Counsel Robert F. Kennedy. Hoffa's reputed connection with organized crime helped foster organized labor's corrupt image. Hoffa later served four years in prison on jury tampering and bribery charges. He disappeared in 1975 and was never found; he is widely believed to have been murdered.

The intense debate over skills led United Mine Workers President John L. Lewis to punch Carpenters Union President Bill Hutcheson at a 1935 AFL convention. Lewis formed the Committee for Industrial Organizations (CIO), renamed the Congress of Industrial Organizations. It broke away from the AFL in 1938 and remained separate from the AFL for two decades.

President Franklin D. Roosevelt's administration tried to impose some rules for the union-organizing process. In 1935, the administration persuaded Congress to pass the National Labor Relations Act, which established the National Labor Relations Board (NLRB) to organize government-supervised, secret-ballot elections for workers at their jobs.

The Supreme Court upheld the law's constitutional-ity in 1937.[58] A year later, the landmark Fair Labor Standards Act banned children under 14 from working at all, while restricting those under 18 from "hazardous" positions in mining and factories. It limited the work-week to 44 hours (revised to 40 hours in 1940), and set the first minimum wage, at 25 cents an hour (around $4.25 in today's dollars).[59]

In December 1936, one of the first sit-down strikes — in which workers take control of their work place,

CHRONOLOGY

1880s–1947 *Workers organize into unions as the country industrializes.*

1886 Unionization of skilled "trade" workers such as printers and cigar makers leads to founding of the American Federation of Labor (AFL).

1890s Bitter strikes at Homestead Steel in Pennsylvania (1892) and the Pullman railway car company in Illinois (1894) lead to riots, killing several workers.

1935 National Labor Relations Act gives workers the right to join unions, prohibits "unfair labor practices."

1938 Formal split in the AFL leads to creation of the Congress of Industrial Organizations (CIO). . . . Fair Labor Standards Act bans children under 14 from working, limits the work week to 44 hours and sets the first minimum wage at 25 cents an hour.

1947 Congress passes the Taft-Hartley Act, restricting union activity.

1950s–1970 *Public-sector unions advance as private-sector unions create controversy.*

1955 AFL and CIO merge, representing some 15.5 million workers.

1959 Wisconsin is first state to pass collective-bargaining law for government workers. . . . Congress passes Landrum-Griffin Act, which aims to root out organized crime in unions.

1967 Teamsters Union leader Jimmy Hoffa is imprisoned on multiple charges and serves four years before President Richard M. Nixon commutes his sentence. . . . Hoffa vanishes in 1975.

1970 Occupational Safety and Health Act includes numerous worker-protection measures.

1980s–1990s *Unions are on losing end of air-traffic controllers strike and North American Free Trade Agreement (NAFTA).*

1981 Republican President Ronald Reagan fires 11,000 striking air- traffic controllers and decertifies their union.

1993 Congress and Democratic President Bill Clinton override labor's opposition and approve NAFTA.

2002-Present *Unions face internal struggles and political setbacks.*

2002 At President George W. Bush's insistence, Department of Homeland Security (DHS) is created, with president given authority to waive collective-bargaining rights.

2005 Service Employees International Union and the Teamsters pull out of the AFL-CIO, followed by the United Food and Commercial Workers Union.

2006 Federal appeals court says Bush administration went too far in curbing collective bargaining with DHS employees.

2009 Lilly Ledbetter Fair Pay Act restores the rights of working women to sue over pay discrimination. . . . Employee Free Choice Act, which requires employers to recognize a union as soon as a majority of workers say they want one, passes the House but stalls in the Senate amid Republican opposition.

2011 Republican Govs. Scott Walker in Wisconsin and John Kasich in Ohio win passage of bills to curb collective bargaining for state and local workers. The Ohio law is repealed, while Walker survives a recall election over the issue.

2014 Walker and Kasich are re-elected; New Jersey Republican Gov. Chris Christie also is re-elected despite tangling with public-employee unions. Republicans also win governors' races in Massachusetts and Illinois despite union opposition.

2015 Unions fail to stop approval of Trans-Pacific Partnership agreement with 11 Pacific Rim countries. . . . President Obama expands the number of people qualifying for overtime pay. . . . Pressed by SEIU, Los Angeles City Council votes in June to raise the minimum wage to $15 by 2020. . . . U.S. Supreme Court will hear arguments this fall in *Friedrichs v. California Teachers Association*, over whether government workers must continue to pay fees to finance public-sector unions if they choose not to become full union members.

preventing management from replacing them with other workers — occurred at a General Motors plant in Flint, Mich. The autoworkers sought to establish the United Auto Workers (UAW) as the only bargaining agent for GM employees. The strike lasted 44 days, with workers winning a pay raise and other concessions.[60]

A series of massive strikes in the 1940s against the automobile, steel and meatpacking industries, as well as others, angered business and conservative groups and led to passage of the Taft-Hartley Act in 1947. The law imposed sharp limits on strikes and enabled states to enact right-to-work laws.[61]

In 1950, historian Arthur M. Schlesinger ranked the "upsurge of labor" before the two world wars as among the 10 events that most "profoundly shaped and shook history" during the first half of the 20th century.[62] But in 1950–51 the reputation of organized labor in the United States was stained by televised hearings chaired by Sen. Estes Kefauver, D-Tenn., that detailed organized crime's influence on unions. A later hearing featuring an aggressive investigator named Robert F. Kennedy, who in the 1960s became attorney general in the administration of his brother, Democratic President John F. Kennedy, further explored the links between the two.[63]

The AFL and CIO resolved their differences and agreed to reunite in 1955. Two years later, the group expelled two of its affiliate unions — the Teamsters and Bakery and Confectionary Workers International Union — for corruption. The Teamsters were readmitted in 1987.[64]

Postwar Growth

During the same post-World War II period, the growth of state and local governments led to a greater recognition of collective-bargaining rights for their employees. Liberals had worried that bargaining rights for public employees could affect government's ability to serve citizens. But in 1958, New York City's Democratic mayor, Robert F. Wagner Jr., granted such rights to city workers.[65] And in 1959, Democratic Wisconsin Gov. Gaylord Nelson won enactment of the first statewide collective bargaining law.[66]

When he ran for president in 1960, Kennedy successfully drew on public-sector workers for support. Kennedy issued an executive order in 1962 giving federal workers the right to organize.[67] But union leaders remained hostile to Attorney General Kennedy.

"Bobby Kennedy wanted to use the Teamsters as a vehicle to get the Kennedy name out front with something that was probably the greatest thriller that ever appeared on TV," Teamsters leader Hoffa recalled, referring to the congressional hearings. "And when he couldn't bull me, he couldn't take over the Teamsters, why, it became a vendetta between he and I."[68]

During the presidency of Richard M. Nixon, unions scored some big legislative victories, including the 1970 Occupational Safety and Health Act (OSHA) that included numerous worker-protection measures.[69] Congress also adopted minimum standards for employee pension plans under the Employee Retirement Income Security Act (ERISA) in 1974.[70]

But unions found a far less sympathetic Republican president in Ronald Reagan. In 1981, more than 11,000 members of the Professional Air Traffic Controllers Organization (PATCO) went on strike, demanding a pay raise and better working conditions. Reagan fired the controllers and permanently replaced them.

"Reagan wanted to really turn back the clock, you might say, to an approach to American government and politics that was pre-New Deal," said Joseph McCartin, a Georgetown University history professor and author of a book on the dispute. "And part of that meant reorganizing the relationship between government and the labor movement. . . . He sent a powerful message that many employers even in the private sector acted upon after that, and it was a period of getting tough with the union movement that really marked a profoundly important turning point."[71]

Reagan, however, remained popular among many union members who had become disillusioned with what they saw as the Democratic Party's growing elitism. The president handily won re-election in 1984 with the backing of many "Reagan Democrats."

NAFTA's Effects

In 1992, many saw Bill Clinton as having a mixed record on labor as Arkansas' governor.[72] Though he was able to gain enough union support to win the presidency that year, he incensed unions with his successful push for the 1994 North American Free Trade Agreement (NAFTA) between Canada, Mexico and the United States. Unions said the pact didn't adequately protect against job losses.

Advocates Seek More Black Female Union Leaders

"Who has the most money and seniority? It's the white men."

As unions seek to expand their ranks, labor organizers and supporters say they must provide more leadership opportunities to one of their most loyal constituencies — African-American women.

Many black women belong to unions; in 2014, their representation rate was 13.5 percent. Only black men, at 15.8 percent, had a higher representation rate among specific race and gender groups.

But an April report by the Institute for Policy Studies, a liberal think tank in Washington, surveyed more than 450 black women and found that even though 65 percent aspired to become union leaders, less than 3 percent reported having held elected positions and less than 5 percent had served as a union president.[1]

Black men have held high-ranking positions in unions for decades. Among the most prominent are civil rights leader A. Philip Randolph, who led the first African-American union in 1925 and became an AFL-CIO vice president 30 years later; William Lucy, secretary-treasurer of the American Federation of State, County and Municipal Employees from 1972 to 2010; and William Burrus, who in 2001 was elected president of the American Postal Workers Union — the first African-American to head a national union.[2]

"African-American women are the most underutilized leadership resource in the U.S. labor movement despite the fact that they belong to unions at higher rates than all other women," said the report.[3]

The report's authors, Kimberly Freeman Brown and Marc Bayard, said they focused on black women "because we know that they are, and always have been, 'the miner's canary' for workers in America. Black women have experienced for decades many of the economic and social ills now faced by others. Making black women whole raises the floor for all women — and likely for all workers."[4]

Nikki Lewis, the African-American executive director of DC Jobs With Justice, a coalition of labor groups and community organizations in Washington, says the report's findings came as no surprise. "I see it when I go to local unions — who has the most money and the most seniority? It's the white men," Lewis says.

Many of the leaders featured in the report have high-ranking jobs in public-sector unions, such as teachers' unions, and the health care field. One of them is Dr. Luella Toni Lewis, a former president of the Committee of Residents and Interns, the largest physicians' union in the Service Employees International Union (SEIU). She is now chair of SEIU Healthcare, which represents more than 1 million doctors, nurses and other health care workers.

In the two decades since NAFTA's enactment, its effects have been sharply debated. Its supporters, and many economists, see a positive impact on U.S. employment and note that new export-related jobs in the United States pay 15 to 20 percent more on average than those focused on domestic production. But others say wages haven't kept pace with labor productivity and that the pressures on the U.S. manufacturing base have contributed to income disparity in the United States.

The AFL-CIO's Silvers says that since NAFTA, "the purpose of U.S. trade policy has been to use it as a lever to push wages down." But many economists say the trade deal can't be blamed for weak wage growth, citing instead broader global shifts away from manufacturing and toward services.[73]

The Republican takeover of Congress in 1994, and the election of Republican George W. Bush as president in 2000, further weakened unions' power. Bush made several moves to cultivate union support, such as imposing tariffs on foreign steel and joining the Teamsters in calling for oil drilling in Alaska's Arctic National Wildlife Refuge. But in 2002 he invoked the Taft-Hartley

"When you look at some senior staff leadership positions, or the management of the hospitals, or who is making decisions on finances, I see fewer and fewer people who look like me," Lewis said in the report.[5]

Unions have not effectively made specialized appeals to demographic groups in the past, says John Delaney, a professor of business administration at the University of Pittsburgh and former dean of its graduate business school who studies labor issues. "The labor movement is going to have to demonstrate to a demographic that they actually care about that demographic, not just about having them pay union dues," Delaney says.

But there is some evidence of change. AFL-CIO President Richard Trumka said in a recent speech that he endorsed the Institute for Policy Studies' findings. "There are too few women, and particularly black women, in leadership roles in the labor movement," Trumka said. "That's about justice and success."[6]

The AFL-CIO held an event in June on race and the labor movement. Lewis, who participated in a town-hall discussion at the event, says she regarded it as "a sign of hope that they would have a bunch of people of color come in and talk about the challenges we face."

A 2007 study by Cornell University's School of Industrial and Labor Relations found that black women statistically have a better track record than others in organizing successful union elections. When black females are the lead organizers, it said, the election win rate was 89 percent, compared to 53 percent overall for female organizers and 42 percent for male organizers.

"Developing more lead organizers who are female, people of color, and especially women of color, when combined with a comprehensive union-building strategy, is a formula for success," said the study by Kate Bronfenbrenner, director of labor education research at the Cornell labor school, and Dorian T. Warren, an assistant professor of political science at Columbia University.[7]

The Institute for Policy Studies' report called for creating and expanding mentorship programs, bolstering public education and crafting pilot organizing projects focused on black women.[8]

— *Chuck McCutcheon*

---

[1] "And Still I Rise: Black Women Labor Leaders' Voices/Power/ Promise," Institute for Policy Studies, April 2015, http://tinyurl.com/ p7q8nqe.

[2] "Asa Philip Randolph (1889-1979)," AFL-CIO, http://tinyurl.com/ qbk4hh2; David Moberg, "Public Worker Union Leader William Lucy Steps Down, Speaks Out," *In These Times*, June 30, 2010, http:// tinyurl.com/o947s8h; "William Henry 'Bill' Burrus, 1936-," *Encyclopedia.com*, http://tinyurl.com/ok3otuv.

[3] "And Still I Rise: Black Women Labor Leaders' Voices/Power/Promise," *op. cit.*

[4] Kimberly Freeman Brown and Marc Bayard, "How Black Women Can Rescue the Labor Movement," *TheRoot.com*, May 1, 2015, http:// tinyurl.com/ mju6fzw.

[5] "And Still I Rise: Black Women Labor Leaders' Voices/Power/Promise," *op. cit.*

[6] "At the 2015 And Still I Rise Event," transcript of Richard L. Trumka remarks, AFL-CIO website, June 26, 2015, http://tinyurl.com/ o8f4d8p.

[7] Kate Bronfenbrenner and Dorian T. Warren, "Race, Gender and the Rebirth of Trade Unionism," Cornell University School of Industrial and Labor Relations, June 2007, http://tinyurl.com/p8q2ykf.

[8] "And Still I Rise: Black Women Labor Leaders' Voices/Power/Promise," *op. cit.*

Act — which had not been used since the 1970s — in ending the labor dispute that had drastically slowed work at 29 West Coast shipping ports.[74]

Congress' swing back to Democratic control in 2007, along with Democrat Obama's election a year later, improved unions' political fortunes. One of Obama's first moves was to sign the Lilly Ledbetter Fair Pay Act, which restored the rights of working women to sue over pay discrimination.[75] Unions lobbied in favor of the president's Affordable Care Act that overhauled the health care payment system.

But Republicans and their allies in the business community sharply stepped up their attacks on unions. One of their chief targets was the National Labor Relations Board (NLRB), which is made up of five members — three from the president's party and two from the opposing party, all of whom are subject to Senate confirmation.

For the first several years of Obama's presidency, the board functioned without a full slate as he fought with Congress over who should serve on it, leading many labor experts to say it was rudderless and unable to function properly.[76]

"Works Councils" Viewed as Alternative to Unions

European concept seeks to improve ties between workers, management.

An oft-discussed alternative to unions is the establishment of "works councils" — employer-employee groups common in Germany and other European countries. Supporters say such entities can empower workers, but critics say the United States lacks the laws and conditions to make them viable here.

Unlike unions, which handle negotiations over wages and benefits, works councils use a formal process to improve communication between workers and management. They cover such areas as company finances, job safety, productivity and operational plans.

"They don't bargain for wages, that's done by the unions; but they have all sorts of rights that relate to working time, who gets laid off, even whether the store is going to close or not," said Thomas Geoghegan, a labor lawyer in Chicago and author of several books on the labor movement. "They can go in and look at the books. The management has to enter into agreements. The works council can't dictate, but they have enormous influence over what working hours will be, who's going to work when and how."[1]

Some U.S. labor leaders support the concept, including Damon Silvers, the AFL-CIO's policy director. "We think that if the U.S. is to be successful at being a high-wage economy, it will be an important part of our competitive advantage to have systems like works councils that are more like what the rest of the world has," Silvers says.

Conservatives generally support the idea as long as the councils are independent of unions. "Many companies do want to hear their employees' concerns," said James Sherk, a senior policy analyst in labor economics at the Heritage Foundation, a conservative think tank in Washington. "Rank-and-file workers know things that senior management does not . . . Shouldn't workers have more options than a union or nothing?"[2]

Works councils exist in the United Kingdom, France and Belgium, but they are most closely associated with Germany, where they are allowed in any workplace employing at least five people. Members are not required to join a union, but more than three-quarters belong to one.[3]

Works councils are hailed as "one of the best, most innovative features" of Germany's labor system, according to labor experts Matthew Finkin, a law professor at the University of Illinois and a member of the governing board of the Institute for Labor Law and Labor Relations in the European Union in Trier, Germany, and Thomas Kochan, a professor of management and co-director of the Institute for Work and Employment Research at the MIT Sloan School of Management.

"They have been shown to enhance efficiency, adaptability and cooperation," Finkin and Kochan wrote. "By supporting the use of work sharing (agreeing to reduce everyone's hours rather than laying some people off), for example, these councils helped Germany experience less unemployment during the Great Recession and a faster, more robust recovery since then."[4]

But exporting the concept to the United States faces multiple challenges. The National Labor Relations Act bans companies from "dominat[ing] or interfer[ing] with the formation or administration of any labor organization."[5] Many labor experts say the law would have to be changed

Since July 2013, the board has been at full strength, and those criticisms have diminished.[77] But Republicans have continued to complain about the agency, saying its rules unfairly tilt the playing field against industry. They pointed to an NLRB mandate to shorten the length of time between a union's filing a request to hold an election and the actual date of the election, which they said gives employers less time to make their case against unionization.

They also criticized NLRB General Counsel Richard Griffin's legal recommendation in 2014 that McDonald's, as a "joint employer," could be held liable if one of its franchises engaged in anti-union activities. Republicans said the decision left the fast-food giant — and potentially to allow works councils because they say the current law is construed to mean that companies cannot take part.

"These kinds of strategies do not migrate well across the Atlantic Ocean," says Carl Van Horn, a professor of public policy at Rutgers University and director of its John J. Heldrich Center on Workforce Development. "We live in a very different world. Our labor market policies are very pro-employer."

Finkin and Kochan said U.S. works councils could be lawful if their main purpose isn't to address wages, hours or working conditions. Kochan said they could be "informal employee involvement groups like quality circles or team-based workplace systems," along with task forces making recommendations on health, safety or absenteeism. But, Finkin acknowledged, that setup creates a "Swiss cheese" effort to remain legal.[6]

Other labor observers note that as Germany's economy moves from manufacturing to services and from larger companies to smaller ones, representation on works councils has been declining.

A study by the Institute of Economics and Social Research, an independent German research organization, found that the biggest declines between 2009 and 2013 in that country came in the fields of finance/insurance, transportation/logistics and construction.[7]

Works councils drew considerable attention last year when the United Auto Workers (UAW), as part of its effort to unionize a Volkswagen plant in Chattanooga, Tenn., sought to create a works council that it said wouldn't violate the Labor Relations Act because it was a union-driven effort.

Workers voted down the union, but the UAW later created a smaller-scale "union local," in which worker participation is voluntary and will not receive formal recognition from VW until a majority of plant workers agree to join. Since then, it has continued to try to form a works council that is not company-organized, thus enabling it to avoid the federal ban.[8]

"This is the appropriate time to put this model forward," UAW Secretary-Treasurer Gary Casteel said in May. He noted that the Chattanooga facility was the only Volkswagen assembly plant worldwide that lacked a works council.[9]

A rival union to the UAW, the American Council of Employees (ACE), said it also was working with VW to create a works council at the plant.[10] It called UAW's effort "nothing more than a Trojan horse created to distract employees" from the progress it said it was making.[11]

— **Chuck McCutcheon**

[1] Terrence McNally, "Why Germany Has It So Good — and Why America Is Going Down the Drain," *Alternet.org*, Oct. 13, 2010, http://tinyurl.com/298w4jv.

[2] James Sherk, "How To Give Workers A Voice Without Making Them Join a Union," *The Atlantic*, March 11, 2014, http://tinyurl.com/p67vlqd.

[3] Douglas Williams, "Are 'Works Councils' Really Such a Good Idea For Workers and Unions?" *In These Times*, Dec. 15, 2014, http://tinyurl.com/pvosor2.

[4] Matthew Finkin and Thomas Kochan, "The Volkswagen Way to Better Labor-Management Relations," *Los Angeles Times*, Jan. 20, 2014, http://tinyurl.com/lbtsm2p.

[5] Sherk, *op. cit.*

[6] Bryce Covert, "How VW Workers Could Still Get A Voice After A Vote To Unionize Failed," ThinkProgress.org, Feb. 18, 2015, http://tinyurl.com/qfnzhm8.

[7] Birgit Kraemer, "Germany: Continued decline in collective bargaining and works council coverage," Institute of Social and Economic Research, Feb. 2, 2015, http://tinyurl.com/nj7ahd8.

[8] Peter Moskowitz, "Volkswagen and UAW to create union at Tennessee plant," Al Jazeera America, July 10, 2014, http://tinyurl.com/mm5nk9d.

[9] David Barkholz and Ryan Beene, "UAW Pushes to Form Works Council at VW Chattanooga Plant," *Automotive News*, May 7, 2015, http://tinyurl.com/poymxts.

[10] Chloé Morrison, "UAW rival reveals specifics of works council proposal," Nooga.com, May 29, 2015, http://tinyurl.com/nnej2vh.

[11] "ACE's Works Council Concept Summary — April 2015," American Council of Employees website, http://tinyurl.com/pub7ju7.

other companies with franchises — vulnerable to unions' claims.[78]

Even before Obama's election, unions conducted internal battles over the movement's direction. Some unions accused the AFL-CIO of spending too much time on politics and too little on organizing employees into unions. The SEIU and Teamsters split from the AFL-CIO in 2005, with SEIU President Andrew Stern charging: "Our world has changed, our economy has changed, employers have changed. But the AFL-CIO is not willing to make fundamental change."[79] AFL-CIO officials, however, said they had accepted many of the critics' ideas and countered that the dissidents simply wanted to dominate the labor coalition.[80]

Former United Mine Workers president and veteran labor activist Richard Trumka, elected AFL-CIO president in 2009, has sought to enlarge the number of causes with which the organization could ally with nonunions. He opened the group's 2013 convention to a wide range of groups ranging from the NAACP and Sierra Club to gay and immigrants' rights organizations.

"We are in a crisis right now," Trumka said just before the convention. "None of us are big enough to change the economy and make it work for everybody. It takes all progressive voices working together."[81]

CURRENT SITUATION

Expanded Outreach

Under AFL-CIO president Trumka, the organization is widening its outreach to Wal-Mart workers as well as to other new fields of workers, such as taxi drivers. He is continuing to seek closer relations with nonunion groups and to appeal to minority groups, who are seen as an important part of the labor movement. The organization also is supporting Coworker.org, a nonprofit group that seeks to make technology easily available to those seeking to organize unions.

"We're involved in a whole wide range of different efforts to work with workers to increase bargaining power in innovative ways," the AFL-CIO's Silvers says.

Representatives of other unions, including AFSCME, SEIU and various teachers unions, in May began an alliance with community groups called Bargaining for the Common Good. In addition to minimum labor standards and greater transparency on governmental financial transactions, the alliance's priorities include expanded after-school programs and investments in affordable housing.[82]

Unions are part of another recent coalition, the Hedge Clippers Campaign, which started in March. It argues that hedge funds — increasingly popular limited partnerships of wealthy investors that use high-risk methods, such as investing with borrowed money — hurt the economy and that its managers enjoy outsized political influence.[83] Stephen Lerner, a veteran labor organizer involved in the campaign, says it is aimed at avoiding what he says was unions' lax response during the 2007–09 recession.

"Many of us believe that it was a failure of the labor movement to take action during the financial crisis,"

Lerner says. "Obama said to Wall Street at one point, 'I'm what stands between you and the pitchforks.' But there were no pitchforks. . . . You had a total redistribution of wealth to the top, and our response was pathetic."

Despite being unable to defeat the Trans-Pacific trade deal, the AFL-CIO and other unions vow to continue pushing the issue. "We're in the middle of the fight to change the direction of U.S. trade and international economic policy, and we're going to be in the middle of it for years to come," Silvers says. "What's fundamentally at stake is whether trade policy will act as an accelerant of inequality or not."

Support for Obama

Unions approve of Obama's rule change in June — similar to an executive order — to make significantly more workers eligible to earn overtime pay. The rule change, which awaits further procedural steps, is expected to guarantee overtime pay to most salaried workers earning less than an estimated $50,440 next year, or nearly 5 million workers.[84]

Obama had discussed the possibility of such a move last year, leading labor activists and Democrats to push for as broad an expansion as possible. "If what they want to do is have an impact on wages, they need to go big here," said Kelly Ross, the AFL-CIO's deputy policy director.[85]

Apart from trade, unions have supported many of Obama's other actions. The AFL-CIO and National Education Association, the nation's largest teachers union, with 3 million members, filed friend-of-the-court briefs in April backing the president's decision last year to issue a controversial executive order on immigration that extended protections against deportation and that 27 states challenged in U.S. District Court.[86] And Obama in March rejected a congressional resolution that would have overturned the NLRB's rule on streamlining the timing of union elections.[87]

Feuding in the States

The latest bitter feud between unions and a Republican governor is unfolding in Illinois, traditionally a Democratic state. A series of scandals involving Democratic governors helped pave the way in 2014 for the election of GOP business executive Bruce Rauner, whose moves have angered unions and their allies in state government.

Rauner has sought to limit vacation time for state workers, raise state workers' health insurance payments and repeal a "prevailing wage" law that he argues forces private contractors to pay high union wages. He also has sought to reduce state workers' pension benefits, citing a pension system that is more than $100 billion in debt.[88]

"We have pensions that are unaffordable that don't really occur in the real world." Rauner said in June.[89]

Massachusetts Gov. Charlie Baker, another Republican elected in 2014 in a typically Democratic state, also has tangled with unions. The National Association of Government Employees, which represents 43,000 state and federal workers nationwide, sued Baker's administration in July alleging that it blocked some state employees from an early-retirement incentive program aimed at reducing state payroll costs.[90]

In New York, unions picked up support from Democratic Gov. Andrew Cuomo in their fight for a higher minimum wage for fast-food workers. A Cuomo-appointed state panel recommended in July that the workers' minimum wage be raised to $15 an hour over the next few years.[91]

Court Action

The U.S. Supreme Court is scheduled to take up a case this fall, *Friedrichs v. California Teachers Association*, that could decide whether government workers must continue to pay fees to finance public-sector unions regardless of whether they choose to become full members of those unions. The practice is standard in many states, but critics of unions contend it is unfair.[92]

Non-members' fees fund negotiations with local school districts over salary and benefits. The fees do not support such political activities as lobbying state governments on education policy.

Unions and their allies argue that they represent the interests of all employees and that even non-members benefit from negotiations and thus should continue to pay the fees. But the 11 educators who filed the lawsuit contend that the government is violating their free-speech rights by forcing them to provide financial support for unions' actions. "Unions like to call us 'free riders,' " said Rebecca Friedrichs, a California teacher and the lead plaintiff in the case. "I like to call myself a 'forced rider,' because I didn't ask the union to represent me."[93]

Fair-pay activist Lilly Ledbetter speaks during an event at the White House on April 8, 2014, marking Equal Pay Day. Early in his first term, President Obama, at right, signed the Lilly Ledbetter Fair Pay Act, which restored the rights of working women to sue over wage discrimination. Unions have applauded several labor-related actions by Obama recently, including a rule change in June to make significantly more workers eligible to earn overtime pay.

Meanwhile, two state supreme courts have taken actions that public-sector unions have sharply criticized.

New Jersey's court in July upheld three municipalities' cost-cutting measures made outside of collective bargaining, including mandatory furloughs and demotions of city workers. That decision came a month after the court accepted the argument of Republican Gov. Chris Christie administration's that it did not have to honor a series of state contributions to New Jersey's ailing pension system.[94]

In July the Illinois Supreme Court refused to take up a request from Democratic Attorney General Lisa Madigan to address whether state workers could be paid in full during the ongoing budget showdown between Democratic lawmakers and Rauner. Republican Comptroller Leslie Munger has been sending out paychecks as Rauner has sought to avoid political problems from that fight.[95]

Presidential Race

Hillary Clinton's efforts to reach out to unions early in the presidential race yielded an endorsement in July from the American Federation of Teachers (AFT), the nation's second-largest teachers union, representing 1.6 million educators. When she ran for president in 2008, the union did not endorse her until October 2007.

Should workers have to pay union fees if they don't join the union?

YES
Lily Eskelsen García
President, National Education Association

NO
Terry Pell
President, Center for Individual Rights

Written for *CQ Researcher*, August 2015

Written for *CQ Researcher*, July 2015

Just as collective decisions have made our country a beacon of progress throughout the world, public services work best when workers have real input into how they are delivered and managed. That input is strongest in states where all who benefit from collective representation pay their fair share of the costs of that representation. Twenty-three states allow for such fair-share fee arrangements, under which individuals can choose not to be union members but do have to contribute their fair share of the costs of their collective representation.

Fair-share fees, also known as agency fees, are a commonsense way to protect equity, individual rights and fair pay for educators, police officers, firefighters and other public servants. Fair share helps to ensure that all employees receive collective-bargaining benefits.

Under these arrangements, no one is forced to join a union. And nonmembers do not have to pay even a penny for a union's political activities, endorsements or other ideological activities. But when a union bargains for smaller class sizes, comprehensive mentoring and peer-assistance programs, it is only fair that everyone who benefits from those programs pays for them.

Nearly 40 years ago, the Supreme Court ruled unanimously in *Abood v. Detroit Board of Education* that these types of fair-share arrangements are consistent with the First Amendment and that states may allow unions to collect fees from nonmembers to pay for collective-bargaining costs, but not for political spending.

Abood has stood the test of time. The court has had many opportunities to overrule the decision, but it has not. In *Friedrichs v. California Teachers Association*, to be argued in the fall and decided next year, the Supreme Court should reject the reactionary invitation by conservatives to read into the First Amendment a bar against such long-settled arrangements.

As educators, the 3 million members of the National Education Association know that schools work best when everyone is heard. The tiny percentage of individuals who opt not to join the union — and it is a very tiny number — should not be allowed to silence that collaboration by declining to pay their modest share of the costs of the basic representation services that their employer has found to have value.

We are confident that the Supreme Court will do the right thing and continue to allow these effective labor-management relationships by reaffirming *Abood* and its progeny.

Rebecca Friedrichs and her eight coplaintiffs are fed up with paying $1,000 per year in compulsory dues to support a union with which they disagree on almost everything it tries to negotiate on their behalf. And they are about to get their day in court.

On June 29, the Supreme Court agreed to hear their challenge to compulsory dues. Friedrichs and her coplaintiffs, whom my organization is helping to represent, is asking the court to overturn *Abood v. Detroit Board of Education*, a 1977 case that allows states to require all public employees to pay an "agency" or "fair-share" fee to support the union's collective bargaining activities.

Abood attempts to soften this compelled speech by requiring dissenting employees to opt out of the portion of dues that have nothing to do with collective bargaining and are purely political. In Friedrichs' view, though, the collective bargaining activities of a public-employee union are inherently political, too — just as political as the union's overt electioneering and lobbying.

When a teachers' union negotiates with local officials for better wages or benefits, it is asking officials to allocate a greater share of tax dollars to education, as opposed to other activities such as parks or welfare. These are inherently political questions about which public employees can, and do, reasonably disagree.

Under well-established First Amendment precedent, a state may not compel individuals to support speech. While many teachers support the union's negotiating efforts, not all do, and those who don't cannot be forced to subsidize an organization with which they disagree.

Unions reply that it's only fair to make all employees pay their share of what it costs the union to represent them in contract negotiations, especially since unions represent the interests of all employees But it is the unions that wish to represent "all or none," not the employees themselves.

If the court releases teachers from agency fees, our clients are willing to negotiate their own contracts, procure other union benefits on their own or rely on standard civil service protections. Many teachers would prefer to negotiate employment terms themselves rather than be forced to support a union's political views with which they fundamentally disagree.

Under the First Amendment, public employees have the constitutionally protected right to decide for themselves whether to support speech with which they disagree. The Constitution does not authorize state legislators or even judges to make that choice on their behalf.

The AFT drew criticism this summer from other unions that noted the endorsement came as Sen. Bernie Sanders of Vermont, a Clinton rival, was picking up momentum among liberals. Even some AFT members said the Clinton endorsement was premature, with nearly 4,000 signing a petition on Change.org calling for the union to withdraw it.

AFT President Randi Weingarten, a friend of Clinton's, defended the timing of the endorsement, saying it came on the heels of a meeting of the union's executive council. Weingarten also said she had made it clear that she supported unions "going our own ways" on when they could make endorsements.[96]

Larry Cohen, outgoing president of the 700,000-member Communications Workers of America, said he would serve as an unpaid volunteer for Sanders' campaign, citing Clinton's refusal to publicly oppose The Trans-Pacific trade deal.[97] Sanders introduced a bill in June seeking to protect the pensions of government retirees from budget cuts.[98]

On the Republican side, Wisconsin Gov. Walker has been stating his disdain for unions as being out of touch with Americans' concerns. He said in April he would back a federal right-to-work law: "Really what we did wasn't just fight unions," he said of his standoff with public employees in Wisconsin. "It was fight the stranglehold that big government special interests had on state and local governments. I think in Washington we need that even more."[99]

But Ohio Republican Gov. John Kasich, who joined the presidential race in July, is expected to court union support. After Ohio voters in 2012 resoundingly repealed a law Kasich signed a year earlier limiting collective bargaining, he took a more accommodating approach by not raising collective bargaining again and by joining unions in backing public-works projects creating union jobs.

"For too long, there's been a disconnect between people like me and organized labor," he said in a speech before winning re-election last November.[100]

Meg Mott, a professor of politics at Vermont's Marlboro College who studies unions and other mass movements, says she is interested to see how often candidates use the word "union" and related terms in the race.

"That can bring up images [to voters] of mobsters or shady deals or backroom deals or corrupt politics," she says. "Are they going to use terms like 'collective bargaining' or 'organizing for economic justice'? Hillary's going to be cautious about how she talks about it."

OUTLOOK
Coming Resurgence?

In assessing the future, many union officials, academics and others draw a distinction between the labor movement, which some say looks promising, and that of unions, which they agree are murkier.

"All of the groundwork is laid for a resurgence of workers' organization in American society; I just don't know how it's going to happen," the AFL-CIO's Silvers says. "Richard Trumka is trying to transform our institutions so that they are helpful in that process, but what exactly is that going to mean? If we knew, we would be there already."

Lerner, the labor organizer, says the current focus on low-wage workers makes him optimistic about the labor movement as a whole. But he said it still must address "the financialization of the economy," citing a widely publicized report that showed that the bonuses paid to Wall Street bank employees in 2014 were about double the annual earnings of all of the nation's full-time minimum-wage workers.[101]

"'Will unions, in their current form and structures, survive?' It's the wrong question," Lerner says. "I'm optimistic about what's going on, but not that the set of unions and leaders that currently exist will be successful in changing their institutions."

However, Georgetown's McCartin says the support among younger Americans for unions is encouraging. He pointed to the concerns among that demographic about student debt and the role it plays in where their paychecks go.

"This generation is really primed to understand it in a way that people 20 years ago were not," he says. "There is a growing awareness among younger people around these issues. That fueled the energy of the Progressive era" — the period of activism and social reform in the United States from the 1890s to the 1920s.

Other experts say any positive effects could be limited in terms of boosting specific types of unions. Marlboro College's Mott says the broad alliances that unions form with other organizations mean that growth could be "more city-based than industry-based," flourishing in union-friendly urban areas rather than among particular unions nationally.

The University of Pittsburgh's Delaney says workers with specialized skills who belong to unions could fare well in the years ahead. He cited Delta Airlines' recent tentative agreement with its pilots for a three-year contract containing hefty pay increases, although the pilots' union in July rejected that contract because its members said it contained too many concessions apart from salaries. The two sides are expected to try to forge a new deal this fall.[102]

"Unions, in those circumstances, have much more leverage," he says. "What's happened is that in a lot of other industries, the leverage the unions were able to develop no longer exists. . . . So we're going to see this kind of balkanization take place."

As for public-sector unions, many experts say their current conflicts with Republican governors and legislatures will only weaken their stature. But the University of Washington's Rosenfeld sees a brighter future for them than for their private-sector counterparts, saying the public sector's relatively larger membership numbers and the absence of corporate opposition make it easier to organize there.

"This is not a popular view, but in terms of organizing on a mass scale, it's the public sector where I think there's the room to grow. . . . Unions would do well to look to those opportunities where they do exist," he says.

NOTES

1. E. Tammy Kim, "'Fight for $15' workers create recipe for change at convention," Al-Jazeera America, June 6, 2015, http://tinyurl.com/o3ercvf.

2. "Union Members — 2014," U.S. Bureau of Labor Statistics news release, Jan. 23, 2015, http://tinyurl.com/y9tfc7k.

3. Kim Phillips-Fein, "Why Workers Won't Unite," *The Atlantic*, April 2015, http://tinyurl.com/kyv58qr.

4. Melanie Trottman, "Unions Flex Muscle to Fight Pacific Trade Bill," *The Wall Street Journal*, June 10, 2015, http://tinyurl.com/ndhyua3.

5. Jill Lawrence, "A Future for Unions, If They Can Keep It," *The National Memo*, May 21, 2015, http://tinyurl.com/pu98try.

6. Mará Rose Williams, "Doing much of the teaching but struggling financially, adjunct faculty joins unions," *The Kansas City Star*, Feb. 24, 2015, http://tinyurl.com/pb688hm. "Union organizing update: what 4 key industries are unions targeting under the NLRB's new election rules?" *Bingham Greenebaum Doll Blog*, June 17, 2015, http://tinyurl.com/pfadnxb.

7. Lydia DePillis, "The Supreme Court's Threat to Gut Unions Is Giving the Labor Movement New Life," *The Washington Post*, July 1, 2015, http://tinyurl.com/ossdtfo.

8. "Mixed Views of Impact of Long-Term Decline in Union Membership," Pew Research Center, April 27, 2015, http://tinyurl.com/nqjjcka.

9. Peter Jamison, "Why union leaders want L.A. to give them a minimum wage loophole," *Los Angeles Times*, July 27, 2015, http://tinyurl.com/q2rvn2z.

10. Steven Greenhouse, "How Walmart Persuades Its Workers Not to Unionize," *The Atlantic*, June 8, 2015, http://tinyurl.com/nauwdf6.

11. Steven Greenhouse, "Democrats Drop Key Part of Bill to Assist Unions," *The New York Times*, July 17, 2009, http://tinyurl.com/py3zwyh.

12. For background see Barbara Mantel, "Minimum Wage," *CQ Researcher*, Jan. 24, 2014, pp. 73–96.

13. For background see Kenneth Jost, "Public-Employee Unions," *CQ Researcher*, April 8, 2011, pp. 313–336.

14. "Union Members — 2014," *op. cit.*

15. Harold Meyerson, "If Labor Dies, What's Next?" *The American Prospect*, September 2012, http://tinyurl.com/924yz3w.

16. James Queally, "Missouri governor vetoes 'right to work' bill; here's why," *Los Angeles Times*, June 4, 2015, http://tinyurl.com/qyfcq98.

17. Lydia DePillis, "The conservative case against picking on unions, courtesy of Missouri Republicans," *The Washington Post*, May 20, 2015, http://tinyurl.com/op25b4q.

18. "Department for Professional Employees, AFL-CIO," AFL-CIO website, http://dpeaflcio.org/.

19. Mike DeBonis, "D.C. administrative law judges vote to form union, ending two years of labor strife,"

The Washington Post, July 31, 2014, http://tinyurl .com/pkowx5n.

20. Alana Semuels, "White-collar workers are turning to labor unions," *Los Angeles Times*, May 16, 2013, http://tinyurl.com/afjkz2b.

21. John W. Curtis, "The Employment Status of Instructional Staff Members in Higher Education, Fall 2011," American Association of University Professors, April 2014, http://tinyurl.com/nubrhxl.

22. Williams, *op. cit.*

23. Edwin J. Feulner, "Taking Down Twinkies," Heritage Foundation website, Nov. 19, 2012, http://tinyurl.com/pc89el8.

24. Sean Hackbarth, "Los Angeles Shows Us the Real Reason Why Unions are Pushing for Minimum Wage Increases," U.S. Chamber of Commerce blog, May 29, 2015, http://tinyurl.com/qz9m688.

25. James Panero, "Don't Let Unions Call the Tune," *The Wall Street Journal*, Oct. 3, 2013, http://tinyurl .com/ojovbkw.

26. James Sherk, "Do Americans Today Still Need Labor Unions?" Heritage Foundation, April 1, 2008, http://tinyurl.com/826qg26.

27. Jeremy Neuner, "40% of America's workforce will be freelancers by 2020," *Quartz.com*, March 20, 2013, http://tinyurl.com/caf3yka.

28. Daniel DiSalvo, "The Trouble With Public-Sector Unions," *National Affairs*, Fall 2010, http://tinyurl .com/2emx7co.

29. Noam Scheiber, "Labor's Might Seen in Failure of Trade Deal As Unions Allied to Thwart It," *The New York Times*, June 13, 2015, http://tinyurl.com/oknte88.

30. Lauren French, "Labor runs ads slamming Rep. Kathleen Rice for backing trade bill," *Politico*, June 8, 2015, http://tinyurl.com/q5z58ck.

31. Steven Greenhouse, "After Push for Obama, Unions Seek New Rules," *The New York Times*, Nov. 8, 2008, http://tinyurl.com/prekfee.

32. Nate Silver, "The Effects of Union Membership on Democratic Voting," *FiveThirtyEight.com*, Feb. 26, 2011, http://tinyurl.com/pz8pv4z.

33. "General Election: McCain vs. Obama," *RealClearPolitics*, http://tinyurl.com/2yke8u.

34. Harry Enten, "How Much Do Democrats Depend on the Union Vote?" *FiveThirtyEight.com*, July 1, 2014, http://tinyurl.com/q5pyjeo.

35. Amy Chozick, "Hillary Clinton Blames Republicans for Promoting Inequality," *The New York Times*, July 13, 2015, http://tinyurl.com/nopx7a8.

36. Nelson Lichtenstein, "Two Roads Forward for Labor: The AFL-CIO's New Agenda," *Dissent*, Winter 2014, http://tinyurl.com/nzl64cd.

37. Max Ehrenfreund, "A reminder that Democrats still need unions for campaign cash," *The Washington Post*, March 11, 2015, http://tinyurl.com/pfxfxpu.

38. "Benjamin I. Sachs," Harvard Law School website, http://tinyurl.com/pj3sbzp.

39. Benjamin I. Sachs, "A New Kind of Union," *The New York Times*, Sept. 1, 2013, http://tinyurl.com/pcj3suc.

40. For background, see Kenneth Jost, "Campaign Finance Debates," *CQ Researcher*, May 28, 2010, pp. 457–480.

41. "Super PACs," Center for Responsive Politics, http://tinyurl.com/q8df5wu.

42. "State Right to Work Timeline," National Right To Work Committee, http://tinyurl.com/qcug3nj.

43. Tom Kertscher, "Right to work: How past claims have fared on the Truth-O-Meter," *PolitFact Wisconsin*, Dec. 4, 2014, http://tinyurl.com/p274nqa.

44. Mark Trumbull, "Wisconsin going 'right to work': What's the impact for jobs and incomes? *The Christian Science Monitor*, March 3, 2015, http://tinyurl.com/q6a33e3.

45. Michael B. Sauter, Charles B. Stockdale and Douglas A. McIntyre, "The 10 Biggest Strikes in American History," Fox Business News, Aug. 9, 2011, http://tinyurl.com/qcdmoxx.

46. Josh Harkinson, "Walmart Is Seeing Its Biggest Black Friday Protests Ever Today," *Mother Jones*, Nov. 28, 2014, http://tinyurl.com/oe8v5wf; Lydia DePillis, "Under pressure, Wal-Mart upgrades its policy for helping pregnant workers," *The Washington Post*, April 5, 2014, http://tinyurl.com/kuo6s88.

47. Jonathan Rosenblum, "SeaTac's Fight for 15: Why Faith Was Key," *LaborNotes.org*, June 9, 2015, http://tinyurl.com/p6m5pgu.

48. Monica Davey and Steven Yaccino, "Teachers End Chicago Strike on Second Try," *The New York Times*, Sept. 18, 2012, http://tinyurl.com/8h48y3s.

49. Matt Phillips, "American labor-union strikes are almost completely extinct," *Quartz*, Feb. 11, 2015, http://tinyurl.com/ohalhfp.

50. Lydia DePillis, "Labor fight at West Coast ports comes to an end — for now," *The Washington Post*, Feb. 21, 2015, http://tinyurl.com/o3kyu2h.

51. Lichtenstein, *op. cit.*

52. David Brody, *Workers in Industrial America: Essays on the 20th Century Struggle* (1993), pp. 14–15.

53. "A Pictorial Walk Through the 20th Century," U.S. Mine Safety and Health Administration, http://tinyurl.com/5t55qr6.

54. "Samuel Gompers (1850–1924)," AFL-CIO website, http://tinyurl.com/oureqcs.

55. Brody, *op. cit.*, p. 24.

56. "The Ludlow Massacre," PBS.org, http://tinyurl.com/n46b73c.

57. Judson MacLaury, "A Brief History: The U.S. Department of Labor," U.S. Department of Labor, http://tinyurl.com/pdbb9ot.

58. Richard B. Freeman and Kelsey Hilbrich, "Do Labor Unions Have a Future in the United States?" from Robert S. Rycroft (ed.), *The Economics of Inequality, Poverty and Discrimination in the 21st Century* (2013), http://tinyurl.com/pbh8rub.

59. "Fair Labor Standards Act of 1938," *Encylopedia.com*, http://tinyurl.com/nca55nj.

60. "1936: Sit-down strike begins in Flint," *History.com*, http://tinyurl.com/8vcpc58.

61. Holly A. Reese, "Taft-Hartley Act," *Encyclopedia.com*, http://tinyurl.com/oyudz65.

62. Brody, *op. cit.*, p. 157.

63. Philip Dray, *There Is Power in a Union: The Epic Story of Labor in America* (2011), pp. 529–530.

64. "Labor History Timeline," AFL-CIO website, http://tinyurl.com/778bued.

65. Fred Siegel, "How Public Unions Took Taxpayers Hostage," *The Wall Street Journal*, Jan. 25, 2011, http://tinyurl.com/p6378pn.

66. Steven Greenhouse, "Wisconsin's Legacy for Unions," *The New York Times*, Feb. 22, 2014, http://tinyurl.com/pksya3l.

67. Siegel, *op. cit.*

68. G. Barry Golson, ed., "Jimmy Hoffa," *The Playboy Interview* (1981), p. 428.

69. "Summary of the Occupational Safety and Health Act," U.S. Environmental Protection Agency, http://tinyurl.com/nvtyrb7.

70. "Employee Retirement Income Security Act (ERISA)," U.S. Department of Labor, http://tinyurl.com/6b6kzdv.

71. "The Consequences of Reagan Breaking the '81 Air Traffic Controllers Strike (1/2)," *TheRealNews.com*, Oct. 3, 2014, http://tinyurl.com/pweh8q7.

72. B. Drummond Ayres Jr., "The 1992 Campaign: Candidate's Record; Unions Are Split on Backing Clinton," *The New York Times*, March 15, 1992, http://tinyurl.com/p3y6lpg.

73. Mohammed Aly Sergie, "NAFTA's Economic Impact," Council on Foreign Relations, Feb. 14, 2014, http://tinyurl.com/k2t56fv.

74. "George Bush, Union Basher?" *The Economist*, Oct. 10, 2002, http://tinyurl.com/nl2go38.

75. "Remarks of President Barack Obama on the Lilly Ledbetter Fair Pay Restoration Act Bill Signing," White House Press Office, Jan. 29, 2009, http://tinyurl.com/orylbdw.

76. Mark Landler and Steven Greenhouse, "Vacancies and Partisan Fighting Put Labor Relations Agency in Legal Limbo," *The New York Times*, July 15, 2013, http://tinyurl.com/nek4vnt.

77. Ramsey Cox, "Senate Confirms All Five NLRB Members," *The Hill*, July 30, 2013, http://tinyurl.com/k4fs95j.

78. Tim Devaney, "NLRB hits McDonald's as joint employer," *The Hill*, Dec. 19, 2014, http://tinyurl.com/q93qgg6.

79. Thomas B. Edsall, "Two Top Unions Split From AFL-CIO," *The Washington Post*, July 26, 2005, http://tinyurl.com/2cugmj9.

80. Jill Lawrence, "Two rebel unions split from AFL-CIO," *USA Today*, July 25, 2005, http://tinyurl.com/okwya55.

81. Lichtenstein, *op. cit.*

82. "What We Do," Bargaining For the Common Good, http://tinyurl.com/p4ntpxn.

83. Ginia Bellafante, "Exposing Hedge Fund Politics in New York," *The New York Times*, March 27, 2015, http://tinyurl.com/nrovwvp.

84. "Middle Class Economics Rewarding Hard Work by Restoring Overtime Pay," White House Office of the Press Secretary, June 30, 2015, http://tinyurl.com/qafeh87.

85. Noam Scheiber, "Obama Making Millions More Eligible for Overtime," *The New York Times*, June 29, 2015, http://tinyurl.com/pthrvhc.

86. Unions fight to preserve Obama's immigration actions, their members," Fox News.com, April 12, 2015, http://tinyurl.com/ppxzq4c.

87. Peter Baker, "Obama Rejects Republican Bid to Overturn New Union Rules," *The New York Times*, March 31, 2015, http://tinyurl.com/pncyowy.

88. Rick Pearson and Kim Geiger, "Illinois Supreme Court Rules Landmark Pension Law Unconstitutional," *Chicago Tribune*, May 8, 2015, http://tinyurl.com/kjll4xp.

89. Anna Giles and Andy Shofstall, "Unions Organize Statewide Protests Against Rauner Agenda," WSIL-TV, June 10, 2015, http://tinyurl.com/nvm6nxo.

90. Joshua Miller, "Union sues Baker administration over early retirement plan," *The Boston Globe*, July 6, 2015, http://tinyurl.com/nvkeb8m.

91. Patrick McGeehan, "New York Plans $15-an-Hour Minimum Wage for Fast-Food Workers," *The New York Times*, July 22, 2015, http://tinyurl.com/qbvjs59.

92. DePillis, "The Supreme Court's Threat to Gut Unions Is Giving the Labor Movement New Life," *op. cit.*

93. Chris Haire, "Should workers pay union fees even if they don't join? O.C. teachers' case goes to U.S. Supreme Court," *The Orange County Register*, June 30, 2015, http://tinyurl.com/ojb8xbo.

94. John Reitmeyer, "NJ Supreme Court deals 2nd blow to public worker unions," Newsworks.com, July 15, 2015, http://tinyurl.com/pakaec6.

95. Kim Geiger, "High court denies Lisa Madigan bid for ruling on state worker paychecks," *Chicago Tribune*, July 17, 2015, http://tinyurl.com/nhpl5hl.

96. Annie Karni, "Unions seethe over early Clinton endorsement," *Politico*, July 16, 2015, http://tinyurl.com/opq89jz.

97. Dave Jamieson, "Labor Leader Joins Bernie Sanders' Campaign, Citing Clinton's 'Silence' On Fast Track," *The Huffington Post*, July 1, 2015, http://tinyurl.com/pds4fcx.

98. Eric Lichtblau, "Bernie Sanders Draws Union Support Pressing Pensions Issue," *The New York Times*, June 18, 2015, http://tinyurl.com/p489oea.

99. O. Kay Henderson, "Governor Walker: a national right-to-work law a 'legitimate' goal," Radio Iowa .com, April 25, 2015, http://tinyurl.com/ogf6bpw.

100. Mark Niquette, "John Kasich Charms Unions as Scott Walker Embodies New Republican Antipathy," *Bloomberg Politics*, April 15, 2015, http://tinyurl.com/pnxnty9.

101. Justin Wolfers, "All You Need to Know About Income Inequality, in One Comparison," *The New York Times*, March 13, 2015, http://tinyurl.com/l94kwny.

102. Susan Carey, "Large Majority of Delta Pilots Reject Three-Year Contract," *The Wall Street Journal*, July 10, 2015, http://tinyurl.com/q3afjox; Carey, "Chief of Pilots Union at Delta Airlines to Resign," *The Wall Street Journal*, July 22, 2015, http://tinyurl.com/pl9tbx2.

BIBLIOGRAPHY

Selected Sources
Books

Geoghegan, Thomas, *Only One Thing Can Save Us: Why America Needs a New Kind of Labor Movement,* **The New Press, 2014.**
A labor lawyer argues that a revived labor movement is crucial for America's economic future.

Hogler, Raymond L., *The End of American Labor Unions: The Right-to-Work Movement and the*

Erosion of Collective Bargaining, Praeger, 2015.
A Colorado State University professor of labor law looks at the legal history of regulating unions.

Neff, James, *Vendetta: Bobby Kennedy Versus Jimmy Hoffa*, Little, Brown & Co., 2015.
An investigative reporter chronicles the disputes between the Senate investigator who became U.S. attorney general and the notorious International Brotherhood of Teamsters leader.

Rosenfeld, Jake, *What Unions No Longer Do*, Harvard University Press, 2014.
A University of Washington sociologist studies the implications of the decline of unions on the economy and on politics.

Walker, Scott, and Marc Thiessen, U*nintimidated: A Governor's Story and a Nation's Challenge*, Sentinel, 2014.
Wisconsin's Republican governor, now a 2016 presidential candidate, describes his battles with his state's public-sector unions.

Articles

DePillis, Lydia, "The Supreme Court's Threat to Gut Unions Is Giving the Labor Movement New Life," *The Washington Post*, July 1, 2015, http://tinyurl.com/ossdtfo.
A reporter looks at union recruiting.

Donahue, Thomas J., "The Truth Behind the Labor Agenda," U.S. Chamber of Commerce, March 23, 2015, http://tinyurl.com/olse352.
The president of the influential business lobbying group details his problems with unions and the National Labor Relations Board.

Greenhouse, Steven, "How Walmart Persuades Its Workers Not to Unionize," *The Atlantic*, June 8, 2015, http://tinyurl.com/nauwdf6.
A veteran labor journalist chronicles how the nation's largest private employer discourages unionization at its stores.

Kaufman, Dan, "Scott Walker and the Fate of the Union," *The New York Times Magazine*, June 15, 2015, http://tinyurl.com/ornjwu3.
A writer explores the impact of the 2016 presidential candidate's attempts to rein in unions in Wisconsin.

Lawrence, Jill, "A Future for Unions, If They Can Keep It," *The National Memo*, http://tinyurl.com/pu98try.
A political reporter examines recent developments involving unions and whether they will translate into more support.

Lerner, Stephen, and Jono Shaffer, "25 Years Later: Lessons from the Organizers of Justice for Janitors," *TalkPoverty.org*, June 16, 2015, http://tinyurl.com/ojp9nwt.
Two organizers of a national 1990 movement aimed at improving custodians' pay and working conditions reflect on the implications of their work.

Lichtenstein, Nelson, "Two Roads Forward for Labor: The AFL-CIO's New Agenda," *Dissent*, Winter 2014, http://tinyurl.com/nzl64cd.
A University of California, Santa Barbara labor historian examines the country's largest umbrella group for unions and its attempts to broaden its appeal.

Phillips-Fein, Kim, "Why Workers Won't Unite," *The Atlantic*, April 2015, http://tinyurl.com/kyv58qr.
A New York University labor historian argues that unions face serious challenges in remaining relevant.

Reports and Studies

"And Still I Rise: Black Women Labor Leaders' Voices/Power/Promise," Institute for Policy Studies, 2015, http://tinyurl.com/lgnsejl.
A liberal policy research group argues unions must do better at promoting African-American women to leadership roles.

"Mixed Views of Impact of Long-Term Decline in Union Membership," Pew Research Center, April 27, 2015, http://tinyurl.com/nqjjcka.
A research group finds in its annual survey that the public is split over the decline in union membership, but that public support for unions exceeds that of opposition.

Chambers, Michael, "An Exploration into Challenges Facing Public Sector Labor Relations: A Literature

Review and Analysis," *Journal of Public Administration and Governance* (Vol. 3, No. 4), 2013, http://tinyurl.com/pxpc7za.
A Northcentral University business and technology researcher investigates the challenges facing managers in their relationships with public-sector unions.

Vedder, Richard, Joseph Hartge and Christopher Denhart, "The Economic Impact of a Right-to-Work Law on Wisconsin," **Wisconsin Policy Research Institute, March 4, 2015, http://tinyurl.com/qa2zcq3.**
A nonpartisan think tank that promotes free-market policies finds that over the last 30 years, states with right-to-work legislation have had greater per-capita personal income growth than other states.

For More Information

AFL-CIO, 815 16th St., N.W., Washington, DC 20006; 202-637-5000; www.afl-cio.org. Umbrella organization representing 12.5 million workers in 56 unions.

Economic Policy Institute, 1333 H St., NW, Suite 300, Washington, DC 20005; 202-775-8810; www.epi.org. Labor-backed think tank that researches labor conditions, jobs, trade and globalization.

National Association of Manufacturers, 733 10th St., N.W., Suite 700, Washington, DC 20001; 202-637-3000; www.nam.org. Influential lobbying group representing small and large manufacturers.

National Education Association, 1201 16th St., N.W., Washington, DC 20036; 202-833-4000; www.nea.org. Nation's largest teachers union, representing 3 million members from pre-school to university graduate programs.

National Right to Work Legal Defense Foundation, 8001 Braddock Rd., Springfield, VA 22160; 703-321-8510;

www.nrtw.org. Nonprofit providing free legal aid to workers who feel their rights have been violated by "compulsory unionism abuses."

Service Employees International Union, 1800 Massachusetts Ave., N.W., Washington, DC 20036; 202-350-6600; www.seiu.org. Represents 2 million U.S. and Canadian workers in health care, property services and other fields.

U.S. Bureau of Labor Statistics, 2 Massachusetts Ave., N.E., Washington, DC 20212; 202-691-5200; www.bls.gov. Department of Labor agency providing information about wages, work stoppages, collective bargaining and unionization rates.

U.S. Chamber of Commerce, 1615 H St., N.W., Washington, DC 20062; 202-659-6000; www.uschamber.org. Influential business-lobbying group that opposes many union priorities.

5

Free Speech on Campus

Sarah Glazer

University of Maryland President Wallace D. Loh said he was torn between wanting to suppress a "reprehensible" racist and misogynistic email that surfaced on campus in March and his belief in the First Amendment. "Where do free speech and hate speech collide?" he asked, echoing debates on campuses across the country following a spate of recent free-speech controversies.

From *CQ Researcher*,
May 8, 2015.

When a racist and misogynistic email from a University of Maryland fraternity member surfaced on the College Park campus in March, university President Wallace D. Loh found himself in a bind.

The email told fellow fraternity brothers seeking sex with young women to "f--- consent" and instructed them not to "invite n----- gals or curry monsters or slanted eyed chicks, unless they're hot."[1]

As the campus erupted in anger, Loh said the email expressed views "reprehensible to our campus community."[2] But he confessed to being torn between regarding the email as hate speech that should be suppressed and statements that — no matter how vile — are protected under the First Amendment to the Constitution.

"It is one of our nation's core values that the government should not be able to tell us what we can and cannot say," Loh tweeted. "Protecting speech, however, does not mean agreeing with it. And quite honestly, I am struggling with justifying this email as speech. Where do free speech and hate speech collide? What should prevail? What justification can we have that tacitly condones this kind of hate?"[3]

A university investigation decided that question for Loh on April 1 when it found that the email merited First Amendment protection.[4]

To legal experts, the implication of the university's conclusion was clear: Expelling the student who wrote the email could have been ruled a violation of the student's constitutional right to free expression if the issue came to court. Instead, Loh announced that, by mutual consent, the student would not return to campus that semester.[5]

Group: Most Colleges Suppress Speech

More than half of U.S. colleges and universities in 2014 had speech codes that "clearly and substantially" violated students' and teachers' First Amendment rights, according to the Foundation for Individual Rights in Education (FIRE), a civil liberties advocacy group.

FIRE Ratings of University Speech Codes, 2014

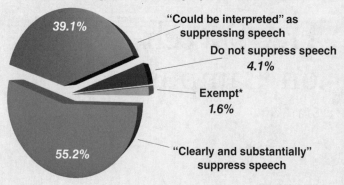

* Private universities that say they prioritize certain values above commitment to freedom of speech

Source: "Spotlight on Speech Codes 2015," Foundation for Individual Rights in Education, Dec. 12, 2014, http://tinyurl.com/o6xlps6

The two incidents have helped place in stark relief a much broader debate about free speech at public colleges and universities: When it comes to inappropriate speech, where does one draw the line?

In recent decades, colleges have tried to restrict racist, sexist or otherwise offensive speech by issuing written student codes of conduct, computer codes of conduct and other policies. Many of these prohibitions are required by federal law guaranteeing equal rights on the basis of gender and race. University administrators say they are simply following the law and trying to protect students from genuine harassment.

However, civil liberties groups have attacked many of these policies as unconstitutional "speech codes" that prohibit and penalize even the most minor offensive remarks or jokes, and violate students' and teachers' First Amendment rights. Speech codes at more than half of U.S. campuses violate the amendment, according to the Foundation for Individual Rights in Education (FIRE), a civil liberties advocacy group and nonprofit foundation in Philadelphia funded by private donors and organizations from "across the political spectrum," according to a FIRE spokesperson.

Complicating the discussion is the fact that while public universities and colleges comprise more than 80 percent of the nation's higher education student body, about 16 percent attend private institutions, which are not bound by the First Amendment.*[8]

The Maryland email appeared the same week that a media storm broke over University of Oklahoma fraternity members filmed singing a racist song about refusing admission to blacks, including lyrics that seemed to condone lynching. "You can hang him from a tree, but he can never sign with me," chanted the members, whose singing on a bus taking them to a black-tie fraternity event was captured on cell-phone video and released on the Internet. Oklahoma's president, David L. Boren, swiftly expelled two students who led the singing and later disciplined 25 others. A subsequent university investigation discovered the fraternity members had learned the song four years ago on a fraternity leadership cruise, signaling a long-standing pattern of racial exclusion in the fraternity.[6]

Many educators praised Boren's action, but civil libertarians and legal experts on both the right and left criticized it on grounds that the song was protected under the First Amendment. If the expelled students were to sue the university for violating their free-speech rights, they would probably win, according to most legal experts queried by *The New York Times.*[7]

---

* As tax-supported institutions, public universities are legally considered extensions of the government and therefore bound by the First Amend- ment's restrictions on government interference with freedom of speech. By contrast, private col- leges and universities, which are not "state actors," are not strictly bound by the First Amendment. However, because most private universities also accept government funds, they must abide by federal anti-discrimination laws.

The recent incidents have escalated the controversy. Some educators and college administrators argue that it's more important to send a strong signal, through disciplinary measures, that certain kinds of speech — especially if racist or sexist — won't be tolerated on campus. And often the students themselves are pushing for even stronger measures against sexually harassing or emotionally disturbing speech.

Yet some administrators say it's unclear whether the recent incidents are constitutionally protected from university discipline. Both the Oklahoma and Maryland students' words "could be perceived as a direct threat," and threats are not protected by the First Amendment, says Kevin Kruger, president of Student Affairs Administrators in Higher Education (NASPA), an association in Washington, D.C., that represents 13,000 administrators. The Oklahoma song could be viewed as condoning lynching, and the Maryland email could be interpreted as advocating sexual assault, Kruger says.

But the legal status is "cloudy," he acknowledges. "There may not be a clear-cut case here, so it may take the courts to decide what is a direct threat and what is protected speech."

On a similar front, a small but growing movement is demanding that professors give students "trigger warnings" about curriculum material that might traumatize them and provide "safe spaces" free of trauma-inducing speech. Critics say these trends are signs that colleges are becoming overly protective of students.[9]

Freedom of expression concerns also have been raised about American universities that accept financial support from autocratic governments. Critics say such arrangements inevitably result in censorship of topics that offend the donor countries.

Conflicts About Speech Are Widespread

Speech-related incidents at U.S. colleges have led to punishment ranging from student expulsions to revocation of faculty tenure.

Institution	Description
U of Maryland, 2015	University declines to suspend student after investigating racist, misogynistic email sent by student to fraternity brothers
Duke, 2015	School says student who admitted hanging a noose on a campus tree was disciplined but can return next semester
Bucknell, 2015	School expels three students who used racial slurs against African-Americans in campus radio broadcast
U of Oklahoma, 2015	University expels two students and disciplines 25 filmed singing racist chant, closes fraternity chapter
Marquette, 2015	Administrators notify professor of plans to revoke his tenure over blog post in which he claimed a student's opposition to same-sex marriage was suppressed by another teacher.
California State, Fullerton, 2014	University sanctions sorority for practicing "indecent" and "obscene" conduct after it hosts Mexican-themed recruitment event
Ohio U, 2014	Student sues after administrators ban sexually suggestive T-shirt; university agrees to revise student conduct code and pay legal fees in 2015 settlement
U of Kansas, 2013	Administrators suspend tenured journalism professor after he tweets anti-gun message
Modesto Junior College, 2013	Student sues college for preventing him from distributing copies of the Constitution outside "free speech zone;" college later agrees in settlement to pay $50,000, abolish zone

Source: Greg Lukianoff, "Free Speech on Campus: The 10 Worst Offenders of 2014," *The Huffington Post*, March 2, 2015, http://tinyurl.com/nqs7lnm; other news sources

For instance, New York University's new satellite campus in Abu Dhabi, built with funding from the United Arab Emirates (UAE), came under press scrutiny in March when an NYU professor critical of UAE labor conditions was barred from entering the country.

"The lack of respect for freedom of speech permeates the whole enterprise," said Marjorie Heins, a former

NYU adjunct professor who serves on the academic freedom and tenure committee of the American Association of University Professors (AAUP).[10]

At the time of the incident, NYU spokesman John Beckman said the university supported "the free movement of people and ideas" but that the UAE government "controls visa and immigration policy."[11]

Additionally, Rep. Chris Smith, R-N.J., has questioned whether academic freedom is threatened on American campuses that receive money from the Chinese government. Approximately 100 colleges in the United States house Chinese language and cultural institutes, known as Confucius Institutes, funded in part by China, which also provides teachers. In addition, some American universities are setting up satellite campuses in China as joint ventures with Chinese educational institutions.

"Is American higher education for sale?" Smith asked at a House Foreign Affairs subcommittee hearing in December. "And, if so, are U.S. colleges and universities undermining the principle of academic freedom — and, in the process, their credibility — in exchange for China's education dollars?"[12]

Confucius Institute teachers are trained in China to discourage discussion of controversial issues, such as Tibetan independence or the 1989 Tiananmen Square massacre, and to paint a rosy picture of China, charges Marshall Sahlins, a professor emeritus of anthropology at the University of Chicago who has written a book on the institutes.[13]

American universities that accept funding from Hanban, the Chinese government agency that controls the institutes, "have become dependent branches of policymaking that starts at the highest reaches of the Chinese [Communist] Party state and runs through the Confucius Institutes," says Sahlins. "It seems incredible to me that we would subcontract teaching and give research control to this operation. That's a violation of academic freedom, integrity and anything a university is based on."

Defenders of the institutes say they provide much-needed Chinese language training that American universities can't afford and that such exchanges are important for international understanding — for both Chinese and Americans. And part of that means accepting the reality that China is an authoritarian state.

Edward A. McCord, a professor in modern Chinese history at George Washington University (GWU), in Washington, D.C., says his university, which has a Confucius Institute, retains control over the political content taught at GWU but is willing to accept language teachers trained by Hanban. "We would have to cut off relations if we want no Chinese control or can't accept any Chinese scholars or students because they might be monitored" by the Chinese government, he says. "Can we live with that?"

As students, faculty and government officials debate campus free-speech policies, here are some of the questions being debated:

Should university conduct codes ban offensive speech?

In the fall of 2013, Ohio University junior Isaac Smith wore a T-shirt to a campus activities fair advertising an organization that helps students at disciplinary proceedings. The shirt bore the student group's slogan, a play on words meant to be humorous: "We get you off for free."

A dean from the Athens, Ohio, institution was not amused, however. Administration officials later told Smith the shirt "objectified women" and encouraged prostitution, and ordered him to stop wearing it, according to a legal complaint filed by Smith against the university. Smith says he obeyed for fear of punishment under the university's code of student conduct.[14]

Smith sued the publicly owned university, claiming violation of his constitutional right to free expression. In court, the university denied that its administrators had made the comments cited by Smith about the shirt's sexual innuendo or that it had forbidden the organization's members from wearing the shirt.[15] Nevertheless, in February, the university settled the suit, promising to revise its student code to conform to the First Amendment and specifying that speech or written communication must meet the legal standard of being "severe, pervasive and objectively offensive" in order to be considered punishable harassment.[16]

The settlement is the fourth resulting from nine First Amendment suits brought by FIRE, which argues that "more than half of America's top colleges maintain speech codes that blatantly violate First Amendment standards."[17]

While most universities deny having speech codes, critics like FIRE say colleges' sexual harassment policies, computer policies, codes of conduct and restrictions on where students can stage protests amount to the same thing. The AAUP shares these concerns, according to Henry Reichman, chair of the association's Committee on Academic Freedom and Tenure.

"Generally there is no right to not be offended in society as a whole or in a university," he says. "Speech codes are a bad idea. . . . It's not surprising to us that speech codes are repeatedly found in violation of the First Amendment in public universities." Reichman adds that "the answer to speech you disagree with is more speech" to express that disagreement, rather than stifling some viewpoints.

Timothy C. Shiell, author of a book on hate speech and professor of philosophy and ethics at the University of Wisconsin, Stout, says 25 years ago he agreed with universities cracking down on hate speech.[18] "But the more you look into how these things actually get implemented, the scarier it all looks," he says. "A lot of these terms are not well defined, so it becomes very subjective."

However, NASPA's Kruger contends the situation is not as dire as FIRE makes out and that "most universities have expunged their hate-speech codes over the last five to seven years," given all the court cases that have come up. He noted: "There's been a fair amount of [court] precedents that hate speech and the most repugnant speech possible has been deemed to be [constitutionally] protected."

Many observers say universities play an important role in drawing a line at the kind of inappropriate speech that violates campus community values. "If students want to learn biology and art history in an environment where they don't have to worry about being offended or raped, why shouldn't they?" University of Chicago law professor Eric Posner wrote recently.[19]

In an interview with *CQ Researcher*, Posner says he was talking mainly about private universities, which do not fall under the same First Amendment protections as public universities. Private, religiously affiliated universities, he points out, have frequently restricted students' behavior — from Catholic universities banning premarital sex to Mormon universities regulating personal grooming. The private institution, he says, "has a right to send a message to the world about what its values are, and it can therefore control students and employees if it wants to."

Some legal experts say, however, that private universities that restrict students' speech may violate their

Ohio University student Isaac Smith displays the T-shirt that led to his free- speech lawsuit against OU in 2014. University officials had ordered Smith and other members of the Students Defending Students campus organization to stop wearing shirts bearing the organization's slogan, "We get you off for free." Administration officials said the shirt "objectified women." Free-speech advocates said the university's actions violated Smith's rights. In February, OU settled the suit, promising to revise its student speech code to conform to the First Amendment.

Foundation for Individual Rights in Education

contractual obligations if they have written policies promising freedom of expression. Meanwhile, because most private universities receive federal money, they are bound by federal laws forbidding discrimination on the basis of gender under Title IX, or race under Title VI, Posner notes.[20] Under those laws, even a private university must not create a "hostile environment," which counts as discrimination, he says.

Starting in 2011 the Department of Education has issued a series of mandates that universities define sexual harassment as including verbal conduct. Since then more campuses have been adopting restrictive speech codes, FIRE contends.

The Education Department's definition of sexual harassment is "breathtakingly broad," says FIRE Vice President Will Creeley, because the department has removed the requirement that speech be "objectively offensive" from the perspective of a "reasonable person" — the widely recognized legal standard. "If all that is required is subjective offense on the part of a listener to classify speech as sexual harassment, then discourse on campus will be severely constrained," he says.

But Kruger calls the department's recent guidance "sound policy" because some speech "is just not tolerable."

He says he agrees with the Obama administration that offensive speech among students can create an environment where "someone cannot function as a student" and that such cases "can have enormous impact on the victim."

Although many university policies forbid verbal harassment, that doesn't mean they're applying the rule so broadly that it violates the First Amendment, says W. Scott Lewis, co-founder of the Association of Title IX Administrators, a Malvern, Pa., group whose members administer the gender discrimination law on campuses. "It happens periodically, but I wouldn't characterize it as a major problem," he says.

Recent guidelines from the departments of Justice and Education encourage schools to enact policies aimed at restricting sexually themed jokes and unwelcome requests for dates, some critics charge. The guidelines could effectively "ban dating (since no one is a mind reader)," objected the free market Competitive Enterprise Institute.[21]

Lewis counters that asking someone out on a single date and being rejected "is never going to constitute sexual harassment under any policy that I've seen applied."[22] Harassment would involve persistently asking for a date or exercising a power imbalance like that between a teacher and student, Lewis added.

Shiell expresses concern that while free speech may have won the legal war in the courts, it has lost the "culture war," as universities continue to ban speech they find objectionable, he says, pointing to FIRE's annual surveys.

As the Ohio University T-shirt incident illustrates, one person's joke can be another's intolerable insult. And FIRE's recent list of 2014's "10 worst" colleges for abusing free-speech rights shows that both liberals and conservatives can be targets. The incidents cited include a University of Kansas professor suspended for tweeting an anti-National Rifle Association message and a Marquette University professor whose tenure was revoked after he objected that a student's opposition to same-sex marriage was suppressed in another teacher's class.[23]

An important question for Shiell is, "Do you want a higher education system where people are coerced to conform to some cultural norm or where they can push back against conformity?"

Public universities can still condemn racist and sexist speech and promote politeness — within limits, Shiell says. "Courts routinely say you can have these aspirational goals of respect and civility but you can't require such things."

Should students be protected from language they find offensive?

Last April, a student approached Northwestern University film professor Laura Kipnis and told her she couldn't watch the film to be discussed in class because it "triggered" upsetting emotions for her.

Kipnis was baffled: The film had some sexual content, but it wasn't "particularly explicit," she wrote. How, she wondered, would this student survive in the film industry? "I had an image of her in a meeting with a bunch of execs, telling them that she couldn't watch one of the company's films because it was a trigger for her."[24]

Although Kipnis had never heard of "trauma trigger warnings," the incident made more sense when a news story appeared the following week reporting that similar advisories — warnings that teachers put on reading assignments or upcoming class discussions — were migrating from the Internet to colleges. Last year The Associated Press reported that students asked six colleges — the University of Michigan, Bryn Mawr, Oberlin, Rutgers, Scripps and Wellesley — for such warnings. So far, no school has required the warnings, although some professors have provided them voluntarily, according to the AP and experts interviewed for this report.[25]

Bailey Loverin, a literature major at the University of California, Santa Barbara, first proposed that professors at her school provide a warning if they were teaching material that could cause flashbacks in students who had been sexually assaulted or suffered other trauma. Loverin, 19, acknowledged that many people had told her, "You are going to get your feelings hurt, and you should just suck it up and meet it head-on." However, she pointed out, "a girl raped just a month ago and sitting in a classroom for the first time again isn't ready to face that head-on."[26]

Like Kipnis, other faculty members have criticized such warnings, describing them as "silly" and "ridiculous."[27]

The AAUP last year condemned the idea of mandating trigger warnings on the grounds that "they interfere with academic freedom in the choice of course reading materials and teaching methods." A report issued by the association's academic freedom committee said, "The presumption that students need to be protected rather than challenged in the classroom is at once infantilizing and anti-intellectual. It makes comfort a higher priority than intellectual engagement."[28]

Former Barnard College President Judith Shapiro wrote of the trigger warning movement: "Aside from this being an insult to the intelligence and good sense of students and faculty members alike, it also threatens to spoil the thrill of discovery." Would a first-time reader of *Anna Karenina* want to be told ahead of time, she asked, that Anna kills herself at the end?[29]

Apparently yes. A columnist for the Rutgers University student paper in New Jersey wrote that teachers should warn students that F. Scott Fitzgerald's 1925 novel *The Great Gatsby* "possesses a variety of scenes that reference gory, abusive and misogynistic violence."[30]

"I'm treating college students like the adults they are, and institutions increasingly treat college students like medicalized children," objected Laurie Essig, associate professor of Gender, Sexuality and Feminist Studies at Middlebury College in Vermont. She said some of her students have criticized her for showing photos of anorexic fashion models in her sociology and gender course without first warning students with eating disorders.[31]

University of Chicago law professor Posner said critics haven't considered "the justification for these policies: . . . that students are children." Perhaps, he wrote, "overprogrammed children engineered to the specifications of college admissions offices no longer experience the risks and challenges that breed maturity."[32]

In an interview, he said 18- and 19-year-olds arriving at college after a lifetime under parental control can find themselves in a "vulnerable" situation. "Universities should take these things into account," he said, whether through student codes of conduct or other means like trigger warnings.

Yet by the time teenagers get to college, they "need to confront new ideas," counters FIRE's Creeley, who supports the Supreme Court's long-held view that a university is a "marketplace of ideas." "If you haven't once been offended you should ask for your money back."

"Safe spaces" on campus — rooms where students can take refuge during debates about "triggering" issues such as

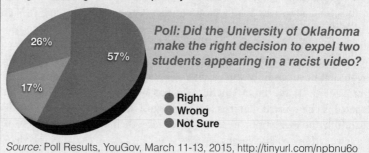

Most Support Oklahoma Expulsions

Fifty-seven percent of Americans said the University of Oklahoma was correct in expelling two fraternity members filmed singing a racist song, according to a March poll by YouGov.

26%

57%

17%

Poll: Did the University of Oklahoma make the right decision to expel two students appearing in a racist video?

● Right
● Wrong
● Not Sure

Source: Poll Results, YouGov, March 11-13, 2015, http://tinyurl.com/npbnu6o

sexual assault — have also come under criticism. Adam Shapiro, a Columbia University junior, protested this trend by printing a flier declaring his room a "dangerous" space. A safe-space mentality has begun infiltrating classrooms, Shapiro objected, making both professors and students reluctant to say anything that might hurt someone's feelings.[33]

While trigger warnings and safe spaces have attracted controversy, many commentators agreed a tough university response was required after the University of Oklahoma video surfaced. For many free-speech advocates, Oklahoma is turning out to be one of those "hard cases" epitomized by the phrase, "I disapprove of what you say, but I will defend to the death your right to say it."[34]

Notably, liberal outlets like *Slate* aligned with libertarian (*Reason*) and conservative (*National Review*) voices to condemn the expulsions as an inappropriate squelching of free speech.[35] In a *New York Times* roundup of opinions, most legal experts agreed that this kind of racist speech by students at a public university is protected by legal precedents, unless it can be proven to threaten actual physical harm or creates a "racially hostile environment."[36]

However, maintains Samantha Harris, director of policy research at FIRE, "the standard for what constitutes a 'hostile environment' goes well beyond one chant on a bus." For instance, she points out, "the chant was not done in front of a dorm of African-American students." While university President Boren was "absolutely right to condemn it," Harris says, without a proof of imminent physical danger to African-American students the expulsions likely violated the expelled students' free-speech and due process rights.

But both black and white students supported the expulsion. "What they said was not just offensive," said Maggie Savage, 20, a sophomore. "If you do anything to make students in a community feel unsafe, you lose the privilege of being able to attend the university."[37]

Boston College Law School professor Kent Greenfield expressed discomfort with the right-left consensus that the racist song was constitutionally protected speech. Writing in *The Atlantic*, he agreed the fraternity students "would almost certainly win" a First Amendment case but added, "If the First Amendment has become so bloated, so ham-fisted that it cannot distinguish between such filth and earnest public debate about race, then it is time we rethink what it means."

And he expressed dismay that, under the First Amendment, fear of being targeted "counts hardly at all"; what matters is a "murderous frenzy then and there."[38]

Do universities that accept money from autocratic governments compromise academic freedom?

As global demand for higher education rises, some foreign governments are offering financial incentives to attract prominent American universities to build branch campuses in their countries.[39] The practice has raised questions about how much independence such campuses have to ensure free debate — especially about subjects uncomfortable for host governments.

Abu Dhabi made an initial donation of $50 million to host a branch of New York University within the emirate, paid for a luxurious new campus and pays most students' tuition and living costs, which could total over $100 million a year.[40]

In March, the government of the UAE (which includes Abu Dhabi and six other emirates) barred NYU professor Andrew Ross from entering the country to conduct research. A professor of social and cultural analysis, Ross has published research critical of exploitative labor conditions for migrant workers in Abu Dhabi.[41]

NYU officials have said that the Abu Dhabi campus will have the same kind of academic freedom as the Manhattan campus. But "it's not at all clear if that's the case," in light of the Ross incident, says the AAUP's Reichman. "If a faculty member of NYU can't go to the campus in Abu Dhabi, that's a problem."

Universities accepting money from autocratic governments raises "a growing and complicated question,"

Reichman says, both on American campuses and overseas. NYU law professor Rick Hills, who teaches at the university's Shanghai campus, has argued that while his students may not enjoy freedom of expression off campus, they can engage in free discussion inside the classroom. "If NYU were to insist that its constituents must be able to pursue in Shanghai every expressive activity that they are entitled to pursue at Washington Square [in New York], then the Chinese government would simply refuse to allow us to teach in the PRC [People's Republic of China]. Such an uncompromising posture would [deprive students] of the benefits of an education that the Chinese eagerly seek," he wrote.[42]

NYU-Shanghai Vice Chancellor Jeffrey Lehman concurs. "The written ground rules are: We have academic freedom . . . at NYU-Shanghai. We can talk about the Dalai Lama, Tiananmen Square, Taiwan and Tibet and anything we want to — and we do," he says. But, that "does not mean I somehow have a special badge that lets me walk around Shanghai exempt from Chinese law or Chinese culture or practice."

The nearly 100 Confucius Institutes established in the last decade at American campuses are equally contentious. Last year, *Foreign Policy* magazine published a forum on whether the institutes stifle academic freedom. Some experts expressed concern that their curricula amount to Chinese government propaganda and the instructors recruited in China were trained to parrot the government line — on issues such as the independence of Tibet and the outlawed spiritual sect Falun Gong.[43] However, experts vigorously disagree on whether the American universities or the Chinese government controls the curriculum and faculty.

Reichman says concern goes beyond the Chinese. "I'm in Russian history, and there's growing concern about Russian oligarchs pouring money into Russian studies" on American campuses. "Are they going to inordinately attempt to influence the research agenda?"

Other academics say such cultural exchanges are nevertheless vital to encourage freedom of thought on both sides. George Washington University's McCord, who helped negotiate GWU's Confucius Institute, says, "Even if [Chinese instructors] can't speak freely, they're here and they see our society, and I think that's good." China is "an authoritarian dictatorship, and they watch their people and punish them if they slip up," so it's understandable if Chinese instructors avoid speaking about politically controversial issues.

Kristin Stapleton, a historian specializing in China at the State University of New York, Buffalo, who served as the first director of her university's Confucius Institute from 2010–13, said the institute "is no different from the initiatives of corporations and other private entities [that] encourage scholarship and academic programs in their areas of interest." Such arrangements should also be scrutinized, she says.

However, Bruce Lincoln, a University of Chicago history professor who organized a successful petition by 100 professors to shut down the Confucius Institute at Chicago, sees the institutes as a symptom of the "corporatization" of universities. "Money is scarce, and institutions are hungry for donors claiming ever more influence as a result of donations. We risk becoming a shopping mall where we rent out space," he says.

BACKGROUND

Academic Freedom

Academic freedom was not a "coherent concept" in America before the late 19th century, for either teachers or students, writes Heins, a civil liberties lawyer and author of *Priests of Our Democracy*, a history of academic freedom.[44]

From the 17th to the 19th century, freedom of thought was neither valued nor practiced, and the teacher was "not to permit any novel opinions to be taught," according to educators from that period. Instead, students were drilled in Latin and Greek and were not to deviate from religious doctrine — nor were their professors. In 1654, the president of Harvard, which trained many of the era's Puritan ministers, was forced to resign because he denied baptism's scriptural validity.[45]

In the last decades of the 19th century (1870–1900), a revolution occurred in American higher education that opened the door to a freer quest for knowledge. Charles Darwin's theory of evolution challenged traditional religious thinking. In addition, German universities were becoming increasingly influential, with their belief that the independent search for truth is the main purpose of a university education and their tradition of affording professors freedom in teaching and intellectual exploration.[46]

Taking that new, enlightened view to heart, the University of Chicago's first president, William Rainey

New York University President John Sexton shakes hands with East China Normal University President Yu Lizhong at a groundbreaking ceremony for NYU's Shanghai satellite campus on March 28, 2011. Lizhong is now chancellor of NYU Shanghai. NYU is one of several American universities setting up satellite campuses in China as joint ventures with Chinese educational institutions. But critics question whether such arrangements inevitably result in censorship of topics that offend the host countries.

Harper, said in 1892: "When for any reason . . . the administration [of a university] attempts to dislodge a professor because of his political or religious sentiments, at that moment the institution has ceased to be a university,"[47]

However, in the late 19th century, professors who expressed their political views outside the classroom came into conflict with wealthy businessmen who were donating to universities on an unprecedented scale and serving as trustees. In 1895, University of Chicago economics professor Edward Bemis was fired after supporting striking railroad workers, which Chicago businessmen saw as "treasonous."[48]

In the early 1900s, socially conscious professors objected that boards of trustees dominated by business executives saw universities as for-profit businesses and felt free to fire teachers for their political views. This struggle was exemplified by the widely publicized firing in 1915 of Scott Nearing, a popular economics professor at the University of Pennsylvania and an outspoken campaigner for decent wages and an end to child labor.

The Nearing dismissal and similar incidents at the universities of Utah, Colorado and Montana spurred the newly formed AAUP to write its founding document on academic freedom in 1915.[49] The "Declaration of Principles on Academic Freedom and Academic Tenure" declared

C H R O N O L O G Y

1915–1950s *State and federal governments suppress campus speech by targeting professors suspected of being communists.*

1915 Professors form American Association of University Professors to protect academic freedom; group investigates University of Pennsylvania's firing of radical economist Scott Nearing.

1949 New York's Feinberg law bans public schools from employing members of groups advocating overthrow of the government.

1950–1954 Sen. Joseph R. McCarthy, R-Wis., alleges that 205 State Department officials are communists; he later holds hearings accusing government employees, civilians and members of the U.S. Army of being communists. Senate censures McCarthy for his reckless tactics and unsubstantiated allegations.

1952 U.S. Supreme Court upholds New York's Feinberg law; Justice William O. Douglas' dissenting opinion marks first time a justice calls academic freedom a right protected by First Amendment.

1957 Supreme Court blocks New Hampshire legislators from investigating the political views of Paul Sweezy, a Marxist Harvard economist.

1964–1970s *Campus free-speech movement spreads nationwide, spurs protests against Vietnam War.*

1964 Students at University of California, Berkeley, protest campus limits on free speech, spawning national movement.

1966 Ronald Reagan elected governor of California promising to clean up "mess" at Berkeley.

1967 U.S. Supreme Court overturns New York's Feinberg law.

1972–1990s *Campuses adopt speech codes, which courts say violate the First Amendment.*

1972 President Richard M. Nixon signs Title IX prohibiting sex discrimination in education.

1981 University of Wisconsin, Madison, adopts the first campus anti-harassment speech code.

1989 Federal court invalidates University of Michigan's ban on racist comments. . . . University of Wisconsin institutes "hate-speech" ban.

1991 University of Wisconsin's 1989 hate-speech ban is declared unconstitutional.

1999 Supreme Court rules in *Davis v. Monroe County* that public schools are liable for student-on-student harassment if it is "severe, pervasive and objectively offensive."

2000s *Free-speech suits against colleges prompt revisions to speech codes; Chinese government funds Confucius Institutes on U.S. campuses.*

2003 California's Citrus College eliminates most speech codes after Foundation for Individual Rights in Education (FIRE) files lawsuit.

2004 Chinese government starts Confucius Institute program on overseas campuses.

2005 Palestinian groups call for boycott of Israeli academic institutions to protest occupation.

2010 Rutgers student Tyler Clementi dies by suicide after roommate posts video of sex encounter on Twitter.

2011 New Jersey enacts nation's toughest anti-bullying law.

2014 Rep. Chris Smith, R-N.J., holds congressional hearings on Chinese influence on academic freedom at American universities.

2015 University of Oklahoma expels two students for racist song; racist speech incidents follow at Duke, Bucknell, University of Maryland and University of South Carolina. . . . Sen. Patty Murray, D-Wash, introduces bill banning harassment of college students based on race, gender, religion or sexual orientation. . . . FIRE claims fifth settlement victory in free-speech suits against colleges.

that universities are not merely businesses driven by profit or by the "resentments" of their trustees.

The declaration proposed that American universities be governed by three basic principles: freedom of inquiry and research, freedom of teaching and "freedom of extramural utterance" (speech uttered outside the classroom). Those three tenets came to define American academic freedom.[50]

McCarthyism

While universities gradually accepted the AAUP's founding principles, those values were trumped by the anti-communist fervor that gripped the country in the late 1940s and early '50s. State governments sought to keep communists or their sympathizers from teaching in tax-supported institutions. New York's 1949 so-called Feinberg law, for instance, required detailed procedures for investigating the loyalty of public school teachers and prohibited employing anyone who belonged to a group advocating the overthrow of the government.

The period between 1950 and 1954 is widely known as the McCarthy era, after Sen. Joseph R. McCarthy, R-Wis., who created a national climate of fear with sensational accusations and congressional hearings in which he denounced U.S. government officials and others as communists. In reality, anti-communist activity had started well before then. In 1947 the House Committee on Un-American Activities had begun holding its infamous hearings in which Hollywood personalities were subpoenaed to testify about known or suspected members of the Communist Party. The hearings resulted in the creation of a blacklist of suspected communists, many of whom lost their jobs and became unemployable.[51]

In this atmosphere, the U.S. Supreme Court generally upheld the ban on hiring communists. In a 1952 decision, *Adler v. Board of Education*, the court found that the Feinberg law did not violate teachers' First Amendment rights. Teachers have no right to their jobs, the court said, and because they worked "in a sensitive area" — forming young minds — their employers were entitled to investigate their political beliefs.[52] In dissent, however, Justice William O. Douglas wrote that academic freedom was a "distinct, identified subset" of the First Amendment right to free speech.[53]

The first Supreme Court case to embrace the idea of academic freedom came amid the continuing atmosphere of the Red Scare. In *Sweezy v. New Hampshire* in 1957, the court blocked New Hampshire legislators from investigating the political views of Paul Sweezy, a Marxist economist at Harvard, based on an allegedly subversive lecture he gave at the University of New Hampshire.[54] Justice Felix Frankfurter, himself a former academic, found the state's national security justification for questioning Sweezy "grossly inadequate" when "weighed against the grave harm resulting from governmental intrusion into the intellectual life of a university."

Chief Justice Earl Warren emphasized the importance of academic freedom for students as well: "Teachers and students must always remain free to inquire, to study and to evaluate, to gain new maturity and understanding; otherwise, our civilization will stagnate and die."[55]

However, the court did not declare loyalty oaths for professors unconstitutional until 1967, in *Keyishian v. Board of Regents*. Harry Keyishian, who taught English at the State University of New York, Buffalo, refused to sign a loyalty oath affirming he was not a member of the Communist Party. In a decision that finally overturned the 1949 Feinberg law, Justice William J. Brennan Jr. wrote that academic freedom is "a special concern of the First Amendment, which does not tolerate laws that cast a pall of orthodoxy over the classroom."[56]

Student Speech

In the early 1960s, students hawked political pamphlets and raised money for the civil rights movement and other causes from a lively strip of sidewalk at the Telegraph Avenue entrance to the University of California, Berkeley. Such political activity was forbidden on the campus itself, and most people thought the sidewalk was not university property.

However, in September 1964 a dean told students they could no longer conduct political activity there because the walkway was university property. Students protested by setting up tables for their political causes not just on the walkway but also on campus.

Eventually, the protest expanded and hundreds of students conducted a campus sit-in. Inspired by the civil disobedience tactics of the civil rights movement, the protest would become known as the Free Speech Movement and would trigger a decade of student protests. "I think about the Free Speech Movement as helping to end the

Yik Yak Tests Campus Speech

Phone app "is being used by young people in a really destructive way."

A popular cellphone app sometimes used to spew racist rants, sexually graphic posts — and worse — has touched off a controversy over whether and how to police speech on campus.

Called Yik Yak, the app allows people to post Twitter-like messages (Yaks) anonymously to users within a 1.5-mile radius.[1] Introduced a little over a year ago, Yik Yak has been used to threaten mass violence at more than a dozen colleges. At Kenyon College in Gambier, Ohio, a "yakker" suggested a gang rape at the school's women's center.[2]

"It is being increasingly used by young people in a really intimidating and destructive way," said Danielle Keats Citron, a law professor at the University of Maryland and author of *Hate Crimes in Cyberspace*.[3]

Violent threats on Yik Yak had led to arrests on at least nine campuses as of December 2014.[4]

Some universities have blocked Yik Yak from their servers because it has been used to cyberbully students or teachers. In December Utica College, in Utica, N.Y., blocked the app in response to a growing number of sexually graphic posts aimed at the school's transgender community.[5]

Opponents of this approach say it's ineffective and may violate students' constitutional guarantee of free speech.

They also note that even if a university blocks Yik Yak, students can still access it on their cell service or find other methods for making the same kinds of comments publicly through the Internet.[6]

The app's privacy policy prevents schools from identifying users without a subpoena, a court order, search warrant or emergency request from a law enforcement official.[7]

The University of Rochester, in New York state, faced that issue in March when it said it would be asking its county district attorney to issue a subpoena in response to racially offensive language. However, for the subpoena to be issued it would have to be part of an investigation of possible criminal wrongdoing "and not just hate speech that's offensive," a local newspaper pointed out.[8]

Yik Yak users defend the app, saying it represents a broad community, which, just like real life, inevitably includes some racist behavior and jeering insults.

The tech website Techdirt said universities' "shoot the messenger" efforts weren't just futile but also bad preparation for the nastiness students will face in the outside world. "By providing shelter rather than pushing students to take control of these situations, these universities are doing their students — and the future of this country — a huge disservice," Techdirt said.[9]

McCarthy era and paving the way for the anti-war protests that came later," said New York University professor of history Robert Cohen, the author of a book about 1960s-era student activist Mario Savio.[57]

In December 1964, after the Berkeley administration failed to reach a compromise with students, a mass sit-in ensued, as more than 1,000 students stormed the administration building, led by folk singer Joan Baez singing "We Shall Overcome." Savio, a 21-year-old philosophy major who had just returned from registering black voters in Mississippi, galvanized students with his electric rhetoric. The sit-in ended with 814 arrests.

Large student protests against the Vietnam War soon erupted in San Francisco, New York and other cities, and by 1968 students worldwide were protesting the war.

Since then, the Berkeley campus has been the site of hundreds of political demonstrations.

But the movement also created a backlash. After his election in 1966, Gov. Ronald Reagan vowed to "clean up the mess at Berkeley" and directed that university president Clark Kerr, seen as soft on students, be fired.

While the seminal Supreme Court decisions on academic freedom, such as *Keyishian* in 1967, had focused on the rights of university faculty, in 1972 the U.S. Supreme Court extended academic freedom to students. The president of a Connecticut state college had refused to recognize the radical group, Students for a Democratic Society, or to let it use campus facilities, claiming its "philosophy was antithetical to school policies." Justice Lewis Powell, writing in a unanimous decision, echoed the 1967 *Keyishian* decision in declaring the college cam-

A better approach, some say, is to counter hate speech by going onto Yik Yak with opposing comments, as a group of 50 professors did at Colgate University, flooding the app with positive posts after the upstate New York campus experienced a rash of racist comments.[10]

"Yik Yak allows for up-and-down voting of 'Yaks' and their related comments," a recent article in *Wired* explained. "If a Yak or a comment receives 5 down votes, it is removed permanently from Yik Yak. Yik Yak also has a robust offensive/abusive content reporting system."[11] The administrators can then take down a post if someone reports it as breaking one of Yik Yak's rules. According to cofounder Brooks Buffington, "People that are consistently posting negative material get suspended or banned."[12] In February, Yik Yak updated its system by adding options for flagging posts, including "offensive content" and "This post targets someone."[13]

The *Wired* article's author, Rey Junco, associate professor of education and human computer interaction at Iowa State University, says research has found that anonymous bystanders are actually more likely to intervene if they see bullying online than if they had to confront the bully in person.

As an active Yakker himself, he says he has seen only one case of harassment — and other Yakkers had promptly criticized it. Rather, he says, Yik Yak reflects how the community is feeling in all its diversity of opinion.

"Some of the same administrators suggesting blocking Yik Yak would do well to learn what their students are talking about — what campus culture is like," he says.

— *Sarah Glazer*

[1]Elizabeth Nolan Brown, "Schools Banning Phone App Yik Yak for Promoting Hate Speech," *Reason.com*, Feb. 6, 2015, http://tinyurl.com/k3hsntm.

[2]Jonathan Mahler, "Who Spewed that Abuse?" *The New York Times*, March 8, 2015, http://tinyurl.com/m3ln755.

[3]*Ibid.*

[4]Alexandra Svokos, "Yik Yak Threats Lead to Charges for Students," *The Huffington Post*, Nov. 25, 2014, http://tinyurl.com/lfr4rjt.

[5]Mahler, *op. cit.*

[6]See Brown, *op. cit.*, and David Sessions, "Colleges should stop worrying about Yik Yak and Start Respecting their Students," *The New Republic*, March 9, 2015, http://tinyurl.com/lgtgvq3.

[7]Mahler, *op. cit.*

[8]James Goodman, "UR to seek subpoena of Yik Yak," *Democrat and Chronicle*, March 12, 2015, http://tinyurl.com/knr6jrk.

[9]Tim Cushing, "University Thinks Yik Yak Ban It Can't Possibly Enforce Will Fix Its 'Hate Speech' Problem," *Free Speech, Techdirt*, Feb. 10, 2015, http://tinyurl.com/kctetu8.

[10]Mahler, *op. cit.*

[11]Rey Junco, "Yik Yak and Online Anonymity Are Good for College Students," *Wired*, March 17, 2015, http://tinyurl.com/jwxek7z.

[12]Courtney Linder, "A Knack for Yik Yak," *The Pitt News*, March 19, 2015, http://tinyurl.com/lxvdvc2.

[13]Roberto Baldwin, "Yik Yak updated with improved reporting system for abusive posts," *TNW* (*The Next Web*), Feb. 19, 2015, http://tinyurl.com/n4dmb67.

---

pus a "marketplace of ideas." Powell wrote: "We break no new constitutional ground in reaffirming this Nation's dedication to safeguarding academic freedom."[58]

Speech Codes

In 1972 a landmark gender-equality clause — known as Title IX — of the Federal Education Amendments became law. It said "no person in the United States shall, on the basis of sex, be excluded from participation in, be denied benefits of, or be subjected to discrimination under any education program or activity receiving Federal financial assistance."[59]

Under the law, all schools receiving any federal funds (which is most of them) must have policies that prohibit sexual harassment. The law laid the groundwork for lawsuits in which parents and students sued school boards for permitting sexual harassment on the grounds that such behavior constituted sex discrimination under Title IX.

In the 1980s and '90s as more women and minorities entered college, universities began prohibiting harassing or hateful speech aimed at them. By 1995, about 350 campuses had adopted such policies.[60]

These so-called speech codes soon faced lawsuits, and courts invalidated some of them. Conservatives also claimed that such "political correctness" was a new form of censorship fostered by liberals.

In a 1989 case, *Doe v. University of Michigan*, a federal court invalidated Michigan's campus hate-speech ban on any expression that "stigmatizes or victimizes an individual" on the basis of race, ethnicity, religion, gender or sexual preference. The university had instituted the ban in response to a rash of racist incidents on

Academic Groups Spar Over Israeli Boycott

Protest over Palestinian policy sparks debate on academic freedom.

When a professor at Tel Aviv University tried to recruit experts at American universities last year to comment on his student's Ph.D. thesis in American studies, the Americans refused.

The student was the first casualty of a boycott of Israeli academic institutions passed by the American Studies Association in December 2013 to protest Israeli occupation of Palestinian land, wrote Michael Zakim, a professor of history at Tel Aviv University. But the episode had a surprising twist: The student is Palestinian.[1]

Probably no academic-freedom issue has divided American faculty as bitterly as the boycott of Israeli academic institutions. No American college has adopted the boycott, according to David C. Lloyd, a member of the organizing committee of the U.S. Campaign for the Academic & Cultural Boycott of Israel (USACBI).[2] But several small associations of professors in academic specialties, including the Association for Asian American Studies and the Native American and Indigenous Studies Association, have adopted resolutions supporting it.

Proponents of the boycott claim it already is affecting public opinion in the United States and Israel. Critics, including the American Association of University Professors (AAUP), say such boycotts, which generally bar exchanges between American and Israeli universities, squelch academic freedom.

The American Studies Association's endorsement drew immediate condemnation from university presidents, and four institutions said they were withdrawing their membership from the association. "Academic boycotts subvert the academic freedoms and values necessary to the free flow of ideas, which is the lifeblood of the worldwide community of scholars," said Drew Gilpin Faust, president of Harvard University.[3] The Tel Aviv incident illustrates another problem with boycotts besides squelching academic freedom: It's not entirely clear how they will be carried out. For instance, most boycott supporters say it is aimed at Israeli institutions, not individuals, so it shouldn't affect a Ph.D. student looking for outside reviewers, according to Feisal G. Mohamed, a professor of English at the University of Illinois who supports the boycott.[4]

But it's difficult to separate individuals from institutions, says David M. Rosen, an anthropologist at Fairleigh Dickinson University in Teaneck, N.J., who helped organize an anti-boycott petition at the American Anthropological Association last December. "The way it really happens is, individual scholars, unless they abide by a political litmus test, will be barred" from academic exchanges, he says, including conferences in the United States and publication in journals.

Even boycott opponents expect the American Anthropological Association to pass a pro-boycott resolution at its annual meeting this November after its overwhelming rejection of an anti-boycott resolution last year. If the resolution passes, and is then approved by the entire membership, the association would be the largest to approve a boycott so far.

Ilana Feldman, a pro-boycott anthropologist at George Washington University, contends that if the boycott is

campus.[61] The court said efforts to assure equal opportunity for all students "must not be at the expense of free speech."[62]

In 1991, a federal district court declared the University of Wisconsin's 1989 hate-speech ban unconstitutional. Wisconsin's 1981 code barring harassing speech, one of the nation's first, remained in place until 1999, when the faculty voted to end it.[63] That same year, University of Pennsylvania history professor Alan Charles Kors and Boston civil liberties attorney Harvey Silverglate founded the Foundation for Individual Rights in Education (FIRE) to litigate against attacks on

academic speech. Their book, *The Shadow University: The Betrayal of Free Speech on America's Campuses*, was highly critical of hate-speech bans.

"I watched with growing concern and fear and moral uneasiness as I saw the generation that had given us the free-speech movement now give us speech codes," said Kors, whose book stimulated public debate on the issue and received kudos from conservatives.[64]

FIRE scored its first victory in June 2003, when California's Citrus College agreed to eliminate most of its speech codes in response to a FIRE lawsuit.[65] In recent litigation, FIRE has succeeded in getting five colleges successful in ending the Israeli occupation, it would improve academic exchanges with Gaza, where she has conducted research.

"Many people's first question is about the consequence for Israelis, but the boycott seeks to support the academic freedom of Palestinians, which is constrained by the Israeli government at the moment," she says, through travel restrictions preventing Gazans from leaving the Gaza strip.*[5] "As a scholar, a tremendous amount is lost in our capacity to engage with Palestinian scholars and do research there," Feldman says, because the Israeli government has also barred many foreigners from access to Gaza.

An AAUP statement in 2006 declared that academic boycotts "strike directly at the free exchange of ideas even as they are aimed at university administrations."[6]

But Lloyd, a professor of English at the University of California, Riverside, counters that the boycott has actually encouraged more discussion and more press — at least about the Palestinian issue. "Until these resolutions were promoted, discussion was rare and one-sided; the Israeli view was the only view you saw," he says.

Marjorie Heins, a member of the AAUP committee on academic freedom, points out that Israeli professors and scholars who disagree with Israel's positions on Palestine also are penalized.[7]

Some academics say Israel is being singled out while China, for instance, is not boycotted for its crackdowns on civil rights in Tiananmen Square or Tibet.[8]

---

* The only legal ways in and out of Gaza are through official bordercrossings with Israel and Egypt, which for security reasons have severelyrestricted movement of people and goods across the borders.

As for the Palestinian student who couldn't find outside readers, Feldman says, "We saw very similar questions in the South Africa boycott" — an economic boycott aimed at ending apartheid that gained worldwide support starting in the 1960s. "The argument was [that] black South Africans were harmed by the boycott," she says. "I don't think there's any way around the fact that individuals can suffer negative consequences in the pursuit of much broader transformation that will be beneficial to them in the long run."

— *Sarah Glazer*

[1]Michael Zakim and Feisal G. Mohamed, "The Best of Intentions: Debating the ASA Boycott," *Dissent*, Nov. 5, 2014, http://tinyurl.com/pc2rv2b.

[2]The proposed boycott of Israeli academic institutions is part of a broader international campaign, the Boycott, Divestment and Sanctions movement (BDS), which began in 2005 with a call from Palestinian civil society organizations demanding, among other things, that Israel end its "occupation and colonization of Arab lands." See BDS website: http://tinyurl.com/3fnrncc.

[3]Tamar Lewin, "Prominent Scholars, Citing Importance of Academic Freedom, Denounce Israeli Boycott," *The New York Times*, Dec. 26, 2013, http://tiny url.com/pgmujcz.

[4]Zakim and Mohamed, *op. cit.*

[5]See Eline Gordts, "Why Don't Palestinians Just Leave Gaza? They Can't," *The Huffington Post*, June 31, 2014, http://tinyurl.com/p8fkl3e.

[6]Marjorie Heins, "Rethinking Academic Boycotts," *AAUP Journal of Academic Freedom*, 2013, p. 3, http://tinyurl.com/nftld9x.

[7]*Ibid.*

[8]Ernst Benjamin, "Why I Continue to Support the AAUP Policy in Opposition to Academic Boycotts: A Response to the AAUP Journal of Academic Freedom," 2013, http://tinyurl.com/m45ys5d.

---

to modify their speech codes, with the most recent victory being a settlement announced May 4 with Western Michigan University.[66]

University of Wisconsin professor Shiell contends that hate-speech codes have "lost the legal war." Between 1989 and 2012 speech codes were struck down in at least 14 cases, including California, Michigan, New Hampshire, Pennsylvania and Texas.[67]

"Plenty of people have been arguing in the last 20 years that the First Amendment has been in error in defending offensive speech. [But] in the courtroom they have always lost," Shiell says. "Our system, as judges understand it, not only permits, but even encourages, robust and offensive actions."

Defining Punishable Speech

The U.S. Supreme Court and other courts have ruled that to be punishable, speech must constitute genuine harassment, a true threat, disorderly conduct or fit some other category of constitutionally unprotected speech. And for speech between students, the Supreme Court has ruled that to constitute harassment, speech must be "severe" and "pervasive" and "objectively offensive" — that is, judged offensive by a "reasonable person."[68]

In the recent University of Oklahoma case, for example, the university president said the students' actions had created a "hostile environment" under federal anti-discrimination law. However, the Supreme Court has set a high bar for meeting the definition of "hostile environment."

In *Davis v. Monroe* (1999), the court said harassment must be "so severe, pervasive and objectively offensive that it can be said to deprive the victims of access to the educational opportunities or benefits provided by the school." In other words, the harassment must be serious enough to have a systemic effect on equal access to education. Thus, it was unlikely that a single act of peer harassment would qualify, experts such as Shiell say.[69]

The *Davis* case centered on LaShonda Davis, a fifth-grader in Monroe County, Ga. Another student was accused of attempting to fondle her and using offensive sexual language on numerous occasions. When the school refused to take disciplinary action, LaShonda's mother sued the school board under Title IX. A lower court had ruled that the board was not liable for student-on-student sexual harassment, but the Supreme Court overturned the decision.

The court also has ruled that to constitute a true threat, a speaker must mean "to communicate a serious expression of an intent to commit an act of unlawful violence to a particular individual or group of individuals."[70]

In a 1997 case, *U.S. v. Alkhabaz*, Abraham Jacob Alkhabaz indicated an interest in violence against women through fictitious stories he posted to an Internet group. One of the stories used the name of a female classmate at the University of Michigan, although Alkhabaz did not communicate any of the stories to her. The court held there was no true threat, since there was no direct intimidation.[71]

By contrast, Richard Machado, a student at the University of California, Irvine, was convicted of a true threat when he sent and re-sent an email to 59 Asian students threatening to "hunt you down and kill your stupid asses."[72]

CURRENT SITUATION
Anti-Harassment Legislation

A bill is pending in the Senate and the House aimed at preventing harassment of lesbian, gay, bisexual and transgender (LGBT) students. It requires all colleges that receive federal money to establish policies against taunting LGBT students.

Introduced by Democratic Sens. Patty Murray, Wash., and Tammy Baldwin, Wis., and Rep. Mark Pocan, Wis., the measure also would require colleges to prevent cyber-bullying and harassment based on students' race, color, national origin, gender, disability or religion. Called the Tyler Clementi Higher Education Anti-Harassment Act of 2015, the measure would amount to a federal expansion of New Jersey's anti-bullying law, considered the strongest in the nation.[73]

The bill is a response to the suicide of Clementi, a Rutgers student who jumped off a bridge in 2010 after discovering his roommate had used a webcam to spy on him having sex with another man. The roommate also encouraged others — via Twitter — to watch the sexual encounter via a video chat room.

LGBT students are more likely to be harassed in school than other students, Murray said, "yet there is no federal requirement for colleges and universities to protect their students from discrimination based on sexual orientation or gender identity."[74]

Murray had introduced a similar version of the bill, which some education-policy experts said was too broadly worded, in 2011, but it died in Congress. Supporters believe the new bill has a better chance now that Murray is the most senior Democratic member of the Education Committee.[75]

Laura Bennett, president of the Association for Student Conduct Administration, which represents deans and other administrators, says "the bill focuses on ensuring every institution has a harassment policy, which I think is good practice." She adds, "I've seen inappropriate sexual comments depriving a student of the ability to go to class," particularly when it is "severe, persistent and pervasive," the definition used in the bill.

But FIRE's Harris said the term "bullying" is not well-defined, and the bill fails to include the standard legal requirement that the conduct be "objectively offensive" to count as harassment. Harris also questions the need for a new law.

"Tyler Clementi is the impetus for these bills, but what happened to him is already illegal," she says. "Every existing university student code of conduct and state laws prohibit surreptitiously videoing someone engaged in sexual conduct and distributing it."

In fact, Clementi's roommate Dharun Ravi was found guilty in 2012 of all 15 counts on which he was charged, including bias intimidation — a hate crime carrying up

Does an academic boycott of Israel threaten academic freedom?

YES

David M. Rosen
PROFESSOR OF ANTHROPOLOGY, FAIRLEIGH Dickinson University

Written for *CQ Researcher*, April 2015

The central objective of the Boycott, Sanction and Divestment movement and its academic allies is the suppression of dissent and free speech in America's colleges and universities. As BDS grows stronger, it becomes more strident. BDS founder Omar Bargouti's recent call for dismantling the Jewish homeland in Israel makes plain that BDS's vision for the Jews of Israel is not a two-state solution or even the one-state solution — but rather a no-state solution. BDS's radical anti-normalization campaign is designed to shut down debate and communication surrounding the Israel-Palestinian conflict and drive out the voices of dialogue and moderation.

The BDS assault on academic freedom is two-pronged: First, BSD is rebranding academic freedom not as a right but as a privilege conditioned upon accepting the BDS perspective. Second, BDS seeks to marginalize and demonize those whose views render them unprivileged to speak. The move to boycott Israeli academic institutions is part of this assault.

The leadership of my professional association, the American Anthropological Association, has embraced the boycott ethos, although a formal boycott vote won't take place until December. At last year's annual meeting of anthropologists, AAA leadership gave center stage to numerous panels of boycott advocates. This year, it refused to sponsor a panel and roundtable submitted by the only organized group of boycott opponents. An openly anti-Semitic blog post calling Israel a "criminal nation" populated by a "nation of criminals" was allowed to stand on a supposedly moderated AAA website. De facto, a boycott is in place, and its discriminatory animus is spreading across the profession.

Boycotters claim that academic boycotts target institutions, not people; but here is how it works in real life: At last year's annual meeting, an Israeli anthropologist was accosted on an elevator and denounced for wearing a nametag that identified his Israeli university affiliation. Another, long opposed to the occupation of the West Bank and Gaza, was publically mocked for suggesting at a session that there might be countries with worse human rights records than Israel's. One pro-boycott anthropologist declared scholarly objectivity to be a Zionist agenda; another celebrated the politicization of teaching, making plain the overtly prejudicial atmosphere in her classroom.

We are witnessing the emergence of the first major political blacklisting since the McCarthy era. When academic freedom is reduced from a "right" to a "privilege," it becomes meaningless. No one can speak truth to power if they need permission to speak.

NO

David Lloyd
Distinguished Professor of English, University of California, Riverside; Founding member, U.S. Campaign for the Academic and Cultural Boycott of Israel

Written for *CQ Researcher*, April 2015

Most discussions of the boycott of Israeli academic institutions ignore Israel's actual violations of Palestinian academic freedoms. This is not a hypothetical matter of what might happen were a boycott imposed, but an ongoing assault on Palestinian educational capacities that threatens their survival.

On the West Bank, several hundred checkpoints hamper access to schools. Campuses undergo military incursions and closures; scholars are denied the right to travel. Israeli authorities deny Gazan students the right to complete their studies on the West Bank. Worse, Israel's devastating military campaigns against Gaza have consistently targeted educational institutions, from the Islamic University to U.N.-run schools. Discrimination within Israeli educational institutions is subtle, but pervasive. Palestinian Israelis make up about 20 percent of the population but only 1 percent of university faculty.

These conditions constitute the real threat to academic freedom. Israeli universities are not bystanders, but are integrated in every aspect of Israel's regime of occupation and discrimination. Universities develop weapon systems and surveillance technology, host institutes that shape strategies like the Dahiya Doctrine, which plans the destruction of civilian infrastructure, and furnish the hydrological and topographical studies that determine the route of the illegal separation wall on Palestinian land or the sites of settlements. Israeli universities occupy land from which Palestinians were expelled or that is intended to be part of a future Palestinian state.

Nonetheless, the guidelines for the academic boycott of Israel are remarkably restrained. The Palestinian call explicitly targets institutions, not individuals. Israeli academics' right to research, teach, travel, attend conferences and express their views is fully respected. We are asked to refrain from collaborating with institutions that actively contribute to the systemic violation of international law and human rights. We are asked not to engage in joint institutional projects or host administrators acting as ambassadors for the state of Israel. Withholding consent from the violation of fundamental rights and refusing to normalize it by our collaboration is not a threat to academic freedom, but its clearest exercise.

The academic boycott will not prevent Israeli scholars from working or exchanging ideas. It will not destroy their institutions. The boycott has specific goals, consistent with human rights conventions and international law, and can be short-lived. Israel's dispossession of the Palestinians threatens to be permanent and irreversible.

Levi Pettit, right, a former University of Oklahoma fraternity member who was expelled from the university after being filmed leading a racist song, appeared at a news conference at Fairview Baptist Church in Oklahoma City on March 25, 2015. Pettit apologized for his role in the incident and said he is upset and embarrassed that he failed to stop it. Oklahoma state Sen. Anastasia Pittman, D-Oklahoma City, left, looks on.

to 10 years in prison in New Jersey — as well as invasion of privacy, witness tampering and hindering arrest. He was sentenced to 30 days in county jail, of which he served 20.[76]

However, the New Jersey Supreme Court in March found the state's "bias intimidation" law unconstitutional, portending a potential reversal in Ravi's case, which is on appeal. The law is the only one in the nation saying a defendant can be convicted if the victim "reasonably believed" the harassment or intimidation was based on race, color, ethnicity, gender or sexual orientation.

The court ruled the statute was "unconstitutionally vague" because it does not give defendants fair notice of when they are crossing a line to commit a crime. The court struck down the provision that bases a conviction on the victim's state of mind — i.e., his belief that he was targeted for a bias crime — ruling that it criminalizes "a defendant's failure to apprehend the reaction that his words would have on another."[77]

New Incidents

Since the video of Oklahoma students singing bigoted lyrics appeared online in early March, racist incidents have proliferated on campuses across the country. Most colleges have followed Oklahoma President Boren's lead in swiftly denouncing the acts and disciplining the students involved.

Bucknell University in Lewisburg, Pa., a private institution, expelled three students who made racist comments during a campus radio broadcast. Then the University of Mary Washington in Fredericksburg, Va., dissolved its men's rugby team and ordered anti-sexual assault training for the team after players were observed singing a sexist song at an off-campus party.

On April 1, Duke University announced that a student alleged to have hung a noose on the university grounds was "no longer on campus" and that "potential criminal violations" were being explored. However, after releasing a public apology from the student, the school said on May 1 that the student has been disciplined, will not face criminal charges and can return to campus next semester.[78] In April, the University of South Carolina (USC) suspended a female student and began a code of conduct investigation after she used the "N" word when writing a list of reasons "why USC WiFi Blows."[79]

The disciplinary actions have provoked almost as much controversy as the incidents themselves. "Colleges have seized on the University of Oklahoma's unconstitutional actions as a signal that they have an 'all clear' to toss free speech and basic fairness out of the window," Robert Shibley, executive director of FIRE, said in a statement April 9. By contrast, FIRE praised University of Maryland President Loh for "bucking the trend" and recognizing that the First Amendment protected the racist student email that popped up on his campus in March.[80]

But speaking from an administrator's viewpoint, NASPA's Kruger says, "Having a president make a strong statement may be worth the risk of a First Amendment suit that would follow."

China Influence

In Congress, Rep. Smith is expected to hold additional hearings on the impact on American universities of the Chinese government's involvement through Confucius Institutes on American campuses and through partnerships on satellite campuses in China. He also has asked the Government Accountability Office (GAO) to investigate whether a two-tier system exists at U.S. satellite campuses, whereby Chinese students and faculty are more restricted in their activities and research than U.S. students and faculty.

"I will also ask whether Communist Party committees operate on campus, whether fundamental freedoms are protected for both Chinese and U.S. students and faculty — religious freedom, Internet freedom, freedom of speech, freedom of association — and whether the universities are required to enforce China's draconian population control policies," Smith said at a Dec. 4 hearing.[81]

Experts at the hearing said potential solutions included more federal funding for Chinese language training so colleges won't need help from China and requiring greater openness in agreements between U.S. colleges and China.

Smith also responded favorably to a suggestion by China scholar Perry Link of University of California, Riverside: withholding visas for Confucius Institute teachers until China agrees to grant visas to American scholars, such as Link, who has been barred from China since 1995 for political reasons. During the 1989 Tiananmen Square uprising Link had smuggled a dissident astrophysicist into the U.S. Embassy in Beijing and helped to edit the "Tiananmen Papers," a 2002 collection of leaked Chinese official documents revealing how Chinese leaders responded to the protest.[82]

OUTLOOK
Open Questions

The recent student expulsions and suspensions for racist incidents on college campuses shows that both public and private university administrators are moving swiftly to punish those responsible. But whether those actions would be upheld, if challenged on First Amendment grounds, remains an open question.

Whether such casas will even come before a court is partly a practical matter: When it comes to students' free-speech rights, a student must have the will and resources to sue the university, notes FIRE's Creeley.

Some critics say college presidents are too focused on taking tough punitive actions in order to avoid suits by the victims of harassment. In the future, FIRE hopes to change that "risk-management calculation," turning the possibility of a First Amendment suit into an equal risk

by continuing to file suits where it sees free speech threatened, according to Creeley.

Meanwhile, many of the recent questions raised about academic freedom will only intensify as American universities continue to expand their global reach. Referring to the recent barring of NYU professor Ross from entering the UAE, NYU-Shanghai Vice Chancellor Lehman says, "We have not had an Andrew Ross situation yet, but I expect we will at some point." If that day comes, he says, the university will do what it does when the U.S. government blocks a visa for a foreign scholar that NYU invites to New York — make a plea for the importance of bringing the scholar over.

"I happen to believe that movement [of scholars between countries] is good," Lehman says. "I hope that over time all governments will make it easier to move across borders. But that's not the world we're in right now."

America's uniquely liberal constitutional stance on free speech — unlike in France, which has outlawed anti-Semitic speech or in Germany where Holocaust denial is a crime — will continue to present challenges when hard cases arise.

"Americans may laud [the French satirical magazine] *Charlie Hebdo* for being brave enough to publish cartoons ridiculing the Prophet Muhammad, but, if Ayaan Hirsi Ali is invited to campus, there are often calls to deny her a podium," observed *New York Times* columnist David Brooks, referring to Muslim students' opposition to Yale University's speaking invitation to Ali, a Somali-born political-rights activist and former Muslim who has been fiercely critical of Islam.[83]

While Americans pride themselves on their free-speech rights, it can be hard to hold to that standard when faced with speech that seems abominable. As journalist George Packer pointed out in a recent comment for *The New Yorker*, "the loathsomeness of an incident in which University of Oklahoma students were caught on video singing a racist song made it seem churlish to argue that their expulsion from a public institution might be unconstitutional."

The difficulty, he observed, is that "hate-speech regulations put actual feelings, often honorable ones, ahead of abstract rights — which seems like common sense. It takes an active effort to resist the impulse to silence the jerks who have wounded you."[84]

NOTES

1. Jake New, "Free Speech or Inciting Violence?" *Inside Higher Ed*, March 16, 2015, http://tinyurl.com/p9gut6r.

2. "An Important Statement from President Wallace Loh," University of Maryland, March 12, 2015, http://tinyurl.com/ldzv3k4.

3. Jake New, "Punishment, Post-Oklahoma," *Inside Higher Ed*, April 1, 2015, http://tinyurl.com/oh2d6uz. See also, Sonali Kohli, "Read this university president's candid reaction on Twitter to frat-house racism on his campus," *Quartz*, March 13, 2015, http://tinyurl.com/lh37y9k.

4. "Rising Above Odious Words," statement by Wallace D. Loh, Office of the President, University of Maryland, April 1, 2015, http://tinyurl.com/lfdessv.

5. *Ibid.*

6. Jamelle Bouie, "Don't Expel Members of Sigma Alpha Epsilon for Racism," *Slate*, March 10, 2015, http://tinyurl.com/m5moa5u. Also see Allie Bidwell, "Racist Fraternity Chant Learned during Leadership Cruise," *U.S. News*, March 27, 2015, http://tinyurl.com/nksv376.

7. Manny Fernandez and Erik Eckholm, "Expulsion of Two Oklahoma Students Over Video Leads to Free Speech Debate," *The New York Times*, March 11, 2015, http://tinyurl.com/ox4ge3p.

8. Lynn O'Shaughnessy, "20 Surprising Higher Education Facts," *U.S. News & World Report*, Sept. 6, 2011, http://tinyurl.com/4y5v8o2.

9. Laura Kipnis, "Sexual Paranoia Strikes Academe," *The Chronicle of Higher Education*, Feb. 27, 2015, http://tinyurl.com/kq9aerc.

10. Stephanie Saul, "N.Y.U. Professor Is Barred by United Arab Emirates," *The New York Times*, March 16, 2015, http://tinyurl.com/kxqm4om.

11. *Ibid.*

12. "Hearing Probes China's Influence on U.S. Universities," Rep. Chris Smith, news release, U.S. House of Representatives, Dec. 4, 2014, http://tinyurl.com/ppu97a4.

13. For more detail see, Marshall Sahlins, Confucius Institutes: Academic Malware (2014).

14. *Isaac Smith v. McDavis*, Jones and Compton, Complaint for Injunctive and Declaratory Relief and Damages, U.S. District Court Southern District of Ohio Eastern Division, July 1, 2014, http://tinyurl.com/ogpevhf.

15. *Isaac Smith v. Roderick J. McDavis, et al.*, Defendants' Answer to Plaintiff's Complaint, Oct. 24, 2014, U.S. District Court for the Southern District of Ohio, Eastern Division.

16. Settlement agreement in *Smith v. McDavis*, Feb. 2, 2015, http://tinyurl.com/q4mtxuv. See also Alyssa Pasicznyk, "OU Reaches Settlement in Freedom of Speech Lawsuit," WOUB Public Media, Feb. 2, 2015, http://tinyurl.com/l29fqhk.

17. "Western Michigan U. Settles Boots Riley 'Speech Tax' Lawsuit," Foundation for Individual Rights in Education, May 4, 2015, http://tinyurl.com/m8l5h5w.

18. Timothy C. Shiell, *Campus Hate Speech on Trial* (2009).

19. Eric Posner, "Universities Are Right — and Within Their Rights — to Crack Down on Speech and Behavior," *Slate*, Feb. 12, 2015, http://tinyurl.com/qbcr226.

20. Title IX is part of the Education Amendments of 1972. Title VI is part of the Civil Rights Act of 1964. See, "Overview of Title VI of the Civil Rights Act of 1964," http://tinyurl.com/leaxlfr.

21. Hans Bader, "Federal Title IX Enforcers Effectively Define Dating and Sex Education as 'Sexual Harassment,' " Competitive Enterprise Institute, May 10, 2013, http://tinyurl.com/qeplvpw.

22. "Dating Imperiled by Government Speech Mandate," Foundation for Individual Rights in Education, May 13, 2013, http://tinyurl.com/kaoxbuf.

23. Greg Lukianoff, "Free Speech on Campus: The Ten Worst Offenders of 2014," *The Huffington Post*, March 2, 2015, http://tinyurl.com/nqs7lnm.

24. Kipnis, *op. cit.*

25. "Trauma Warnings Move from Internet to Ivory Tower," The Associated Press, April 26, 2014, http://tinyurl.com/kwsbhzg.

26. *Ibid.*

27. *Ibid.*

28. Edward J. Graham, "Mandated Trigger Warnings Threaten Academic Freedom," American Association of University Professors, November-December 2014, http://tinyurl.com/lcurfs9.

29. Judith Shapiro, "From Strength to Strength," *Inside Higher Ed*, Dec. 15, 2014, http://tinyurl.com/kd8xgb2.

30. "Trauma Warnings Move from Internet to Ivory Tower," *op. cit.*

31. *Ibid.*

32. Posner, *op. cit.*

33. Judith Shulevitz, "In College and Hiding From Scary Ideas," *The New York Times*, March 21, 2015, http://tinyurl.com/l4ne9ye.

34. Although this phrase is often attributed to Voltaire, he apparently never said it.

35. See Bouie, *op. cit.*; Robby Soave, "To Safeguard All Students' Rights, SAE Should Sue Oklahoma U.," *Reason*, March 19, 2015, http://tinyurl.com/k73sjt4; and David French, "Congratulations, Oklahoma, In Your Outrage You Just Violated the Law," *National Review*, March 10, 2015, http://tinyurl.com/krgcnso.

36. Fernandez and Eckholm, *op. cit.*

37. *Ibid.*

38. Kent Greenfield, "The Limits of Free Speech," *The Atlantic*, March 13, 2015, http://tinyurl.com/n43twsn.

39. "Excellence v. Equity," in "Special Report: Universities," *The Economist*, March 28, 2015, p. 4, http://tinyurl.com/k863uxj. For background, see Reed Karaim, "College Rankings," *CQ Researcher*, Jan. 2, 2015, pp. 1–24; and, Robert Kiener, Future of Public Universities, *CQ Researcher*, Jan. 18, 2013, pp. 53–80.

40. "A Pearl in the Desert," in "Special Report: Universities," *The Economist*, March 28, 2015, p. 11.

41. Stephanie Saul, "N.Y.U. Professor Is Barred from United Arab Emirates," *The New York Times*, March 16, 2015, http://tinyurl.com/kxx3qaj.

42. Rick Hills, "Is it legitimate to compromise on academic freedom abroad?" *PrawfsBlawg*, March 20, 2015, http://tinyurl.com/qd2579o.

43. Stephen I. Levine, *et al.*, "The Debate Over Confucius Institutes in the United States," *Foreign Policy*, July 11, 2014, http://tinyurl.com/le7yobw.

44. Marjorie Heins, *Priests of Our Democracy* (2013), p. 17.

45. Geoffrey R. Stone, "A Brief History of Academic Freedom," in Akeel Bilgrami and Jonathan R. Cole, eds., *Who's Afraid of Academic Freedom?* (2015).

46. *Ibid.*, pp. 3–4.

47. *Ibid.*, p. 5.

48. Heins, *op. cit.*, p. 18.

49. *Ibid.*, pp. 20–23.

50. Marjorie Heins, "An Old Story: The Corporate University," *Dissent*, Nov. 14, 2012, http://tinyurl.com/pnxfy77.

51. Heins, *Priests of Our Democracy*, *op. cit.*, p. 74.

52. *Ibid.*, p. 3.

53. Marcia Clemmitt, "Academic Freedom," *CQ Researcher*, p. 846.

54. Heins, Priests of Our Democracy, *op. cit.*, p. 179.

55. *Ibid.*, p. 180.

56. *Ibid.*, p. 4.

57. Lisa Leff, "What Was the UC Berkeley Free Speech Movement?" *The Huffington Post*, Dec. 2, 2014, http://tinyurl.com/lbj8kg7; Robert Cohen, *Freedom's Orator: Mario Savio and the Radical Legacy of the 1960s* (2009).

58. Heins, *Priests of Our Democracy*, *op. cit.*, p. 240.

59. "Title IX," *Encyclopaedia Britannica*, http://tinyurl.com/bhfkweu.

60. Clemmitt, *op. cit.*, p. 847.

61. "Harvard Law Review: Recent Case," LexisNexis, April 1990, http://tinyurl.com/qhrdetg.

62. Clemmitt, *op. cit.*, p. 847.

63. *Ibid.*

64. "Alan Charles Kors," National Endowment on Humanities, http://tinyurl.com/ntsb3c4.

65. *Ibid.*

66. "Western Michigan U. Settles Boots Riley 'Speech Tax' Lawsuit," *op. cit.*

67. Timothy C. Shiell, "The Case of the Student's Racist Facebook Message," *AAUP Journal of Academic Freedom*, 2014, http://tinyurl.com/ohy48pv.

68. *Ibid.* For "reasonable person" legal definition, see Cornell University Law School Legal Information Institute, http://tinyurl.com/nsjx6gz.

69. *Davis v. Monroe*, cited in Shiell, *op. cit.* Also see "Davis v. Monroe County Board of Education," *Encyclopaedia Britannica*, http://tinyurl.com/qdg97of.

70. Shiell, *op. cit.*

71. *Ibid.*

72. *U.S. v. Machado* (1999), cited in *ibid.*

73. "Tyler Clementi Higher Education Anti-Harassment Act of 2015," govtrac.u.s., http://tinyurl.com/p5dr35x.

74. "Murray, Baldwin, Pocan Introduce Tyler Clementi Anti-Harassment Act," press release, Sen. Patty Murray, U.S. Senate, March 18, 2015, http://tinyurl.com/p236x28. Also see, Carlos P. Zalaquett, "Cyberbullying in College," SAGE Open, March 19, 2014, http://tinyurl.com/ndeehfe; the study found 19 percent of college students experienced cyberbullying.

75. Tyler Kingkade, "Democrats Renew Push for Colleges to Establish Cyberbullying Policies That Cover LGBT Students," *The Huffington Post*, March 18, 2015, http://tinyurl.com/kdrnsv8.

76. Kate Zernike, "Jail Term Ends After 20 days for Ex-Rutgers Student," *The New York Times*, June 19, 2012, http://tinyurl.com/pbewfqj.

77. Kate Zernike, "Part of New Jersey's Bias Intimidation Law Is Ruled Unconstitutional," *The New York Times*, March 18, 2015, http://tinyurl.com/qhztk5r.

78. The Associated Press, "North Carolina: Investigation into Noose at Duke Ends," *The New York Times*, May 1, 2015, www.nytimes.com/2015/05/02/us/north-carolina-investigation-into-noose-at-duke-ends.html.

79. Peter Holley, "University of South Carolina student suspended after racist photo goes viral," *The Washington Post*, April 5, 2015, http://tinyurl.com/kcg83ro.

80. "Colleges Rush to Violate Free Speech, Due Process in Response to Speech Controversies," Foundation for Individual Rights in Education, April 9, 2015, http://tinyurl.com/kcnyhw5.

81. Rep. Chris Smith, Opening Statement, House of Representatives, Dec. 4, 2014, http://tinyurl.com/pskomnx.

82. Daniel Golden and Oliver Staley, "China Banning U.S. Professors Elicits Silence from Colleges," *Bloomberg Business*, Aug. 10, 2011, http://tinyurl.com/orazy7n. Also see Andrew J. Nathan, "The Tiananmen Papers," *Foreign Affairs*, January/February 2001, http://tinyurl.com/oxr2r6o.

83. David Brooks, "I Am Not Charlie Hebdo," *The New York Times*, Jan. 8, 2015, http://tinyurl.com/nhpxtsc. Also see, Rich Lizardo, "We Invited Ayaan Hirsi Ali to Yale — and Outrage Ensued," *The American Spectator*, Sept. 16, 2014, http://tinyurl.com/nm9ttge; Richard Pérez-Peña and Tanzina Vega, "Brandeis Cancels Plan to Give Honorary Degree to Ayaan Hirsi Ali, a Critic of Islam," *The New York Times*, April 8, 2014, http://tinyurl.com/mc2w2sq.

84. George Packer, "Comment: Mute Button," *The New Yorker*, April 13, 2015, http://tinyurl.com/nf987xg.

BIBLIOGRAPHY

Selected Sources

Books

Bilgrami, Akeel, and Jonathan R. Cole, eds., *Who's Afraid of Academic Freedom?* Columbia University Press, 2015.
A sociology professor (Akeel) and a philosophy professor (Cole) from Columbia University provide academic essays, some of which discuss the boycott of Israeli higher education institutions.

Fish, Stanley, *Versions of Academic Freedom: From Professionalism to Revolution*, University of Chicago Press, 2014.
A law professor at Florida International University asks whether academic freedom authorizes professors to question the status quo inside and outside of the university.

Heins, Marjorie, *Priests of Our Democracy: The Supreme Court, Academic Freedom and the Anti-Communist Purge*, New York University Press, 2013.
A civil liberties lawyer traces the history of academic freedom from the late 19th century to today.

Articles

Bouie, Jamelle, "Don't Expel Members of Sigma Alpha Epsilon for Racism," *Slate*, March 10, 2015, http://tinyurl.com/m5moa5u.
An African-American columnist says the University of Oklahoma should educate students about a 1921 anti-black race riot in Tulsa, Okla., so they "see what their words actually mean," instead of expelling them.

Fernandez, Manny, and Erik Eckholm, "Expulsion of Two Oklahoma Students over Video Leads to Free Speech Debate," *The New York Times*, March 11, 2015, http://tinyurl.com/ox4ge3p.
Numerous legal experts say racist singing by University of Oklahoma students, two of whom were later expelled, was constitutionally protected speech.

Greenfield, Kent, "The Limits of Free Speech," *The Atlantic*, March 13, 2015, http://tinyurl.com/n43twsn.
A law professor at Boston College asks whether Americans should rethink the First Amendment if it protects racist chants such as those sung by University of Oklahoma students, some of whom were later expelled.

Kipnis, Laura, "Sexual Paranoia Strikes Academe," *The Chronicle of Higher Education*, Feb. 27, 2015, http://tinyurl.com/kq9aerc.
A film professor at Northwestern University says university sexual-harassment codes and "trigger warnings" leave students ill-prepared for the outside world.

McCord, Edward A., "Confucius Institutes: Hardly a Threat to Academic Freedoms," *The Diplomat*, March 27, 2014, http://tinyurl.com/q3qzeym.
A historian of China at George Washington University finds little evidence that Confucius Institutes threaten academic freedom on American campuses.

New, Jake, "Punishment Post-Oklahoma," *Inside Higher Ed*, April 1, 2015, http://tinyurl.com/oh2d6uz.
After the University of Oklahoma expelled students for a racist song caught on video, other college presidents quickly disciplined students involved in similar incidents.

Sahlins, Marshall, "China U.," *The Nation*, Oct. 29, 2013, http://tinyurl.com/kdkmr53.
A professor emeritus of anthropology at the University of Chicago says Confucius Institutes censor political discussion of China on American campuses.

Schiell, Timothy, "The Case of the Student's Racist Facebook Message," *Journal of Academic Freedom*, 2014, http://tinyurl.com/ohy48pv.
A professor of philosophy at the University of Wisconsin-Stout examines a racist Facebook message through the lens of landmark court decisions to determine if it is constitutionally protected free speech.

Scott, Joan W., "Changing My Mind about the Boycott," *Journal of Academic Freedom*, 2013, http://tinyurl.com/kn5xltc.
A professor emerita of social science at the Institute for Advanced Study, in Princeton, N.J., explains why she supports a boycott of Israeli academic institutions.

Reports and Studies

"Spotlight on Speech Codes 2015: The State of Free Speech on Our Nation's Campuses," Foundation for Individual Rights in Education, 2015, http://tinyurl.com/o6xlp56.
A report by a group advocating free speech on college campuses concludes that more than 55 percent of colleges restrict speech protected by the Constitution.

"Subcommittee Hearing: Is Academic Freedom Threatened by China's Influence on American Universities?" U.S. House of Representatives, Dec. 4, 2014, http://tinyurl.com/plp6t9j.
Foreign Affairs Subcommittee Chairman Rep. Christopher Smith, R-N.J., leads a hearing on whether Confucius Institutes on American campuses and satellite campuses in China undermine academic freedom

For More Information

Association of American University Professors, 1133 19th St., N.W., Suite 200, Washington, DC 20036; 202-737-5526; www.aaup.org. Professional association representing faculty at American colleges and universities that promotes academic freedom and shared governance.

Association of Title IX Administrators (ATIXA), 116 E. King St., Malvern, PA 19355-2969; 610-644-7858; https://atixa.org. Professional association for school and college Title IX administrators responsible for coordinating the anti-sex discrimination law.

Foundation for Individual Rights in Education (FIRE), 170 S. Independence Mall W., Suite 510, Philadelphia, PA 19106; 215-717-3473; https://www.thefire.org. Educational foundation that works across the ideological spectrum on behalf of individual rights, freedom of expression, academic freedom, due process and freedom of conscience at colleges and universities.

Human Rights Watch, 350 Fifth Ave., 34th Floor, New York, NY 10118-3299; 212-290-4700; www.hrw.org. International organization that defends human rights worldwide.

International Campaign for Tibet, 1825 Jefferson Place, N.W., Washington, DC, 20036; 202-785-1515; www.savetibet.org. Advocacy group that promotes human rights and democratic freedoms for the people of Tibet.

Scholars at Risk, 194 Mercer St., Room 410, New York, NY, 10012; 212-998-2179; scholarsatrisk.nyu.edu. International network of education institutions and individuals hosted at New York University that promotes academic freedom and defends scholars' human rights.

Student Affairs Professionals in Higher Education (NASPA), 111 K St., N.E., 10th Floor, Washington, D.C. 20002; 202-265-7500; www.naspa.org. Association of professionals in student affairs at the college and university level.

6

Housing Discrimination

Kenneth Jost

Demonstrators march in Baltimore in May, a day after authorities said criminal charges would be filed against six police officers in connection with the death of 25-year-old Freddie Gray. Explosive clashes between inner-city residents and police in Baltimore, Ferguson, Mo., and other cities have been linked to the isolation of African-Americans in racially segregated, high-poverty neighborhoods.

From *CQ Researcher*, November 16, 2015.

K imberly grew up in public housing in the 1990s in one of Baltimore's predominantly African-American neighborhoods with her single, drug-abusing mother. Two decades later, living in a modest home in a racially mixed Baltimore suburb, she looks back on those years unhappily.

"My mom got me into the public housing system," Kimberly (whose last name was not made public) told researchers studying the court-ordered Baltimore Housing Mobility Program, which was aimed at breaking up racially based housing patterns in one of the nation's most segregated cities. "I don't want that for my children."[1]

Kimberly had a troubled adolescence in the kind of dysfunctional social system characteristic of many of the barracks-style public housing projects. She was expelled from school, got pregnant at 15 and moved from one housing project to another.

Kimberly left the inner city for a suburban single-family home thanks to a lawsuit under the federal Fair Housing Act (FHA), the landmark 1968 law prohibiting discrimination in the sale or rental of housing. The law has helped reduce, but by no means eliminate, racial segregation in U.S. cities and suburbs. Enforcement of the law by the U.S. Department of Housing and Urban Development (HUD) and local public housing authorities has lagged. Experts blamed inadequate funding and political opposition at the local level to demographic changes viewed as threatening the character of established, predominantly white neighborhoods.

Public housing tenants in Baltimore had joined in a federal lawsuit in 1995 charging HUD, the Baltimore housing authority and other city officials with perpetuating racial segregation by concen-

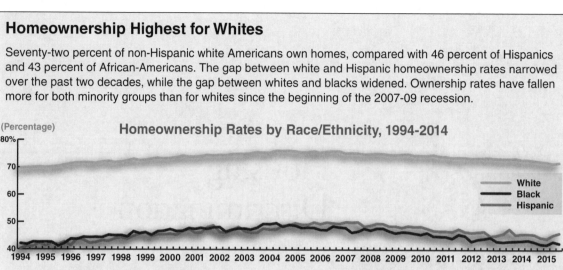

Homeownership Highest for Whites

Seventy-two percent of non-Hispanic white Americans own homes, compared with 46 percent of Hispanics and 43 percent of African-Americans. The gap between white and Hispanic homeownership rates narrowed over the past two decades, while the gap between whites and blacks widened. Ownership rates have fallen more for both minority groups than for whites since the beginning of the 2007-09 recession.

Homeownership Rates by Race/Ethnicity, 1994-2014

(Percentage)

White
Black
Hispanic

Source: Graphic from "Where You Live Matters: 2015 Fair Housing Trends Report," National Fair Housing Alliance, April 30, 2015, p. 9, http://tinyurl.com/neuq462; data downloaded from "Housing Vacancies and Homeownership" Historical Tables, Table 16, U.S. Census Bureau, http://tinyurl.com/kxxz82g

trating public housing in predominantly African-American neighborhoods. The suit, *Thompson v. HUD*, resulted in 2003 in the creation of a program to provide federal housing vouchers to low-income families to move from the crime-ridden projects to low-poverty, racially mixed neighborhoods.[2]

Kimberly hesitated when she first heard about the Section 8 voucher program but eventually decided to participate, as did 2,400 others in Baltimore so far. Today, Kimberly lives with her two daughters, a half-sister and her grandfather and says she feels more in control of her life. "It's only in leaving that I started growing and wanting to do different things, learn different things and be something different," she told the researchers.

The Baltimore anti-discrimination suit was one of more than a dozen filed in the 1990s, aimed at breaking up persistent patterns of black-white residential segregation in the United States. Housing advocates and experts across the ideological spectrum agree that the federal government bears much of the blame for the growth of housing segregation in the first half of the 20th century by steering tax-supported housing to minority neighborhoods. And most also fault the government for doing too little to promote desegregation after passage of the 1968 law.

"There is a broad consensus that intentional discrimination is unlawful and immoral, but there's also a growing understanding that government policy and institutional structures have fostered segregation in this country," says Philip Tegeler, executive director of the Poverty & Race Research Action Council in Washington, a civil rights think tank. "But I don't think there's political will really to confront that legacy of segregation and do what needs to be done to reverse it."

The Fair Housing Act prohibits discrimination in the sale, rental or financing of housing on the basis of race, national origin or other characteristics. One provision, largely disregarded until now, according to critics, requires HUD to administer its programs in a manner that "affirmatively" furthers the law's goals.[3]

In a report issued in 2008 on the 40th anniversary of the law, a bipartisan commission convened by four major civil rights groups described HUD's enforcement efforts as "failing." The seven-member commission was co-chaired by two former HUD secretaries: Republican Jack Kemp and Democrat Henry Cisneros.[4]

In the Baltimore case, U.S. District Judge Marvin Garbis found HUD guilty of consigning the poor to the inner city instead of dispersing public housing throughout the region. "It is high time that HUD live up to its statutory mandate to consider the effect of its policies on the racial and socio-economic composition of the surrounding area," Garbis wrote in a stinging decision.[5]

Fair-housing advocates blame the private sector as well for the lagging progress in combating residential segregation. "We still have barriers in the real estate market," says Lisa Rice, executive vice president of the National Fair Housing Alliance (NFHA), a consortium of fair-housing groups. "We still have barriers in the lending market. We have barriers in the rental market."

Rice says housing authorities have mixed records in promoting racial integration. "Some housing authorities have not done what they should, and some are doing exactly what they should," she says." The "mosaic of housing authorities" in most cities also prevents breaking up urban seg-

Disability Complaints Most Common

Allegations of discrimination against people with disabilities represented more than half of complaints filed in 2014 with local, state and federal housing agencies, private fair-housing groups or the U.S. Department of Justice. Complaints alleging racial discrimination accounted for about 20 percent of the total.

Percentage of Housing Discrimination Complaints, by Type, 2014

(Percentage of complaints)

Disability 51.8%
Race 22.0%
Families with Children 11.0%
National Origin 10.6%
Sex 6.5%
Color 1.4%
Religion 1.3%
Other 7.8%

* Percentages add to more than 100 because some complaints involve multiple categories.

Source: "Where You Live Matters: 2015 Fair Housing Trends Report," National Fair Housing Alliance, April 30, 2015, p. 21, http://tinyurl.com/neuq462

regation and diversification in the suburbs, according to Jacob Vigdor, a professor of public policy and governance at the University of Washington in Seattle.

In the pre-civil rights era, the real estate industry openly blocked African-Americans from moving into predominantly white neighborhoods either as homeowners or renters. The federal government created a program in 1934 to promote homeownership by insuring home mortgages, thus lowering interest rates on the loans. But the program effectively blocked use of the loans in African-American neighborhoods by "redlining" those areas — designating them on maps in red as credit-unworthy. White Americans used those loans after World War II to create suburbs, which then adopted restrictive zoning laws that still effectively operate to make many homes unaffordable for lower-income black families.

On the positive side, residential segregation has been declining since fair housing became law nationwide. The number of metropolitan areas categorized by one of the leading experts as either highly or, in his terminology, "hypersegregated" has declined from 40 in 1970 to 21 in 2010. Still, Douglas Massey, a professor of sociology at

Princeton University, says one-third of all African-American city dwellers were living in highly or hypersegregated neighborhoods as of 2010.[6]

Despite the decline, "Many of our metro areas remain largely segregated," says Bryan Greene, a 25-year HUD veteran now serving as deputy assistant secretary for fair housing and equal opportunity.

Recent HUD enforcement actions indicate that tenants and homebuyers still encounter discrimination. HUD won settlements with housing authorities in Medina, Ohio, over alleged discrimination in administering the Section 8 voucher program and in Hazelton, Pa., over restrictive terms on would-be Hispanic tenants. The Wisconsin-based Associated Bank agreed in May to provide minority customers $200 million in mortgage loans to settle charges of redlining.[7]

Massey and others link the recent explosive clashes with police in Baltimore and Ferguson, Mo., to the isolation of African-Americans in cities. The riots and protests "have occurred in racially segregated, high-poverty neighborhoods," writes Paul Jargowsky, a professor of public policy at Rutgers University in Camden, N.J.[8]

The decline in segregation has coincided with a shift in public housing policies away from construction of large, publicly owned "projects." Instead, the government began providing the Section 8 subsidies for private rentals for the poor and tax credits to encourage developers to build affordable housing. The low-income housing tax credits (LIHTCs, pronounced lie-techs) required developers to build a certain percentage of units for low-income tenants, with rents no more than 30 percent of the area's median income.

Judge Garbis faulted HUD and the Baltimore housing authority for concentrating subsidized units in the inner city, even as the old-style projects in minority neighborhoods were being demolished.

In a case that reached the Supreme Court this year, fair-housing advocates in Dallas similarly challenged the Texas state housing agency for awarding tax credits primarily to developers who built in predominantly minority neighborhoods. The issue in *Texas Department of Housing and Community Affairs v. Inclusive Communities Project, Inc.* was whether to apply the Fair Housing Act not only to intentional discrimination but also to government policies that adversely affect minorities — so-called disparate impact.[9]

The justices appeared to have a strong interest in re-examining lower court decisions that had adopted the broader disparate-impact view of discrimination under the housing law. Twice the court had accepted cases posing the issue, in 2011 and 2012, but the cases settled instead. Fair-housing advocates were pleased in June when the court issued a 5–4 decision reaffirming the broader view of the law.

"Recognition of disparate-impact claims is consistent with the FHA's central purpose," Justice Anthony M. Kennedy wrote in the June 25 decision joined by the court's four liberal members. "It permits plaintiffs to counteract unconscious prejudices and disguised animus that escape easy classification as disparate treatment [intentional discrimination]."[10]

Just two weeks later, on July 8, HUD issued a long-awaited rule requiring state and local housing agencies to "affirmatively further" the fair-housing law's goals of banning housing discrimination and promoting housing desegregation. HUD Secretary Julián Castro called the rule "the most serious effort" ever to require communities to reduce housing segregation.[11]

As HUD implements the new regulation, the National Association of Housing and Redevelopment Officials (NAHRO), which opposed the rule, continues to criticize it. The Republican-controlled House of Representatives voted on June 9 to block implementation of the rule on grounds that it would threaten local control of housing issues.

Fair-housing advocates applaud the rule but continue to fault HUD for what they see as its lagging enforcement of the law. Federal programs are "perpetuating this long pattern of segregation," Tegeler says. HUD relies on state and local housing authorities and private fair-housing groups to bring most individual cases. Interestingly, just over 50 percent of complaints received in 2014 involved possible discrimination against persons with disabilities — coverage added to the law in 1988.

With racial issues in U.S. cities still roiling, here are some of the fair-housing questions being debated:

Are current government policies contributing to residential segregation?

Texas' Department of Housing and Community Affairs is responsible for approving applications from builders for the federal tax credits for building low-income housing. Over the 10-year period from 1999 to 2008, 92 percent of the tax-credit units built in the Dallas area were in mostly nonwhite neighborhoods. The state agency, applying a complex formula, approved just under half of the applications to build in areas with 90 percent minority populations but only 37 percent of the applications in areas with 90 percent or more white population.

U.S. District Judge Sidney Fitzwater made those findings as part of his March 2012 ruling that the state agency had failed to justify the concentration of housing built with tax credits in minority neighborhoods. The Supreme Court's decision in the case left those findings in place but sent the case back to Fitzwater for further proceedings.[12]

Demetria McCain, executive vice president of the Inclusive Communities Project (ICP), the plaintiff in the case, says the state used the tax credits "not only to recreate racial segregation but to make it worse. It will be a long time before there's even a modicum of units in white areas," she says.

Tegeler, with the poverty research group, says the Texas pattern can be found nationwide. "The vast majority of housing programs are steering housing to minority neighborhoods," he says.

In defending its policies, the Texas agency noted that federal law requires housing agencies to give a preference to tax-credit applicants proposing to build in low-income areas. The state said it was neutrally applying a set of factors in acting on applications for the tax credits, including a state provision that a project's financial viability was to be the major criterion. In his ruling, however, Fitzwater ordered the state to give additional points for projects in areas with good schools and to disqualify projects proposed in high-crime areas or near landfills.

Commenting after the Supreme Court decision, a lawyer with the Washington Legal Foundation, a conservative public-interest law firm that backed Texas in the case, continued to defend concentrating affordable housing in low-income neighborhoods. Cory Andrews, a senior legal counsel at the foundation, argued that it makes sense to allocate tax credits to lower- instead of higher-income communities — "where, presumably, fewer low-income minorities will stand to benefit. If the goal is to provide affordable housing to people," Andrews explains, "you would presumably provide it in places where those people live."[13]

In its comment after the ruling, the National Association of Housing and Redevelopment Officials emphasized portions of Kennedy's majority opinion upholding housing authorities' discretion in policy priorities. "Disparate-impact theory does not override the permissibility of basing decisions on market factors, issues that contribute to quality of life, or other legitimate business interests," NAHRO said in a written statement.

Housing advocates and experts across the ideological spectrum join in condemning the federal policies that cut African-Americans out of federally subsidized home loans in the 1930s and during the critical post-World War II years. In a recent appearance on NPR's "The Diane Rehm Show," Richard Rothstein, a research associate with the liberal Economic Policy Institute, noted that the Federal Housing Administration insured loans for homebuyers "on the explicit condition" that no loans be approved for African-Americans. On the same program, Edward Pinto, a housing expert with the conservative American Enterprise Institute (AEI), called the policies of that era "abhorrent."[14]

Even after passage of the Fair Housing Act, the federal government failed to develop policies to affirmatively promote desegregation, according to Rutgers professor

A joyous Sallie Sanders stands in front of her new home in Hamtramck, Mich., in March 2010, more than 50 years after her family was forced out of their rental home in the same suburban Detroit neighborhood. In 1971, a federal judge found that Hamtramck officials had used urban-renewal projects to raze black areas, displacing Sanders' family and hundreds of others. After years of delays following the ruling, the city has built more than a hundred homes for the children and grandchildren of the displaced Hamtramck residents who initially sued the city.

Jargowski. "They could have required every new suburban community to have some element of affordable housing," Jargowski says. "We could have desegregated as we suburbanized. That's not what happened."

HUD now has a critical role to play in getting state and local housing authorities to break down segregated housing patterns, according to Fred Underwood, director of diversity at the National Association of Realtors. "The proof is going to be in how HUD and the local communities handle it," says Underwood, who previously worked on fair-housing enforcement for HUD and a private civil rights group. The test, he says, is whether policies "really do focus on a more holistic approach. It's not simply enforcing the law."

HUD official Greene says the department's new rule is intended to help housing authorities comply with the law. "Communities need for HUD to inform them what is necessary to meet these requirements," he says. In explaining the rule, however, HUD Secretary Julián Castro said that cutting off funds to agencies that fail to comply would be a "last resort."[15]

Rice, of the National Fair Housing Alliance, says her organization is working with local agencies to develop policies to promote integration. "We are making

Federal Discrimination Investigations Decline

The Department of Housing and Urban Development (HUD) investigated 1,710 housing-discrimination complaints in 2014, roughly 20 percent of all those received. It was the fewest investigations since HUD was given additional enforcement authority under 1988 amendments to the Fair Housing Act. Investigations declined sharply from 1992 to 1997 as HUD increasingly referred complaints to state and local housing agencies for investigation.

(No. of HUD Investigations)

Investigations of Discrimination Complaints by HUD, 1990-2014

Source: "Where You Live Matters: 2015 Fair Housing Trends Report," National Fair Housing Alliance, April 30, 2015, p. 27, http://tinyurl.com/neuq462; data for the total number of cases provided by HUD

progress," Rice says. "The government is moving in the right direction." But institutional inertia and lack of funds hamper progress at the local level, she says.

"You're trying to change the way that these agencies do business," Rice says. "That's a heavy lift. That heavy lift becomes even heavier if those agencies don't have the funding to implement them."

Are current real estate and lending practices contributing to residential segregation?

New Jersey's largest savings bank agreed in September to pay $32.5 million to settle federal charges that it violated the Fair Housing Act by concentrating branches and mortgage loans in white neighborhoods while avoiding predominantly black and Hispanic areas.

"Redlining is not a vestige of the past," Vanita Gupta, head of the Justice Department's Civil Rights Division, told reporters in announcing the action against Hudson City Savings Bank.[16]

Rice, with the fair-housing alliance, is especially critical of what she sees as continued redlining of minority communities by mainstream lenders. "There's never been a time in U.S. history when the mainstream credit market has been the primary provider of credit for certain communities of color," she says.

"Redlining was very much practiced as official policy," HUD official Greene says. "Those kinds of practices don't go away overnight."

Minorities also continue to face discrimination at the hands of real estate brokers who screen racial and ethnic minorities from buying or renting in non-minority areas, according to a HUD-commissioned study released in 2013. Researchers from the Washington-based Urban Institute, a nonpartisan research organization, found that racial and ethnic minorities continue to face "subtle forms of housing denial" by real estate brokers and apartment owners, even though "blatant" acts of racial discrimination are declining.

"Discrimination still persists," HUD's then-secretary, Shaun Donovan, told reporters in releasing the study in mid-June.[17]

Minority communities also "got flooded with subprime loans" offered by so-called predatory lenders during the housing bubble and subsequent financial crisis of 2007–09, according to Gregory Squires, a professor of sociology and public policy at George Washington University in Washington, D.C. "And minority communities were hardest hit by foreclosures when the housing bubble burst."

In response, Pete Mills, a senior vice president with the Mortgage Bankers Association, says the industry has taken "dramatic steps . . . in strengthening its fair-lending performance," and the government has "ample tools" to ensure compliance with nondiscriminatory lending laws. But Mills says credit-tightening rules adopted after the financial crisis now put lenders at risk of running afoul of HUD's disparate-impact rule.

The regulations require lenders to closely examine factors such as a borrower's income and debt levels, which indicate an applicant's ability to repay, Mills explains. "The unintended consequence, he says, "is that these factors are often correlated by race, ethnicity and some of the other prohibited factors."

Real estate brokers often are caught up in small-scale HUD enforcement actions, many of them resulting from the use of black and white "testers" to uncover different treatment of would-be customers based on race. In one recent example, the Philadelphia real estate firm Brotman Enterprise agreed in June 2014 to pay $25,000 in damages to settle charges that it referred the white testers posing as customers to a "safe" neighborhood while the supposed customers who were black were shown properties in a less desirable, high-crime area.

To conduct such testing, HUD contracts with private groups such as the National Fair Housing Alliance (NFHA), which filed the complaint in the Brotman case. "Testing remains one of our most effective tools for exposing unlawful housing discrimination," Greene said in a release announcing the settlement.[18]

The 2013 study was based on similar testing in 28 metropolitan areas. It found that African-Americans, Hispanics and Asians seeking apartments to rent were told about or shown fewer units than white testers. Among would-be homebuyers, African-Americans and Asians were shown fewer houses than whites, with no difference between Hispanics and whites.

Rice, the NFHA executive director, says discrimination by real estate agents is hard to detect. "It's discrimination with a smile," Rice says. "It's no one telling you that they're not going to service you because you're a person of color. It's discrimination that happens behind cloak and veil."

On the industry side, National Association of Realtors' official Underwood acknowledges that violations still occur and says violators should be punished. "There is a strong commitment to eliminating discrimination in the market," he says.

Underwood says, however, that the incidence of "bad actors" is decreasing. "The focus on one particular point of the transaction obviously will uncover problems as long as problems exist in our society," Underwood says. "The question is how impactful are those situations."

Rice acknowledges that the real estate industry is itself increasingly diversified and calls the Realtors' commitment to fair housing "genuine." But she says fair-housing enforcement is difficult because victims may not recognize discrimination when it occurs or may simply move on to another broker without ever filing a complaint.

She agrees with HUD that using testers is an important tool, but complains that Congress does not provide enough funding for the purpose. "There is a funding problem," Rice says. "Congress doesn't want to appropriate the funds necessary to deal with this particular issue."

Housing activists in New York City hold a "die-in" on Sept. 17, 2015, to demand more affordable housing options for the homeless and the poor. Public-housing policies in the United States have shifted away from the construction of large, publicly owned "projects." Instead, the federal government began providing Section 8 subsidies for private rentals for the poor and tax credits to encourage developers to build affordable housing.

The Office of Fair Housing and Equal Opportunity budget for fiscal 2015 was $63.2 million — down from a peak of $71.3 million in 2011, according to a spokesman in the agency's press office.

Can local officials do more to reduce racial segregation in housing?

Crystal Wade had hoped to use a federal housing voucher to move out of her run-down townhouse in Ferguson, the predominantly black St. Louis suburb roiled by police-citizen tensions over the past year, and into a better neighborhood elsewhere in St. Louis County. But after looking all over the county this summer for a big enough place that was affordable and available to tenants paying with Section 8 vouchers, she came up mostly empty.

Wade, who lives with her boyfriend and three daughters, ended up with a house in somewhat better condition but in another racially segregated neighborhood with a higher crime rate, although one with fewer vacant lots. Boyfriend Bryant Goston was philosophical about the move. "I can adapt, yeah," he told a *New York Times* reporter. "Because, to be honest, that's what all black people have to do."[19]

Many housing policy experts on both sides of the ideological fence are similarly downbeat about the short-term potential for desegregating U.S. cities. "Inserting subsidized housing into suburban neighborhoods is going to be a drop in the bucket," says Peter Salins, a professor of political science at Stony Brook University in New York and a senior fellow at the Manhattan Institute, a conservative think tank.

"Massive investments went into creating segregated housing," Sherilyn Ifill, president and director-counsel of the NAACP Legal Defense and Educational Fund, said on "The Diane Rehm Show." "You cannot undo the damage simply by no longer making those investments."

The Section 8 housing voucher program — now officially called the Housing Choice Voucher Program — has built-in limitations, with a long waiting list — 25,000 in the city of St. Louis — and a $2,200-per-month rental cap, which limits options for finding housing in better neighborhoods. In addition, landlords are generally under no obligation to accept Section 8 tenants. The city of St. Louis has a law requiring landlords to accept Section 8 vouchers, but the county does not.

Some housing experts also suggest that many people in minority neighborhoods are reluctant to move from familiar surroundings into majority-white neighborhoods. "While expanding choice has a lot of appeal," University of Washington professor Vigdor explains, "it doesn't necessarily mean they're going to make different choices."

The researchers who studied the Baltimore program argue, however, that "intensive counseling" can overcome that reluctance. "Residential preferences can shift over time as a function of living in higher-opportunity neighborhoods," they write.[20]

Political obstacles, including resistance from majority-white neighborhoods, may also limit the potential for desegregation. "If you allow this to be a purely local decision about where to put these projects," Vigdor says, "there's just going to be a natural gravitation toward neighborhoods that offer the least amount of resistance."

Jargowsky, the Rutgers professor, says HUD itself has lacked the political will to force desegregation on communities. "They work so much with the housing authority, and the housing authority works with the developers," he says. "Over time, many of the programs that were designed to make housing more dispersed, they ended up replicating the existing patterns."

HUD official Greene concedes that the statutory command to "affirmatively further fair housing" is "probably the greatest unfinished business" at the department. "It's a new rule but not a new requirement," he explains, citing the language from the original 1968 law. "HUD had an obligation to affirmatively further fair housing, and by extension recipients of federal financial assistance from HUD had an obligation." The new regulation, Greene says, "is intended to make sure that communities know the path forward and to help communities make sure that they're dotting their i's and crossing their t's." But the housing authorities' national organization views the rule less favorably.

In comments submitted to HUD in mid-August, NAHRO said the new rule and the related "Assessment of Fair Housing" tool, which housing authorities must complete to show their compliance with the law, create "administrative burdens" while ignoring local community conditions. "Program participants are being pressured to set goals that do not fully reflect the needs and priorities of their communities and ignore the real-world constraints under which they operate," NAHRO argued.

At the Supreme Court, NAHRO joined a brief that said housing authorities risked facing legal liability whether they placed affordable housing in minority neighborhoods or in majority-white communities. NFHA executive director Rice says the fear is misplaced, however.

"You have to have a multipronged approach to achieving fair housing," Rice says. "The law makes it clear it's not either-or," she says. "You have do both."

Greene agrees. "HUD has steadfastly maintained that communities need to pursue a balanced approach," he says.

BACKGROUND
Separate Worlds

White and black Americans have lived mostly in separate worlds from the post-slavery era until at least the mid-20th century. After slavery was outlawed, residential segregation resulted from law, custom and market forces as well as, significantly, mid-20th-century federal policies promoting homeownership and urban renewal that benefited whites but significantly disadvantaged blacks. The passage of the Fair Housing Act in 1968 made racial discrimination illegal, but racially identifiable neighborhoods continued to be the norm in U.S. cities and suburbs.

African-American slaves lived side by side with white slave owners, but they had no legal rights and gained neither income nor wealth from the fruits of their labor. Despite the abolition of slavery in 1865, most blacks in the South continued to live in a form of indentured servitude, many as sharecroppers on the onetime slave plantations. They still effectively were denied legal, political or economic rights. Few African-Americans lived in the North before the Civil War, and immediately after the war their numbers grew only slightly. Some migrated westward along with white settlers seeking land and new lives in the American frontier.

After emancipation, some self-segregated themselves, establishing about 60 all-black townships across the country.[21] Two of those communities were destroyed by white rioters in the early 1920s following accusations of interracial sexual assaults. The Greenwood district in Tulsa, Okla. — proudly proclaimed as "the Black Wall Street" — was burned to the ground in a 15-hour assault that lasted from May 31 to June 1, 1921. The official death toll of 36 is believed to be low. Two years later, the all-black community of Rosewood, Fla., was razed in an incident known as the Rosewood massacre. The official death count of six blacks and two whites is similarly thought to be low.[22]

In the 20th century, the lure of jobs in the industrialized North and Midwest, combined with the harshness of the Jim Crow era, led more than 6 million African-Americans to move out of the South in a phenomenon now called the Great Migration.[23] But law, custom and market forces continued to limit black Americans' ability to choose where to live.

Some cities enacted ordinances segregating neighborhoods by race — ostensibly to preserve racial harmony — although the Supreme Court ruled such ordinances unconstitutional in a 1917 Louisville, Ky., case.[24] Smaller communities — "sundown towns" — enforced, by custom, rules requiring African-Americans to leave by nightfall.[25] And real estate firms continued to use racial covenants, contractual terms that prohibited the sale of a property to African-Americans or, in some instances, to Jews. Only in 1948 did the Supreme Court rule that those restrictions could not be enforced in court.[26]

Racial segregation in housing also was enforced by anti-black intimidation and in some instances violent confrontations. A riot broke out in the all-white Chicago suburb of Cicero on July 11–12, 1951, after an

Demonstrators at U.S. District Court in Manhattan on Aug. 8, 1988, protest a judge's decision to heavily fine Yonkers, N.Y., because its City Council refused to accept his housing desegregation order. Judge Leonard Sand ordered Yonkers to build public housing for minority residents in a white section, but the city resisted right up to the brink of municipal bankruptcy. More than 200 new townhouses for low-income minority families were finally opened for occupancy in 1992.

African-American family moved into an apartment building. There were no deaths, but the building suffered at least $20,000 in damage. A Cook County grand jury indicted the apartment owner for inciting a riot, but the charges were eventually dropped. The police chief and two officers were convicted in federal court for failing to protect the family's rights.[27]

The federal government undertook major policies to promote homeownership as part of President Franklin D. Roosevelt's New Deal, but the policies fortified patterns of residential segregation. The federal Home Ownership Loan Corp.'s practice of designating predominantly minority neighborhoods in red as uncreditworthy created the new word "redlining." The Federal Housing Administration and Veterans Administration (VA) adopted the same practice, limiting the availability of federally insured home mortgages for African-Americans. Federal support for urban renewal in the post-World War II era cleared predominantly minority slums in many cities, but the displaced minorities got little by way of relocation assistance. Meanwhile, the real estate and credit industries continued many of the practices that disadvantaged would-be African-American tenants or homebuyers even after the demise of legally enforceable racial covenants.[28]

The midcentury civil rights revolution brought housing discrimination issues to the fore. President John F. Kennedy

CHRONOLOGY

1930s–1950s *Racial segregation in housing is legal, widespread and buttressed by federal policy.*

1933–34 Federal government establishes home loan assistance programs; "redlining" limits loans to African-Americans.

1948 In a landmark ruling, Supreme Court holds that courts cannot enforce racial covenants on real estate.

1951 A race riot breaks out in Cicero, Ill., when an African-American family moves into an apartment building, drawing worldwide condemnation after being broadcast on television.

1960s–1970s *Government moves to bar racial discrimination in housing.*

1962 President John F. Kennedy issues executive order prohibiting racial discrimination in housing owned or financed by federal government.

1968 President Lyndon B. Johnson signs Fair Housing Act into law one week after assassination of the Rev. Martin Luther King Jr. . . . Supreme Court says racial discrimination in housing had been illegal under Civil Rights Act of 1866.

1974 Fair Housing Act is amended to prohibit gender-based discrimination. . . . Equal Credit Opportunity Act broadly prohibits discrimination by lenders. . . . Section 8 program is established to provide subsidies for low-income renters.

1975 Home Mortgage Disclosure Act is enacted to gather demographic data from mortgage lenders.

1977 Community Reinvestment Act requires federally regulated financial institutions to meet the credit needs of their communities.

1980s–1990s *Congress strengthens fair-housing enforcement.*

1985 Federal judge orders Yonkers, N.Y., to build public housing for minorities in a predominantly white neighborhood; the homes open for occupancy in 1992.

1986 Low-Income Housing Tax Credit program is created under the Tax Reform Act of 1986 to help finance construction of low-income housing.

1988 Fair Housing Act is amended to cover familial status, disabilities; amendments also strengthen Department of Housing and Urban Development's (HUD) enforcement authority.

1995 Public housing tenants sue HUD and Baltimore officials for concentrating public housing in minority neighborhoods; similar suits are filed in more than a dozen cities during the decade.

2000–Present *Residential segregation declines overall, but persists in many U.S. cities.*

2005 Federal judge finds HUD guilty in Baltimore case of failing to disperse affordable housing throughout the metropolitan region.

2008 Bipartisan commission calls for reorienting federal housing programs to help minorities move to less racially and economically segregated communities.

2009 Federal judge says Westchester County, N.Y., misrepresented desegregation efforts in seeking federal funds.

2012 Federal judge faults Texas housing agency for awarding tax credits for low-income housing mostly in minority neighborhoods in Dallas; state's appeal eventually reaches Supreme Court. . . . Wells Fargo agrees to pay $175 million to settle charges that it discriminated against minorities in its mortgage lending practices.

2013 A HUD-commissioned study finds racial screening by real estate brokers is still widespread.

2015 Supreme Court upholds "disparate impact" liability for housing policies that result in segregation. . . . HUD issues "Affirmatively Furthering Fair Housing" rule to enforce long-standing obligation under 1968 law; National Association of Housing and Redevelopment Officials calls for rule to be scrapped. . . . New Jersey's largest savings bank agrees to pay more than $30 million to settle "redlining" charges. . . . Judge in Dallas housing case sets briefing schedule for further proceedings.

issued an executive order in 1962 directing federal agencies to prevent racial discrimination in housing owned or financed by the federal government. It took six more years for Congress to pass and President Lyndon B. Johnson to sign the Fair Housing Act. The legislation stalled even after the passage of the omnibus Civil Rights Act of 1964 and the Voting Rights Act of 1965, but Johnson helped push it across the congressional finish line just one week after the assassination of the Rev. Martin Luther King Jr. in April 1968. King had helped dramatize the issue by focusing on fair housing as one of the goals after he allied with the grassroots Chicago Freedom Movement, beginning in late 1965.[29]

The Fair Housing Act prohibited private discrimination in housing on the basis of race, religion or national origin, with some exceptions — for example, for small boarding houses. It included a provision requiring local governments to affirmatively further integration, but gave HUD only limited enforcement authority. In an ironic postscript, the Supreme Court ruled two months later that private discrimination in housing had been illegal for more than a century under the Civil Rights Act of 1866, which guaranteed blacks the same contract rights as white persons.[30]

Slow Changes

Congress and the federal judiciary expanded fair-housing protections under federal law through a succession of statutes and judicial decisions beginning in the 1970s. Over time, enforcement combined with voluntary compliance and affirmative efforts by some local housing authorities to reduce black-white residential segregation somewhat, but most African-Americans still lived in highly segregated metropolitan neighborhoods. And resistance to integration persisted, as demonstrated by one high-profile clash over public housing in Yonkers, N.Y.

The Supreme Court set the stage for strengthening fair-housing enforcement by interpreting the job discrimination provisions of the Civil Rights Act of 1964 to cover not only intentional discrimination but also employment practices that had an adverse or disparate impact based on race. The 1971 ruling in *Griggs v. Duke Power Co.* allowed a civil rights challenge to a supposedly race-neutral job requirement for a high school diploma — without adequate justification — based on its adverse impact on African-Americans. Over the next four decades, federal appeals courts uniformly held that practices by housing authorities, real estate firms or lenders could

similarly be challenged under a theory of disparate-impact liability without proof of intentional discrimination.

Earlier, however, President Richard M. Nixon had squelched a politically treacherous plan by his housing secretary, George Romney, to use HUD funds to force cities, counties and states to try to break up residential segregation. Romney ordered HUD officials to withhold grants for water, sewer or highway projects from jurisdictions with policies that fostered segregation. Once opposition reached the Oval Office, Nixon ordered the policy rescinded in a 1972 memo to his domestic policy director, John Ehrlichman.[31]

Congress expanded the Fair Housing Act in 1974 to prohibit discrimination on the basis of sex and again in 1988 to prohibit discrimination on the basis of family status or disabilities. HUD used the sex and family status provisions as the basis of a non-statutory regulation issued in 2012 to prohibit discrimination on the basis of sexual orientation or gender identity in HUD-assisted housing.[32] The disabilities provision required builders to construct new, multifamily dwellings to meet specified adaptability and accessibility requirements. The 1988 law also authorized HUD to file discrimination complaints, gave individuals more time to file an administrative complaint or a lawsuit and somewhat expanded available remedies. Significantly for the eventual Supreme Court case, the law included language that appeared to adopt judicial decisions recognizing disparate-impact liability under the law.

HUD's major low-income housing programs began taking shape in the 1970s and '80s. The Housing and Community Development Act of 1976 replaced an existing rent-subsidy program with the Section 8 voucher program. Qualified low-income tenants found their own housing but had to pay no more than 30 percent of their adjusted gross income for rent; public housing authorities made up the difference with direct payment to landlords. A decade later, Congress aimed at the supply side of the issue by authorizing, as part of the Tax Reform Act of 1986, dollar-for-dollar tax credits for developers to build or rehabilitate affordable housing. Over time, it was estimated that the tax credits were responsible for 90 percent of the affordable housing built in the country.

Meanwhile, Congress strengthened fair-housing protections with three laws aimed at preventing discrimination in the mortgage industry. The Equal Credit Opportunity Act, enacted in 1974, prohibited discrimination in the

Fewer Metro Areas Seens as "Hypersegregated"

All-white neighborhoods "extinct," but inner-city poverty worsens.

Residential segregation along racial lines has declined in the United States since passage of the Fair Housing Act in 1968, but experts who have crunched the numbers disagree on exactly how much.

One leading researcher using 2010 census figures counts 21 U.S. metropolitan areas as "hypersegregated," or extremely segregated, down from 40 in 1970.

"Despite evidence of progress in many metropolitan areas, therefore, the United States has not become a race-blind society," concluded Princeton University sociology professor Douglas Massey. The United States "has not been able to eradicate hypersegregation from its urban areas."[1] Massey defined the degree of residential segregation in an area using a methodology that weighs several criteria, rather than setting specific percentages of people of varying races.

Two other researchers, using a different methodology to analyze the same census figures, proclaimed "the end of the segregated century."[2] Harvard economics professor Edward Glaeser and University of Washington public policy professor Jacob Vigdor say all-white neighborhoods in nonrural areas used to be common but are now "effectively extinct." The scholars, affiliated with the free market-oriented Manhattan Institute, cite as evidence the migration to the suburbs of higher-income African-Americans.

"There's been a dramatic change in the number of neighborhoods where you find exactly zero African-American residents," says Vigdor. "These used to be very common and are very rare now."

Massey and co-author Jonathan Tannen, a PhD student in urban and population policy at Princeton, say 26 percent of the nation's African-Americans live in hypersegregated metropolitan areas, compared with 47 percent in 1970.

Residential segregation can be quantified in five different ways. The most commonly used method calculates the relative number of blacks and whites who would have to exchange neighborhoods to achieve an even distribution. On average, in the eight most segregated cities, seven out of every 10 blacks and seven out of every 10 whites would have to swap neighborhoods to have an even residential distribution. Other methods calculate the relative isolation of African-Americans, the degree of clustering around racially defined neighborhoods, the relative amounts of space occupied by whites and blacks and the degree of racial concentration around the metropolitan center.

In Massey's calculation, eight cities are hypersegregated on all five of those measures and 13 others on four of the five. Together, those 21 cities account for about one-third of African-Americans living in metropolitan areas. Six of the eight most segregated cities are in the Midwest's Rust Belt: Milwaukee, Detroit, St. Louis, Chicago, Cleveland and Flint, Mich. The two others also are once heavily industrialized cities: Birmingham, Ala., and Baltimore.[3]

Hispanics and Asians have not experienced anywhere near the high degree of residential segregation from whites experienced by African-Americans, according to Massey. The 2010 census figures show that three-fourths of urban

approval of credit applications on the basis of race, sex national origin, marital status or receipt of public assistance. Adopted a year later, the Home Mortgage Disclosure Act required lenders to disclose data on loan applications and approvals to address the concern about credit shortages in some urban neighborhoods. The Community Reinvestment Act, passed in 1977, added an affirmative obligation for federally regulated financial institutions to address financing needs of communities they served.

Over time, Americans generally came to accept the principle of fair housing, but concrete steps to integrate neighborhoods still stirred controversy. In one dramatic

example, a federal judge provoked a political standoff in Yonkers, an exurban area just north of the Bronx in New York; Judge Leonard Sand found the city guilty of discrimination in 1985 because all public housing was sited in a small, predominantly African-American section. Sand ordered the city to build public housing for minority residents in a white section, but the city resisted right up to the brink of municipal bankruptcy. The 230 townhouses were finally opened for occupancy in 1992; they now house about 200 low-income minority families.[33]

The nation's demographics were changing rapidly in the late 20th century because of increased immigration

Hispanics and 100 percent of Asian urbanites are in cities with moderate or low segregation. Those figures "underscor[e] the continued distinctiveness of black segregation in metropolitan America," Massey and Tannen write.

Another leading expert on the issue criticizes Glaeser's and Vigdor's decision to use the migration of Asians and Hispanics into predominantly black neighborhoods to suggest reduced segregation. "They calculated segregation as black versus non-black," says Paul Jargowsky, a professor of public policy at Rutgers University in Camden, N.J. "I feel that when we're talking about segregation, what we're really concerned about is how segregated a particular minority group is from the majority."

All of the experts agree that despite reduced segregation, predominantly black neighborhoods are suffering from increased concentration of poverty. "Once the barriers to free housing choice were lessened, the first to leave these neighborhoods were the more affluent," Vigdor says.

Jargowsky calculated that the number of people living in high-poverty ghettos, barrios and slums has nearly doubled since 2000 — from 7.2 million to 13.8 million today. "We are witnessing a nationwide return of concentrated poverty that is racial in nature," he wrote in an article for The Century Foundation, a liberal think tank in Washington.[4]

In their article, Massey and Tannen say poverty is particularly concentrated in hypersegregated areas. "Owing to the important role that it plays in concentrating poverty," they wrote, "segregation is critical to understanding racial stratification in the United States today."

— *Kenneth Jost*

[1]See Douglas S. Massey and Jonathan Tannen, "A Research Note on Trends in Black Hypersegregation," *Demography*, Population

Harvard economics professor Edward Glaeser contends all-white neighborhoods in nonrural areas, once common, are now "effectively extinct." Other experts disagree, saying many cities are still extremely segregated.

Association of America, June 2015 [published online March 20, 2015], http://tinyurl.com/odta3bf.

[2]Edward Glaeser and Jacob Vigdor, "The End of the Segregated Century: Racial Separation in America's Neighborhoods, 1890-2010," *Civic Report, No. 66*, Manhattan Institute, January 2012, http://tinyurl.com/7sz2hjh.

[3]For a complete list of the cities designated as "hypersegregated" in 1970 and in 2010, see Tanvi Misra, "America Has Half as Many Hypersegregated Metros as It Did in 1970," *City Lab* (blog of *TheAtlantic.com*), May 21, 2015, http://tinyurl.com/oca9f7s.

[4]Paul A. Jargowsky, "Architecture of Segregation: Civil Unrest, the Concentration of Poverty, and Public Policy," The Century Foundation, Aug. 7, 2015, http://tinyurl.com/q2uzvyt.

from Latin America and Asia under liberalized country-of-origin rules enacted by the landmark Immigration and Nationality Act of 1965.

With the Fair Housing Act in effect, the newly arriving Latino- and Asian-Americans encountered less overt discrimination than immigrants had experienced in the past; some found homes in predominantly white neighborhoods, but many moved into predominantly black neighborhoods. By the end of the century, black-white residential segregation had also decreased, but only slowly. The number of "hypersegregated" metropolitan areas in the United States declined from 40 as of 1970 to 21 in

2010, according to Massey, and within those areas, the degree of black-white segregation had fallen only slightly.[34]

Unsettled Times

Racial segregation in housing decreased further in the 21st century, but migration patterns combined with an economic downturn to leave many cities with significantly higher degrees of concentrated poverty in predominantly minority neighborhoods. Fair-housing advocates complained about lagging federal enforcement under President George W. Bush and about the disproportionate effect that the 2007–09 housing bust had on minority

Pet-Policy Dispute Lands in Court

Tenants with disabilities have right to "support animals."

Armed with a prescription from her doctor, Chelsy Walsh called one of the owners of her Sioux Falls, S.D., apartment complex in January 2014 to say she would be buying a dog as a "support animal" for her mental health. But Linda Christensen told Walsh that animals were not allowed at the Viking Villas and warned Walsh that she would have trouble finding another place to live because she was receiving a federal subsidy under the Section 8 voucher program.

Today, the seemingly everyday landlord-tenant dispute over pets is literally a federal case after the Department of Housing and Urban Development (HUD) charged Linda and her husband Robert with violating the Fair Housing Act by discriminating against Walsh on the basis of her disability. The Christensens are disputing the charge, which is pending in a federal court in South Dakota.

Congress expanded the landmark 1968 law in 1988 by also prohibiting discrimination based on disabilities. The law initially prohibited discrimination in the sale, rental or financing of housing on the basis of race, national origin or other characteristic. Today, disability-related claims account for just over half of the Fair Housing Act complaints received by HUD, state or local agencies or nongovernmental organizations that fight housing discrimination.[1] A majority of the complaints — 57 percent — stem from allegations

that landlords or apartment owners failed to make "reasonable accommodation" for individuals with disabilities, as the law requires, according to HUD statistics.[2]

"I don't think that housing providers even this far after the Fair Housing Act have totally realized that people with disabilities are a protected class and they can't be discriminated against," says Kenneth Shiotani, a senior staff attorney with the Washington-based National Disability Rights Network, an umbrella organization for state and local disability rights groups.

The National Apartment Association says it "strongly supports" the right of tenants with disabilities to request reasonable accommodations, but says requests for emotional support animals are "a particular area of concern." "A lack of clarity in the law . . . allows for abuse and imposes an unfair burden on property owners," the association told *CQ Researcher* in a written statement supplied on request.

Walsh, who suffers from post-traumatic stress disorder and bipolar disorder, formalized her phone call with a written request a week later and then filed an administrative complaint with HUD. In June she bought a seven-year-old, 10.5-pound shih tzu-lhasa apso mix.

Robert Christensen allegedly responded by asking Walsh to sign a "Companion Animal/Pet Policy Agreement"

neighborhoods. Those groups cheered, however, when the Supreme Court in June upheld the broader, disparate-impact definition of housing discrimination and HUD issued its rule in July detailing local governments' affirmative duty to promote integrated housing.

The number of discrimination complaints filed by HUD "spiraled downward" during the Bush administration, according to data in the 2008 report of the private National Commission on Fair Housing, a bipartisan group convened by civil rights organizations and headed by two former HUD secretaries: Democrat Henry Cisneros and Republican Jack Kemp. The number had fallen under President Bill Clinton from 125 in fiscal 1995 to 88 in fiscal 2001, and then fell sharply under Bush to only 31 in fiscal 2007. Data from the fair-housing alliance showed

the number rose under President Obama to a peak of 55 in fiscal 2011 but fell by more than half to only 27 in fiscal 2014. Both reports faulted HUD for its slow pace in processing complaints.[35]

Meanwhile, federal judges had signaled impatience with housing desegregation efforts in two high-profile cases on the East Coast. In his 2005 ruling in the Baltimore case, Garbis accused HUD of "effectively wearing blinders" by placing low-income housing only in minority neighborhoods. Four years later, U.S. District Judge Denise Cote faulted suburban Westchester County, N.Y., for misrepresenting its desegregation efforts when applying for federal funds by leaving the location of low-income housing up to individual villages and towns. The county settled the case six months later by promising to site low-income that included inspection and property damage provisions and allowed the owners to revoke permission for the animal at their "sole discretion." Walsh considered the agreement overly burdensome and moved out.

After failing to conciliate the dispute, HUD turned the case over to the Justice Department, which filed the federal suit on Sept. 15 seeking damages for Walsh and an injunction to prevent the Christensens from future discrimination on the basis of disability.

Michael Paulson, an attorney representing the Christensens, says the dispute resulted from "a communication issue" with Walsh. "My clients have done absolutely all that they can to make reasonable accommodations," Paulson says. The lawyer also agrees with the apartment owners' association that the disabilities provision is subject to abuse because the language is vague and the requirements for proving a disability too lax.

Requests for service or emotional support animals are "a fairly routine problem," according to Shiotani, a 10-year veteran with the disability rights network. Under the law, tenants with disabilities cannot be denied permission or charged a fee for having a service or support animal live with them. Among other examples, HUD's website explanation of the law says apartment owners cannot refuse to rent because they are uncomfortable with an individual's disability and can be required to make such accommodations as a reserved parking space or some structural modifications at the resident's expense. [3]

The HUD summary also explains that most multifamily buildings constructed after March 13, 1991, must meet seven design and construction requirements, including accessible entrances and common spaces. Individual units must have "usable doors" — that is, wide enough for a wheelchair; "usable" kitchens and bathrooms; reinforced bathroom walls and accessible light switches and other controls. Construction-related complaints account for under 5 percent of all cases, according to HUD statistics. [4]

The increasing number of disability-related fair-housing complaints reflects the effect of education and outreach efforts by HUD itself and advocacy organizations, according to Bryan Greene, HUD's deputy assistant secretary for fair housing.

"Discrimination against people with disabilities remains much more in the open than many other forms of discrimination," he says. "It's very important for people with disabilities that you stand up for your fair-housing rights."

— *Kenneth Jost*

[1] "Where You Live Matters: 2015 Fair Housing Trends Report," National Fair Housing Alliance, April 30, 2015, http://tinyurl.com/neuq462.

[2] "Annual Report on Fair Housing," U.S. Department of Housing and Urban Development, November 2014, p. 6, http://tinyurl.com/o4mxboh.

[3] See "Disability Rights in Housing," U.S. Department of Housing and Urban Development, undated, http://tinyurl.com/3ujp6fx.

[4] "Annual Report on Fair Housing," *op. cit.*

housing in predominantly white neighborhoods, but the county is now facing possible penalties for failing to follow through on the accord.[36]

The big housing story of the early 21st century, however, was the foreclosure crisis, brought on by the bursting of a decades-long housing bubble. African-Americans were hurt the worst, according to experts and advocacy groups, because mainstream lenders made them targets for risky subprime loans. In the 2008 report, the national commission charged that "predatory lenders" had steered minority homebuyers into subprime loans, with appealing but ultimately risky features, even when they could have qualified with mainstream mortgage lenders. The commission urged a federal crackdown on unscrupulous lenders. In 2012, Wells Fargo, the nation's largest mortgage lender, agreed to pay $175 million to settle charges that its independent brokers discriminated against black and Hispanic borrowers.[37]

Over time, the Supreme Court generally upheld broad applications of the Fair Housing Act — for example, in a 1982 decision allowing "testers" to sue real estate firms for racial screening.[38] The court's unsuccessful moves in the 2011 and 2012 to reconsider the question of disparate-impact liability stirred fears that the conservative majority was about to limit the law to intentional discrimination. Civil rights forces instead applauded the 5–4 decision, issued on June 25, to uphold the broader definition.

The Legal Defense Fund's Ifill called the ruling "a crucial victory for all Americans who care about the continuing impact of segregation." But Roger Clegg,

Getty Images/*The Washington Post*/Joshua Lott

Tracy Carrithers and Carla Cathion search for suitable rental housing in Chicago on June 27, 2015. The two women planned to pay their rent with vouchers from the federal government's Section 8 program for low-income families. The program has built-in limitations, including long waiting lists and a $2,200-per-month rental cap, which limits options for finding housing in better neighborhoods. In addition, landlords generally are not obligated to accept Section 8 vouchers.

general counsel of the conservative Center for Equal Opportunity, warned the decision would encourage "race-based decision-making in the housing area, exactly what the Fair Housing Act was meant to prohibit."[39]

Two weeks after the Supreme Court decision, HUD announced its long-under-development rule aimed at strengthening the requirement that state and local agencies affirmatively reduce residential segregation. Speaking to *The New York Times*, HUD Secretary Castro stressed cooperation over confrontation as the goal in dealing with local agencies. Enforcement "is possible," Castro said, "but our preference is to work cooperatively and steadfastly with communities."[40]

The Republican-controlled House of Representatives voted 239–191 on June 9 to try to block implementation of the rule, and Republicans and conservatives renewed criticism of the rule after it was issued. The Senate has not acted on the House measure.

Pinto, of the American Enterprise Institute, called the rule "the latest of a series of attempts by HUD to social-engineer the American people." But Marc Morial, president of the National Urban League, a New York-based civil

rights organization, called it "a serious effort by the administration to, in effect, enforce one of the legacy civil rights laws."

CURRENT SITUATION
Stepping Up Efforts

HUD's fair-housing enforcement unit is stepping up efforts to desegregate U.S. cities, even as its staffing has fallen to historically low levels and it is outsourcing many of its cases to state and local civil rights agencies.

"Our numbers and staff have been declining," says Greene, second in command in HUD's Office of Fair Housing and Equal Opportunity. "We do have a great challenge ahead of us, and it's very much on the resource effort."

"There is a funding problem," says NFHA Executive Director Rice. "Congress doesn't want to appropriate the funds necessary to deal with this particular issue."

Congress authorized funds in fiscal 2015 for only 516 employees at the fair-housing office, the lowest number since HUD was given additional enforcement authority in 1988 and far below the 750 recommended by the Kemp-Cisneros commission in 2008, according to NFHA's most recent annual report. The understaffing "has increased the number of aged cases, delaying justice for victims of discrimination and resolution for respondents," the alliance states.[41]

The alliance also faults as "insufficient" the funding for HUD's Fair Housing Initiatives Program, which awards grants to private organizations for education, outreach, testing, investigation and mediation. During the Obama administration, funding for the program has risen from $27.5 million in fiscal 2009 to $40.1 million in fiscal 2015 — far short of the $75.4 million in applications from fair-housing groups in fiscal 2009. The amount still is insufficient to "monitor local housing markets or address the overall incidence of housing discrimination," the alliance says.[42]

Greene says present-day discrimination is more subtle and thus harder to detect or even recognize than the blatant refusal to sell or rent in the days before the Fair Housing Act. "Our tools to uncover that kind of discrimination have to be sharper today," he says.

Should Congress block HUD's new fair-housing rule?

YES
Rep. Paul Gosar, R-Ariz.

Written for *CQ Researcher*, November 2015

As President Obama reaches the end of his second term, he has made it clear that his top priority during his waning days is to further his far-left political agenda by forcing big government programs on the American people. The calling card of this administration has been to use overreaching executive mandates and regulations to force American families, businesses and consumers into complying with its misguided utopian ideology.

The Affirmatively Furthering Fair Housing (AFFH) rule, introduced by the Department of Housing and Urban Development (HUD) this past July, is no different. This overreaching new rule is an attempt to extort communities into giving up control of local zoning decisions and reengineer the makeup of our neighborhoods. Important federal housing grants will be stripped away if communities do not fit the racial and economic standards concocted by D.C. bureaucrats. Just as the president has used the Department of Justice, Internal Revenue Service and Department of Homeland Security as a political weapon, he has now expanded his arsenal to include HUD as a way of punishing neighborhoods that don't fall in line with his liberal view of where Americans should live.

Let me be clear: This new Washington mandate has nothing to do with race, as housing discrimination has been illegal for more than 40 years. The 1968 Fair Housing Act already makes discrimination illegal in the "sale, rental and financing of dwellings based on race, religion, sex or national origin." Apparently, it's not enough to provide everyone with equal opportunity in housing matters. What the Obama administration wants is equal outcomes, and the only possible way to produce this is for the federal government to force itself upon local jurisdictions.

Similar to other big-government policies from this administration, the flawed AFFH rule will result in more harm than good by way of increased taxes, depressed property values and further harm to impoverished communities. Local zoning decisions have always been, and should always be, made by local communities and municipalities. American citizens should be free to choose where they would like to live and not be subject to neighborhood engineering and gerrymandering at the behest of an overreaching federal government. Congress must remain vigilant in opposing this new edict, and I am pleased that, so far, many of my colleagues have recognized the perils associated with this looming threat that will negatively impact homeownership.

NO
Rep. Keith Ellison, D-Minn.

Written for *CQ Researcher*, November 2015

For decades, our nation has prohibited housing discrimination based on race, sex, religion, national origin and disability. The law prohibits landlords from discriminating and precludes discrimination by towns, cities, counties and states receiving federal housing funds.

Our nation faces an alarming rental-housing crisis. Our limited federal housing assistance must provide more than shelter; it must provide opportunities for families to thrive in communities with jobs and access to high quality education, health care and transportation.

Despite having more than 11 million households spending more than 50 percent of their income on rent, fewer than one in four who qualify for housing assistance receive it. Limited federal housing funds should provide housing and reduce racial segregation and concentrated poverty.

HBO's miniseries "Show Me a Hero" vividly depicted what happens when federal housing dollars are spent exclusively in low-income and minority communities. These communities are at a higher risk for crime, poor schools and limited access to jobs and health care.

The Affirmatively Furthering Fair Housing rule requires local governments to use their funds to actively increase fair housing. They must provide options for those who receive housing assistance to live in supportive communities that provide opportunities to their families. Federal housing funds should afford low-income families, people with disabilities and the elderly access to community resources. By providing low-income families access to jobs, health care and good schools, we can reduce racial segregation and concentrated poverty.

We must resist Republican attacks to end the Fair Housing requirements for federal funds. Despite arguments that fair-housing rules are about "unrealistic utopian ideas of what every community should resemble," we must be proactive and use limited housing resources to reduce segregation. Everyone benefits when people with disabilities, African-Americans, Latino Americans, families with children, immigrant families and the elderly live in safe communities with access to jobs and quality services.

For too long, ZIP codes have been the defining factor in determining access to quality education, jobs and health care. Unequal access to vital resources results in unequal access to opportunity, undermining our nation's prosperity and success. We should expand housing assistance and ensure that our families and communities can thrive.

Many subtle real estate practices of old continue, Greene explains. "Many of the people in the real estate industry were trained under the old guidelines," he says. Testing evidence "amply illustrates some of the practices that go on today," Greene adds.

Redlining by lenders also continues, Greene says, with some banks choosing not to make loans or establish offices in minority neighborhoods. He cites the pending Hudson City case as an example. He notes that the complaint quotes Hudson City executives as favoring European or Asian ethnic groups when opening offices on predominantly white Staten Island, and ignoring African-Americans and Hispanics.

HUD itself had come under criticism in the 2008 Kemp-Cisneros commission report. The three major federal programs — Section 8 vouchers, public housing and low-income housing tax credits (LIHTCs) — "do very little to further fair housing and, in some cases, work to create and/or maintain segregated housing patterns," the report stated. "These programs must be reoriented to focus, in part, on helping families move to less racially and economically segregated communities."[43]

The report also said HUD had "failed" in ensuring that state and local recipients of federal housing assistance comply with the obligation to "affirmatively further" fair housing. The new rule is aimed in that direction, but NAHRO, the housing officials' organization, is unhappy with HUD's promise of help in meeting the obligation.

NAHRO noted in its mid-August statement that HUD is promising to supply some data for the new Assessment of Fair Housing tool, but it called the information "unwieldy and hard to understand." Some of the information "relies on complex social science indices . . . whose meaning is largely unintelligible to most users," NAHRO added.

Even as NAHRO and other groups are calling for rewriting the rule, the Dallas fair-housing group Inclusive Communities Project hopes the new rule will help reorient housing policies there. ICP vice president McCain says she hopes HUD will get "very serious" about enforcing the rule — by withholding federal funds if necessary.

Squaring Off in Court

The Inclusive Communities Project is back before a federal trial judge in Dallas challenging the Texas Department of Housing and Community Affairs (TDHCA) to award more federal tax credits for affordable housing in white neighborhoods.

The Supreme Court's decision to recognize disparate-impact liability under the Fair Housing Act sent the seven-year-old case back for a decision on the merits of ICP's allegation that state policies were causing discrimination against African-Americans. But Justice Kennedy's opinion for the majority included several comments and instructions that could help housing authorities or private developers being sued on the grounds of disparate impact.

ICP and the state squared off over how Judge Fitzwater should conduct future proceedings. As part of a Sept. 10 joint status report, ICP argued that it had already proved, "using uncontested evidence," the discriminatory effect of the housing authority's policies. The only remaining issues, the group argued, were whether the state could justify its policies or there were fewer discriminatory alternatives.

The TDHCA, however, said the judge should reconsider his earlier summary judgment in ICP's favor, noting that the Supreme Court had "repeatedly questioned" whether ICP had even alleged a disparate-impact claim and had "strongly suggested" that the state had "a valid defense." The agency said Fitzwater "did not have the benefit of the Supreme Court's explanation of what is required to establish a disparate-impact cause of action" when he made his earlier ruling.

On Oct. 8, Fitzwater said he would reconsider whether ICP had established a prima facie case of discrimination, needed to proceed to the other issues, and said either side could present additional evidence. "The judge is trying to be eminently fair," says Michael Daniel, the attorney representing ICP. In his opinion, Kennedy stressed that housing authorities and private developers should be given "leeway to state and explain the valid interest served by their policies" when sued on the grounds of disparate impact. "Entrepreneurs must be given latitude to consider market factors," he explained, and zoning officials must consider "a mix of factors" affecting a community's "quality of life."

Kennedy also said a statistical disparity alone was insufficient to make a case unless a plaintiff could cite policies by the defendant causing the disparity. The TDHCA reasserted that federal law, not its own policies, create a preference for building tax-credit units in minority neighborhoods. But ICP says the state agency's formula failed to give points to developments that would further what it called "a concerted community revitalization plan."

Fitzwater's eventual ruling could be delayed until 2016. The losing party will probably appeal his decision to the Fifth Circuit appeals court.

Meanwhile, ICP has a separate lawsuit pending against the U.S. Department of the Treasury and the Office of Comptroller of the Currency for allegedly failing to promote fair housing in its policies regarding low-income housing tax credits. Treasury administers the LIHTC program; the Comptroller oversees portions of it to make sure national banks don't invest in LIHTC projects unless they would primarily promote the public welfare, including housing for low- and moderate-income families.

ICP's complaint, filed in August 2014, alleges that neither Treasury nor the Comptroller has regulations related to the perpetuation or elimination of racial segregation. The two sought to have the case dismissed, but Fitzwater issued an opinion on Aug. 4, allowing most of the suit to proceed. The government's answer on the merits was to be filed on Oct. 30.[44]

OUTLOOK
Political Challenges

As mayor of Seattle, Ed Murray is pushing a multipronged plan to provide affordable housing in a city now ranked among the 10 most expensive in the United States. Murray's plan includes an array of tax breaks and land use changes, but he retreated in the face of strong political opposition from a proposal to allow multifamily buildings in parts of the city now zoned for single-family houses only.[45]

Murray's about-face on the so-called upzoning proposal underscores the volatile nature of housing policy debates even when race is not an explicit issue. As Stony Brook professor Salins notes, the low-density zoning laws that created the modern American suburb lead inevitably to higher housing prices and thus economic segregation.

Salins favors easing those zoning restrictions but cautions against linking any changes to breaking down residential segregation. 'If you want to kill any chance of economic integration and racial integration," he says, "tie the two together."

Despite progress on fair housing, experts and advocates alike agree that institutional barriers to residential desegregation are still daunting. "We've come quite a bit of a way in terms of achieving fair housing, but we still have a long way to go," says NFHA Executive Director Rice.

Rothstein, the Economic Policy Institute researcher, agrees with HUD official Greene that case-by-case enforcement of fair-housing laws is not enough to break down the barriers that created and now to some extent maintain residential segregation. "Prohibiting ongoing discrimination can't undo that," Rothstein remarked on "The Diane Rehm Show." Legal Defense Fund President Ifill said on the same program: "If you have massively invested in the creation of white suburbs . . . you cannot undo the damage of that simply by no longer making those investments."[46]

The housing officials group's opposition to the new HUD rule indicates that the government can expect local resistance as it seeks to enforce the long-standing obligation to affirmatively further fair housing. Political opposition seems certain if communities are required to put housing that minority buyers and tenants can afford into predominantly white neighborhoods. "The greatest opposition is going to be from neighborhoods that don't have any of that housing yet," says Vigdor, the University of Washington professor.

"We have a long way to go," says Tegeler, with the Poverty & Race Research Action Council. "These structures are not easy to undo. They require a lot of courage from officials and a lot of work from people at the local and regional level."

Like others, Vigdor and Tegeler profess at least a measure of cautious optimism about future trends. At HUD, Greene sees reason for optimism in changing preferences across racial and ethnic lines about where to live. "I'm very hopeful that we're going to see the dial turn toward more integrated communities in this country," Greene says. "I see more people moving into cities because they want to live in an integrated community."

In its annual report, the fair-housing alliance stressed that housing patterns have far-reaching consequences — on schools, air quality, access to jobs and transportation and the ability to accumulate wealth through homeownership.

"Inequality persists in all of these areas along racial and ethnic lines," Shanna Smith, the group's president and CEO, wrote in an accompanying press release, "which means that we need an all-out strategy to build up neighborhoods and provide a range of safe and affordable housing options for all Americans."[47]

NOTES

1. All quotes and background drawn from Stefanie DeLuca and Jessi Stafford, "Voices of the Baltimore Housing Mobility Program," The Century Foundation, March 2014, http://tinyurl.com/p9tajgt. Kimberly's last name and other details were omitted in the multimedia presentation. For an academic paper based on the investigation, see Jennifer Darrah and Stefanie DeLuca, " 'Living Here Has Changed My Whole Perspective': How Escaping Inner-City Poverty Shapes Neighborhood and Housing Choice," *Journal of Policy Analysis and Management*, Vol. 33, Issue 2 (spring 2014), http://tinyurl.com/qyu5x56 ($$). A pre-publication version of the article is available at http://tinyurl.com/pwyhvxv. For a more positive view about public housing, see David Madden, "Five Myths About Public Housing," *The Washington Post*, Sept. 13, 2015, p. B3, http://tinyurl.com/oltzg8l.

2. The suit was filed initially by the American Civil Liberties Union of Maryland (ACLU) and joined by the NAACP Legal Defense and Educational Fund (LDF). For legal and other materials, see the ACLU's website, http://tinyurl.com/nlqjer7, or the LDF's website, http://tinyurl.com/pc8f7x6.

3. The law is codified at 42 U.S.C. §§3601–3619, http://tinyurl.com/ph2td8b; the "affirmatively further" provision is section 3608(e)(5).

4. "The Future of Fair Housing: Report of the National Commission on Fair Housing and Equal Opportunity," http://tinyurl.com/qaeunt5. The commission was convened by the Lawyers' Committee for Civil Rights Under Law, the Leadership Conference on Civil Rights, the NAACP Legal Defense and Educational Fund and the National Fair Housing Alliance.

5. The full text of the decision is at: http://tinyurl.com/pe85hx4. For coverage, see Eric Siegel, "Judge criticizes pooling poor in city," *The Baltimore Sun*, Jan. 7, 2005, http://tinyurl.com/p7jx4vj.

6. Douglas S. Massey and Jonathan Tannen, "A Research Note on Trends in Black Hypersegregation,"

Demography, Population Association of America, June 2015 (published online March 20, 2015), http://tinyurl.com/odta3bf.

7. See "Fair Housing and Equal Opportunity," undated, accessed October 2015, http://tinyurl.com/4a9ku8b.

8. Paul A. Jargowsky, "Architecture of Segregation: Civil Unrest, the Concentration of Poverty, and Public Policy," The Century Foundation, Aug. 7, 2015, http://tinyurl.com/q2uzvyt.

9. For an account, see Kenneth Jost, "Fair Housing Law Held to Apply Broadly," in *Supreme Court Yearbook 2014–2015*. http://tinyurl.com/po8ks9n. For case materials and pre- and post-decision coverage, see *SCOTUSblog*, http://tinyurl.com/n2o892m.

10. *Texas Department of Housing and Community Affairs v. Inclusive Communities Project, Inc.*, http://tinyurl.com/o5xfdsk. Kennedy's opinion was joined by Justices Ruth Bader Ginsburg, Stephen G. Breyer, Sonia Sotomayor and Elena Kagan; the main dissenting opinion was written by Justice Samuel A. Alito Jr. and joined by Chief Justice John G. Roberts Jr. and Justices Antonin Scalia and Clarence Thomas.

11. See "HUD Announces Final Rule on Affirmatively Furthering Fair Housing," http://tinyurl.com/ov4z4j5. The press release includes a link to the text of the rule. Castro is quoted in Emily Badger, "Long-awaited rules aim to strengthen housing act," *The Washington Post*, July 8, 2015, http://tinyurl.com/qcd8eck.

12. For comprehensive compilation of materials from plaintiff's side, see the website of the law firm Daniel & Beshara, http://tinyurl.com/ofhvejh.

13. Cory Andrews, "Supreme Court's Victory for Disparate Impact Includes a Cautionary Tale," *SCOTUSblog*, June 25, 2015, http://tinyurl.com/nkd3pf6.

14. "Housing Discrimination, Racial Segregation, and Poverty in America," The Diane Rehm Show, Sept. 16, 2015, http://tinyurl.com/ou4ysbf.

15. See Julie Hirschfeld Davis and Binyamin Appelbaum, "Obama Unveils Stricter Rules on Fair Housing," *The New York Times*, July 9, 2015, http://tinyurl.com/px3xqf4.

16. "CFPB and DOJ Order Hudson City Savings Bank to Pay $27 Million to Increase Mortgage Credit

Access in Communities Illegally Redlined," Consumer Financial Protection Bureau, Sept. 24, 2015, http://tinyurl.com/q9uec68. The settlement also includes a $5.5 million penalty. The press release includes links to the complaint and proposed consent decree. For coverage, see Richard Newman, "Hudson City Settling Case," *Herald News* (Passaic County, N.J.), Sept. 25, 2015, http://tinyurl.com/nnvnff7.

17. Margery Austin Turner *et al.*, "Housing Discrimination Against Racial and Ethnic Minorities 2012," Urban Institute, prepared for U.S. Department of Housing and Urban Development, June 2013, http://tinyurl.com/oqn74wl. For coverage, see Shaila Dewan, "Discrimination in Housing Against Nonwhites Persists Quietly, U.S. Study Finds," *The New York Times*, June 12, 2013, p. B3; web version: http://tinyurl.com/p83kolr.

18. "HUD, Philadelphia-Area Real Estate Company Reach Agreement Resolving Racial Steering Allegations," U.S. Department of Housing and Urban Development, June 24, 2014, http://tinyurl.com/ncue7lu.

19. John Eligon, "An Indelible Black-and-White Line," *The New York Times*, Aug. 9, 2015, http://tinyurl.com/pnlfczv.

20. Darrah and DeLuca, *op. cit.*

21. "The Black Towns Project," http://tinyurl.com/np8jppc; Larry O'Dell, "All-Black Towns," *Encyclopedia of the Great Plains*, The University of Nebraska Lincoln, 2011, http://tinyurl.com/q2g3mhj.

22. James H. Hirsch, *Riot and Remembrance: The Tulsa Race War and Its Legacy* (2002); R. Thomas Dye, "Rosewood, Florida: The Destruction of an African American Community," *The Historian*, Vol. 58, No. 3 (spring 1996), pp. 605–622.

23. For a compelling account, see Isabel Wilkerson, *The Warmth of Other Suns: The Epic Story of America's Great Migration* (2010).

24. The decision is *Buchanan v. Warley*, 245 U.S. 60 (1917). The Supreme Court's unanimous decision sustained a challenge to the ordinance brought by a white property owner who had sought to sell his home to an African-American.

25. For an account, see James W. Loewen, *Sundown Towns: A Hidden Dimension of American Racism* (2005).

26. The decision is *Shelley v. Kraemer*, 334 U.S. 1 (1948).

27. See Arnold R. Hirsch, *Making the Second Ghetto: Race and Housing in Chicago 1940–1960* (1998).

28. For an overview, see Ta-Nehisi Coates, "The Case for Reparations," *The Atlantic*, June 2014, http://tinyurl.com/nopprgt.

29. HUD's website has a celebratory account of the enactment: "History of Fair Housing," http://tinyurl.com/6f7exxg.

30. The decision is *Jones v. Alfred H. Mayer Co.*, 392 U.S. 409 (1968).

31. Account drawn from Nikole Hannah-Jones, "Living Apart: How the Government Betrayed a Landmark Civil Rights Law," *ProPublica*, Oct. 29, 2012 (updated June 25, 2015), http://tinyurl.com/8jzwt3w. See also Christopher Bonastia, *Knocking on the Door: The Federal Government's Attempt to Desegregate the Suburbs* (2006).

32. The statutes have been codified as indicated: Equal Credit Opportunity Act, 15 U.S.C. §§1691 *et seq.*; http://tinyurl.com/pvhrt53; Home Mortgage Disclosure Act, 12 U.S.C. §§ 2801 *et seq.*, http://tinyurl.com/2wb8xpx; Community Reinvestment Act, 12 U.S.C. §§ 2901 *et seq.*, http://tinyurl.com/4w74td. The LGBT rule, formally entitled "Equal Access to Housing in HUD Programs — Regardless of Sexual Orientation or Gender Identity," was issued on Jan. 27, 2012, and took effect after formal publication on March 5, 2012, http://tinyurl.com/6s3jj8p.

33. See Lisa Belkin, "The Painful Lessons of the Yonkers Housing Crisis," *The New York Times*, Aug. 14, 2015, http://tinyurl.com/nhnqpg7.

34. Massey and Tannen, *op. cit.*

35. See "Fair Housing Enforcement at HUD Is Failing," in "The Future of Fair Housing: Report of the National Commission on Fair Housing and Equal Opportunity," December 2008, http://tinyurl.com/phzn4c6; National Fair Housing Alliance, "Where You Live Matters: 2015 Fair Housing Trends Report," April 30, 2015, p. 28, http://tinyurl.com/neuq462.

36. See Fernanda Santos, "Judge Faults Westchester County on Desegregation Efforts," *The New York Times*, Feb. 27, 2009, http://tinyurl.com/pyho9ja; Sam Roberts, "Housing Accord in Westchester," *The*

New York Times, Aug. 11, 2009, http://tinyurl.com/
lgl36q; Mark Lungariello, "Feds: Housing accord
violated," *The Journal News* (Westchester County,
N.Y.), July 23, 2015, http://tinyurl.com/ph8osw3.

37. See "Fair Housing and the Foreclosure Crisis,"
Future of Fair Housing, *op. cit.*, http://tinyurl.com/
czpj9b; Charlie Savage, "Wells Fargo Will Settle
Mortgage Bias Charges," *The New York Times*, July
13, 2012, http://tinyurl.com/mdoqvqo.

38. The decision is *Havens Realty Corp. v. Coleman*, 455
U.S. 363 (1982).

39. Quoted in Jost, *op. cit.*

40. Davis and Appelbaum, *op. cit.*

41. "Where You Live," *op. cit.*, pp. 41–42.

42. *Ibid.*, pp. 43–44.

43. See "Summary of Recommendations," in Future of
Fair Housing, *op. cit.*

44. For text of complaint and other materials, see website of the law firm Daniel & Beshara, http://tinyurl
.com/o6ruldg.

45. See Daniel Beekman, "Mayor Murray backs off plan
to increase density in single-family zones," *The
Seattle Times*, July 30, 2015, http://tinyurl.com/
pnsn9r2. Seattle ranked 7th in a list of the United
States' 25 most expensive cities compiled by
Vanessa Ho, "The 25 most expensive cities in the
United States," *Expatistan*, Jan. 25, 2014, http://
tinyurl.com/n2pzjkf.

46. "Housing Discrimination, Racial Segregation, and
Poverty in America," *op. cit.*

47. "National Fair Housing Alliance Report Links Fair
Housing to Health, Education, Transit, Wealth, and
Job Opportunities," April 30, 2015, http://tinyurl
.com/q2r77nd.

BIBLIOGRAPHY

Selected Sources

Books

Jackson, Kenneth T., *The Crabgrass Frontier: The
Suburbanization of the United States*, Oxford
University Press, 1985.

This comprehensive history of the development of the
modern American suburb by a professor of history and
social science at Columbia University traces some of the
barriers that contributed to residential segregation in
metropolitan areas. Includes detailed notes.

**Oliver, Melvin L., and Thomas M. Shapiro, *Black
Wealth/White Wealth: A New Perspective on Racial
Inequality*, Routledge, 2006 (10th anniversary edition).**
The authors link homeownership patterns to the persis-
tent wealth inequality between white and black
Americans. Includes detailed notes, list of references.
Oliver is professor of sociology and dean of social sci-
ences at the University of California, Santa Barbara;
Shapiro is a professor of law and social policy at the
Heller School for Social Policy and Management at
Brandeis University.

**Sharkey, Patrick, *Stuck in Place: Urban Neighborhoods
and the End of Progress toward Racial Equality*,
University of Chicago Press, 2013.**
An associate professor of sociology at New York
University details political decisions and social policies
that he says have led to severe disinvestment from
African-American neighborhoods, persistent segregation
and declining economic opportunities. Includes detailed
notes, list of references.

Articles

**Bridegam, Martha, "Fair Housing: Talking Past Each
Other About Cities and Segregation," *California
Planning & Development Report*, Aug. 30, 2015,
http://tinyurl.com/oh4o87l.**
The article discusses the conflicting reactions to the
Supreme Court's decision recognizing "disparate impact"
liability for housing policies by government or the pri-
vate sector that contribute to racial or ethnic segregation.

**Coates, Ta-Nehisi, "The Case for Reparations," *The
Atlantic*, June 2014, http://tinyurl.com/nopprgt.**
A senior writer for *The Atlantic* details what he calls "35
years of racist housing policy" in a widely noticed call for
compensatory payments to African-Americans.

**Eligon, John, "A Year After Ferguson, Housing
Segregation Defies Tools to Erase It," *The New York
Times*, Aug. 8, 2015, http://tinyurl.com/pnlfczv.**

A journalist examines efforts to reduce residential segregation in St. Louis against the backdrop of police-citizen clashes in the predominantly black suburb of Ferguson and indicates that barriers "remain very much a thing of the present."

Hannah-Jones, Nikole, "Living Apart: How the Government Betrayed a Landmark Law," *ProPublica*, June 25, 2015 (originally published Oct. 29, 2012), http://tinyurl.com/8jzwt3w.
The nonprofit investigative-reporting website critically examines the lagging enforcement of the Fair Housing Act under both Republican and Democratic presidents.

Reports and Studies

Glaeser, Edward, and Jacob Vigdor, "The End of the Segregated Century: Racial Separation in America's Neighborhoods, 1890–2010," Manhattan Institute, January 2012, http://tinyurl.com/7sz2hjh.
The report by the conservative, New York City-based think tank finds U.S. cities more integrated today than at any time since 1910 and all-white neighborhoods all but nonexistent. Glaeser is a senior fellow at the institute and an economics professor at Harvard University; Vigdor is an adjunct fellow at the institute and a professor of public policy and governance at the University of Washington.

Jargowsky, Paul A., "The Architecture of Segregation: Civil Unrest, the Concentration of Poverty, and Public Policy," The Century Foundation, August 2015, http://tinyurl.com/pbjyqhe.
A Rutgers University professor describes the increasing concentration of poverty in racially and ethnically segregated ghettos and barrios in U.S. cities and links the trend to the increased civil unrest in the wake of violent confrontations between police and residents.

Massey, Douglas, and Jonathan Tannen, "A Research Note on Trends in Black Hypersegregation," *Demography*, Population Association of America, June 2015, http://tinyurl.com/odta3bf.
The number of "hypersegregated" cities has declined since 1970, the researchers find, but those cities house one-third of the country's black city dwellers. Massey is a professor of sociology and Tannen a Ph.D. candidate at Princeton University.

Rothstein, Richard, "From Ferguson to Baltimore: The Fruits of Government-Sponsored Segregation," Working Economics Blog (Economic Policy Institute), April 29, 2015, http://tinyurl.com/nqs2q5x.
A researcher with the liberal think tank traces the history of government-sponsored residential segregation in Baltimore.

Swarns, Rachel L., "Biased Lending Evolves, and Blacks Face Trouble Getting Mortgages," The New York Times, Oct. 30, 2015, http://tinyurl.com/qcuxtj5.
The article recounts the increased attention to racial discrimination in the mortgage industry in the wake of the 2007–2009 recession.

For More Information

Housing and Civil Enforcement Section, NWB, Civil Rights Division, U.S. Department of Justice, 950 Pennsylvania Ave., N.W., Washington, DC 20530; 202-514-4713; www.justice.gov/crt/housing-and-civil-enforcement-section. Enforces the Fair Housing Act, the Fair Lending Act and the public accommodations provisions in Title II of the Civil Rights Act of 1964.

Manhattan Institute for Policy Research, 52 Vanderbilt Ave., New York, NY 10017; 212-599-7000; www.manhattan-institute.org. A conservative think tank, renamed in 1981 from the International Center for Economic Policy Studies, that supports market-oriented policies in, among other areas, housing and land use.

Mortgage Bankers Association, 1919 M St., N.W., 5th floor, Washington, DC; 20036; 202-557-2700; www.mba.org. Represents all segments of the real estate finance industry on legislative and regulatory issues and works to develop open and fair standards and practices for the industry.

NAACP Legal Defense and Educational Fund, 40 Rector St., 5th floor, New York, NY 10006; 212-965-2200; www .naacpldf.org. Civil rights organization that has been involved in fair-housing litigation through much of its history.

National Association of Housing and Redevelopment Officials, 630 I St., N.W., Washington, DC 20001; 202-289-3500; www.nahro.org. Represents housing and redevelopment officials who administer federal housing programs, including public housing and section 8 housing choice vouchers.

National Association of Realtors, 500 New Jersey Ave., N.W., Washington, DC 20001; 202-383-1000; www .realtor.org. An influential trade association with 1 million members in the commercial and residential real estate industries.

National Disability Rights Network, 820 1st St., N.E., Suite 740, Washington, DC 20002; 202-408-9514; www.ndrn.org. Advocates for basic rights for persons with disabilities, including nondiscrimination in housing.

National Fair Housing Alliance, 1101 Vermont Ave., N.W., #710, Washington, DC 20005; 202-898-1661; www .nationalfairhousing.org. A consortium of more than 220 private, nonprofit fair housing organizations, state and local civil rights agencies and individuals.

Office of Fair Housing and Equal Opportunity, U.S. Department of Housing and Urban Development, 451 7th St., S.W., Washington, DC 20410; 800-669-9777; www .hud.gov/fairhousing. The office responsible for the administration, enforcement, development and public understanding of federal fair-housing provisions.

Poverty & Race Research Action Council, 1200 18th St., N.W., #200, Washington, DC 20036; 202-906-8023; www .prrac.org. Civil rights policy organization convened by major civil rights, civil liberties and anti-poverty groups in 1989-90 to connect social science research to advocacy in those fields.

7

Religious Freedom

Reed Karaim

Kim Davis, the clerk of Rowan County, Ky., became a national figure last summer when, despite a Supreme Court ruling that same-sex marriage is legal, she said her religious beliefs would not allow her to issue marriage licenses to gay couples. Davis was briefly jailed in September when she refused to comply with a federal court order to provide the licenses.

Getty Images/ABC/Ida Mae Astute

L ast June, Kim Davis was toiling in obscurity in the eastern reaches of Kentucky. As clerk of Rowan County, she signed public documents, registered various legal records and issued marriage licenses. But on June 29, three days after the U.S. Supreme Court ruled that same-sex marriage is legal in the United States, Davis stepped onto the nation's front pages, saying her religious beliefs would not allow her to issue marriage licenses to gay couples.[1]

Although Davis was one of several county clerks who objected last summer to issuing such licenses, she quickly became a national figure. Her story went viral when she was jailed briefly in September after refusing to comply with a federal court order directing her to provide the licenses. In a statement released by her attorneys, Davis said, "To issue a marriage license which conflicts with God's definition of marriage, with my name affixed to the certificate, would violate my conscience. It is not a light issue for me. It is a heaven or hell decision."[2]

But in his ruling requiring her to issue the licenses, U.S. District Judge David Bunning found the state was not restricting Davis' religious activities or beliefs; it was asking her to fulfill her duties as an elected official. "She may continue to attend church twice a week, participate in Bible study and . . . she is even free to believe that marriage is a union between one man and one woman, as many Americans do," Bunning wrote. "However, her religious convictions cannot excuse her from performing the duties that she took an oath to perform as Rowan County clerk."[3]

Davis' case highlights an emotional debate over how far religious freedom in the United States should extend. The central question is whether religious convictions give someone the right to refuse to

From *CQ Researcher*,
January 1, 2016.

Majority Say Islamic, American Values Clash

More than half of Americans say Islamic values conflict with Americans' values and way of life. About four in 10 disagree.

Percentage of Americans who Agree or Disagree that Islamic Values Are "At Odds" with American Values and Way of Life

- 56%
- 3%
- 41%

● Agree
● Disagree
● Don't know/refused

Source: "Anxiety, Nostalgia, and Mistrust: Findings from the 2015 American Values Survey," Public Religion Research Institute, Nov. 17, 2015, p. 27, http://tinyurl.com/qgk4wob

participate in activities they believe are contrary to God's commands, such as same-sex marriage, abortion or birth control, and how that right is to be honored when it clashes with the rights of others.

The debate also reflects a fundamental question about government's role in religion: In its effort to remain religiously neutral and to maintain a wall between church and state, has the government gone too far by, among other things, barring prayer in public schools and restricting the use of religious symbols, such as displays of the Ten Commandments in courtrooms or nativity scenes on public property?

Some Christians, Hasidic Jews and others answer yes. They say the government's actions have gone beyond neutrality in religion to hostility toward it, with some Christians complaining about a "war on Christmas" or government forcing them to compromise their beliefs. Many others disagree, saying the government remains accommodating to religious faith, particularly Christianity.

Muslims, meanwhile, have faced a wave of anti-Islam sentiment in the United States following November terrorist attacks in Paris and a December mass shooting in San Bernardino, Calif., both initiated by followers of the Islamic State, also known as ISIS and ISIL. Muslims have reported a sharp increase in vandalism and threats to mosques, while some commentators, including two of the leading Republican presidential candidates, Donald Trump and Ben Carson, have disparaged the religion as

incompatible with American beliefs. In early December, Trump said the United States should deny entry to all Muslims until the nation's leaders "can figure out what's going on."[4]

Scholars say much of the tension over religious freedom and conflicting rights can be traced to the Constitution's First Amendment. The opening clauses declare, "Congress shall make no law respecting an establishment of religion, or prohibiting the free exercise thereof."[5] The first part of the amendment is known as the Establishment Clause, the second part as the Free Exercise Clause.

Thus, scholars note, one clause gives Americans the right to exercise their religious beliefs, while the other sets a limit on how far that exercise can go.

"These two tracks are in conflict with each other: the deep religious convictions Americans have held from the beginning . . . and the understanding that you cannot base America on any particular religious faith," says history professor Raymond Haberski Jr., director of American studies at Indiana University-Purdue University Indianapolis.

William Burgess, senior staff attorney at the Council on American-Islamic Relations, a Washington-based group that works to educate the public about Islam, says the traditional American vision of religious liberty establishes the right to religious expression but acknowledges limits to that practice. Religious liberty "starts with the freedom to believe whatever you like to believe," he says. "There's absolute freedom of belief and limited freedom of practice. The protection for the actual practices of religion — attendance at services, religious dress — need to be quite strong. But in areas where they impact third parties, religious liberty may need to be limited to make way for other values."

The contemporary debate over religious freedom grew more heated after the Supreme Court's ruling on same-sex marriage and the implementation of the Patient Protection and Affordable Care Act, commonly known as Obamacare. The 2010 law requires businesses to offer health insurance that includes access to contraceptives, an obligation which some businesses and religiously affiliated institutions object to on religious grounds.

In a case involving the Hobby Lobby retail chain and Conestoga Wood Specialties, a cabinet-making firm in East Earl, Pa., the Supreme Court ruled that closely held corporations — those with only a limited number of shareholders — can be exempt from providing certain contraceptives based on the owners' religious beliefs.[6] The justices recently agreed to consider another religious freedom claim from several nonprofit entities closely affiliated with religious denominations, such as Little Sisters of the Poor, a Catholic order that provides care for the elderly. The groups argue that they should not be required to provide contraceptive care to their employees.[7]

Despite conservative Christians' recent successes in the Supreme Court, many still say government directives threaten religious liberty. "It's under unprecedented assault, and I think it's only going to get worse with this issue of same-sex marriage," says Mat Staver, chairman of Liberty Counsel, a nonprofit Christian law firm and advocacy group in Orlando, Fla., that represented Davis in her case. Staver says churches could lose their tax exemption and Christian colleges their accreditation if they refuse to comply with laws regarding same-sex marriage.

But the Rev. Barry Lynn, head of Americans United for Separation of Church and State, a nonprofit group based in Washington that works to preserve church-state separation, believes the Supreme Court, the federal government and the states have bent over backward to accommodate religious beliefs, particularly those of conservative Christians. "I think we're absolutely awash in religious accommodations and exceptions," Lynn says. "The idea that there's a war against religion or Christianity or Christian holidays is all truly nonsensical."

The battle over religious freedom comes at a time when Americans are becoming less religious. A survey of more than 35,000 U.S. adults conducted by the nonpartisan Pew Research Center in Washington found that "the percentages who say they believe in God, pray daily and regularly go to church or other religious services all have declined modestly in recent years."[8] Pew said, however, that the 89 percent of Americans who say they

Muslim shopkeeper Sarkar Haq was beaten in an alleged hate crime at his shop in New York City on Dec. 7, 2015. Muslim-American leaders accused Donald Trump, the front-runner for the Republican presidential nomination, of inciting anti-Muslim violence when he said all Muslims should be banned from entering the United States. Trump's call for a ban followed a mass shooting in San Bernardino, Calif., on Dec. 2 by a Muslim-American couple who supported the Islamic State.

believe in God remains "remarkably high" compared with other industrial nations.

Still, a growing number of Americans are religiously unaffiliated — those who describe their religion as "nothing in particular" or who identify as atheists or agnostics. The biggest shift is among the Millennial Generation, those born between 1980 and about 2005. They are far less likely to attend church or say religion is very important in their lives compared with older generations, the survey indicated.[9]

Pew also found that although Christianity remains the dominant faith in the United States, its share of the population is declining while those of other faiths, particularly Islam and Hinduism, are growing. Since 2007, the percentages of Muslims and Hindus in the United States have roughly doubled, although members of both faiths each still represent slightly less than 1 percent of the U.S. population. (The Jewish population is about 1.9 percent.)[10]

Some scholars say the combination of these two trends — a decline in church attendance, especially among the young, and the growth of non-Christian religions — may account for the fervor with which some Christians are asserting their religious rights.

21 States Have Religious Freedom Laws

Arkansas and Indiana are the most recent states to enact laws patterned after the federal Religious Freedom Restoration Act limiting restrictions on religious expression. Nineteen states have passed such laws since 1997, when the U.S. Supreme Court ruled that the federal act did not apply to state or local governments.

States With Religious Freedom Restoration Acts

Source: "State Religious Freedom Restoration Acts," National Conference of State Legislatures, Oct, 15, 2015, http://tinyurl.com/jbtq4dv; David Johnson and Katy Steinmetz, Time.com, April 2, 2015, http://tinyurl.com/q3svxwd

"I think what's happening is, majority Christian religions are losing their position of privilege, and we're shifting to a position of greater religious equality," says Frederick Gedicks, a law professor at Brigham Young University in Provo, Utah, and an expert on the intersection of law and religion. "If you formerly enjoyed privilege, that probably feels like an assault. But if we take a step back . . . it's not an assault, it's the latest iteration of equality in America."

As courts, politicians, religious institutions and the public wrestle with how far religious liberty should extend, here are some of the questions being debated:

Should public officials be allowed to place their religious convictions ahead of their civic duty?

The Supreme Court's ruling this year in *Obergefell v. Hodges* that same-sex marriage is legal across the United States was met with resistance by local officials in several states. Judges in Oregon and Alabama, magistrates in North Carolina and county clerks in Texas and Kentucky objected on religious grounds to either issuing marriage licenses or marrying couples.

The case that became emblematic of these objections revolved around Davis' refusal to grant marriage licenses in Rowan County. County clerk is an elected position in Kentucky. Couples who wish to get married must appear in person to receive their licenses, which bear the county clerk's signature.

In 2004, Kentucky voters passed a state constitutional amendment banning same-sex marriage, and the state's law was one of those before the Supreme Court when the justices ruled that the U.S. Constitution guarantees the right of same-sex couples to marry.[11] After the ruling, then-Kentucky Democratic Gov. Steve Beshear directed state agencies and county officials to comply.[12]

Many experts in law and religion say Davis' role, not just as a government employee but as an elected official, meant she had a clear responsibility to follow the nation's laws. "I do not believe that public officials do or should have the right to pick and choose who they serve," says Brigham Young University's Gedicks. "They're elected to serve all of the people. And if they can't do that, then a person of integrity doesn't seek a religious exemption; he or she resigns and seeks another position, because the essence of the position is service to the public."

But defenders of Davis and other public officials say the right of government workers to express their religious beliefs deserves consideration regardless of their position. "Public officials, whether they're an employee or whether they're an elected official, don't lose their constitutional rights when they take office or employment," says Staver, founder of Liberty Counsel, which represented Davis in federal court.

Stanley Fish, a law professor at Florida International University, said those who say Davis is free to practice her religion in other ways — such as attending church and doing charitable work — ignore that many religions, including Christianity in its traditional interpretation, demand an obedience to their beliefs that does not allow for exceptions. "She cannot cast off the tenets of her religion when they conflict with worldly mandates," Fish wrote of Davis. "She cannot, that is, exercise her religion intermittently, on weekends and sacred holidays, and dance to secular tunes for the rest of the time."[13]

Kentucky is one of 21 states with a state Religious Freedom Restoration Act (RFRA), modeled after a 1993 federal law that says the government "should not substantially burden religious exercise without compelling justification."[14] Kentucky's act says government at the state and local levels should seek to make accommodations to faith unless the government has a clear and compelling interest in infringing on religious expression.[15] The law, Fish noted, does not rule out making religious accommodations for state officials.[16]

But others say ensuring that all members of the public are legally served at a government office is a compelling state interest. "You can believe anything you want about matters of faith and the existence of God or Gods or no God," says Lynn of Americans United for Separation of Church and State. "What you can't do is expect that your right to practice what you believe always prevails when it comes into conflict with someone else's legitimate claim to their rights."

Some legal analysts also say that allowing claims such as Davis' to prevail would violate the Establishment Clause in the First Amendment. "By claiming 'God's authority' as the basis for denying the license — rather than any man-made law — Davis effectively established her religion in the Rowan County clerk's office and imposed on the religious liberty of those who hold other (or no) faiths," wrote Randal John Meyer, a legal associate at the Center for Constitutional Studies at the Cato Institute, a libertarian think tank in Washington.[17]

After initially closing her county office so it couldn't issue marriage licenses to anyone, Davis sought a compromise that Staver says would have allowed same-sex couples to marry. When her office reopened, deputy clerks handled marriage licenses, and Davis asked that her name not appear on any licenses, believing her signature would be a de facto endorsement of same-sex marriage. "Marriage licenses are issued under the name

AP Photo/Brennan Linsley

Following the Supreme Court's ruling that same-sex marriage is legal, cake shop owner Jack Phillips of Lakewood, Colo., refused on religious grounds to provide goods or services for the marriage ceremonies of gay or lesbian couples. A rejected couple sued Phillips, arguing their civil rights had been violated, and a state court ruled in their favor.

and authority of the county clerk. She's only asking for her name and her title to be removed from the licenses," says Staver.

Texas, Louisiana and North Carolina have announced they will allow elected officials to opt out of issuing licenses or performing weddings to which they have a religious objection, but will require that other officials be available to perform these duties — an accommodation they say protects the religious liberty of the officials and the rights of those who wish to be married.[18]

But critics say these approaches still subject same-sex couples to uncertainty and possible rejection and imply their marriages are of a different or lesser status, when the U.S. government has recognized same-sex marriages as equal under the law.[19] The accommodations tilt the balance toward religion over individual rights, says the Rev. Carolyn Davis, an analyst with the Faith and Progressive Policy Initiative at the Center for American Progress, a liberal Washington think tank. "This question of how far people can go to express their religious beliefs seems to be getting more and more stretched," she says, "and real people suffer on the other side."

In Kentucky, Davis has appealed her case. But Matt Bevin, Kentucky's newly elected Republican governor who took office in December, has promised to issue an executive order removing the names of country clerks from marriage forms. That essentially would grant Davis' request for accommodation of her religious beliefs.[20]

Should business owners be required to provide goods or services if it violates their religious beliefs?

Since the Supreme Court's ruling on same-sex marriage, some small-business owners have asserted the right, based on their religious beliefs, not to provide goods or services to the marriage ceremonies of gay or lesbian couples.

In two cases that received considerable attention, Elane Photography in Albuquerque, N.M., refused to take pictures at the wedding of a lesbian couple, and Masterpiece Cakeshop in Lakewood, Colo., would not provide a cake for a same-sex wedding. In both cases, the rejected couples sued, arguing their civil rights had been violated, and state courts ruled in favor of the couples.[21]

In a similar case in Gresham, Ore., the state labor commissioner ruled that Sweet Cakes by Melissa, a bakery that refused to cater a same-sex wedding because of the owner's religious beliefs, had violated a state law barring businesses from discriminating or refusing service based on sexual orientation, age, race, sex, disability or religion. The commissioner ordered the bakery's owners to pay the couple $135,000 in damages.[22]

Oregon, Colorado and New Mexico are among 21 states with anti-discrimination laws that include sexual orientation.[23] To make exceptions to those laws to accommodate religious belief would set a troubling precedent, says Robert Tuttle, a professor of law and religion at George Washington University in Washington, D.C., who compares the current debate to earlier civil rights battles over racial equality.

"Do we really want a business to say, sorry, for religious reasons, we can't serve women who aren't accompanied by men; we cannot serve people of a particular faith?" Tuttle asks. "Public-accommodation laws were important achievements of the civil rights era, and to start creating exceptions to them, even if people have deeply held religious beliefs, raises the serious problem of a slippery slope."

But Liberty Counsel's Staver says the photographer and the baker were not discriminating against the couples based on sexual orientation. They don't concern themselves with whether their customers are gay or lesbian, he says, and serve whomever comes through their doors. But, he says, participating in a same-sex wedding is different. "They don't want to participate in a ceremony that signifies something that directly collides with their deeply held religious convictions," Staver says. "That's different from discriminating because someone is gay or lesbian. It's a really major point that needs to be understood."

Anthony Caso, a law professor at Chapman University in Orange, Calif., which is affiliated with the Christian Church (Disciples of Christ), agrees the photography or bakery businesses had the right to turn down same-sex weddings. Because the couples could easily procure photography and baking services elsewhere, he says, the injury wasn't significant enough to provide the compelling government interest required to overcome the Free Exercise of Religion Clause. "If you can make the argument that there's nobody else to take pictures at your wedding or bake your cake, then, maybe, it's different. But this isn't the case," Caso says. "There's going to be lots of bakers more than willing to bake that cake."

However, Louise Melling, director of the American Civil Liberties Union Center for Liberty in New York City, says a compelling societal interest is at stake. "This isn't just about a cake; this is about equality," Melling says. "What does it mean if I go into a store and I get sent away because of who I am? Every time I walk into a store from then on I think I'm going to have a different feeling — will I be served, will I be treated fairly?"

Melling notes that earlier generations cited religion to defend discrimination, including racial and sexual discrimination. Many advocates of slavery and, later, racial segregation quoted the Bible to justify their actions, and some faiths still believe God grants men authority over women, she points out. "If we reject religious exemptions in the context of other models of discrimination, why would we do differently here?" Melling asks.

Granting business owners a religious right to turn away gay and lesbian couples undercuts the basic premise of the Supreme Court ruling on same-sex marriage, says Melling. "The [court] is saying, 'We are going to have a rule that says you are embraced in our society instead of being treated like an outcast.' This really undermines that notion."

Brigham Young's Gedicks agrees that "conceptually and legally, if you're offering services to the public, you should adhere to public values, and same-sex marriage is now legal and a public value." But in the cases of small, individually owned businesses, he says, "I do have sympathy for services that require presence on the premises [for a same-sex wedding], for the photographer or the florist," he says, adding that the gay rights movement should be willing to "find some accommodation they can live within these cases. These are really sympathetic plaintiffs. When people provide services at a wedding, it's reasonable for them to feel implicated."

Public opinion surveys indicate that most Americans are less sympathetic to the claim of religious liberty in such cases. A 2015 poll by the Public Religion Research Institute, a nonpartisan organization in Washington that studies public opinion on religious issues, found that 60 percent of Americans "oppose allowing a small-business owner to refuse products or services to gay and lesbian people, even if doing so violates their religious beliefs," while 34 percent support such a policy.[24]

White evangelical Christians were the only religious group that expressed majority support for allowing small businesses to refuse to serve gay and lesbian people, according to the poll; Catholics felt most strongly that businesses must provide goods or services to gay or lesbian people.[25]

Fewer Americans Belong to a Religion

The percentage of American adults who are not affiliated with a particular religion rose nearly 7 points from 2007 to 2014, while the share who identify as Christian fell nearly 8 percentage points. The non-Christian population grew slightly, with Hindus and Muslims accounting for most of the increase.

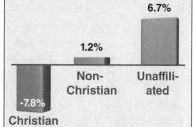

Percentage Change in U.S. Population, by Religious Affiliation, 2007 to 2014

6.7% Unaffiliated
1.2% Non-Christian
-7.8% Christian

Source: "America's Changing Religious Landscape," Pew Research Center, May 12, 2015, p. 4, http://tinyurl.com/ppz6qv2

Should businesses, doctors and others be allowed to refrain from dispensing contraceptives on religious grounds?

Lawsuits by Hobby Lobby and Conestoga Wood Specialties challenging the contraceptive requirement in the Affordable Care Act attracted national attention in 2014 when the Supreme Court ruled that they did not have to provide certain kinds of contraception.

Some pharmacies, individual pharmacists and doctors in recent years also have refused to provide birth control to customers or patients based on religious convictions. Pharmacists have refused to fill prescriptions for contraceptives in at least 25 states, according to reports compiled by the National Women's Law Center, a Washington-based nonprofit that advocates for women's rights.[26] Citing their Catholic faith, several doctors also have refused to write birth-control prescriptions.[27]

The Catholic Church considers the use of contraceptives "objectively immoral" because they weaken the bonds of marriage and work "against the natural gift of fertility, treating pregnancy as if it were a disease and fertility as if it were a pathological condition," the United States Conference of Catholic Bishops said.[28] Some evangelical and conservative Protestant denominations, including Baptist churches, also oppose certain contraceptives, such as the "morning-after pill," because they believe they are akin to abortion.[29]

But organizations that back women's access to contraceptives say the Supreme Court ruling and other accommodations on religious grounds have tilted the balance between religious freedom and individual rights too far toward religion.

"We're really concerned about allowing an individual or corporation's religious belief to trump the health and welfare and rights of other individuals," says Gretchen

Demonstrators rally outside the U.S. Supreme Court during oral arguments on March 25, 2014, in a case involving the Hobby Lobby retail chain and Conestoga Wood Specialties, a cabinet-making firm in East Earl, Pa. The Supreme Court ruled that corporations with limited numbers of shareholders can be exempt from providing certain contraceptives based on the owners' religious beliefs.

Borchelt, vice president for health and reproductive rights at the National Women's Law Center.

Supreme Court Associate Justice Samuel Alito, writing for the majority in the *Hobby Lobby* case, based the decision on the 1993 Religious Freedom Restoration Act. Critics of the ruling believe Congress never intended the act to apply to businesses or to deprive individuals of legal, government-mandated services. It was intended, they say, to protect the individual practice of religion from government interference. "The Hobby Lobby case has been a turning point. . . . It seems as though RFRA, which was intended as a shield, is now being used as a sword," says Borchelt.

But Chapman University's Caso says the government doesn't have a compelling justification to force companies to provide insurance that includes all the listed contraceptives, when it could have provided them to women through other means. "There are a lot of ways to provide contraceptives to people. The government could just hand them out. They could have provided a voucher to people for purchasing them at the drugstore," he says.

Borchelt counters this would amount to relegating women to "a separate [health care] system. It's not fair, and it probably wouldn't work for a lot of women." Several of the proposals, she says, would require women to arrange their own contraceptive care and to even bear

upfront costs. "The whole reason the birth control mandate was put into place," she says, "was to help women who couldn't afford those upfront costs."

Hobby Lobby objected to morning-after pills and intrauterine devices, saying they cause abortions by blocking a fertilized egg from implanting in the uterus.[30] (Supporters of reproductive rights say the drugs and devices prevent fertilization and are not abortions.) Hobby Lobby was willing to provide other contraceptives through its health plan. But some religiously affiliated universities and charities, including the Little Sisters of the Poor, have balked at providing any contraceptives to their employees.

Churches that object to contraceptive care are exempt from the mandate; affiliated organizations are not. In response to complaints from the University of Notre Dame in Indiana and other religiously affiliated institutions, the Obama administration offered an accommodation through which these institutions could opt out of paying for contraception by submitting a form that notified the government of their objection. Their health insurance companies would still provide contraceptives to their employees, but the institution would no longer be supporting it.

Supporters of such institutions reject the accommodation, saying it still leaves them responsible for setting in motion a chain of events that leads to contraception being available through their health care plans. By submitting the form requesting accommodation, they cause something to happen to which they religiously object.

"It goes far beyond just signing the form. It's the effect of the form. It's the power of the form," says Adéle Keim, counsel for the Becket Fund for Religious Liberty, a Washington-based nonprofit law firm that works on religious liberty cases and that filed the original lawsuit for the Little Sisters of the Poor. "When the government says, 'The Little Sisters just have to sign the form,' that doesn't answer the question: What does the form do?" Keim says.

In the end, Keim says, the government wants these institutions "to provide something that they believe is morally wrong."

Borchelt disagrees, arguing that the accommodation removes the employer from the process of providing contraceptives. "The insurance company provides it directly to the employee and they [the employers] aren't paying for it," she says. "Yes, it's the same insurance company, but the

Getty Images/Chip Somodevilla

employer has been carved out of the process. If there's any connection, it's so attenuated and so indirect that to say the provision of birth control services is a violation of their beliefs is incredible."

The battle has worked its way through the federal courts, where the lower courts have mostly ruled that the approach would not unduly burden religiously affiliated institutions.[31] The Supreme Court will settle the debate: On Nov. 6, it announced it will hear the case of the Little Sisters of the Poor and six other religiously affiliated institutions that have rejected the Obama administration's accommodation.

BACKGROUND

Freedom Seekers

From Pilgrims who landed at Plymouth Rock to Catholic migrants who settled Maryland, many American colonists came to the New World in search of a place to practice their religion without government interference.

England, which many of the settlers had fled, had a state-sponsored religion in the Church of England, and authorities persecuted Catholics and Protestant dissenters, including Puritans, in the 16th and much of the 17th centuries. Religious minorities in other European countries also endured persecution that caused many to migrate to British North America and elsewhere.[32]

But if many settlers arrived in the New World seeking religious freedom, they often established intolerant regimes of their own. The Puritans, in what is now Massachusetts, expelled dissenters from their colonies and hanged four Quakers in the mid-17th century for practicing their faith.[33] In Virginia, where the Church of England became the established church, the colony's assembly passed a series of anti-Quaker laws in the mid-17th century, and the colony was later hostile to evangelical migrants, including Baptists.[34]

Religious oppression in the American colonies created a new set of exiles — colonists who fled to other parts of the Eastern seaboard to establish their own communities. Roger Williams, expelled from Massachusetts for opposing religious coercion, founded Rhode Island in 1636 as a colony based on religious freedom, welcoming Jews, Quakers, Baptists and other religious minorities. In a letter written later in life, he expressed his enduring belief that "forced worship stinks in God's nostrils."[35]

Pennsylvania, under the leadership of Quaker William Penn, and Maryland were also more religiously welcoming and tolerant than many other colonies.[36]

Even as toleration of dissenting faiths slowly took hold in the 18th century, Americans during and after the American Revolution remained ambivalent about religious freedom. In 1786, after a heated debate about the role of the church in the new state, the Virginia General Assembly passed the Virginia Statute for Religious Freedom, written by Thomas Jefferson, which would serve as a model for the religious freedom clauses in the Constitution's First Amendment.[37]

Before the states approved the first 10 amendments, known as the Bill of Rights, the Constitution included only one direct reference to religion, in the third clause of Article 6, which states, "[N]o religious Test shall ever be required as a Qualification to any Office or public Trust under the United States."[38]

John Fea, a professor of American history at Messiah College, an institution in Mechanicsburg, Pa., that was founded by the Brethren in Christ Church, says the Founders varied widely in their religious beliefs. They included agnostics, deists (who believed in a distant Supreme Being not directly involved in daily life) and Christians of varying beliefs.

But Fea, the author of *Was America Founded as a Christian Nation?*, says Christian beliefs were deeply embedded in early American culture. "The most fascinating part of the American founding is that the defenders of the separation of church and state, the skeptics, are the ones who win the day with the document that's going to define this country, despite the fact that it's an overwhelmingly Christian society," he says.

Other historians question the depth of religious feeling at the nation's founding. David Sehat, a cultural historian at Georgia State University in Atlanta, in *The Myth of American Religious Freedom*, cites records indicating only 17 percent of the national population belonged to a church in 1776. "It appears that an official religion governed an indifferent population for much of the colonial period," he wrote.[39]

Many Americans believe the First Amendment's religion clauses created a dividing line in U.S. history by neatly separating church and state. But historians note the amendment initially applied only to the federal government. "Some states — most prominently Massachusetts

CHRONOLOGY

1791-1802 *The United States seeks to separate church and state at the federal level.*

1791 States ratify Constitution's First Amendment, which states, "Congress shall make no law respecting an establishment of religion, or prohibiting the free exercise thereof. . . ."

1802 President Thomas Jefferson writes a letter to a Baptist congregation in which he says the First Amendment has built "a wall of separation between Church and State."

1878–1940 *Supreme Court determines extent of religious liberty, extending First Amendment protections to the state level.*

1878 Supreme Court rules that banning polygamy does not violate Mormons' religious freedom.

1940 Supreme Court holds that rights of Jehovah's Witnesses were violated when they were arrested for proselytizing in a Catholic neighborhood. The case extends the Free Exercise Clause to the states.

1948–1985 *Supreme Court rules on the role of religion in public schools.*

1948 Providing space for religious teaching during school hours violates the First Amendment's Establishment Clause prohibiting government endorsement of religion, Supreme Court decides.

1962 In *Engel v. Vitale*, a landmark case that severely limits prayer in schools, the Supreme Court rules that New York state violated the Establishment Clause by providing a voluntary, nondenominational prayer in public schools.

1985 High court strikes down an Alabama statute providing for a moment of "meditation or voluntary prayer" in public schools.

1988–1997 *After a Supreme Court ruling narrows the right to exercise religious freedom, Congress steps in to pass the Religious Freedom Restoration Act (RFRA).*

1990 Supreme Court says members of a Native American church do not have the right to use peyote as part of religious rituals.

1993 Congress passes bipartisan RFRA, intended to return the nation to a more expansive interpretation of the Free Exercise Clause.

1997 Supreme Court rules RFRA does not apply to states; 21 states eventually adopt their own versions.

2002–2015 *Supreme Court allows state money to go to religious schools, says some corporations have religious rights and legalizes same-sex marriage.*

2002 Supreme Court rules that vouchers do not constitute state support for religion because they have a nonreligious purpose: greater school choice.

2010 Voters amend Oklahoma constitution to say that state courts cannot consider Islamic (Sharia) law in decision-making. A federal court strikes down the amendment as discriminatory, but other states adopt similar bans. . . . Patient Protection and Affordable Care Act becomes law, including contraceptive coverage.

2014 Supreme Court, in *Burwell v. Hobby Lobby*, grants religious rights to a closely held corporation, freeing it from having to offer contraceptive coverage.

2015 Supreme Court grants same-sex couples the right to marry and rules in *Holt v. Hobbs* that Arkansas cannot bar a Muslim prisoner from growing a beard in accordance with his religion. . . . Kentucky county clerk Kim Davis refuses to grant marriage licenses to same-sex couples, citing her religious beliefs. . . . In November the Supreme Court announced it will decide in 2016 whether the birth control mandate in the Affordable Care Act constitutes an improper burden on religiously affiliated groups that do not believe in contraception, despite a government accommodation that relieves them from directly paying for it.

and Connecticut — maintained state-supported churches for decades after the Constitution was adopted," wrote Stephen D. Smith, a professor of law at the University of San Diego, in *The Rise and Decline of American Religious Freedom*.[40]

Revolutionary-era state constitutions often guaranteed religious freedom to Protestants only and placed restrictions on Catholics, Jews and other religious minorities. In New Jersey, for instance, Article XIX of the 1776 constitution stipulated "that no Protestant inhabitant . . . shall be denied the enjoyment of any civil right, merely on account of his religious principles." And it limited office-holding in the state government to those "professing a belief in the faith of any Protestant sect."[41]

State backing for religion included levying taxes to support churches and requiring oaths of office that acknowledged a divine being. The states discarded many of these provisions early in the 19th century as recognition of the need to protect religious pluralism gained acceptance. But the nation's religious fervor grew during the same period, in what historians call the Second Great Awakening, which arose in the 1790s and peaked in the 1830s,[42] (The First Great Awakening began in the 1730s and lasted until the mid-1740s.)

The outpouring of religious expression that swept across the young nation in the Second Great Awakening was evangelical in nature, with preachers proclaiming the road to salvation at camp meetings that drew large crowds.[43]

The movement, many historians agree, also had a political component, as evangelical Christianity, combined with American nationalism, led to the view that the United States was a special nation blessed by God and had a mission to spread liberty and Protestant Christianity, a moral responsibility that extended to its public institutions. "The Second Great Awakening saw the government itself as the vehicle for religious transformation, and that, I think, is a departure from the ideas of the founding," says George Washington University's Tuttle.

First Amendment Defined

On April 26, 1938, Newton Cantwell and his two sons were proselytizing for the Jehovah's Witnesses in a heavily Catholic neighborhood in New Haven, Conn. The Cantwells carried a portable record player on which they played an anti-Catholic message for people who agreed to listen to it.[44]

Two pedestrians who consented became angry when its purpose became clear and told the Cantwells to leave the neighborhood. They refused and were arrested for soliciting without a permit shortly afterward.

Cantwell v. Connecticut made its way to the Supreme Court in 1940. The Cantwells argued the arrests violated their right to proclaim their religious message. The court unanimously agreed and overturned their convictions.[45]

The court cited the Constitution's 14th Amendment, which prohibits the states from depriving "any person of life, liberty, or property, without due process of law."[46] The states ratified the 14th Amendment after the Civil War, but it had not been applied to questions of religious liberty until the *Cantwell v. Connecticut* decision. In their decision, the justices ruled that the principal of liberty espoused in the 14th Amendment applied to the free expression of religion guaranteed in the First Amendment.[47]

The court also found the Connecticut law under which the Cantwells were prosecuted to be unconstitutional because it allowed the state, when determining whether someone qualified for the right to solicit, to decide what religious exercise it considered legitimate. This, in effect, was establishing favored religions in violation of the Establishment Clause of the First Amendment.[48]

Constitutional scholars consider *Cantwell v. Connecticut* a landmark because it extended the guarantee of religious freedom and the prohibition against an established religion to the state level. It also brought the federal courts more deeply into the struggle to define the relationship between religion and government, a struggle that would soon center on public schools.

Throughout much of the 19th century, religious expression, almost exclusively Christian and Protestant, had been commonplace in schools. "For the first half of the century, the point of disagreement was not whether public schooling should be religious or secular, but how religious that schooling should be," wrote Steven K. Green, a professor of law at Willamette University in Salem, Ore., and the author of *The Bible, the School, and the Constitution: The Clash that Shaped Modern Church-State Doctrine*.[49]

Even as public education grew more secular in the late 19th and early 20th centuries, daily prayers and other observances of Christian faith remained a part of many school days.[50] But in 1948, in *McCollum v. Board of Education*, the Supreme Court ruled that public schools

Hostility Toward Muslims Remains Strong

"The First Amendment for Muslims has been violated" throughout the U.S.

In a contentious city council meeting in the Detroit suburb of Sterling Heights last year, several residents voiced strong objections to allowing a mosque to be built in a largely residential neighborhood.

Some speakers linked the mosque to Islamic extremists in the Middle East, with one warning that the mosque could be used "to store weapons."[1] Another said "what they should probably do is have Homeland Security check these people out, just in case. . . . You know, they're cutting people's heads off. They killed our soldiers and everything. They scare me. They scare everybody."[2]

Many opponents said their objections had nothing to do with the Islamic faith but with concerns about traffic and property values. Others, however, including Chaldean Christians who have settled in the area, did not hide their animosity toward Islam.[3] (Chaldean Christians are members of a Catholic sect originally from Iraq.)

According to press reports, a resident, Saad Antoun, brought a picture of a woman covered in a niqab, a head covering worn by some Islamic women that covers everything but the eyes. "This mosque is going to bring . . . people like this," Antoun said, displaying the image to the crowd. "I don't want to be near people like this. This is not humanity. . . . This is scary and disgusting."[4]

Three weeks later, when the city planning commission voted 9-0 against the mosque, saying it was unsuitable for that street, a large crowd gathered outside to sing "God Bless America" and boo local Muslim leaders as they left the meeting.[5]

Among the most basic freedoms enshrined in the Constitution's First Amendment is the right to gather in worship. But in recent years, American Muslims seeking to build or open mosques have faced stiff public opposition in numerous places around the United States, including in California, Florida, Georgia, New York and Texas.

Opposition to a proposed interfaith community center in Manhattan that would have included prayer space for Muslims two blocks from the former World Trade Center — destroyed by Islamist extremists on Sept. 11, 2001 — attracted the most media attention. (The developer has abandoned his plans for the interfaith center and is planning on building a 70-story tower of luxury condos on the location.) But in many communities, local authorities have refused to grant construction permits to mosques.[6]

Dawud Walid, executive director of the Michigan chapter of the Council on American-Islamic Relations, based in suburban Detroit, says the local group that hoped to open the mosque in Sterling Heights hasn't determined whether it will go to court, but he has no doubt what is happening. "I think the First Amendment for Muslims has been violated not only in Sterling Heights but in varying localities throughout these United States of America," he says. Walid calls much of the opposition "Islamophobic."

The resistance to mosques appears to reflect a larger animosity toward Muslims that has grown in the United States since the 9/11 terrorist attacks. The FBI typically recorded 20 to 30 anti-Muslim hate crimes per year before members of al Qaeda attacked the United States in 2001. In the years since, the annual total has averaged 100 to 150. (However, Jews continue to be the target of the largest number of hate crimes in the United States, according to the FBI statistics.)[7]

In many recent cases, citizens worked to block mosques from coming to their cities. In Katy, Texas, a small city within the greater Houston metropolitan area, residents held pig races on Fridays, Islam's holy day, next to a proposed mosque site. Pork is forbidden to Muslims, and some residents said the races were meant to send a message the mosque was not welcome.[8]

---

violated the Establishment Clause when they provided space for religious teaching during school hours.[51]

In 1962, the court followed with a landmark ruling in *Engel v. Vitale* that state-sponsored prayer in schools was unconstitutional, a decision that reverberates politically and socially to this day. The justices went further in 1985,

overturning an Alabama state law setting aside a moment of voluntary prayer or meditation in schools, saying that by including voluntary prayer the statute violated the separation of church and state.[52]

Tuttle says those Supreme Court rulings were critical in defining the modern conception of the separation

In several cases, the U.S. Department of Justice sued on behalf of the right of Islamic groups to open mosques, including in Pittsfield Township, Mich., where the department said local authorities were placing an "undue burden" on the free exercise of religion by those who wished to open the mosque.[9]

Adherents to the Islamic faith also have faced discrimination in lesser ways. Muslims have had to sue for the right of Muslim women to wear a headscarf at work and for Muslim prisoners to be allowed to grow a half-inch beard in accordance with Islam. (Authorities claimed the beard would be a security risk because it provided a possible way of concealing dangerous items.) In both instances, the U.S. Supreme Court ruled on behalf of the plaintiffs' religious rights.[10]

While distrust of Muslims seems tied to terrorist attacks by jihadist groups claiming to represent Islam, historians say hostility toward religious minorities dates to colonial days. Protestants in early America viewed many newly arriving religious groups as strange foreigners who threatened their way of life; persecution often followed. Later Americans of all faiths sometimes exhibited the same kind of intolerance.

Quakers were originally viewed with hostility, says history professor Raymond Haberski Jr., director of American studies at Indiana University-Purdue University Indianapolis. And, he adds, "Catholics were seen in that light. Jews were seen in those terms. Mormons were targeted by the federal government, if not for annihilation, at least for marginalization. Today, Islam is just, in many ways, the latest group to be targeted in this way."

— *Reed Karaim*

AP Photo/The Free Lance-Star/Peter Cihelka

Sister Munira Salim Abdalla, chief administrator for the Islamic Ummah of Fredericksburg, Va., said she heard threats against Muslims during a heated public meeting on Nov. 17, 2015, about the possible construction of a new Islamic Center.

[5] Robert Snell and Candace Williams, "Sterling Hts. panel rejects proposed mosque on 15 Mile," *The Detroit News*, Sept. 10, 2015, http://tinyurl.com/oepmlz9.

[6] "Nationwide Anti-Mosque Activity," American Civil Liberties Union, undated, http://tinyurl.com/nu27t28. " 'Ground Zero Mosque' site to become ultra-luxury condos," *The New York Post*, Sept. 27, 2015, http://tinyurl.com/pvxgqdm.

[7] Christopher Ingraham, "Uniform Crime Report: Anti-Muslim hate crimes are still five times more common today than before 9/11," *The Washington Post*, Feb. 11, 2015, http://tinyurl.com/q2awkqh; "2013 Hate Crime Statistics," FBI, 2013, http://tinyurl.com/oxryagg.

[8] Cindy Horswell, "Not Ground Zero, but Katy mosque also stirs passions," *The Houston Chronicle*, Sept. 7, 2010, http://tinyurl.com/nmdbufj.

[9] Tom Perkins, "Justice Department sues Pittsfield Township over rejection of Islamic School plans," *Mlive.com*, Oct. 27, 2015, http://tinyurl.com/gvgp6gn.

[10] Simran Jeet Singh, "A Muslim woman beat Abercrombie & Fitch. Why her Supreme Court victory is a win for all Americans," *The Washington Post*, June 1, 2015, http://tinyurl.com/np9s5fs; David Savage, "Muslim prisoner wins Supreme Court case to keep his beard," *Los Angeles Times*, Jan. 20, 2015, http://tinyurl.com/oz7oly6.

[1] Niraj Warikoo, "Proposed mosque in Sterling Heights stirs opposition," *The Detroit Free Press*, Sept. 10, 2015, http://tinyurl.com/q7t6n64.

[2] Gus Burns, "Muslim fear grows in Sterling Heights: 'They scare me, they scare everybody,'" *Mlive.com*, Aug. 30, 2015, http://tinyurl.com/oycjzn4.

[3] Warikoo, *op. cit.*

[4] *Ibid.*

between church and state. "The prayer-in-school cases were important milestones in the sense of fulfilling the promise that the government was not going to be the agent of religious formation," he says. "That was going to be something that was left to parents and their children."

But the rulings also gave birth to the idea still popular in conservative Christian circles that the courts and government in general had gone beyond being neutral to being actively hostile to their beliefs. "It did set off a counter-reaction among those who felt like the war on Christianity had started," Tuttle says. "A lot of people do

Abroad, Echoes of U.S. Struggles Over Religious Liberty

Many democracies seek to define limits of free expression.

A Christian airline attendant's crucifix in England, a Hindu student's nose stud in South Africa and a Muslim university student's head scarf in Turkey — all have been the center of religious-rights cases decided by courts around the world.

So have the actions of bed-and-breakfast owners in Canada who have refused accommodations to same-sex couples and of doctors, midwives and pharmacists in several countries who have refused to provide contraceptives or participate in abortions.[1]

The different courts' decisions — allowing the crucifix and the nose stud but denying the bed-and-breakfast owners' objections and barring the student's head scarf — illustrate the varying approaches democracies are taking, often based on long-standing tradition, as they sort through claims of religious free expression.

In many autocratic nations, religious freedom is highly restricted or nonexistent. Nearly 75 percent of the world's inhabitants live in countries that curtail religious freedom, even though it is a fundamental human right under international law. Draconian anti-blasphemy laws, threats of imprisonment and physical attacks are some of the tools used to stifle religious expression.[2]

Elsewhere, civil wars and insurgencies have led to violent assaults on religious minorities. "In the Middle East, sub-Saharan Africa and throughout Asia, a range of nonstate actors, including terrorist organizations, have set their sights on destroying religious diversity," a 2014 U.S. State Department report concluded.[3]

But many of the world's democracies are struggling to define the extent of religious liberty, echoing current debates in the United States, although with differences. The U.S. Constitution's First Amendment prohibits the government from establishing a state religion or favoring one religion over another, while some countries — including England, Denmark and Greece — have state-established churches that have long-standing relationships with the government. In England, for example, the queen appoints the church's senior clergy in consultation with the prime minister. Countries such as Italy and Spain accord special privileges to the Roman Catholic Church.[4]

In centuries past, minority religions faced government-sanctioned discrimination in many Western countries. Today, however, most democracies promote tolerance of other faiths and recognize the right of people of different religious beliefs to gather together to worship. Declining

trace it back to that decision [against official prayer in schools]. It was 'taking God out of schools.'"

Some conservatives formed the Moral Majority and other groups in the 1970s and '80s to mobilize Christian voters to fight what they saw as the secularization of American society.[53]

Religious Freedom Restoration Act

In 1990, the Supreme Court tightened the standard it had been using when considering cases involving the First Amendment guarantee of the free exercise of religion.

Since the early 1960s, the court had generally held that the government should accommodate sincerely held

religious beliefs unless it had a "compelling interest" (that is, an overriding reason) not to do so. But in 1990, the Supreme Court ruled against two Native American guidance counselors at an Oregon drug rehabilitation center who claimed the right to ingest peyote during their traditional religious ceremonies. Peyote — a hallucinogenic drug containing mescaline — was illegal in Oregon, and the center had fired them.[54]

A lower court ruled in favor of the counselors, saying the state's drug laws did not provide a compelling interest to deny them the freedom to practice their religion. But the Supreme Court disagreed. In doing so, it threw church attendance across Europe has also fostered tolerance or a lack of interest in religious differences.[5]

Still, Europe has no exact equivalent to the U.S. First Amendment ban on governmental prohibitions against the free exercise of religion. The European Convention on Human Rights, which 47 European nations have signed, includes a declaration of religious freedom but says freedom can be limited in the interest of "public safety . . . [,] the protection of public order, health or morals, or for the protection of the rights and freedoms of others."[6]

Orthodox Christianity and Catholicism remain strong in Eastern Europe, where mainly Catholic Poland, for example, allows doctors to refuse to participate in medical procedures, such as abortion, that conflict with their religious beliefs, but physicians must refer patients to a doctor who will provide the service.

France and Turkey are among the nations with political traditions that limit what people of faith can do in public. Both countries prohibit overtly wearing religious apparel such as headscarves or crucifixes in schools and public institutions.[7] In the United States, the constitutional right of religious free expression means such visible signs of faith are generally allowed for all religions, including in schools and other public buildings.

"France offers an interesting point of comparison. The concept of secular in the U.S. means the government is neutral to religion, but also that it protects minority religious views, whereas in France, they have this view of secularism that means keeping religion [completely] out of the public sphere," says William Burgess, a senior staff attorney for the Washington-based Council on American-Islamic Relations, which promotes education on Islam and mutual understanding among faiths. "That simply would not fly here."

On another hot-button issue, the United States is part of a movement across much of the democratic world toward ensuring that the religious beliefs of others do not infringe on the rights of lesbian, gay, bisexual and transgender (LGBT) individuals, according to a study by an international network of civil liberties groups.[8]

"I was surprised by what did appear to be a trend where courts [in many nations] were refusing to grant religious exemptions when it came to LGBT cases," says Louise Melling, director of the American Civil Liberties Union Center for Liberty and one of the study's authors.

— *Reed Karaim*

[1]Louise Melling *et al.*, "Drawing the Line: Tackling Tensions Between Religious Freedom and Equality," The International Network of Civil Liberties Organizations, September 2015, http://tinyurl.com/j6s5nrp.

[2]For background, see Michelle Johnson, "Religious Repression," *CQ Researcher*, Nov. 1, 2013, pp. 933-956.

[3]"International Religious Freedom Report for 2014," U.S. Department of State, http://tinyurl.com/bor9yjm.

[4]"How Europe defines religious freedom," *The Economist*, March 31, 2014, http://tinyurl.com/zaaqcdc.

[5]Naftali Bendavid, "Europe's Empty Churches Go on Sale," *The Wall Street Journal*, Jan. 2, 2015, http://tinyurl.com/o9ouue3.

[6]"How Europe defines religious freedom," *op. cit.*

[7]"Why the French are so strict about Islamic head coverings," *The Economist*, July 6, 2014, http://tinyurl.com/k6got25.

[8]Melling *et al.*, *op. cit.*

out the compelling-interest standard and said what mattered was that a law was religiously neutral, treating all religions equally.[55]

Many liberal and conservative lawmakers felt the ruling went too far in weakening the protection afforded religious belief and could prevent individuals from freely practicing their faiths. In 1993, Congress passed the Religious Freedom Restoration Act (RFRA), which restored the compelling-interest standard by requiring strict scrutiny of any laws that sought to override religious conviction. The bill was sponsored in the Senate by Edward M. Kennedy, D-Mass., one of the preeminent liberals of the era, and the Senate passed it 97–3.[56]

But RFRA ended up having consequences that many of the act's supporters hadn't foreseen, analysts say. The Supreme Court's ruling in favor of Hobby Lobby's right not to provide certain contraceptives to its employees was based in part on the justices' interpretation of RFRA.

Supporters of the decision hailed the law's impact. "RFRA has proven true to its promise. It has succeeded in providing critical protections for religious freedom," the Becket Fund for Religious Freedom, which provided legal representation for Hobby Lobby, states on its website.[57]

Others say the courts have badly misinterpreted the law. Lynn of Americans United for Separation of Church

Getty Images/Aaron P. Bernstein

Gov. Mike Pence of Indiana signed the state's Religious Freedom Restoration Act (RFRA), making Indiana, along with Arkansas, two of the most recent states to enact a state-level law patterned after the federal RFRA, which limits restrictions on religious expression. Nineteen states have passed such laws since 1997, when the U.S. Supreme Court ruled that the federal RFRA did not apply to state or local governments.

and State helped to draft the act's language as a member of the American Civil Liberties Union staff at the time. "No one ever talked about this applying to for-profit companies," Lynn says. "This was unthinkable. Sen. Kennedy would literally have blown up. It would have been the end of the coalition [supporting the bill] if there was any chance that this would be the case."

But Tuttle says the language used in the bill established a stricter test for restricting religious liberty than some supporters realized. "Are we really going to make every law subservient to claims of religious exemption? That's what they did," he says. "Nothing major happened with it until Hobby Lobby, and the Supreme Court said that's what Congress said. So now the [religious] rights argument has this really powerful footing."

CURRENT SITUATION
Anti-Muslim Proposals

The question of religious freedom is at the forefront of the battle for the Republican presidential nomination following November's terrorist attacks in Paris by followers of the Islamic State and December's mass shooting in San Bernardino, Calif., by a couple inspired by the terrorist group.

The issue has particular resonance in Iowa, which is holding the first presidential caucus early next year. More than half of the state's Republican caucus-goers are evangelical Christians.[58]

Previously, candidate Carson had expressed doubts about the suitability of a Muslim serving as president of the United States, describing the tenets of the religion as un-American.[59] But after the Paris attacks, several Republicans went further. Former Florida Gov. Jeb Bush suggested the United States should take in only Christian refugees from war-torn and predominantly Muslim Syria, where the Islamic State controls part of the country.[60] Sen. Ted Cruz of Texas said he would introduce a bill to ban Muslim Syrian refugees from entering the United States.[61] Trump, leading in the polls for the nomination, went furthest of all: Besides barring entry to all Muslims, he said the United States should "strongly consider" shutting down mosques in the country and even create a database to track U.S. Muslims — proposals decried by candidates in both parties.[62]

President Obama responded forcefully to the suggestion that Muslim refugees, who make up a majority of those fleeing Syria, should be banned. "When I hear folks say that maybe we should just admit the Christians but not the Muslims, when I hear political leaders suggesting that there would be a religious test for which person who is fleeing from a war-torn country is admitted . . . that's not American. That's not who we are," Obama said.[63]

The three Democratic candidates for president — former Secretary of State Hillary Clinton, Sen. Bernie Sanders of Vermont and former Maryland Gov. Martin O'Malley — support accepting Syrian refugees of all faiths after government screening, and all have spoken out against demonizing Muslims based on the actions of a few.[64]

But a new poll indicates that a majority of the U.S. population shares the doubts expressed by Republican candidates. The Public Religion Research Institute found that 56 percent of Americans "agree that the values of Islam are at odds with American values and way of life, while roughly four in 10 (41 percent) disagree."

Americans' fears were on display in Virginia in mid-November, when the Islamic Center of Fredericksburg's plan to build a bigger mosque led to protests. "Nobody, nobody, nobody wants your evil cult in this county," a man who identified himself as a former Marine said at a community meeting about the mosque. "I will do

Should someone be able to deny others service based on religious beliefs?

YES
Mat Staver
Founder and Chairman, Liberty Counsel

Written for *CQ Researcher*, January 2016

The first freedom enshrined in the Bill of Rights is religious freedom. In the Virginia Statute on Religious Freedom, Thomas Jefferson wrote that "Almighty God hath created the mind free." He directed that his tombstone acknowledge this statute as one of the three most important things he did in his life. Religious freedom and the right of conscience were among Jefferson's top priorities.

While religious freedom is not absolute, in America we have always sought to make reasonable accommodations to protect the right of conscience when a law, policy or practice conflicts with deeply held religious beliefs. Those opposed to combat, for instance, are exempt from using a weapon to take the life of a human being.

Because of the unique circumstances among the Amish, they are exempt from compulsory education upon reaching age 16. Unemployment laws do not require people to work on their Sabbath. Churches are exempt from religious-discrimination laws, thus allowing a Catholic Church to hire Catholics and an evangelical church to hire those who affirm the church's doctrine.

Like private individuals, public officials and employees also have the right to conscience. People do not lose their constitutional rights when they accept public employment or run for office. The question is whether a person has a sincerely held religious belief that is substantially burdened by a law, policy or practice. If yes, then we have required some effort to accommodate that belief if reasonable alternatives are available. Obviously not every religious belief can be accommodated, but where the objective can still be achieved without violating a person's conscience, we have required that accommodation.

A prominent case involving religious accommodation is that of County Clerk Kim Davis of Kentucky. She sought an accommodation for her religious beliefs regarding marriage. She requested that her name and title be removed from all marriage licenses. The Kentucky Clerks Association made a similar request. The newly elected governor, Matt Bevin, stated that he would issue an executive order, upon taking office in December, to accommodate Davis and other clerks.

The right of conscience is a preeminent right that must be protected where possible. No one should trample upon another person's conscience when there are reasonable alternatives. A free society is best judged by how it protects the right of conscience. In repressive societies, the first freedom to suffer is religious freedom and the right of conscience.

NO
The Rev. Barry Lynn
Executive Director, and

Natacha Lam,
Constitutional Litigation Fellow, Americans United for Separation of Church and State

Written for *CQ Researcher*, January 2016

Since the U.S. Supreme Court on June 26 struck down laws banning marriage for gay or lesbian couples, marriage equality is now the law of the land. But some people continue to resist full equality for lesbian, gay, bisexual and transgender Americans.

Among other challenges, we've seen businesses attempt to violate state and local civil rights laws and deny service to same-sex couples. For instance, a wedding venue in New York, a florist in Washington state and bakers in Oregon and Colorado have refused service to same-sex couples and then argued in court that their religious beliefs entitled them to discriminate. So far, most judges have rejected these arguments, but the battle will continue in courts across the country.

This is not the first time business owners have attempted to use their religion as an excuse to discriminate. Those who now seek to deny service to same-sex couples are making the same arguments as those who sought to deny service to African-Americans or interracial couples 50 years ago. Although many people of faith supported desegregation and opposed discrimination, some people invoked religion as a basis for denying service to African-American customers. For example, after the Supreme Court struck down laws barring interracial marriage, a restaurant owner argued that he had a constitutional right — under the First Amendment's ban on any law "prohibiting the free exercise" of religion — to exclude African-Americans from his business and a religious obligation to prevent the mixing of the races. Unsurprisingly, the Supreme Court rejected his argument — unanimously.

Just as our right to swing our fists does not include the right to punch someone else's nose, our right to free exercise of religion does not include the right to injure someone else. When a business refuses to serve a same-sex couple, it injures that couple severely. There are practical harms: In some places, the number of service providers is limited, so same-sex couples may have nowhere else to turn.

And as we learned during the era of segregation, serious harms result from discrimination. Even if a couple has somewhere else to go, a profound stigma accompanies being told that "we don't serve your kind." The civil rights era illustrated the harm that occurs when someone is denied service based on who they are. The same holds true when someone is denied service based on whom they love.

everything in my power to make sure that [a new mosque] doesn't happen, because you are terrorists."[65]

On Capitol Hill, both sides of the debates over religious freedom and same-sex marriage have introduced legislation to bolster their causes.

The Equality Act, a House bill that has attracted 171 sponsors, all Democrats, would amend the 1964 Civil Rights Act to include sexual orientation and gender identity among the prohibited categories of discrimination or segregation in places of public accommodation. Such places would include stores, restaurants, retailers and other establishments that provide goods or services.[66]

On the other side of that debate, the First Amendment Defense Act, which has 151 House Republican sponsors and one Democratic sponsor, would protect people who refuse to provide services to gays and lesbians seeking to marry. The legislation would prohibit the federal government from acting against individuals who, in accordance with their religious faith, believe that marriage should be the union of one man and one woman, or that sexual relations are properly reserved to such a marriage.[67]

Although the backers of both bills point to the number of sponsors as evidence that their legislation can pass, the likelihood of either measure making it through a divided Congress appears remote.

In the Courts

The Supreme Court's decision to hear the objection of the Little Sisters of the Poor and other religiously affiliated groups to the Affordable Care Act's contraception mandate means the case will be the next major test of religious freedom. The court is expected to hear arguments in March, with a ruling likely coming by the end of the court's term on June 30.[68]

The question is whether the accommodation offered by the Obama administration — in which institutions with a religious objection do not have to pay for contraception but do have to sign a form that allows their employees to receive it — still constitutes a substantial burden on religious liberty under the Religious Freedom Restoration Act. Supporters of the religious institutions say triggering contraceptive coverage and allowing their health care plans to be used to provide it violate their religious rights. Opponents say the accommodation is

fair and add that if the courts rule it a heavy burden on religious freedom, it will open the door to far more religious liberty claims.

Meanwhile, since 2014, some 24 religiously affiliated colleges and universities across the United States have received exemptions from the civil rights protections provided under Title IX — the federal law that prohibits discrimination on the basis of sex in federally funded educational programs, according to *The New York Times*. The waivers exempt schools from provisions of the law that they say violate their religious beliefs on gender identity, sexual orientation and other issues. Critics say the exemptions allow the schools to discriminate against students and employees.[69]

At the State Level

The ongoing struggle to balance civil rights with religious freedom was evident in November when Republicans in the Indiana Senate unveiled a bill to extend civil rights protections to include sexual orientation and gender identity. The state currently has a patchwork of county and local ordinances providing such protections, but no statewide law.[70]

However, the legislation also would provide exemptions for religious institutions and some small businesses that object to providing services on religious grounds. For example, religiously affiliated adoption agencies could reject same-sex couples, and businesses with fewer than four employees that cater weddings wouldn't have to perform work for a gay or lesbian couple.[71]

By overriding local and county ordinances, the measure would guarantee equal treatment under the law, supporters say. But opponents say it would weaken civil rights guarantees in many areas in the name of religious freedom.

Republican Senate President Pro Tem David Long called the bill a good "first attempt," saying it attempts to balance competing interests.[72] But Jennifer Pizer, law and policy project director for Lambda Legal, a gay, lesbian, bisexual and transgender (LGBT) civil rights organization, said the measure is "a road map for discrimination against LGBT people."[73]

The debate parallels earlier battles in Arkansas and Indiana over those states' Religious Freedom Restoration Acts that critics said would allow businesses to discriminate against gay and lesbian couples. Legislatures in both states revised their laws to lessen their impact after objections poured in, including from several major corporations.[74] In Indiana, conservative groups are pushing back: On Dec. 10, the Indiana Family Institute, a family advocacy group in Indianapolis, Ind., and others sued Indianapolis and Carmel, arguing that those revisions are unconstitutional because they remove legal protections for religious beliefs.[75]

State Religious Freedom Restoration Acts continue to be the basis for lawsuits from an array of religious groups in other states. Among the religious groups citing RFRA are Satanists in Missouri, who claim on religious freedom grounds that they do not need to meet state counseling requirements to receive abortions, and members of the First Church of Cannabis, who say their beliefs require that their members be shielded from Indiana laws against possession of marijuana.[76] An Amish man from Lancaster County, Pa., recently sued for the right to buy a gun without having to show a photo ID, saying his faith prohibits members from having their pictures taken. (Although pacifists, some Amish use guns for hunting.)

In other legal battles, the ACLU has gone to court several times to fight the teaching of creationism, the biblically inspired belief that the Earth is only a few thousand years old, in public schools. In recent years, creationists have been invited into public schools in Kansas, while some teachers have promoted creationist views in class.[77] Muslim women continue to fight in court for the right to wear the hijab, a headscarf, in public, including at places of work and other locations. In two cases, Muslim women have sued, saying law enforcement officers forced them to remove their hijabs while holding them in custody. The police and sheriff's departments say they have a right to remove a hijab for security reasons.[78]

OUTLOOK

Tolerance to Grow?

The Pew Research Center's polling on religion in America has found a significant decline in religious commitment and belief among Millennials (those born between 1980 and about 2004). The question is whether that change will be matched by a greater tolerance for alternative views among those who continue to adhere to a faith.

The center's study finds evidence that could happen, particularly when it comes to same-sex marriage. In the survey Millennials expressed far more acceptance of gay relationships than did older adults. The trend was true even among a key Christian demographic. "Fully half of Millennials who identify as evangelical Protestants, for instance, now say homosexuality should be accepted by society," Pew reported.[79]

Messiah College's Fea sees further signs of a generational shift. "The evangelical kids I talk to as a teacher at a religious college . . . are tired of the old culture wars that their parents and grandparents fought," he says. "They're very much tired of the politicization of Christianity, the way in which their faith and religion has been co-opted by the GOP. As these young people come of age, I don't think they're going to change their deeply held moral convictions, but they're going to seek common ground with people they disagree with."

Burgess, the attorney for the Council on American-Islamic Relations, says he hopes acceptance of Islam and other minority religions will grow over time as the country's population becomes more diverse. "I think the tolerance will get worse for a while and then get better as people come to accept that we live in a more multicultural nation," he says. "I think we're heading to a better place in the long run."

Liberty Counsel's Staver believes, however, that same-sex marriage will prove to be an enduring issue among some Christians, much the way that opposition to abortion has remained strong 43 years after the Supreme Court made it legal in *Roe v. Wade.*

"Anybody who thinks this will fade or go away is naïve about the future," Staver says. "I think it will get worse. I think there's going to be significant pushback." The country will have to find ways to accommodate the religious freedom of those who cannot support same-sex marriage, despite the Supreme Court ruling, Staver adds, which he says will become more unpopular over time.

Chapman University's Caso says the Affordable Care Act's guarantee of contraceptive benefits is a harbinger of growing governmental interference in private realms. If that happens and government requires institutions and individuals to conform to other ideas that violate their beliefs, he says, claims of religious freedom are likely to grow. "It's going to be a source of continuing friction until we find a way to work it out, find a way to protect people's religious beliefs," Caso says. "These issues are going to continue to be with us for a while."

But Haberski of the Center for the Study of Religion and American Culture believes shifting public attitudes have Christian conservatives on the defensive, forcing them to pursue religious freedom claims in the courts.

"It seems to me this is almost an over-reaction among religious conservatives because they know they are losing ground," Haberski says. "[So] they want to enforce a religious view legally because American society in general is changing and becoming less beholden to that view."

NOTES

1. "Kim Davis timeline from Supreme Court to jail," *The Louisville Courier-Journal*, Sept. 3, 2015, http://tinyurl.com/ojfogr8.

2. "Davis Releases Statement, Lawyer Acknowledges Divorces," LEX18.com, Sept. 1, 2015, http://tinyurl.com/nl6xdas.

3. Mike Wynn, "Judge: Clerk must issue gay marriage licenses," *The Louisville Courier-Journal*, Aug. 12, 2015, http://tinyurl.com/oz8vg7t.

4. Dave Collins, "U.S. Muslims on Edge," *U.S. News & World Report*, Nov. 18, 2015, http://tinyurl.com/q8holkh; "GOP rhetoric on Muslims seen as having little cost," The Associated Press, *The New York Times*, Nov. 28, 2015, http://tinyurl.com/ovew5yq; and Jenna Johnson and David Weigel, "Donald Trump calls for 'total' ban on Muslims entering the United States," *The Washington Post*, Dec. 8, 2015, http://tinyurl.com/odxlzqv.

5. "Amendment 1, Freedom of Religion, Speech, Press, Assembly, and Petition," The National Constitution Center, undated, http://tinyurl.com/py1d73v.

6. Adam Liptak, "Supreme Court Rejects Contraceptives Mandate for Some Corporations," *The New York Times*, June 30, 2014, http://tinyurl.com/q9g4gbw.

7. Adam Liptak, "Supreme Court to Hear New Case on Contraception and Religion," *The New York Times*, Nov. 6, 2015, http://tinyurl.com/okvca6u.

8. "U.S. Public Becoming Less Religious," Pew Research Center, Nov. 3, 2015, http://tinyurl.com/pcyjbot.

9. *Ibid.*

10. "America's changing religious landscape," Pew Research Center, May 12, 2015, http://tinyurl.com/ldnxabw.

11. "Kentucky voters approve same-sex marriage ban amendment," *USA Today*, Nov. 3, 2004, http://tinyurl.com/a3nq68v; Jess Bravin, "Supreme Court Rules Gay Marriage Is a Nationwide Right," *The Wall Street Journal*, June 26, 2015, http://tinyurl.com/nboemyv.

12. Andrew Wolfson, "Kentucky moves quickly to adopt gay marriage ruling," *The Louisville Courier-Journal*, June 26, 2015, http://tinyurl.com/q4aygko.

13. Stanley Fish, "The Case for Kim Davis, Part Two," "The Blog," *The Huffington Post*, Sept. 14, 2015, http://tinyurl.com/n9nctqn.

14. "2015 State Religious Freedom Restoration Legislation," National Conference of State Legislatures, GovTrack.us, Sept. 3, 2015, http://tinyurl.com/qgh7opz; "Text of the Religious Freedom Restoration Act of 1993," Nov. 3, 1993, http://tinyurl.com/qxakosa.

15. "Kentucky House Bill 279," *Legiscan*, March 27, 2013, http://tinyurl.com/jy2yaqa.

16. Fish, *op. cit.*

17. Randal John Meyer, "Kim Davis Also Raised an Establishment Clause Issue," *Cato @ Liberty* blog, Cato Institute, Sept. 14, 2015, http://tinyurl.com/gwwy6xe.

18. Kara Loewentheil and Katherine Franke, "Proposed Conscience or Religion-Based Exemption for Public Officials Authorized to Solemnize Marriages," Memorandum, Public Rights/Private Conscience Project, Columbia University School of Law, June 30, 2015, http://tinyurl.com/jd97zv4.

19. Mike Wynn, "Couples want Kim Davis to stop altering marriage forms," *USA Today*, Sept. 21, 2015, http://tinyurl.com/ovexfky.

20. Steve Bittenbender, "Governor-elect to remove clerk names from Kentucky marriage licenses," Reuters, Nov. 6, 2015, http://tinyurl.com/jgcq7wl.

21. Sarah Larimer, "Colorado court rules against baker who refused same-sex marriage cake order," *The Chicago Tribune*, Aug. 15, 2015, http://tinyurl.com/glltwpl; "Court rules against photographer in gay

bias case," The Associated Press, *The Albuquerque Journal*, Aug. 22, 2013, http://tinyurl.com/ny3yzfb.

22. George Rede, "Sweet Cakes final order: Gresham bakery must pay $135,000 for denying service to same-sex couple," *The Oregonian/OregonLive*, July 2, 2015, http://tinyurl.com/qzrfqyg.

23. "Non-Discrimination Laws: State by State Information — Map," American Civil Liberties Union, undated, http://tinyurl.com/zngm46c.

24. "Survey: Majority Favor Same-sex Marriage; Two-thirds Believe Supreme Court Will Rule to Legalize,' Public Religion Research Institute, June 11, 2015, http://tinyurl.com/zzzwbaq.

25. *Ibid.*

26. "Pharmacy Refusals 101," National Women's Law Center, Aug. 4, 2015, http://tinyurl.com/oykejxs.

27. Patricia Miller, "When the Catholic Church owns your doctor: the insidious new threat to affordable birth control," *Salon*, May 11, 2015, http://tinyurl.com/k2fnub9; Wesley Smith, "MD Wins Right Not to Prescribe Contraceptives," "The Corner blog," *The National Review*, Aug. 17, 2015, http://tinyurl.com/hezu9ev.

28. "Belief and Teachings, What we Believe: Love and Sexuality," United States Conference of Catholic Bishops, undated, http://tinyurl.com/j3b6fzt.

29. Pam Belluck and Erik Eckholm, "Religious Groups Equate Some Contraceptives with Abortion," *The New York Times*, Feb. 16, 2012, http://tinyurl.com/6nrcfpg. According to the Mayo Clinic, a morning-after pill prevents pregnancy through one of three methods: "delaying or preventing ovulation, blocking fertilization, or keeping a fertilized egg from implanting in the uterus." The clinic says the pill does not abort an established pregnancy. See "Tests and Procedures, Morning-After Pill," Mayo Clinic, undated, http://tinyurl.com/jgdmdsm.

30. Jayne O'Donnell, "Hobby Lobby case: What birth control is affected?" *USA Today*, June 30, 2014, http://tinyurl.com/qarrfmj. For background, see William Wanlund, "Abortion Debates," *CQ Researcher*, March 21, 2014, pp. 265–288.

31. Laurie Sobel and Alina Salganicoff, "Round 2 on the Legal Challenges to Contraceptive Coverage: Are Nonprofits 'Substantially Burdened' by the "Accommodation?" Henry J. Kaiser Family Foundation, Nov. 9, 2015, http://tinyurl.com/nrw52by.

32. "Religion and the Founding of the American Republic, America as a Religious Refuge, the 17th Century, Part 1," Library of Congress, undated, http://tinyurl.com/4hhwk.

33. "Religion and the Founding of the American Republic, America as a Religious Refuge, the 17th Century, Part 2," Library of Congress, undated, http://tinyurl.com/lflm5xw.

34. *Ibid.*

35. Roger Williams, "Letter to Major John Wilson and [Connecticut] Governor Thomas Prence," World Policy Institute, June 22, 1670, http://tinyurl.com/owqklfr.

36. "Religion and the Founding of the American Republic, America as a Religious Refuge, The 17th Century, Part 2," *op. cit.*

37. "Thomas Jefferson and the Virginia Statute for Religious Freedom," Virginia Historical Society, undated, http://tinyurl.com/npjkzd2.

38. "Constitution of the United States," National Archives, undated, http://tinyurl.com/yqm97q.

39. David Sehat, *The Myth of American Religion Freedom* (2011), p. 5.

40. Steven D. Smith, *The Rise and Decline of American Religious Freedom* (2014), p. 3.

41. Constitution of New Jersey, 1776, http://tinyurl.com/z3gokrp.

42. "Religious Transformation and the Second Great Awakening," Ushistory.org, undated, http://tinyurl.com/45rdfbt.

43. *Ibid.*

44. Samuel Walker, "Cantwell Family Arrested; Case Establishes Free Exercise of Religion," *Today in Civil Liberties History*, http://tinyurl.com/p7l4kea.

45. "Cantwell v. Connecticut (1940)," Bill of Rights Institute, http://tinyurl.com/qcq7b4f.

46. "Amendment XIV: Citizenship Rights, Equal Protection, Apportionment, Civil War Debt, National Constitution Center, undated, http://tinyurl.com/qaedlnq.

47. *Cantwell v. Connecticut*, Legal Information Institute, Cornell University Law School, undated, http://tinyurl.com/nbeytov.

48. *Ibid.*

49. Steven K. Green, *The Bible, the School, and the Constitution: The Clash that Shaped Modern Church-State Doctrine* (2012), p. 18.

50. Jeff Nilsson, "Atheists v. Evangelists: The School Prayer Decision of 1962," *The Saturday Evening Post*, June 16, 2012, http://tinyurl.com/p9hy3xe.

51. *Illinois ex rel. McCollum v. Board of Education of School District*, Legal Information Institute, Cornell University Law School, http://tinyurl.com/q57t3yu.

52. *Wallace v. Jaffree*, Oyez, Chicago-Kent College of Law, Illinois Institute of Technology, accessed Nov. 18, 2015, http://tinyurl.com/pxrzbwk.

53. Doug Banwart, "Jerry Falwell, The Rise of the Moral Majority, and the 1980 Election," *Western Illinois Historical Review*, Spring 2013, http://tinyurl.com/owlsa56.

54. Jeff Guo, "How religious freedom laws were praised, then hated, then forgotten, then, finally, resurrected," *The Washington Post*, April 3, 2015, http://tinyurl.com/nbomyaa.

55. *Ibid.*

56. *Ibid.*

57. "History of RFRA," Becket Fund for Religious Liberty, undated, http://tinyurl.com/pg4e39u.

58. Michael Patrick Leahy, "Evangelicals Again Poised to Play Key Role in Iowa GOP Caucus," *Breitbart.com*, Aug. 21, 2015, http://tinyurl.com/hnwjpa7.

59. Ed Demaria, "Ben Carson does not believe a Muslim should be president," "Meet the Press," NBC News, Sept. 20, 2015, http://tinyurl.com/pbpja78.

60. Ed O'Keefe, "Jeb Bush: U.S. assistance for refugees should focus on Christians," *The Washington Post*, Nov. 15, 2015, http://tinyurl.com/gpmslqr.

61. Jonathan Swan and Julian Hattem, "Cruz to offer bill banning Syrian refugees," *The Hill*, Nov. 16, 2015, http://tinyurl.com/qcc6y7p.

62. Gregory Krieg, "Donald Trump: 'Strongly consider' shutting mosques," CNN, Nov. 16, 2015, http://tinyurl.com/hy58vqd.

63. Tessa Berenson, "President Obama Hits Jeb Bush and Ted Cruz Over Syrian Refugees," *Time*, Nov. 16, 2015, http://tinyurl.com/jx3hs6s.

64. John Wagner, "Bernie Sanders launches petition drive to preserve Syrian refugee program," *The Washington Post*, Nov. 20, 2015, http://tinyurl.com/jnrunkn.

65. Rachel Weiner, "Meeting about Virginia mosque exposes deep divide," *The Washington Post*, Nov. 22, 2015, http://tinyurl.com/hvasjbh.

66. "H.R. 3185 — Equality Act," Congress.gov, Sept. 9, 2015, http://tinyurl.com/o46poac.

67. "H.R. 2802 — First Amendment Defense Act," Congress.gov, June 17, 2015, http://tinyurl.com/qhrjn5c.

68. Ariane de Vogue, "Supreme Court to hear new challenge to Obamacare contraception mandate," CNN, Nov. 6, 2015, http://tinyurl.com/phcxjks.

69. Liam Stack, "Religious Colleges Obtain Waivers to Anti-Discrimination Law," *The New York Times*, Dec. 10, 2015, http://tinyurl.com/gs92tmr.

70. "Indiana GOP bill on LGBT rights has religious exemptions," The Associated Press, *The South Bend Tribune*, Nov. 18, 2015, http://tinyurl.com/hjm-mm3s.

71. Tony Cook, Stephanie Wang and Chelsea Schneider, "Republicans' LGBT protections bill draws criticism on both sides," *The Indianapolis Star*, Nov. 17, 2015, http://tinyurl.com/o3sw482.

72. "Indiana GOP bill on LGBT rights has religious exemptions," *op. cit.*

73. "Trudy Ring, Indiana Bill Would Ban Anti-LGBT Bias . . . Unless It's Faith-Based," *The Advocate*, Nov. 18, 2015, http://tinyurl.com/jhfynqw.

74. Wesley Lowery, "Gov. Pence signs revised Indiana religious freedom bill into law," *The Washington Post*, April 2, 2015, http://tinyurl.com/zklrjj9; Kevin Trager and Alyse Eady, "Arkansas governor signs new 'religious freedom' bill," *USA Today*, April 3, 2015, http://tinyurl.com/jsw8b3x.

75. "Suit challenges limits on Indiana's religious objections law," The Associated Press, *South Bend Tribune*, Dec. 11, 2015, http://tinyurl.com/oscgmuy.

76. Lucien Grieves, "The Satanic Temple just filed a lawsuit against abortion restrictions," "Bloggytown blog," *Orlando Weekly*, May 8, 2015, http://tinyurl.com/kmea6as; Stephanie Wang and Michael Anthony Adams, "Church of Cannabis suit raises religious liberty issues," *The Indianapolis Star*, July 8, 2015, http://tinyurl.com/o5gjy5r.

77. Heather Weaver, "Creationism Follies: the 2012–2013 Edition," American Civil Liberties Union, June 27, 2013, http://tinyurl.com/jq9rh3w.

78. Niraj Warikoo, "Muslim woman sues Dearborn Police over headscarf removal," *The Detroit Free Press*, June 30, 2015, http://tinyurl.com/jhcd65t.

79. "U.S. Public Becomes Less Religious," *op. cit.*

BIBLIOGRAPHY

Selected Sources

Books

Fea, John, *Was America Founded As a Christian Nation? A Historical Introduction*, Westminster John Knox Press, 2011.
A professor of American history at Messiah College, a Christian school in Pennsylvania, finds a complicated relationship between religious belief and the establishment of self-government in America's early days.

Lupu, Ira C., and Robert Tuttle, *Secular Government, Religious People*, Wm. B. Eerdmans Publishing Co., 2014.
Two legal and religious scholars from George Washington University in Washington argue that the secular nature of American government has allowed religious liberty and diversity to flourish in a highly religious nation.

Sehat, David, *The Myth of American Religious Freedom*, Oxford University Press, 2010.
A history professor at Georgia State University in Atlanta assembles evidence showing that a Protestant majority in America has frequently used government power to punish free thinkers and religious dissenters.

Staver, Mathew, *Eternal Vigilance: A Complete Handbook for Defending Your Religious Rights*, B&H Publishing Group, 2005.
The co-founder of the Liberty Council, a nonprofit legal and policy group that works to advance religious liberty, explains how people can protect their religious rights, which the author believes are threatened by government and other secular forces.

Articles

Allen, John Jr., "Pope Francis could reframe the US religious freedom debate," *The Crux*, Sept. 21, 2015, http://tinyurl.com/oj4kglt.
Pope Francis' comments on religious freedom could be broadening the scope of the issue and moving it beyond the Catholic Church's focus on abortion, same-sex marriage and contraception.

Eckholm, Erik, "Context for the Debate on 'Religious Freedom' Measures in Indiana and Arkansas," *The New York Times*, March 31, 2015, http://tinyurl.com/hhbmdxl.
A journalist examines the differing state religious freedom laws in the United States, which began proliferating after the federal government passed a similar law in 1993.

Ingraham, Christopher, "Anti-Muslim hate crimes are still five times more common today than before 9/11," "Workblog," *The Washington Post*, Feb. 11, 2015, http://tinyurl.com/q2awkqh.
Anti-Muslim hate crimes in the United States have jumped 500 percent since the 9/11 terrorist attacks, averaging 100 to 150 incidents a year, according to an examination of FBI crime reports.

Volokh, Eugene, "When does your religion legally excuse you from doing part of your job?" "The Volokh Conspiracy blog," *The Washington Post*, Sept. 4, 2015, http://tinyurl.com/o9r5hgf.
A UCLA law professor and widely read legal-affairs blogger (*The Volokh Conspiracy*), examines employees' requests to be excused from certain responsibilities because of religious convictions.

Reports and Studies

Cooperman, Alan, Gregory Smith and Stefan Cornibert, "U.S. Public Becoming Less Religious," Pew Research Center, Nov. 3, 2015, http://tinyurl.com/pcyjbot.

Although the nation's overall rate of religious belief remains high, a survey finds that the percentages of U.S. adults who say they believe in God or attend church regularly have declined, and that younger Americans are far less religious than their elders.

Davis, Carolyn, *et al.*, "Restoring the Balance: A Progressive Vision of Religious Liberty Preserves the Freedoms of All Americans," Center for American Progress, October 2015, http://tinyurl.com/o27fpsx.
A liberal Washington think tank studied the implications of recent assertions by the religious right that, on religious freedom grounds, businesses do not have to provide some services to the public. The center argues that laws should be changed to better protect the rights of those who are denied services.

Melling, Louise, *et al.*, "Drawing the Line: Tackling Tensions Between Religious Freedom and Equality," The International Network of Civil Liberties Organizations, September 2015, http://tinyurl.com/ondsnmw.

Civil rights groups from around the world look at the struggle to balance religious and civil rights in various countries.

Messner, Thomas, "From Culture Wars to Conscience Wars: Emerging Threats to Conscience," The Heritage Foundation, April 12, 2011, http://tinyurl.com/hc5ymcw.
A visiting fellow at a conservative Washington think tank argues that government mandates concerning abortion, same-sex marriage and nondiscrimination threaten religious liberty.

Shackelford, Kelly, *et al.*, "Undeniable: The Survey of Hostility to Religion in America, 2014 Edition," Liberty Institute, 2014, http://tinyurl.com/p3cccy4.
A conservative legal think tank in Plano, Texas, publishes its latest compendium of attacks on religious liberty in the United States, and argues such incidents are on the rise.

For More Information

American Civil Liberties Union, 125 Broad St., 18th Floor, New York, NY 10004; 212-549-2500; www.aclu.org. National organization that works to protect the individual rights and liberties guaranteed by the U.S. Constitution, including the First Amendment right of religious freedom.

Americans United for the Separation of Church and State, 1901 L St., N.W., Suite 400, Washington, DC 20036; 202-466-3234; www.au.org. Nonpartisan educational organization dedicated to preserving the constitutional principle of church-state separation as the only way to ensure religious freedom for all Americans.

Becket Fund for Religious Liberty, 1200 New Hampshire Ave., N.W., Suite 700, Washington, DC 20036; 202-955-0095; www.becketfund.org. Public-interest legal and educational institute that seeks to protect the free exercise of all faiths; supports the principle that religious freedom is a fundamental human right.

Council on American-Islamic Relations, 453 New Jersey Ave., S.E., Washington, DC 20003; 202-488-8787; www.cair.com. Advocacy group that seeks to enhance understanding

of Islam, encourage dialogue, empower American Muslims and support the civil rights of all groups regardless of faith.

Freedom From Religion Foundation, PO Box 750, Madison WI 53701; 608-256-8900; http://ffrf.org. Nonprofit dedicated to defending and promoting the constitutional principle of separation of state and church and to educating the public on nontheism (the absence of belief in a god or gods).

Liberty Counsel, PO Box 540774, Orlando, FL 32854; 800-671-1776; www.lc.org. Nonprofit Christian litigation, education and policy group dedicated to advancing its vision of religious freedom, the sanctity of life and the traditional family by providing pro bono assistance and representation on these and related topics.

United States Conference of Catholic Bishops, 3211 Fourth St., N.E., Washington, DC 20017; 202-541-3000; www.usccb.org. Assembly of clerical leadership in the United States and the Virgin Islands that promotes the Catholic Church's vision of social and spiritual issues, including religious freedom and toleration.

8

Transgender Rights

Alan Greenblatt

American transgender actress Mya Taylor attests to the increasing visibility of transgender people in popular culture. Taylor won a 2015 Gotham Award for her portrayal of a trans sex worker in the independent film "Tangerine," making her the first transgender actress to win the award. "The Danish Girl," a new film about Danish transgender pioneer Lili Elbe, stars Eddie Redmayne as one of the first-known recipients of sex-reassignment surgery.

Getty Images/David Livingston

From *CQ Researcher*, December 11, 2015.

An increasing number of young Americans are identifying as transgender, and perhaps nowhere more than in Madison, Wis. Researchers in the liberal college town found that 250 high school students in Dane County, home to Madison, identify as transgender — that is, their sense of their own gender identity does not match up with their birth sex.[1] That's about 1.5 percent of all high school students in the county, or five times the estimated share of the transgender population nationwide.[2]

The community in some ways has embraced this expression of gender identity among students. In October, Madison West High School (the district's largest) announced that it was making its homecoming court gender neutral after nearly 1,000 students and staff signed a petition requesting the change. Students would not be identified as prom "king" or "queen" or even necessarily be chosen by gender.

"I think this gets us closer on a whole variety of fronts to making each and every student in our building feel like a valued, recognized member of our community," said Madison West Principal Beth Thompson.[3]

But many transgender students in Dane County continue to find life difficult. One survey found that 17 percent had attempted suicide, compared with 3 percent of non-transgender students.[4] Mindy Fabian, a transgender senior at Madison West, took her own life in 2013.[5] Skylar Marcus Lee, a transgender junior at the school, killed himself in September.

Guide to Transgender Terms

Term	Definition
Cisgender	People who are not transgender.
Cross-dresser/ transvestite	People who wear clothes associated with the opposite sex but who do not necessarily identify with the opposite gender. (The older term "transvestite" is now widely viewed as pejorative.) Many male cross-dressers prefer female sex partners.
Gender dysphoria	Condition in which a person's birth gender and gender identity differ.
Gender identity	Internal, deeply held sense of one's gender.
Gender expression	Outward portrayal of a person's gender through name, pronouns, clothing, behavior, voice or body characteristics.
Gender nonconforming	People — not necessarily transgender — whose gender expression differs from conventional femininity or masculinity.
Sex-reassignment (or gender-confirmation) surgery	Surgery to change one's genital organs to those of the opposite sex; not undertaken by all transgender people.
Genderqueer	People who do not identify as either male or female.
Sex	Bodily characteristics — including chromosomes, hormones and reproductive organs — that define a person as male or female.
Sexual orientation	A person's enduring physical, romantic or emotional attraction to other people.
Transgender	People whose gender identity and/or gender expression differs from conventions associated with their sex at birth. Transgender people can be straight, homosexual or bisexual.
Transition	Period in which transgender people change their name and appearance.
Pronoun usage	Some transgender people prefer to be referred to by gender-neutral pronouns such as "they" and honorifics such as "Mx."

Sources: "GLAAD Media Reference Guide — Transgender Issues," undated, GLAAD, http://tinyurl.com/6u7k67c; "Gender Dysphoria," Diagnostic and Statistical Manual of Mental Disorders (DSM-5), American Psychiatric Association, 2013, http://tinyurl.com/kxaf3m6

"This bill reinforces the societal norm in our schools that students born biologically male must not be allowed to enter facilities designated for biological females and vice versa," the bill's two lead Republican sponsors wrote to their colleagues.[6]

Fear about transgender individuals using the "wrong" bathroom or locker room has become the most visible expression of societal discomfort about the transgender movement. In November, voters in Houston rejected an anti-discrimination ordinance that would have provided legal protections to individuals on the basis of race and sex, as well as gender identity, following a campaign that turned on the question of bathroom use. "No men in women's bathrooms," Texas GOP Gov. Greg Abbott tweeted the day before the election.[7]

"They do not have gender identity dysphoria because they chose to," says Brad Dacus, president of the Pacific Justice Institute, a Sacramento, Calif., organization that promotes religious freedom, referring to the condition in which people feel discomfort or distress because their biological sex does not match their gender identity. "They need to have respect and reasonable accommodations," he says. But that "needs to be balanced with the need to have privacy for boys and girls in bathrooms and locker rooms and showers." His group is collecting signatures for a California ballot measure that would impose $4,000 fines on people who use bathrooms that don't align with their sex at birth.

An individual with gender dysphoria may have been born anatomically female but knows herself to be male, often from a young age. Researchers are unsure

And the same week the high school made its homecoming court gender neutral, Wisconsin lawmakers introduced a bill to require students to use restrooms and locker rooms that correspond to the sex listed on their birth certificates rather than their current gender identity.

what causes gender dysphoria, but when it persists the person may transition to the opposite gender.

The number of transgender Americans is unknown, with many afraid to come out publicly. The most widely cited estimate — from the Williams Institute, a think tank at the University of California, Los Angeles, law school — suggests that about 700,000 Americans are transgender.[8] That estimate is 100 times as many as was believed during the 1980s.

Some, but not all, transgender people are gay. Someone who transitions from being female to being male — or male to female — might be attracted to either women or men. When individuals transition to the opposite sex, the change typically entails coming out to family and friends and adopting a different appearance in dress and hair, changing their name and possibly receiving psychiatric and medical treatment. Some take hormones or have cosmetic surgery, but only a minority have surgery to change genitalia.

In addition, some individuals reject the idea that gender can be split neatly into categories. Those who do not identify as either male or female are known as "genderqueer," while those whose outward expression of gender differs from conventional femininity or masculinity are regarded as "gender noncomforming." In rare cases, intersex people are born with genitalia of both sexes.

On the whole, transgender individuals are gaining broader acceptance, or are on the cusp of doing so. A YouGov poll in June found that less than one-third of Americans (31 percent) believed that being transgender was morally wrong. Just 18 percent of those under the age of 30 believed it was wrong.[9]

Transgender figures such as Caitlyn Jenner — who was known as Bruce Jenner, an Olympic star — are celebrated in popular culture. Politicians, at least on the Democratic side, are insisting on anti-discrimination

18 States Ban Transgender Discrimination

Eighteen states and the District of Columbia prohibit gender-identity and sexual-orientation discrimination in housing, employment and public accommodations. Three states ban only sexual-orientation bias, and Utah bans both gender-identity and sexual-orientation discrimination, but not in public accommodations.

Ban gender-identity and sexual-orientation discrimination in employment, housing and public accommodations

Ban only sexual-orientation discrimination, or ban gender-identity and sexual-orientation discrimination, but not in public accommodations

Source: American Civil Liberties Union (ACLU)

protections based on gender identity. Major corporations and local chambers of commerce are endorsing legal protections for transgender people and in some cases supporting expansion of health coverage for them.

Transgender advocates are, by and large, optimistic about the increase in social acceptance. Nonetheless, they note that serious problems remain. Transgender individuals are far more likely than the population as a whole — or even other members of the LGBT (Lesbian, Gay, Bisexual, Transgender) community — to suffer discrimination in areas such as employment and housing. In addition, transgender individuals often live in fear of violence, with about two dozen transgender women having been killed in the United States so far in 2015.

And transgender individuals have not gained full legal and political acceptance, despite the Obama administration's efforts to extend transgender rights, including a likely move next year to allow them to serve openly in the military. Vice President Joseph Biden frequently calls transgender rights "the civil rights issue of our time."

Congress and most states, however, remain reluctant to protect transgender rights. A bill to offer such protection is supported by nearly all House Democrats but lacks a single co-sponsor among the majority Republicans. Fewer than half the states offer legal protection to transgender people against discrimination.

Many mainstream politicians, including social conservatives, have avoided publicly discussing transgender issues. Some describe gender identity and all that entails as a personal matter.

This year, Pope Francis rejected an academic theory that says gender exists along a changeable spectrum, calling it a denial of the "order of creation" and arguing that "the design of the Creator is written in nature."[10] Other conservative denominations, such as the Southern Baptist Convention and Assemblies of God, criticize "transgender confusion."[11] Some other denominations, such as the Episcopal Church, the Evangelical Lutheran Church and the United Church of Christ, are welcoming to transgender individuals.[12]

"For people who have had much more conservative gender norms and sexual norms, the world must look like a very scary place" after the Supreme Court decision on gay marriage and all the recent movies and television shows depicting transgender people, says Virginia Sapiro, a political scientist at Boston University who has written about gender politics.

Pop culture — which often has depicted transgender people, or "trans," as flamboyant cross-dressers or as mentally ill — is now lavishing more positive attention on them. TV shows such as "Transparent," "Sense8," "Orange Is the New Black" and "Becoming Us" all offer sympathetic portrayals of transgender characters. Transgender advocates say the positive reception will encourage more people to come out.

"There are hundreds of thousands of trans people who are out now, and there weren't 20 years ago," says Mara Keisling, executive director of the National Center for Transgender Equality, an advocacy group in Washington. "The most important work that's going on is when people educate their families and classmates and people they go to religious services with."

A survey released this summer by GLAAD (a group formerly known as Gay & Lesbian Alliance Against Defamation), which tracks media portrayals of LGBT people, found that 16 percent of Americans personally know or work with someone who is transgender — double the percentage in 2008.[13] In addition, 27 percent of Millennials — those 18 to 34 years old — say they know a transgender person.[14]

As people get to know more about transgender issues, they tend to become more sympathetic, according to a recent Williams Institute study.[15] "It's hard to be prejudiced against people they know," says Robin McHaelen, executive director of True Colors, a nonprofit that provides social services to LGBT youths in Connecticut.

As transgender equality looms larger on the national radar, here are some of the issues under debate:

Should anti-discrimination laws be extended to transgender people?

Comedian and playwright Jill Soloway created "Transparent," a comedy available via streaming on Amazon, that portrays a family's adjustment when its patriarch comes out as a transgender woman. In September, when she received an Emmy award for directing, Soloway pointed out that the central character could easily face discrimination in real life.

"She could, tomorrow, go and try to find an apartment and in 32 states it would be legal for the landlord to say, 'We don't rent to trans people,'" Soloway said.[16]

There's a saying these days in the transgender community: You can get married on Sunday, but fired on Monday. The Supreme Court made same-sex marriage rights universal last June, but most states and cities offer no legal protections for transgender people when it comes to employment, housing, lending or health insurance.

Jamie Hileman, president of the Metro Trans Umbrella Group, a support and advocacy group for transgender people in St. Louis, says, "Almost every single woman in the group has experienced or is experiencing work discrimination. I find myself, all too often, sharing the painful advice of how to deal with the situation," says Hileman, who says she lost her previous job in the liquor wholesale business after coming out.

Over the past couple of years, the departments of Justice and Education have issued numerous opinions that transgender rights fall under the protection of Title IX, the sex discrimination section of the Civil

Rights Act. Eighteen states and about 200 cities have laws protecting transgender individuals in employment and housing, but the levels and types of protection vary by locality.[17]

"People are just plain fired because they transition," says Amy Eisen Cislo, a senior lecturer in women, gender and sexuality studies at Washington University in St. Louis. "People transition on the job and that's it; the boss can just say, 'This isn't going to work for our company.'"

The result is widespread unemployment and poverty among transgender Americans. According to a survey by the National Center for Transgender Equality and the National Gay and Lesbian Task Force, transgender people are four times as likely to have a household income under $10,000 and are twice as likely as the average American to be unemployed. And nearly half of transgender individuals (47 percent) reported unfavorable employment outcomes, such as not being hired, being fired or being denied promotion.[18]

Autymn Williams, a 20-year-old transgender woman who is a student at the University of Central Oklahoma, says she consistently gets turned down for part-time jobs, even at restaurants and stores where she knows employees and managers. "You know me, and you're still doing this," she says she complained to one prospective employer.

The inability to find or keep a job can have serious consequences. An Indiana University study found that transgender people who face discrimination are more likely than the public as a whole to attempt suicide, abuse drugs or engage in other destructive behavior.[19]

Despite polls showing that most Americans support workplace protections for transgender individuals, anti-discrimination laws have been a tough sell in Congress and the 32 states without anti-discrimination laws.[20]

Bathrooms are one reason. Most Americans are uncomfortable with the idea of someone who is anatomically male using a women's restroom or locker room. "The focus is on the right of a young girl not to feel herself as having her privacy violated in the most intrusive way by having to dress and shower and be naked, potentially, and be visually violated by someone who is 100 percent biologically the other sex," the Pacific Justice Institute's Dacus says.

A CBS News poll found that 59 percent of Americans believe students should use the bathrooms that conform to their gender at birth, as opposed to 26 percent who

Six-year-old Coy Mathis and her mother appear at the Colorado statehouse in Denver on June 24, 2013, to announce that the Colorado Civil Rights Division ruled against her elementary school and said she could use the girls' bathroom because she is a transgender person. Since an early age, Coy, who was a male at birth, has said that she identified as a female.

say students should be able to pick according to their current gender identity.[21]

Transgender advocates bemoan what they call bathroom panic, saying that for all the fear about supposedly predatory transgender people, they are the ones who are likely to be harassed or abused in public facilities. "People just want to pee in peace," True Colors' McHaelen says.

Concerns about bathrooms and other public accommodations seem to come up in every discrimination debate. Bills mandating bathroom use according to birth gender have been proposed in Arizona, Florida, Kentucky and other states. The Houston ordinance would have extended anti-discrimination protections in areas such as public accommodations, housing, employment and city contracting to people on the basis of sex, race, sexual identity and gender orientation. But voters rejected it in November, largely due to TV ads and other messages that warned about the bathroom issue.

"Most people think it's gross to force little girls to share a bathroom with grown men," tweeted Sean Davis, co-founder of *The Federalist*, a conservative online magazine.[22]

Those opposed to extending anti-discrimination protections to transgender individuals believe this would burden businesses, as well as schools, hospitals and churches. Some argue it could be harder to ban discrimination on the basis of gender identity because it is more malleable than race. "The basic idea here is that race is something much more identifiable and definable," says Ryan T. Anderson, a senior research fellow at The Heritage Foundation, a conservative think tank in Washington. In addition, he says, "it's unclear what the costs for protecting on the basis of sex identity would be."

Many corporations, however, support transgender rights. According to the Human Rights Campaign, two-thirds of the nation's 500 largest corporations have adopted gender-identity nondiscrimination policies — up from just 3 percent in 2002. A third of the companies now offer transgender-inclusive health insurance, including coverage on procedures specifically related to gender identity, up from zero in 2002.[23]

Some companies are dealing with the bathroom issue by allowing employees to use whatever restroom they are comfortable with, while others are providing single-stall or gender-neutral restrooms. Some transgender individuals, however, equate gender-neutral restrooms with the "separate but equal" approach to school segregation that existed in the South during the Jim Crow era.

Still, Anderson says, the government should not rush into an area where research is needed. An anti-discrimination law protecting LGBT individuals in areas such as employment and lending, known as the Equality Act, has stalled in Congress. It has 170 co-sponsors in the House, but none belongs to the majority Republican Party.

Nonetheless, given the speed at which pop culture and public opinion are changing, some opposed to making gender identity a protected class worry that they're losing momentum.

"We're definitely fighting an uphill battle," says Andrew Beckwith, president of the Massachusetts Family Institute, a socially conservative group. "Proponents have the media and a lot of big business and a lot of politicians on their side."

Should transgender individuals serve openly in the military?

Jennifer Peace is an Army intelligence officer who has served in Iraq and Afghanistan. Her performance evaluation in April named her one of her battalion's top captains. "Capt. Peace's potential is unlimited," the evaluation reads. "Promote to major and send to [an academy for majors] now."[24]

Nevertheless, Peace — who was born a male — remains nervous about her career. Her commanders have known since she came out as a woman three years ago, but her peers have been ordered to refer to her as a man. She worries that a new commander could view her as unfit for duty as a transgender woman. Under current Pentagon rules, transgender soldiers and sailors are considered medically unfit and can be honorably discharged if diagnosed with "psychosexual conditions" such as "transsexualism" and "transvestism."[25]

The question of whether the military might pay for gender-confirmation surgery has also been a point of controversy, especially since Bradley Manning — an Army sergeant convicted in 2013 for leaking sensitive documents — came out shortly after his conviction as Chelsea Manning and successfully pressed the government to pay for hormone therapy. If the Pentagon decides to allow transgender individuals to serve openly, it is likely the military will pay for such treatment, estimated to cost the military $5.6 million annually.[26]

Official military policy appears likely to change in the coming months. In July, Defense Secretary Ashton Carter ordered a six-month review of policies regarding transgender personnel, making clear his desire to allow them to serve openly.

"The Defense Department's current regulations regarding transgender service members are outdated," Carter said. "We have transgender soldiers, sailors, airmen and Marines — real, patriotic Americans — who I know are being hurt by an outdated, confusing, inconsistent approach that's contrary to our value of service and individual merit."[27]

Carter said a policy change should move forward, barring discovery of "objective, practical impediments." A Defense Department memo suggested the ban on transgender troops could be lifted as early as May 27, 2016.[28]

This change has drawn criticism, notably from Republican presidential aspirants. "The military is not a social experiment. The purpose of the military is [to] kill people and break things," former Arkansas Gov. Mike Huckabee said at the first GOP presidential debate in August. "I'm not sure how paying for transgender surgery for soldiers, sailors, airmen, Marines makes our country safer."[29]

At an October presidential campaign stop in Iowa, Sen. Ted Cruz of Texas made similar points: "We shouldn't view the military as a cauldron for social experiments."[30] Cruz said he would listen to the "expert judgement" of generals and admirals. But they have not been speaking out against the policy change. "The lack of vocal opposition isn't an accurate indication of the majority of military members," says Beckwith of the Massachusetts Family Institute. "I served in the Marine Corps for a tour. I can tell you, the nature of the military is to follow orders."

On a recent afternoon, a small group of veterans and active-duty personnel was sitting at the bar at the Veterans of Foreign Wars (VFW) post in Richmond Heights, Mo., watching "Jeopardy." When the topic of transgender individuals serving in the military came up, a man who said his "road name" is "Wrench" commented, "I wouldn't want one in my freaking foxhole."

Wrench said he served six years in the Army, including in Vietnam. "I just feel that if they're male-to-female or female-to-male, there's something wrong with their genetic code, and maybe their psyche," he said.

Although transgender individuals are often subject to verbal taunting and abuse, many already serve or have served in the military. UCLA's Williams Institute estimated in 2014 that 15,500 transgender people were serving in the military, with 134,300 others retired from duty. That is 21 percent of the nation's overall transgender population and double the 10 percent enlistment rate for the general population.[31]

However, only a couple of dozen transgender individuals — such as Capt. Peace, Army Sgt. Shane Ortega and Army Staff Sgt. Patricia King — are serving openly in the U.S. military, hoping to draw attention to the issue.

That's the opposite approach of most transgender soldiers and sailors. Some serve specifically because they don't accept their gender identity, say some psychologists. They have coined the term "flight into hypermasculinity" as part of the possible diagnoses for transgender women who enlist in the military or pursue other traditionally masculine careers, such as police officer or firefighter.[32] "It's very common for trans women [who are born male] to try to prove that masculinity when they're in denial," says Hileman, the Metro Trans Umbrella Group president.

Paula Sophia, a transgender woman who served in the Army as a man and had a 21-year career on the Oklahoma City police force, says it's true some join the military to prove something to themselves and to search for — or deny — their own identities. "We're attracted to those roles that seem definite," she says.

She notes that the debate about transgender individuals serving openly echoes earlier debates about whether gays should serve in the military or whether women should serve in combat. Gays have been allowed to serve in the military since 2001. And in September, President Obama nominated Eric Fanning to become the first openly gay secretary of the Army.

And early this month, Defense Secretary Carter announced he was lifting the ban on women serving in combat. Carter said the military will open all combat jobs to women early next year with "no exceptions."

"When it comes down to it, if you can physically hack the demands of that job, then you ought to be able to do it, whether you're male or female, whether you're trans or [nontrans]," Sophia says. "The military is a very pragmatic organization, and that's how they ought to judge people across the board. If they can do the job, that's it."

Should children receive medical treatment for gender identity issues?

Due to stigma and fear, transgender people in earlier generations would often wait until well into adulthood to come out. Former Olympic star Jenner was 65 when she announced this year that she was transgender. Increasingly, however, people are coming out in their teens or even earlier.

Jazz Jennings, a transgender girl, has been in the media spotlight since giving an interview to ABC News in 2007, when she was 6.[33] Last summer, at age 14, she had her own reality TV show.[34]

Not all parents accept the idea that the child they've known as their son is now their daughter. But levels of parental support, while not universal, appear to be increasing, according to therapists. Families must decide not only whether to support a child's social transition — changes in hair, dress and name — but whether to allow medical intervention.

Some doctors will prescribe puberty-blocking hormones, delaying the development of secondary sex characteristics such as breasts, facial hair and a more pronounced Adam's apple. Some describe this as hitting a "pause" button — giving a child more time to explore gender issues before the body undergoes developmental changes. "It provides a longer window for a person to really explore their gender identity before you undergo puberty," says Cislo, the Washington University lecturer.

Doctors have used such hormones for several decades to treat children who were entering puberty too early. Treating transgender children is what's known as an "off-label" use of the medication, meaning it hasn't been approved by the Food and Drug Administration. But some doctors offer such treatment. In fact, the Endocrine Society, the largest professional association devoted to endocrinology and hormone health, has recommended use of puberty-blocking hormones for children with gender dysphoria since 2009.[35]

However, the society does not recommend surgery and cross-sex hormones (estrogen and testosterone) for preadolescents.

"What the medical standard is now is that you don't do anything that's irreversible for people under 18, and in some jurisdictions, 21," says Jamison Green, president of the World Professional Association for Transgender Health (WPATH), which represents health providers and sets standards of care. "They're not getting their sex changed, they're not getting surgery."

But little research has been done about potential long-term effects of children taking hormones. Some physicians worry about the potential impact on growth, bone density and the brain. "My approach as a physician is that it's much more important to get it right than to get it fast," says Fred Berlin, a psychiatrist at Johns Hopkins University in Baltimore.

He notes that children are not trusted with major decisions such as voting or buying or selling the family car. Their brains are still developing, and their sense of

Americans Divided on Restroom Use

American adults are almost evenly split on whether transgender people should be allowed to use restrooms and other public facilities that don't match their birth gender, according to a June 2015 poll; one in four were undecided.

Should Transgender People Be Allowed to Use Public Restrooms, Dressing Rooms and Locker Rooms Not Designated for Their Birth Gender?

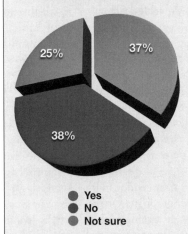

- ● Yes
- ● No
- ● Not sure

Source: "Poll Results: Transgender," YouGov/*The Huffington Post*, June 3-4, 2015, http://tinyurl.com/odk8s8x. The poll of adults 18 and over featured 1,000 respondents.

identity — including gender identity — is fluid, he says.

Some studies indicate that only a minority of children who express gender dysphoria identify as transgender later in life.[36] A 2014 study by the Hastings Center, a bioethics research institute in Garrison, N.Y., found that only 6 to 23 percent of boys and 12 to 27 percent of girls treated in gender clinics continued to experience gender dysphoria as adults.[37] "The overwhelming majority of pre-pubescent children who express these feelings of gender dysphoria don't persist in these feelings later in life," Berlin says.

Some doctors and therapists believe that an early medical approach to gender transition will result in more children persisting in feelings of gender dysphoria, rather than growing out of them or potentially becoming more comfortable with the sex they were at birth.[38] "Even a social transition back to one's original gender role can be an emotionally difficult experience for children," writes Debra W. Soh, a sex researcher and neuroscientist at York University in Toronto.[39]

Critics of the "watch and wait" approach, however, warn that not offering hormone therapy poses its own dangers. What might sound like a simple thing, such as a transgender male binding his breasts, can scar the lungs by making breathing more difficult.[40] More significantly, they point to potential mental health issues. Transgender children can become anxious and even suicidal during puberty as their bodies seem to betray them by becoming more masculine or feminine, in contrast to their gender identity.

"People with gender dysphoria that did not receive treatment had a much higher rate of hospitalizations or ER visits or doctors' visits for depression and anxiety," said Ariel Smits, medical director of a commission that recommended Oregon's Medicaid program pay for puberty-suppressing hormone treatments. "And they had a pretty significantly high suicide rate — some studies found about 30 percent."[41]

Clinicians and advocates say children who are "consistent, persistent and insistent" in saying that their bodies do not match their gender identity should receive treatment.

"If you socially transition a child, and all of a sudden they're thrilled to go to school, and they're not self-hating, that's a pretty good indication you've made the right decision," says Nick Adams, director of transgender media at GLAAD. "There's a small cabal of sexologists who continue to think children can be talked out of being transgender, but they're on their way out as a treatment model."

Hileman, of the Metro Trans Umbrella Group, counters that most kids under 18 who go through "gender variant behavior" may be "gender playing" and are not truly transgender. "It would be wrong to prescribe them puberty blockers," she says. But Hileman, a 49-year-old transgender woman who lives in Alton, Ill., adds that children who are likely to remain transgender in adulthood would benefit greatly from hormone treatments because it would save them so much angst. "It's impossible to express what a boon it would have been, not having to go through the wrong adolescence," she says. "There's not a trans person I know who, if they had a chance, wouldn't take it."

Of course, not all transgender people pursue medical interventions, at any age.

"People are realizing that a lot of people live their whole life as a different sex than they were born, without hormones and surgery," says Green, the World Professional Association for Transgender Health president.

BACKGROUND
Outlawed

Although the term transgender has been in use for only the last couple of decades, there have always been some men who act or identify as women — or women as men. They have been mostly vilified throughout human history.

A man urges people to vote against the Houston Equal Rights Ordinance outside an early voting center in Houston on Oct. 21, 2015. In November, voters rejected the anti-discrimination ordinance, which would have provided legal protections to individuals on the basis of race and sex, as well as gender identity. The anti- ordinance campaign turned on the question of bathroom use. "No men in women's bathrooms," Texas GOP Gov. Greg Abbott tweeted the day before the election.

"The woman shall not wear that which pertaineth unto a man, neither shall a man put on a woman's garment: For all that do so are [an] abomination unto the LORD thy God," the King James version of the Bible states in Deuteronomy 22.

From their earliest days in the Western Hemisphere, European colonizers noticed that in various Native American cultures, some males assumed women's dress and duties, and vice versa. They sometimes called such people "berdache," a derogatory French term, while Native Americans used the expression "Two-Spirits."[42]

Although native cultures accepted such people, European colonizers found them an abomination. During his 1513 expedition across Panama, the Spanish explorer Vasco Núñez de Balboa, enraged by cross-dressing men, sicced dogs against a tribal king and others; 40 died.[43]

But cross-dressers became part of American life. By the mid-19th century, industrialization meant more people were living on their own in cities and enjoying more freedom, anonymity and independence from their families and closer-knit rural communities. Starting in the 1850s, dozens of cities passed laws prohibiting individuals from wearing clothes associated with the opposite sex.[44]

Hundreds of Civil War soldiers were born women, including Dr. Mary Edwards Walker, who began cross-dressing in the 1850s and received a congressional Medal

CHRONOLOGY

1940s–1980s *Transsexual movement gains little progress in legal rights.*

1949 The term "transsexual" is coined. . . . California's attorney general rules that surgeons can be prosecuted for genital modification.

1952 American Christine Jorgensen completes sex-change surgery in Denmark.

1962 The California Supreme Court strikes down laws against cross-dressing.

1966 Compton's Cafeteria riot in San Francisco is one of the early protests for transgender rights. . . . Johns Hopkins University opens the first U.S. clinic offering sex-change operations.

1968 Gore Vidal's *Myra Breckenridge*, a sensational novel about a transsexual, becomes a best-seller.

1975 The diagnosis of "transsexualism" first appears in an international psychiatric classification, followed in 1980 by its appearance in the *Diagnostic and Statistical Manual of Mental Disorders* (*DSM*).

1980 The *DSM* defines transsexualism as a disorder.

1990s–2000s *State and local governments begin extending benefits and rights protections to transgender people.*

1993 Minnesota becomes the first state to offer legal protections to transsexuals.

1999 An annual Transgender Day of Remembrance is started to honor the memory of transgender people killed in hate crimes.

2000 Hilary Swank wins the Academy Award for best actress for playing Brandon Teena, a transgender man who was raped and killed in 1993, in "Boys Don't Cry."

2001 San Francisco becomes the first city to offer health benefits, including coverage of gender reassignment surgery, to transgender employees.

2007 Hormones are first prescribed in the United States — at Boston's Children's Hospital — for treating children with gender identity issues.

2009–Present *The Obama administration aggressively moves to protect transgender rights.*

2009 President Obama signs a hate crime bill that includes protections for the LGBT community, the first federal law that addresses a gender identity issue.

2010 The White House appoints the first two openly transgender officials to serve in administrative posts.

2011 The White House hosts its first conference on transgender issues.

2012 Equal Employment Opportunity Commission determines Title VII of the Civil Rights Act protects transgender employees against harassment.

2013 The *DSM* drops "gender identity disorder" as a diagnosis, replaces it with "gender dysphoria." . . . Bradley Manning, an Army soldier convicted of leaking thousands of classified documents, comes out as Chelsea Manning. . . . California becomes the first state to enshrine certain rights for transgender students into law, including access to the sports teams, locker rooms and bathrooms of their choice.

2014 Obama signs an executive order protecting federal employees from discrimination on the basis of gender identity, as well as one barring federal contractors from discriminating against LGBT people. . . . Medicare lifts the ban on coverage of gender reassignment surgery. . . . The Army agrees to recognize the new names adopted by transgender veterans. . . . Attorney General Eric Holder determines that the prohibition against sex discrimination under Title VII of the Civil Rights Act covers transgender rights.

2015 Seventeen million viewers watch Caitlyn Jenner come out as a transgender woman on ABC (April). . . . Defense Secretary Ashton Carter announces the Pentagon is moving toward a policy of allowing transgender soldiers and sailors to serve openly (July). . . . Houston voters turn down an anti-discrimination ordinance that would have protected transgender individuals (November). . . . Congress creates a Transgender Equality Task Force to examine transgender rights (November).

of Honor as an assistant surgeon in the Union Army.[45] "People are surprised when I say we have lots of historical evidence of people not necessarily identifying with the sex assigned at birth," says Cislo, the Washington University lecturer. "We have people who fought in the Civil War who we realized later had a vagina, that the soldier was, quote, 'really a woman.'"

Early in the 20th century, researchers coined many terms to describe the phenomenon of people acting or dressing like the opposite sex. *The Transvestites*, a 1910 book by Magnus Hirscheld, a German sexologist, lent its name to a lasting expression that is now considered derogatory.[46] (Some cross-dressers, or transvestites, do not identify as transgender.)

By the 1920s a few doctors, mostly in Germany, performed "sex-change" operations, currently referred to as gender-reassignment or gender-confirmation surgeries.[47] (In 1930, artist Einar Wegener underwent the first of five surgeries in Germany to transition from male to female.[48] She became known as Lily Elbe and is the subject of the new film "The Danish Girl," starring Oscar-winning actor Eddie Redmayne as Elbe.

By the 1950s, a handful of American doctors had performed sex-change operations, but most patients who sought such procedures were rejected. While occasional sensationalistic stories appeared about "transsexuals," as transgenders were known at the time, discussion of treatments virtually disappeared from U.S. scientific journals.[49]

Pat Brown, the attorney general of California, ruled in 1949 that genital modification would cause "mayhem" and surgeons who performed them could face prosecution. "That opinion cast a pall, lasting for years, over efforts by U.S. transgender people to gain access to transsexual medical procedures in their own country," writes Susan Stryker, director of the Institute for LGBT Studies at Arizona State University.[50]

Path to Treatment

In 1952, American George Jorgensen, a World War II Army veteran, completed hormone treatment and two surgeries in Denmark, becoming known as Christine Jorgensen. After *The New York Daily News* broke the story — the famous headline was "Ex-GI Becomes Blonde Beauty" — Jorgensen's experience became one of the most written about news events of the decade.[51] "In the 1950s, Jorgensen made sex change a household term," writes Joanne Meyerowitz, a historian at Yale University.[52]

American transgender woman Christine Jorgensen, shown in 1954, became one of the most written about people in the 1950s when she completed hormone treatment and two surgeries in Denmark to transition from being George Jorgensen. The famous *New York Daily News* headline on the story was "Ex-GI Becomes Blonde Beauty."

That did not open the door to widespread treatment in the United States, however. Things didn't start to change until the mid-1960s. In 1966, endocrinologist Harry Benjamin published *The Transsexual Phenomenon*, arguing that gender identity can't be changed so transsexuals should be helped to lead fuller, happier lives.[53]

Within months of the book's publication, Johns Hopkins University established the nation's first gender reassignment clinic. "Soon afterward, other major medical centers opened their own gender identity programs that offered sex-change operations," Meyerowitz wrote, often with financial backing from a foundation established by Reed Erickson, a wealthy transgender man born in Texas, whose family made a fortune in the petroleum industry. Erickson was born in 1917 but began masculinizing his body in the 1960s, soon after his father's death.[54]

Surgeons were unable — or unwilling — to keep up with the demand. During the first two and a half years of its existence, the Johns Hopkins program received "almost 2,000 desperate requests" for surgery, Meyerowitz wrote, but doctors there operated on only 24 patients.[55]

The medical profession saw transsexualism as a disorder, while insurers considered treatment for the disorder as cosmetic or elective. Thus, insurance coverage for the

Transgender Movement Hails Jenner as Pivotal

"She gave people a chance to tell their stories."

For many transgender people, the huge amount of media attention paid to former Olympic athlete Caitlyn Jenner has been a breakthrough. Many compare her coming out as a transgender person to comedian and TV star Ellen DeGeneres' 1997 announcement on "The Oprah Winfrey Show" that she is a lesbian.[1]

Jenner — who had long been famous as Bruce Jenner, the 1976 Olympic gold medal winner in the men's decathlon — is "a pivotal figure. She's our generation's and trans people's Ellen DeGeneres in many ways," says Paula Sophia, a transgender woman who lives in Oklahoma City and unsuccessfully ran for the state House of Representatives in 2014. "Caitlyn Jenner has made it so trans people aren't invisible anymore, more than any one person."

Jenner has helped draw attention to the lives of ordinary transgender individuals, says Mara Keisling, executive director of the National Center for Transgender Equality, an advocacy group in Washington, D.C. "She gave us an opportunity to tell the story," Keisling says. "Hundreds of trans people got interviewed by local media all over the country. She gave people a chance to tell their stories."

At the same time, Keisling stresses that no one person can serve as spokesperson for a population as diverse as the transgender community. Some transgender people worry that Jenner — a wealthy celebrity able to afford expensive surgeries — will give people the wrong impression about transgender life. (Jenner, 65, has had breast implants, had her Adam's apple shaved and has had cosmetic surgery to feminize her face.[2])

Indeed, Jenner likely had the most visible coming out of any transgender person in history. In an interview with longtime ABC News anchor Diane Sawyer last April — watched by 17 million people — Jenner discussed her long struggle with gender identity and announced, "For all intents and purposes, I'm a woman. My brain is much more female than it is male," Jenner said. "It's hard for people to understand that, but that's what my soul is."[3]

In the months since the interview, Jenner has been featured in thousands of news articles, including a flattering profile in *Vanity Fair*.[4] She appeared on the cover in a glamorous photo by celebrated portrait photographer Annie Leibovitz, under the headline "Call me Caitlyn." Jenner received an ESPN award for courage and was named one of *Glamour*'s women of the year.[5] Jenner, who has said she never met a transgender person until this year, also has raised awareness of transgender individuals and the issues they face on "I Am Cait," her documentary series on E! network that was renewed for the 2016 season despite weak ratings.[6]

The Jenner phenomenon has had "a weird backlash effect on the kids we serve," says Robin McHaelen, executive director of True Colors, a Connecticut nonprofit that provides mentoring and other services to LGBT youths. "We've got one kid who won't go to school because she doesn't have the same access to resources [as Jenner], and she's never going to look like Caitlyn does."

It's not just a question of being able to afford enough plastic surgery to look good on a magazine cover. Not all transgender people want surgery, including gender confirmation surgery to alter genitalia.

"The Caitlyn Jenner thing has been a point of controversy because for people who know nothing about trans identity, it seems to solidify the idea that it's a person who fully wants to change their bodily appearance and appear as the opposite sex through surgeries," says Amy Eisen Cislo, who lectures on gender issues at Washington University in St. Louis. "Transgender is so much broader than that."

surgeries — which currently average about $20,000 — was for the most part nonexistent.

Psychiatrists and surgeons who did offer treatment took a rigid "gatekeeper" approach. A person seeking to change genders would have to see a therapist for months before being referred to an endocrinologist, then would have to live socially as the desired gender for at least a year.[56] To get treatment, people with gender dysphoria learned to lie about their conditions, leading providers to distrust them.[57]

"You had to fit the narrative of what they called successful, willing to have every step of the process, up to and including [gender reassignment] surgery," says Adams of GLAAD. "The critical part, their idea of a successful

Some conservatives are mystified or even outraged that a paragon of masculinity such as an Olympic athlete now identifies as a woman. "Is it him? Her? It? I don't even know what to call it," a resident of Osceola, Iowa, told *The Washington Post*. "You know, don't shove this down my throat."[7]

For the most part, however, prominent conservative politicians are steering clear of the transgender issue. "It's a personal decision," Republican Gov. Scott Walker of Wisconsin told ABC News, when asked about Jenner during his recent unsuccessful presidential run. "I don't know that there's anything more to comment on."[8]

Some conservatives complain the Republican Party is making a mistake by not voicing disapproval of the transgender movement. "The rapidly growing acceptance of the previously marginal idea that underlies the transgender moment was only made possible by the Republican decision to opt out of this debate entirely," wrote Sean Fieler, chairman of the American Principles Project, a Washington organization that promotes conservative social positions.[9]

— Alan Greenblatt

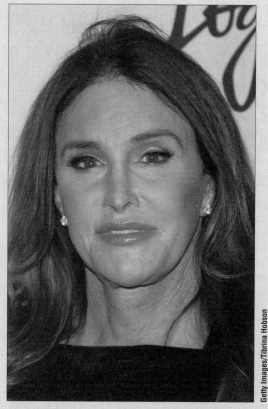

Caitlyn Jenner, the former Olympic decathlon champion Bruce Jenner, has been featured in thousands of news articles since she came out, at age 65, as a woman.

[1]Joyce Chen, "Ellen DeGeneres on Coming Out as Gay: 'I Didn't Think I Was Going to Come Out, Period,' " *Us Weekly*, Oct. 23, 2015, http://tinyurl.com/o4jy3nv.

[2]Charlotte Wareing, "Caitlyn Jenner 'left in constant pain' following gender transition surgeries," *Mirror*, Sept. 21, 2015, http://tinyurl.com/jnvln6a.

[3]Rick Kissell, "Bruce Jenner Interview Ratings: 17 Million Watch ABC Special," *Variety*, April 25, 2015, http:// tinyurl.com/qgrggqf. The interview is available online at http:// tinyurl.com/n2e4s43. "Bruce Jenner: 'My brain is much more female than male,' " ESPN.com News Services, April 24, 2015, http://tinyurl.com/hqr hyfu.

[4]Buzz Bissinger, "Caitlyn Jenner: The Full Story," *Vanity Fair*, June 30, 2015, http:// tinyurl.com/n9awbct.

[5]"Glamour's Women of the Year 2015," *Glamour*, Oct. 29, 2015, http://tinyurl.com/o6x gqzf.

[6]Pooja Bhagat, " 'I Am Cait' Season 2 Set To Premiere in 2016: Get The Details," *Yibada*, Oct. 26, 2015, http://tinyurl.com/no3udzm.

[7]Philip Rucker and Robert Costa, "In a Fast-Changing Culture, Can the GOP Get in Step With Modern America?" *The Washington Post*, June 27, 2015, http://tinyurl.com/o8whxua.

[8]" 'This Week' Transcript: Gov. Scott Walker," June 7, 2015, http:// tinyurl.com/ owyqebd.

[9]Sean Fieler, "What Republicans Should Learn From the Transgender Moment," *The Daily Signal*, May 27, 2015, http://tinyurl.com/ q5o2xfh.

transition, was that you would be a passable, heterosexual person and would never tell anyone you were trans."

Outside the clinics, meanwhile, police routinely harassed and arrested transsexuals. Presaging the 1969 Stonewall riots — protests in New York City against police raids that sparked the modern gay rights movement — people now called transgender had participated in a series of similar, spontaneous protests. The demonstrations were at spots such as Dewey's lunch counter in Philadelphia in 1965 and Compton's Cafeteria in San Francisco in 1966.[58]

From Rejection to Inclusion

People known as transvestites at the time were at Stonewall, but they were marginalized by the gay rights movement.

Killings of Transgender People on Rise

The increase worries LGBT community as experts debate causes.

Zella Ziona was just 21 when she was killed outside a laundromat in Gaithersburg, Md., in October. The transgender woman had been surrounded by a group of young adults, one of whom has been charged in Ziona's shooting death. Authorities say the suspect possibly acted out of embarrassment that his relationship with her had become known.[1]

Among transgenders, Ziona's story is tragically familiar. Nearly all the transgender individuals killed in 2015 were women of color. "Most Americans think it's been an amazing year for transgender rights," said Mara Keisling, executive director of the National Center for Transgender Equality, an advocacy group in Washington. "But for the transgender community, it's been one of the most traumatic years on record."[2]

The exact number of killings is unknown. Police and media reports sometimes "misgender" victims, failing to account for their transgender status. Nevertheless, activists in the lesbian, gay, bisexual, transgender and queer (LGBTQ) community believe that at least 22 transgender individuals have been killed so far this year, up significantly from the 12 trans women killed in each of the previous two years, according to the National LGBTQ Task Force, an advocacy group in Washington.[3]

Transgender individuals have long been subject to violence. The 1999 film "Boys Don't Cry" dramatized the real-life rape and murder of Brandon Teena, a transgender man, bringing widespread attention to the problem.[4] In 2009, President Obama signed a hate-crime law that included gender identity as a protected category.[5]

The increase in killings has drawn attention from the White House and other politicians, primarily Democrats. Democratic presidential candidate Hillary Clinton called it a "national crisis" in a private meeting with activists from the Black Lives Matter movement.[6] Believing that their causes overlap, some African-American and transgender activists are working together on criminal justice issues.[7]

As more transgender people come out, and as the movement gains prominence, more may be targeted for violence, experts say. "In general, if you look at history, a lot of times whenever there are positive moves for historically marginalized groups, there tends to be a backlash," said Kevin Nadal, head of the Center for LGBTQ Studies at the Graduate Center at the City University of New York.[8]

A recent study by the National Coalition of Anti-Violence Programs, an advocacy group for the LGBTQ and HIV communities, found that transgender and gender nonconforming people (who reject the idea of a binary split between male and female) are twice as likely to face violence from a partner than those in the gay community.[9]

"Financial dependence can make it more difficult to leave an abusive relationship," write Nick Gorton and Hilary Maia Grubb, California physicians who work with transgender patients. They are "less likely to be employed and financially independent than cisgender people" and may need to stay with abusive partners in order to have food and shelter.[10]

About half of transgender individuals killed in 2015 worked in the sex trade.[11] Some transgender people who have been kicked out of their homes or have trouble finding

"For a long time, this sense of an identity opposite of what was assigned at birth was not accepted in the gay community," Washington University's Cislo says. Seeking wider acceptance, some gays and lesbians looked down on masculine women and feminine men. Some lesbians in particular expressed hostility toward transgender women, whom they saw as appropriating women's bodies and insisting on regressive and oppressive dress and stereotypes.

"As lesbian feminists saw it, transvestites were mocking women by mimicking what demeaned them," wrote historian Lillian Faderman.[59]

In 1979, women's studies scholar Janice Raymond argued in her influential book *The Transsexual Empire: The Making of the She-Male* that "transsexuals rape women's bodies by reducing the real female form to an artifact."[60] Such attitudes were not universal, but through the 1990s transgender people were excluded from several gay festivals and parades.

work turn to prostitution, which can lead to violence, drug use and incarceration.[12]

A 2011 survey of 6,450 transgender and gender nonconforming people found that one-fifth of them had experienced homelessness in their lifetimes.[13] The survey also found that 41 percent of transgender people have attempted suicide, compared with 1.6 percent of the general population. A more recent analysis of that survey showed that suicide risk was especially high among people who had experienced violence or family rejection. "Seventy-eight percent of survey respondents who suffered physical violence at school reported suicide attempts, as did 65 percent of respondents who experienced violence at work," according to the analysis.[14]

Jamison Green, president of the World Professional Association for Transgender Health, a providers' network, says suicide risk among this population can sometimes be exaggerated, but he adds that many transgender people have thought about killing themselves. Some suicides take on a special resonance, such as the death of 17-year-old Leelah Alcorn of Union Township, Ohio, who killed herself by walking into Interstate traffic three days after Christmas in 2014.

Alcorn's death, which followed an attempt by her parents to use Christian-based conversion therapy aimed at returning her to her biological sex, sparked vigils and calls for Congress and state legislatures to pass a "Leelah's Law" to ban such treatments. Some conservatives complain the law could prevent therapists from exploring whether gender identity issues can be addressed in ways other than transitioning to another gender. Still, in August, Illinois became the fourth state to ban doctors and therapists from attempting to change a minor's sexual orientation.[15]

— *Alan Greenblatt*

[1]"Transgender Woman's Family Believes Murder Was Hate Crime," WUSA, Oct. 17, 2015, http://tinyurl.com/ochte23.

[2]David Crary, "Homicides of Transgender Women in U.S. Reach Alarming High," The Associated Press, Nov. 23, 2015, http://tinyurl.com/prnjx6l.

[3]"Stop Trans Murders," National LGBTQ Task Force, Oct. 16, 2015, http://tinyurl. com/na5hdsp.

[4]Stephanie Fairyington, "Two Decades After Brandon Teena's Murder, A Look Back at Falls City," *The Atlantic*, Dec. 31, 2013, http://tinyurl.com/k9pt74m.

[5]"National Defense Authorization Act for Fiscal Year 2010," Government Printing Office, http://tinyurl.com/ovzvdos.

[6]Darren Sands, "Activists: Hillary Clinton Called Violence Against Black Trans Women A 'National Crisis,' " *BuzzFeed News*, Oct. 9, 2015, http://tinyurl.com/oxmd8qs.

[7]Cleis Abeni, "Trans Lives Matter and Black Lives Matter Join Forces for Justice," *Advocate*, Sept. 10, 2015, http://tinyurl.com/of5o8ts.

[8]Zach Stafford, "Transgender Murders in US Have Nearly Doubled Since Last Year, Activists Say," *The Guardian*, Nov. 6, 2015, http://tinyurl.com/qhh9dbs.

[9]Chai Jindasurat and Emily Waters, "Lesbian, Gay, Bisexual, Transgender, Queer and HIV-Affected Intimate Partner Violence in 2014," National Coalition of Anti-Violence Programs, Oct. 27, 2015, http://tinyurl.com/nwwdkv2.

[10]Laura Erickson-Schroth, ed., *Trans Bodies, Trans Selves* (2014), p. 225.

[11]Zach Stafford, "Two LGBT murders within 24 hours leaves community in 'state of emergency,' " *The Guardian*, Oct. 11, 2015, http://tinyurl.com/ok8df5k.

[12]Erickson-Schroth, *op. cit.*, p. 169.

[13]Jaime M., Grant, Lisa A. Mottet and Justin Tanis, "Injustice at Every Turn," National Center for Transgender Equality and the National Gay and Lesbian Task Force, 2011, http://tinyurl.com/4hy6rb6.

[14]Ann P. Haas, Philip L. Rogers and Jody L. Herman, "Suicide Attempts Among Transgender and Gender Non-Conforming Adults," American Foundation for Suicide Prevention and the Williams Institute, January 2014, http://tinyurl.com/mxnamkb.

[15]Aditya Agarwal, "Illinois Bans Gay Conversion Therapy for Minors," *Time*, Aug. 21, 2015, tinyurl.com/qygbb2m.

Also in 1979, a study by the director of the Johns Hopkins clinic showed "no objective improvement" among those who had undergone sex-change surgery. Although the study was later shown to be biased, the clinic announced that it would no longer offer sex-reassignment surgeries.[61] Other clinics followed suit.[62]

Ostracized by an array of groups — social conservatives, some on the left and much of the medical and psychiatric communities — and with the outbreak of the AIDS epidemic, many transgender communities became "very inwardly focused by the 1980s," Stryker of the Institute for LGBT Studies wrote, as they concentrated more "on providing mutual aid and support to their members than broader social activism."

Then in the 1990s, transgender people began using the Internet to reach out to one another. Suddenly a world of information was easily shared online. "The most significant factor in the development of a national

Brooke Guinan, the only transgender firefighter in New York City, has become, literally, the poster child for transgender rights since a poster of her in a tight T-shirt reading "So Trans So What" went viral as part of an awareness campaign for the LGBTQ advocacy group V.O.I.C.E. (Vocal Organization for International Courage and Equality).

trans movement may have been the rise of the Internet in the mid-1990s," wrote Genny Beemyn, who runs an LGBT center at the University of Massachusetts, Amherst.[63]

In recent years treatment protocols have become more patient-friendly. In 2013, the American Psychiatric Association's *Diagnostic and Statistical Manual of Mental Disorders* (*DSM*) was revised so that "gender dysphoria" replaced "gender identity disorder," offering a less stigmatizing diagnosis.[64]

The latest standards of care, released in 2011, "acknowledge that there's no one way to be trans. Each case needs to be treated individually," says the World Professional Association for Transgender Health's Green, whose group sets treatment standards.[65]

Some people can successfully transition without medical or psychological care of any kind, he says. But treatment can help.

"We know through historical data that people will be more successful in their transition if they have some social support, a very highly developed sense of their self in relation to the world and that they're not socially or emotionally impaired," Green says.

Despite recent advances, it took time for gays, lesbians and transgender people to join forces politically. In 2007, then-Rep. Barney Frank, D-Mass., a prominent openly gay member of Congress, introduced the Employment

Non-Discrimination Act, or ENDA, which offered legal protection to employees on the basis of sexual orientation but not gender identity. "We'll never get the votes" if transgender people were included in the measure, Frank said. Members of Congress will "think about people who haven't had a physical change and at work there are communal showers — they'll think, what if some male pervert wants to [come into] the women's shower and says, 'Well, I just decided — I'm transgender.'"[66]

A poll conducted in 2007 by the Human Rights Campaign, which backed Frank's position, found that 70 percent of LGBT respondents preferred passage of an anti-discrimination law that excluded transgender people over no law at all.[67] Still, more than 300 groups formed a coalition known as United ENDA to press for transgender inclusion. "It was the first time mainstream organizations raised united voices for transgender rights," Faderman writes.[68]

Over the past 20 years major gay rights groups, including the Human Rights Campaign in 2001 and GLAAD in 2013, have slowly added transgender people to their mission statements.[69] Although long neglected and sometimes spurned by the "LGBs," transgender people are starting to benefit from the successes of the larger gay-rights movement.

CURRENT SITUATION
Federal and State Actions

The Equality Act, which would prohibit discrimination in employment, housing and public accommodations on the basis of gender identity or sexual orientation, remains stalled in Congress. Although the measure, introduced in July by Rep. David Cicilline, D-R.I., has nearly universal support among Democrats, it has not been embraced by Republicans.

But the Obama administration is moving forward to extend rights to transgender people on several fronts, and about 20 states are sympathetic to the cause.

Last January Obama became the first president to use the word "transgender" in a passage in the State of the Union address about respecting human dignity.[70] In August, the White House appointed its first openly transgender staff member: Raffi Freedman-Gurspan, a former official at the National Center for Transgender Equality, who is director of outreach and recruitment for the White House personnel office.

Should transgender rights be legally protected?

YES
Jamison Green
President, World Professional Association for Transgender Health

Written for *CQ Researcher*, December 2015

NO
Ryan T. Anderson
Senior Research Fellow, The Heritage Foundation

Written for *CQ Researcher*, December 2015

Transgender people are not new. We have existed among every race, class and culture since human beings first appeared. What's new is that people who experience the hallmark condition of transgender people — that their gender identity or expression does not match their sex as assigned at birth — are no longer content to live in fear and shame, and they are talking about their experiences.

Knowledge about human sexual and gender diversity that was once suppressed, or that was closely held by scientists who feared being ostracized by their peers, is now more openly shared and discussed. And transgender people themselves are becoming some of the researchers, physicians, lawyers, clergy, educators and policymakers helping to shape the discourse.

Transgender people are not a threat to anyone simply for being transgender. We apparently are seen as a threat because other people would rather believe their own prejudices; they are afraid of other people's difference, and they refuse to give up those beliefs. Transgender people should be protected against discrimination because we are vulnerable to bias, prejudice, hatred and misunderstanding.

All people are deserving of respect and equality under the law. We understand that your rights end at the tip of my nose, and my rights end at the tip of yours. You can think whatever you want, you can say whatever you want, but you cannot impede my rights to peaceable assembly; my rights to freely practice my religion; my rights to an education; my rights to a job for which I am qualified; my rights to all the benefits of society, including access to health care, public accommodations, routine commerce such as shopping for groceries and clothing and access to the public restrooms that comport with my gender identity — the same rights that everyone else has.

These are not special rights; these are equal rights.

Nondiscrimination statutes exist because certain people hold opinions about us because of the way some transgender people look, or because of false propaganda about what being transgender means. Just as some people are racially targeted and suspected of conforming to negative stereotypes, transgender people are similarly targeted, and transgender people of color have even more difficulty. Nondiscrimination laws and policies give everyone hope that we can learn to overcome our worst prejudices. When we live in a society that can respect others and accommodate difference, perhaps we won't need nondiscrimination laws anymore.

Government should not take sides in the transgender debate. That's what the citizens of Houston made clear in November when they voted to repeal a local law requiring businesses to allow biological men to use women's bathrooms if they identify as women. The implications for the privacy and safety rights of adults and children are extremely serious.

The issue is not limited to Houston. The Department of Education (DOE) told an Illinois school district that it is violating Title IX, a 40-year-old law designed to guarantee women's access to education, by setting rules on transgender use of locker rooms. DOE is now interpreting the law to create special protections based on "gender identity."

At issue is the school district's decision to allow a male student who identifies and dresses as a girl to use bathrooms with private single-stalls, but to not allow him into the girls' locker rooms unless he changes behind a curtain out of respect for the privacy concerns of the surrounding students. Even this commonsense compromise was attacked by the federal government, and DOE is threatening to deny federal funding to the district if it does not drop the curtain requirement.

Virtually ignored amid these debates about gender identity are children who should not be confronted with such questions before they reach an appropriate age, as determined by their parents. Gender-identity laws would prevent schools, parents and employers from protecting children from these adult debates about sex. These situations are best handled locally, by the parents and teachers closest to the children — not by government mandates.

The Department of Health and Human Services has also gotten into the act. In September, it published a notice of proposed rulemaking to extend Obamacare's ban on sex discrimination in health care to gender identity. If implemented, this would force doctors to participate in gender-reassignment therapies and surgeries even when doing so would go against their considered medical judgment, their consciences or their religious beliefs. It also seems that it would force nearly all health care plans to cover such reassignment treatments.

Americans should respect the dignity of their neighbors. How to do so in situations related to transgender students, sex-reassignment surgeries and bathrooms is just emerging as a matter of public concern. Many concerns must be weighed by citizens immediately affected where such issues arise. The government is not justified in imposing its own ideological, one-size-fits-all "solution."

"Her commitment to bettering the lives of transgender Americans — particularly transgender people of color and those in poverty — reflects the values of this administration," Obama adviser Valerie Jarrett said.[71] More broadly, the administration is trying to shift the government's understanding of gender by making it easier for people to change their sex classification on Social Security cards and other government documents.[72]

The Pentagon is expected to allow transgender soldiers and sailors to serve openly in the coming months. Both the Equal Employment Opportunity Commission and the Justice Department have found that transgender rights are protected under federal sex discrimination statutes.

In September, the administration proposed a rule that would forbid most health insurers from discriminating against transgender patients.[73] Often, transgender patients have been denied coverage for basic services, such as prostate exams for transgender women and Pap smears for transgender men.

"Rather than mandating that insurers provide certain treatments, like gender-confirming surgeries, the proposed policy requires insurers to make sure that their policies are not designed to discriminate based on gender identity, and provides transgender patients with legal options to seek legal recourse if they are denied trans-inclusive health services," according to the *Advocate*, a gay-interest publication.[74]

In October, after the New York Legislature failed to extend legal protections to transgender people in areas such as housing and employment, Democratic Gov. Andrew Cuomo announced he would do so, joining the 18 states that already offer such protection. He noted that existing state laws protecting gay and bisexual individuals do not cover people on the basis of gender identity.

"The law left out the 'T,' so to speak," Cuomo said, alluding to the acronym LGBT. "Transgendered individuals deserve the same civil right that protects them from discrimination."[75]

California Democratic Gov. Jerry Brown signed a package of bills in October designed to help LGBT individuals. On Jan. 1, California will become the first state to require major contractors — those who do more than $100,000 worth of business with the state — to offer equal benefits to their employees, regardless of gender identity.[76]

Also in October — in response to a lawsuit — California's prison system announced the nation's first guidelines for allowing surgical sex-reassignment procedures sought by transgender inmates.[77]

Despite these political and legal victories, transgender people have yet to gain much traction as political candidates. In Maryland, Democrat Kristin Beck, a celebrated former Navy SEAL, faces an uphill battle in her effort to unseat Rep. Steny Hoyer, the second-ranking Democrat in the House. And in 2014, Sophia, the transgender woman who served in the Army as a man, came close to winning election as the first openly transgender state legislator, but lost — by only 22 votes — in a runoff in an LGBT-friendly district in Oklahoma City.

"I just let my presence in the race be statement enough about my trans status," she says.

Bathroom Bills

Lawmakers in Republican-controlled state governments have been more skeptical about transgender equality. Legislators in Florida, Nevada, Texas, Wisconsin and elsewhere have introduced bills that would limit students or adults to using bathrooms for the gender listed on their birth certificates.

Bill sponsors say their intent is to protect the privacy and modesty rights of other individuals who object to the presence of someone with male anatomy walking into a women's room. "I've got four granddaughters, and I'm not interested in anybody that has a question about their sexuality to be stepping in on them," said Texas state Rep. Dan Flynn, a Republican.[78]

Transgender advocates argue that the bathroom issue amounts to fearmongering. Allowing transgender individuals to use the bathrooms of their choice poses no public safety issue, they say. And health and human-rights officials in states that have passed laws offering equal access to public accommodations say they have not seen an increase in assaults or harassment.[79]

"It's turning things on their head — it's not the trans people who are doing the assaulting; it's trans people who are being victimized," says Beemyn of the University of Massachusetts. "The important thing is, obviously, that everyone wants to be able to go to the bathroom and not have to fear being attacked or harassed for doing so."

But November's lopsided vote in Houston against an anti-discrimination ordinance, following a debate that largely focused on bathroom issues, underscored both the political sensitivity of the issue and the concerns that many people have about transgender access to intimate public spaces.

Despite the Obama administration's insistence that transgender students must be allowed to use the facilities of their choice, some schools are asking transgender students to use unisex single-stall bathrooms or faculty lounges. In September, U.S. District Judge Robert Doumar ruled against a female-to-male transgender student in Virginia who sought to have access to the boys' bathroom at school.[80] Justice and Education department attorneys argued in the case that not allowing transgender students to use the facilities of their choice represents discrimination on the basis of sex.[81]

In November, federal education officials found that by not allowing a transgender girl access to girls' locker and bathrooms an Illinois school district had violated Title IX, which prohibits discrimination on the basis of gender in any education program that receives federal funding.[82]

After a transgender male-to-female student in Missouri insisted on having access to the girls' restroom at her high school this year, more than 150 of her fellow students staged a walkout in protest.[83] The student argued she should not have to use separate accommodations from her peers.

Although the transgender bathroom debate is a recent flashpoint, it echoes earlier civil rights debates. Nervousness about mandated unisex bathrooms fueled some of the opposition to a federal Equal Rights Amendment to protect women in the 1970s. African-Americans in the 1950s and '60s were seeking not just voting and employment rights but the right to use the same swimming pools, drinking fountains, lunch counters — and bathrooms — as white people.

In 2011, Massachusetts extended protections to transgender people in areas such as employment and housing, but the law excluded public accommodations, due to the bathroom issue. However, state lawmakers in recent months have been considering legislation to cover public spaces.

"The argument that a nontransgender person feels uncomfortable with a transgender person using the same bathroom . . . is the same argument that was once made of people of color using public bathrooms, seating on public transportation, [using] public drinking fountains and more," writes Massachusetts state Rep. Paul Heroux, a Democrat. "It is a lack of understanding at best and hateful at worst."[84]

Beckwith, of the Massachusetts Family Institute, says he "strenuously objects" to the equating of gender identity and race.

"There is not a rational basis to distinguish between people based on the color of their skin," he says. "There is, however, a very rational basis for distinguishing between biological males and females when it comes to the sharing of intimate spaces."

OUTLOOK
Turning Point

Despite the enormous hurdles many transgender people continue to face — discrimination, poverty, homelessness, violence and abuse — advocates say they are more hopeful than they have ever been.

"I'm incredibly optimistic," says Keisling of the National Center for Transgender Equality. "We've come so far, so fast. The pace at which change is happening is invigorating, in general."

It's becoming increasingly unusual for Republicans to voice opposition to transgender rights as prominent transgender individuals receive more positive portrayals in the media and major Democratic politicians voice support for their rights.

That could mean that only supportive voices will be heard. "You'll see a groundswell of support for transgender rights," says Beemym, director of the Stonewall Center. "Even people who don't support it are going to find themselves having to be tolerant. It's going to become like same-sex marriage, where there's going to be more liability in opposing it than supporting it."

Beemyn suggests acceptance will take longer among individuals from conservative religious traditions. Indeed, conservatives such as the Massachusetts Family Institute's Beckwith worry that there already is a "chilling effect," with those opposed to greater transgender rights being portrayed as misguided or bigoted. "Many people of faith believe the Bible states God has made us male and female, and they believe this is nonbiblical behavior," Beckwith says.

Conservatives also fear that the rush to extend greater rights to transgender people will cut off dissenting viewpoints. "There's a risk that only one viewpoint becomes politically correct," says Anderson of The Heritage Foundation. "Anyone marshalling any sort of argument that we need to address this coolly and calmly becomes marginalized."

Even some transgender advocates say it might be too much to hope that Congress will pass a law granting people protection from discrimination on the basis of gender identity in the coming years. "People who object will heighten the rhetoric, but I believe that will be a last gasp," says Cislo, the Washington University lecturer.

More jurisdictions and companies appear certain to extend health benefits to transgender people, including coverage of hormone treatments and gender confirmation surgery. More research into the causes and treatment of gender dysphoria is also likely. "We're going to have more of a medical understanding than we do now," says Sophia, the former political candidate in Oklahoma. "By virtue of that, there will be more empathy from mainstream society."

Adams, of GLAAD, agrees that the emergence of additional facts about "the actual trans experience" will inform more discussions. Both political attitudes and media portrayals, as a result, will become more favorable, he says.

Adams hopes that in time, being transgender will be accepted as simply a part of someone's life or his or her character. "That's the point I hope we get to, that it becomes one among many facts about them," Adams says. "I'll disclose to someone that I'm trans, and they'll want to know what books I read or whether I ski."

As sociologists and other scholars have long noted, members of every minority group have hoped to gain sufficient acceptance that people will see past their ethnicity, skin color or sexual orientation. Transgender people, like members of other groups, want to be seen as something more than just transgender. "Passing becomes everything, everything," Fallon Fox, a transgender mixed martial arts athlete, told *GQ*. "Every time you go into a Starbucks and there's nothing in someone's eyes, it feels great."[85]

Paula Ison, a 64-year-old transgender woman in Cincinnati, recalls that when she came out in 1993, she and other transgender individuals were pessimistic about their chances of gaining acceptance. "We were at best an oddity," says Ison, who retired recently after a long career in the insurance industry. "Fast-forward to today, and kids go to the Internet and they get everything," Ison says. "They turn on the TV and they get role models.

It's more than day and night; it's just an amazing change that we've had in 50 years."

Polls back up Ison's assertion, showing that more people have grown tolerant of the transgender movement over time.

"I had a business client say this to me seven years ago: 'You're a whole person who just happens to be trans,'" Ison says.

NOTES

1. Doug Erickson, "New Transgender Research Filling in Gaps," *Wisconsin State Journal*, Jan. 26, 2014, http://tinyurl.com/pduvew8.

2. Gary J. Gates, "How Many People Are Lesbian, Gay, Bisexual and Transgender?" Williams Institute, UCLA School of Law, April 2011, http://tinyurl.com/77bdant.

3. Doug Erickson, "Blazing a Trail, West Madison High School Makes Homecoming Court Gender Neutral," *Wisconsin State Journal*, Oct. 8, 2015, http://tinyurl.com/nzkssaa/.

4. Erickson, "New Transgender Research," *op. cit.*

5. Doug Erickson, "With Death of Transgender Student, a Community Mourns and Redoubles Its Efforts," *Wisconsin State Journal*, Jan. 26, 2014, http://tinyurl.com/mljufyx.

6. Jesse Opoien, "Rep. Jesse Kremer Says His Bill to Place Gender Restrictions on School Bathrooms Will Increase Safety, Dignity," *Capital Times*, Oct. 7, 2015, http://tinyurl.com/na99gf7.

7. Twitter account of Greg Abbott, Nov. 2, 2015, http://tinyurl.com/oexga4l.

8. Gates, *op. cit.*

9. Peter Moore, "One Third Think It Is Morally Wrong to Be Transgender," YouGov, June 5, 2015, http://tinyurl.com/qbw4qmx.

10. Joshua J. McElwee, "Francis Strongly Criticizes Gender Theory, Comparing It to Nuclear Arms," *National Catholic Reporter*, Feb. 13, 2015, http://tinyurl.com/lys5dtl.

11. Vanessa Vitiello Urquhart, "Conservative Christianity's Discovery of Transgender Issues Worries Trans Christians," "Outward" blog, *Slate*, Oct. 7, 2015, http://tinyurl.com/z4l5l4s.

12. Aleksandra Sandstrom, "Religious Groups' Policies on Transgender Members Varies Widely," Pew Research Center, Dec. 2, 2015, http://tinyurl.com/zb3mas9.

13. The acronym LGBT is sometimes lengthened to include other initials representing other identities, such as "Q" for "queer," "I" for "intersex" and "A" for "asexual."

14. Zeke Stokes, "New Poll: Number of Americans Who Report Knowing a Transgender Person Doubles," GLAAD, Sept. 17, 2015, http://tinyurl.com/p8g7wmb.

15. Andrew R. Flores, "Attitudes toward Transgender Rights: Perceived Knowledge and Secondary Interpersonal Contact," *Politics, Groups and Identities*, March 30, 2015, http://tinyurl.com/qxxgu9o.

16. Soraya Nadia McDonald, "Jill Soloway and Jeffrey Tambor of 'Transparent' Highlight Trans Issues in Emmy Acceptance Speeches," *The Washington Post*, Sept. 20, 2015, http://tinyurl.com/nlc6n6u.

17. "Transgender People and the Law," American Civil Liberties Union, undated, http://tinyurl.com/nc84hm3.

18. Jaime M. Grant, Lisa A. Mottet and Justin Tanis, "Injustice at Every Turn," National Center for Transgender Equality and the National Gay and Lesbian Task Force, 2011, http://tinyurl.com/4hy6rb6.

19. Lisa R. Miller and Eric Anthony Grollman, "The Social Costs of Gender Nonconformity for Transgender Adults: Implications for Discrimination and Health," *Sociological Forum*, September 2015, http://tinyurl.com/p3js2yb.

20. See Parker Marie Malloy, "Poll: Majority of Americans Support Trans-Inclusive ENDA," *Advocate*, Dec. 14, 2013, http://tinyurl.com/l562qqu; Maggie Haberman, "Poll: Anti-Discrimination Law Support," *Politico*, Sept. 30, 2013, http://tinyurl.com/po5kpou; and "Infographic: U.S. House of Representatives and ENDA," Williams Institute, Nov. 19, 2013, http://tinyurl.com/mnklpqr/.

21. "CBS News Poll: Transgender Kids and School Bathrooms," CBS News, June 8, 2014, http://tinyurl.com/mhd3z63.

22. Twitter account of Sean Davis, Nov. 3, 2015, http://tinyurl.com/pryf4ju.

23. Claire Zillman, "Changing Genders at Work," *Fortune*, July 13, 2015, http://tinyurl.com/onmgfr6.

24. Adam Ashton, "JBLM Transgender Soldier Endures Excruciating Wait for Army Reforms," *Tacoma News Tribune*, Oct. 3, 2015, http://tinyurl.com/p7g3g8e.

25. Andrew Tilghman, "Transgender Troops Policy Change Raises Many Questions," *Navy Times*, July 19, 2015, http://tinyurl.com/nmuetml.

26. Haimy Assefa, "Study estimates cost of care for transgender troops," CNN, Aug. 14, 2015, http://tinyurl.com/qb7o58w.

27. "Statement by Secretary of Defense Ash Carter on DOD Transgender Policy," news release, Department of Defense, July 13, 2015, http://tinyurl.com/nqfmvw4.

28. Tom Vanden Brook, "Military Transgender Ban Set to End Next May," *USA Today*, Aug. 25, 2015, http://tinyurl.com/p4azd8b.

29. "Annotated Transcript: The Aug. 6 GOP Debate," *The Washington Post*, Aug. 6, 2015, http://tinyurl.com/oytls99.

30. Katie Zezima, "Ted Cruz: The Military Shouldn't Be a 'Cauldron for Social Experiments,'" *The Washington Post*, Oct. 12, 2015, http://tinyurl.com/p7p2fdz.

31. Gary J. Gates and Jody L. Herman, "Transgender Military Service in the United States," Williams Institute, May 2014, http://tinyurl.com/nup8r2a.

32. Alan Zarembo, "Why Do Transgender People Join the Military in Such High Numbers?" *Los Angeles Times*, Sept. 4, 2015, http://tinyurl.com/ocxekc7.

33. Alicia Menendez, Meagan Redman and Lauren Effron, "I Am Jazz: Transgender Teen on Grappling with High School, Puberty," abcnews.go.com, July 14, 2015, http://tinyurl.com/pxxexb7.

34. Yezmin Villarreal, "I Am Jazz: 14, Transgender, and the Star of My Own Docu-Series," *Advocate*, July 29, 2015, http://tinyurl.com/ncv9l2n.

35. Wylie C. Hembree *et al.*, "Endocrine Treatment of Transsexual Persons: An Endocrine Society Clinical Practice Guideline," *The Journal of Endocrinology and Metabolism*, June 4, 2009, http://tinyurl.com/poy37wt.

36. Madeleine S.C. Wallien and Peggy T. Cohen-Kettenis, "Psychosexual Outcome of Gender Dysphoric Children, " *Journal of the American Academy of Child and Adolescent Psychiatry*, December 2008, http://tinyurl.com/nudr5pu.

37. Jack Drescher and Jack Pula, "Ethical Issues Raised by the Treatment of Gender-Variant Prepubescent Children," *Hastings Center Report*, September-October 2014, http://tinyurl.com/qce5cjy.

38. See "Sunday Dialogue: Our Notions of Gender," "Sunday Review Letters," *The New York Times*, June 29, 2013, http://tinyurl.com/kca8llc.

39. Debra W. Soh, "Why Transgender Children Should Wait to Transition," *Pacific Standard*, Sept. 1, 2015, http://tinyurl.com/o2566v7.

40. Martha Bebinger, "Uncertainty Surrounds Medical Treatments for Transgender Youth," WBUR, Jan. 24, 2014, http://tinyurl.com/lqlg73s.

41. Kristian Foden-Vencil, "The Medical Pros and Cons of Suppressing Puberty in Transgender Teens," Oregon Public Broadcasting, March 26, 2015, http://tinyurl.com/ph9wjjw.

42. Leslie Feinberg, *Transgender Warriors* (1996), p. 21.

43. Walter Williams, *The Spirit and the Flesh* (1986), p. 137.

44. Susan Stryker, *Transgender History* (2008), p. 32.

45. Feinberg, *op. cit.*, p. 111.

46. Stryker, *op. cit.*, p. 39.

47. Joanne Meyerowitz, *How Sex Changed* (2002), p. 5.

48. Laura Erickson-Schroth, ed., *Trans Bodies, Trans Selves* (2014), p. 216.

49. Meyerowitz, *op. cit.*, p. 49.

50. Stryker, *op. cit.*, p. 45.

51. Erickson-Schroth, *op. cit.*, p. 508.

52. Meyerowitz, *op. cit.*, p. 51.

53. Stryker, *op. cit.*, p. 73.

54. Meyerowitz, *op. cit.*, p. 9.

55. *Ibid.*, p. 142.

56. Stryker, *op. cit.*, p. 112.

57. Meyerowitz, *op. cit.*, p. 158.

58. Lillian Faderman, *The Gay Revolution* (2015), pp. 116, 119.

59. *Ibid.*, p. 231.

60. Janice Raymond, *The Transsexual Empire* (1994), p. 104.

61. Meyerowitz, *op. cit.*, p. 268.

62. Erickson-Schroth, *op. cit.*, p. 519.

63. *Ibid.*, p. 528.

64. *Ibid.*, p. 520.

65. Eli Coleman *et al.*, "Standards of Care for the Health of Transsexual, Transgender, and Gender-Nonconforming People, Version 7," *International Journal of Transgenderism*, 2011, http://tinyurl.com/pxlcmxc.

66. Faderman, *op. cit.*, p. 568.

67. "Poll: 70% of LGBT Respondents Support Noninclusive ENDA," *Advocate*, Nov. 7, 2007, http://tinyurl.com/h3nt8ot.

68. Faderman, *op. cit.*, p. 569.

69. Erickson-Schroth, *op. cit.*, p. 530.

70. Tessa Berenson, "Obama Made History By Using This Word in the State of the Union," *Time*, Jan. 20, 2015, http://tinyurl.com/nemj9mc.

71. Abby Ohlheiser, "Meet the White House's First Transgender Staffer," *The Washington Post*, Aug. 18, 2015, http://tinyurl.com/nlz8rvp.

72. Juliet Eilperin, "Obama's Quiet Transgender Revolution," *The Washington Post*, Dec. 1, 2015, http://tinyurl.com/pzsalo7.

73. Abby Goodnough and Margot Sanger-Katz, "Health Care Rules Proposed to Shield Transgender Patients From Bias," *The New York Times*, Sept. 3, 2015, http://tinyurl.com/q9sswrr.

74. Cleis Abeni, "New HHS Rule Could Change the Game for Trans Health Care," *Advocate*, Sept. 3, 2015, http://tinyurl.com/o6ore9t.

75. Jesse McKinley, "Cuomo Planning Discrimination Protections for Transgender New Yorkers," *The New York Times*, Oct. 22, 2015, http://tinyurl.com/qdtluzw.

76. Trudy Ring, "California Gov. Signs Four LGBT-Supportive Bills," *Advocate*, Oct. 7, 2015, http://tinyurl.com/omscjze.

77. Bob Egelko, "California Prisons Break New Ground With Sex-Reassignment Policy," *San Francisco*

Chronicle, Oct. 23, 2015, http://tinyurl.com/qbx69jz.

78. Edgar Walters, " 'Bathroom Bills' Pit Transgender Texans Against GOP," *The Texas Tribune*, April 4, 2015, http://tinyurl.com/mpdg96j.

79. "15 Experts Debunk Right-Wing Transgender Bathroom Myth," Media Matters for America, March 20, 2014, http://tinyurl.com/pnxl4jw.

80. Julie Zauzmer, "Judge Denies Transgender Student's Request to Use Boys' Bathroom," *The Washington Post*, Sept. 4, 2015, http://tinyurl.com/pabqw7a.

81. Lisa Leff, "Feds Back Transgender Teenager in School Restroom Dispute," The Associated Press, Oct. 29, 2015, http://tinyurl.com/pvqrd4r.

82. Mitch Smith and Monica Davey, "Illinois District Violated Transgender Student's Rights, U.S. Says," *The New York Times*, Nov. 2, 2015, http://tinyurl.com/pjluetf.

83. Dan Greenwald, "Hillsboro High School Students Stage Walkout in Dispute Over Transgender Student," KMOV.com, Aug. 31, 2015, http://tinyurl.com/nvbxn3m.

84. Paul Heroux, "Transgender Rights and Public Bathrooms," "The Blog," *The Huffington Post*, Oct. 12, 2015, http://tinyurl.com/jocc59k.

85. Nancy Hass, "Fallon Fox: The Toughest Woman in Sports," *GQ*, Dec. 23, 2013, http://tinyurl.com/oxmhezq.

BIBLIOGRAPHY

Selected Sources

Books

Erickson-Schroth, Laura, *Trans Bodies, Trans Selves: A Resource for the Transgender Community*, Oxford University Press, 2014.
This guide for transgender people covers such issues as coming out, employment, identity changes and hormone therapy.

Faderman, Lillian, *The Gay Revolution: The Story of the Struggle*, Simon and Schuster, 2015.
A historian traces the evolution of gay rights since World War II, including tensions between gays and lesbians and transgender people and their eventual political collaboration.

Stryker, Susan, *Transgender History*, Seal Press, 2008.
The director of the LGBT Center at Arizona State University surveys legal and medical issues throughout U.S. history.

Articles

Ashton, Adam, "JBLM Transgender Soldier Endures Wait for Army Reforms," *Tacoma News Tribune*, Nov. 1, 2015, http://tinyurl.com/p7g3g8e.
A highly regarded intelligence officer is serving openly as a transgender woman in the Army, awaiting changes in policy that will ensure she won't be discharged.

Bissinger, Buzz, "Caitlyn Jenner: The Full Story," *Vanity Fair*, July 2015, http://tinyurl.com/n9awbct.
A journalist spent months with Caitlyn Jenner during her transition period, before she came out publicly as transgender.

Fieler, Sean, "What Republicans Should Learn From the Transgender Moment," *The Daily Signal*, May 27, 2015, http://tinyurl.com/q5o2xfh.
The chair of the conservative policy group American Principles Project argues that Republicans have surrendered without a fight in the push for transgender recognition and rights.

Holden, Dominic, "After Winning Marriage, The LGBT Movement Faces An Unexpectedly Tough Battle In Houston," *BuzzFeed News*, Nov. 2, 2015, http://tinyurl.com/p2z7c5k.
An ordinance in Houston would have provided anti-discrimination protections to a wide variety of groups, but the campaign against it succeeded because of voters' fears about transgender women entering women's bathrooms.

McHugh, Paul, "Transgender Surgery Isn't the Solution," *The Wall Street Journal*, June 12, 2014, http://tinyurl.com/ovuvubs.
Gender dysphoria is a mental disorder that should not be treated by amputating normal genital organs, argues a retired psychiatrist from Johns Hopkins University.

Rochlin, Margy, "In 'Transparent,' a Heroine Evolves Further Still," *The New York Times*, Nov. 27, 2015, http://tinyurl.com/h3mdw59.
Jill Soloway, the creator of "Transparent," is using its success to create training and job opportunities for transgender people in entertainment.

Soh, Debra W., "Why Transgender Children Should Wait to Transition," *Pacific Standard*, Sept. 1, 2015, http://tinyurl.com/o2566v7.
A sex researcher and neuroscientist argues that most children with gender dysphoria outgrow it and thus should wait to undergo gender transition.

Reports and Studies

Drescher, Jack, and Jack Pula, "Ethical Issues Raised by the Treatment of Gender-Variant Prepubescent Children," Hastings Center, September 2014, http://tinyurl.com/qce5cjy.
Only about a quarter of children treated at gender clinics identify as transgender as adults; most boys instead identify as gay.

Flores, Andrew R., "Attitudes toward Transgender Rights: Perceived Knowledge and Secondary Interpersonal Contact," Williams Institute, June 5, 2015, http://tinyurl.com/qxxgu9o.
A researcher finds that as people become more familiar with transgender issues and individuals, they grow more supportive.

Grant, Jaime M., Lisa A. Mottet and Justin Tanis, "Injustice at Every Turn," National Center for Transgender Equality and the National Gay and Lesbian Task Force, 2011, http://tinyurl.com/4hy6rb6.
A survey of 6,450 transgender and gender nonconforming Americans finds they face pervasive discrimination and high levels of unemployment and poverty. Results from an updated survey will be released in 2016.

Miller, Lisa R., and Eric Anthony Grollman, "The Social Costs of Gender Nonconformity for Transgender Adults: Implications for Discrimination and Health," Sociological Forum, September 2015, http://tinyurl.com/p3js2yb.
Gender nonconforming adults are more likely to engage in harmful activities, such as smoking and abusing drugs and alcohol, because of the discrimination they face.

"Where We Are on TV," GLAAD, Oct. 27, 2015, http://tinyurl.com/nmqp7xz.
An LGBT advocacy group's annual survey of LGBT depictions on TV finds that no scripted broadcast prime time shows have recurring transgender characters but that there are three on cable and four on streaming series, including two series leads.

For More Information

American Principles Project, 1130 Connecticut Ave., N.W., Suite 425, Washington, DC 20036; 202-503-2010; americanprinciplesproject.org. Conservative group that studies social issues, supports religious liberty and traditional marriage.

American Veterans for Equal Rights, PO Box 94376, Atlanta, GA 30377; 718-849-5665; aver.us. Veterans service organization that advocates for equal rights for current and retired LGBT members of the military.

GLAAD, 5455 Wilshire Blvd., Suite #1500, Los Angeles, CA 90036; 323-933-2240; www.glaad.org. Works with media outlets to promote positive portrayals of the LGBT community; originally known as the Gay and Lesbian Alliance Against Discrimination.

National Center for Transgender Equality, 1400 16th St., N.W., Suite 510, Washington, DC 20036; 202-642-4552; www.transequality.org. Advocacy group that promotes policy changes to ensure transgender rights at the local, state and federal levels.

Trans Kids Purple Rainbow Foundation, 7000 W. Palmetto Park Road, Boca Raton, FL 33433; 561-750-8311; transkidspurplerainbow.org. Supports children with gender dysphoria in schools through media outreach and advocacy.

The Williams Institute, UCLA School of Law, Box 951476, Los Angeles, CA 90095; 310-267-4382; williamsinstitute.law.ucla.edu/. Think tank that conducts research on law and public policy concerning sexual orientation and gender identity.

The Witherspoon Institute, 16 Stockton St., Princeton, NJ 08540; 609-688-8779; winst.org. Conservative research center that publishes *Public Discourse*, an online publication that covers transgender health and legal issues.

World Professional Association for Transgender Health, 2575 Northwest Parkway, Elgin, IL 60124; 847-752-6245; wpath.org. Professional and educational organization that promotes transgender health.

9

Campus Sexual Assault

Barbara Mantel

Columbia University senior Emma Sulkowicz carries a mattress around campus to raise awareness of campus sexual assault and to protest the handling of her rape charge against a fellow student. A school disciplinary panel found the male student "not responsible."
Sulkowicz said: "At the end of the day, my rapist still goes to this school, and they haven't done anything about that."

Since early September, Columbia University student Emma Sulkowicz has attracted international media attention as she carries a 50-pound mattress around campus. "Carry That Weight" is both a performance piece for her senior art thesis and a protest against sexual assault, including, she says, her own.

Sulkowicz was starting to have consensual sex with a fellow student in her dorm room two years ago when, she alleges, he suddenly hit, choked and anally penetrated her while she resisted and repeatedly said no, according to a police report. Sulkowicz eventually complained to the university, and a school disciplinary panel found the male student "not responsible," a decision upheld on appeal.

Frustrated, Sulkowicz filed a criminal complaint in May but has not followed through because the police encounter was so upsetting, she told *The New York Times*.[1]

The university does not comment on the specifics of cases, but Sulkowicz contends that school administrators made serious errors during their investigation, including misrepresenting her statements to them.[2] "At the end of the day, my rapist still goes to this school, and they haven't done anything about that," Sulkowicz said.[3]

The issue of how colleges handle sexual assault complaints has received unprecedented attention in the past two years, as young women with stories of mishandled cases formed advocacy groups, the White House created a special task force and Congress passed legislation to strengthen schools' sexual violence policies and procedures.

When students file a sexual assault complaint with their school, federal law compels the school to investigate and decide whether the

From *CQ Researcher*,
October 31, 2014.

Rights of Student Victims of Sexual Assault

When a college student files a sexual assault complaint with school authorities, federal law compels the school to investigate and decide whether the accused student is "responsible" for sexual misconduct, which can result in a maximum penalty of expulsion. The accuser also can file a criminal complaint with the local police. While victims may have additional rights under federal and state law, here are key provisions under Title IX of the Education Amendments of 1972:

Victims and the accused have the right to:

- Present witnesses and evidence.
- Have an adviser of their choosing, including a lawyer.
- Have proceedings documented, including through written findings of fact, transcripts or audio recordings.
- Reject mediation in place of an investigation.

Schools must:

- Resolve complaints based on a preponderance-of-the-evidence standard of proof — that is, what is more likely than not to have happened. Schools cannot use a higher standard of proof.
- Notify victims and the accused in writing of the outcome of a complaint and any appeal.
- Provide an appeal process equally available to both parties.

Remedies:

- If the school determines that sexual violence created a hostile environment, the school must take prompt steps to eliminate the hostile environment, prevent its recurrence and remedy its effects.
- Remedies include disciplinary action against the perpetrator and educational assistance for victims, such as providing academic support, allowing penalty-free retaking of classes and offering counseling.
- Schools may also have to provide prevention training for the student population or change their services or policies to prevent other incidents.

Source: "Know Your Rights: Title IX Requires Your School to Address Sexual Violence," Office for Civil Rights, United States Department of Education, http://tinyurl.com/n2puexs

But as momentum builds to hold colleges and universities to greater account, advocates for civil liberties on campus and lawyers for students accused of sexual assault say this pressure is leading some schools to rush to judgment. There is debate about whether some men have been wrongly expelled and whether the standard of evidence used by colleges and universities is too low. And there is resistance among some students and civil libertarians as an increasing number of schools require students to get "affirmative consent" from their partner at every stage of sex.

"The core problem is that campuses are not really equipped to be adjudicating these cases in the first place, and they're being asked to do something that's well outside of their competence," says Joseph Cohn, legislative and policy director at the Philadelphia-based advocacy group Foundation for Individual Rights in Education (FIRE). Cohn says schools should leave the investigating and adjudicating of sexual assault cases to law enforcement.

But the founders of new advocacy groups such as SurvJustice, Know Your IX and End Rape on Campus (EROC) disagree and want the government to force schools to do a better job. They have filed, and are helping others to file, complaints with the U.S. Department of Education, charging colleges and universities with violating two federal laws.

One is Title IX, the landmark 1972 federal law barring sex discrimination in education, best known for fostering equality in school sports. The law also requires schools receiving federal funds to investigate sexual assault complaints, and to do so fairly and equitably. The other law is the 1990 Clery Act, which establishes a bill of rights for campus sexual assault victims and requires

accused student is "responsible" for sexual misconduct, which can result in a maximum penalty of expulsion.* The accuser can also file a criminal complaint with the police.

---

* Schools use the term "responsible" rather than "guilty" to make clear that their proceedings are different from those of criminal courts.

colleges that take federal funds to make crime statistics public.[4]

"Victims have a variety of complaints against their schools," says Laura Dunn, founder and executive director of SurvJustice. Dunn says schools sometimes do nothing after a sexual assault complaint, untrained administrators ask humiliating questions or disciplinary panels dispense weak punishment, such as summer suspensions or essay assignments.

As a result, the Education Department currently is investigating 86 colleges and universities under Title IX over their handling of sexual assault and harassment allegations, including Ivy League institutions such as Princeton and Harvard, public universities such as the University of Virginia and the University of Idaho and small private colleges such as Amherst and Occidental. The department also has an undisclosed number of Clery Act investigations ongoing at schools for possible faulty reporting of crime statistics or other issues involving compliance with the Clery Act.

According to the Education Department, last year Yale University was fined $155,000, one of the largest penalties under the Clery Act, for inadequately reporting campus crime statistics more than a decade ago, including omitting four forcible sex offenses from 2001 and 2002.

Even after decades of research on the extent of sexual assault among college students, the numbers are disputed. "One in five women is sexually assaulted in college," states an April report from the White House task force.[5] The same statistic appears on the websites of government agencies, advocacy groups and members of Congress. And that's a problem, say critics, who point out that the figure is the result of one survey. The actual rate of campus sexual assault could be higher, or lower, they say.

Hard numbers are difficult to come by because women rarely report sexual assault. For instance, researchers estimate that only about 12 percent of rapes

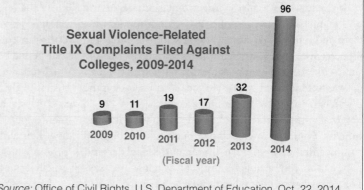

Complaints Against Colleges Triple

The Department of Education received 96 complaints in fiscal 2014, which ended Sept. 30 — up threefold from fiscal 2013 — from individuals claiming their institutions had mishandled a sexual assault allegation. It had 81 open school investigations in fiscal 2014. Complaints began to rise sharply after the Department of Education in April 2011 reminded universities that Title IX of the 1972 Education Amendments requires them to investigate all student reports of sexual violence.

Sexual Violence-Related Title IX Complaints Filed Against Colleges, 2009-2014

2009	2010	2011	2012	2013	2014
9	11	19	17	32	96

(Fiscal year)

Source: Office of Civil Rights, U.S. Department of Education, Oct. 22, 2014

among college women are reported to law enforcement. Women don't want others to know, fear retaliation, believe there isn't enough evidence or aren't sure a crime was committed, researchers say.[6]

"Very often in college the victims of sexual assault who are raped know their perpetrator . . . and in their mind, they can't fathom that someone they know could rape them," says Christopher Krebs, senior research social scientist with North Carolina-based RTI International, a major research institute.

Underreporting means that the number of forcible rapes reported to campus security or local police that schools must publicize under the Clery Act — 4,837 in 2012, the latest year for which data are available — is unreliable. And trying to compare that number to other years, say the 3,613 forcible rapes reported in 2010, is also a problem for a different reason: The numbers may have risen because schools are under pressure to do a better job of encouraging victims to come forward and not because of an increase in crime.[7]

So researchers must rely on confidential surveys. The one-in-five statistic comes from a survey conducted by RTI at two public universities in the winter of 2006 for the U.S. Justice Department. Krebs, who led the research team, says: "We don't claim that this is representative of all college women in the country, by any means." But critics say politicians and advocates do.

"Anyone who believes that a statistic taken at two schools out of the thousands around the United States can reliably be generalized to a national figure is on very shaky ground," says James Fox, a criminologist at Boston's Northeastern University.

In fact, while 5,446 young women answered the online questionnaire, the one-in-five number is culled from an even smaller sample: 1,402 seniors.[8] Plus, only 42 percent of college women who were asked to take the survey did so, making it possible that those who chose to answer were students who cared the most. Krebs says the researchers tried to take that into account.

Finally, the researchers defined sexual assault fairly broadly, from unwanted kissing, touching and fondling to unwanted oral sex, sexual intercourse, anal sex and penetration with a finger or object.[9] "That's fine," says Fox, "but you see many headlines over the past months that one in five college students are raped, and it's not the case." It's true that one in five, or 20 percent, of surveyed seniors did not indicate they were raped. However 15 percent did so, according to Krebs.

Even without precise data, schools are recognizing they must do more to prevent sexual assaults among students. And recent highly publicized cases of schools failing to thoroughly investigate complaints — especially if the accused is a star athlete — are adding to the pressure. For instance, Florida State University star quarterback and Heisman Trophy winner Jameis Winston was accused by a freshman nearly two years ago of rape. A local prosecutor said he did not have enough evidence to charge Winston, but an investigation by *The New York Times* revealed that police detectives did not interview a witness who had videotaped part of the encounter and did not attempt to get a sample of Winston's DNA.

"There was virtually no investigation at all, either by the police or the university," concluded *The Times*.[10] Florida State is one of the 86 schools under investigation for possible Title IX violations by the Department of Education.

Winston's attorney has said the encounter was consensual. Florida State recently launched its own investigation.[11]

Against this backdrop, here are some of the questions that advocates, lawyers, students, elected officials and school administrators are debating:

Do colleges handle sexual assault allegations fairly?

Dissatisfied students not only are filing complaints with the U.S. Department of Education, they are taking their schools to court. United Educators, an insurer owned by more than 1,000 colleges and universities that covers schools' legal costs, reports that its members filed 262 claims in connection with such lawsuits over the five-year period ending in 2010.

"Students accused of perpetrating a sexual assault are just as likely to sue the institution as accusing students," said Alyssa Keehan, a United Educators risk-management expert. Both sides complain that colleges don't follow their written policies and procedures, don't respond promptly or properly to an assault report and treat them cruelly or unfairly.[12]

College and university staffs are not properly trained, says Christina Brandt-Young, a senior staff attorney at New York-based Legal Momentum, a women's defense and legal education fund. "People need to understand the dynamics of sexual assault and . . . the dynamics of forensic interviewing, so that they don't retraumatize people while they investigate," says Brandt-Young.

Some advocates for the accused say better training also is needed for those deciding these cases, usually deans or hearing panels consisting of staff, professors and sometimes students. There must be "people that are trained and objective triers of fact, that have experience deconstructing testimony and complex factual scenarios with competing versions of events," said Andrew Miltenberg, an attorney whose firm represents at least three students accused of sexual assault who say their schools violated their rights.[13]

In a recent survey of 440 four-year institutions of higher learning, one-fifth reported they provided no training for their faculty and staff about how to respond to student complaints of sexual assault, and one-third failed to provide specialized training to personnel who investigate and decide sexual assault cases.[14]

Beginning this year, all schools receiving federal funds must provide such training under provisions of the Campus Sexual Violence Elimination Act of 2013.

Once a hearing concludes, however, the problems often continue, says Brandt-Young. "Schools are not issuing punishments proportionate to the offenses found," she says.

For example, at one university, a group of men caught on video groping a woman as she said no were banned from attending homecoming. Another school suspended for less than an academic year a student found responsible for choking and sexually assaulting a client of Brandt-Young's. "That's not a proportionate discipline," she says.

"We've had cases where . . . the person is found responsible for nonconsensual sex and then assigned to watch a video that everyone watched during freshmen orientation, or they're just sent to counseling," says Dunn of SurvJustice.

"I do believe that universities are not always fair to people who bring accusations forward," says Sherry Warner-Seefeld, president of the advocacy group Families Advocating for Campus Equality (FACE), formed by three mothers of students accused of sexual assault. "I do believe that there have been years and years of this being swept under the rug, and that's wrong."

However, she continues, "what I hear, and what we experienced firsthand with my son, Caleb, is that in many cases the person is assumed guilty from the moment an accusation is made."

In 2010, a female student accused Caleb of sexual assault. The University of North Dakota expelled him after a panel found Caleb responsible. But three months later, the police charged the young woman with filing a false report, and the university invited Caleb to return. Warner-Seefeld says he was traumatized and chose instead to remain at work.

In 2011, the Department of Education's Office for Civil Rights (OCR) wrote to colleges and universities clarifying their responsibilities when handling allegations of sexual assault and harassment and followed up with a 53-page FAQ (frequently asked questions) this year. Many campus officials took this guidance to mean they should side with victims, according to Brett Sokolow, president of the Pennsylvania-based law and consulting firm National Center for Higher Education Risk Management. But Catherine Lhamon, assistant secretary for civil rights at the Education Department, said in July that was not OCR's intent.[15]

Nevertheless, Cohn of FIRE says OCR guidance leads schools to treat accused students unfairly. The

Erin Cavalier, 19, has filed a complaint with the federal government charging that Catholic University in Washington, D.C., responded inadequately to her report of being raped on campus in December 2012, when she was a freshman. Meanwhile, the White House created the Special Task Force on Campus Sexual Assault, and a bipartisan group of senators has proposed legislation incorporating many of its recommendations, including providing confidential advisers to victims and conducting surveys of students about their experience with sexual violence and harassment.

Campus Sexual Violence Elimination Act requires schools to allow students to have advisers of their choice, including lawyers, present at all proceedings. But Cohn says schools should go further and allow lawyers to actively participate, for instance by objecting to panel questions they believe are unfair and by cross-examining the accuser. The OCR strongly discourages cross-examination by the accused because it may be "traumatic or intimidating."[16]

Cohn says if that extends to the accused's lawyer as well, it "would be deeply troubling."

In its 2011 letter, the OCR also instructed schools to use a preponderance-of-evidence standard — that it is more likely than not that the accused is guilty — when deciding sexual assault and harassment cases. In other words, schools would need to be 51 percent sure. Using the more rigorous clear-and-convincing standard — that it is highly probable or reasonably certain that the accused is guilty, or about 70 percent certain — violates Title IX, the letter said. That sent some schools, including Duke, Stanford and the University of Virginia, scrambling to change their policies. Most schools now use the lower preponderance-of-evidence standard, which is also used in civil court proceedings.

"It's absolutely ridiculous," says Warner-Seefeld of FACE, who thinks the lower standard is resulting in the expulsion of innocent men. "In civil courts, a preponderance of evidence standard is acceptable because there is a full complement of due process rights." At schools, however, there is no discovery, no ability to subpoena witnesses and no legally trained judge, critics say.

And the stakes are high for accused students, who can be expelled, branded a rapist and denied entry to other colleges, says Warner-Seefeld.

But victims' advocates say she and Cohn are misunderstanding Title IX. "Title IX requires schools to have policies preventing sex discrimination," says Dunn of SurvJustice, and schools are deciding whether a student violated those policies and can be found responsible for sexual misconduct. It's a misconduct hearing, she says, not a court, and "the process requires only minimal due process."

Dunn also doesn't buy the argument that the consequences are life altering. Schools don't send anyone to jail, she says. "The idea that it ruins the accused's life is completely made up," says Dunn. "They easily go to other schools."

Should colleges hand off all investigations of sexual assault to police?

While Title IX requires colleges and universities to investigate and adjudicate sexual assault complaints through disciplinary proceedings, nothing prevents a student from also going to the police. In fact, schools must advise students of their right to file a criminal complaint and help them contact law enforcement, if that is what the student wishes. However, schools cannot delay their own inquiry while awaiting the results of a police investigation.

FIRE and others propose amending federal law to require colleges to routinely send sexual assault complaints to local law enforcement, especially those that could be considered a felony, such as rape, and refrain from handling such complaints themselves.*

"A dean from the English Department, a physics professor and an anthropology sophomore — without the court procedures that go into screening out facts from fiction — have very little possibility of reaching reliable determinations that are fair," says FIRE's Cohn.

---

* Crimes are classified as either felonies, the most serious, or misdemeanors.

But S. Daniel Carter, director of the Virginia-based 32 National Campus Safety Initiative, says Cohn's concern is invalid. "Fights occur between students all the time, and they are often handled internally without the police, and no one is in an uproar over that," he says. "Colleges and universities are dealing with serious crimes like robberies and aggravated assault every day."

But sexual assault, especially rape, is different, say critics of the school process. The FBI ranks forcible rape the second-most-serious crime after homicide.

"Universities have been taking policies and procedures that were meant to respond to plagiarism and trying to adapt them for a serious felony," says David Lisak, a clinical psychologist and forensic consultant to defense attorneys, prosecutors and law enforcement, "but the complexities are enormous." It takes extensive training and experience to understand a victim's behavior and statements, how to conduct sensitive interviews and how to search for evidence, says Lisak, who also trains sex crimes detectives and U.S. military investigators.

"Very often the issue of incapacitation [of the accuser] comes up, and that's another terribly complicated thing to determine," says Lisak. "You have to interview witnesses, and you have to get blood alcohol levels." In RTI International's survey at two universities, 60 percent of undergraduates who reported being sexually assaulted said they had been incapacitated after having voluntarily consumed alcohol or drugs.[17] According to state laws and college codes, someone who is incapacitated is not able to consent to sex.

But Lisak disagrees with Cohn's solution. In an ideal world, a serious violent crime is handled by the criminal justice system, says Lisak. "But we don't have a functioning criminal justice system when it comes to sexual assault," he contends. It's rare to have both specially trained police detectives and district attorneys in one jurisdiction, says Lisak. Thus, he adds, "I see instance after instance of local district attorneys' offices just declining and declining these cases."

One research study shows that of every 100 rapes committed in the United States, fewer than 20 are reported to police, fewer than five are prosecuted and result in conviction, and fewer than three lead to jail time. Police may not take acquaintance rape seriously, victims may have second thoughts about pursuing someone they know and prosecutors may take only the strongest cases, said the study's authors.[18]

Lisak says instead of deferring to law enforcement, schools should hire specially trained, professional investigators with solid track records.

Tracey Vitchers, a board member at the New York-based advocacy group Students Active for Ending Rape (SAFER), agrees with Lisak about the current state of the criminal justice system. "Unfortunately, many survivors know that the criminal justice system is not kind to survivors of sexual assault in many cases, and many investigators are not well trained in trauma-informed report taking," she says. "Many students also come from communities that have been the target of police violence or police harassment, and they don't believe that [going to] the police is a safe alternative for them."

Both Vitchers and Lisak say requiring students to go to local law enforcement would have a chilling effect on student reporting.

But Roger Canaff, a fellow at the National District Attorneys Association in Alexandria, Va., says most fears of humiliation by investigators and of prosecutors' unwillingness to "take the case" do no prove true. The criminal justice system's response "is improving steadily in most places," he says.

Canaff says schools need to learn how to work closely with local law enforcement because a school's investigation can have ramifications if the accuser does file a criminal complaint. "Pretty much anything that's uncovered or discussed in the [school's] adjudication of a case can, and likely will, become relevant in the criminal case," Canaff says.

District attorneys complained at a roundtable discussion held by members of Congress that if students view the school process as an alternative to the police and then are disappointed with the outcome and contact law enforcement, the delay may mean that evidence gets stale and witnesses' memories fade.

Cohn says going late to the police with a complaint of sexual assault or not going at all is simply dangerous. "Campus judiciaries can't put people behind bars. Only law enforcement can," he says, "and that matters because research shows that a vast majority of rapes are committed by a very few repeat offenders. Leaving perpetrators on the streets is not sound policy."[19]

In September, hospital worker Jesse Matthew was charged with abducting University of Virginia student Hannah Graham, 18, missing since Sept. 13. Graham's

Former hospital worker Jesse Matthew is charged with the abduction of University of Virginia student Hannah Graham, whose remains were found on Oct. 18. He had been accused of sexually assaulting female Virginia students twice before, at Liberty University and Christopher Newport University, but he left each school after the accusations, and no criminal complaints were filed. Matthew also was indicted on Oct. 20 in the 2005 abduction, sexual assault and attempted murder of another Virginia woman.

remains were found on Oct. 18. Matthew was also indicted in the 2005 abduction, sexual assault and attempted murder of another Virginia woman. Matthew had been accused of sexually assaulting female students twice before, while a football player between 2002 and 2003 at Liberty University in Lynchburg, Va., and at Christopher Newport University in Newport News, Va. He left each school on his own after the accusations, and no criminal complaints were filed, university officials said.[20]

Cohn says colleges have a strong role to play in educating students about sexual assault, providing victim resources and making immediate accommodations, such as requiring the accused student to change classes or housing in order to avoid contact with and possible retaliation against the accuser. "And if an accused student who later turns out to be innocent [in criminal court] is forced to take a class online or remotely, or is forced to move to a different dorm building, FIRE isn't going to lose any sleep over that," says Cohn.

But attorney Brandt-Young at Legal Momentum says the accused student deserves a timely resolution, "and these police investigations can literally go on for many months or even years."

Most schools complete their investigation and adjudication within 60 days, and if that student is cleared, "their life will go back to normal," she says.

Should all colleges adopt "affirmative consent"?

Title IX and the Clery Act do not define consent, which is the basis for determining whether sexual assault occurred. As a result, it is being left up to schools, and "colleges are defining consent in radically different ways," says Fatima Goss Graves, vice president for education and employment at the Washington-based National Women's Law Center.

"There are places that really don't have much of a definition at all, and so people are relying on either the local criminal law, or it's an issue that's contested in each individual case," she explains.

And some schools, such as Harvard, prohibit "unwelcome conduct of a sexual nature." In a published Q&A, Harvard's Title IX officer, Mia Karvonides, said, "essentially conduct is unwelcome if a person did not request or invite it and regarded the conduct as undesirable or offensive."[21]

But advocates for alleged victims of sexual assault say Harvard's consent policy is outdated and inappropriate, a standard that the U.S. Department of Education was recommending 13 years ago in a guidance letter to schools. Legal Momentum's Brandt-Young says people can't have signs around their necks saying, "You can touch me here, you can grab me there," and so the only way to let someone know that sexual conduct is "unwelcome" is to say "no."

"And that's the problem with it. It's entirely reactive," says Brandt-Young. "You have to wait for the other

Many Colleges Lack Reporting Tools

Just over half of colleges and universities have 24-hour hotlines and 44 percent have websites for reporting sexual assaults at their schools, according to a survey of 440 four-year colleges. Additionally, only 16 percent of four-year colleges conduct anonymous student surveys about sexual violence at their schools.

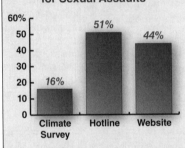

Percent of Colleges With Research and Reporting Tools for Sexual Assaults

Source: "Sexual Violence on Campus," U.S. Senate Subcommittee on Financial and Contracting Oversight — Majority Staff, July 9, 2014, pp. 5–6, http://tinyurl.com/lv5p84k

person to engage in some sexual conduct you don't like, and then you let them know afterward." The burden of consent is on the recipient.

She and other advocates would like to shift that burden to the initiator by having colleges and universities adopt so-called affirmative consent, also known as "yes means yes," a standard that the new White House task force is encouraging.[22]

Antioch College in Ohio was the first college to adopt affirmative consent 20 years ago, and it's one of the strictest policies, requiring unambiguous verbal consent for students engaging in sexual activity. The policy was widely mocked at the time and inspired a "Saturday Night Live" skit about a college game show called "Is It Date Rape?"[23]

Dartmouth, Yale, the University of California system and other schools have recently overhauled their sexual assault policies to require affirmative consent, although unlike Antioch, consent does not have to be verbal. A nonverbal "yes" could be indicated with a "vigorous head nod, or active engagement in the sexual activity, as long as it is 'unambiguous and voluntary,' " Dianne Klein, a University of California spokeswoman, told *The New York Times*.[24]

On Sept. 28, Democratic California Gov. Jerry Brown signed the nation's first affirmative consent legislation. It applies to all public and private postsecondary schools that receive state funds and follows the adoption of affirmative consent earlier this year by the University of California and California State University systems.

Under the law, California colleges must require students to obtain "affirmative, conscious and voluntary agreement to engage in sexual activity." Lack of protest or resistance does not mean consent; neither does silence.

Consent can be verbal or nonverbal, must be ongoing throughout the encounter, and can be revoked at any time. Previous sexual relations or a dating relationship do not imply consent.[25]

Critics of the California law, and of affirmative consent in general, say the approach micromanages students' sex lives and is vague and confusing, and some students agree.

"Are there guidelines? Are we supposed to check every five minutes?" asked Henry Mu, a 24-year-old biology major at California State University, Long Beach a few months before the bill became law. "If you were to do that, it would definitely kill the vibe," Mu's friend and fellow student, Sue Tang, 27, said with a laugh.[26]

John Banzhaf, a professor of public-interest law at George Washington University in Washington, D.C., says students' bewilderment is well placed. Nonverbal signals can be ambiguous and easily misinterpreted and the extent of consent given not be clear, he says. If a young woman lying with a young man on a dorm room bed raises her hips, "I assume she's consenting to letting him pull her jeans down, but is she also consenting for him to pull her underwear down? To have him touch her?" asks Banzhaf.

Students just have to speak up in that situation, says Vitchers of SAFER. "I don't think it's so complicated to say, 'I don't understand if you want to do this or not. Are you cool with this, or do you want to do that?' "

Banshaf says it's more efficient to require students to say one "no" than five or six or seven "yeses" as the encounter progresses. And Warner-Seefeld of FACE says young women can handle that responsibility. "I have a problem infantilizing women by taking all responsibility for their choices away from them," she says.

But that doesn't take into account the fear that a young woman may feel that may prevent her from saying "no," says Legal Momentum's Brandt-Young. "Freezing in fear is a totally legitimate response to danger," she says.

The California law, and most college affirmative consent policies, also state that consent can't be given by a student who is incapacitated by drugs, alcohol or medication. But students often have difficulty figuring out exactly what incapacitated means, said Scott Berkowitz and Rebecca O'Connor, executives with the Rape, Abuse & Incest National Network (RAINN), in a letter to the White House task force.

"Some campaigns and websites claim that the ingestion of even a single drink renders someone unable to legally consent, while conversely others explain that anyone short of unconscious can consent," they wrote. Schools need to do a better job of explaining, and videos, interactive apps and websites could help, they said.[27]

To clear up confusion about its disciplinary procedures for sexual assault, Yale University a year ago released eight different "sexual misconduct scenarios," using gender-neutral first names, including three in which students were drunk. After each capsule description, the school then described the likely punishment.[28]

Schools must go beyond defining consent and give concrete examples, as Yale did, said Emily Greytak, another SAFER board member. "These scenarios are commonly what happens on college campuses . . . and what people want to know," she said.[29]

BACKGROUND
Campus Activism

Feminists formed the country's first rape crisis centers in the 1970s, with volunteers guiding victims through fraught encounters with police, doctors and prosecutors. Activists were responding to shortcomings in the criminal justice system, which often blamed women for being raped. The feminists also sought to redefine rape as an act of violence often perpetrated by acquaintances and resulting from women's unequal status in society.

In 1970, Bay Area Women Against Rape founded a rape crisis center in Berkeley, Calif., and similar centers were soon established in Washington, D.C.; Ann Arbor, Mich; New York City, and Pittsburgh. By 1976, 400 rape crisis centers were operating in cities across the country. Although these centers were based in the community rather than on campuses, the movement influenced "the first forms of campus anti-rape activism," wrote psychiatrist Jodi Gold and public health expert Susan Villari in *Just Sex: Students Rewrite the Rules on Sex, Violence, Activism, and Equality.*[30]

Two of the earliest campus rape crisis centers were established at the University of Maryland and the University of Pennsylvania, in 1972 and 1973, respectively, following a series of rapes on those campuses. And in 1976, after a rape at the University of California, Berkeley, the entire University of California system adopted anti-rape education for students.[31]

CHRONOLOGY

1970s–1980s *Congress passes landmark sex discrimination law; anti-rape activists compel change on campuses.*

1972 Title IX of the Education Amendments Act prohibits sex discrimination at schools receiving federal financial aid. The law becomes the basis for mandating how schools handle campus sexual violence. University of Maryland students establish campus-based rape crisis center.

1976 A rape at the University of California, Berkeley, prompts UC system to adopt anti-sexual assault programs.

1980 Department of Education is established; Office for Civil Rights is given oversight of Title IX.

1985 *Ms.* magazine publishes "Date Rape: The Story of an Epidemic and Those Who Deny It," citing controversial survey results showing that one in four college women have been victims of rape or attempted rape, mostly by acquaintances. . . . Student protests prompt University of Michigan (and later the University of Minnesota) to provide comprehensive sexual assault services.

1990s *Congress passes laws to make campuses safer and to protect women from sexual violence.*

1990 Student-Right-to-Know and Campus Security Act, commonly known as the Clery Act, requires colleges and universities receiving federal funds to collect and publicize statistics on campus crime.

1992 Campus Sexual Assault Victim's Bill of Rights affords rape victims certain basic rights and requires schools to notify victims that they may file a report with local law enforcement. . . . Ohio's Antioch College is the first to require students to give step-by-step consent during sexual encounters.

1994 Violence Against Women Act (VAWA) holds offenders accountable and funds programs to help victims.

1998 Congress amends the Clery Act to require schools to identify whether crimes occur on campus, in certain

non-campus buildings, such as fraternity housing, or in adjacent public places.

2000s *Surveys continue to find high rates of sexual violence on campus; Congress strengthens Clery Act.*

2006 A paid dancer at a Duke University lacrosse team party tells police three team members sexually assaulted her; campus protests follow, and three players are arrested. Eventually, all charges are dropped, and the district attorney is charged with prosecutorial misconduct.

2007 University of Colorado-Boulder pays a record $2.85 million settlement to two female students who were gang-raped during a football recruiting program. . . . "Campus Sexual Assault Study" by RTI International finds that one in five surveyed female college seniors experienced a sexual assault since entering college.

2011 Office of Civil Rights tells colleges and universities they must use the lower "preponderance-of-evidence" standard in sexual violence proceedings.

2012 Department of Education raises (from $27,500 to $35,000) the fine for violating Clery Act reporting rules.

2013 Campus Sexual Violence Elimination Act expands campus crime reporting, requires training of campus nvestigators, allows both accuser and accused to have advisers and requires colleges to have ongoing sexual violence prevention programs. . . . Yale University is fined $155,000, one of the largest penalties under the Clery Act, for inadequately reporting campus crime statistics more than a decade ago, including omitting four forcible sex offenses from 2001 and 2002.

2014 White House Task Force to Protect Students from Sexual Assault calls for bystander intervention programs at schools (April). . . . Eight senators introduce Campus Safety and Accountability Act, which would increase Clery Act penalties and require schools to conduct student surveys on sexual violence (July). . . . Gov. Jerry Brown, D-Calif., signs legislation requiring "affirmative consent" during sex at colleges (September).

At about the same time, Congress held hearings to examine reports of employment discrimination against women and other forms of sex discrimination at the nation's colleges and universities. In response, Congress passed Title IX of the Education Amendments of 1972, which President Richard M. Nixon signed into law on June 23, 1972.

The landmark legislation prohibited discrimination based on gender in education programs and activities, from kindergarten through graduate level schooling, that receive federal funds. The law banned sexual harassment as well as unequal opportunity in athletics, science, technology, engineering and math programs, employment discrimination in schools and discrimination based on pregnancy.[32] Schools violating the law could be forced to revise their policies and lose federal financial aid, although the government has never applied financial punishment. Students and employees also could sue their schools for alleged Title IX violations.

It would take more than two decades and several federal court cases before sexual assault was considered a form of sexual harassment under Title IX and for the law to become a basis for regulating college policies around sexual violence.

Date Rape

Anti-rape activism continued on college campuses through the 1980s. Feminists said "epidemic levels" of young college women "were being subjected not only to the physical and emotional horrors of being raped or sexually assaulted by dates and acquaintances (primarily college men) but also to the horror of having college or university administrators disbelieve, discredit or attempt to silence them in an effort to preserve the public images of their colleges and universities," wrote criminal justice professors John Sloan III and Bonnie Fisher in *The Dark Side of The Ivory Tower: Campus Crime As a Social Problem.*[33]

In the first half of the decade, however, little empirical data existed to support such claims, so they were considered "largely rhetorical and were fairly ineffective in capturing the attention of either policy makers or the public," said Sloan and Fisher.[34] That changed dramatically in 1985, when *Ms.* magazine published "Date Rape: The Story of an Epidemic and Those Who Deny It." The article was based on preliminary results of a national study of female students at 32 colleges and universities, conducted by clinical psychologist Mary Koss, then teaching at Ohio's Kent State University and now at the University of Arizona.

Carly Mee, a student at Occidental College, center, talks with other students during the Oxy Sexual Assault Coalition awareness night campout at the Los Angeles college on April 19, 2013. A group of Occidental students and alumni filed a Title IX complaint with the Education Department, saying the school does not meet federal standards for preventing and responding to rapes and other sexual assaults on campus.

Two years earlier, the National Institute of Mental Health had agreed to sponsor Koss's study to assess sexual victimization among female college students. Koss did not ask women if they had been raped or sexually assaulted, since those general terms can mean different things to different people. Instead, she devised a 10-question survey that asked women about specific behaviors, such as giving in to unwanted sex play, experiencing unwanted attempted sexual intercourse or unwanted completed intercourse because of a man's verbal pressure, use of his position of authority, threats or use of physical force or because a man had given them alcohol or drugs.[35]

"If Koss's study yielded the conclusion that a substantial proportion of these women were being victimized, it would be a bombshell," wrote Bonnie Fisher, Leah Daigle and Francis Cullen in *Unsafe in the Ivory Tower: The Sexual Victimization of College Women.* Besides revealing a hidden problem, such a result would raise questions "about why women were being subjected to such aggression and why nobody was doing much to address it."[36]

In fact, Koss's findings were "startling," said Fisher, Daigle and Cullen. Koss found that one in four of the surveyed women said they had been a victim of behaviors since age 14 that met the legal definition of rape or

Most Campus Assaults Linked to Alcohol, Drugs

But women's advocates say don't blame the victim.

Alcohol and sex can be a dangerous combination, research shows. Sixty percent of undergraduate women who reported being sexually assaulted in a survey at two universities said they had been incapacitated after voluntarily consuming alcohol or drugs. Less than 1 percent thought they had been surreptitiously given a drug.[1]

"But discussing alcohol in the context of sexual assault is the third rail of discourse," says Christopher Krebs, senior research social scientist with North Carolina-based RTI International, a major research institute, who led the survey. "It's very difficult to talk about without upsetting or offending somebody." In fact, Krebs says some people were "furious" that his team asked about alcohol use in its survey.

That's because a victim's drinking is irrelevant, say women's advocates. Advising women to change their behavior and cut down on drinking, as some pundits have suggested, is unfair, advocates argue. "The burden should not be solely on victims to prevent their own assaults," says Christina Brandt-Young, a senior staff attorney at New York-based Legal Momentum, a women's defense and legal education fund. "Nobody should be trying to stop rape single-handedly."

"The cost of any form of self-policing — not walking alone in the dark, watching what you drink and what you wear — is that you live under a self-inflicted form of fear," said recent Columbia University graduate Ayushi Roy, who told *The Chronicle of Higher Education* that she resented the idea that she should monitor her behavior in order to stay safe.[2]

Besides, advising college women to cut down on drinking won't reduce overall sexual assaults on campus, say advocates. "Most campus rapists are repeat offenders, . . . who intentionally target women they perceive as vulnerable," says Brandt-Young, referring to research conducted at a large commuter college.[3] So they'll focus on women who continue to drink, she says.

Many college administrators agree. Instead of concentrating on potential victims' behavior, "we need to be talking about perpetrators who are using alcohol to be able to perpetrate sexual assault," said Jessica Ladd-Webert, director of victim assistance at the University of Colorado, Boulder. Educating students in this way could help them intervene, she said.[4] A growing number of schools are embracing education programs that encourage students to step in if they think that another student is in danger of being sexually assaulted.

attempted rape, and nearly 17 percent had experienced rape or attempted rape in the past academic year. These rates were 10–15 times greater than those from government crime surveys. In addition, almost 90 percent of the women in Koss's survey knew their assailants.[37]

The "one in four" statistic became a rallying cry and proof to feminists that sexual violence on campus was epidemic, though largely hidden, in part because society did not view rape by known assailants as "real" rape, a view apparently held by victims themselves. Nearly three-fourths of the women whose experience met the legal definition of rape failed to identify it as rape.[38]

Over the next several years, other journalists followed up the *Ms.* article with books, such as Robin Warshaw's *I Never Called It Rape*, and articles in *The Boston Globe*, *Newsweek*, *Time*, CNN and *The New York Times*.

However, critics charged that some of Koss's questions were vague and her numbers inflated. Over time, Koss and other researchers, including Fisher, have refined the research methods, and several surveys during the past 25 years have arrived at significant rates of college sexual violence, although not quite as high as "one in four."

New Laws

In the late 1980s and '90s, parents began pressuring colleges and universities to create freshmen orientation programs to reduce alcohol abuse and sexual victimization. Students began to organize "Take Back the Night" marches protesting sexual violence against women. And post-secondary institutions began to invest in computer-controlled or key-card access to dormitories, closed-circuit television

Krebs says he understands why victims' rights advocates say the intoxication of the victim is irrelevant, but he thinks college women should be warned that consuming alcohol can degrade their judgment and ability to perceive risk.

Often, a woman starts out in a safe situation, say drinking with friends in an apartment, but then the risk suddenly changes, and alcohol prevents her from picking up on the cues, says Krebs. Perhaps the guys from the downstairs apartment come in, guys she has never met before, he says. "She may go into a bedroom to crash, and the next thing she knows, someone is sexually assaulting her," says Krebs.

"Is it her fault? Absolutely not. Nowhere under the sun is that the woman's fault," says Krebs, but having drunk to excess may have made her vulnerable.

"Fear of blaming the victim may prevent us from doing something that we should be doing," says James Fox, a criminologist at Boston's Northeastern University. He says schools should discuss alcohol and sexual assault, warning both men and women about the risks they each face. "Men can still be charged with sexual assault if they are drunk. The fact that both are drunk does not establish consent." In addition, it's difficult for bystanders to intervene if they're inebriated, he says.

At the University of Michigan all incoming students take an online educational course that includes discussions about how alcohol affects the ability to consent to sex and to clearly understand when consent has not been given. The course is part of a multi-stage sexual violence prevention program at the school, which has required unambiguous affirmative consent for student sexual activity for years.

"We're really trying to always push this message that we want students to be engaging in mutually consensual, sober, enthusiastically engaged sex," says Holly Rider-Milkovich, director of the university's Sexual Assault Prevention and Awareness Center.

When the school gets pushback from students, it's often that they don't think the message is realistic. "They actually can't imagine a situation where they would be comfortable in expressing their sexuality or engaging in sexual activity without first having alcohol to drink," says Rider-Milkovich.

— *Barbara Mantel*

---

[1]Christopher P. Krebs, *et al.*, "College Women's Experiences with Physically Forced, Alcohol- or Other Drug-Enabled, and Drug-Facilitated Sexual Assault Before and Since Entering College," *Journal of American College Health*, May/ June 2009, http://tinyurl.com/ood2lzk.

[2]Robin Wilson, "Why Campuses Can't Talk About Alcohol When It Comes to Sexual Assault," *The Chronicle of Higher Education*, Sept. 4, 2014, http://tiny url.com/qfxa5w2.

[3]David Lisak and Paul M. Miller, "Repeat Rape and Multiple Offending Among Undetected Rapists," *Violence and Victims*, January/February 2002, p. 78, http:// tinyurl.com/kv5qf3m.

[4]"Third Roundtable on Sexual Assault on College Campuses with Sen. Claire McCaskill," C-Span, June 23, 2014, http://tinyurl.com/khk98qe.

---

surveillance systems in parking garages and upgraded security practices.[39]

In 1990 Congress passed the groundbreaking Student-Right-to-Know and Campus Security Act, known as the Clery Act, after Jeanne Clery, the 19-year-old Lehigh University student who was brutally raped, tortured and killed in April 1986. Her murderer, fellow student Josoph Henry, 20, whom she did not know, entered Clery's dormitory on the college's Bethlehem, Pa., campus through a series of unlocked doors while she slept.

During Henry's trial, in which he was convicted and sentenced to death, evidence showed that between 1984 and the murder, 38 incidences of robberies, rapes and assaults in or near the dormitory had been reported to campus authorities, who took no extraordinary action to protect students.[40]

Clery's parents sued Lehigh and settled out of court, then used the money to form the group Security on Campus (SOC) to advocate for safer campuses. The Clery Act was largely a result of intense lobbying by the Clerys and SOC.

The act requires postsecondary institutions receiving federal funds to compile three years' worth of statistics about on-campus alcohol, drug and weapons arrests; crimes such as homicide, forcible sex and robbery reported to campus security or local police; and descriptions of school security policies. The information is collected and published in annual campus security reports that allow prospective students and their families to consider campus crime rates when choosing schools, thereby pressuring institutions to improve students' safety.

The U.S. Department of Education's Federal Student Aid (FSA) office, which enforces the act, can

Training Bystanders May Help Stop Sexual Violence

It's "the only program that has promising evidence."

Each new academic year, college freshmen undergo orientation, where they make friends, register for classes, buy books, sign up for clubs, navigate the campus and generally absorb a sense of school spirit. It's also where they learn about the school's conduct code and hear warnings about underage drinking and sexual assault.

The sexual assault portion of the orientation usually lasts about an hour, during which college officials review the definition of consent, describe the resources available for sexual assault victims and explain school procedures for investigating and adjudicating sexual assault accusations.

But experts say these brief sessions don't necessarily reduce sexual assault among students. "All of the evidence . . . suggests that they are, at best, ineffective, and in some cases may actually be harmful," says Sarah DeGue, a behavioral scientist with the Division of Violence Prevention at the Centers for Disease Control and Prevention (CDC). That might be, she notes, because "people who are participating in the [session] might actually feel defensive . . . and it might actually make their attitudes worse."

Starting this year, the Campus Sexual Violence Elimination Act of 2013 requires schools to implement more extensive and ongoing prevention programs. "If it's done right, and if schools are doing the types of programs that are going to make a difference, I think that's going to be really great," says Fatima Goss Graves, vice president for education and employment at the Washington-based National Women's Law Center. However, there is little research about which prevention programs actually reduce campus assault rates.

"The only thing we have to date that has promising evidence . . . is Bringing in the Bystander," says DeGue. A study shows that the program can increase the participants' knowledge of sexual violence, their understanding of bystander intervention and their willingness to intervene when someone is at risk of sexual assault. [1] But it remains unknown whether the program reduces the rates of sexual assault. Such research is just beginning.

Bringing in the Bystander is a four-and-a-half-hour program, usually split into two sessions in one week and is also available in a condensed 90-minute version. It provides

penalize schools up to $35,000 per reporting infraction, raised in 2012 from $27,500. Since the law was enacted, 22 postsecondary schools have paid a total of $2.4 million in fines, according to the Department of Education.

As a result of SOC lobbying over the next two decades, the federal government expanded the law. For example, in 1992, Congress passed the Campus Sexual Assault Victim's Bill of Rights, which requires schools to have procedures for:

- Students to report sexual violence to school officials;
- Notifying students of their right to report an incident to law enforcement;
- Instructing students on how to preserve evidence of an assault;

- Notifying students of options to change living arrangements and class schedules if they feel threatened after an alleged sexual assault.

In addition, schools must have a disciplinary process that treats both accuser and accused equally. [41]

In 1998, Congress required schools to state whether reported crimes occurred on campus, in certain non-campus buildings, including fraternity or sorority housing, or in public places adjacent to campus. In 2008, Congress required schools to notify the campus community by email or prerecorded telephone message within 30 minutes of a "critical incident" deemed a significant safety threat. [42]

But campus security reports filed under the Clery Act have serious flaws, say campus crime experts. For example, they grossly underestimate college sexual information about the prevalence, causes and consequences of sexual violence; explains the concept of bystander responsibility in preventing sexual violence; conducts role-playing exercises so students can practice safe intervention and provides information about community resources. Students also pledge to be active bystanders in their communities.[2]

Bringing in the Bystander was developed at the University of New Hampshire and has been adopted at colleges and universities elsewhere. Some schools, such as Clark University in Worcester, Mass., put all incoming students through the program. Others wait until the second semester after students have settled into school and may feel more comfortable intervening in a risky situation. Still others conduct the program among specific groups, such as athletes or fraternity and sorority members.

"Bystander intervention isn't just about intervening and telling people that their behavior is wrong and they need to stop," says Jane Stapleton, co-director of Prevention Innovations, a research and development unit at the University of New Hampshire. "It can also be distracting the perpetrator away from the victim or the potential victim."

Stapleton says program coordinators help students devise safe ways to do that. Students have suggested turning the lights up or turning off the music at a party if someone is trying to lead an intoxicated friend out of the room. "We've had women students say if that was happening to their friend, they would go up to her and say, 'Here's the tampon you asked for.' It's a way to interrupt the intensity of the moment and to get people away from a situation," says Stapleton.

But more often, bystander intervention occurs before any immediate risk is present. "Interventions are much more likely to be along the lines of speaking up when you hear people saying things that are supportive of rape, or that are sexually harassing, that sort of thing," says DeGue. Or it may mean not promising a friend he can use your room if he plans to get a young woman really drunk at a party, says Stapleton.

Bystander intervention is important, she says, because the vast majority of rapes on campus are perpetrated by a small number of repeat offenders, men who are likely immune to efforts to change their behavior, according to a study at a large commuter college. [3]

"The way you're going to stop those men . . . is not to necessarily get them in a room and put them through an educational program," Stapleton says. "It's to get to the people who surround these perpetrators."

— *Barbara Mantel*

[1]Victoria L. Banyard, *et al.*, "Sexual Violence Prevention Through Bystander Education: An Experimental Evaluation," *Journal of Community Psychology*, May 2007, p. 463, http://tinyurl.com/p3r2wna.

[2]"Bringing in the Bystander," National Institute of Justice, http://tinyurl.com/ meqad5x.

[3]David Lisak and Paul M. Miller, "Repeat Rape and Multiple Offending Among Undetected Rapists," *Violence and Victims*, January/February 2002, p. 78, http://tinyurl.com/ofqjm6a.

violence because, research shows, most incidents go unreported. Secondly, statistics are limited to mostly on-campus incidents, even though much sexual violence occurs in off-campus housing.

In addition, higher reported crime statistics may reflect a school committed to preventing sexual violence by encouraging victims to come forward, while low crime statistics could indicate a school trying to preserve its reputation by discouraging reporting.[43] In any case, experts say most prospective students and their families don't know about the campus security reports.

Clarification and Reform

A series of court cases and communications from the Department of Education since the late 1990s has clarified that peer sexual violence is now considered a form of sexual harassment under Title IX. Courts also have established standards of proof for cases in which students sue their schools for not properly responding to an allegation of sexual violence. For a school to be found in violation of Title IX in court, the school must have acted with "deliberate indifference" in the face of "actual knowledge" of the violent act.

It's a difficult standard to meet, and most private suits are settled out of court. The largest settlement to date was $2.85 million paid by the University of Colorado, Boulder in 2007 to two female students who were gang-raped during a football recruiting program that the university knew was dangerous to women.[44]

When cases have gone to court, schools have been found to have acted with deliberate indifference for:

Many Schools Fail to Provide Training

About 20 percent of 440 surveyed four-year colleges and universities did not train faculty or staff in how to respond to allegations of sexual assault. For students, 77 percent of large schools provided prevention or response training, compared to less than half of small schools (with fewer than 1,000 students).

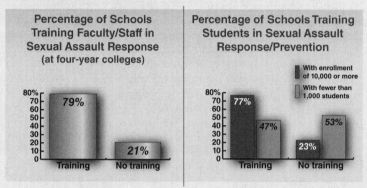

Source: "Sexual Violence on Campus," U.S. Senate Subcommittee on Financial & Contracting Oversight — Majority Staff, July 9, 2014, p. 7, http://tinyurl.com/lv5p84k

• Doing nothing at all;
• Doing nothing after the accused student denies the allegation;
• Investigating too slowly;
• Investigating in a biased way;
• Finding that sexual violence occurred but failing to discipline the assailant for retaliatory harassment;
• Finding that sexual violence occurred and then removing the victim, but not the assailant, from classes and housing;
• Requiring the alleged victim and perpetrator to face each other in mediation before a complaint can be filed.[45]

Nancy Chi Cantalupo, the associate vice president of equity, inclusion and violence prevention for the National Association of Student Personnel Administrators, said the "actual knowledge" standard may provide an incentive for schools "to suppress [victim] reporting, at least passively," to reduce their exposure to lawsuits.

However, the Department of Education's Office for Civil Rights (OCR) uses a "constructive knowledge" standard, which asks whether a school knew or reasonably should have known about a risk of sexual harassment or violence. That standard provides an incentive for schools to encourage students to report incidents, said Cantalupo.[46]

If a school is accused of violating Title IX, the OCR will conduct a comprehensive review of the school's policies and procedures along with past sexual harassment cases. Schools found to have violated Title IX "can be, and often are, required to change their entire response system to peer sexual violence and harassment," said Cantalupo.[47]

Sometimes, the OCR will issue guidance to all schools at once, as it did in its 2011 letter reminding schools of their obligations under Title IX and, in a controversial move, telling them to use the lowest standard of proof. Then Congress sent colleges and universities scrambling again in 2013, when it required schools to significantly reform their sexual violence policies.

The Campus Sexual Violence Elimination Act, an update of the Clery Act, required, among other things, campus crime reports to include statistics about stalking, dating and domestic violence and required colleges and universities to have ongoing violence prevention, bystander intervention and risk reduction programs for students, staff and faculty.[48]

In April the White House Task Force to Protect Students from Sexual Assault issued its first report, calling for colleges to conduct student "climate" surveys assessing the extent of sexual violence on campus, institute programs to promote bystander intervention and provide trained advocates to victims of sexual violence.[49] The task force also issued a checklist for campus sexual misconduct polices that recommended defining sexual assault as "non-consensual sexual contact, and non-consensual sexual intercourse." It also suggested a minimum definition of consent that comes very close to affirmative consent.[50]

CURRENT SITUATION

Proposed Legislation

In late July, a bipartisan group of eight senators led by Claire McCaskill, D-Mo., introduced the Campus Safety and Accountability Act (CASA), which, if passed, would enshrine many of the White House Task Force recommendations into law. CASA is one of three measures introduced in Congress this year to deal with campus sexual assault. It has four GOP sponsors.

"This represents a rare thing in Washington — a truly collaborative, bipartisan effort — and that bodes well for our shared fight to turn the tide against sexual violence on our campuses," said McCaskill.[51]

The legislation would require colleges and universities to:

- Conduct annual, standardized, anonymous, Web-based surveys of students about their experience with sexual violence and harassment, with the results to be published online;
- Provide confidential advisers to victims to help them obtain services and, if desired, report crimes to campus authorities and/or law enforcement;
- Train confidential advisers, investigators and participants in disciplinary proceedings about the nature of sexual violence and how to properly interview students bringing complaints of sexual assault;
- No longer allow athletic departments to handle complaints of sexual violence against athletes; and
- Enter a memorandum of understanding with local law enforcement to clearly delineate their respective responsibilities.

The Department of Education would be required to publish the names of schools with pending Title IX investigations and the final resolution of those cases; moreover, the department could fine a school up to 1 percent of its operating budget for noncompliance with certain provisions. In addition, the penalty for each Clery Act violation would increase from $35,000 to $150,000.[52]

"SurvJustice has endorsed the bill, although there are definitely some issues with it that we hope will be improved when it goes to committee," says SurvJustice's Dunn, who thinks the student climate surveys "will really force colleges to recognize the scope of the problem."

Vice President Joseph Biden introduces Lilly Jay, who says she was raped at Amherst College when she was a freshman, during the Sept. 19 launch of the White House "It's on Us" campaign against campus sexual assault. "Using your experience to protect others from rape is so empowering and so important, but it also tethers you to your pain," said Jay. "In order to be heard, I had to talk about the night in which violence silenced me."

Dunn disagrees with the bill's provision making the confidential adviser both the victim's advocate and forensic interviewer. "Anyone who is involved in an investigation can be subpoenaed by a court, and if you have to testify about your conversations with a victim, it's not really confidential," she says.

Groups such as FIRE, which advocate for more due process protections for the accused, also have mixed feelings about CASA. They support increased cooperation with local law enforcement, better training for campus personnel, a ban on special treatment for athletes and increased transparency at the Department of Education. But they also want support services for accused students and provisions to advance their due process protections. And they prefer that all sexual assault allegations be referred to local law enforcement. They also criticize the bill's use of the word "victim."[53]

"McCaskill's word choice suggests that she and her colleagues believe that an accuser is automatically a 'victim,' thereby abandoning the presumption of innocence for the accused," said history professor KC Johnson, author of *Until Proven Innocent: Political Correctness and the*

Should colleges hand off all sexual assault cases to the police?

YES

Robert David "KC" Johnson
*Professor of History, Brooklyn College and
City University of New York Graduate Center;
Author,* Until Proven Innocent: Political
Correctness and the Shameful Injustices of
the Duke Lacrosse Rape Case

Written for *CQ Researcher*, October 2014

Few people would contend that colleges and universities should investigate students charged with attempted murder or armed robbery. Colleges cannot subpoena evidence or place witnesses under oath. Few universities employ forensic or medical analysts, prosecutors who can sift through complex evidence or defense attorneys who can safeguard accused students' rights.

Yet, regarding one serious felony — sexual assault — a powerful coalition has demanded that colleges not only adjudicate the issue but also implement procedural changes to increase the likelihood of guilty findings. The coalition includes the Obama administration, which has ordered universities to evaluate sexual assault claims under a preponderance-of-evidence standard, which is weaker than the beyond-a-reasonable-doubt criterion used in criminal trials.

California now requires colleges (but not the courts) to determine "affirmative consent" in sexual assault cases. When asked how an innocent student could prove that he obtained the necessary ongoing consent, the law's co-sponsor, Assemblywoman Bonnie Lowenthal, replied, "Your guess is as good as mine."

On campus, self-described survivors and their faculty allies have pressured schools to further erode due process. Cornell stripped the accused of the right to cross-examine their accusers, even when the complainant is the only witness. Stanford no longer requires unanimous findings of guilt. Swarthmore forbids an accused student to tell anyone outside of the disciplinary process, including his parents, of the specific evidence compiled against him. Too many colleges vaguely define the relationship between intoxication and sexual assault in ways that invite arbitrary decisions.

The rationale behind these changes is that prosecutors tend not "to bring charges in college-acquaintance rape cases" — in short, that letting police and prosecutors do their jobs is somehow objectionable. Under universities' parallel judicial systems — which have lower burdens of proof, minimal due-process protections and wildly incomplete evidentiary bases — surely more undergraduates will be branded as rapists. As to how many of these students will actually be innocent? Due-process opponents seem unconcerned with that question.

But colleges cannot serve the interests of justice by adjudicating serious criminal offenses such as sexual assault.

NO

Nancy Chi Cantalupo, Esq.
*Associate Vice President of Equity, Inclusion and Violence
Prevention, NASPA Student Affairs Administrators;
author,* 'Decriminalizing' Campus Institutional Responses
to Peer Sexual Violence

Written for *CQ Researcher*, October 2014

Requiring campuses to rely exclusively on the criminal justice system to address gender-based violence undermines our commitment to equality and our effectiveness in ending this violence. My research confirms that noncriminal laws that apply to campus gender-based violence — including Title IX, the Clery Act and constitutional law on administrative due process — help both victims and schools while protecting the rights of students accused of perpetrating violence.

Criminal law has failed to deter gender-based violence. Today less than 3 percent of rapists are incarcerated.

However, even if the criminal law worked perfectly, it cannot ensure students' equal access to educational opportunity, because that is not its goal. To protect equality, both survivors and schools must look to Title IX, the groundbreaking civil rights statute prohibiting gender discrimination in education. Unlike the criminal law, Title IX gives schools multiple methods to assist their students in continuing with and succeeding in their education after the trauma of violence. These include a wide range of academic accommodations and services to help survivors overcome the trauma of violence.

My research shows that both the Clery Act — as recently amended by the 2013 Violence Against Women Act — and court rulings on accused students' administrative due-process rights support Title IX. Neither conflicts with Title IX, and Clery explicitly protects the rights of victims of gender-based violence. Supreme Court and lower court precedents allow schools to use equal, Title IX-compliant procedures when disciplining students and to take temporary actions, pending a hearing, when a student may pose a threat to the community. All of these laws use civil, not criminal, legal procedures, including the preponderance-of-evidence standard of proof. Moreover, just as employers discipline or fire employees for assaulting coworkers when such assaults also violate criminal law, schools may use noncriminal parallel proceedings to enforce their rules.

In fact, Title IX, the Clery Act and administrative due-process laws help schools protect all students' rights — the accused and survivors alike — as well as prevent gender-based violence and its awful aftermath. Criminal law is not designed to accomplish the equality goals, nor is it historically effective at fulfilling the prevention objectives.

Shameful Injustices of the Duke Lacrosse Rape Case, which reviews the highly publicized prosecution and subsequent dropping of sexual assault charges against three players.[54]

Northeastern University criminologist Fox worries that the online climate surveys might not accurately reflect sexual violence on campus. "Students who have been sexually assaulted might be more likely to respond; students who are unconcerned might not respond," potentially skewing the results, says Fox. There is also nothing to prevent a student from taking a survey twice by filling one out for someone else, Fox adds. "The one thing you don't want to do is embark on a very expensive, large-scale annual survey that can very easily be criticized, and then publicize the results school by school."

RTI International researcher Krebs agrees that methodological rigor is crucial to credibility and says his firm is exploring how such surveys can "produce school-level estimates that engender the confidence needed to really make decisions based on them."

Those in the prevention field are dismayed that McCaskill's bill focuses exclusively on reacting to sexual violence. "It's pretty much devoid on anything about prevention," says Jane Stapleton, co-director of the University of New Hampshire's Prevention Innovations: Research and Practices for Ending Violence on Campus. Some prevention programs, such as bystander intervention, have been shown to change attitudes and may reduce sexual violence, she says.

The two other pending bills, both introduced in late July, share some of CASA's components. One is the Survivor Outreach and Support Campus Act (SOS Act), introduced in the Senate by Sen. Barbara Boxer and in the House by Rep. Susan Davis, both California Democrats.

The other is the Hold Accountable and Lend Transparency on Campus Sexual Violence Act (HALT Act), introduced by Reps. Jackie Speier, D-Calif., and Patrick Meehan, R-Pa. It would allow individuals to bring private lawsuits against schools they believe are violating the Clery Act. (Currently, private lawsuits can be filed only under Title IX.) The HALT Act also would require the Education Department to publicly list the schools investigated under Clery, just as CASA would do for Title IX.[55]

State Action

Sponsors of California's new affirmative consent standard for sex on campus are celebrating Gov. Brown's signing of the measure late last month.

"Every student deserves a learning environment that is safe and healthy," said state Sen. Kevin de León, D-Los Angeles. "The State of California will not allow schools to sweep rape cases under the rug. We've shifted the conversation regarding sexual assault to one of prevention, justice and healing."[56]

"This is amazing," said UCLA student Savannah Badalich, founder of 7000 in Solidarity, an organization educating the campus community about sexual assault. "It's going to educate an entire new generation of students on what consent is and what consent is not . . . that the absence of a 'no' is not a 'yes.'"[57]

Critics of the law continue to argue that the definition of affirmative consent, which can be nonverbal, is vague and confusing and inappropriately shifts the burden of proving consent onto men.

Four days after Gov. Brown signed the measure, New York Democratic Gov. Andrew Cuomo announced that the State University of New York (SUNY) would make affirmative consent the rule on all of its 64 campuses within 60 days. Campus sexual assault "is not SUNY's problem by origination," Cuomo said. "I would suggest it should be SUNY's problem to solve and SUNY's place to lead."[58]

As in California, SUNY's affirmative consent means both partners must express unambiguous desire to engage in each sexual act, either verbally or nonverbally. Silence cannot be interpreted as consent, previous consent is not sufficient, and people who are physically helpless, incapacitated or asleep are considered unable to give consent.

According to *The New York Times*, many of SUNY's 64 campuses "already require some form of affirmative consent, but often with varying degrees of specificity." Some have a single paragraph explaining their consent policy, while others have pages, complete with suggestions for gaining consent, such as asking, "Is it O.K. if I take off my pants?"[59]

OUTLOOK
More Lawsuits?

Stapleton of Prevention Innovations at the University of New Hampshire believes more colleges will adopt affirmative consent in the future.

"But this will take a while, as I believe that there will be a lot of resistance," she says. Stapleton also believes colleges will do more to educate students about consent.

"However, I am a little bit concerned about all of the emphasis on consent," she says, because research shows that "the majority of sexual assault is not about miscommunication," but rather is perpetrated by repeat offenders.

Legal Momentum's Brandt-Young agrees that more colleges will adopt affirmative consent. Both she and Stapleton say schools will also be doing more bystander intervention programs in the future, and more schools will be consistently following more transparent investigation processes, Brandt-Young predicts.

Dunn of SurvJustice expects more attention to be paid to the relationship between campus and police investigations. "There will be more reporting to police, and I'm hoping that that will draw more attention to the ways that police mishandle these cases."

She also hopes "schools will bring only suspensions and expulsions for sexual misconduct, rather than essays and campus counseling. Those will be a thing of the past." And because starting this year schools must allow students to have an adviser of their choice present at proceedings, including a lawyer, she expects victims to bring more lawsuits against schools they believe are violating federal law.

FIRE's Cohn agrees there will be more lawsuits filed, by both sides. "If the lawsuits by accused students succeed, campus administrators will likely start adding procedural protections like the right to active participation of counsel," says Cohn. "But if the lawsuits fail, campus judiciaries will continue to be shams where fundamental notions of fairness remain absent."

While it's difficult to predict which, if any, of the three bills pending in Congress will pass, many observers predict that Congress will, at a minimum, mandate that schools conduct annual climate surveys of their students about their experiences with sexual assault.

However, Krebs of RTI International thinks the government may want to consider helping to develop a centralized system that would survey students using a well-researched, rigorous methodology, analyze the data and produce individual university reports.

"Such a system could ultimately produce the information universities and the nation need to better understand the prevalence and nature of sexual assault on college campuses," says Krebs. It will also reveal "what can be done to prevent and respond to incidents, which will ultimately improve academic performance, student satisfaction and public health and safety."

NOTES

1. Emma Bogler, "Frustrated by Columbia's inaction, student reports sexual assault to police," *Columbia Spectator*, May 16, 2014, http://tinyurl.com/p64cekp. Roberta Smith, "In a Mattress, a Lever of Art and Political Protest," *The New York Times*, Sept. 21, 2014, http://tinyurl.com/qgnva88.

2. Vanessa Grigoriadis, "Meet the College Women Who Are Starting a Revolution Against Campus Sexual Assault," *New York Magazine*, Sept. 21, 2014, http://tinyurl.com/lmzdg6q.

3. Bogler, *op. cit.*

4. For background, see the following *CQ Researcher* reports: Peter Katel, "Crime on Campus," Feb. 4, 2011, pp. 97–120; Chanan Tigay, "Women and Sports," March 25, 2011, pp. 265–288; and Barbara Mantel, "Sexual Harassment," April 27, 2012, pp. 377–400.

5. "Not Alone: The First Report of the White House Task Force to Protect Students From Sexual Assault," The White House, April 2014, p. 2, http://tinyurl.com/lb6vqgj.

6. Dean G. Kilpatrick, *et al.*, "Drug-facilitated, Incapacitated, and Forcible Rape: A National Study," U.S. Department of Justice, July 2007, p. 3, http://tinyurl.com/3lv7jjz.

7. "The Campus Safety and Security Data Analysis Cutting Tool," Office of Postsecondary Education, U.S. Department of Education, http://tinyurl.com/okk7drb.

8. Christopher P. Krebs, et al., "College Women's Experiences with Physically Forced, Alcohol- or Other Drug-Enabled, and Drug-Facilitated Sexual Assault Before and Since Entering College," *Journal of American College Health*, May/June 2009, p. 644, http://tinyurl.com/ood2lzk.

9. Glenn Kessler, "One in five women in college sexually assaulted: the source of this statistic," *The Washington Post*, May 1, 2014, http://tinyurl.com/kt6rsjp.

10. Walt Bogdanich, "A Star Player Accused, and a Flawed Rape Investigation," *The New York Times*, April 16, 2014, http://tinyurl.com/lkcac78.

11. "Florida State University Finally Launches Investigation Into Jameis Winston Rape Report,"

The Associated Press/*The Huffington Post*, Sept. 5, 2014, www.huffingtonpost.com/2014/09/04/florida-state-winston-rape_n_5769652.html.

12. Alyssa S. Keehan, "Student Sexual Assault: Weathering the Perfect Storm," United Educators, pp. 1, 2, http://tinyurl.com/n899s67.

13. Ashe Schow, "Four better ideas to fight campus sexual assault," *Washington Examiner*, Aug. 6, 2014, http://tinyurl.com/n3nwzl2.

14. "Sexual Violence on Campus," U.S. Senate Subcommittee on Financial and Contracting Oversight — Majority Staff, July 9, 2014, pp. 6, 11, http://tinyurl.com/lv5p84k.

15. Robin Wilson, "Presumed Guilty," *The Chronicle of Higher Education*, Sept. 1, 2014, http://tinyurl.com/kbqvxq8.

16. "Dear Colleague Letter," Office of the Assistant Secretary, U.S. Department of Education, April 4, 2011, http://tinyurl.com/k3u5k99.

17. Krebs, *et al.*, p. 641, *op. cit.*

18. Kimberly A. Lonsway and Joanne Archambault, "The 'Justice Gap' for Sexual Assault Cases: Future Directions for Research and Reform," Violence Against Women, March 28, 2012, pp. 152–153, 155, 157, http://tinyurl.com/mloq5ow.

19. David Lisak and Paul M. Miller, "Repeat Rape and Multiple Offending Among Undetected Rapists," *Violence and Victims*, January/February 2002, p. 78, http://tinyurl.com/ofqjm6a.

20. Jennifer Steinhauer, "Virginia Cases Show Vulnerability of Women on Campus," *The New York Times*, Oct. 3, 2014, http://tinyurl.com/m47qckv. Also see Ashley Dejean, "UVA Abduction Suspect Jesse Matthew Faced Previous Sexual Assault Allegations," WAMU, Oct. 2, 2014, http://tinyurl.com/l6lv2tc. Michale Martinez, "Remains found last week are those of UVA student Hannah Graham," CNN, Oct. 24, 2014, http://tinyurl.com/p489gza.

21. Stacy Teicher Khadaroo, " 'Rape culture' on campus: why Harvard's new policy is 'really important,' " *The Christian Science Monitor*, July 2, 2014, http://tinyurl.com/lxsvjsr.

22. "Checklist for Campus Sexual Misconduct Policies," White House Task Force to Protect Students from Sexual Assault, April 2014, pp. 4–5, http://tinyurl.com/kabl5g7.

23. "Is It Date Rape?" "Saturday Night Live," http://tinyurl.com/lbhsgwt.

24. Ian Lovett, "California Bill Sets Sights on Curbing Campus Sexual Assaults," *The New York Times*, Sept. 10, 2014, http://tinyurl.com/mnjkk7b.

25. "SB-967 Student safety: sexual assault," California Legislative Information, Sept. 28, 2014, http://tinyurl.com/of6sdq8.

26. Josh Dulaney, "Students question 'affirmative consent' bill designed to combat sexual assaults," *Long Beach Press Telegram*, June 8, 2014, http://tinyurl.com/qx8tzyo.

27. "Dear Members of the Task Force," Rape, Abuse & Incest National Network, Feb. 28, 2014, http://tinyurl.com/mtttzcf.

28. "Sexual Misconduct Scenarios," Sexual Misconduct Response at Yale, http://tinyurl.com/lktlwo7.

29. Tara Culp-Ressler, "Yale University Works to Strengthen Its Sexual Assault Policy By Clarifying 'Consent,' " Think Progress, Sept. 13, 2013, http://tinyurl.com/o4yj8u4.

30. Jodi Gold and Susan Villari, *Just Sex: Students Rewrite the Rules on Sex, Violence, Activism, and Equality* (2000), pp. 5–6.

31. *Ibid.*

32. "Sex Discrimination: Overview of the Law," U.S. Department of Education, http://tinyurl.com/qh8mhp7.

33. John J. Sloan III and Bonnie S. Fisher, *The Dark Side of The Ivory Tower: Campus Crime As a Social Problem* (2011), p. 82.

34. *Ibid.*, p. 86.

35. Bonnie S. Fisher, Leah Daigle and Francis Cullen, *Unsafe in the Ivory Tower: The Sexual Victimization of College Women* (2010), pp. 12–13.

36. *Ibid.*, p. 15.

37. *Ibid.*, pp. 15–17.

38. *Ibid.*, p. 14.

39. Sloan and Fisher, *op. cit.*, p. 25.

40. *Ibid.*, pp. 56–57.

41. Bonnie S. Fisher and John J. Sloan III, *Campus Crime: Legal, Social, and Policy Perspectives* (2013), p. 101; *The Dark Side of the Ivory Tower, op. cit.*, pp. 75–77.

42. *Ibid., The Dark Side of the Ivory Tower.*

43. Fisher, *et al., op. cit.*, p. 187.

44. Fisher and Sloan, *Campus Crime: Legal, Social, and Policy Perspectives, op. cit.*, p. 95.

45. *Ibid.*, pp. 95–96.

46. *Ibid.*, p. 98.

47. *Ibid.*, pp. 98–99.

48. "Campus Sexual Violence Elimination Act of 2013," http://clerycenter.org/campus-sexual-violence-elimi-nation-save-act.

49. Nick Anderson and Katie Zezima, "White House issues report on steps to prevent sexual assaults on college campuses," *The Washington Post*, April 29, 2014, http://tinyurl.com/n8acluq.

50. "Checklist for Campus Sexual Misconduct Policies," *op. cit.*

51. "Bipartisan Bill Takes Aim at Sexual Assault on College and University Campuses," Press Release, U.S. Sen. Claire McCaskill, July 30, 2014, http://tinyurl.com/lnjmsmj.

52. *Ibid.*; "Summary and Analysis of the Campus Accountability and Safety Act," Stop Abusive and Violent Environments (SAVE), Aug. 1, 2014, http://tinyurl.com/przyuab.

53. *Ibid.*, "Summary and Analysis of the Campus Accountability and Safety Act"; Joseph Cohn, "Third Campus Sexual Assault Bill Introduced in Congress: Still No Provisions Addressing Due Process," Foundation for Individual Rights in Education (FIRE), Aug. 1, 2014, http://tinyurl.com/kt3h23g.

54. KC Johnson, "Campus 'Due Process Has No Lobby,'" *Minding the Campus*, July 31, 2014, http://tinyurl.com/ndhea2b.

55. See the "Hold Accountable and Lend Transparency on Campus Sexual Violence Act," www.opencongress.org/bill/hr5269-113/text.

56. "California Gov. Jerry Brown Signs Nation's First Affirmative Consent Standard Into Law," The Associated Press, Sept. 29, 2014, http://tinyurl.com/m67sxde.

57. *Ibid.*

58. Ariel Kaminer, "Cuomo Orders SUNY to Overhaul Its Sexual Assault Rules," *The New York Times*, Oct. 2, 2014, http://tinyurl.com/nf364dq.

59. *Ibid.*

BIBLIOGRAPHY

Selected Sources

Books

Fisher, Bonnie S., *et al., Unsafe in the Ivory Tower: The Sexual Victimization of College Women*, Sage, 2010.
Three criminologists examine the research into sexual violence against college women.

Fisher, Bonnie S., and John J. Sloan III, *Campus Crime: Legal, Social, and Policy Perspectives*, Charles C. Thomas, Ltd., 2013.
Two criminologists examine student crime rates and laws governing campus crime.

Gold, Jodi, and Susan Villari, *Just Sex: Students Rewrite the Rules on Sex, Violence, Activism, and Equality*, Rowman & Littlefield, 2000.
A psychiatrist and a public health expert present writings of student activists and scholars about campus sex and sexual violence.

Articles

"California Gov. Jerry Brown Signs Nation's First Affirmative Consent Standard Into Law," The Associated Press, Sept. 29, 2014, http://tinyurl.com/m67sxde.
A new law requires California colleges and universities to adopt an affirmative consent policy for student sex.

Anderson, Nick, and Katie Zezima, "White House issues report on steps to prevent sexual assaults on college campuses," *The Washington Post*, April 29, 2014, http://tinyurl.com/n8acluq.
A special White House task force advises colleges to survey students about sexual assault.

Bogler, Emma, "Frustrated by Columbia's inaction, student reports sexual assault to police," *Columbia Spectator*, May 16, 2014, http://tinyurl.com/p64cekp.

A Columbia University student filed a police report and began carrying a mattress around campus in protest after the university found her accused rapist not responsible.

Grigoriadis, Vanessa, "Meet the College Women Who Are Starting a Revolution Against Campus Sexual Assault," *New York Magazine*, Sept. 21, 2014, http://tinyurl.com/lmzdg6q.
The author profiles several young sexual assault survivors who have started an anti-rape advocacy movement.

Kaminer, Ariel, "Cuomo Orders SUNY to Overhaul Its Sexual Assault Rules," *The New York Times*, Oct. 2, 2014, http://tinyurl.com/nf364dq.
New York's governor orders the state's public colleges and universities to adopt affirmative consent policies.

Kessler, Glenn, "One in five women in college sexually assaulted: the source of this statistic," *The Washington Post*, May 1, 2014, http://tinyurl.com/kt6rsjp.
The statistic that one in five college women will be sexually assaulted before graduation is controversial.

Wilson, Robin, "Why Campuses Can't Talk About Alcohol When It Comes to Sexual Assault," *The Chronicle of Higher Education*, Sept. 4, 2014, http://tinyurl.com/lqvtdgz.
Talking about binge drinking's link to sexual assault stirs passions.

Reports and Studies

"Not Alone: The First Report of the White House Task Force to Protect Students From Sexual Assault," The White House, April 2014, http://tinyurl.com/lb6vqgj.
A special White House task force recommends schools change their sexual assault policies and procedures.

"Sexual Violence on Campus," U.S. Senate Subcommittee on Financial and Contracting Oversight — Majority Staff, July 9, 2014, http://tinyurl.com/lv5p84k.
Senate Democrats issue survey results from hundreds of schools about sexual assault policies and procedures.

Banyard, Victoria L., *et al.*, "Sexual Violence Prevention Through Bystander Education: An Experimental Evaluation," *Journal of Community Psychology*, May 2007, p. 463, http://tinyurl.com/p3r2wna.
Researchers find that a bystander education program makes individuals more willing to stop potential sexual assaults.

Krebs, Christopher P., *et al.*, "College Women's Experiences with Physically Forced, Alcohol- or Other Drug-Enabled, and Drug-Facilitated Sexual Assault Before and Since Entering College," *Journal of American College Health*, May/June 2009, http://tinyurl.com/ood2lzk.
A survey of female students at two public universities finds that one in five seniors has been sexually assaulted.

Lisak, David, and Paul M. Miller, "Repeat Rape and Multiple Offending Among Undetected Rapists," *Violence and Victims*, January/Februry 2002, www.davidlisak.com/wp-content/uploads/pdf/RepeatRapein UndetectedRapists.pdf.
A survey of men at a commuter university finds that a small percentage of males account for most rapes on campus and are repeat offenders.

Lonsway, Kimberly A., and Joanne Archambault, "The 'Justice Gap' for Sexual Assault Cases: Future Directions for Research and Reform," Violence Against Women, March 28, 2012, http://tinyurl.com/mloq5ow.
Researchers review what is known about rates of reporting and prosecuting sexual assaults.

For More Information

Centers for Disease Control and Prevention, Division of Violence Prevention, 1600 Clifton Rd., Atlanta, GA 30329; 800-232-4636; www.cdc.gov/ViolencePrevention? index. html. Works to prevent injuries and deaths from violence.

End Rape on Campus, 424-777-3762; http://endrapeon campus.org. Works to end sexual violence through survivor support, education and legislative reform.

(Continued)

(Continued)

Families Advocating for Campus Equality (FACE), P.O. Box 5448, Spartanburg, SC 29304; 701-491-8554; www.facecampusequality.org. Promotes due process in college sexual assault investigations.

Foundation for Individual Rights in Education (FIRE), 170 S. Independence Mall West, Suite 510, Philadelphia, PA 19106; 215-717-3473; www.thefire.org. Advocates for individual rights at colleges and universities.

Know Your IX, http://knowyourix.org. National survivor-run, student-driven campaign to end campus sexual violence.

Legal Momentum, 5 Hanover Square, Suite 1502, New York, NY 10004; 212-925-6635; www.legalmomentum.org. Defense fund advancing women's and girls' rights.

National Women's Law Center, 11 Dupont Circle, N.W., #800, Washington, DC 20036; 202-588-5180; www.nwic.org. Researches and advocates for opportunity and advancement for women and girls.

Students Active for Ending Rape (SAFER), 222 Broadway, 19th Floor, New York, NY 10038; 347-465-7233; www.safercampus.org. Supports student-led campaigns to reform college sexual assault policies.

SURVJustice; survjustice.org. Works to reduce sexual violence by assisting survivors, empowering activists and supporting institutions.

10

Reforming Juvenile Justice

Christina L. Lyons

Eighteen-year-old Rodney Stallworth of East Baltimore spent eight months in detention at the J. DeWeese Carter Center in Chestertown, Md., on a drug charge. He said fights would break out among the young inmates that sometimes turned into melees. Maryland juvenile detention centers have had problems with violence and excessive use of force by the staffs, according to the state's Juvenile Justice Monitoring Unit.

Getty Images/*The Baltimore Sun*/Kenneth K. Lam

Fifteen-year-old Adrian Jere Gonzalez of Santa Cruz, Calif., lured his 8-year-old neighbor to his family's apartment last July, then raped and killed her, according to police.[1]

Gonzalez was soon arrested, and the district attorney charged him as an adult for murder, sexual assault and kidnapping. Youth advocacy groups immediately criticized the prosecutor's decision to send the boy to criminal court, where he could be subject to a much longer sentence than in juvenile court.[2]

"When you have somebody as young as 15, this shouldn't just be decided arbitrarily by a district attorney but by a judge in a hearing hopefully informed by experts in adolescent psychology and psychiatry," says Barry Krisberg, director of research and policy at the University of California-Berkeley's Chief Justice Earl Warren Institute on Law and Social Policy.

But victims' rights advocates say a teen accused of such a heinous act should be tried in adult court. "He knew what he was doing; he has to be held accountable," says Harriet Salarno, board chairperson of Crime Victims United of California, a nonprofit in Auburn that advocates on behalf of crime victims. She says a jury — not available in juvenile court — should be able to decide the case.

The dispute highlights a growing debate about how state judicial systems handle minors who get into trouble. At a time of declining youth crime, many lawmakers, psychologists and advocates for juveniles want to reform heavily punitive systems to take into account neuroscientific research showing adolescents have limited reasoning abilities but are greatly amenable to rehabilitation. The reformers are lobbying for states to focus on the juvenile justice

From *CQ Researcher*, September 11, 2015.

Juvenile Detentions Down Sharply

About 54,000 juveniles were housed in detention centers, shelters, group homes, wilderness camps and other residential correctional facilities in 2013, roughly half the number detained in 1999. Some experts have attributed the drop to the deterrence effect of get-tough approaches to juvenile crime; others link the drop to fewer school referrals to police of misbehaving students and states' increased use of community programs instead of detention facilities.

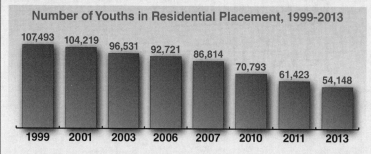

Number of Youths in Residential Placement, 1999-2013

1999	2001	2003	2006	2007	2010	2011	2013
107,493	104,219	96,531	92,721	86,814	70,793	61,423	54,148

Source: Melissa Sickmund *et al.*, "Easy Access to the Census of Juveniles in Residential Placement," Office of Juvenile Justice and Delinquency Prevention, 2015, http://tinyurl.com/qendwcp

system's founding ideal of keeping young offenders in family courts, where their sentences can involve rehabilitation rather than simply punishment and incarceration in large state prisons far from home.

"Kids are not just small adults," says Nate Balis, director of the Juvenile Justice Strategy Group for The Annie E. Casey Foundation, a private Baltimore-based philanthropy that focuses on issues affecting children. "Not only do they look different, but they are different."

Yet some prosecutors, legal experts and victims' rights advocates contend that youth crime is down precisely because of the deterrence of harsh punishments. Juvenile offenders, particularly the most violent, must be held accountable and public safety must remain a priority, they say.

"Even a 5-year-old knows it's wrong to kill people," says Steven Erickson, a forensic scientist in York, Pa.

State laws vary on when and how juveniles can be sent to adult criminal court, where they could face the same punishment as adults, including life in prison. For example, in Wisconsin, 10-year-olds charged with murder can be sent to adult criminal court. New York and North Carolina treat all 16- and 17-year-olds as adults,

regardless of the crime. California allows prosecutors to decide whether to charge a 14-year-old as an adult for murder or other violent offenses, while juvenile court judges in Alaska and Washington can send a child of any age to adult court for any criminal offense. Often, juveniles convicted as adults begin their sentences in a juvenile facility and are transferred, usually at age 18 or 21, to an adult facility.[3]

In the early 20th century, most states automatically dealt with youths under 18 in juvenile court, where judges could decide to transfer them to adult court. Then, in the early 1990s after juvenile crime began to rise and some political scientists warned of a coming wave of "brutally remorseless" young "super-predators," legislatures began cracking down on young offenders.[4]

However, the predicted wave of super-predator criminality never developed, and juvenile crime in fact began declining after spiking in the mid-1990s. By 2010, the number of juveniles arrested was down 21 percent from 2001. By 2003, homicides committed by youths had dropped to the lowest level since 1980. And after an uptick between 2003 and 2006, juvenile arrests fell in 2012 to their lowest level in 33 years.[5] Likewise, the number of youths detained in juvenile facilities fell about 50 percent between 1999 and 2013.[6]

Theories vary on the reasons for the declines. "Crime rates are down because we've had a system of increasing consequences," says Michael Rushford, president of the Sacramento, Calif.-based Criminal Justice Legal Foundation, a group of legal and academic experts that supports tougher prosecution and sentencing. But Krisberg cites improved economic circumstances, more early-childhood education, fewer gangs and less reliance by schools and law enforcement on 1990s-era "zero tolerance" policies in dealing with juvenile delinquency.[7]

Experts cite similar reasons for the drop in juvenile detentions, and they say dwindling state budgets made authorities more willing to divert youths to community rehabilitation programs instead of expensive state-run detention facilities. In addition, lawsuits alleging overcrowding or abuse in such facilities forced some states to seek other alternatives.[8]

Meanwhile, reports indicate that juvenile detainees are often physically or sexually abused by guards or other inmates. For example:

• The Casey foundation recently found systemic "maltreatment" of youths in juvenile facilities in 29 states since 2000.
• The U.S. Department of Justice in 2014 reported that male juveniles at New York City's Rikers Island detention facilities were routinely abused by guards and other inmates.
• Also in 2014, the American Civil Liberties Union reported about harm caused by solitary confinement, widely used as a punishment in juvenile facilities and to protect juveniles in adult facilities from the regular prisoner population.[9]

Nell Bernstein, an investigative reporter and author of the 2014 book *Burning Down the House*, found that youth in juvenile facilities receive limited education and counseling — and even less in adult facilities — although judges often believe teens will be rehabilitated so they can re-enter their communities.[10]

Punitive sentencing of young offenders is contrary to the founding principle of the juvenile justice system to rehabilitate delinquent youths, reform advocates say. And, recent neuroscientific research bolsters their argument that young people should be handled differently than adults, they say.

Magnetic resonance imaging (MRI) of the adolescent brain has shown that the prefrontal cortex — responsible for cognitive processing, reasoning and self-regulation — does not fully develop until youths are in their early- to mid-20s, researchers say. Thus, they add, adolescents are highly susceptible to peer pressure and unlikely to consider long-term consequences, making them potentially less culpable for their crimes.[11]

"There's a reason that kids do incredibly stupid things, especially when they are in a group," says Kathleen R. DeCataldo, executive director of the New York State Permanent Judicial Commission on Justice for Children.

But some prosecutors and psychologists say brain research does not prove that youths who commit violent crimes cannot control their actions and shouldn't be punished as adults. Further, such a philosophy "doesn't lead people to be able to take responsibility for their actions and choices in life," says Nita Farahany, a law and philosophy professor at Duke University.

Temple University psychology professor Laurence Steinberg says that while the research may not prove juveniles lack culpability, it shows promise that they can be rehabilitated. In his 2014 book, *Age of Opportunity: Lessons from the New Science of Adolescence*, Steinberg described adolescence as a period of "brain reorganization," when the mind is easily influenced and shaped by outside factors.[12]

Such research shows that youths should not be punished the same as adults and need counseling to change their behavior, says Michael Harris, senior attorney for the Oakland, Calif.-based National Center for Youth Law, which provides legal resources for child advocates. "No young person should be tried in adult court," he says. "It's more counterproductive than going through the juvenile justice system, and nothing is done to help them become productive citizens."

Youth advocates also say juveniles should not face life sentences without the possibility of parole. Given young peoples' "unique capacity to change," accountability measures "should focus on rehabilitation," says Jody Kent Lavy, director and national coordinator of the Baltimore-based Campaign for the Fair Sentencing of Youth.

But Charles "Cully" Stimson, a senior legal fellow with the conservative Heritage Foundation think tank, stands by his opposition to that approach, as reflected in his 2009 report: "Adult Time for Adult Crimes."

In 2012 the U.S. Supreme Court, in *Miller v. Alabama*, declared it unconstitutional for states to make it mandatory for juveniles found guilty of certain crimes to receive life in prison without the possibility of parole.[13] Since then, states and courts have disagreed on whether that ruling should apply to sentences imposed before 2012. The high court is expected to rule on that issue this fall.[14]

As reform advocates, legislators, psychologists and lawyers continue to debate how the justice system should handle youths, they are focusing on these key issues:

Does brain research prove adolescents are less culpable for their crimes?

Wallace Mlyniec, senior counsel at Georgetown University's Juvenile Justice Clinic, says advances in brain imagery have helped researchers understand that the human brain continues to mature until about age 25, meaning adolescents are less able to make rational decisions.

"The cognitive part really is pretty good by the age of 16," he says. "Most 16-year-olds have the cognitive capacity of adults, but they don't have the impulse control, the decisionmaking ability, the experience to understand what is the consequence of their behavior, and they are influenced by peers in the ways adults are not."

"The future, for a 15-year-old, is Friday night," he says. Therefore, adolescents should not be held to the same standards of culpability as an adult, he contends.

The Supreme Court began suggesting that in its 1998 ruling in *Thompson v. Oklahoma* barring capital punishment for anyone under 16. "The susceptibility of juveniles to immature and irresponsible behavior means 'their irresponsible conduct is not as morally reprehensible as that of an adult,' " the court stated. It reiterated this statement in 2005, when it banned the death penalty for juveniles under 18, and reaffirmed that stance in 2012, when it barred mandatory life sentences without parole for youths.

Harris, of the National Center for Youth Law, points out: "What we have learned . . . over the last couple of decades through research on adolescent brain development is that teenagers and adolescents are very susceptible to peer influence. They are very much thrill-seeking. And they do not have the ability to consider long-term consequences the same way an adult can."

UC-Berkeley's Krisberg is a strong proponent of adolescent brain research, saying it "puts a fine point on what we knew for a long time" about adolescent behavior. But, he warns, it should not be the only factor considered at trial. Lawyers on both sides in a case should be able to also provide psychological and psychiatric evaluations of the youth involved and information about his or her family and social background, and prior criminal convictions and evidence of motive, he says.

Sally Satel, a resident scholar at the conservative American Enterprise Institute think tank in Washington and co-author of the 2013 book *Brainwashed: The Seductive Appeal of Mindless Neuroscience*, says lawyers and psychologists rely too heavily on the rhetorical power of science to sway juries. "What we know from neuroscience does not deepen the picture" of why adolescents behave a certain way but only "adds new vocabulary," she says. Further, she argues, neuroscience is not well enough advanced to explain culpability on a case-by-case basis.[15]

Erickson, the forensic scientist, agrees. "Most people in the system are impulsive, risk takers, [who] don't see the future," he says. "The Supreme Court said these qualities are what make juveniles less morally culpable. Then who in the criminal justice system is morally culpable?"

Likewise, says Duke's Farahany, who serves on the Presidential Commission for the Study of Bioethical Issues, the brain science "doesn't tell us what competency an individual has, nor what competencies you have to have to be answerable to the law."

Stephen Morse, a professor of law and psychiatry at the University of Pennsylvania, warns against "brain-overclaim syndrome," in which "people make claims based on the neuroscience that don't follow from the neuroscience." The "criteria for responsibility are entirely behavioral — meaning acts and mental states," he says. "We don't hold brains responsible; we hold people responsible."

Society already knew that juveniles tend to be more impulsive and susceptible to peer pressure, he says. He objects to the argument that neuroscience shows that certain legal policies are necessary. Whether sentences for juvenile offenders should be mitigated is "not a scientific argument or question; it's a moral and legal question."

Temple psychology professor Steinberg agrees the science has only bolstered what society long knew about adolescent behavior, and that the science doesn't mitigate youths' culpability. Like Erickson, he asks, "If we argue that young people are less able to control their impulses, what do we do about adults who for some demonstrable reason have less ability to control their impulses?"

However, Steinberg says, "It's not just that adolescents are less mature, it's that adolescents are transient. A 30-year-old who has poor judgment and is short-sighted is always going to be that way." But an adolescent could change, he maintains. Thus, he says, when deciding sentences, courts should consider research showing brains are malleable, and therefore youths can reform.[16]

"The brain's malleability makes adolescence a period of tremendous opportunity — and great risk," Steinberg wrote in 2014. "If we expose our young people to positive, supportive environments, they will flourish. But if the environments are toxic, they will suffer in powerful and enduring ways."[17]

DeCataldo, of New York's commission on justice for children, uses adolescent brain research to teach legislators, educators and policymakers "that we can really change these kids." She says the research shows that a youth development approach that involves input from a school and community "is so much more effective than a punitive approach."

She adds: "I think people can come back from doing the most heinous acts."

Should states raise the age at which juveniles can be charged as adults?

Based on recent brain research, justice reform advocates have been pushing states to raise the age at which juveniles can be charged for any offense in adult court, where they can be subject to lengthy or lifelong prison sentences,

"With all the research on the adolescent brain, the idea of treating a 16-year-old as an adult is a hard case to make," says the Casey Foundation's Balis.

Many advocates cite inconsistencies in U.S. laws regarding teens and young adults. "A society that tries 12-year-olds who commit serious crimes as adults because they are mature enough to 'know better,' but prohibits 20-year-olds from buying alcohol because they are too immature to handle it, is deeply confused about how to treat people in this age range," Temple University's Steinberg wrote in 2014.[18]

Youth advocates say when children under 18 are held in adult facilities they are exposed to harmful conditions, ranging from physical abuse by adult inmates to lengthy periods of solitary confinement. In 2010, for example, 16-year-old Kalief Browder was sent to Rikers Island, an adult prison in New York City, after being accused of stealing a backpack. While awaiting trial in the adult system, he spent three years in jail, including nearly two in solitary confinement. He was released in late 2014 and committed suicide several months later.[19]

The Bureau of Justice Statistics estimated that about 7,600 youths under 18 were held in adult facilities in 2010. That is far more than the 2,300 held in June 1999 but 20 percent fewer than the 9,500 held in 1990, when the juvenile population in adult prisons peaked. However, observers on both sides of the issue say reliable estimates are hard to collect because few courts keep records of the number of juveniles incarcerated with adults.[20]

Americans have "a deep cultural instinct to punish as a way of changing behavior," says Jeffrey Butts, director of the Research and Evaluation Center at the John Jay College of Criminal Justice in New York. "And most people making decisions about policy are thinking about someone else's kid," not their own.

Such severe punishment for young people also doesn't reliably change behavior, Butts and others say. The Department of Justice reported that six major studies found higher recidivism rates among juveniles convicted for violent offenses in criminal court when compared with similar offenders tried in juvenile court.[21]

Moreover, says DeCataldo of New York state's commission on justice for children, "when kids go through adult facilities, they aren't getting any type of education." New York requires imprisoned youths to attend classes only until they are 16, she says.

Mlyniec, of the Juvenile Justice Clinic at Georgetown University, says the juvenile system should change how it deals with typical adolescent behavior that can result in mistakes. He cites the experience of 19-year-old Zachery Anderson of Elkhart, Ind. Anderson met a girl on an online dating website who said she was 17 — a year above the age of consent in her home state of Michigan. Anderson eventually traveled to Michigan where the two had sex. However, it turned out she was 14. Originally convicted of criminal sexual conduct, Anderson would have been placed on a sex offender registry. Mlyniec asks, "Should it even be a crime?" — a question many observers asked, prompting a district court judge in September to vacate the sentence. A new judge will consider whether to sentence Anderson under a Michigan law for youthful offenders and not place his name on the state's sex offender registry.[22]

Judges sometimes impose overly harsh sentences, and youths should not be incarcerated with adults, says Heritage's Stimson. But "first-degree murder is still first-degree murder," he says. "It's not debatable the brain is developing, but whether at some point in the development [adolescents] can appreciate the difference of right and wrong."

Few States Ban Juvenile Life Sentences

Fourteen states — most recently Vermont, Hawaii and West Virginia — have banned life sentences for juveniles without the possibility of parole.

States that Ban Juvenile Life Sentences without Parole

Source: "States that have eliminated JLWOP," The Campaign for the Fair Sentencing of Youth, undated, http://tinyurl.com/p2anypr

raped, you have got a family member that's dead at the hands of another person."

Texas state Sen. John Whitmire, a Democrat and strong proponent of justice reforms, says legislators should carefully consider the consequences of changing laws. "Advocates say the poor 17-year-old shouldn't be in [facilities] with adults," Whitmire says. "But if you put him in a juvenile facility, what about my 12-, 13-, 14-year-olds? You want to protect them from 17-year-olds."

Further, if all 17-year-olds typically charged as adults in Texas — about 26,000 last year — are handled in the juvenile system, he says, "it will crash the system. I'm actually trying to depopulate the juvenile system."

Should juveniles be sentenced to life in prison without parole?

Many youth advocacy groups balk at the prospect of young people facing life sentences without the possibility of parole. "The idea that they would get effectively a death sentence, that they will die in prison, without ever having the opportunity to prove that they could change just seems wrong," says the Casey Foundation's Balis.

Advocacy groups such as the Campaign for the Fair Sentencing of Youth want a ban on life sentences for juveniles. Currently, there are about 2,500 prisoners nationwide who were sentenced as juveniles to life in prison, according to The Sentencing Project, a Washington-based research group that opposes life without parole for juveniles.[24]

According to the fair sentencing campaign, 14 states have banned life sentences without parole for juveniles, nine after the Supreme Court's 2012 ruling in *Miller v. Alabama* that mandatory life sentences for juveniles are unconstitutional. Also following the ruling, five states abolished life without parole as an option for juveniles "in most cases," the campaign said.[25]

Many juveniles serving life in prison "have demonstrated that, even with limited programming on the inside,

Forensic scientist Erickson doesn't entirely agree. He says, "It's fine to have a system that wants to treat juveniles differently" for such crimes as theft. "But when you are talking about murder, that's different. Retribution has to be part of the criminal justice system; we punish them because they deserve it."

Juries should consider each case individually, says Rushford of the Criminal Justice Legal Foundation. "A major focus of the trial is the age of the defendant," he says. "So let the jury look at the case on its own merits."

A major worry is that a violent youth could hurt someone else, says Steve Doell, president of the Oregon chapter of Crime Victims United. In a recent Oregon case, a juvenile who had been charged with burglary and harassment was treated as a low-level offender, but later raped a 39-year-old woman and killed a 29-year-old woman, he says.[23]

For a crime victim, or for the surviving family members, "it really doesn't make any difference if the person is 16, 24 or 66 years old," Doell says. "You have got the same result; you have got the family member that's been they have been able to grow and change," says Jody Kent Lavy, the campaign's director and national coordinator. "It's important to check on them later in life to determine that they have been rehabilitated."

She adds, "We know young people can commit serious crimes, and the consequences are no less tragic. But the question we face as a society is, how do we hold them accountable as youth? Do we want to encourage them to better themselves while in prison and prove they can come home as productive members of their community?"

Many young criminals have been exposed to violence as a child, she explains, an argument Associate Justice Elena Kagan made in the Supreme Court's *Miller* ruling. "Mandatory life without parole . . . prevents taking into account the family and home environment that surrounds him — and from which he cannot usually extricate himself — no matter how brutal or dysfunctional."[26]

Moreover, says The Sentencing Project, housing juveniles for life "requires decades of public expenditures," averaging $34,135 per year — and double that for an inmate over 50.[27]

Lavy says the United States does not align with the rest of the world on this issue. She says the U.N. Convention on the Rights of the Child, ratified by 140 signatory countries but not the United States, prohibits life sentences for juveniles.[28] Yet, she says, the United States has ratified the International Covenant on Civil and Political Rights, considered an international bill of rights, and the International Convention on the Elimination of All Forms of Racial Discrimination — relevant because a disproportionate percentage of juveniles of color are incarcerated.[29] The Campaign for the Fair Sentencing of Youth says life without parole for juveniles also undermines the U.N. convention against torture.[30]

"There's no merit to those arguments," says \the Heritage Foundation's Stimson, a former deputy

Case	Year	Court decision/effect of ruling
Stanford v. Kentucky	1989	Upheld Kentucky and Missouri supreme court rulings that juveniles age 16 or older can be sentenced to death.
Roper v. Simmons	2005	Overturned *Stanford v. Kentucky* on the ground that executing minors is "cruel and unusual punishment" under the Eighth Amendment.
Graham v. Florida	2010	Determined that state laws permitting life imprisonment for juveniles without parole for non-homicidal crimes are unconstitutional.
Miller v. Alabama	2012	Determined that state laws permitting life imprisonment without parole for juveniles who commit homicide are unconstitutional.
Montgomery v. Louisiana	2015	Will hear case involving question of whether the court's previous ruling in *Miller v. Alabama* should apply retroactively to prisoners serving life sentences without parole for crimes committed as juveniles.

Key Supreme Court Rulings on Juveniles

Source: Case pages at The Oyez Project at IIT Chicago-Kent College of Law, www.oyez.org/cases

assistant secretary of Defense who in 2006 helped defend the department's compliance with the convention against torture before the United Nations. That convention and the International Covenant on Civil and Political Rights are silent on the issue of life without parole sentences, he says.

"States are fully within their rights and their decision-making fully within the debate of the social science experts to offer life without parole sentences for those convicted of first degree murder," he says.

State justice systems allow judges to use discretion, as the Supreme Court directed in its 2012 ruling in which it stated that "the judge must take youth and experience and other factors into consideration," Stimson points out. "So they get an individualized sentencing procedure." In any case, he adds, most juveniles convicted of murder are not given life sentences, and prosecutors "are sensitive to the unique circumstances of each case."

Salarno, of Crime Victims United, says, "We aren't making anybody accountable and responsible." She contends there is a "movement . . . going on in this country" in which "the victim has become the perpetrator and the perpetrator has become the victim."

Her group opposed a California measure, ultimately passed in 2013, to allow those sentenced to life without parole before age 18 to ask for a rehearing. "Those families went through all that trauma and all that fear, and a jury gave them that sentence," Salarno says. "And now they live in fear because [the inmate] is going to get out. That is wrong to do that to those families."

In his dissent in the *Miller* case, Chief Justice John G. Roberts Jr. said the court had confused decency with leniency. "It is a great tragedy when a juvenile commits murder — most of all for the innocent victims," Roberts wrote.

Erickson, the forensic scientist, warns, "If the Supreme Court eventually decides we will have a categorical ban, is that not at war with the doctrine that juries get to decide?"

Rushford of the Criminal Justice Legal Foundation opposes banning life without the possibility of parole (LWOP), and says some murderers, even those under 18, "should never see the light of day." However, he adds, "the juveniles on LWOP who are performing well, behaving and making themselves productive should be in a different kind of housing from the hard-core gang banger."

Moreover, he continues: "There is a guaranteed way to reduce sentences for 17-year-old multiple murderers. There is something called a commutation by the governor. In California, we have a governor who has done that. He's putting his butt on the line every time when he makes those calls."

Muhammad, of Impact Justice, says paroled inmates released in recent years by Democratic Gov. Jerry Brown have become productive citizens. He says those convicted at 14 and sentenced to life terms likely didn't have a brain that had fully developed yet. "Thirty years later they would be a human being."

He supports banning life-without-parole sentences. He warns, however, that courts can impose sentences that are not termed life without parole but are effectively the same. "There are courts and judges who get around [a ban on mandatory life without parole] by giving 150-year sentences. That hasn't been outlawed."

Erickson and others explain, however, that such sentences typically provide for a parole hearing after a certain number of years.

BACKGROUND
Early Sentencing

Juveniles were treated as adults in the criminal system until the start of the 18th century, when the Roman Catholic Church said children under age 7 could not form the intent to commit a crime. In 1704 Pope Clement XI created a center for "profligate youth," and over the next two centuries governments began creating separate judicial systems for youths.[31]

In the 1760s legal scholar William Blackstone refined judicial guidelines for children. In his *Commentaries on the Laws of England*, Blackstone said an individual must meet two criteria to be accountable for a crime: He must have committed the crime and have had a "vicious will" to commit the crime. Children 6 and under could not be found guilty, he said, while children 15 and older could be tried and sentenced as adults.[32]

In the American colonies, children under 14 were incarcerated or even executed for certain crimes such as murder or rape well into the 18th century.[33] The Society for the Prevention of Pauperism formed in 1818 to oppose the sentencing of youths to adult jails and prisons, and in 1825 New York City established the first House of Refuge, where children ages 8 to 17 who were accused of a range of offenses attended classes and did carpentry, sewing or housework. Those sent to the facility were thought to include "children of poor and often vicious emigrants; from the intemperance of parents, and the frequent want, misery and ignorance of their children."[34] Dozens more such facilities opened around the country over the next 15 years.

For many years some states tried "reform schools" for law-breaking youths, the first of which opened in Massachusetts in 1849. But the schools proved ineffective and later were determined to have subjected inmates to severe abuse, sometimes leading to death. Recent investigations have revealed, for instance, that boys held at the Arthur G. Dozier School for Boys, which operated for more than 100 years in Marianna, Fla., suffered "unspeakable abuses" at the hands of authorities there. The bodies of at least 51 who died there have recently been discovered.[35]

States tried other methods to deal with wayward juveniles. In 1876, the U.S. Navy transferred the ship *Jamestown* to San Francisco's Industrial School for Boys to provide training for work on merchant ships. But three years later the school returned the *Jamestown* to the Navy after public complaints that it was being used as a training ship for criminals.[36]

In 1899 the Illinois Legislature created the first juvenile court in Cook County (Chicago), where judges ruled on cases ranging from truancy to major crimes. Other states followed suit, creating juvenile systems based on the philosophy that children should be treated differently from adults. By the 1930s, with urban populations and crime rates growing, community leaders tried to determine the cause of juvenile misbehavior.[37] Lawmakers and civil reformers sought ways to reform youths rather than just punish them.

The California Youth Correction Authority Act, passed in 1941 and applicable to anyone under 23, was the first law to state that the purpose of juvenile corrections was rehabilitative rather than punitive.[38] By the end of 1950, Wisconsin, Minnesota, Massachusetts and Texas had enacted similar laws.[39]

In 1950 Congress passed the Youth Corrections Act, which gave judges flexibility in sentencing youths, such as imposing probation or requiring special services for incarcerated juveniles. The law also allowed a youth's record to be cleared.[40] And the Justice Department in 1954 set aside six federal corrections facilities for programs aimed at turning "young law violators into useful citizens."[41] During the 1850s, many states built "work camps" and "training schools" for youths who ran afoul of the law.[42]

Urban crime rates rose drastically in the 1960s and '70s, as post-World War II Baby Boomers reached their teens and 20s. In 1962, arrests of juveniles under 18 for serious crimes had risen three times faster over the previous six years than the rate of growth of the youth population.[43] The rate of juvenile arrests for homicide doubled during the decade after 1964.[44]

Meanwhile, news reports on overcrowding and abuse in training schools and detention facilities led to a push for reforms. The Supreme Court issued a series of rulings giving juveniles the right to due process and limiting the use of the death penalty, although in 1971 it ruled that youths were not entitled to a jury trial in juvenile court.[45]

In 1968, Congress passed the Juvenile Delinquency and Prevention Act to encourage states to create delinquency prevention and rehabilitation programs. Yet reports of abuse continued.

Sen. Birch Bayh Jr., D-Ind., in 1973 opened a series of hearings to investigate a growing trend of youth incarceration, estimating that at least 500,000 youths were in detention centers at the time. And he said he would look into reports of abuse of young inmates, citing reports that four cellmates in a Louisiana parish jail had reportedly gang-raped a 17-year-old, and a 15-year-old boy being held in a Niles, Mich., jail hanged himself.[46]

The hearings culminated in renewal of the Juvenile Justice and Delinquency Prevention Act, providing funds for community delinquency-prevention programs if states pledged to house convicted juveniles separately from adults and not to imprison them for minor felonies. Under the law, states also had to try to reduce the disproportionate number of minority youths caught up in the justice system.[47]

'Get Tough' Approach

For a while, the juvenile arrest rate for violent crimes stopped rising. From 1975 to 1987, it hovered at around 300 arrests per 100,000 youths ages 10 to 18. But over the next seven years, at the height of the urban crack cocaine epidemic, the rate rose by more than 60 percent, to about 500 per 100,000.[48] The growing illegal drug trade and gang activity contributed to the rise.[49] Meanwhile, the number of school discipline cases that ended up in state and federal courts increased between the 1960s and '90s.[50]

In the 1970s and '80s, states cracked down hard on juvenile criminals. New York passed new laws in 1978 in response to two murders by 15-year-old Willie Bosket Jr., who, despite a history of violent crimes, was subject to a maximum five-year placement in a juvenile facility. The new law made 14- and 15-year-olds criminally responsible in adult court for 14 different crimes and allowed 13-year-olds to be prosecuted for murder in adult court.[51]

By 2000, 45 states and Washington, D.C., allowed prosecutors to file adult charges against juveniles for serious felonies.[52] Many states lowered the age at which youths could be tried in adult court, expanded the eligible offenses for transferring juveniles to adult courts and increased the severity of penalties available in juvenile court. In Illinois, the legislature in 1995 lowered from 13 to 10 the age limit at which youths could be sentenced to prison. Subsequently, a 12-year-old convicted (with a 13-year-old

CHRONOLOGY

1825-1950 *States devise methods to charge and detain delinquent and criminal youths separately from adults.*

1825 New York House of Refuge, nation's first known juvenile reformatory, opens with nine youths.

1899 Illinois establishes first juvenile court.

1941 California passes Youth Corrections Authority Act, declaring that the purpose of juvenile corrections is rehabilitation, not punishment.

1950 Congress passes Youth Corrections Act, giving judges flexibility in sentencing juveniles.

1968-1974 *As juvenile crime rises, states impose tough penalties on juvenile offenders; Supreme Court, Congress uphold juvenile rights.*

1968 Congress passes Juvenile Delinquency and Prevention Act, encouraging states to create new ways to handle youthful offenders.

1970 Supreme Court in *In Re Winship* says criminal charges against youths must be proved "beyond a reasonable doubt."

1971 Supreme Court in *McKeiver v. Pennsylvania* rules juveniles are not entitled to trial by jury in juvenile court proceedings.

1974 Congress passes Juvenile Justice and Delinquency Prevention Act, authorizing the first federal oversight of justice systems governing youths.

1989-1996 *In the wake of rising crime during crack cocaine epidemic, states allow teens to be tried as adults; juvenile crime spikes, then drops.*

1989 Supreme Court of Missouri upholds death penalty for 16- and 17-year-olds.

1994 Violent Crime Control Act authorizes millions of dollars for boot camps and other private juvenile justice services. . . . Youth crime rate begins to drop.

1996 Drug czar William J. Bennett and think tank director John P. Walters warn of era of ultra-violent youths. . . . Youth crime rate continues to drop.

2003-Present *Adolescent brain research advances; lawmakers provide protections for juvenile offenders; Justice Department investigates state juvenile justice systems.*

2003 Congress passes Prison Rape Elimination Act, requiring 17-year-old prisoners to be separated from adults.

2005 In 5-4 ruling, Supreme Court in *Roper v. Simmons* rules death sentence for juveniles under 18 is unconstitutional.

2008 President George W. Bush signs Second Chance Act authorizing funding for states and communities to help incarcerated or released juveniles re-enter society.

2010 In *Graham v. Florida*, Supreme Court bars mandatory sentences of life without the possibility of parole for juveniles under 18 in noncapital cases.

2012 In *Miller v. Alabama*, Supreme Court bars mandatory sentence of life without possibility of parole for all juveniles, regardless of offense.

2013 Juvenile prison inmates in Michigan file class action lawsuit alleging abuse.

2014 Sens. Charles Grassley, R-Iowa, and Sheldon Whitehouse, D-R.I., propose reauthorization of Juvenile Justice and Delinquency Prevention Act. . . . U.S. secretary of Education and U.S. attorney general send letter to schools and attorneys calling for reduction in youth contact with adult criminal justice system.

2015 Rep. Robert Scott, D-Va., introduces reauthorization of Juvenile Justice and Delinquency Prevention Act. . . . Supreme Court agrees to hear case this fall to determine if ruling in *Miller v. Alabama* is retroactive. . . . Several states debate legislation to raise the age at which juveniles can be charged as adults. . . . Federal investigators report abuse of juveniles at Rikers Island jail in New York City.

friend) for the murder of a 5-year-old became the nation's youngest prison inmate.[53]

California voters in 1994 supported a "three strikes and you're out" law, which imposed a life sentence for almost any crime if the defendant had two prior convictions for serious or violent crimes.[54] Juvenile convictions counted.[55]

The Comprehensive Crime Control Act of 1984 had repealed the 1950 Youth Corrections Act, which had provided sentencing benefits to defendants up to the age of 26, including the potential clearing of records for those paroled early.[56] A decade later, the Violent Crime Control Act of 1994 authorized millions of dollars for boot camps, and jurisdictions began privatizing criminal justice services.[57] And between 1992 and 1997, 45 states made it easier to transfer juveniles to the criminal justice system.[58]

The public backed tough-on-crime laws in part because a group of academics had predicted an impending surge of youth violence. In a 1996 report to the U.S. attorney general, Northeastern University criminology professor James A. Fox reported that while overall violent crime was going down, youth violence was rising.[59] And the rates would continue to increase as the Baby Boomers' offspring grew up, he said, noting that a record 39 million children were under age 10.

"Millions of them live in poverty. Most do not have full-time parental supervision at home," wrote Fox. "They will reach their high-risk years before too long [and] we likely face a future wave of youth violence that will be even worse than that of the past ten years." He also reported that a growing proportion of perpetrators ages 14 to 24 were black males, and warned the percentage would increase.[60]

That same year, another academic, Princeton political science professor John J. DiIulio Jr., forecast the rise of "super-predators," described as "radically impulsive, brutally remorseless youngsters, including ever more preteenage boys, who murder, assault, rape, rob, burglarize, deal deadly drugs, join gun-toting gangs and create serious communal disorders." He predicted that "By the year 2010, there will be approximately 270,000 more juvenile super-predators on the streets than there were in 1990."[61] But the predicted super-predator onslaught never occurred.

However, the country witnessed a rise in school shootings in the 1990s, prompting schools to adopt zero-tolerance discipline policies and provide more police officers on campus.[62] That presence was boosted after a mass shooting at Columbine High School in Colorado in 1999, during which two seniors killed 12 students and a teacher before committing suicide.[63]

Pushback

By the time the super-predator warnings were issued, the rate of homicides committed by youths had already started to decline, and they continued to decrease through the 1990s and during the subsequent decade — apart from a brief increase between 2004 and 2006.

By 2005, the number of homicide arrests of suspects under 18 had dropped by two-thirds since 1994.[64] By 2011, violent juvenile crime had declined to levels "not seen since 1970," said Butts of John Jay College and Douglas N. Evans, an assistant professor of criminal justice at Mercy College in Dobbs Ferry, N.Y.[65]

Liberals opposed the new harsh penalties, arguing that the juvenile system had failed to fulfill its promise of rehabilitation and that recidivism rates were high. In the 1990s, newspaper reporters portrayed physical and sexual abuse of juveniles by staff and other inmates, long-term solitary confinement and lack of educational opportunities in California Youth Authority facilities.

The stories led to the *Farrell v. Harper* ruling in 2003, in which a teen inmate's aunt charged the California Youth Authority with subjecting inmates to illegal and "inhumane" treatment.[66] The case resulted in a consent decree that closed many juvenile detention facilities, increased the use of probation, established rules on solitary confinement and assigned some juvenile offenders to community-based rehabilitation programs.[67]

In 2002, Congress reauthorized the Juvenile Delinquency and Prevention Act and in 2003 enacted the Prison Rape Elimination Act, which required 17-year-olds to be separated from adult prison inmates. And in 2005, the Supreme Court ruled, 5–4, in *Roper v. Simmons*, that executing a minor violated the Constitution's Eighth Amendment protection against "cruel and unusual punishment" and the 14th Amendment's guarantee to "equal protection of the laws," as well as "the evolving standards of decency that mark the progress of a maturing society."[68]

States Urged to Protect Juveniles' Confidentiality

Call for secrecy conflicts with public's right to know.

Craig Sparks finds himself in a quandary: how to protect the confidentiality of youths entering the juvenile detention center under his supervision in Bernalillo County, N.M., while honoring the public's desire to know about violent criminals in their community.

As director of the Youth Services Center, Sparks convinced the county in May to halt its longstanding practice of releasing teenagers' arrest information. He and the county attorney believed that releasing the records violated the New Mexico Children's Code, which bars public access to juvenile records — from arrest through probation.[1]

But the county reversed course again in July, after news organizations and open-government advocates demanded copies of the arrest information and booking photos of six teens charged with murdering a 60-year-old man.[2]

"These are records of alleged criminal activity in our community," said Gregory Williams, board president of the New Mexico Foundation for Open Government, "and nothing in New Mexico law prevents their release."[3] The children's code says that "all records pertaining to the child" be kept confidential but does not specifically require that arrest records be kept secret.

Laws on the confidentiality of juvenile arrest and court records vary by state, often depending on the age of the youth and the type of alleged offense. Cases involving juveniles under 17 or 18 typically are considered in juvenile court before a judge in closed proceedings, depending on the youth's age and the alleged offense. Many states allow, or even mandate, prosecutors or judges to send youths charged with violent crimes such as murder or rape to adult criminal court, where cases are considered by a jury and typically are open to the public.

But youth advocates are pushing agencies to keep law enforcement and juvenile court records confidential and to comply with laws mandating that such records be sealed or physically destroyed, or "expunged," which usually occurs when the individuals finish their probation or reach a certain age between 21 and 25. Such policies — which governed the handling of juvenile records in the past — are designed to enable juvenile offenders, as adults, to seek education, housing and employment without being stigmatized as criminals, say youth advocates.[4]

"What many of us are trying to do with young adult justice is reduce the level of consequences for youth up to 25, so when they come out, they don't have a felony on their record," says David Muhammad, vice president of Impact Justice, a new advocacy and research center in Oakland, Calif.

However, prosecutors, victims' rights advocates, open government groups and news media organizations contend that public safety could be at stake and that the public has a right to know how its juvenile justice system is being administered. "I believe that juveniles who commit any degree of homicide, first-degree violent crimes and first-degree sex offenses should not be able to have their records expunged and that the conviction should not be sealed," says Steve Doell, president of Crime Victims United of Oregon.

Sparks says limiting information available to the public will "help youth with their future" but acknowledges that "the public also wants to know . . . what kinds of crimes kids are allegedly committing. I can see both sides of it. It's not simple."

Early juvenile justice systems kept court records confidential, says Wallace Mlyniec, senior counsel at

That case introduced neuroscience into legal and policy debates on juvenile justice. The American Medical Association wrote in a friend-of-the-court brief that "to a degree never before understood, scientists can now demonstrate that adolescents are immature not only to the observer's naked eye but in the very fibers of their brains."[69]

In the late 1990s, studies began showing what many already presumed: The adolescent brain was not as anatomically mature as the adult brain,

Georgetown University's Juvenile Law Center. And courts sought to avoid labeling youths as criminals by having juvenile offenses adjudicated in civil rather than criminal courts, according to James B. Jacobs, director of New York University School of Law's Center for Research in Crime and Justice.[5]

By the 1920s, most states had restricted the disclosure of juveniles' arrest and court records, and some required a case to be automatically sealed when an individual turned 21 so he "could embark upon adulthood without a criminal stigma," Jacobs said. In 1950, Congress passed the Federal Youth Corrections Act, allowing certain individuals ages 18 through 26 to have their convictions expunged.[6]

In the 1970s, the Supreme Court ruled in two cases that a state cannot bar the media from publishing the name of a juvenile who is arrested if the information was acquired legally. [7] And as juvenile crime spiked in the 1980s and '90s, "those confidentiality rules began to go away," Mlyniec says, "because even liberals believed the community should know that a juvenile delinquent was among them."

Today, laws still exist governing the confidentiality of juvenile records, but they often are ineffective, the Juvenile Law Center, a nonprofit law firm based in Philadelphia, found in a 2014 study.[8] And the National Center for Juvenile Justice reported that in 20 states, delinquency hearings are open to the public depending on the age of the juvenile and the alleged offense.[9]

Individuals with juvenile records often face difficulty gaining access to college, military service or employment, say attorneys for the Juvenile Law Center, because an applicant must release that information or a prospective employer, for instance, can search online for the records.[10] "Permanent open records are like a ball and chain that prevent young people from becoming productive adults," said Riya Saha Shah, an attorney at the center.[11]

Some states are complying with juvenile confidentiality laws. For example, the Washington Supreme Court in June ruled that state juvenile court records must be sealed. [12] The Juvenile Law Center's study gave New Mexico the strongest rating for protecting juvenile records, but Sparks says the

state legislature should make the law clearer. A state statute requires juvenile court records to be sealed after a certain amount of time, typically at the end of a probationary period, Sparks says. Yet the county has been releasing arrest records.

"To me, it didn't make sense that one part of the statute would allow the juvenile detention center to release records on a kid pre-adjudication, yet another agency [the judicial probation office], can't release anything" about the case, he says.

— *Christina Lyons*

[1]New Mexico statute 32A-2-32 (2013), http://tinyurl.com/o8rzvt8.

[2]Ryan Boetel, "County refuses to release teens' booking mugs," *Albuquerque Journal*, July 10, 2015, tinyurl.com/onllkv5; Dan McKay, "Bernalillo County agrees to release juvenile arrest information," *Albuquerque Journal*, July 29, 2015, http://tinyurl.com/p3243yb.

[3]*Ibid.*, McKay.

[4]See for example, Laurie Parise, "Know Your Rights," Legal Action Center, http://tinyurl.com/q3mptdr.

[5]James B. Jacobs, "Juvenile Criminal Record Confidentiality," in Franklin E. Zimring and David S. Tanenhaus (eds.), *Choosing the Future for American Juvenile Justice* (2014), p. 150; also available at http://tinyurl.com/qapnmzl.

[6]*Ibid.*, p. 151.

[7]*Oklahoma Publishing v. District Court*, no. 76-867, March 7, 1977, http:// tinyurl.com/nmjxau9; *Smith v. Daily Mail Publishing*, No. 78-482, June 26, 1979, http://tinyurl.com/pa8y6vw.

[8]Riya Saha Shah and Lauren Fine, "Juvenile Records: A National Review of State Laws on Confidentiality, Sealing and Expungement," Juvenile Law Center, 2014, p. 6, http://tinyurl.com/nosh4hx.

[9]Melissa Sickmund and Charles Puzzanchera (eds.), "Juvenile Offenders and Victims: 2014 National Report," National Center for Juvenile Justice, December 2014, p. 97, http://tinyurl.com/nvepoan.

[10]Jacobs, *op. cit.*, pp. 157-165.

[11]Lynn Anderson, "States Are Failing to Protect Juvenile Records, Study Shows," Juvenile Justice Information Exchange, Nov. 13, 2014, http:// tinyurl.com/nc6wcvt.

[12]Mike Carter, "State ruling affirms easier sealing of juvenile-court records," *The Seattle Times*, June 11, 2015, http://tinyurl.com/o59mw7e.

Temple University's Steinberg says. Then, in the first decade of the 21st century, magnetic resonance imaging (MRI) technology showed that adolescent brains are less mature, both anatomically and developmentally, he says.

Yet some psychologists warned against overemphasizing the science. A "careful look at relevant data shows that the teen brain we read about in the headlines — the immature brain that supposedly causes teen problems — is nothing less than a myth," Robert Epstein, a senior

Youth Advocates Seek Alternatives to Prison

"Our goal should be to change their behavior."

Five boys sued the Idaho Juvenile Corrections Department in March, alleging they were abused by a staff nurse and an intern at a state juvenile corrections facility.[1]

Their complaints echo those made in cases involving other youths held in both juvenile and adult facilities across the country. For example:

• Officials in Palm Beach County, Fla., in August terminated a contract with a private company operating a youth corrections facility for high-risk males ages 13-18 after many reported they had been "sexually victimized" or forced to fight with other inmates.[2]

• In Michigan, hundreds of plaintiffs await action on their 2013 suit against the state Department of Corrections and several employees for not protecting them from alleged rape and other abuse at the hands of older inmates while the plaintiffs were incarcerated at adult facilities while minors.[3]

Such stories are spurring support for alternative juvenile justice programs designed to keep troubled youths — including, sometimes, those convicted of violent crimes — out of large, state- or privately operated juvenile or adult prisons where they may be vulnerable to abuse or rape or placed in solitary confinement. Victims' advocate groups, however, warn that some youths, particularly the most violent, should remain in high-security facilities to ensure the public's safety.

Among the alternatives being tried by states and communities are "positive youth development" or "restorative justice" programs, which offer options ranging from home-based approaches to locked community residential facilities. Such programs are designed to keep youths engaged with their schools and community services, provide therapy for the juveniles and their families and sometimes allow victims to provide input on how an offender should be sentenced.

"We are working to help kids change," says Michael Harris, senior attorney for the Oakland, Calif.-based National Center for Youth Law, which provides legal aid for youth advocates. "So everything we do for them is about that, . . . even for kids who committed the most serious offenses."

Community programs, typically funded by federal or private grants, are based on brain research showing that adolescents have limited reasoning ability, heightened susceptibility to peer pressure and greater amenability to rehabilitation than adults. The programs also acknowledge that many youths in the juvenile justice system have a history of trauma or abuse.[4]

The aim is to limit incarceration and reduce recidivism. Program specialists evaluate the delinquents' behavior and home and school environments to determine whether they should be placed in a locked or unlocked residential facility or released on probation at home with community supervision or in supervised foster care with therapeutic treatment.[5]

For instance, The Baltimore-based Annie E. Casey Foundation provides funds for communities to divert juvenile offenders to local rehabilitation programs, closely oversee incarcerated juveniles and encourage collaboration among community agencies to monitor youths on probation.[6] The foundation and others cite the so-called Missouri model, which provides for a variety of youth facilities: day treatment centers for the least serious offenders; group homes that house 10 to 12 offenders who have committed less-serious acts; moderately secure facilities that house 20 to 50 youths; and highly secure facilities for the most violent offenders.[7]

The New York State Permanent Judicial Commission on Justice for Children oversees partnerships between schools and justice systems to determine sentencing for juvenile offenders and allows victims to play a role in determining punishment and treatment, says Kathleen R. DeCataldo, executive director of the commission. The Vera Institute of Justice, a nonprofit research firm, operates a similar program in Brooklyn for 16- to 24-year-olds charged with violent felonies and their victims.[8]

Such efforts have helped reduce the number of youths in large state prisons. In 2012, more juvenile offenders were in local facilities than in state-operated ones for the first time since 2000, according to the Department of Justice.[9] California, for example, had 10,000 juveniles in the state system in 1997, more than any other state, says David Muhammad, former chief probation officer of Alameda County, Calif. "Now there's less than 700," he says.

Some victims' advocates say alternative programs must be careful in determining which juveniles can be rehabilitated and which should be placed in high-security detention facilities. "A sociopath cannot be rehabilitated," says Harriet Salarno, chairperson and co-founder of Crime Victims United of California, which represents victims and their families. She contends many juvenile offenders are not rehabilitated but instead are released quickly back into the community.

Michael Rushford, president of the Criminal Justice Legal Foundation, which represents prosecutors and victims, says violent repeat offenders and "hard core incorrigibles who won't change" should be kept in secure facilities and "reprogrammed." They should "learn some skills and some values, and when they go out the door, we should not be done watching them," he says. "But that [requires] an investment."

Many youth advocates say courts continue to send juveniles to detention centers for low-level, nonviolent crimes and that a disproportionate number are minorities. The Justice Policy Institute, which advocates changes in the justice system, reported that 62 percent of youths detained in 2011 had committed nonviolent offenses. And the nonprofit National Council on Crime and Delinquency, which supports reforms of the justice system, said the proportion of minority youths sent to "secure" facilities rose from 12.4 percent in 2002 to 22.3 percent a decade later; the proportion of whites increased less than 3 percentage points.[10] The report called for research into the cause of disparities.

The Casey Foundation in June reported continued "widespread maltreatment" of youths in state-run juvenile corrections facilities. It called for states to close all such prisons in favor of community prevention and intervention methods.[11]

"We are putting young people in large facilities, far away from their homes, that are punitive in nature," says Nate Balis, director of Casey's Juvenile Justice Strategy Group. "Relationships take a back seat to coercion to behave, and everything is based on compliance in order to keep order. . . . It's hard to walk into a place like that and see it as some place that will help people to turn their lives around and be better than when they walked in."

— Christina Lyons

Terrence Jones, a counselor and probation officer, works with a young detainee at the Fairfax County (Va.) Juvenile Detention Center school, which serves youths serving sentences or awaiting trial.

"FDLE to review Palm Beach County juvenile facility," *Orlando Sentinel*, May 30, 2015, http://tiny url.com/ntrkqpr.

[3]Jim Lynch, "Juvenile prisoners in Michigan allege abuse, rape," *The Detroit News*, April 1, 2015, http://tinyurl.com/nwj5vr8;

[4]Vanessa Sacks *et. al.*, "Adverse Childhood Experiences: National and State-level Prevalence," *Child Trends*, July 2014, http://tinyurl.com/nh2oaka; also see "A Hidden Crisis: Findings on Adverse Childhood Experiences in California," Center for Youth Wellness, 2014, http://tinyurl.com/ntrkqpr.

[5]Robert Butters, "Community-Based Treatment Interventions," in Wesley T. Church II *et al.* (eds.), *Juvenile Justice Sourcebook* (2014), pp. 313-336.

[6]Richard A. Mendel, "Juvenile Detention Alternatives Initiative: Progress Report 2014," The Annie E. Casey Foundation, 2014, http://tinyurl.com/pafp9ys.

[7]Richard A. Mendel, "The Missouri Model: Reinventing the Practice of Rehabilitating Youthful Offenders," The Annie E. Casey Foundation, 2010, http://tiny url.com/oyd454u.

[8]"Common Justice," Vera Institute of Justice, www.vera.org/project/common -justice.

[9]Sarah Hockenberry *et. al.*, "Juvenile Residential Facility Census, 2012: Selected Findings," U.S. Department of Justice, March 2015, http://tinyurl.com/n957etn.

[10]Antoinette Davis, Angela Irvine and Jason Ziedenberg, "Stakeholders' Views on the Movement to Reduce Youth Incarceration," National Council on Crime and Delinquency, April 2014, p. 4, http://tinyurl.com/osmbwcg.

[11]"Annie E. Casey Foundation CEO Calls for States to Close 'Youth Prisons,' " The Annie E. Casey Foundation, June 24, 2015, http://tinyurl.com/nnmsuwj; Richard A. Mendel, "Maltreatment of Youth in U.S. Juvenile Corrections Facilities: An Update," The Annie E. Casey Foundation, 2015, http://tinyurl.com/ofamoao; "Sticker Shock: Calculating the Full Price Tag for Youth Incarceration," Justice Policy Institute, December 2014, http://tinyurl.com/pwagd33.

[1]John Sowell, "Suit alleges five more teen victims of sexual abuse at state juvenile detention center," *The Idaho Statesman*, March 22, 2015, http://tinyurl. com/mn3w5t4.

[2]"State Seeks New Provider at Troubled Juvenile Correctional Facility," CBS12, Aug. 21, 2015, http://tinyurl.com/pn9s3qv; Margie Menzel,

research psychologist at the American Institute for Behavioral Research and Technology, wrote in 2007. He said the images of the brain "do not necessarily provide useful information about the causes of thought, feeling and behavior."[70]

In *New Mexico State v. Garcia*, defense attorneys failed to persuade the state Supreme Court in 2007 that automatically transferring juveniles charged with murder to adult court represented a "rejection of biology."[71]

Then in *Graham v. Florida* in 2010, the high court barred mandatory sentences of life without parole for juveniles in noncapital cases — a ruling New York University Law School professor Martin Guggenheim called the most significant case to advance children's rights.[72]

And in 2012 in *Miller v. Alabama*, the court barred states from employing a mandatory sentence of life without parole for juveniles, regardless of the offense. It said "a sentencer needed to examine all [the] circumstances before concluding that life without any possibility of parole was the appropriate penalty."[73]

CURRENT SITUATION
Federal Efforts

Lawmakers across the political spectrum are proposing an array of criminal justice reforms in response to stories of harsh sentencing and abusive prison conditions for juveniles as well as adults. The Obama administration is pushing to end the so-called school-to-prison pipeline, in which children arrested for minor school infractions end up in prison, and to reform a juvenile system that relies heavily on incarceration.[74] Meanwhile, an unlikely coalition of advocacy groups created by the conservative billionaire Charles Koch and including the liberal Center for American Progress is battling what Koch calls the "overcriminalization of America."[75]

At the same time, some House and Senate lawmakers are pushing for reauthorization of the Office of Juvenile Justice and Delinquency Prevention (OJJDP), which hasn't been reauthorized since 2002 and whose appropriations fell by 50 percent between 2003 and 2010.[76]

In April the Senate Judiciary Committee held a hearing to review allegations that states receiving juvenile justice grants were violating federal law governing those grants by incarcerating juveniles for minor offenses.[77]

Chairman Charles Grassley, R-Iowa, and Sen. Sheldon Whitehouse, D-R.I., responded by proposing reauthorization of the Juvenile Delinquency and Prevention Act, approved by the Judiciary Committee in July. The measure would authorize $159 million annually for five years for grants to help states crack down on juvenile system abuses and provide prevention and rehabilitation services. It also would phase out a provision in the law allowing children convicted of "status offenses" — such as truancy, running away or curfew violation — to be incarcerated.[78]

Rep. Robert Scott, D-Va., offered a companion bill in the House in June. He is also pushing a measure that would provide funding for local grants aimed at keeping youths out of prison. As of early September, Republican Party leaders had not scheduled any hearings or action on the measure.[79]

Approval of the grant funding could be difficult. In June Republican House appropriators pushed through a bill to fund the departments of Commerce, Justice and State in fiscal 2016 that reduced spending on several programs in each agency, including a $68 million cut for juvenile justice, mostly by eliminating funding for state delinquency prevention grants.[80] Due to those cuts and other reductions in the spending bill, the Obama administration has threatened to veto the legislation if it is not changed.[81]

Although the Supreme Court has prohibited states from mandating that children guilty of certain violent crimes, such as first-degree murder, be sentenced to life in prison without the possibility of parole, neither the House nor Senate has proposed legislation to prevent states from allowing such sentences. However, Rep. Tony Cardenas, D-Calif., in late July introduced a resolution, which does not carry the force of law, calling for an end to the practice.[82]

Meanwhile, the Justice Department is investigating state juvenile justice systems for possible violations of youths' due process rights. In March, for example, the department said it was looking into juvenile district courts in Texas and the Dallas County Truancy Court to determine whether they deprived about 20,000 children of their due process rights in 2014 by prosecuting them for failure to attend school.[83]

In June the Justice Department reached a settlement with Mississippi calling for the overhaul of the state's juvenile justice system, after federal investigators found that youths' due process rights were being violated and that some ended up in the system for such minor infractions as truancy.[84] In New York City, a recent U.S. attorney's report found abuses and poor conditions at juvenile detention facilities on Rikers Island.[85]

Many advocacy groups are pushing officials to find ways to reduce adolescent recidivism and prevent juvenile crime. In a 2014 report, the National Academy of Sciences, a private, Washington-based organization representing researchers nationwide, called for increased funding for state and local juvenile rehabilitation programs and increased OJJDP staffing and employee training.[86]

Youth advocates also are calling for more research on racial disparities in the juvenile justice system and the increase in girls being arrested. In 2010 African-American youths — who represented about 15 percent of the nation's youth population — made up a disproportionate share (40 percent) of juvenile detentions; all minority youths made up 75 percent of those held for violent offenses. The proportion of girls arrested has risen from 17 percent in 1980 to 29 percent in 2010, largely attributed to more arrests for aggravated assault, often related to domestic violence.[87]

Meanwhile, the President's Commission for the Study of Bioethical Issues is considering the role of neuroscience in criminal law and has called for guidance for the criminal justice system on the proper use of brain science.[88]

Youth advocates believe the prospects for change are promising. They point, for example, to bipartisan support for reforming the criminal justice system from groups such as the Koch-backed coalition. It has begun a multimillion-dollar campaign to advocate for reducing prison populations, overhauling sentencing procedures and reducing recidivism.

In the Courts

State lawmakers, courts and youth advocates await the Supreme Court's decision — following arguments scheduled for this fall — in *Montgomery v. Louisiana*. The case involves lower court discrepancies on whether the 2012 *Miller* decision barring mandatory life sentences without parole for juveniles should apply to sentences handed down before 2012.

The case follows the appeal of Henry Montgomery of Louisiana, who in 1963 at age 17 killed a police officer in Baton Rouge and was sentenced to life in prison without the possibility for parole. He now argues that, based on the court's 2012 ruling, he should have a chance at parole.[89]

Several appeals courts have allowed individuals to file petitions in federal court for their sentences to be reconsidered, while two others have ruled that the *Miller* decision already applies retroactively to sentences imposed before the decision. Meanwhile, supreme courts in 14 other states have ruled that it does apply retroactively, while seven have ruled it does not.[90]

Since the 2012 decision, supreme courts in California, Massachusetts, Mississippi, Nebraska and Wyoming have ruled that various portions of the states' juvenile sentencing statutes were unconstitutional. The Wyoming court also said a state law that allows for parole only after a certain term of years is unconstitutional.

In Michigan, a lawsuit is pending against the Department of Corrections on behalf of several juveniles, age 17 and younger, who charge the department did not protect them from sexual assaults in the adult prison system.[91]

State Efforts

Legislatures continue to debate changing their juvenile justice laws, focusing on the effects of the *Miller* ruling and proposals such as those to raise the age at which juveniles can be charged as adults — all with mixed success.

According to the Campaign for the Fair Sentencing of Youth, 14 states bar the life-without-parole sentencing option for youths, nine of which abolished the sentence after the *Miller* ruling. Five states ban the sentencing option for youth "in most cases," according to the campaign.[92]

In California, lawmakers continue to change sentencing laws to provide juveniles more leniency, and in 2013 Democratic Gov. Brown signed a law that established a new parole process for those who initially were charged as juveniles.[93] This year, the legislature expanded the law to apply to those who were 23 or younger at the time of their crimes.[94]

After reports of abuses at Rikers Island, New York City juvenile advocates and lawmakers are pushing for reforms, including raising the age of criminal responsibility to 18 (from 16 and 17), except for certain violent crimes, such

Should life-without-parole sentences for juveniles be banned?

YES

John Hambrick
Vice Chair, Nevada Assembly Ways and Means Committee

John Ellem
Former Member, West Virginia House of Delegates

Written for *CQ Researcher*, September 2015

as conservative Republican legislators, we helped lead the efforts in our states to end life-without-parole sentences for juveniles and replace them with age-appropriate sentences that consider children's capacity to change and become rehabilitated. In West Virginia and Nevada, the states we represent, the legislatures overwhelmingly passed these measures.

The impact of serious crimes is no less tragic because a child is involved, and youths must be held accountable for their conduct. However, as a modern society we must balance protecting public safety and justice for victims with the psychological and developmental differences between children and adults. In fact, many victims' families who have come to know the child offenders in their cases have found healing when the children were given the possibility of a second chance. Not everyone should be released from prison, but children who change and become rehabilitated should be given that hope, and we should support healing for the victims' families and their communities.

Adolescent-development research has shown children do not possess the same capacity as adults to think through the consequences of their behaviors, control their responses or avoid peer pressure. Often the children who commit serious offenses have suffered abuse, neglect and trauma, which affect their development and play a role in their involvement in the justice system. Drawing in part on this research, the U.S. Supreme Court has said children are "constitutionally different" and should not be subject to our harshest penalties.

But our motivation goes beyond what the court said. Redemption is a basic tenet of nearly every religion. When we sentence a child to die in prison, we forestall the possibility that he or she can change and find redemption. In doing so, we ignore Jesus' fundamental teachings of love, mercy and forgiveness. As the Rev. Bernard Healey, director of the Rhode Island Catholic Conference, recently pointed out, Moses, David and the Apostle Paul were all guilty of killing but found redemption and purpose through the grace of God. Shouldn't we show this same mercy to our nation's children, allowing them a chance at redemption?

Fourteen states have abolished life-without-parole sentences for children. All states should do so, and as Congress looks to criminal justice reform, it would do well to make banning these sentences a priority.

NO

Kent Scheidegger
*Legal Director,
Criminal Justice Legal Foundation*

Written For *CQ Researcher*, September 2015

what punishment should society impose on the very worst 17-year-old murderers? Punishment in the worst cases is the real question when someone proposes an absolute, no-exceptions ban on a given punishment for a given group. Limitations already in place will result in lesser sentences in typical cases. What about the atypical, exceptionally heinous crimes?

Take, for example, Renaldo Adams. In 1997, when he was 17 years old, Adams put on a stocking mask and gloves and broke into the Montgomery, Ala., home of the Mills family, where the two parents and three young children were sleeping. He held Mrs. Mills, who was four months pregnant, hostage at knifepoint and forced Mr. Mills to go out to get money. While he was out, Adams raped Mrs. Mills and stabbed her multiple times. She and her unborn child both died.

A jury decided, appropriately, that Adams should die for this crime. His sentence was reduced to life without parole when the U.S. Supreme Court imposed a blanket ban on the death penalty for anyone who has not reached his 18th birthday, regardless of how heinous the crime, how extensive his criminal record, or how close he was to the magic day. Now it is proposed that heartless, raping murderers such as Adams receive a double discount on murder, making them exempt from life without parole as well.

Such a simplistic rule would be both bad science and bad policy. It is one thing to say younger people generally have a greater capacity to change for the better, and it is quite another to say we must draw a bright line at the 18th birthday and treat 17-year-olds radically different from 18-year-olds. The science of brain development that is so often cited in support of more lenient treatment of youths does not remotely support such a bright-line cut off.

Age should be considered, but it should not be a trump card. It is already the law that a person under 18 cannot be sentenced to life in prison without parole for any crime less than murder. For murder, it is already the law that the sentencing judge must consider the defendant's age along with other valid factors and have the option of a lesser sentence. The law presently provides plenty of room for leniency when it is appropriate.

We do not need a simplistic cutoff.

as first-degree murder. After a similar measure failed earlier this year, Democratic Gov. Andrew Cuomo ordered that individuals younger than 18 be transferred from adult prisons to juvenile detention centers.[95]

Many states continue to debate raising the age for prosecuting juveniles as adults to 18 for all or most offenses, and since 2005 at least 29 states and the District of Columbia have made it harder to prosecute and sentence juveniles as adults. New Jersey in August raised from 14 to 15 the age at which teenagers can be charged as adults, and increased from 16 to 18 the age at which they can be placed in adult facilities. In some states they can stay in juvenile facilities until age 21.[96]

South Dakota is changing its juvenile justice system to abide by a measure passed this year calling for only "serious" juvenile offenders — those charged with violent crimes — to be incarcerated in adult facilities.[97]

In Texas — after removing a provision that would have raised the age at which juveniles could be charged as adults from 17 to 18 — the legislature passed a broad juvenile justice reform bill that aims to place juveniles being punished for lesser crimes in regional facilities close to their homes.[98] The bill's author, Democratic Sen. Whitmire, says he will study how raising the age affects the juvenile system.

Meanwhile, youth advocates continue to push other measures that would end solitary confinement, protect the confidentiality of juvenile records, ban registries for youths who commit sex offenses and end courtroom shackling, among other things.

OUTLOOK
Window of Opportunity

Broad bipartisan support exists to pass criminal justice reform measures in light of reduced crime rates and an ongoing desire to tighten government budgets. But some reform advocates say lawmakers should act quickly, before the economy changes.[99]

"Let's take advantage of all these opportunities right now," says Butts of John Jay College, "because the heat has turned down on the crime issue in the last 15 years. As soon as crime starts to go back up, the support and bipartisan consensus will go away again. The punitive forces are still in the trees, and they will run back out as soon as the time is right."

U.S. Attorney General Loretta Lynch addresses the federal Coordinating Council on Juvenile Justice and Delinquency Prevention on June 22, 2015. The Obama administration is pushing to end the so-called school-to-prison pipeline, in which children arrested for minor school infractions end up in prison, and to reform a juvenile system that relies heavily on incarceration.

Getty Images/Alex Wong

Cully, of the Heritage Foundation, fears a long campaign to weaken sentencing standards. "What's really going on here is a long-term effort by some to not only eliminate the death penalty . . . for everyone . . . but then to get rid of life sentences without parole, then long sentences."

But observers on all sides agree on a need for rehabilitative services for young people. Rushford, of the Criminal Justice Legal Foundation, says the focus should be on improving rehabilitation services for incarcerated youths so they can become productive members of society.

UC-Berkeley's Krisberg says he expects the "large-scale secure juvenile facility" to become "a dinosaur. It will be like the Confederate flag" and fully removed in favor of home-based care or community programs. "There is an overwhelming consensus bubbling its way up to the courts and to the legislators," Krisberg says. He predicts the number of incarcerated youths will dwindle as governors and legislators become reluctant to spend more on prisons. The next step, he says, will be a focus on reinventing probation.

"Some common-sense recognition that something is wrong with locking children up will move us forward," says Mlyniec, of Georgetown University. "But it's going to take money, and it will take money out of communities that want jails built [for] employment. Jails employ an incredible number of people."

Muhammad, of Impact Justice, warns that even with some reforms, changing the attitudes of justice system workers will be difficult.

Members of the Research Network on Adolescent Development at the John D. and Catherine T. MacArthur Foundation plan to issue studies on the adolescent brain and juveniles' culpability.[100]

The University of Pennsylvania's Morse, a member of the MacArthur research network led by Temple University's Steinberg, is participating in research to distinguish between two mental states, one in which individuals commit a crime knowingly or one in which they commit a crime recklessly. Further research could help pinpoint a neural marker that could enhance the accuracy of predictions about recidivism, he says.[101]

Some justice professionals call for more study of the brains of 18- to 25-year-olds, although many predict that reforming sentencing standards for that age group would be difficult to push through legislatures.[102] "Tradition and custom is so deeply inbred about adulthood being 18 or 21," says Harris, of the Center for Youth Law. "It would be hard across the board to go there."

NOTES

1. Stephen Baxter, "Maddy Middleton murder: A teen's turbulent family life and the death of a Santa Cruz 8-year-old," *Santa Cruz Sentinel*, July 31, 2015, http://tinyurl.com/oh3hcdr.

2. Janie Har, "Youth Advocates decry trying teen as adult in girl's death," *San Jose Mercury News*, The Associated Press, July 31, 2015, http://tinyurl.com/nhcyldq.

3. Melissa Sickmund and Charles Puzzanchera (eds.), "Juvenile Offenders and Victims: 2014 National Report," National Center for Juvenile Justice, December 2014, pp. 99–101, http://tinyurl.com/q7vn64g; and Wisconsin Statutes Sec. 938,183, "Statutory Exclusion," http://tinyurl.com/qesn57a; Yamiche Alcindor, "N.Y., N.C. consider changes to juvenile justice laws," *USA Today*, March 1, 2014, http://tinyurl.com/kllewtj.

4. *Ibid.*, p. 84; for background, see Peter Katel, "Juvenile Justice," *CQ Researcher*, Nov. 7, 2008, pp. 913–936; and Thomas J. Billitteri, "Youth Violence," *CQ Researcher*, March 5, 2010, pp. 193–216.

5. Sickmund and Puzzanchera, *op. cit.*, p. 120; "New Data: Population At Youth Facilities Cut In Half

Since 1999," The Sentencing Project, May 8, 2015, http://tinyurl.com/phtukny.

6. "New Data: Population at Youth Facilities Cut in Half Since 1999," *op. cit.*; also see Sarah Hockenberry, Melissa Sickmund and Anthony Sladky, "Juvenile Residential Facility Census, 2012: Selected Findings," Juvenile Offenders and Victims: National Report Series, Office of Juvenile Justice and Delinquency Prevention, U.S. Department of Justice, March 2015, pp. 2, 121.

7. For background, see Kathy Koch, "Zero Tolerance for School Violence," *CQ Researcher*, March 10, 2000, pp. 185–208; and Anne Ferris Rosen, "School Discipline," *CQ Researcher*, May 9, 2014, pp. 409–432.

8. Claire Wiseman, "Young criminals, old practices: Reforming the juvenile justice system," *Chattanooga Times Free Press*, Feb. 3, 2015, http://tinyurl.com/oe5kknc.

9. Richard A. Mendel, "Maltreatment of Youth in U.S. Juvenile Correction Facilities: An Update," The Annie E. Casey Foundation, 2015, http://tinyurl.com/ofamoao; Joel Rose, "'Culture of Violence' Pervades Rikers' Juvenile Facilities," NPR, Oct. 15, 2014, http://tinyurl.com/otymzbh; "Alone & Afraid: Children Held in Solitary Confinement and Isolation in Juvenile Detention and Correctional Facilities," American Civil Liberties Union, June 2014, http://tinyurl.com/nma9m2p.

10. Nell Bernstein, *Burning Down the House* (2014).

11. See for example: "The Teen Brain: Still Under Construction," NIH Publication No. 11–4929, National Institutes of Mental Health, 2011, http://tinyurl.com/qf4w5fg.

12. See Laurence Steinberg, *Age of Opportunity: Lessons from the New Science of Adolescence* (2014), p. 22.

13. *Miller v. Alabama* (2012), p. 16, http://tinyurl.com/73nz3fp.

14. David G. Savage, "High court to decide whether young murderers can one day go free," *Los Angeles Times*, March 23, 2015, http://tinyurl.com/q36ez95.

15. See Sally Satel and Scott O. Lilienfeld, *Brainwashed: The Seductive Appeal of Mindless Neuroscience* (2013).

16. For additional background, see Laurence Steinberg, "Should the Science of Adolescent Brain Development Inform Public Policy?" *Issues*, Spring 2012, http://tinyurl.com/nb43fj6.

17. Steinberg, *Age of Opportunity*, p. 9.

18. *Ibid.*, p. 1.

19. Michael Schwirtz and Michael Winerip, "Kalief Browder, Held at Rikers Island for 3 Years Without Trial, Commits Suicide," *The New York Times*, June 8, 2015, http://tinyurl.com/nlnodmx; also see Peter Katel, "Solitary Confinement," *CQ Researcher*, Sept. 14, 2012, pp. 765–788.

20. Melissa Sickmund and Charles Puzzanchera, eds., *op. cit.*, p. 220.

21. Richard E. Redding, "Juvenile Transfer Laws: An Effective Deterrent to Delinquency?" *Juvenile Justice Bulletin*, June 2010, http://tinyurl.com/nt5as5d.

22. Julie Bosman, "Teenager's Jailing Brings a Call to Fix Sex Offender Registries," *The New York Times*, July 4, 2015, http://tinyurl.com/nwwcy94. Julie Bosman, "Michigan: New Sentencing for Teenager in Sex Crime," *The New York Times*, Sept. 8, 2015, http://tinyurl.com/o5er94u.

23. Steve Doell, "Oregon's Juvenile Justice Failure," *The Oregonian*, April 18, 2015, http://tinyurl.com/p86a6qx.

24. Joshua Rovner, "Juvenile Life Without Parole: An Overview," The Sentencing Project, May 2015, http://tinyurl.com/q4xwchm.

25. "Facts and Infographics about Life Without Parole for Children," The Campaign for the Fair Sentencing of Youth, updated 2015, http://tinyurl.com/odcsdqt. (Note: these figures may not include recent state legislative changes).

26. Adam Liptak and Ethan Bronner, "Justices Bar Mandatory Life Terms for Juveniles," *The New York Times*, June 25, 2012, http://tinyurl.com/nsc2385.

27. Rovner, *op. cit.*

28. "Convention on the Rights of the Child," United Nations Treaty Collection, http://tinyurl.com/nem6owo.

29. "FAQ: The Covenant on Civil and Political Rights," ACLU, updated April 2014, http://tinyurl.com/pctr4b5.

30. "Convention against Torture and Other Cruel, Inhuman or Degrading Treatment or Punishment, United Nations Treaty Collection, 1984, http://tinyurl.com/pdhvjqe.

31. James B. Nolan, "Police and Youth," *Journal of Law and Criminology*, Vol. 43, Issue 3, 1952, http://tinyurl.com/pl38nxy.

32. William Blackstone and Thomas M. Cooley, "The Commentaries on the Laws of England in Four Books," Vol. 4, 2006, p. 432, http://tinyurl.com/oombjvu.

33. "Juvenile Justice History," Center on Juvenile and Criminal Justice, undated, http://tinyurl.com/qb2u7mf; Frances E. Jensen, *The Teenage Brain* (2015), p. 261.

34. "Our City Charities; The New-York House of Refuge for Juvenile Delinquents," *The New York Times*, Jan. 23, 1860, http://tinyurl.com/nvyzkz2.

35. Ben Montgomery and Waveney Ann Moore, "The Dozier Saga: The Lost Bones: A Two-Part Series," *The Tampa Bay Times*, Dec. 18, 21, 2014, http://tinyurl.com/qfpweje; The Associated Press, "Florida boys raped in 'dungeon,' beaten to death in Arthur G. Dozier school: report," *New York Daily News*, Feb. 6, 2015, http://tinyurl.com/oa2xfka.

36. "History of the DJJ," California Department of Corrections and Rehabilitation Division of Juvenile Justice, http://tinyurl.com/pfq32km.

37. For background, see Christina Lyons, "Media Violence," *CQ Researcher*, Feb. 14, 2014, pp. 145–168.

38. Nell Bernstein, *Burning Down the House: The End of Juvenile Prison* (2014), p. 236; Karl Holton, "Youth Correction Authority in Action: The California Experience," *Law and Contemporary Problems*, Fall 1942, pp. 655–666, http://tinyurl.com/p4s9f6q.

39. "Federal Youth Corrections Program," Address by Honorable Herbert Brownell Jr., Attorney General of the United States, Cincinnati Bar Association, April 20, 1956, http://tinyurl.com/ooeopu4.

40. Michael J. Fusz, "Probation Under the Federal Youth Corrections Act," *Chicago-Kent Law Review*, Vol. 53 (1), April 1976, http://tinyurl.com/oo3jdzc.

41. "Address by Honorable Herbert Brownell Jr.," *op. cit.*

42. See H. B. Shaffer, "Reform of Delinquents," *Editorial Research Reports*, July 17, 1957; Bernstein, *op. cit.*, p. 45.

43. *American Peoples Encyclopedia 1964 Yearbook* (1964), p. 192.

44. Franklin E. Zimring, "American Youth Violence: A Cautionary Tale," in Franklin E. Zimring and David S. Tanenhaus, eds., "Choosing the Future for American Juvenile Justice," 2014, pp. 14–15, 24–25.

45. *Kent v. United States*, 383 U.S. 541 (1966), http://tinyurl.com/qjlbch7; *In re Gault*, 387 U.S. 1 (1967), http://tinyurl.com/lugw5qq; *In re Winship*, 397 U.S. 358 (1970), http://tinyurl.com/pdusct8; *Breed v. Jones*, 421 U.S. 519 (1975), http://tinyurl.com/pvgemhk; *Eddings v. Oklahoma*, 455 U.S. 104 (1982), http://tinyurl.com/py86hbd; 1971, *In McKeiver v. Pennsylvania*, 403 US 582 (1971), http://tinyurl.com/oc3sbnc.

46. "The detention and jailing of juveniles: Hearings before the Subcommittee to Investigate Juvenile Delinquency of the Committee on the Judiciary," U.S. Senate, 1974, p. 3, http://tinyurl.com/ohy5f6d.

47. Lauren Kirchner, "Protecting Juvenile Offenders from Adult Inmates, and from Themselves," *Pacific Standard*, May 7, 2015, http://tinyurl.com/ohnalg2; C. Aaron McNeece and Tiffany Ryan, "Juvenile Justice Policy: Current Trends and 21st Century Issues," in Wesley T. Church, II, David W. Springer and Albert R. Roberts, eds., *Juvenile Justice Sourcebook*, 2nd ed. (2014), pp. 37–59.

48. Jeffrey A. Butts and Howard N. Snyder, "Too Soon to Tell: Deciphering Recent Trends in Youth Violence," Chapin Hall Center for Children, University of Chicago, November 2006, p. 4, http://tinyurl.com/oej84eu.

49. See Billitteri, *op. cit.*

50. See Rosen, *op. cit.*; The Supreme Court permitted tighter control over juveniles in its 1985 ruling in *New Jersey v. T.L.O.*, permitting students' lockers and belongings to be searched if "reasonable grounds" existed that they may have violated school rules or the law. *New Jersey v T.L.O.*, 469 U.S. 325, http://tinyurl.com/m7b5nc6.

51. John P. Woods, "New York's Juvenile Offender Law: An Overview and Analysis," *Fordham Urban Law Journal*, Vol. 9, Issue 1, 1980, http://tinyurl.com/p2m5kat.

52. Franklin E. Zimring, "The Power Politics of Juvenile Court Transfer in the 1990s," in Zimring and Tanenhaus, *op. cit.*, p. 42.

53. "Boy, 12, to be Nation's Youngest Prison Inmate," *The New York Times*, Jan. 30, 1996, http://tinyurl.com/nnrn7se.

54. For background, see Patrick Marshall, "Three-Strikes Laws," *CQ Researcher*, May 10, 2002, pp. 417–432.

55. Bob Egelko, "Court: juvenile case still counts in three strikes," *SFgate.com*, May 22, 2012, http://tinyurl.com/pmjb9m5.

56. William R. Colson, "Federal Juvenile Law and Practice," Gold & Associates. Ltd., 1990, http://tinyurl.com/ndx4d9j. The act remains available for offenses committed prior to Oct. 12, 1984.

57. Wesley T. Church II *et al.*, *Juvenile Justice Sourcebook*, Second Ed. (2014), p. 41.

58. Sickmund and Puzzachera, *op. cit.*, p. 86.

59. James Alan Fox, "Trends in Juvenile Violence: A Report to the United States Attorney General on Current and Future Rates of Juvenile Offending," March 1996, http://tinyurl.com/nuqye3g.

60. *Ibid.*, p. 1.

61. Quoted in Elizabeth Becker, "As ex-Theorist on Young 'Superpredataors,' Bush Aide Has Regrets," *The New York Times*, Feb. 9, 2001, http://tinyurl.com/menmaa.

62. For background, see Rosen, *op. cit.*; Thomas J. Billitteri, "Discipline in Schools," *CQ Researcher*, Feb. 15, 2008, pp. 145–168; Kathy Koch, "Zero Tolerance for School Violence," *CQ Researcher*, March 10, 2000, pp. 185–208; and Kathy Koch, "School Violence," *CQ Researcher*, Oct. 9, 1998, pp. 881–904.

63. Rosen, *op. cit.*

64. Zimring, "American Youth Violence: A Cautionary Tale," *op. cit.*

65. Jeffrey A. Evans and Douglas N. Evans, "The Second American Crime Drop: Trends in Juvenile and Youth Violence," in Church *et al.*, *op. cit.*

66. The case was later called *Farrell v. Cate.*

67. Barry Krisberg *et al.*, "A New Era in California Juvenile Justice: Downsizing the State Youth Corrections System," Berkeley Center for Criminal Justice and National Council on Crime and Delinquency, October 2010, http://tinyurl.com/pj9nlzu; "Juvenile Corrections Reform in California," Center on Juvenile and Criminal Justice, http://tinyurl.com/nbxj9g3.

68. *Roper v. Simmons*, No. 03–633, http://tinyurl.com/qgmnw6k.

69. Church *et al.*, p. 125.

70. Robert Epstein, "The Myth of the Teen Brain," *Scientific American Mind*, April/May 2007, http://tinyurl.com/q7up4f6.

71. *New Mexico State v. Garcia* (2007).

72. *Graham v. Florida*, 130 S. Ct. 2011 (2010), http://tinyurl.com/os3yvyp; Martin Guggenheim, "Graham v. Florida and a Juvenile's Right to Age-Appropriate Sentencing," *Harvard Civil Rights-Civil Liberties Law Review*, June 2012, Vol. 47 (2), http://tinyurl.com/pek4b34.

73. *Miller v. Alabama* (2012), p. 16, *op. cit.*

74. "Smart on Crime: Reforming the Criminal Justice System for the 21st Century," U.S. Department of Justice, August 2013, http://tinyurl.com/p790mus.

75. Michael Hirsh, "Charles Koch, Liberal Crusader?" *Politico*, March/April 2015, http://tinyurl.com/o2k9ksa.

76. *Implementing Juvenile Justice Reform: The Federal Role* (2014), National Research Council, p. 2, http://tinyurl.com/o5pk8vw.

77. Susan Ferriss, "Hearing airs charges that states took grant money while violating laws," Center for Public Integrity, April 22, 2015, http://tinyurl.com/qc898jv.

78. Sarah Barr, "Senate Judiciary Committee Approves JJDPA Update," Juvenile Justice Information Exchange, July 23, 2015, http://tinyurl.com/pf9m72y.

79. Rep. Robert Scott, "Youth Justice Act of 2015," Congress.gov, http://tinyurl.com/pwqmlul; Rep. Robert Scott, "Youth Promise Act," Congress.gov, http://tinyurl.com/qh6w7j6; Christina Wilkie, "A Bill to Keep Kids Out of Prison Gets A New Lease on Life, Thanks to Conservatives," *The Huffington Post*, May 7, 2015, http://tinyurl.com/nqktvnp; Press Release, "Scott Introduces Bill to Reauthorize Juvenile Justice and Delinquency Prevention Act," June 11, 2015, http://tinyurl.com/qakp78h; Sen. Charles Grassley, "Major Provisions of Juvenile Justice Reauthorization Act of 2015," http://tinyurl.com/pmvjd7s.

80. John Kelly, "House Appropriators Zero Out Juvenile Justice Appropriations," *Chronicle of Social Change*, May 13, 2015, http://tinyurl.com/qaguemr; Austin Igleheart, "House subcommittee Funds Critical County Law Enforcement Programs, Cuts Juvenile Justice Funding," National Association of Counties, May 16, 2015, http://tinyurl.com/pgv8vt5.

81. "Statement of Administration Policy," Executive Office of the President, June 1, 2015, http://tinyurl.com/o93qflf.

82. Michael Oleaga, "Rep. Tony Cardenas Introduces Resolution Eliminating Juvenile Life Sentences," *Latin Post*, July 28, 2015, http://tinyurl.com/q9bvnfu.

83. "Department of Justice Announces Investigation of the Dallas County Truancy Court and Juvenile District Courts," U.S. Department of Justice, March 31, 2015, http://tinyurl.com/pj45kgt.

84. Carrie Johnson, "Settlement Reached to Overhaul Mississippi Juvenile Courts," NPR, June 19, 2015, http://tinyurl.com/njsqvzw.

85. "CRIPA Investigation of the New York City Department of Correction Jails on Rikers Island," U.S. Attorney, Southern District of New York, Aug. 4, 2014, http://tinyurl.com/osb35uc.

86. Richard J. Bonnie *et al.*, *Implementing Juvenile Reform: The Federal Role, National Research Council* (2014), http://tinyurl.com/o5pk8vw.

87. Sickmund and Puzzanchera, *op. cit.*, pp. 121, 196.

88. Owen D. Jones *et al.*, "Law and neuroscience: recommendations submitted to the President's Bioethics Commission," *Journal of Law and the Biosciences*, Aug. 29, 2014, pp. 224–236, http://tinyurl.com/otuy3py.

89. Savage, *op. cit.*, 2015.

90. Michelle Kirby, "Juvenile Sentencing Laws and Court Decisions After Miller v. Alabama," Connecticut General Assembly Office of Legislative Research, March 16, 2015, http://tinyurl.com/o2z96j3.

91. Jim Lynch, "Juvenile prisoners in Michigan allege rape, abuse," *The Detroit News*, April 1, 2015, http://tinyurl.com/nwj5vr8.

92. "Facts and Infographics about Life Without Parole for Children," The Campaign for the Fair Sentencing of Youth, http://tinyurl.com/q6fe5uh/.

93. "California: New Youth Parole Law Promises Hope," Human Rights Watch, Sept. 17, 2013, http://tinyurl.com/pug4jqp.

94. Alton Pitre, "California Measure Is Step Toward True Justice," Youth Transition Funders Group, June 5, 2015, http://tinyurl.com/pvggkfm; "SB 261 Youth offender parole hearings," California Legislation Information, http://tinyurl.com/qfqfeyg.

95. Jackie Davis, " 'Raise the Age' effort fails; youth can still be prosecuted and tried as adults," *Legislative Gazette*, June 29, 2015, http://tinyurl.com/outuj49.

96. Michael Booth, "Christie OK's Juvenile Justice Reforms," *New Jersey Law Journal*, Aug. 11, 2015, http://tinyurl.com/ocqg8bg.

97. Randy Dockendorf, "SD Begins Implementing Juvenile Justice Changes," *Yankton Daily Press & Dakotan*, July 10, 2015, http://tinyurl.com/qjp5asw.

98. Matt Smith, "Texas Juvenile Justice Reformers: 'Raise the Age' Will Rise Again," Juvenile Justice Information Exchange, June 1, 2015, http://tinyurl.com/pbcazw5.

99. See Bernstein, *op. cit.*

100. "Bringing Research to Policy and Practice in Juvenile Justice," The MacArthur Foundation, Research Network on Adolescent Development and Juvenile Justice, Sept. 21 and 22, 2006, http://tinyurl.com/p2jvwco.

101. Eyal Aharoni *et al.*, "Neuroprediction of future rearrest," *Proceedings of the National Academy of Sciences*, Vol. 110 (15), April 9, 2013, http://tinyurl.com/oodfnzs; Dustin A. Pardini *et al.*, "Lower Amygdala Volume in Men Is Associated with Childhood Aggression, Early Psychopathic Traits, and Future Violence," *Biological Psychology*, Jan. 1, 2014, Vol. 75 (1), http://tinyurl.com/nkkv3ks.

102. George Timberlake, "More Data Needed On New Group 'Emerging Adults,' " Juvenile Justice Information Exchange, July 6, 2015.

BIBLIOGRAPHY

Selected Sources

Books

Bernstein, Nell, *Burning Down the House: The End of Juvenile Prison*, The New Press, 2014.
A Berkeley, Calif.-based investigative reporter portrays incidents of abuse, rape and solitary confinement of incarcerated youths and advocates community-oriented youth-rehabilitation programs.

Church II, Wesley T., David W. Springer and Albert R. Roberts, *Juvenile Justice Sourcebook: 2nd Ed.*, Oxford University Press, 2014.
Scholars in law, criminal justice and social work explain the juvenile justice system, research into the causes of juvenile delinquency and the use of adolescent-brain research in courtroom proceedings.

Satel, Sally, and Scott O. Lilienfeld, *Brainwashed: The Seductive Appeal of Mindless Neuroscience*, Basic Books, 2013.
A scholar at the conservative American Enterprise Institute think tank (Satel) and an Emory University psychology professor consider the consequences of relying on neurology rather than psychology to explain behavior.

Steinberg, Laurence, *Age of Opportunity: Lessons from the New Science of Adolescence*, Eamon Dolan/Houghton Mifflin Harcourt, 2014.

A Temple University psychology professor argues that neuroscience brain research shows that adolescence is a prime time to influence behavior at home, school and in the justice system.

Zimring, Franklin E., and David S. Tanenhaus (eds.), *Choosing the Future for American Juvenile Justice*, New York University Press, 2014.
Two scholars on juvenile justice, along with other experts in law and psychology, review a range of issues affecting youthful offenders, including the impact of neuroscience on sentencing, the school-to-prison pipeline, the impact of immigration, the privacy of juvenile records and policies for juvenile sex offenders.

Articles

DeRuy, Emily, "Killing Them Softly: The Juvenile Justice System Is Complicit in Lost Lives," *The National Journal*, July 31, 2015, http://tinyurl.com/occj6ua.
A reporter examines the growing debate about how youths are handled in the juvenile justice system.

Goshe, Sonya, "Moving Beyond the Punitive Legacy: Taking Stock of Persistent Problems in Juvenile Justice," Youth Justice, 2015, Vol. 15, pp. 42–56.
A lawyer and now assistant professor of criminal justice at Wilmington College in Ohio warns of potential hurdles for juvenile justice reformers.

"This is Rikers," The Marshall Project and *New York* magazine, June 28, 2015, http://tinyurl.com/oqu-w9fm.
Following federal reports of widespread abuse at Rikers Island jail in New York City, this news feature details the history and conditions at Rikers and Mayor Bill de Blasio's plans for reform.

Reports

"Implementing Juvenile Justice Reform: The Federal Role (2014)," National Research Council, http://tinyurl.com/o5pk8vw.
Committees of the National Research Council, the research arm of the National Academies of Sciences,

recommend ways Congress and other federal policy-makers can help states and communities overhaul their juvenile justice and rehabilitation systems.

Porter, Nicole D., "The State of Sentencing: 2014," The Sentencing Project, 2015, http://tinyurl.com/nbvuw3f.
The director of advocacy for a Washington-based group that advocates for criminal sentencing reforms outlines state legislative changes — including those related to juvenile justice — made during 2014 that were aimed at reducing levels of incarceration.

Shah, Riya Saha, and Lauren Fine, "Juvenile Records: A National Review of State Laws on Confidentiality, Sealing and Expungement," Juvenile Law Center, 2014, http://tinyurl.com/nosh4hx.
A staff attorney (Shah) and a former fellow of a public-interest law firm in Philadelphia review state laws and policies on confidentiality, sealing and expungement of juvenile records and evaluate their effectiveness. The report also recommends policies and standards to improve confidentiality.

Sickmund, Melissa, and Charles Puzzanchera (eds.), "Juvenile Offenders and Victims: 2014 National Report," National Center for Juvenile Justice, December 2014, http://tinyurl.com/nvepoan.
The research division of the National Council of Juvenile and Family Court Judges provides data through 2010 on juvenile offenders and victims, including demographics of juvenile victims and offenders, arrest and incarceration trends and juvenile court cases.

Video

Haberman, Clyde, "When Youth Violence Spurred 'Superpredator' Fear," *The New York Times*, April 6, 2014, http://tinyurl.com/opvlh4n.
A reporter describes the effect on the nation's juvenile justice systems of the inflammatory — and incorrect — mid-1990s prediction that a wave of youth violence would sharply increase the crime rate.

For More Information

Annie E. Casey Foundation, 701 St. Paul St., Baltimore, MD 21202; 410-547-6600; aecf.org. Finances rehabilitation programs for convicted youths.

Campaign for Fair Sentencing of Youth, 1319 F St., N.W., Suite 303, Washington, DC 20004; 202-289-4677; fairsentencingofyouth.org. Advocates a ban on life-without-parole sentences for juveniles.

Criminal Justice Legal Foundation, 2131 L St., Sacramento, CA 95816; 916-446-0345; www.cjlf.org. Advocates for victims' rights.

Equal Justice Initiative, 122 Commerce St., Montgomery, AL 36104; 334-269-1803; www.eji.org. Provides legal representation for youthful offenders and inmates.

National Center for Juvenile Justice, 3700 S. Water St., Suite 200, Pittsburgh, PA 15203; 412-227-6950; www.ncjj.org.

Studies juvenile crime and gathers statistics on state juvenile justice activities.

National Organization for Victims of Juvenile Murders, 248-736-1737; www.teenkillers.org. Advocates for the rights of family members of those murdered by juveniles.

Rosenberg Foundation, 131 Steuart St., Suite 650, San Francisco, CA 94105; 415-644-9777; www.rosenbergfound.org. Finances efforts to reform the criminal justice system in California.

The Sentencing Project, 1705 DeSales St., N.W., 8th Floor, Washington, DC 20036; 202-628-0871; www.sentencingproject.org. Promotes sentencing reform and alternatives to incarceration.

11

Racial Conflict

Peter Katel

Following a hung jury in December, Baltimore police officer William G. Porter, right, here with his lawyer, will be retried on charges stemming from the death of Freddie Gray, 25, last April. Gray died from spinal cord injuries allegedly sustained while he was being transported in a police van after his arrest for carrying a pocket knife. Porter is one of six officers charged in Gray's death.

Getty Images/Rob Carr

Chicago's Magnificent Mile, a 13-block stretch of upscale shops, sleek office towers and tony hotels, usually buzzes with post-Thanksgiving holiday shopping. But late last year it became a focal point of perhaps the most urgent social issue wracking the nation: relations between whites and minorities, particularly African-Americans.

"Sixteen shots! Thirteen months!" demonstrators shouted as they virtually shut down "Black Friday" commerce in Chicago's main shopping zone. The catalyst was a just-released video showing a Chicago police officer shooting 17-year-old Laquan McDonald 16 times on a city street, killing him. City officials had kept the video under wraps for 13 months until a reporter forced its release through a freedom-of-information request.[1]

Then, one day after Christmas, Chicago police accidentally shot and killed an unarmed grandmother while also fatally shooting an allegedly mentally troubled 19-year-old college student who was reportedly threatening family members with a baseball bat. The Chicago events followed other deadly incidents — in Ferguson, Mo., New York City, North Charleston, S.C., and elsewhere — in which white police officers used deadly force against black suspects, many of them unarmed. Tensions over these deaths ratcheted up again at year's end when a Cleveland grand jury declined to indict a policeman who shot to death 12-year-old Tamir Rice, who had been holding a toy replica of a pistol. What's more, those incidents have followed decades of frustration over large gaps between African-Americans and whites in household wealth, housing, education and employment.[2]

From *CQ Researcher*,
January 8, 2016.

More than 50 years after the official end of segregation and efforts by the Rev. Martin Luther King Jr. and other leaders to protect minorities' civil rights, many activists and some scholars charge that nothing less than institutional racism still grip the nation.

"We still have segregation across America geospatially, with housing practices and banking practices that actually retarded if not prevented integration opportunities," says Maya Rockeymoore, president and CEO of Global Policy Solutions, an advocacy think tank on racial and economic inequality. "And students who have been systematically impoverished are attending impoverished schools in inner-city neighborhoods [and] are never prepared to even qualify to get into higher education. They are victims of structural barriers to opportunity."

Others deny that racism is institutionalized, saying such characterizations are designed to mask the black community's failure to meet the challenges that came after legal discrimination ended in the 1960s. They note that as the nation's first African-American president winds up his second term, a record 48 black lawmakers are serving in Congress and countless more African-Americans preside as big-city mayors, police chiefs and even the U.S. attorney general.[3]

"There is no de jure [legal] segregation in the United States anymore," says Walter E. Williams, an African-American economics professor at George Mason University in Fairfax, Va. "At one time, black Americans did not have the guarantees that everyone else did, but the civil rights struggle is over and won. That does not mean there are not major problems in the black community. When blacks were no more than a generation or more out of slavery, there was greater family stability and there weren't all these problems we see among black folks today."

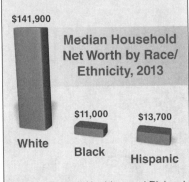

Wealth Gap Divides Whites, Minorities

The median net worth of white households in 2013 was more than 10 times that of Hispanics and nearly 13 times that of blacks, according to the latest federal data.

Median Household Net Worth by Race/ Ethnicity, 2013

$141,900 — White
$11,000 — Black
$13,700 — Hispanic

Source: Rakesh Kochhar and Richard Fry, "Wealth inequality has widened along racial, ethnic lines since end of Great Recession," Pew Research Center, Dec. 12, 2014, http://tinyurl .com/kww2vpoa

As the debate continues, a new generation of activists is challenging racial inequities that have lingered long after pundits declared a "post-racial America" following Barack Obama's 2008 election. Police encounters with black citizen are only one impetus for renewed activism. Also key, advocates say, are the socioeconomic differences between black and white Americans:

- The $11,000 median net worth of black households is about 13 times less than the median white household net worth of $141,900.
- African-Americans die 3.6 years earlier, on average, than whites.
- Only 22 percent of African-Americans earn college degrees, compared with 34 percent of whites.
- About one in 12 black men ages 25–54 are in jail or prison, versus one in 60 white men; and
- Black Americans are almost eight times more likely than white Americans to die by homicide.[4]

For the activists, these outcomes show that America has not shaken off a legacy of race-based oppression. "The [1965] Voting Rights Act and desegregation gave [blacks] more access to a still-racist system," says DeRay Mckesson, a Baltimore-based organizer with the Black Lives Matter movement, which emerged in response to widely publicized cellphone videos of police shootings or violent arrests of African-Americans in the past year.

In a year-long investigation of nearly 1,000 fatal shootings by police in the United States in 2015 (as of late December) *The Washington Post* showed stark racial disproportion in the use of deadly force. Although African-American males account for only 6 percent of the U.S. population, they represent 40 percent — or 37

— of the 90 unarmed men shot to death by police, *The Post* reported. Overall, however, fatal shootings of unarmed black men by white officers accounted for less than 4 percent of such events. (*The Guardian*, a London newspaper, reported its own figure of 1,134 deaths at police hands — including deaths from Taser stun guns and deaths in custody — with African-American 15-to-34-year-old males accounting for 15 percent of the deaths.)[5]

Cellphone, dashboard and other videos, however, do not convey the complexities of America's racial history, many scholars say. They point to what they see as a systematic preference for whites encoded in America's institutional DNA.

Joe R. Feagin, a sociology professor at Texas A&M University, traces the socioeconomic racial divide to centuries of government policies that implicitly or explicitly provided preferential treatment for whites, especially when it came to land grants, government-guaranteed mortgages and college tuition aid — government largesse that has been the foundation of upward mobility for millions of families.

"We white families have had 20 generations to unjustly enrich ourselves," Feagin says. "Even whites who came from working-class backgrounds like mine had access to the marvelous aspects of this country — programs and services."[6]

Many black conservatives, however, reject the notion of present-day institutional racism. "Many times, people use the term when they can't find a racist," Williams says. "A lot of times they can't show you a live, breathing individual or company, so now they call it institutionalized racism." Williams continues, "Next year, I'll be 80 years old. I saw racial discrimination."

Williams blames "the welfare state" for many problems in the black community, saying that government assistance to single mothers "has done what slavery and Jim Crow could not have done: destroy the black family and create a high rate of illegitimacy and family breakdown."

He and other African-American conservatives say that with racial discrimination outlawed for a half-century, ongoing law enforcement issues and poverty in black communities stem from a breakdown of values. "One of the reasons that relations between police and poor blacks are so bad," says Derryck Green, a doctoral candidate at Azusa Pacific University, near Los Angeles, and a member of the National Leadership Network of Black Conservatives, an online think tank for the African-American political right, "is the number of children who grow up in families without a male authority figure."

Jack Hunter, a white libertarian conservative and the political editor of the online news site *Rare*, says many conservatives "cannot wrap their heads around" discriminatory police practices. "Part of that is a lack of recognition that black Americans do have it worse — something that many conservative Republicans are not willing to accept."

For example, "young white men and black men use marijuana at the same rate," he says. "But young black men are jailed at four times the rate for whites" for marijuana violations.[7]

Some scholars cite historical and economic forces for concentrated black poverty, including deficient schools and a loss of manufacturing jobs that once provided a decent living to people with limited education — leaving criminal activities as a major alternative. "Youth unemployment is not some magical problem that dropped from the sky," Feagin says. "When you suffer discrimination on a large scale, where do you go for a job? The crime economy."

In the view of some liberal academics, think tanks and Democratic presidential candidates, government programs to boost employment, educational opportunities and homeownership for all low-income Americans are among the antidotes to racial inequality. And generations of activists and writers — most recently best-selling African-American author Ta-Nehisi Coates — have proposed preferential programs (or reparations) for victims of past institutional discrimination in the distribution of land, home mortgage guarantees and college tuition grants.[8]

But providing racial preferences in anti-poverty programs is widely seen as politically impossible — and unfair, given that many poor people are white. The standard white American's response to racially based criteria would be, " 'My tax dollars shouldn't be used to fix something I'm not responsible for,' " says Leslie Hinkson, a sociology professor at Georgetown University in Washington. Hinkson says most people do not know that "structural racism . . . limits the life chances of people because of their race."

Blacks Highest in Police Stops

African-Americans make up less than a third of Chicago's population but represented nearly three-fourths of the people stopped and frisked by Chicago police over a four-month period in 2014. In New York City, where blacks make up less than a fourth of the population, they accounted for more than half of police stops.

Percentage of Whites, Blacks and Hispanics Stopped and Frisked in Chicago and New York City
(from May-August 2014)

NYC

White	11.8% / 32.7%
	54.2%
Black	22.6%
Hispanic	26.5% / 28.8%

Chicago

White	9.0% / 32.2%
Black	72.0% / 31.5%
Hispanic	17.0% / 28.9%

Percentage of People Stopped

Percentage of Population

Sources: Chicago stop-and-frisk data from ACLU Chicago affiliate, http://tinyurl.com/zpepgmd; New York City stop-and-frisk data from ACLU New York City affiliate, http://tinyurl.com/8vuhkp2; population data from 2014 American Community Survey, U.S. Census Bureau, http://tinyurl.com/o8op597

That idea had wide acceptance in the mid-1960s. The landmark civil rights laws enacted then "helped a lot of black middle-class folks, but didn't do much for the urban black poor," says Michael Javen Fortner, urban studies director at the City University of New York's School of Professional Studies. "Middle-class people could use . . . laws and policies to leave neighborhoods, to get into schools that in the past they couldn't get into."

Paradoxically, the renewed attention to black-white racial tensions comes as the non-Hispanic white majority is becoming a minority.[9] Hispanics have long endured discrimination (reflected in a history of 547 documented lynchings of Mexicans and Mexican-Americans between 1848–1928 in the West and Midwest), and American Indians have been the targets of military campaigns, mass removals and massacres that modern tribal leaders call genocide.[10]

But the African-American experience occupies a unique place in U.S. life because of slavery's legacy and the fact that the nation's culture is partly a black creation. The Smithsonian National Museum of African American History and Culture, due to open this fall on the National Mall in Washington, is designed to introduce a mass audience to that often-hidden side of the American story.[11]

As activists, scholars and others debate race relations, here are some of the questions being asked:

Would improving police interactions with African-Americans significantly advance race relations in America?

Today's conflicts between police and African-Americans have stirred debate about the larger issue of race in America, just as urban riots in the 1960s — often triggered by confrontations between police and black citizens — led to similar soul-searching.[12]

With cellphone video now ubiquitous, the public is seeing what happens in police-citizen interactions that turn ugly. In the past year alone, videos have shown, among other incidents:

- A white police officer at a Columbia, S.C., school overturning an allegedly disobedient black student's chair with her in it before handcuffing her;
- A white officer in McKinney, Texas, slamming a black, bikini-clad girl to the ground at a pool party, then drawing his gun on her companions; and
- A white, Charlotte, N.C., officer shooting and killing an unarmed black man after a one-car accident.[13]

Videos, or "the C-Span of the streets," according to Paul Butler, a professor at Georgetown University Law School and a former prosecutor, corroborate "what African-Americans have been saying for years."[14]

Some police chiefs have accepted video as evidence of misconduct. In South Carolina, the North Charleston chief — saying he was "sickened" by the video of a cop shooting an unarmed black to death — fired the officer, who was later charged with murder.[15]

But videos also can be used unfairly against officers, said Bill Johnson, executive director of the National Association of Police Organizations. "Even if we do everything right, if we do it by the law and the investigation shows that we did, we can still just be so dragged through the mud unfairly and inaccurately by community activists, by the media," he said.[16]

Johnson said the omnipresence of videos today makes police reluctant to be "as aggressive as we used to be," something FBI Director James Comey has said might be causing an uptick in crime. But Comey conceded that police can fall into a habit of linking criminal behavior to race. "The two young black men on one side of the street look like so many others the officer has locked up," Comey said in a speech last February. "Two white men on the other side of the street — even in the same clothes — do not."[17]

Despite the outrage generated by videos, some in the Black Lives Matter movement — which emerged after the 2014 police shooting of Michael Brown, 18, in Ferguson, Mo. — say discriminatory law enforcement is not the worst problem facing African-Americans.[18] Schools, health care and other structures and institutions affect people "along the lines of race and class," says Black Lives activist Mckesson, who has co-authored a plan to limit police use of deadly force.[19]

Nevertheless, Mckesson says, the potentially deadly consequences of confrontations with police make changing relations with cops a priority. "The impact of the criminal justice system, because it means jail for people, means the police are violently interacting with your body. That is a loss of freedom and safety right now."

Some black conservatives argue that confrontations between police and African-Americans typically reflect high crime rates and moral decay in black communities. Williams of George Mason cites statistics showing that most homicide victims are black people killed by other African-Americans.[20] From 1980 to 2008, according to FBI data, 93 percent of black homicide victims were killed by other African-Americans. Overall, 28 percent of the FBI's "known offenders" are black, significantly above the black population share, the data show.[21]

"This is not a civil rights problem," Williams says. "It's not the Klan murdering blacks."

But for others, the high crime rates in poor black neighborhoods do not justify discriminatory police action. Rockeymoore of Global Policy Solutions says police and others in the criminal justice system often automatically link race with criminality. "You have

Brandon Risher is comforted at the casket of his grandmother, Ethel Lance, 70, who was one of nine victims killed in a mass shooting at historic Emanuel African Methodist Episcopal Church in Charleston, S.C., on June 17, 2015. Dylann Roof, 21, a white supremacist, is accused in the shootings, which occurred during a prayer meeting.

Getty Images/Joe Raedle

situations where innocents are being slaughtered or wrongly arrested," she says.

Last October, *The New York Times* — using data from police traffic stops and arrests in Greensboro, N.C. — concluded that African-Americans accounted for 54 percent of drivers pulled over even though they made up only 39 percent of the city's driving-age population. Cars driven by blacks were searched more than twice as often as cars driven by whites, and force was used more frequently with blacks than with whites. Statistics from six other states showed similar results.[22]

Nevertheless, Rockeymoore, who lives in Baltimore — a black-majority city plagued by violence — acknowledges that the high crime rates in poor, African-American neighborhoods mean those neighborhoods need more police. "It's not a function of race, but of class," she says. "When you combine poor people with primary needs and no way to meet those immediate needs outside of what they perceive as criminality, . . . that increases the rate of people wanting and needing police officers."

Lisa L. Miller, a political scientist at Rutgers University in New Brunswick, N.J., who specializes in crime and race, goes further, arguing that the Black Lives Matter movement's intense focus on policing reinforces fundamental distrust of government, a vision that doesn't match the concerns of people in impoverished minority communities. "My worry about the fixation on state violence is that it reinforces the anti-statist narrative," Miller says. "But we don't need the state to do less; we need it to do more."

Would new laws and government programs reduce institutional racism?

Experts representing all political persuasions agree that the landmark 1954 Supreme Court decision *Brown v. Board of Education* outlawing school segregation, along with three major civil rights laws of the 1960s, were essential to correcting injustices that persisted 100 years after slavery ended.*

But experts are divided over how the government can narrow today's racial gaps in education and employment.

Hillary Clinton, the leading candidate for the Democratic presidential nomination, debated the issue in New Hampshire last summer during a meeting with Black Lives Matter activists.

Clinton acknowledged that a 1994 crime law — endorsed by her husband, President Bill Clinton — brought unintended negative consequences, including a vast increase in imprisonment, especially for African-Americans convicted of drug use.

After candidate Clinton's comments, activist Julius Jones of Worcester, Mass., referring to racism's historical roots, said: "America's first drug [was] free black labor. . . . Until someone . . . speaks that truth to white people in this country so that we can finally take on anti-blackness as a founding problem in this country, I don't believe there's going to be a solution."[23]

Clinton said that approach would accomplish little because too many whites would say, "We get it, we get it, we're going to be nicer." But she added, "That's not enough in my book, that's not how I see politics."

To address racial inequality, Clinton has called for measures intended to fight poverty and reduce income inequality — measures, she says, that would begin to curb disparities in the criminal justice system. Mass incarceration condemns ex-prisoners and their families to poverty, Clinton said.[24]

But citing persistent housing segregation despite the 1968 Fair Housing Act, which banned racial discrimination in housing, Hinkson of Georgetown says, "Hillary Clinton believes too much in the power of the law to effect substantial change. With laws, you have a possibility of change, but you can't have actual change

without having mechanisms in place to ensure that the law is upheld."

Furthermore, she continued, "you also need to effect cultural shifts so that people don't feel, 'You're forcing me to do something. I'm going to find ways around it.'"[25]

Without white acknowledgment of racism, Hinkson argues, the majority white view will continue to be: "Sure we understand that racism exists, but we're not willing to have our government do anything to alleviate it because we have this understanding that if I do not overtly discriminate against someone because of their race, then I do not contribute to racism."

Even during slavery times, official, systematic discrimination has led some to argue that the government owes compensation to black victims of government policies. In more recent decades, some activists and politicians have called for "reparations." But even author Coates, among the latest to take up the cause, acknowledges that getting today's lawmakers to agree on a compensation system might be impossible — though, he writes, the debate would be worth it.[26]

Global Policy Solutions, Rockeymoore's organization, proposes a series of government programs aimed at closing the racial wealth gap, including financing infrastructure projects that would provide jobs and subcontracts in the African-American community. But the programs, despite their racial-justice impulse, would be open to all, regardless of color. "I don't think that there has been much political will or public will for racially specific solutions," Rockeymoore says.

Nevertheless, another of the center's proposals calls for reviving the "10–20–30 plan" — a provision of the American Recovery and Reinvestment Act of 2009.[27] The so-called "economic stimulus" poured federal money into food stamps and other aid, as well as infrastructure projects that designated 10 percent of stimulus money toward communities with at least 20 percent of the population living below the poverty line for at least 30 years.

But Green of the National Leadership Network of Black Conservatives, organized by the conservative advocacy group the National Center for Public Policy Research, which supports environmental deregulation, opposes expanding government-funded health care and works to get black conservatives elected, doubts that programs and laws will do much good. "Racism and racial

---

* The three laws were the Civil Rights Act of 1964, the Voting Rights act of 1965 and the Fair Housing Act of 1968.

discrimination are a manifestation of sin," he says. "We have to deal with it from a moral perspective."

Green dismisses a major liberal policy proposal — raising the minimum wage nationally to $15 an hour — because, he says, doing so would kill jobs. "Increasing the minimum wage increases the unemployment of black people, whether teens or adults," he says. "If you increased to $15 for entry-level workers, business owners are not going to hire those who need employment the most. . . . [So] how are they going to develop work skills and overcome the socioeconomic differences between black and white?"

Those who favor government activism acknowledge that government programs can hurt some intended beneficiaries. "The ghetto has become a slum," says William Sampson, chair of the public policy studies department at DePaul University in Chicago. "When it was a ghetto, everybody black lived in it; it didn't matter if you were a lawyer or a dentist or on welfare, the folkways and mores were determined by the middle-income folks. Integration allowed them to leave, and they did, which took away the role models and compass of those communities."

Sampson stresses that he doesn't mean ending legal segregation was bad. "But there was a downside," he says. Some of that negative effect could be counteracted by a massive government program to train families in effective child-rearing techniques, he says.

"Kids who do well in school have quiet, orderly, structured home environments," Sampson says, "and are disciplined, with high self-esteem, internally controlled and responsible."

Does government need to recommit to school desegregation?

Desegregation of public schools, a major victory of the 20th-century civil rights movement, essentially ended after 1991, when the Supreme Court allowed the termination of plans based on busing students to schools outside their neighborhoods to achieve racial balance.[28]

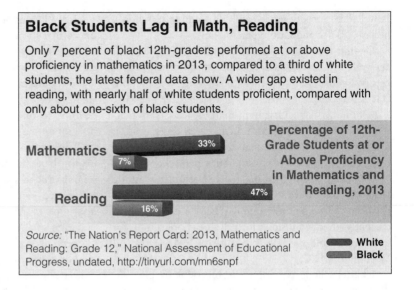

Black Students Lag in Math, Reading

Only 7 percent of black 12th-graders performed at or above proficiency in mathematics in 2013, compared to a third of white students, the latest federal data show. A wider gap existed in reading, with nearly half of white students proficient, compared with only about one-sixth of black students.

Percentage of 12th-Grade Students at or Above Proficiency in Mathematics and Reading, 2013

Mathematics: White 33%, Black 7%
Reading: White 47%, Black 16%

Source: "The Nation's Report Card: 2013, Mathematics and Reading: Grade 12," National Assessment of Educational Progress, undated, http://tinyurl.com/mn6snpf

White
Black

School integration levels began dropping after the decision, in part because blacks and whites remained residentially segregated. But by 1997, even black families who moved to suburbs found public schools there increasingly divided by race.[29]

As a result, according to the Civil Rights Project, a research organization at the University of California, Los Angeles, a statistically typical white student's class of 30 in 2011–12 had 22 whites, two blacks and four Latinos, while the class of a typical black or Latino student had at least 20 blacks or Latinos and eight whites.[30]

"Black and Latino students tend to be in schools with a substantial majority of poor children," a research report concluded, "but white and Asian students are typically in middle-class schools."[31]

Standardized test results also reflect sharp racial divisions. The most recent report of the National Assessment of Educational Progress shows that in 2013, only 7 percent of black 12th-graders — compared with 33 percent of their white counterparts — were at or above proficiency in math. In reading, 16 percent of black students were proficient, compared with 47 percent of whites.[32]

Some education experts link blacks' poor academic performance to the resegregation of public schools. Sampson of DePaul says schools serving black and Latino students don't get the same level of resources that go to predominantly white schools. "White parents can move" if they are dissatisfied with their children's schools, he says. "Black and Latino parents can't."

George Theoharis, chair of the teaching department at Syracuse University's School of Education and a former Wisconsin school principal, advocates integration. "Certainly, there are other things that matter," he says. "Teaching matters, curriculum matters, leadership matters. But we have disregarded the fact that desegregation really matters. We have enough history in this country of being unable to achieve separate but equal schools."

But rather than pushing for reintegrating public schools, some education experts call for more publicly financed charter schools or more school vouchers, which currently provide subsidies for private-school tuition for low-income and special-needs students in 13 states and Washington, D.C.

Charter schools typically focus on trying to raise academic performance rather than on integration. "Charter schools make no bones" about their focus on academics over race, says Theoharis, who sees charter schools as "part of the whole reform agenda of the past 30 years that has really moved away from desegregation."

Proponents of charter schools, in fact, call those institutions the best way to eliminate academic-performance gaps. Charter schools provide "exciting and viable education in an inclusive, individual manner," said the Center for Education Reform, a leading charter-advocacy organization, citing statistics that show charter students in New York City outperform their public school counterparts.[33]

"In theory, charter schools make some sense," Sampson says. "In practice, they're horrible. They take only the best students. But charter schools on the whole don't outperform public schools." Lotteries that some school districts hold for charter school admissions don't avoid that selection bias, he says, because parents who enter lotteries are by definition more involved in looking for the best schools for their children.

Sampson says having black and white students mix is socially positive for all the students. Georgetown's Hinkson also supports reintegration, pointing out that in her doctoral research at Princeton she found that in the armed forces — often called the most integrated part of America — racial test score gaps at schools for children of military personnel "were smaller there than in any other state in this country."[34]

But Williams of George Mason says, "There is no evidence that in order for black kids to get a high-quality education, we have to capture white kids to sit beside them."

Theoharis says resuming desegregation would be difficult, although "magnet" schools — public schools devoted to one field — could help accomplish more integration, he says, if they were available to all students.

Williams says the need for alternatives is far more urgent than changing schools' racial makeup. He favors school vouchers or tuition tax credits so black parents could have "some kind of alternative to these rotten public schools in many of these neighborhoods."

Green of the National Leadership Network of Black Conservatives argues that public schools should get the kind of scrutiny that Sampson applied to charters. "Some charter schools are going to be terrible and should fail," he says, "and [bad] public schools should fail, too."

BACKGROUND
Slavery and Jim Crow

Today's racial tensions were born in the trans-Atlantic slave trade, which forcibly brought as many as 388,000 Africans to colonial America and the United States between 1619 and 1865, when Congress abolished slavery nationwide by passing the 13th Amendment to the Constitution.[35]

Seventy-eight years earlier, when delegates gathered in Philadelphia in 1787 to write the Constitution, they compromised on slavery in order to keep the South in the Union. Delegates from the North, where several states had banned slavery within their borders years before the constitutional convention convened, wanted to end the trans-Atlantic slave trade. But Southerners refused to accept an immediate ban. The compromise allowed the trade to continue until 1808 and slavery to survive in states where it already existed.[36]

Historians still debate whether the United States was founded as a "slave" nation. Sean Wilentz of Princeton University argued that toleration of regional slavery "did not sanction slavery in national law, as a national institution."[37] But Patrick Rael, of Bowdoin College in Brunswick, Maine, wrote: "If slavery was not legal in every state, it was nonetheless 'national law,' protected and upheld by the Constitution."[38]

The Constitution did contain sections favorable to slave owners, particularly Article 4, Section 2, which held that slaves who escaped to states that had abolished slavery remained slaves and had to be returned to their owners.[39] In 1850 Congress passed a law strengthening slave owners' rights to seize their fugitive "property."[40] Then, in 1857, the Supreme Court ruled in the *Dred Scott* decision that Scott, a slave born in Virginia, did not become free when his master took him temporarily to the free states of Illinois and Wisconsin because he was not a U.S. citizen — nor was any other person of African ancestry.[41]

During the Civil War, President Abraham Lincoln issued the Emancipation Proclamation of 1863, freeing the slaves in Confederate states. In 1865 the 13th Amendment abolishing slavery was ratified, followed three years later by the 14th Amendment, defining anyone born in the United States as a citizen entitled to "equal protection of the laws."[42]

Lincoln's successor, President Andrew Johnson, embarked on Reconstruction, the attempt to establish social and political racial equality in the South. But white resistance won out, with the acquiescence or support of some Northern politicians and judges. The post-Civil War system of white domination became known in the 1890s as Jim Crow. Southern state governments also adopted laws that decreed the arrest of all jobless black people. The penalty was forced labor — essentially, slavery.[43]

In response to white resistance, President Ulysses S. Grant stationed federal troops in nine South Carolina counties.[44] And in 1870 Congress adopted the 15th Amendment, prohibiting states from denying or limiting the right to vote because of "race, color, or previous condition of servitude." Congress followed up with the Enforcement Act, which defined racist violence as a federal crime.[45]

But anti-black violence continued, and in the 1870s, the national political tide shifted against Reconstruction, as Southern white resistance solidified and many Northern politicians proved unwilling to crush the opposition.[46] In 1877, disputed presidential election results led to a Democratic-Republican deal: The Democrats would recognize Republican Rutherford B. Hayes as the winner, and Hayes would pull federal troops out of Louisiana and South Carolina. As a result, white-supremacist politicians' power was cemented throughout the South.[47]

The end of Reconstruction took a deadly toll: Nearly 4,000 blacks were lynched in 12 Southern states between 1887 and 1950, according to the Equal Justice Initiative in Montgomery, Ala.[48]

In several Deep South states — notably Alabama, Florida and Georgia — a forced-labor system was developed in which thousands of black men were worked, often to death, in mines, steel mills and lumber camps. *Slavery by Another Name*, a Pulitzer Prize-winning 2008 book by reporter Douglas A. Blackmon, chronicled how black men were trapped in the labor system by arrests for crimes such as "vagrancy," then "leased" to companies by county sheriffs.[49]

'White Affirmative Action'

After Democrat Franklin D. Roosevelt became president in 1933, his administration's "New Deal" sought to revive the Depression-crippled economy and protect workers' rights through such laws and regulations as the Social Security Act, the Fair Labor Standards Act, the Civilian Conservation Corps, the Works Project Administration and dozens of other efforts.[50]

But whites were the primary beneficiaries, according to historians such as Ira Katznelson of Columbia University, author of the 2005 book, *When Affirmative Action Was White*. Maids and farmworkers — the two kinds of jobs disproportionately held by black people — were excluded from laws protecting unionization and establishing minimum wages and work hours as well as coverage under the new Social Security system. Social Security did not cover those two job categories until the 1950s.[51]

Although Roosevelt and many Northern Democrats didn't share Southerners' racial prejudices, the administration accommodated their racial attitudes because FDR needed support from Southern Democrats to pass New Deal measures.[52] The black press argued that African-Americans were paying the price for the New Deal. Nonetheless, some black commentators did credit FDR and his allies — particularly his wife, Eleanor — with trying to advance racial equality.[53]

After World War II, the GI Bill of Rights — which financed college educations, home mortgages and business ventures — vastly expanded the American middle class.[54] But the bill ensured that Southern black veterans received only minimal benefits — if any. Moreover, blacks were significantly under-represented in the armed forces during

CHRONOLOGY

1789-1863 *Founders compromise on slavery; issue eventually tears country apart.*

1789 Constitution allows slavery and return of fugitive slaves as "property."

1857 Supreme Court rules in *Dred Scott* case that slaves are not citizens.

1863 In midst of Civil War, President Abraham Lincoln issues Emancipation Proclamation, freeing slaves in 10 Confederate states.

1865-1940 *Civil War ends; racist Jim Crow regime in South survives New Deal labor and welfare laws.*

1865 13th Amendment frees all slaves. As Reconstruction attempts to establish racial equality in the South, ex-Confederate Gen. Nathan Bedford Forrest founds Ku Klux Klan to terrorize black population.

1877 Rutherford B. Hayes is recognized as the winner of presidential election in return for pulling federal troops from the South; Jim Crow system follows.

1915 African-Americans begin their "Great Migration" out of the South; the number eventually reaches 6 million.

1933 Compromises with segregationist Southern Democrats restrict black access to New Deal labor benefits.

1940 The number of African-Americans lynched in the South since 1887 approaches 4,000.

1944-1980 *Anger over obstacles to black access to veterans' benefits helps fuel civil rights movement, which wins landmark legislation.*

1944 Local administrators restrict black access to veterans' education grants and business and mortgage loans.

1954 Supreme Court unanimously rules school segregation unconstitutional in *Brown v. Board of Education.*

1964 Civil Rights Act outlaws job, school and public facilities discrimination.

1965 Voting Rights Act prohibits discriminatory obstructions to voting.

1967 Civil disorders erupt in 160 cities.

1968 National commission studying causes of urban riots concludes the nation is moving toward two "separate and unequal" societies. . . . Civil rights leader Rev. Martin Luther King Jr. is assassinated, sparking urban riots. . . . Congress passes Fair Housing Act, banning racial discrimination in housing. . . . Richard M. Nixon is elected president on promise to restore law and order to cities.

1974 Supreme Court rules against combining urban and suburban school districts to desegregate, dealing a blow to desegregation plans.

1994-Present *Crack epidemic prompts harsher sentencing laws for drug-related crimes, later viewed as impetus to mass incarceration of African-Americans.*

1994 Congress and states pass tough anti-crime bills.

2000 Incarcerated population reaches nearly 2 million, up from 474,000 in 1980, with disproportionally high black imprisonment rate.

2008 Democratic Sen. Barack Obama of Illinois is elected president, leading to hopes that America had overcome its racist past.

2012 A neighborhood watch volunteer kills black teenager Trayvon Martin in Florida, focusing new attention on dangers to black males.

2014 Death of Michael Brown at the hands of police in Missouri sparks Black Lives Matter protests and "All Lives Matter" backlash.

2015 President Obama defends Black Lives Matter slogan and movement. . . . Black Lives activists disrupt Democratic candidates' primary speeches, force changes in their campaigns. . . . Demonstrations at the University of Missouri, Yale and elsewhere raise issues of racial discrimination on campus. . . . Chicago police officer is charged with murder in shooting death of 17-year-old Laquan McDonald. . . . Justice Department opens investigation of Chicago police. . . . Chicago Mayor Rahm Emanuel fires police chief; protesters call for Emanuel's resignation.

World War II, with only half of military-age African-Americans serving. The military, which remained segregated until 1948, cited poor performance on health, literacy and aptitude tests for many of the rejections, although the all-black 477th Bombardment Group of airmen performed with distinction.[55]

Three years after the GI Bill was enacted, a report on how black vets were faring said it was "as though the GI Bill had been earmarked 'For White Veterans Only.' "[56]

While the South remained the African-American heartland, about 6 million blacks fled Jim Crow to cities in other regions during the "Great Migration" of 1915 to 1970. The politics and culture of Chicago, New York, Detroit, Los Angeles and many other cities soon reflected the effects of this massive population shift.[57]

In some places, the GI Bill was more equitably administered than in the South. But well into the 1960s, federal housing policy effectively blocked black home-ownership — even outside the South — by preventing homes in those areas from qualifying for government-backed mortgages.

"Neighborhoods where black people lived . . . were usually considered ineligible for FHA [Federal Housing Administration] backing," journalist Coates wrote last year, centering his reporting on Chicago. In effect, black people were denied access to mortgages or sometimes forced to rely on extortionate "contract" home purchases, which allowed the sellers to evict families for missing a single payment, leaving the buyers with no equity in the property, Coates reported.[58]

Civil Rights

In the 1950s, the civil rights movement gained fresh momentum, spurred in part by the Supreme Court's 1954 *Brown v. Board of Education* ruling, which called segregated schools inherently unequal.[59]

Then African-Americans and their white allies began a campaign of nonviolent disobedience against state segregation laws, with marches, boycotts and sit-ins that sought to register black voters and end discriminatory practices that, among other things, forced blacks to sit in backs of buses and prevented them from getting served at lunch counters.[60] By the mid-1960s, the movement was challenging racist housing, school and job policies and laws throughout the country.

Within five years of the epic 1963 March on Washington, when 250,000 white and black Americans gathered on the National Mall to demand an end to segregation and job discrimination, Congress had passed the three landmark civil rights laws. They prohibited discrimination in employment, housing, schools and all other public facilities, and mandated that states provide equal access to the polls, with Justice Department prior review — or preclearance — required of any laws that might impede voting in four Deep South states.*[61]

School desegregation efforts begun after the *Brown v. Board of Education* ruling prompted major resistance, including in the North. In Boston, years of sometimes violent protests followed a federal court order in 1974 that both white and black students be bused to schools outside their neighborhoods in order to achieve racial integration.[62]

The busing order was based on a 1970 Supreme Court decision. But four years after the 1974 court order, the high court blocked lower courts from combining city and suburban school districts as part of desegregation plans.[63] Because housing patterns were often racially defined, neighborhood schools remained largely segregated by race.[64]

While residential patterns changed little, national politics were transformed because of the civil rights movement. Democratic President Lyndon B. Johnson, a Texan proud of his Southern roots, championed civil rights and pushed the landmark legislation through a Democratic-controlled Congress; as a result, his party became identified with the movement, and Republicans successfully appealed to Southern white Democrats to switch political allegiances.[65]

"The more Negroes who register as Democrats in the South, the sooner the Negrophobe whites will quit the Democrats and become Republicans," a strategist for Republican President Richard M. Nixon, elected in 1968, later told *The New York Times*. "That's where the votes are."[66] By the 1980s, Republican presidential candidates were winning an average of 67 percent of the white Southern vote.[67]

A major factor in the anti-civil rights backlash was riots in largely black and poor inner-city districts that erupted in Los Angeles, Newark, Detroit and about 160 other cities in 1967. A report by a commission appointed

---

* This "preclearance" requirement was later extended to Alaska and Arizona and selected counties and townships in California, New York and Michigan.

'Black Lives Matter' Slogan Praised and Condemned

Backers point to police brutality, but critics say the slogan is anti-cop.

Three words — Black Lives Matter — have sparked a new argument over race in America. Demonstrators chanting and tweeting that slogan have protested the deaths of African-Americans, many of them unarmed, at the hands of police officers — most of them white — in cities across the country in the past two years. As Black Lives Matter activist Melina Abdullah, Pan-African studies chair at California State University in Los Angeles, said on CNN, the slogan first showed up in media reports of demonstrations after the Aug. 9, 2014, shooting death of black teenager Michael Brown by then-Ferguson, Mo., police officer Darren Wilson.[1]

A series of ensuing demonstrations evolved into the Black Lives Matter movement after unarmed black men or boys were killed by police in New York City; Beavercreek, Ohio; North Charleston, S.C.; and Baltimore. Then, a young white supremacist was charged in the shooting deaths of nine parishioners at a historic African-American church in Charleston, S.C., last July.[2]

The slogan reflects reality, says Leslie L. Hinkson, a sociology professor at Georgetown University in Washington. "We're told in so many ways that 'no, your lives don't matter,'" she says, "You don't have good services, your schools are horrible. There are constant reminders."

Some police officials and political conservatives argue, however, that the slogan and movement behind it are anti-cop. Even some sympathizers say the movement is ignoring the fact that most black homicides are perpetrated by African-Americans (as most homicides of whites are white-on-white).[3]

President Obama has defended the slogan, saying the organizers used the phrase "not because . . . they were suggesting nobody else's lives matter. Rather, what they were suggesting was there is a specific problem that is happening in the African-American community that's not happening in other communities. And that is a legitimate issue that we've got to address."[4]

Criticism of the movement, however, grew more heated after a handful of African-Americans were accused of attacking police. Those incidents included the December 2014 killing of two New York City officers and the September 2015 shooting death of Houston Deputy Sheriff Darren Goforth. "Police Lives Matter" was the rallying cry for a memorial march in his honor.[5]

"Black Lives Matter has blood on their hands . . . blue blood on their hands," Fox News host Eric Bolling said in November, accusing the movement of stoking violence against police.[6]

On the political front, the slogan has given Democratic presidential primary candidates some trouble. In June, at a speech to a black church audience in Missouri, Hillary Clinton said, paraphrasing her mother, "All lives matter." After push-back from activists, she was embracing the slogan by July. "This is not just a slogan, this should be a guiding principle," Clinton said in South Carolina. "We have some serious problems with race and justice and systemic racism."[7]

Among Republican primary candidates, the strongest reaction to Black Lives Matter has come from New Jersey Gov. Chris Christie, who accused members of calling for the killing of police officers, apparently a reference to a chant during a Minneapolis demonstration that one activist said was a joke.[8]

But some conservatives back the slogan. Jack Hunter, a libertarian former aide to Republican presidential primary candidate Rand Paul, says Obama had it right. "It's not that all lives don't matter," Hunter says. "Black Lives Matter is saying that there is something specifically wrong with our society, our criminal justice system, and that is a fact. That is what that phrase means."

Still, the movement could trigger a backlash if critics persuade enough non-African-Americans that the slogan means that only black lives matter, and only when black people are killed or injured by police.

Citing the high death-by-homicide rate for African-Americans at the hands of African-Americans, Hinkson of Georgetown asks, "Don't people within the [black] community also need to be reminded that black lives matter?"

John McWhorter, a linguistics professor at Columbia University in New York, agreed. Calling himself sympathetic to the movement, he said the movement should also direct its "fierceness" at preventing the "minority of black men from killing one another all the time."[9]

Filmmaker Spike Lee spoke in even tougher terms. "We as a people can't talk only about Black Lives Matter," he told *Chicago* magazine, "and then not talk about this self-inflicted genocide. . . . Only by talking about both and addressing both can we bring change."[10]

About two weeks after Lee's interview, a 9-year-old Chicago boy, TyShawn Lee, was shot to death in an alley in the city's largely black South Side. Police said the boy was executed because of his father's alleged gang ties; they later charged 27-year-old African-American gang member Corey Morgan with first-degree murder.[11]

Then attention shifted back to police killings after the release of a video showing a Chicago police officer fatally shooting a black 17-year-old, Laquan McDonald, 16 times; protests led to the early December firing of the police chief.[12]

Black Lives activist DeRay Mckesson, organizer of "Campaign Zero," which advocates new restrictions on police use of force and related measures, says Lee and McWhorter are missing the point. "To see people with such exposure and intellect not be able to grasp the fundamental difference between community violence and police violence is nothing short of stunning," he says. "Police are powerful not only because they have guns but because they are allowed to use guns and have protection when they use them. That makes them different from anyone else."[13]

— Peter Katel

A demonstrator on the National Mall on Oct.10, 2015, holds a sign that answers critics who see racism in the Black Lives Matter slogan. The Justice or Else! rally was held to commemorate the 20th anniversary of the Million Man March.

AFP/Getty Images/Andrew Caballero-Reynolds

[1]"CNN Newsroom," Oct. 2, 2015, Nexis.

[2]Matt Apuzzo, "Dylann Roof, Charleston Shooting Suspect, Is Indicted on Federal Hate Crime Charges," *The New York Times*, July 22, 2015, http://tinyurl.com/qcwlj8b; Sheryl Gay Stolberg, "Trial Set for First of 6 Baltimore Officers Charged in Freddie Gray Case," *The New York Times*, Sept. 29, 2015, http://tinyurl.com/pnfc22m; Al Baker, J. David Goodman and Benjamin Mueller, "Beyond the Chokehold: The Path to Eric Garner's Death," *The New York Times*, June 13, 2015, http://tinyurl.com/nflggzh. For background, see Barbara Mantel, "Far-right Extremism," *CQ Researcher*, Sept. 18, 2015, pp. 769-792.

[3]Amy Sherman, "An updated look at statistics on black-on-black murders," *Politifact Florida*, May 21, 2015, http://tinyurl.com/nmvpj4l.

[4]"Remarks by the President in Arm Chair Discussion on Criminal Justice with Law Enforcement Leaders," the White House, Oct. 22, 2015, http://tinyurl.com/qguv37k.

[5]Radley Balko, "Once again: There is no 'war on cops,' " *The Washington Post*, Sept. 10, 2015, http://tinyurl.com/ohbeune; "Community holds 'Police Lives Matter' march in memory of slain deputy," KHOU-TV, *USA Today*, Sept. 12, 2015, http://tinyurl.com/q5lz2ho; Larry Celona et al., "Gunman executes 2 NYPD cops in Garner 'revenge,' " *New York Post*, Dec. 20, 2014, http://tinyurl.com/lgubufb.

[6]"Quentin Tarantino defends anti-cop comments," Fox News, Nov. 5, 2015, http://tinyurl.com/pzrd7te.

[7]Cameron Joseph, "'Black Lives Matter': Hillary Clinton addresses nation's racial inequality in meeting with South Carolina Democrats," *New York Daily News*, July 23, 2015, http://tinyurl.com/otyrq4m; Tamara Keith, "Hillary Clinton's 3-Word Misstep: 'All Lives Matter,' " NPR, June 24, 2015, http://tinyurl.com/nc4ndro.

[8]Quoted in Caitlin Dickson, "Chris Christie doubles down on Black Lives Matter claims," Yahoo News, Oct. 31, 2015, http://tinyurl.com/h4pa59v; "Black Lives Matter Activist: 'Pigs in a Blanket' Chant was 'More Playful Than Anything,' " *Breitbart*, Sept. 1, 2015, http://tinyurl.com/phsasgl; Rich Zeoli, "Executive Director of the FOP: Comey Wrong About Ferguson Effect," CBS News, Oct. 28, 2015, http://tinyurl.com/hp7r9d3.

[9]"CNN Tonight," CNN, Sept. 29, 2015; John McWhorter, "Black Lives Matter should also take on 'black-on-black crime,' " *The Washington Post*, Oct. 22, 2015, http://tinyurl.com/jjfqpys.

[10]Bryan Smith, "Spike Lee Sounds Off on Chi-Raq, Gun Violence, and Rahm," *Chicago* magazine, Oct. 22, 2015, http://tinyurl.com/zsmlhsv.

[11]Sarah Kaplan, "Chicago police: Slain 9-year-old was targeted, lured into alley," *The Washington Post*, Nov. 6, 2015, http://tinyurl.com/hts7spv. See also Jason Keyser, "Charges Filed In Murder Of 9-Year-Old Chicago Boy Tyshawn Lee," The Associated Press, *The Huffington Post*, Nov. 29, 2015, http://tinyurl.com/qfm62o6.

[12]"Chicago mayor fires police chief in wake of video release," The Associated Press, Yahoo! News, Dec. 1, 2015, http://tinyurl.com/j7z7zxx.

[13]"Campaign Zero," undated, http://tinyurl.com/p6vknog.

Race Becomes Big Issue in Upcoming Primaries

Activists demand more action from Democrats.

Race is becoming — again — a headline issue in U.S. life just as the two main political parties are preparing to nominate presidential candidates.

Democratic candidates' speeches have been interrupted by demonstrators demanding more responsiveness on race questions, prompting some changes in how the Hillary Clinton and Bernie Sanders campaigns deal with the issue.

Most members of the larger Republican field have devoted little time to the causes associated with Black Lives Matter — above all, the issue of law enforcement in minority communities.

Nevertheless, the only black candidate from either party is Republican Ben Carson, a retired pediatric neurosurgeon. He had written earlier in his career that blacks and whites received different treatment from the law enforcement system. Now, he is calling the focus on criminal justice a mistake. "I just don't agree that that's where the emphasis needs to be," he said.[1]

The Democratic Party's relations with the black community, forged in the civil rights battles of a half century ago, have not guaranteed an easy ride with the new generation of activists.

Since Democratic front-runner Clinton argued politely with Black Lives Matter activists last summer, she has stepped up her attacks on racial inequities. "Race still plays a significant role in determining who gets ahead in America and who gets left behind," Clinton said in a speech in Atlanta in October. "Racial profiling is wrong." Her campaign website does not single out racial inequality as an issue. But, in her criminal justice proposals she calls for legislation to end racial profiling by federal, state and local law enforcement officials.[2]

Clinton's leading primary opponent, Sen. Sanders of Vermont, a "democratic socialist," had his own tussles with Black Lives Matter activists. He started his campaign by stating that more jobs are the answer to racial injustice. But after activists disrupted some of his speeches, Sanders unveiled a criminal justice policy to address "violence waged against black and brown Americans: physical, political, legal and economic." He advocates "community policing," which promotes closer ties between officers and neighborhood residents; more racial and ethnic diversity on police forces; and aggressive prosecution of lawbreaking police.[3]

Clinton and Sanders' decisions to embrace the activists' cause was good politics, some analysts say. "For Democrats to win the White House in 2016, African-Americans must give 90 to 95 percent of our votes to that party's nominee," wrote Van Jones, the president of two social justice advocacy groups, Dream Corps and Rebuild the Dream, which promote innovative solutions for America's economy. "Given that fact, younger African-Americans rightfully expect each and every Democratic candidate to explicitly, loudly and enthusiastically address the pain and needs of black lives — to their satisfaction."[4]

Donald Trump, the New York real estate developer who has polled highest among the GOP candidates, has a troubled history on racial matters. In July, he reprised his past support of the conspiracy theory — embraced by white supremacists — that President Obama was not U.S.-born.[5]

When Trump opened his presidential campaign in June, he said of Mexican immigrants: "They're bringing drugs, they're bringing crime, they're rapists."[6]

Then in November, Trump defended the punching of a Black Lives Matter protester who disrupted a speech by the candidate in Birmingham, Ala. "Maybe he should have been roughed up because it was absolutely disgusting what he was doing," Trump said after the incident.[7]

Soon after, Trump announced that 100 black ministers and religious leaders would endorse him at a public event.

to investigate the cause of the riots concluded: "Our nation is moving toward two societies, one black, one white — separate and unequal."[68]

Just after the report was issued, more riots broke out, following the April assassination of the Rev. King, the unquestioned leader of the civil rights movement. Within

But the event instead became a private meeting with a smaller group, where the beating of the protester was discussed. After the session, Trump got one endorsement, from the Rev. Darrell Scott, a Cleveland-area pastor who had helped organize the event.[8]

Before the meeting, the Rev. Al Sharpton, a prominent black civil rights activist, cited the candidate's recent comments about undocumented Mexican immigrants as a reason not to attend. "I don't know how you preach Jesus, a refugee, on Sunday and then deal with a refugee-basher on Monday," Sharpton said.[9]

Two Republican candidates stand apart from their competitors on racial issues. Sen. Marco Rubio of Florida spoke sympathetically of protests against discriminatory policing. "This is a legitimate issue," he said on Fox News in August. "It is a fact that in the African-American community around this country there has been, for a number of years now, a growing resentment toward the way law enforcement and the criminal justice system interacts with the community."[10]

Sen. Rand Paul of Kentucky, spoke along similar lines. "There's no justification for violence, but there is anger," he said, also on Fox. "I am starting to understand where the anger comes from, and that we need to fix things . . . in our system, because [justice] isn't being meted out fairly."[11]

But one other Republican candidate's statements on racial matters have been characterized by some as insulting or hostile. Former Florida Gov. Jeb Bush, asked during a South Carolina appearance how he would attract black voters, said: "Our message is one of hope and aspiration. It isn't one of division and 'get in line and we'll take care of you with free stuff.' "[12] Bush immediately came under fire for seemingly echoing a conservative view that government aid has sapped African-Americans' initiative.

Statistics on race and party affiliation give Republicans little political incentive to reach out to black voters in primary races. Only 11 percent of the black population "lean" Republican, according to a 2015 study by the Pew Research Center. By contrast, 80 percent of African-Americans lean Democratic.[13]

Nevertheless, candidates from both parties have been invited to two February town hall meetings on race-related

issues. DeRay Mckesson, an African-American activist who is helping to organize the sessions, says, "Whoever the next president is will need to engage on a range of issues, including those that don't necessarily align with their viewpoint."

— Peter Katel

[1]Quoted in Kelefa Sanneh, "A Wing and a Prayer," *The New Yorker*, Nov. 30, 2015, http://tinyurl.com/pu9vdsh.

[2]Sabrina Siddiqui, "Black Lives Matter protest interrupts Clinton speech on criminal justice," *The Guardian*, Oct. 30, 2015, http://tinyurl.com/p8dvba3; "Our criminal justice system is out of balance," hillaryclinton.com, undated, http://tinyurl.com/pfneqjb.

[3]"Racial Justice," Bernie 2016, http://tinyurl.com/pp8bfja; Brandon Ellington Patterson, "Black Lives Matter Just Officially Became Part of the Democratic Primary," *Mother Jones*, Oct. 21, 2015, http://tinyurl.com/onc9sjm.

[4]Van Jones, "Disrupting Bernie Sanders and the Democrats: 5 lessons," CNN, Aug. 13, 2015, http://tinyurl.com/ouubgf7.

[5]Meghan Keneally, "Donald Trump's History of Raising Birther Questions About President Obama," ABC News, Sept. 18, 2015, http://tinyurl.com/qdtdlu5; Evan Osnos, "The Fearful and the Frustrated," *The New Yorker*, Aug. 31, 2015, http://tinyurl.com/q4dhgs9.

[6]Adam B. Lerner, "The 10 best lines from Donald Trump's announcement speech," *Politico*, June 16, 2015, http://tinyurl.com/or9bsht.

[7]Jeremy Diamond, "Trump on protester: 'Maybe he should have been roughed up,' " CNN Politics, Nov. 23, 2015.

[8]Michael Barbaro and John Corrales, " 'Love' and Disbelief Follow Donald Trump Meeting With Black Leaders," *The New York Times*, Nov. 30, 2015, http://tinyurl.com/osd7opc.

[9]*Ibid.*

[10]German Lopez, "Marco Rubio shows other Republicans how to respond to Black Lives Matter," *Vox*, Sept. 30, 2015, http://tinyurl.com/otdbvzb.

[11]Katherine Krueger, "Rand Paul: 'Not A Big Fan' Of Black Lives Matter, But I Get 'The Anger,' " TPM Livewire, Oct. 23, 2015, http://tinyurl.com/og9j74m.

[12]Sean Sullivan, "Jeb Bush: Win black voters with aspiration, not 'free stuff,' " *The Washington Post*, Sept. 24, 2015, http://tinyurl.com/nbpnpz8.

[13]"A Deep Dive Into Party Affiliation," Pew Research Center, April 7, 2015, http://tinyurl.com/lbed829.

a week, at Johnson's urging, Congress had passed the Fair Housing Act, outlawing housing discrimination based on race, religion, sex or national origin.

But Nixon — elected months later on a "law and order" platform — blocked efforts by Housing and Urban Development Secretary George Romney to use the new

Acclaimed author Ta-Nehisi Coates, right, discusses racial issues with sociology professor Bruce Western at Harvard University's John F. Kennedy School of Government on Nov. 11, 2015. A MacArthur fellow and national correspondent for The Atlantic, Coates won the 2015 National Book Award for Between *the World and Me,* about the centuries-old legacy of violence inflicted upon African-Americans.

law to "affirmatively further" housing integration. Romney considered the nation's segregated housing patterns a "high-income white noose" around black inner cities and saw poverty in black ghettos as a major cause of the 1967 urban riots.[69]

"Equal opportunity for all Americans in education and housing is essential if we are going to keep our nation from being torn apart," Romney wrote at the time, according to a 2014 investigation by the public interest journalism organization Pro Publica. Romney ordered HUD to reject applications for federal water, sewer and highway projects in places that fostered segregated housing.[70] Nixon promptly shut down Romney's program, explaining in a memo: "I am convinced that while legal segregation is totally wrong, . . . forced integration of housing or education is just as wrong." He acknowledged that his decision would leave blacks and whites living apart and attending separate schools.[71]

Economic Shifts

Major economic shifts followed the civil rights victories of the 1960s. Labor-intensive manufacturing, including textile mills in the South, began moving to Asia and Mexico, putting many unskilled blacks out of work. Many well-paying, blue-collar jobs migrated to predominantly white suburbs.[72]

Drugs, already a presence in some black urban areas, provided steady — albeit illegal — work for some individuals in urban neighborhoods. As addiction spread, so did robberies and burglaries committed by addicts, prompting demands for tougher penalties for users and dealers. In 1973, with strong support from some in the black community, New York Gov. Nelson Rockefeller, a Republican, pushed through tough, new anti-drug laws, the first major attempt to deal with the drug scourge by ratcheting up prison sentences.[73]

Urban crime skyrocketed during a crack cocaine boom in the late 1980s: In Washington, D.C., alone, the rate of homicide deaths of black men jumped eightfold between 1985 and 1991.[74] Congress reacted in 1994 by passing the largest anti-crime bill in U.S. history, mandating life imprisonment without parole after three violent or drug-trafficking convictions and providing nearly $10 billion for prisons.[75]

States adopted similar measures, spurring a major increase in the prison population. From 1990 to 2000, the number of inmates in prisons and jails more than quadrupled, from 474,000 to nearly 2 million. As the prison population rose, so did racial disparity. In 1993, the imprisonment rate among blacks was seven times that of whites. By 2000, nearly 10 percent of all black males ages 25–29 were in prison, compared with 1.1 percent of whites in the same age range.[76]

The skyrocketing prison population led Michelle Alexander, an Ohio State University law professor, to dub the U.S. criminal justice system "the new Jim Crow."[77] She was referring to, among other things, police racial profiling and over-focusing on drug enforcement in African-American communities.[78]

In a forerunner of today's police-violence cellphone videos, a civilian in 1991 recorded four Los Angeles police officers repeatedly kicking and striking an unarmed black motorist, Rodney King, after a high-speed car chase. The video, showing King being struck 56 times with metal batons, aroused nationwide outrage, and the officers were charged with assault and use of excessive force. In 1992, however, an all-white jury acquitted three of them and deadlocked on the fourth, setting off five days of riots in predominantly black South Los Angeles. More than 60 people died in the mayhem. A federal grand jury later indicted the officers on charges of violating King's civil rights; two were convicted and went to prison, and two were acquitted.[79]

Fifteen years later, Obama's election aroused hopes the country had moved into a post-racial era, but reality proved otherwise. A long-running effort on the right to challenge Obama's U.S. citizenship — joined by current Republican presidential candidate Donald Trump — was seen by commentator Fareed Zakaria as "shame[ful] coded racism," a view shared by many others.[80]

Then a series of deaths of black people, mostly at police hands (and one, Trayvon Martin, 17, killed by a neighborhood watch volunteer in Sanford, Fla.), propelled racial issues back to the top of the national agenda.

CURRENT SITUATION

Police on Trial

Police officers face criminal charges in the deaths of two young black men in separate incidents in Baltimore and Chicago. The deaths sparked shock across the nation, riots in Baltimore, dismissal of the Chicago police chief and demands that Chicago's mayor resign.

In Baltimore, six police officers face charges in connection with the death of Freddie Gray, 25, arrested for carrying a knife after running from patrol officers on April 12, 2015. A video showed Gray being dragged, groaning, to a police van, where his hands and legs were shackled but he was not secured with a seatbelt. Hospitalized after losing consciousness, he died from spinal cord injuries allegedly sustained in the van.[81]

In December, William G. Porter was the first officer to go on trial on charges of manslaughter, assault and reckless endangerment — all stemming from his failure to secure Gray with a seatbelt. In mid-December, a mistrial was declared after a jury of seven blacks and five whites deadlocked. Prosecutors said they will retry the officer. The van's driver faces second-degree murder charges, while two other officers are accused of manslaughter and two others with second-degree assault.[82]

Porter's defense focused on his testimony that he had asked Gray if he needed a medic and helped him onto a van bench.[83]

The McDonald shooting in Chicago presents an even starker picture of what can happen in interactions between police and residents of poor, tough neighborhoods. The 17-year-old was shot in Chicago's predominantly black South Side on Oct. 20, 2014, by police responding to a call that a man had punctured a car tire with a knife.

Police reports at the time depicted McDonald advancing on officer Jason Van Dyke and threatening violence by attempting to get up from the ground after being shot.[84]

But a police car dashcam video, released more than a year later, showed McDonald walking away from police and then spinning around and collapsing as he is hit by the first of Van Dyke's 16 bullets.[85] The video became public after a journalist sued to get it released and only hours after Van Dyke was charged with first-degree murder in the death. He was freed on bail, and in late December pleaded not guilty.[86]

A week later, as protests of police practices grew, Mayor Rahm Emanuel fired Police Superintendent Garry F. McCarthy, saying he "had become an issue rather than dealing with the issue." Emanuel later apologized for the killing and took responsibility for it. But protesters demanded that he resign.[87]

Pressure on Emanuel increased again after the post-Christmas police killings of a grandmother and college student. The mayor announced "a major overhaul" of use-of-force policies. Every officer assigned to respond to incidents will be required, by June 1, to carry a non-lethal electric stun gun (Taser).

Meanwhile, new revelations have emerged about the department's treatment of African-Americans. The Cook County prosecutor released another long-held video, of a police shooting of Ronald Johnson III, 25, fatally shot in the back a week before the McDonald incident. Another video, from 2012, showed officers using a stun gun against a jail inmate, then dragging him down a hallway by his handcuffed wrists. The prisoner, Philip Coleman, a University of Chicago graduate with a master's degree from the University of Illinois, was suffering from a mental health crisis when he died in custody, according to his family.[88]

Chicago police shot and killed 70 people, most of them black, in a five-year period ending in 2014 — more than any other of the nation's 10 largest cities, *The New York Times* reported. The city's police oversight panel upheld misconduct claims in only two cases of more than 400 police shootings since 2007. But the city has paid out more than $500 million since 2004 to settle lawsuits or complaints involving police.[89]

In late December, Dean Angelo Sr., president of the Chicago chapter of the Fraternal Order of Police, pointed to the level of violence in some parts of the city, noting

Is Black Lives Matter a valid slogan?

YES
Jack Hunter
Editor, Rare Politics

Written for *CQ Researcher*, January 2016

If I told my fellow allies in the fight against abortion that "unborn lives matter," few would think I was saying that other lives didn't matter. It's hard to imagine abortion opponents even being offended at such an assertion.

They would implicitly understand that I was saying certain lives seem to matter less under our legal system and in our society. If some anti-abortion activists showed poor judgment or even committed violent acts in the name of their cause, few of the like-minded would suggest that this kind of behavior discredited the cause itself.

"Black Lives Matter" makes the same important point.

Overall, it doesn't matter if Black Lives Matter leaders sometimes do questionable things. It doesn't matter if some who champion this slogan sometimes take things to unnecessary and even deplorable extremes.

Those exceptions do not discount certain realities.

Black Lives Matter is an answer to a long-standing societal question: Why are African-Americans targeted and incarcerated at disproportionate rates compared with any other racial group? Why are they more often the victims of police brutality?

And why do more Americans not realize this is happening?

From Ferguson, Mo., and the killing of Michael Brown, to Baltimore, Md., and the death of Freddie Gray, to Charleston, S.C., and the deadly police shooting of Walter Scott, to a Staten Island, N.Y., sidewalk where Eric Garner was choked to death by the police for selling "loose" cigarettes, Americans continue to see incidents, time and again, where black lives do seem to be valued less than others.

Not all of these high-profile incidents are the same. Some are murkier than others, such as in Ferguson. Some are quite clear, such as in Charleston, where a police officer now sits in jail, charged with murder.

But there is a pattern, one that is repeated too often. Many of these incidents that have captured the national imagination and begun important conversations about race have been caught on smartphone cameras.

Smartphone cameras are relatively new, but black Americans are trying to tell us that this type of brutality is not new. These problems did not begin with the advent of smartphones.

What critics like to portray as a movement needlessly stoking racial division is really just an abused minority finally giving voice to the violence they have long faced.

Black Lives Matter is an integral part of the ongoing fight to right unpardonable wrongs.

NO
Derryck Green
Member of Project 21, the National Leadership Network of Black Conservatives

Written for *CQ Researcher*, January 2016

Black Lives Matter is neither a valid slogan nor a legitimate protest movement. The slogan's implication and the movement's emphasis are incongruent; it's an intentional mischaracterization. When one hears the slogan Black Lives Matter, one is led to think of an all-inclusive phrase and social movement that's focused on several pressing issues that have a direct and immediate impact on improving the quality of black lives.

But that's not the intention of the motto. Black Lives Matter isn't all-inclusive. It's very selective, because the only black lives that matter to this protest movement are blacks who were shot and killed by white police officers. Members and supporters continue to propagate the belief, with little evidence, that cops are systematically targeting and unjustly killing black people.

This perspective is thoroughly problematic. First, police shoot more white suspects than black suspects. Second, most of the black suspects who were shot and killed by police in the past year — many of whom were defended by Black Lives Matter — were criminals resisting arrest. Defending black criminals legitimizes and glorifies black criminality. Sanctifying black criminals killed by cops largely comes at the expense of black victims — and the movement's credibility — especially when more serious issues desperately need addressing.

Furthermore, the desire to be singularly identified as people who are targeted only because they're black is to embrace victimization. Black Lives Matter doesn't want any other group intruding on or minimizing its claims of victimhood, which explains the petulant indignation to the phrase "all lives matter." If "all lives matter," blacks' special status as victims is negated and the transparent and dishonest rationale for the existence of this movement is destroyed. The movement uses victimization as leverage for its dishonesty.

The disproportionate focus on the rare, alleged cases of police brutality and shootings intentionally diverts attention from the significant difficulties blacks face. Black women accounted for 37 percent of all abortions in 2012. Black illegitimacy is at 72 percent. Black children are disproportionately trapped in substandard and underperforming schools, preserving the educational gap between black and white students. Black unemployment is twice the national rate. Blacks kill 90 percent of black homicide victims. Don't black lives suffering from these problems matter?

The selective moral outrage that favors black criminals over black lives in general invalidates the social and moral credibility of Black Lives Matter.

that officers seize thousands of guns a year. The department took 6,714 illegal guns off the street as of mid-December, 2015. "That is good policing," he said. "But nobody looks at it that way." Politicians are "throwing us under the bus," he added.[90]

Homicides in Chicago and Baltimore have spiked in recent years. By the end of 2015, Baltimore had suffered 344 homicides, the highest number since 1993, when the city had a population of 100,000 more people. Chicago's homicide number rose by 12.6 percent to 468.[91]

Later, at a meeting of mayors and police chiefs in Washington, Emanuel blamed the rising homicide rate on police second-guessing themselves due to fear of being accused of misconduct. Angelo denied Emanuel's accusation, saying police were "out there working their buns off." But his Baltimore counterpart had said following the Freddie Gray incident that officers were "more afraid of going to jail than getting shot and killed right now."[92]

Campus Revolts

Protests against racism are surging at public and private universities.

At the University of Missouri in Columbia, the entire football team, blacks and whites, refused to play unless university President Tim Wolfe quit or was fired. The players were backing black protesters outraged at what they called Wolfe's failure to respond to their concerns over threats and insults against black students. Wolfe resigned in early November, acknowledging his "inaction" in the face of growing unrest. Chancellor R. Bowen Loftin, who supervised the Columbia campus, stepped down as well (but took another job at the university).[93]

Similar protests spread beyond "Mizzou." At Yale, more than 1,000 students marched in early November after several racially tinged incidents, including the alleged exclusion of students of color from a "White Girls Only" fraternity party — denied by Sigma Alpha Epsilon — and a controversy over a student panel's request that students not don racially or ethnically offensive Halloween costumes, such as blackface or feathered headdresses.[94]

Buildings named for former college presidents whose racism is no longer considered acceptable have become a rallying point for many students. At Georgetown, students held a sit-in over plans to rename two buildings after former Georgetown presidents who had organized slave sales in the 19th century. The university canceled the renamings.[95]

At the University of Maryland in College Park, the state Board of Regents acceded to student demands to remove from the football stadium the name of a former university president, Harry C. Byrd, who had opposed admitting black students.[96]

At Princeton, black students objected to the use of U.S. President Woodrow Wilson's name on several university facilities. Wilson, a former Princeton president, purged many African-Americans from the federal civil service during his years in the White House. In November Princeton President Christopher Eisgruber agreed to consider renaming the facilities, among them the Woodrow Wilson School of International Affairs.[97]

Some see name removal as retroactive judgment. "I don't like Woodrow Wilson any more than they do, but we can't impose modern values on historical figures," said Josh Zuckerman, a Princeton senior and the editor-in-chief of the conservative college magazine, the *Princeton Tory*.[98]

But lawyer Gordon J. Davis of the Venable law firm in New York argued in a *New York Times* op-ed that Wilson's race policies had real and lasting consequences, including for his grandfather, who lost his civil service job. Wilson "ruined the lives of countless talented African-Americans and their families," Davis wrote.[99]

OUTLOOK
Hope and Fear

Those who study race view the near-term future with a mix of hope and fear. For many, the country's demographic shift — already underway — is the key change on the horizon.

By 2060 non-Hispanic whites are expected to decrease from 62 percent of the population to less than 44 percent, as Hispanics come to represent more than one-quarter of the country. African-Americans are expected to be only slightly above their current 13 percent level.[100]

For Texas A&M's Feagin, the demographic transformation and what he sees as stepped-up white hostility toward African-Americans and other nonwhites are "like two trains on the same track headed toward each other," illustrated by what he calls "this dramatic increase in white protectionism to protect our privileges that you see so dramatically in Republican candidates."

Trump's incendiary language about Mexican immigrants is a danger sign for all people of color, Feagin says. "We've had coded language, but to call Mexican immigrants rapists — ordinary working people accused of being rapists — forget all the subtle stuff," he says. "This reflects the levels of white fear of losing privilege and income and wealth."

Yet one view from abroad is that Americans are facing up to their racial issues, in sharp contrast to Western Europe, which has failed to integrate Arab and African immigrants, many of them Muslims who have lived in Europe for three generations. Continuing tensions in Parisian suburbs with big immigrant populations since riots in 2005, and recent anti-immigrant violence in Germany, are only the most obvious signs of the strained relations, aggravated by recent terrorist attacks in France and Belgium.[101]

Damaso Reyes, a black Dominican-American photojournalist from New York now based in Barcelona, says the United States is far more willing than Europe to confront race in its social, political and cultural dimensions. "Black people, white people, brown people are all having conversations about race all the time, in social media, schools and history books," he says. "When a Texas history book says that 'workers' were brought to America from Africa, there is a huge outcry: 'Call slavery, slavery.' To me, that is a positive thing."[102]

For Rockeymoore of Global Policy Solutions, solving institutional racism is the most urgent task facing today's activists. "If we don't address structural racism in this country, within 40 to 50 years we'll look like apartheid South Africa or pre-1950 America in terms of opportunity or lack thereof," she says.

Georgetown's Hinkson doesn't think much is going to change in the next 20 years with regard to deep-seated patterns of racial separation. "The very fact that we haven't been able to say that integrating schools by race and class is the best way to eliminate gaps" in academic performance "tells you that as far as our schools being less segregated 20 years from now, that is not going to happen."

Fortner, of City University of New York, is somewhat more hopeful. "I'm a perpetual optimist when it comes to the American project," he says. However, he adds, he doesn't think improvement will come rapidly, given the polarization and gridlock in the political system.

"Washington is broken. If we find a way out of the current political morass, we could race to a much better future," Fortner says. "But if the system remains so gridlocked, it's going to be a slow walk to progress."

NOTES

1. Quoted in Monica Davey and Mitch Smith, "Anger Over Killing by Police Halts Shopping in Chicago," *The New York Times*, Nov. 27, 2015, http://tinyurl.com/pppahla.

2. "Chicago Mayor Cutting Short Cuba Vacation After Police Shooting," Reuters, *The New York Times*, Dec. 28, 2015, http://tinyurl.com/nhdf5cg; "Prosecutors Defend Urging No Charges in Tamir Rice Shooting," The Associated Press, *The New York Times*, Dec. 30, 2015, http://tinyurl.com/ns9eghq.

3. Maya Rhodan, "Congress Now Has More Black Lawmakers Than Ever Before," *Time*, Jan. 6, 2015, http://tinyurl.com/jqawbw3.

4. Nate Silver, "Black Americans Are Killed At 12 Times The Rate of People In Other Developed Countries," *FiveThirtyEight:Politics*, June 18, 2015, http://tinyurl.com/q6o4n38; Justin Wolfers, David Leonhardt, Kevin Quealy, "1.5 Million Missing Black Men," *The Upshot* blog, *The New York Times*, April 20, 2015, http://tinyurl.com/z7f954b; "Digest of Education Statistics," National Center for Education Statistics, 2014, http://tinyurl.com/qerhs5c; Kenneth D. Kochanek, Elizabeth Arias and Robert N. Anderson, "Leading Causes of Death Contributing to Decrease in Life Expectancy Gap Between Black and White Populations: United States, 1999–2013," U.S. Centers for Disease Control and Prevention, "NCHS Data Brief No 218," November 2015, http://tinyurl.com/jcntjbk; and Rakesh Kochhar and Richard Fry, "Wealth inequality has widened along racial, ethnic lines since end of Great Recession," Pew Research Center, Dec. 12, 2014, http://tinyurl.com/kww2vpo.

5. Kimberly Kindy *et al.*, "A Year of Reckoning: Police fatally Shoot Nearly 1,000," *The Washington Post*, Dec. 26, 2015, http://tinyurl.com/zx95ptf; (with updated statistics) http://tinyurl.com/nrsl3xr; Jon Swaine *et al.*, "Young black men killed by US police

at highest rate in year of 1,134 deaths," *The Guardian*, Dec. 31, 2015, http://tinyurl.com/zc39qv2.

6. Kochhar and Fry, *ibid.*

7. "The War on Marijuana in Black and White," American Civil Liberties Union, June, 2013, p. 49, http://tinyurl.com/jycxybp; David Weigel, "The Avenger Without a Mask," *Slate*, Aug. 5, 2014, http://tinyurl.com/jvc9jkn.

8. Ta-Nehisi Coates, "The Case for Reparations," *The Atlantic*, June 2014, http://tinyurl.com/nopprgt.

9. Sandra L. Colby and Jennifer M. Ortman, "Projections of the Size and Composition of the U.S. Population: 2014 to 2060," U.S. Census Bureau, March 2015, p. 9, http://tinyurl.com/zvobj4q.

10. "National American Indian Holocaust Museum," National Congress of American Indians, Resolution #TUL-13–005, 2013, http://tinyurl.com/j2g4hay; Guenter Lewy, "Were American Indians the Victims of Genocide?" History News Network, September 2004, http://tinyurl.com/nhuz248. William D. Carrigan and Clive Webb, "When Americans Lynched Mexicans," *The New York Times*, Feb. 20, 2015, http://tinyurl.com/n2yruap.

11. "National Museum of African American History and Culture," *Smithsonian*, updated Oct. 2, 2015, http://tinyurl.com/mrxe8b.

12. "Report of the National Advisory Commission on Civil Disorders, Summary, Chapter 2," Homeland Security Digital Library, 1968, http://tinyurl.com/jzsccqz.

13. Eliott C. McLaughlin, John Murgatroyd and Kevin Conlon, "Charlotte jury hears vastly different accounts of Jonathan Ferrell's death," CNN, Aug. 6, 2015, http://tinyurl.com/gv54r2g; Peter Holley, "New video shows Texas police officer pulling gun on teenagers at pool party," *The Washington Post*, June 8, 2015, http://tinyurl.com/okvksap; Emma Brown, T. Rees Shapiro and Elahe Izadi, "S.C. sheriff fires officer who threw student across a classroom," *The Washington Post*, Oct. 28, 2015, http://tinyurl.com/hch2ajo.

14. Quoted in Richard Pérez-Peña and Timothy Williams, "Glare of Video is Shifting Public's View of Police," *The New York Times*, July 30, 2015, http://tinyurl.com/nf57czh.

15. Quoted in Alan Blinder and Marc Santora, "Officer Who Killed Walter Scott Is Fired, and Police Chief Denounces Shooting," *The New York Times*, April 8, 2015, http://tinyurl.com/pow99ay.

16. Quoted in Melanie Eversley and Jessica Estepa, "Across the USA, videos of police killings spark protests, drive conversation," *USA Today*, Dec. 8, 2015, http://tinyurl.com/grt92oq.

17. James B. Comey, Georgetown University, Washington, D.C., Feb. 12, 2015, http://tinyurl.com/mckgtf4.

18. For background, see Peter Katel, "Race Relations," *CQ Researcher*, "Hot Topic" report, May 20, 2015.

19. "We The Protesters, Campaign Zero," Campaign Zero, http://tinyurl.com/p6vknog.

20. According to the most recent statistics, 51 percent of 12,253 homicide victims in 2013 were African-American: "Crime in the United States, 2013," FBI, undated, http://tinyurl.com/oxo5mhu.

21. "FBI Releases 2013 Crime Statistics from the National Incident-Based Reporting System," FBI press release, Dec. 22, 2014, http://tinyurl.com/optoe5d; Amy Sherman, "An updated look at statistics on black-on-black murders," *Politifact Florida*, May 21, 2015, http://tinyurl.com/nmvpj4l.

22. Sharon LaFraniere and Andrew W. Lehren, "The Disproportionate Risks of Driving While Black," *The New York Times*, Oct. 24, 2015, http://tinyurl.com/pj9ukke.

23. "Full Video: Hillary Clinton meets Black Lives Matter," "The Rachel Maddow Show," Aug. 20, 2015, http://tinyurl.com/pn9s2ex.

24. David McCabe, "Clinton focuses on race, inequality," *The Hill*, April 29, 2015, http://tinyurl.com/pfkw3rb.

25. For background, see Kenneth Jost, "Housing Discrimination," *CQ Researcher*, Nov. 6, 2015, pp. 937–960.

26. Coates, *op. cit.*; Joe R. Feagin, *Racist America: Roots, Current Realities, and Future Reparations* (2014 3rd. ed.), pp. 306–308.

27. "A Policy Agenda for Closing the Racial Wealth Gap," Center for Global Policy Solutions, 2015, http://tinyurl.com/ov256s5.

28. *Board of Education of Oklahoma City Public Schools v. Dowell*, 498 U.S. 239 (1991), http://tinyurl.com/qc73rxq; Linda Greenhouse, "Justices Rule Mandatory Busing May Go, Even if Races Stay Apart," *The New York Times*, Jan. 16, 1991, http://tinyurl.com/nbrlw6d.

29. Peter Applebome, "Schools See Re-emergence Of 'Separate but Equal,' " *The New York Times*, April 8, 1997, http://tinyurl.com/om4gtqc.

30. Gary Orfield *et al.*, "Brown at 60: Great Progress, a Long Retreat and an Uncertain Future," The Civil Rights Project, UCLA, May 15, 2014, p. 12, http://tinyurl.com/n9cok4e; for background, see Reed Karaim, "Race and Education," *CQ Researcher*, Sept. 5, 2014, pp. 721–744.

31. *Ibid.*, p. 2.

32. "The Nation's Report Card: 2013 Mathematics and Reading: Grade 12 Assessment," Nation's Assessment of Educational Progress, undated, http://tinyurl.com/mn6snpf.

33. "Why Charter Schools Work," Center for Education Reform, undated, http://tinyurl.com/qdmokdf.

34. Leslie Hinkson, "Racial Issues in Urban Schools," TEDx Talks, Nov. 24, 2015, http://tinyurl.com/oxjklhx.

35. Hugh Thomas, *The Slave Trade: The Story of the Atlantic Slave Trade: 1440–1870* (1997), pp. 804–805; "The Abolition of the Slave Trade," undated, The Schomburg Center for Research in Black Culture, http://tinyurl.com/osj9pn9.

36. *Ibid.*, Thomas, pp. 501–502.

37. Sean Wilentz, "Constitutionally, Slavery Is No National Institution," *The New York Times*, Sept. 16, 2015, http://tinyurl.com/nb99yrp.

38. Patrick Rael, "Sean Wilentz is wrong about the Founders, Slavery, and the Constitution," African American Intellectual History Society, Sept. 29, 2015, http://tinyurl.com/q4oe3jb.

39. James McPherson, *Battle Cry of Freedom: The Civil War Era* (1988), p. 73.

40. *Ibid.*, pp. 78–79.

41. Elizabeth R. Varon, *Disunion! The Coming of the American Civil War, 1789–1859* (2008), pp. 298–304.

42. F. Michael Higginbotham, *Ghosts of Jim Crow: Ending Racism in Post-Racial America* (2013), pp. 64–66.

43. *Ibid.*, p. 64.

44. *Ibid.*, pp. 68–69.

45. Charles Lane, *The Day Freedom Died: The Colfax Massacre, the Supreme Court, and the Betrayal of Reconstruction* (2008), Kindle edition, no page numbers.

46. *Ibid.*

47. *Ibid.*

48. "Lynching in America: Confronting the Legacy of Racial Terror, Report Summary," Equal Justice Initiative, 2015, http://tinyurl.com/pu8gqwd.

49. Douglas Blackmon, *Slavery by Another Name: The Re-Enslavement of Black Americans from the Civil War to World War II* (2008), pp. 395–396.

50. Ira Katznelson, *When Affirmative Action Was White* (2005), pp. 24–52.

51. *Ibid.*, pp. 24–25.

52. *Ibid.*, p. 26.

53. *Ibid.*, p. 29.

54. "History and Timeline," U.S. Department of Veterans Affairs, undated, http://tinyurl.com/mgx-7vzu.

55. Katznelson, *op. cit.*, pp. 126, 129. Also see J. Todd Moye, *Freedom Flyers: The Tuskegee Airmen of World War II* (2012).

56. *Ibid.*, Katznelson, p. 115.

57. Isabel Wilkerson, *The Warmth of Other Suns: The Epic Story of America's Great Migration* (2010), pp. 8–11.

58. Coates, *op. cit.*

59. *Brown v. Board of Education of Topeka*, 237 US 483 (1954), http://tinyurl.com/o2cl9o9.

60. Taylor Branch, *Parting the Waters: America in the King Years, 1954–1963* (1988).

61. For background, see Kenneth Jost, "Voting Controversies," *CQ Researcher*, Feb. 21, 2014, pp. 169–192.

62. Bridget Murphy, "Effects of Desegregation Busing Battles Linger in Boston," The Associated Press, in

The Huffington Post, April 7, 2013, http://tinyurl
.com/p6pwxqj.

63. For background, see Kenneth Jost, "Supreme Court
Controversies," *CQ Researcher*, Sept. 28, 2012,
pp. 813–840.

64. Reed Jordan, "America's public schools remain highly
segregated," Urban Institute, Aug. 27, 2014, http://
tinyurl.com/pp79kye.

65. "President Johnson's Special Message to Congress: The
American Promise," LBJ Presidential Library, March
15, 1965, http://tinyurl.com/qaq4l6p.

66. Quoted in James Boyd, "Nixon's southern strategy:
'It's All in the Charts,' " *The New York Times
Magazine*, May 17, 1970, http://tinyurl.com/
nuusnn8.

67. Earl Black and Merle Black, *The Rise of Southern
Republicans* (2003), p. 220.

68. "Report of the National Advisory Commission on
Civil Disorders," *op. cit.*, "Summary, Introduction."

69. See Nikole Hannah-Jones, "Living Apart: How the
Government Betrayed a Landmark Civil Rights
Law," *ProPublica*, June 25, 2015, http://tinyurl
.com/8jzwt3w.

70. *Ibid.*

71. *Ibid.*

72. Orlando Patterson, with Ethan Fosse, eds., *The
Cultural Matrix: Understanding Black Youth* (2015),
p. 127.

73. Michael Javen Fortner, *Black Silent Majority: The
Rockefeller Drug Laws and the Politics of Punishment*
(2015), Kindle edition, no page numbers.

74. For background, see Peter Katel, "Fighting Crime,"
CQ Researcher, Feb. 8, 2008, pp. 121–144.

75. JoAnne O'Bryant, "Crime Control: The Federal
Response," Congressional Research Service, updated
March 5, 2003, pp. 3–4, http://tinyurl
.com/7x9hhdr.

76. "The Punishing Decade: Prison and Jail Estimates at
the Millennium," Justice Policy Institute, May 2000,
http://tinyurl.com/cp2xa84; Allen J. Beck and Paige
M. Harrison, "Prisoners in 2000," *Bureau of Justice
Statistics Bulletin*, August 2001, p. 11, http://tinyurl.
com/hpucn5l; Allen J. Beck and Darrell K. Gilliard,

"Prisoners in 1994," Bureau of Justice Statistics,
August 1995, p. 1, http://tinyurl.com/z9s6a4q.

77. Michelle Alexander, *The New Jim Crow: Mass
Incarceration in the Age of Colorblindness* (2010).

78. *Ibid.*, pp. 58–88.

79. Lou Cannon, "National Guard Called to Stem
Violence After L.A. Officers' Acquittal in Beating,"
The Washington Post, April 30, 1992, http://tinyurl.
com/zocva6x; "A timeline of events in Rodney King's
life," CNN, June 17, 2012, http://tinyurl.com/
zle595t.

80. Ben Smith and Byron Tau, "Birtherism: Where it all
began," *Politico*, April 24, 2011, http://tinyurl.com/
qcm7uuq; Ari Melber, "The Nation: Confronting
Trump's Coded Racism," *The Nation* (NPR), April
27, 2011, http://tinyurl.com/3qfp93p.

81. "The Latest: Medical Examiner: Gray's spine was
'kinked,' " The Associated Press, Dec. 4, 2015,
tinyurl.com/1o428x7o; Justin Jouvenal, Lynh Bui
and DeNeen L. Brown, "First trial in death of
Freddie Gray begins in a city still on edge," *The
Washington Post*, Nov. 30, 2015, http://tinyurl.com/
j38wwhm.

82. Sheryl Gay Stolberg, "Police Officers Charged in
Freddie Gray's Death to Be Tried in Baltimore," *The
New York Times*, Sept. 10, 2015, http://tinyurl.com/
nanbfwv; Justin Jouvenal and Lynh Bui, "New trial
date isn't set for Baltimore officer accused in Freddie
Gray's death," *The Washington Post*, Dec. 17, 2015,
http://tinyurl.com/hyz9wss.

83. Peter Hermann, "Friends and neighbors remember
Freddie Gray," *The Washington Post*, April 24, 2015,
http://tinyurl.com/mmbvo7p.

84. "Laquan McDonald police reports differ dramatically
from video," *Chicago Tribune*, Dec. 5, 2015, http://
tinyurl.com/nmo4my5; "Crime Trends in Archer
Heights," *Chicago Tribune*, Nov. 19-Dec. 19, 2015,
http://tinyurl.com/gwnlerx.

85. Jason Meisner, Jeremy Gorner and Steve Schmadeke,
"Chicago releases dash-cam video of fatal shooting
after cop charged with murder," *Chicago Tribune*,
Nov. 24, 2015, http://tinyurl.com/nfhhx98.
"Changes to Be Announced in Chicago Police
Training, Tasers," The Associated Press, *The New*

York Times, Dec. 30, 2015, http://tinyurl.com/oqgh2d3.

86. Ashley Southall, "Reporter Who Forced Release of Laquan McDonald Video Is Barred From News Event," *The New York Times*, Nov. 25, 2015, http://tinyurl.com/q6gl2g2.

87. Rick Pearson, Bill Ruthhart and John Byrne, "Emanuel recall bill, council hearing, show political flank-covering in McDonald case," *Chicago Tribune*, Dec. 16, 2015, http://tinyurl.com/joe2523; Amber Phillips, "Rahm Emanuel is in deep, deep trouble," *The Washington Post*, Dec. 10, 2015, http://tinyurl.com/nhg5kos.

88. Don Babwin, "1 After Another, Chicago Police Videos Made Public," The Associated Press, Dec. 10, 2015, http://tinyurl.com/nlhs8em.

89. Monica Davey and Timothy Williams, "Chicago Pays Millions but Punishes Few in Killings by Police," *The New York Times*, Dec. 17, 2015, http://tinyurl.com/ot78klo.

90. Quoted in *ibid.*, "Changes to Be Announced in Chicago Police Training, Tasers."

91. "Josh Sanburn, "Chicago Shootings and Murders Surged in 2015," *Time*, Jan. 2, 2016, http://tinyurl.com/os3q9ay; Kevin Rector, "Deadliest year in Baltimore history ends with 344 homicides," *The Baltimore Sun*, Jan. 1, 2016, http://tinyurl.com/z9dxs5s.

92. Quoted in John Byrne, "Emanuel blames Chicago crime uptick on officers second-guessing themselves," *Chicago Tribune*, Oct. 13, 2015, http://tinyurl.com/ofxw9wp; Josh Sanburn, "What's Behind Baltimore's Record-Setting Rise in Homicides," *Time*, June 2, 2015, http://tinyurl.com/ngdg4pw.

93. Susan Svrluga, "U. Missouri president, chancellor resign over handling of racial incidents," *The Washington Post*, Nov. 9, 2015, http://tinyurl.com/jv6p7kp.

94. Avianne Tan, "The Allegations of Racism at Yale That Culminated in Over 1,000 Marching for Justice on Campus," ABC News, Nov. 10, 2015, http://tinyurl.com/pkcn35y. Liam Stack, "Yale's Halloween Advice Stokes a Racially Charged Debate," *The New York Times*, Nov. 8, 2015, http://tinyurl.com/oxu7y3o.

95. Katherine Shaver, "Georgetown University to rename two buildings that reflect school's ties to slavery," *The Washington Post*, Nov 15, 2015, http://tinyurl.com/jsj3pdq.

96. Yvonne Wenger, "Byrd Stadium to become Maryland Stadium after regents vote," *The Baltimore Sun*, Dec. 11, 2015, http://tinyurl.com/zapmvgb.

97. Mary Hui, "After protests, Princeton debates Woodrow Wilson's legacy," *The Washington Post*, Nov. 23, 2015, http://tinyurl.com/hplwgqs; William Keylor, "The long-forgotten racial attitudes and policies of Woodrow Wilson," *Professor Voices*, Boston University, March 4, 2013, http://tinyurl.com/nas8ok9.

98. Quoted in Hui, *op. cit.*

99. Gordon J. Davis, "What Woodrow Wilson Cost My Grandfather," *The New York Times*, Nov. 24, 2015, http://tinyurl.com/p36bvol.

100. Colby and Ortman, *op. cit.*

101. Angelique Chrisafis, " 'Nothing's changed': 10 years after French riots, banlieues remain in crisis," *The Guardian*, Oct. 22, 2015, http://tinyurl.com/ngd7rerj; Alison Smale, "Anti-Immigrant Violence in Germany Spurs New Debate on Hate Speech," *The New York Times*, Oct. 21, 2015, http://tinyurl.com/oxu7y3o.

102. Manny Fernandez and Christine Hauser, "Texas Mother Teaches Textbook Company a Lesson on Accuracy," *The New York Times*, Oct. 5, 2015, http://tinyurl.com/pwpe3oe.

BIBLIOGRAPHY

Selected Sources

Books

Alexander, Michelle, *The New Jim Crow: Mass Incarceration in the Age of Colorblindness*, *The New Press*, 2010.
An Ohio State University law professor's book helped spur efforts to change the nation's criminal justice system.

Coates, Ta-Nehisi, *Between the World and Me*, *Spiegel & Grau*, 2015.

A journalist's brief but searing memoir-essay explores life as a black man in today's America.

Feagin, Joe R., *Racist America: Roots, Current Realities, and Future Reparations*, Routledge, 2014.
A Texas A&M sociologist specializing in race, describes government policies that implicitly or explicitly provided preferential treatment for whites.

Fortner, Michael Javen, *Black Silent Majority: The Rockefeller Drug Laws and the Politics of Punishment*, Harvard University Press, 2015.
Examining the impact of the country's first drug-crackdown laws, a City University of New York professor of urban studies analyzes anti-crime sentiment in the African-American community.

Oliver, Melvin L., and Thomas M. Shapiro, *Black Wealth/White Wealth: A New Perspective on Racial Inequality*, Routledge Taylor & Francis, 2006.
Sociologists from the University of California, Santa Barbara, and Brandeis University, respectively, updated a 1995 book that drew attention to how profoundly discriminatory practices have affected black asset-building.

Riley, Jason L., *Please Stop Helping Us: How Liberals Make It Harder for Blacks to Succeed*, Encounter Books, 2014.
A senior fellow at the center-right Manhattan Institute sums up the black conservative vision: Personal choices and a culture of "victimhood" — rather than historical and economic forces — explain conditions in poor African-American neighborhoods.

Articles

Domenech, Ben, "Are Republicans For Freedom Or White Identity Politics?" *The Federalist*, Aug. 21, 2015, http://tinyurl.com/nny5h66.
The publisher of a conservative magazine worries that Republican presidential candidate Donald Trump's focus on white grievances could push his party into European-style semi-fascist populism.

Mckesson, DeRay, "Reflections on Meeting with Senator Bernie Sanders and Secretary Hillary Clinton, and the #DemDebate," *Medium*, Oct. 15, 2015, http://tinyurl.com/o5tumj4.

A leading activist reports on how top Democratic candidates greeted proposals from members of the Black Lives Matter protest movement.

Rutenberg, Jim, "A Dream Undone," *The New York Times Magazine*, July 29, 2015, http://tinyurl.com/p8hmfdt.
A veteran correspondent chronicles a long campaign to weaken the 1965 Voting Rights Act based on the argument that discriminatory conditions have changed in the South.

Smith, Jamil, "BlackLivesMatter Protesters Are Not the Problem," *The New Republic*, Aug. 10, 2015, http://tinyurl.com/p5b473e.
An editor at a liberal magazine argues that activists are justified in confronting friendly presidential candidates on racial justice issues.

Walk-Morris, Tatiana, "Blacks Are Challenged to Buy From Black-Owned Businesses to Close Gap," *The New York Times*, Nov. 15, 2015, http://tinyurl.com/pmasdk3.
A Chicago lawyer bought only from black-owned businesses for one year, prompting an examination of the effectiveness of grassroots efforts to close the black-white wealth gap.

Williams, Vanessa, "For Clinton, a challenge to keep black voters energized about her campaign," *The Washington Post*, Nov. 1, 2015, http://tinyurl.com/oxaxqbu.
A political reporter chronicles the Democratic frontrunner's efforts to maintain support of a vital part of the party's constituency.

Reports and Studies

Azerrad, David, and Rea S. Hederman Jr., "Defending the Dream: Why Income Inequality Doesn't Threaten Opportunity," *Heritage Foundation*, Sept. 13, 2012, http://tinyurl.com/d28ppb7.
Two staff members of a conservative think tank conclude that the high rate of single-parent households among African-Americans explains the black-white wealth gap.

Orfield, Gary, *et al.*, "Brown at 60: Great Progress, a Long Retreat and an Uncertain Future," *The Civil*

Rights Project, University of California, Los Angeles, **May 15, 2014, http://tinyurl.com/q8v3t6b.** Four education scholars conclude that public schools increasingly are segregated by race and class, even though legally mandated segregation has disappeared.

Traub, Amy, and Catherine Ruetschlin, "The Racial Wealth Gap: Why Policy Matters," *Demos,* **March 10, 2015, http://tinyurl.com/mxltzn5.** A liberal think tank analyzes government policies that contribute to the wealth gap and others that could narrow the divide.

For More Information

ACLU, 125 Broad St., New York, NY 10004; 212-549-2500; https://www.aclu.org/issues/racial-justice. Litigates on a variety of race-related issues, including discrimination in school discipline and racial profiling by police.

Campaign Zero, www.joincampaignzero.org/#vision. An outgrowth of the Black Lives Matter movement; has proposed ways to help curb police use of force.

Global Policy Solutions, 1300 L St., N.W., Washington, DC 20005; 202-265-5111; http://globalpolicysolutions.com. A research and advocacy organization that focuses on equality of economic opportunity, including racial equity.

Project 21, National Leadership Network of Black Conservatives, www.nationalcenter.org/P21Index.html. Provides an outlet for commentary by African-Americans of the political right on topics such as affirmative action and immigration.

Scholars Network on Black Masculinity, University of Michigan, Department of Sociology, 500 South State St., Ann Arbor, MI 48109; 734-647-4444; http://thescholarsnetwork.org/index.html. Studies how to improve life possibilities for black men.

The Sentencing Project, 1705 DeSales St., N.W., Washington, DC 20036; 202-628-0871; www.sentencingproject.org. A criminal justice reform advocacy think tank.

12

Prisoners and Mental Illness

Sarah Glazer

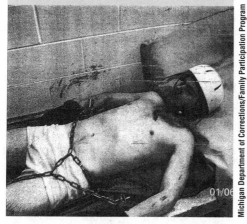

Michigan Department of Corrections/Family Participation Program

Kevin DeMott, 19, is shackled in his cell at a Michigan adult prison in January 2011, a helmet protecting against his head-banging. Kevin's mother says the prison kept him in solitary confinement for four months to punish him for behaviors stemming from his bipolar disorder and did not treat his illness. As states have lost some $4 billion in mental illness treatment funds in recent years, hospitals and mental health clinics have closed, and many mentally ill people ended up in jails and prisons.

From *CQ Researcher*, March 13, 2015.

The photo is shocking. A young man wearing a helmet lies chained to a bed. The wall behind him shows a smear of blood where he had been banging his head.[1]

The helmet and chains were "the treatment that was provided" at the Michigan adult prison where 19-year-old Kevin DeMott had been held in solitary confinement for four months, says his mother, Lois DeMott.

Kevin had long been troubled: a bipolar-disorder diagnosis at 11, juvenile detention for trying to rob a pizza store with a toy gun at 13 and adult prison at 15. In prison he was cited dozens of times for breaking rules and sentenced to more time behind bars for assaulting a guard.

Kevin's mother says the prison imposed solitary confinement to punish behavior rooted in his mental illness — throwing objects off a balcony in a rage, breaking light bulbs to cut himself and ripping a so-called "suicide gown" to make a noose to hang himself.

When photographed in solitary, in January 2011, Kevin was receiving no medication for his condition and "was very depressed," Lois DeMott says.

The plight of mentally ill inmates — and how to treat their condition while holding them accountable for crimes and keeping prisons safe — is receiving new attention from criminal justice and psychiatric experts. Mental health advocates say budget cuts in community mental health services have led police and courts to lock up many troubled individuals in jails and prisons that are ill-equipped to treat them. At the same time, they say, many inmates are inappropriately placed in solitary confinement, causing or exacerbating mental problems.

Even so, some experts say that only a minority of the crimes committed by mentally ill people are due to their illness, citing other factors such as using drugs or associating with criminals. Thus treatment alone will not prevent many mentally ill offenders from returning to jail, they contend. Meanwhile, unions representing prison guards defend the use of solitary confinement as necessary to keep inmates from harming themselves or others.

More than one in five Michigan prisoners in 2009 had severe mental disabilities, according to a University of Michigan study, but 65 percent of those had received no treatment in the previous 12 months.[2]

Echoing a nationwide trend that began in the 1960s, Michigan closed three-quarters of its 16 state psychiatric hospitals between 1987 and 2003. The patients could be better served, it was thought, in community mental health centers. But budget cuts reduced those community services, and Michigan's prisons and jails have become, in effect, its largest mental hospitals.[3]

More people with serious mental illness are now in a prison or jail in 44 states than are housed in those states' largest psychiatric hospitals, according to a survey published last year by the Treatment Advocacy Center, a group in Arlington, Va., that advocates more timely and effective treatment for people with mental illness.[4]

However, states have lost some $4 billion in treatment funds in the last few years, forcing them to close or shrink mental health clinics and hospitals. As that's happened, more mentally ill inmates have wound up in jails and prisons, and corrections officials say they aren't able to deal with the trend.

In the Madison, Wis., area, Dane County Sheriff Dave Mahoney says he must put suicidal or dangerous mentally ill inmates in solitary confinement because he

Jail Inmates Have High Rate of Mental Illness

Women in America's local jails are about six times more likely — and men about 4.5 times more likely — to suffer from a serious mental illness than people in the general population.

Percentage of Serious Mental Illness, in Jails vs. General Population, by Gender

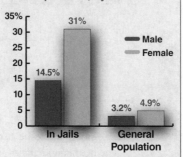

Source: "Incarceration's Front Door: The Misuse of Jails in America," Vera Institute of Justice, February 2015, p. 12, http://tinyurl.com/lyuun67; original research from Henry J. Steadman, *et al.*, "Prevalence of Serious Mental Illness Among Jail Inmates," *Psychiatric Services,* June 2009, http://tinyurl.com/q8j9mke

has no mental health facilities. It's "inhumane" and a "human rights violation," Mahoney says, but he's been unable to persuade the county to provide the more than $100 million needed to update his jail.

About 15 percent of men and 31 percent of women in local jails suffer from serious mental illnesses, such as schizophrenia, bipolar disorder or major depression — rates four to six times that of the general population.[5] Most are in jail for misdemeanors — often petty crimes, such as trespassing, disorderly conduct or drug use, resulting from a combination of homelessness and mental illness.[6]

Sheriff Thomas J. Dart last year proclaimed Chicago's Cook County Jail the state's largest psychiatric hospital.[7] On any given day, about a third of its 10,000 inmates are mentally ill, according to the sheriff.[8]

Jails are the wrong place to treat mentally ill people, Dart wrote, calling it a "nightmare" that rising numbers of mentally ill people have been caught in the web of the criminal justice system ever since the shuttering of mental hospitals and clinics. Those who land in his jail are mainly charged with "crimes of survival," such as prostitution and trespassing, he said. "They are, for the most part, good people who suffer from an illness beyond their control and simply need their government to have its priorities straight."

For a fraction of the cost of incarcerating a mentally ill inmate, he continued, "we can empower new community health centers and establish comprehensive discharge planning. It's humane and fiscally prudent."[9]

The situation has become especially acute in the nation's local and county jails.[10] On one weekend last year, 48 percent of some 1,000 inmates at the Dane County Jail were taking at least one psychotropic medication for a mental illness, according to a snapshot census by the jail. Mahoney says the number of mentally ill inmates has risen since last April, when, to save money, Madison's state hospital closed its unit for people with mental health emergencies brought in by police.

To avoid the five-hour roundtrip to the nearest state mental hospital, in Oshkosh, police instead are charging mentally ill people with crimes and taking them to jail because "they know I have full-time mental health care," Mahoney says.[11]

Often, a mentally ill person lands in jail for disorderly conduct when "the 'crime' is the fact that he's off his medications," Mahoney says.

The Dane County Jail is unusual in providing 24-hour mental health care delivered by a psychiatrist or staff psychiatric social worker. Elsewhere, 83 percent of inmates with mental illness received no treatment for their condition after admission, according to a 2015 report by the Vera Institute of Justice, a research group in New York.[12]

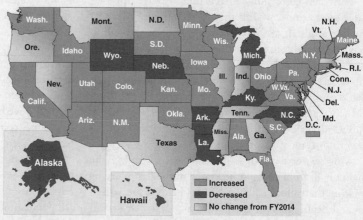

Fewer States to Raise Mental Health Spending

Twenty-eight states and the District of Columbia plan to increase spending on mental health services in fiscal 2015 — seven fewer than in 2014. Eleven states plan no change in their mental health budgets, while 10 say they will cut spending.

Changes in State Mental Health Budgets, Fiscal 2014 to Fiscal 2015

Legend:
- Increased
- Decreased
- No change from FY2014

Source: "State Mental Health Legislation 2014: Trends, Themes & Effective Practices," National Alliance on Mental Illness, December 2014, p. 25, http://tinyurl.com/osoj5c6

Even prisoners who receive treatment can have periods when their symptoms return. They may throw feces at guards or become belligerent. According to a forthcoming Human Rights Watch report, corrections guards respond to such behavior by subjecting mentally ill prisoners — more often than other inmates — to "unnecessary and even gratuitous use of force," ranging from the use of pepper spray and stun guns to outright brutality.[13]

Prison officers "rarely receive training to help them understand mental illness and how it can affect conduct," the report says.

Mentally ill inmates also are more likely than other prisoners to end up in solitary confinement for breaking rules. They can remain isolated for up to 23 hours a day, a form of sensory deprivation that is stressful even for those without mental health issues, say psychiatrists and advocates for the mentally ill.

"Even if they don't get worse, they don't get better because in general they're not given treatment," says

Renee Binder, president-elect of the American Psychiatric Association, which says prolonged solitary should be avoided for the seriously mentally ill.

"You begin to turn on yourself," says James Burns, 27, who spent almost two years of a five-year prison sentence for armed robbery in solitary in an adult prison in Colorado, starting at age 15. "I would punch the walls until my knuckles bled. Hurting myself felt better than feeling nothing at all."

Recent lawsuits on behalf of inmates produced a series of court decisions declaring it a violation of the Constitution's prohibition against "cruel and unusual punishment" to place seriously mentally ill prisoners in solitary. As a result, some prisons have been developing specialized housing and treatment programs for the mentally ill.

This year, Massachusetts became the third state to prohibit solitary for those with serious mental illness. Others, including Montana, New Jersey and New

Mexico, are considering similar laws for psychologically vulnerable populations such as mentally ill or juvenile inmates.[14] As a result of litigation, New York recently became the largest state to limit solitary confinement for young people, declaring it off-limits for those under 18. New York City officials went even further recently, banning solitary for inmates 21 and younger at its Rikers Island jail, effective next year.[15]

However, corrections officers' unions have opposed such restrictions, saying they threaten the safety of inmates and staff. In New Jersey, unions oppose a bill to ban prolonged solitary for those 21 and under. "You'll have a gang member who's going to assault, seriously injure or kill another inmate and then he's going to pass that weapon over to a 21-year-old because the 21-year-old can't get locked up in isolation," says Edward S. Sullivan, president of the New Jersey Superior Officers Law Enforcement Association.

Most experts say the solution lies in keeping the mentally ill from being incarcerated in the first place by treating their illness. That's the idea behind specialized mental health courts, which offer mandated treatment in lieu of a conventional sentence behind bars.

Most such courts once offered alternative sentences only to people charged with misdemeanors, but more now make the same offer to people charged with felonies — sometimes violent felonies. But Jeffrey L. Metzner, clinical professor of psychiatry at the University of Colorado School of Medicine, says that trend raises two concerns: "One is the issue of dangerousness, and there's also an issue the public has, which is not unreasonable: If you do something really bad, you ought to be punished."

Even when mental health courts work well, they handle only a fraction of the thousands of people with mental illness who end up in a big-city jail, says Michael Jacobson, a former New York City corrections commissioner and now director of the Institute for State and Local Governance at the City University of New York.

"In any system, you probably want some of those specialized [mental health and drug] courts; but there has to be some systematic way, aside from boutique courts that handle 20 people a day," of reducing the numbers of mentally ill behind bars, says Jacobson, who is advising the city on how to do that.

As courts, judges, prosecutors, policy-makers and mental health advocates consider the problems of the mentally ill in prisons, here are some questions they are asking:

Is the proportion of mentally ill people in jails and prisons rising?

The number of mentally ill inmates in Chicago's Cook County Jail has doubled in the last eight years, even as the county's overall jail population has been falling.[16]

Nneka Jones, the psychologist in charge of mental health services at the jail, cited recent closures of mental health facilities, which include Mayor Rahm Emanuel's decision in 2012 to close six of Chicago's 12 mental health clinics. "I do believe that there is a correlation," she said. "We have not only seen an increase in the number of mentally ill inmates coming into our custody, we have also seen them coming in in a sicker state."[17]

Jails around the country are reporting similar problems. In some cases, the number of mentally ill inmates has remained relatively constant, but their share of the jail population has risen as crime rates have plummeted. In New York City, the share of mentally ill inmates has doubled over the last eight years, to 38 percent, mainly because the overall jail population has fallen by about half since the 1990s.[18]

However, it's difficult to know whether such a proportion applies nationally or has changed over time. Although the federal Bureau of Justice Statistics has conducted several national surveys, bureau statistician Lauren Glaze says its method for measuring mental illness has differed from survey to survey, so trends cannot be determined.

Indeed, according to psychology professor Craig Haney of the University of California, Santa Cruz, who served on a National Academy of Sciences committee on the growth of incarceration, "we don't have reliable enough data to say with confidence if the actual percentage of prisoners who are mentally ill is increasing or not. Most suspect it has, primarily because of the expanded reach of the prison and jail system over the last 35 years, and corresponding reductions in the size of the public mental health system."

For a prison to calculate its mentally ill population, it must have enough psychiatric staff to identify them, something many prisons lack, Haney says. However, as a result of litigation, "a number of systems are under pressure to at least accurately count for the first time," he says.

The question goes beyond statistics, he continues. "If we're not counting them reliably we're not treating them effectively, and they're certainly not getting better on their own," Haney says.

Many experts blame the deinstitutionalization movement that began during the John F. Kennedy administration in the early 1960s, when states began closing many of their mental health hospitals.[19]

"The absolute numbers of mentally ill in prisons have risen exponentially" since then, says Doris A. Fuller, executive director of the Treatment Advocacy Center. "In the mid-1950s, when there was widespread availability of psychiatric beds, 4 percent of the prison population was estimated to have mental illness. Over the long arc of time, it has risen, and it has never abated."

Experts cite a variety of causes for the rising numbers of mentally ill inmates. Two prominent ones are harsher mandatory sentencing and the nation's so-called war on drugs, which sent jail and prison populations soaring from the 1980s to 2009, when they began to abate. Starting in the 1980s, drug arrests more than tripled, peaking in 2006.[20]

Those trends ensnared many mentally ill people. Nearly three-quarters of jail inmates with mental illness also suffer from drug or alcohol addiction.[21]

In addition, the so-called "broken windows" strategy — in which police in New York and other large cities arrest people for "quality of life" crimes as a strategy for preventing more serious crimes — tend to sweep up more mentally ill people. The homeless are especially vulnerable because "they're peeing in the street, panhandling, sleeping in the subway," says Jacobson at City University of New York.

The mentally ill also swell the local jail population by coming back more often than other offenders. A group of 400 "frequent fliers" returned to New York City's jails more than 18 times over the past five years; 67 percent

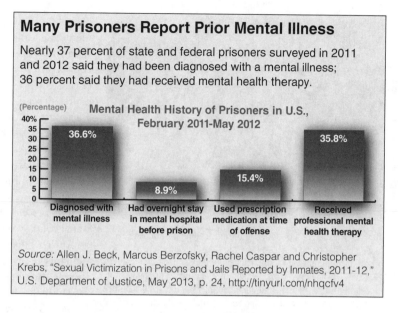

Many Prisoners Report Prior Mental Illness

Nearly 37 percent of state and federal prisoners surveyed in 2011 and 2012 said they had been diagnosed with a mental illness; 36 percent said they had received mental health therapy.

Mental Health History of Prisoners in U.S., February 2011-May 2012

(Percentage)

- Diagnosed with mental illness: 36.6%
- Had overnight stay in mental hospital before prison: 8.9%
- Used prescription medication at time of offense: 15.4%
- Received professional mental health therapy: 35.8%

Source: Allen J. Beck, Marcus Berzofsky, Rachel Caspar and Christopher Krebs, "Sexual Victimization in Prisons and Jails Reported by Inmates, 2011-12," U.S. Department of Justice, May 2013, p. 24, http://tinyurl.com/nhqcfv4

had a mental health need and 99 percent had a substance abuse disorder.[22]

In addition, while most mentally ill jail inmates are picked up for minor nonviolent crimes, they tend to stay longer than the average inmate.[23] According to Homer Venters, assistant commissioner for the Bureau of Correctional Health Services in New York City's Department of Health and Mental Hygiene, mentally ill inmates at the Rikers Island jail stay twice as long as the average inmate, perhaps because they are less skilled at obtaining bail and at working the system and are more likely to commit infractions.

"We have a system that has become brittle and inaccessible for people with mental illness," Venters says.

Some say the perceived rise may simply be the result of jail and prison directors doing a better job of screening and diagnosing those with mental illness upon entry. "We used to put them in the hole [solitary confinement]; now we get a psychiatrist for them," the warden of a California jail told Henry J. Steadman, lead author of a frequently cited survey that found about 17 percent of the 12 million people admitted to jails each year exhibit signs of serious mental illness.[24]

As for historical trends, "the proportion of people with mental illness in U.S. jails may not be much different than it was 20 to 40 years ago," says Steadman, president of Policy Research Associates, a consulting firm

Timothy Heckler says goodbye to program administrator Shari Lewinski after being released from the Court to Community program for people with mental illness in Denver, Colo., on July 17, 2014. "I've learned a lot. I'm still off the drugs; I'm really grateful for that," Heckler told Judge Johnny Barajas. One way the criminal justice system is dealing with mentally ill people is to divert them to specialized mental health courts that allow them to enter mandatory court-monitored treatment programs instead of going to jail.

outside of Albany, N.Y. "Was it 17 percent 30 years ago? No one ever collected the data. Even today, in most jails they can't tell you how many have serious mental illness."

Do programs that offer treatment instead of jail prevent further crime?

It's a heart-warming scene repeated often around the country. The courtroom breaks into applause as smiling defendants march up to the judge's podium to receive a certificate and a hug from the judge. It's graduation day in mental health court, a ceremony to congratulate defendants for completing treatment under the court's supervision.

The first such court opened in 1997 in Ft. Lauderdale, Fla., when suicides of mentally ill people in Broward County jails prompted officials to pursue reforms. As originally conceived, the courts focus on mentally ill people accused of misdemeanors, aiming to get them into treatment and prevent them from committing further, possibly more serious, crimes.[25]

Since then, mental health courts have grown rapidly to between 300 and 400 nationwide, and most operate similarly: In place of a trial and conventional sentence, a

defendant may opt for attending court-mandated treatment that can last 12 to 24 months.[26] The defendant then must appear regularly at status hearings in the courtroom, where a clinical team working with the judge checks on progress and adherence to treatment. The court can send the individuals to jail if they don't comply with a treatment regimen.

Advocates of such courts say evaluations show graduates are less likely to commit new crimes. In a frequently cited evaluation of four mental health courts in California, Minneapolis and Indianapolis, 49 percent of participants were re-arrested after 18 months, compared with 58 percent of mentally ill defendants in the conventional court system.[27]

At first blush, seeing almost half of a program's participants re-arrested may not sound like a resounding success. But evaluation co-author Allison Redlich, an associate professor of criminal justice at the State University of New York, Albany, says, "This population has earned the name 'frequent fliers,'" for the frequency of their arrests, "so any kind of reduction can be a success." Nevertheless, she adds, "mental health courts don't work for everybody. Trying to figure out how and for whom they work is where we should be focusing our efforts."

A new research finding — that less than 20 percent of crimes committed by mentally ill defendants can be directly traced to their illness — might explain the high re-arrest rates.[28]

Jennifer Skeem, co-author of this research and a professor in the School of Social Welfare at the University of California, Berkeley, says mentally ill people often commit crimes for the same reasons as others — hanging out with the wrong crowd, using drugs or not thinking or caring about the consequences of their actions beyond immediate gratification.

The premise of most jail diversion programs — that treating mental illness will stop people from committing crime — is too "simplistic," she says.

"We shouldn't stop investing in specialty programs for that population," says Skeem. But, she cautions, "the emphasis of those programs needs to be broadened" beyond psychiatric treatment, "and we need to pay attention to other risk factors that could relate even more strongly to their involvement in the criminal justice system."

For example, she says a form of cognitive behavioral group therapy that aims to change criminal thinking patterns — such as justifying irresponsible behavior to oneself — in all kinds of offenders, not just the mentally ill, has been shown to reduce subsequent violent acts.

When it comes to reducing crime nationally, mental health courts get "mixed reviews," depending on the courtroom, says Nicole Waters, principal court consultant at the National Center for State Courts, an independent court improvement organization based in Williamsburg, Va. "A court might be very effective in one state and not another, and we don't know why," she says.

Research shows it is important to have a probation officer or judge with a "firm but caring relationship" with the person being supervised, Skeem says. That could explain why success varies so widely from court to court. "You might have a judge who realizes that unless this defendant stops hanging out with their drug-using cousin, all the medication compliance in the world won't make the difference in preventing re-arrests," she says.

Some civil liberties groups and defense lawyers complain that court-supervised treatment often lasts much longer than the conventional sentence a defendant would have received for a misdemeanor — such as probation, a fine or a few weeks in jail.

Steadman, who advises local governments on such programs, agrees that mandated treatment tends to last much longer than the 60 to 90 days typical for a misdemeanor sentence. But, he says, "These are not quick fixes. The people getting into these specialty courts have got longer-term behavioral health problems that take long-term treatment. You don't give them an injection and they're better."

"Most mental health courts are targeted on misdemeanants, many of whom would never be involved with the criminal justice system but for mental health courts," asserts Ira Burnim, legal director of the Bazelon Center for Mental Health Law, a legal advocacy group for the rights of the mentally ill based in Washington.

He describes a Florida mental health court where "they dragged in one guy for drinking coffee on the street and loitering. This was just a homeless guy they were trying to bring in for some services."

Waters agrees that such so-called "net-widening" is a risk for courts that only take misdemeanors. But increasingly mental health courts are accepting felony cases as well, where the defendant is more likely to face a substantial prison sentence, she notes.

Upon hearing the word felony, "the public has the perception these are mass murders, but those are not the types of cases" these courts take, says Waters.

In Miami-Dade County, for example, the majority of felony cases handled by the mental health diversion court are drug possession charges and assaults connected with resisting arrest, which can include even slight physical contact with the officer. In addition, Waters says, the prosecutor has a lot of discretion over which cases to bring: "He can say 'no' to murders, sex offenses, gang affiliations."

Nevertheless, Waters says, prosecutors often fear that a mental health court could release people into the community without adequate supervision, and that they may commit another crime. However, a new study suggests that accepting felony defendants actually improves public safety by reducing the risk of future violence. In a one-year follow-up, felony defendants who went through the San Francisco Mental Health Court were found to be far less likely to have committed violent acts than those from other courts.[29]

The study is consistent with other research that presents a seemingly paradoxical finding: Programs targeting high-risk offenders produce a better payoff in reduced recidivism than those aimed at low-level offenders, who are more likely to get re-arrested for petty offenses.[30] At New York City's Nathaniel Project, which treats court-referred felony defendants, only 3 to 4 percent of graduates are re-arrested for a violent crime two years later, according to project co-founder Ann-Marie Louison.

Violent felonies now comprise more than 40 percent of the caseload at the Brooklyn Mental Health Court, although the court won't take defendants charged with murder or rape. Judge Matthew J. D'Emic, who presides over the court, says the decision to accept violent felonies was based on some early cases in which the crime seemed directly linked to the person's mental illness.

As for releasing dangerous defendants into the community, D'Emic admits, "I'm worried about it every day." But because he receives daily reports on defendants, he says he is alerted right away if someone has violated his or her agreement by dropping out of a treatment program. He can then order that person's arrest.

AP Photo/Michael Rubinkam

Matt Dougherty, a police officer in Lower Merion, Pa., center, undergoes training designed to help police recognize and respond to people suffering from serious mental illness. The trainers, intervention specialist Michelle Monzo and officer Joe Smith, whisper to Dougherty to help him empathize with a mentally ill person who hears voices.

Does solitary confinement induce mental illness?

Kalief Browder was a sociable 16-year-old living in New York when he was falsely accused of stealing a backpack and sent to Rikers Island, the city's huge jail. Browder would spend three years at Rikers awaiting a trial — two in solitary confinement, typically for repeated scuffles with other inmates. After Browder refused numerous offers to plead guilty to a lesser charge, saying he wanted to prove his innocence at trial, prosecutors finally dismissed the case, saying the man who had accused Browder of stealing the backpack had gone back to Mexico and disappeared. Six months after Browder returned home he made two suicide attempts — first by attempting to slit his wrists, second by trying to hang himself.

Browder had frequent flashbacks to the "Bing," as solitary is called at Rikers. Like many inmates who have endured solitary, he no longer felt comfortable around other people, describing himself as having become paranoid, quiet and "distant." He told *The New Yorker*, "I feel like I was robbed of my happiness."[31]

In recent years, stories like Browder's and reports by advocacy groups have called attention to the psychologically damaging effects of solitary confinement, especially on young people.

People in solitary are more likely to commit suicide or deliberately harm themselves than the general prison population.[32] And mentally ill inmates are more likely to land in solitary than other prisoners, according to several studies.[33]

Researchers and psychiatrists agree that solitary confinement can be particularly damaging for the mentally ill. The American Psychiatric Association says prolonged solitary "should be avoided" for those with serious mental illness.[34]

However, psychiatrists and psychologists have long debated whether solitary induces mental illness in people without a mental disorder. In research first published in the 1980s, Harvard Medical School psychiatrist Stuart Grassian examined prisoners being held in solitary confinement and concluded that isolation units tend to induce psychosis. Even inmates who did not become obviously psychotic reported psychosis-like symptoms, including hallucinations and violent outbursts.[35]

Three years after California opened its high-security prison at Pelican Bay, the University of California's Haney interviewed a representative sample of 100 inmates in solitary as an expert consultant to a prisoner lawsuit challenging the unit's constitutionality. Haney found some form of serious psychological or emotional disturbances in nearly every prisoner he interviewed. More than 90 percent reported problems with anxiety; 70 percent felt they were on the verge of an "impending breakdown;" more than 40 percent had hallucinations; and 27 percent had suicidal thoughts. More than three-quarters exhibited social withdrawal, and an almost equal number suffered chronic withdrawal, Haney said in an e-mail to *CQ Researcher*.[36]

Terry Kupers, a psychiatrist at the Wright Institute in Berkeley, Calif., an educational institution for psychologists, has visited many prisoners in solitary confinement as an expert witness. "It is very clear from the research . . . that for just about all prisoners, being held in isolated confinement for longer than three months causes lasting emotional damage, if not full-blown psychosis and functional disability," he writes.[37]

Typically, upon release from solitary, he says, "the first thing most do is shut themselves in a room . . . as if reproducing the conditions of solitary confinement they've become habituated to; they won't go places, can't hold a job and won't talk to others."

However, Jeffrey L. Metzner, a clinical professor of psychiatry at the University of Colorado, disagrees.

"With a few exceptions, long-term segregation," as solitary is often called, "does not cause someone to develop a mental illness. It certainly causes people to feel distressed . . . anxious and depressed and irritable." But, says Metzner, "it doesn't make you psychotic."

Metzner adds, "In the movies you're placed in a cell with no communication with anyone. That doesn't exist. What exists is people locked down in cells who communicate with other people because there may be anywhere from 15 to 20 cells adjacent."

Some inmates say they feel safer in solitary confinement because they have made enemies in the prison yard, notes Joel Dvoskin, a mental health consultant to states, who served on a controversial Colorado prison study of solitary that found no adverse effects. "We don't think it helped mental functioning, but there was no evidence of systematic deterioration," he says.[38]

But the relatively positive results, Dvoskin says, may have occurred because conditions in Colorado may have been better than in other prisons. Many inmates had TVs in their cells, and the corrections officers treated prisoners respectfully. "If the officers are rude, it makes a difference," says Dvoskin.

Critics argued that the results in Colorado could not be generalized to other states. "I agree: All it tells us is that in that study that's what they found," says Dvoskin, adding that the study should be replicated in other states.

Some critics of research by Grassian and Haney say their studies were not well designed because it was unclear how many of the prisoners already had psychiatric symptoms before entering prison. Nor was there a comparison group of prisoners who had not experienced solitary, they said.[39]

However, Haney disputes these criticisms. "I've seen a number of cases in which people with no pre-existing mental illness and no record of family history developed serious forms of psychosis that persisted, even after they were released from prison," he says. "I have absolutely no doubt it can occur. I'd not suggest isolation makes everyone mentally ill, but I've seen it happen."

Corrections officials say solitary confinement is an essential tool for protecting inmates and controlling misbehavior. "Where do you put someone who is hallucinating? If you leave him in general housing, everyone's safety is in jeopardy," says Thomas J. Fagan, a former administrator with the Federal Bureau of Prisons who is now director of the Division of Social and Behavioral Sciences at Nova Southeastern University in Fort Lauderdale, Fla.

"If you take that option away, . . . the other options are going to be costly," Fagan says, because it generally means creating a new, secure mental health facility with more psychiatric staff.

CUNY's Jacobson says surveys indicate that inmates knifing fellow prisoners or committing other types of violence represent a very small percentage of those who end up in solitary. Mainly, he says, "It's prisoners not listening to an order" or possessing a pornographic magazine — infractions for which inmates can go to solitary for weeks, or even months, he says.

Much like with a naughty child, the appropriate answer to misbehavior by a prisoner is a brief timeout in solitary, he asserts. "Whatever benefits come from cooling people off, you can probably get in a week or two."

BACKGROUND
From Jails to Bedlams

With more mentally ill people now housed in prisons and jails than hospitals, many observers have noted a cruel paradox: The United States seems to be returning to 19th-century conditions decried by social reformers at the time.[40]

In the early 1800s, reformers discovered that many mentally ill people were being housed and abused in jails or poorhouses. A Massachusetts preacher, the Rev. Louis Dwight, was delivering Bibles to a Boston jail when he came upon a psychotic inmate imprisoned for nine years despite breaking no laws. The prisoner was dressed in rags, Dwight wrote, and his only bed was "a heap of filthy straw."[41]

Dwight's revelations spurred an investigation by the Massachusetts Legislature and the opening of the first State Lunatic Asylum in 1833, in Worcester. When the hospital opened, more than half of the patients came from jails, prisons and almshouses.[42]

A decade after Dwight's original findings, Dorothea Dix, a Massachusetts teacher, was horrified at finding "insane" prisoners in miserable conditions in unheated jail cells in 1841. She began a campaign, traveling from state to state, urging the humane treatment of the

CHRONOLOGY

1830s–1950s *Wretched prison conditions for the "insane" lead to creation of asylums as humane alternatives.*

1833 Massachusetts lunatic asylum opens.

1841 Prison reformer Dorothea Dix begins campaign to place the mentally ill in asylums — hospitals — not jails.

1900 Asylums exist in every state.

1940s Conscientious war objectors expose abuses they see while working at asylums, helping set the stage for deinstitutionalization.

1954 Thorazine, a schizophrenia drug, is marketed in U.S., spurring pharmacological revolution and crusade for community treatment.

1960s–1970s *Deinstitutionalization movement empties state mental hospitals, while psychotropic drugs revolutionize care.*

1963 Under President John F. Kennedy's prodding, Congress authorizes up to $3 billion in state grants for community mental health centers.

1971 President Richard Nixon declares a "war on drugs."

1973 New York state's "Rockefeller drug laws" start a national trend for mandatory sentences for drug possession.

1980s *Homelessness among the mentally ill rises. . . . States begin building "supermax" prisons.*

1980 Fewer than 800 community mental health centers exist instead of the 2,000 expected.

1988 After a police officer kills a mentally ill man, Memphis, Tenn., pioneers training for police to recognize psychiatric symptoms.

1989 California builds Pelican Bay supermax prison to hold some inmates in solitary 23 hours a day.

1990s *Courts rule solitary confinement for the mentally ill is "cruel and unusual punishment." . . . First mental health courts are founded.*

1993 In *Casey v. Lewis*, federal court finds it unconstitutional for Arizona to place seriously mentally ill prisoners in solitary confinement.

1995 In *Madrid v. Gomez*, federal judge declares holding those with mental illnesses in solitary at California's Pelican Bay prison is unconstitutional.

1997 Broward County, Fla., opens first mental health court.

2000s–Present *Mental health courts grow rapidly, accept more serious crimes; bipartisan support grows for federal legislation to offer treatment and rehabilitation to prisoners.*

2004 Congress passes the Mentally Ill Offender Treatment and Crime Reduction Act to help state and local governments improve responses to the mentally ill in the criminal justice system.

2008 President George W. Bush signs the Second Chance Act, authorizing grants to states to help prisoners re-enter society.

2011 U.N. expert declares putting mentally ill and young people in solitary confinement is "torture." . . . New York state prohibits long-term solitary confinement of people with serious mental illness.

2014 Colorado becomes second state to bar long-term solitary confinement for mentally ill. . . . New York state activists charge that hundreds of mentally ill people remain in solitary. . . . New York City mayoral task force announces $130 million plan to divert the mentally ill from the justice system and treat them.

2015 Massachusetts becomes third state to limit solitary confinement for the mentally ill. . . . To improve funding for treatment, President Obama proposes increasing grants to states and local governments. . . . Montana, New Mexico, New Jersey consider bills to limit solitary confinement for inmates who are mentally ill. . . . At least 300 mental health courts are in existence; study finds they reduce violence among felony defendants.

mentally ill in asylums instead of prisons. Her advocacy led to the opening of 32 state psychiatric hospitals in 18 states.[43]

By 1900, every state had a mental institution.[44]

By the mid-20th century, however, state mental hospitals had become the target of exposés. Conscientious objectors, appalled at the conditions they found while working as attendants in such institutions in 20 states during World War II, turned to the press and testified in Congress about the abusive treatment.

The exposés began a reform movement that became the early impetus for a push toward deinstitutionalization — the movement to shift mentally ill patients from hospitals to outpatient treatment in community mental health clinics.

The movement was aided by the development of antipsychotic drugs, the first of which — Thorazine — was introduced in 1954. The drug set off a pharmacological revolution in the treatment of schizophrenia. The discovery of additional psychotropic drugs created a sense of optimism that the seriously mentally ill could live independently in their own neighborhoods.

Deinstitutionalization was also the result of stronger due process protections against involuntary commitment to mental hospitals, the growing influence of psychiatrists who thought the mentally ill could be cared for outside of institutions and the enactment of Medicaid in 1965, according to the Vera Institute of Justice. Medicaid would not reimburse state mental hospitals for care, leading many state institutions to release droves of patients to nursing homes, general hospitals or the street, where they could obtain Medicaid coverage.

In 1963, President Kennedy proposed a series of federally funded community mental health centers that would function as an alternative to psychiatric hospitals, signing into law the Mental Retardation and Community Mental Health Centers Construction Act. It authorized Congress to provide up to $3 billion in grants to states to establish community mental health centers.[45]

However, the federal government never followed through with adequate funds, and by 1980 only 754 of the 2,000 planned centers had been built.[46]

Mandatory Sentencing

At the same time that the population of state mental hospitals was dropping, the number of people entering the nation's prisons and jails was increasing.

Drastic cuts in the social safety net in the 1980s contributed to rising homelessness and to increasing numbers of mentally ill people on the streets. Growth in prison and jail populations closely mirrored the rate at which state psychiatric institutions were emptying.[47]

One factor during the 1980s was the rise in the prosecution of drug crimes, beginning with President Richard M. Nixon's declared war on drugs in 1971. Another was the growing popularity of mandatory sentences, starting with the so-called Rockefeller drug laws adopted in New York state in 1973, which included mandatory sentences for drug possession.

During the 1970s, crime experts began to question the effectiveness of rehabilitation for convicted criminals, a changing view that would cause prisons to turn away from rehabilitation programs and politicians to support harsher sentencing.

Beginning in the 1980s and continuing into the '90s, more states passed laws mandating long sentences and minimums for certain crimes as well as "three strikes" laws, which imposed a lengthy mandatory sentence for an offender's third conviction.

Between 1970 and 2005, the nation's prison population exploded by 700 percent and continued rising to a peak of 1.6 million in 2009. The increase in incarceration involving drug arrests accounted for about two-thirds of the increase in the federal prison population and one-half of the increase in state prisons between 1985 and 2000.[48]

The 1980s also saw the beginning of a state trend to build so-called supermax prisons, designed to confine the worst of the worst prisoners in solitary confinement. In 1989, California opened the Pelican Bay prison with a Security Housing Unit (SHU) designed to hold prisoners in solitary for 23 hours a day.

In 1995, a federal judge prohibited confinement of mentally ill prisoners at the SHU and concluded that conditions were close to intolerable even for the mentally healthy.[49]

Among the cases of abuse was that of an inmate who refused to return a food tray in protest against an officer who called him derogatory names. He was beaten unconscious until a piece of his scalp had been peeled back.[50]

In his decision, U.S. District Judge Thelton E. Henderson ruled that prison officials "cross the constitutional line when they force certain subgroups of the prison

Innovative Program Diverts Mentally Ill From Jail to Treatment

"We're the biggest crime prevention program in town."

Justin Volpe had stopped taking his medications for psychosis and was addicted to drugs when he heard voices telling him to steal from a co-worker. The 23-year-old was arrested for theft in 2007 and landed in a Miami jail for a month and a half awaiting trial.

But instead of a trial and a sentence, Volpe was offered an eight-month court-mandated course of drug treatment and psychiatric counseling, part of a mental health jail diversion program run by Miami-Dade County and the 11th Judicial Circuit of Florida.[1]

Today, Volpe, 31, says the program helped him turn his life around. Were it not for the jail diversion program, "I would have continued the vicious cycle of drugs and incarceration," says Volpe, who sports a neatly trimmed beard and a ready smile. "If I were still alive, my quality of life would be nowhere near what it is today."

Now the married father of a 4-year-old, Volpe is a full-time employee for the Miami-Dade County courts. As a certified peer specialist, he helps mentally ill defendants on their road to recovery, taking them out for coffee and offering support to help them make it through their mandated treatment.

Although the mental health diversion program operates out of a court, it has some notable differences from a typical mental health court. Defendants who enter the program are not required to plead guilty, as in some courts, and if they successfully complete the program their charges are dismissed so they don't acquire a criminal record.

Recidivism rates — arrests for new offenses — have dropped from 70 percent before the program began in 2000 to about 20 percent for those who finish the program, according to Tim Coffey, coordinator of the court's diversion program. The program also works closely with local and county police who have been trained in crisis intervention, or how to de-escalate conflicts involving mentally ill people. In 2013, out of 10,626 mental health crisis calls answered by police, only nine arrests were made, according to Coffey.

The program has had strong support from public defenders and prosecutors. "We want to stop people from committing crimes," says Jennie Conklin, an assistant state attorney. "You can only lock people up for so long. We can keep arresting them for misdemeanor after misdemeanor or try to get them treatment to reduce recidivism. . . . Just putting them in jail and saying, 'Good luck and we hope you take your meds' won't work."

With the cooperation of prosecutors, the program recently has begun accepting people who have committed low-level felonies, mostly for drug possession and assault related to a physical struggle while resisting arrest, according to Coffey. Recidivism rates for felony offenders who complete the program are just 6 percent.[2]

The program's secret ingredient, many experts say, is the judge who founded it in 2000 and has spearheaded many of its innovations, Judge Steve Leifman, associate administrative judge in the Miami-Dade County Court Criminal Division. Leifman says he became convinced the program was needed because he was appalled at how badly mentally ill people were being treated by the criminal justice system.

"There is so much stigma with mental illness that most judges have no clue," he says, that people can recover from it with appropriate treatment, just like any physical illness. Leifman also works with a national program to train judges to recognize psychiatric symptoms and address mentally ill defendants respectfully. "When I talk to people with mental illnesses, it is striking how abused they are by the mental health system and the criminal justice system," he says. "How you address them in court makes all the difference in the outcome: If they're motivated, and you're offering them help, they're mostly going to do it."

Citing the diversion program's record in reducing re-arrests, he declares, "We're the biggest crime prevention program in town."

Yet, it's difficult to find hospital beds or other aid needed by the people in the program, such as housing, employment and job training.

With 9 percent of the county's population suffering from serious mental illness — the highest rate of any urban center in the country — fewer than 13 percent receive care in the public mental health system, according to the project's website.[3]

Many mental health clinics "don't want to deal with a homeless guy with mental illness," Leifman says. "They haven't bathed; they're difficult. The treatment providers don't get paid enough" to give this population the level of service they need. But he adds, "It's not just about putting them on the right medications; it's about giving them a life where they want to get back up and help themselves again."

Leifman has become so frustrated with the lack of a facility offering appropriate treatment to mentally ill offenders that he decided to create one. He is leading county efforts to convert an abandoned state mental hospital into a comprehensive center for mentally ill offenders. Plans call for 168 beds available for up to 90 days of residential treatment, providing a seamless transition from the courtroom to services — all under one roof.

On a recent tour of the building, Leifman showed off the large institutional kitchen he plans to turn into a culinary job-training program, an area that will be used as a crisis center where police can bring mentally ill people to be evaluated and offices where case managers can help link people up with benefits.

With the help of a $1-a-year lease arrangement with the state and passage of a $22 million bond issue, he hopes the new facility will open within two years. Leifman also has his eye on a neighboring property he would like to see converted into low-cost housing for those coming through the program.

Historically, the nation has gone from warehousing the mentally ill in state mental hospitals with scant treatment

CQ Researcher/Sarah Glazer

Justin Volpe was arrested in Miami after he heard voices telling him to steal. But instead of a jail sentence, he received drug treatment and counseling, helping him turn his life around.

to today's conventional court system, where "we're kicking them all to the street, which is equally horrible," observes Leifman. With the new facility, he says, mentally ill people "will come here and we'll gently reintegrate them back into the community. This will be the crowning jewel; we'll make sure they get everything they need."

— *Sarah Glazer*

[1]The official name of the program is the Eleventh Judicial Criminal Mental Health Project.

[2]"Eleventh Judicial Criminal Mental Health Project — Program Summary," http://tinyurl.com/qg4efnk.

[3]The high rate is thought to be the result of a combination of homeless people attracted by South Florida's warm climate and the legacy of the 1980 Mariel boatlift, when Cuban President Fidel Castro allowed more than 125,000 people to emigrate to the United States, some of whom were from Cuba's mental wards and prisons. See Pete Earley, *Crazy* (2006). Also see Eleventh Judicial Circuit of Florida, Criminal Mental Health Project website, http://tinyurl.com/qdkjb4d.

States Revamping 'Solitary' for the Mentally Ill

"It was a culture change in the beginning."

After 25 years spent mostly locked alone in his cell, a Pennsylvania prisoner identified only as "BB" developed schizophrenia and had difficulty speaking in complete sentences — a condition "principally attributable to his experiences in solitary confinement," according to a 2014 Justice Department report.[1]

But, prompted by a lawsuit filed in March 2013 by the Disability Rights Network of Pennsylvania, the Pennsylvania Department of Corrections is taking steps to drastically curtail solitary confinement for inmates with serious mental illness.

Under a settlement announced Jan. 6, those who have demonstrated "problematic" behavior, such as posing a danger to inmates or staff, must be sent to specialized but still secure treatment units, where they will be allowed at least 20 hours weekly outside of their cell and receive individualized mental health treatment.[2]

The settlement specifies that after July 1, 2016, no seriously mentally ill person can be placed in solitary unless "exceptional circumstances" exist, such as lack of bed space, and cannot be held in solitary longer than 30 days.[3]

Pennsylvania's Department of Corrections says it already has moved hundreds of mentally ill inmates out of solitary and placed potentially dangerous inmates in the newly designed secure treatment units specified in the settlement.

"Even though the cell size and furnishings are similar [to regular solitary prison cells], the experience is very different," says Robert Marsh, director of the psychology department for the Pennsylvania Department of Corrections. The new units include areas where inmates can congregate and cubicles where they can meet privately with therapists.

"The artwork lets you know this is different," Marsh says, alluding to inmates' artwork on themes of recovery adorning the hallways.

The Justice Department initiated its investigation several months after the Disability Rights Network filed its suit and conducted it independently of the advocacy group, says Kelly Darr, legal director of the Disability Rights Network of Pennsylvania. The government investigation "confirmed the allegations" in the advocacy group's lawsuit and "added pressure" on the Pennsylvania Department of Corrections "to address the issue," she says.[4]

The Justice Department report, based on a statewide investigation, concluded last year that hundreds of mentally ill prisoners remained in solitary confinement for months and sometimes years in "harsh" conditions in Pennsylvania's prisons.

"They are routinely confined to their cells for 23 hours a day, denied adequate mental health care, and subjected to punitive behavior modification plans . . . unsettling noise and stench, harassment by correctional officers and the excessive use of full-body restraints," the Justice Department charged.[5]

John Wetzel, secretary of the Pennsylvania Department of Corrections, said last year that the report relied on information from one or two years earlier and thus did "not reflect the reality" of how the department was operating at the time of the report's release in February 2014.[6]

In January, the Pennsylvania Department of Corrections said fewer than 150 people with serious mental illness remained in traditional solitary confinement cells, down from nearly 850 previously.[7] More recently, Susan McNaughton, press secretary for the Department of

population, including the mentally ill, to endure the conditions in the SHU, despite knowing that the likely consequence for such inmates is serious injury to their mental health."[51] Placing mentally ill persons in such conditions is "the mental equivalent of putting an asthmatic in a place with little air to breathe," he wrote.[52]

In December 1995, Henderson followed up by ordering the removal of 100 severely mentally ill prisoners from the SHU by year's end.

Nevertheless, Henderson refrained from declaring solitary unconstitutional for prisoners without mental disorders. Conditions in solitary "may well hover on the

Corrections, said in a March 5 e-mail, "We have no seriously mentally ill inmates who experience solitary confinement."

The corrections department has also undertaken mental health training for its entire custody staff, Marsh says. As part of the training, correctional officers are given ear buds with a tape that simulates the schizophrenic experience of "hearing voices." Officers listening to the tape have to cope with a demanding situation — such as repeating numbers backwards. "It's an eye-opener as to how stressful mental illness can be," Marsh says.

Eldon Vail, secretary of the Washington state Department of Corrections from 2008 to 2011, pioneered the alternative approach of providing secure treatment units as deputy secretary from 1999 to 2006. "Some of those guys are dangerous to themselves or others so you've got to have them in a more restricted environment," he says, but it should be a specialized unit where "mental health staff have significant authority over how it's operated."

Retraining prison guards is crucial, according to Vail. "The orientation for corrections officers for the last 30 or 40 years has been around this notion 'Games Prisoners Play': You're taught that every interaction is a potential effort by the inmate to manipulate you, so you start to look with great suspicion at the folks you're responsible for supervising," he says.

Prisoner BB, who was exhibiting bizarre speech and responding to hallucinations, improved dramatically after he was admitted twice to an offsite inpatient unit, according to the Justice Department. Instead of recognizing this improvement as confirmation that solitary confinement was harming the inmate's mental functioning, Pennsylvania corrections officials viewed it as evidence he had "malingered" or had "faked" his mental illness while in solitary, the Justice Department reported.[8]

Asked if there was a trend of corrections staff accusing inmates of faking mental illness, Marsh says, "It's very difficult to make that conclusion," adding that "Mental illness can wax and wane."

— **Sarah Glazer**

Recovery-themed artwork by mentally ill inmates now adorns the new units Pennsylvania established for state prisoners moved out of solitary confinement in response to a lawsuit.

[1] Department of Justice, letter from Acting Assistant Attorney General Jocelyn Samuels to Gov. Tom Corbett, Feb. 24, 2014, p. 12, http://tinyurl.com/p4ayyja.

See also Elizabeth Daley, "Pennsylvania Agrees to Keep Mentally Ill Inmates out of Solitary," Reuters, Jan. 6, 2015, http://tinyurl.com/k4oyz9a.

[2] "Pennsylvania Department of Corrections Settles Lawsuit with the Disability Rights Network of Pennsylvania," news release, Pennsylvania Department of Corrections Jan. 6, 2015, http://tinyurl.com/pgt9ktm.

[3] *Disability Rights Network of Pennsylvania v. John Wetzel*, U.S. District Court for the Middle District of Pennsylvania, case number 1:13-cv-00635, p. 12, http://tinyurl.com/pn56aop.

[4] The Justice Department initiated its statewide investigation in May 2013. See Department of Justice, *op. cit.*

[5] Department of Justice, *ibid.*

[6] Mark Berman, "The Pennsylvania Prison System Will Stop Putting Mentally Ill Inmates in Solitary," *The Washington Post*, Jan. 8, 2015, http://tinyurl.com/p7zcjlx.

[7] News release, *op. cit.*

[8] Department of Justice, *op. cit.*

edge of what is humanly tolerable for those with normal resilience," he said. However, he added, its use for the general population does not violate the Eighth Amendment's ban on "cruel and unusual punishment."

The Pelican Bay ruling led to a series of lawsuits by the American Civil Liberties Union (ACLU) and other advocacy groups on behalf of prisoners confined in solitary in Arizona, Indiana, New Mexico, New York, South Carolina, Texas and Wisconsin. That litigation has led to settlements or court orders prohibiting confinement of mentally ill prisoners in solitary, albeit only for those prison systems named in the suits.

The ACLU also has waged a campaign outside the courtroom to "stop solitary," likening isolation to "torture" — advocating the adoption of state laws to limit solitary.[53] That effort is a recognition, says the ACLU's Amy Fettig, senior staff counsel for its National Prison Project who directs the Stop Solitary campaign, of the difficulty of achieving change merely by filing suits and enforcing settlements. "Not even the ACLU can sue every state and every single facility that engages in this practice," she says.

Mental Health Courts

In recent years, the second generation of mental health courts has changed the way the specialty courts do business, partly in response to some of the criticisms from civil liberties groups about how they operate. For example, some advocates for the civil rights of the mentally ill object that courts often require a defendant to enter a guilty plea before entering the program, saddling the person with a criminal record that can bar him or her from public housing or make it difficult to get a job.

According to Waters of the National Center for State Courts, at least 43 percent of the nation's mental health courts now allow the defendant to enter the program without pleading guilty.

A tragedy in Memphis, Tenn., in 1988 — a police officer's shooting of a mentally ill man — spurred another type of alternative to incarceration. Memphis pioneered a 40-hour training program for officers on how to recognize signs of mental illness and de-escalate a combative situation with a mentally ill person and provided a drop-off center where an officer could take a person exhibiting psychiatric symptoms for evaluation and treatment.[54]

The approach, known as Crisis Intervention Team (CIT) training, has spread rapidly, with 2,500 programs offered in cities and counties throughout the United States, according to Michele Saunders, vice president of CIT International, a Memphis-based membership organization that provides information to localities on how to start a CIT program. In addition, some jails and prisons have started CIT training to help corrections officers deal with mentally ill inmates more empathetically and to identify when they have a mental disorder, Saunders says.

CURRENT SITUATION
State Action

Montana, New Jersey and New Mexico are considering legislation to protect mentally ill prisoners from long-term solitary confinement, joining New York, Colorado and Massachusetts, which already have such laws, according to the ACLU's Fettig.[55]

However, advocates for the New York law, known as the "SHU Exclusion Law," which took effect in 2011, say they are disappointed with the results. While approximately 200 inmates have been moved from solitary into special mental health units, hundreds of others remain in isolation because of questions over their diagnosis. The law's prohibition applies only to those with "serious mental illness," including schizophrenia, bipolar disorder and major depressive disorder.[56]

> **Court decisions in six states have decreed that holding prisoners with serious mental illness in solitary is unconstitutional under the Eighth Amendment.**

About 700 prisoners in solitary "don't meet this magic line" of serious mental illness, but have been diagnosed with some other more minor form of mental illness, and some may be in solitary because of misdiagnosis, according to Jack Beck, director of the Prison Visiting Project of the Correctional Association of New York, a nonprofit that inspects prisons and reports to the state Legislature.

"They are not receiving any out-of-cell therapy and are still being harmed," he says. "We think the 'serious mental illness' line is not working as well as we would like. People with mental illness [of any kind] shouldn't be in there."

To address this gap, his organization and prisoner advocacy groups are supporting a bill introduced in the New York Legislature to prohibit solitary confinement for inmates with any mental illness.[57]

Legislation in several states, supported by a coalition of religious and civil liberties groups, would prohibit prolonged disciplinary confinement for all prisoners. New Mexico, New Jersey and New York are considering a 15-day limit, while a bill in Montana would place a 14-day limit for the seriously mentally ill and those under 18.[58]

Should prolonged solitary confinement be banned?

YES State Sen. Raymond J. Lesniak, D-N.J.

Written for *CQ Researcher*, March 2015

The United States leads the world in the percentage of its population in prison. Antiquated and counterproductive corrections policies, which often make inmates more likely to commit crimes than when they entered prison, contribute to that high percentage. That's hardly the goal of rehabilitation, which should be in the forefront of corrections policy. Extensive use and misuse of solitary confinement is a prime example of a counterproductive corrections policy.

The vast majority of people subjected to solitary confinement will one day re-enter society. When they return, do we want men and women haunted by that experience, or do we want people capable of making the greatest contributions they can? The humane choice, the one that promotes public safety in and out of our prisons, is to end solitary confinement in its current form.

What makes solitary confinement so traumatic? It entails locking up people in a small cell for 23 hours per day, depriving them of any meaningful human interaction. This leads to self-mutilation, revenge fantasies, rage and irrational anger, heart palpitations, hallucinations and violent nightmares.

Solitary confinement endures despite sound alternatives. And its drawbacks far outweigh its very few perceived benefits.

U.S. courts and international human rights bodies have correctly recognized prolonged isolation as torture, especially among vulnerable populations such as children and prisoners with mental illnesses. The legislation I proposed in New Jersey would eliminate solitary confinement for these groups. A federal judge described solitary confinement for mentally ill individuals as equivalent to "putting an asthmatic in a place with little air to breathe." The developing brains of young people are particularly susceptible to the harms associated with solitary confinement.

Beyond the mental and emotional anguish of the people directly subjected to it, solitary confinement poses dangers to the corrections community, as well as the broader society. The states that have dramatically reduced its use have all seen incredible results. When Maine reduced its reliance on solitary, it saw reductions in inmate violence, use of force and self-mutilation, which went from a weekly occurrence to one almost nonexistent. Mississippi has had even more dramatic results, ultimately leading to the closure of its solitary unit, saving the state millions.

Limiting solitary confinement, as proposed in my legislation, will reduce repeat offenses, provide better safety for correction workers and save taxpayer dollars. It's worked in Maine and Mississippi. It can also work in New Jersey.

NO Michael Powers
President, New York State Correctional Officers & Police Benevolent Association

Written for *CQ Researcher*, March 2015

Those who spend every day working in our prison system — protecting the safety and security of inmates and fellow staff members — understand that solitary confinement cannot be completely eliminated. Opponents of this widely accepted practice tend to be agenda-driven advocacy organizations that demonstrate their lack of experience by relying on Hollywood myths, not real-life situations, to make their case.

Disciplinary separation for inmates of any age is a proven strategy for restoring stability and safety to the often dangerous correctional environment. Implemented thoughtfully, it's a critical tool in today's prisons.

The only inmates put in disciplinary confinement in the special housing unit — known as "solitary" — are those needing to be there for the protection of the staff, other inmates or sometimes even the inmate himself. Solitary is the only mechanism for removing a violent inmate from the general population.

And make no mistake — some need to be removed. In the real world, inmates continue to perpetrate violence after they've lost their freedom and are living behind prison walls.

For example, an inmate serving 15 to 45 years for manslaughter, burglary and attempted arson recently beat a correction sergeant so badly that he was hospitalized with two broken ribs and a punctured lung. An inmate doing 15-to-life for murder and robbery seriously injured two officers who tried to break up a fight he was having with other inmates.

After these incidents, and the subsequent legal hearing process, these inmates were removed from the general population so they could not perpetrate more violence.

In solitary, inmates are closely monitored through constant rounds made by correction officers and other staff. They are allowed reading and legal materials, and they get to exercise.

Keeping those determined to harm others apart from less violent inmates is an important strategy in medium-security facilities, where inmates live in dorms with dozens of other inmates. Violent disruptions also prevent orderly inmates from taking part in the educational and other programs aimed at helping them transition back into society.

Today's disciplinary confinement policies have evolved over decades of experience. While we are always open to identifying new ways to improve public safety and the protection of everyone at our facilities, the smartest and most effective policy changes come from those of us working in the field — not those whose only exposure to the corrections system is "Orange Is The New Black" or Hollywood prison movies.

In support of their efforts, reformers have been citing a 2011 report by the U.N. special rapporteur on torture. It declared that solitary confinement can amount to "torture" for juveniles and for the mentally ill and should be prohibited for both groups, as well as barred for anyone else beyond 15 days.[59]

A bill introduced by Democratic New Jersey State Sen. Raymond J. Lesniak would prohibit solitary confinement for inmates with mental illness and those 21 and under and would limit it to 15 days for others. However, unions representing corrections officers and the New Jersey Department of Corrections oppose the bill, with the latter warning it would be "financially prohibitive."

"The use of restrictive housing is a necessary tool . . . to ensure a safe environment for staff as well as inmates," the department testified.[60]

Court decisions in six states have decreed that holding prisoners with serious mental illness in solitary is unconstitutional under the Eighth Amendment. Several other states, including Pennsylvania, are making changes in response to lawsuit settlements.

In an interim agreement reached last year growing out of litigation filed by the ACLU, New York state agreed to ban solitary confinement for 16- and 17-year olds and restrict it to 30 days for people with developmental disabilities, such as traumatic brain injury or an extremely low IQ.

A final settlement could lead to even more sweeping restrictions. The ACLU has agreed to suspend its litigation until February 2016 while an expert for each side monitors the system and recommends new guidelines for solitary confinement.

Local Action

After a schizophrenic man died last year in an overheated cell at Rikers Island, New York City announced what some experts call the most extensive program of any city aimed at the mentally ill in the criminal justice system.[61]

"The best way to deliver services in jails is to make sure people don't get into jail," says Trish Marsik, executive director of Mayor Bill de Blasio's Task Force on Behavioral Health and the Criminal Justice System, which came up with the $130 million plan last December.

The sweeping program aims to connect mentally ill people with services at every point where they might have contact with the criminal justice system. Starting with drop-off centers, where police can bring mentally ill people for treatment and evaluation rather than jail, the plan would also make sure inmates get treatment upon their release.[62]

An important goal is to identify the mentally ill before they are charged at an arraignment hearing so judges realize that in many cases, "we don't need to send those people to jail," says Marsik. "We've just been using jail because we don't know what else to do."

The plan has so far received favorable reviews from advocates for mentally ill prisoners. But CUNY's Jacobson notes that "even in a place like New York City, which has more community-based [treatment] capacity than most, there's not remotely enough capacity to deal with these folks."

In addition, for people who are mentally ill but pose a threat to other people, "a drop-off center won't do it for them," he says. "You may need secure facilities because you can't deal with them in a 48-hour drop-off center."

The mistreatment of mentally ill inmates at Rikers Island, revealed by press accounts and a two-and-a-half-year investigation by a U.S. attorney in Manhattan, prompted these and other reforms, including a shakeup of the jail leadership by de Blasio and expanded therapy inside the city's jails.[63]

However, last month *The New York Times* reported abuse by guards was persisting at Rikers Island. It documented another 62 cases of inmates, some of them mentally ill, who were seriously injured in conflicts with guards in the six months after the U.S. attorney in Manhattan published a report in August describing in graphic detail widespread brutality against inmates.[64]

New York City corrections officers complain that they now have fewer methods to control inmates. After the state eliminated solitary confinement for 16- and 17-year-olds in December, there was a spike in violence among inmates. And in March, more than half of the inmates at Rikers were locked down in their cells for 34 hours to curb rising gang violence. Previously an inmate could be locked in solitary up to 90 days, but now the limit is 30.[65]

"It appears to me that the inmates are being emboldened to think that there is virtual impunity for their actions," said Sidney Schwartzbaum, president of the union for assistant deputy wardens.[66]

Congressional Action

When it comes to funding a mental health court or training police to recognize mental illness, some state and local governments have been helped by grants under the federal Justice and Mental Health Collaboration Program.

The program, which aims to improve responses to mentally ill people involved with the criminal justice system, is funded under the 2004 Mentally Ill Offender Treatment and Crime Reduction Act, due to expire this year. Sen. Al Franken, D-Minn., is expected to introduce a bill to reauthorize the program under a new title, the Comprehensive Justice and Mental Health Collaboration Act of 2015.

However, at its current funding level of $8.5 million, the program funds only about 15 percent of applicants, according to Ron Honberg, director of policy and legal affairs at the National Alliance on Mental Illness. President Obama's budget would boost funding for this program by 60 percent — to $14 million in fiscal 2016.[67]

"We're hoping to increase funding for this," says Honberg. "We have opportunities for this, because the bigger goal of reducing the number of people who are incarcerated is becoming a bipartisan conversation," as fiscally conservative lawmakers such as Sen. Rand Paul, R-Ky., have joined with liberals to reduce spending on prisons.[68]

In February a bipartisan group, including such conservatives as Sen. Ted Cruz, R-Texas, backed the Smarter Sentencing Act of 2015, which would cut some mandatory sentences in half and give judges greater discretion in sentencing.[69] The bill was introduced in the Senate by Mike Lee, R-Utah, and Dick Durbin, D-Ill., and in the House by Rep. Paul Labrador, R-Idaho. In a meeting with 16 members of Congress on Feb. 24, President Obama reportedly threw his support behind the bill, but the legislation is still expected to face opposition from Senate Judiciary Committee Chairman Chuck Grassley, R-Iowa, who condemned a similar bill last year as "lenient" and "dangerous."[70]

Obama is also seeking more money for two other programs that could help mentally ill people who come in contact with the justice system. He proposes to almost double funding to $120 million for the Second Chance Act, signed into law by President George W. Bush in 2008. It provides grants to states and nonprofits to develop re-entry programs for released prisoners — such as connecting them to jobs, housing and treatment — with the aim of reducing recidivism. This program has strong bipartisan support.

The Justice Reinvestment Initiative — another program that would get a budgetary boost (from $27.5 million to $45 million) — aims to help states reduce their prison populations by investing in recidivism-prevention strategies, such as drug treatment for people on probation and parole.[71]

However, outlays for these programs are tiny when compared with the more than $4 billion that states have cut in mental health funding in recent years.[72]

"The pendulum in funding has swung in the negative territory for a while; a deep hole needs to be filled" in mental health services, says Fred Osher, director of health systems and services policy at the Council of State Government's Justice Center, which advises states on strategies for reducing prison populations.

One thing that could help, Osher says, is Obama's Affordable Care Act (ACA). Under the ACA, childless single men are obtaining insurance for the first time through an expanded Medicaid program. "That's opening up doors in increased expenditures," Osher says.

One of the biggest problems mentally ill prisoners face is the loss of Medicaid while in prison and the difficulty in re-enrolling after their release. Some jails, like Sheriff Mahoney's in Dane County, Wis., sign prisoners up for Medicaid immediately upon their release in an effort to keep them connected to treatment and, ideally, out of jail.

OUTLOOK
Training Judges

As New York City's new top-to-bottom plan for the mentally ill suggests, some localities are trying a new tack. But it may take more tragic stories from inside prisons and jails — and more money from state legislatures and local governments — for this approach to become widespread.

Most of the reform energy is coming from the judicial branch, maintains Steve Leifman, an associate administrative judge in the Miami-Dade County Criminal Division, in Miami, Fla. "Judges are on the front line," he says. Leifman is leading a project with the American Psychiatric Association to train judges in how to recognize mental illness and how to address mentally ill defendants — a program he hopes to expand nationally from the 300 to 400 judges now signed up.

The goal is to get more people into treatment as soon as they show up in the courtroom. But some advocates for the mentally ill say efforts like this are merely a reaction that comes too late to a more serious problem: "Every community needs a local facility where someone with mental problems can go for help *before* he ends up in trouble," writes journalist and advocate Pete Earley. His son was arrested for breaking into a neighbor's house after a hospital had turned him away for treatment of his bipolar disorder during a manic episode. Earley argues the required treatment often means a hospital for someone seriously psychotic — not just an outpatient clinic.[73]

The need for hospital beds after the era of deinstitutionalization is getting renewed attention. Recently a group of medical ethicists from the University of Pennsylvania issued a call to "Bring Back the Asylum."[74] For people with severe psychotic disorders, "who are too unstable or unsafe for community-based treatment," they wrote, "the financially sensible and morally appropriate way forward includes a return to psychiatric asylums that are safe, modern and humane."

Responding to the lack of local treatment facilities in Miami-Dade, Leifman is spearheading an unusual effort to convert an abandoned mental hospital into an inpatient and outpatient treatment center.

But those who have committed violent crimes don't necessarily have any treatment alternatives to prison, as New York City real estate developer Francis J. Greenburger discovered when his oldest son was charged with arson. According to Greenburger, his mentally ill son was convinced a drug dealer was pursuing him, and after getting no response from the police, he set trash on fire on his stove and called the fire department for help.[75]

He was convicted and sentenced to five years. Because there was no alternative to prison that was secure enough to satisfy the district attorney, Greenburger decided to build one of his own. His Greenburger Center for Social and Criminal Justice is negotiating with the New York State Office of Mental Health to license what may be the first treatment center of its kind in the country — a 30- to 60-bed locked facility for mentally ill people facing felony prison sentences of at least two years.

But whether such a facility would pose a danger to the surrounding community remains a concern. "I think that district attorneys and judges would be more inclined to let certain individuals out [of prison for an alternative treatment program] if they were in a secure facility," says D'Emic of the Brooklyn Mental Health Court, commenting on the Greenburger proposal.

Increasingly, judges like D'Emic and Leifman are becoming experts on the root causes — homelessness, drug abuse, mental delusions and poverty — that bring people before them.

"It's like a social services agency more than a court," Cheryl Roberts, executive director of the Greenburger Center, says of D'Emic's mental health court. Indeed, she says, courts have "become, for better or worse, the place where our social problems — homelessness and mental illness — are colliding."

NOTES

1. Jeff Gerritt, "Mentally Ill Get Punishment Instead of Treatment," *Detroit Free Press*, Feb. 5, 2012, http://tinyurl.com/7kk9owc.

2. *Ibid.* Also see Jeff Gerritt, "After Closing Psychiatric Hospitals, Michigan incarcerates Mentally Ill," *Detroit Free Press*, Nov. 27, 2011, http://tinyurl.com/knnf9l7. Brante E. Fries, "Report to the Legislature: Independent Study of Mental Health and Substance Abuse, Final Report," Feb. 16, 2010, http://tinyurl.com/ozku7ro; "Majority of Mentally Ill Inmates Don't Get Treatment," University of Michigan, press release, April 12, 2010, http://tinyurl.com/olcwjes.

3. *Ibid.*

4. "The Treatment of Persons with Mental Illness in Prisons and Jails: A State Survey," Treatment Advocacy Center, April 8, 2014, p. 8, http://tinyurl.com/lnwkj7s.

5. "Incarceration's Front Door: The Misuse of Jails in America," Vera Institute of Justice, February 2015, http://tinyurl.com/lyuun67.

6. Tom Dart, "How We Shaft the Mentally Ill," *Chicago Tribune*, July 29, 2014, http://tinyurl.com/mult5bw.

7. *Ibid.*

8. On March 5, 38 percent of inmates entering Cook County jail self-identified as mentally ill according to Cook County Sheriff Thomas J. Dart webpage, http://tinyurl.com/pefxnlk.

9. Dart, *op. cit.*

10. Jails are locally run facilities, primarily holding people arrested but not yet convicted or serving a sentence of less than a year.

11. Also see Steven Elbow, "City Poised to Sue State Over Closing Mendota Mental Health Institute to Detained Mental Patients," *The Capital Times*, June 28, 2014, http://tinyurl.com/lbvd9hg.

12. "Incarceration's Front Door . . . ," *op. cit.*

13. "Callous and Cruel: The Use of Force Against Inmates with Mental Illness in U.S. Jails and Prisons," Human Rights Watch, forthcoming.

14. See Solitary Watch, http://tinyurl.com/mf8fnhz.

15. Michael Winerip and Michael Schwirtz, "Rikers to Ban Isolation for Inmates 21 and Younger," *The New York Times*, Jan. 13, 2015, http://tinyurl.com/kkjmasv.

16. Mary Cirincione, "Mentally Ill Population Doubled Since 2006; Now 20 Percent," Medill News Service, Oct. 15, 2014, http://tinyurl.com/kzwkl34.

17. *Ibid.*

18. See Elizabeth Glazer, "Breaking Point," Vera Institute of Justice Blog: Current Thinking, Feb. 19, 2015, http://tinyurl.com/m4cgcc8. Also See Mayor's "Action Plan," p. 5. Also See Margaret Hartmann, "Mentally Ill Rikers Inmates are Frequently Attacked by Officers, Says Secret Study," *New York Magazine*, July 14, 2014, http://tinyurl.com/lyfmkzl.

19. Dominic A. Sisti, *et al.*, "Improving Long-Term Psychiatric Care; Bring Back the Asylum," *JAMA*, Jan. 20, 2015, pp. 243–244, http://tinyurl.com/nxmneqa.

20. Sarah Glazer, "Sentencing Reform," *CQ Researcher*, Jan. 10, 2014, pp. 25–48.

21. David Cloud, "On Life Support: Public Health in the Age of Mass Incarceration," Vera Institute of Justice, November 2014, p. 7, http://tinyurl.com/mvewx4f.

22. "Action Plan," Mayor's Task Force on Behavioral Health and the Criminal Justice System, 2014, http://tinyurl.com/mwlpxnr.

23. Vera, "Incarceration's Front Door," *op. cit.*

24. Henry J. Steadman, *et al.*, "Prevalence of Serious Mental Illness Among Jail Inmates," *Psychiatric Services*, June 2009, pp. 761–765.

25. "The Broward County (Fort Lauderdale) Mental Health Court," Emerging Judicial Strategies for the Mentally Ill in the Criminal Caseload, April 2000, http://tinyurl.com/p4d7msj.

26. The National Center for State Courts estimates that there are about 300 courts. A recent article estimates "upwards of 400." See Sisti, *et al.*, *op. cit.*

27. Henry J. Steadman, *et al.*, "Effect of Mental Health Courts on Arrests and Jail Days," *Archives of General Psychiatry*, February 2011, pp. 167–172.

28. J. Peterson, J. Skeem, and P. Kennealy, "How often and how consistently do psychiatric symptoms directly precede criminal behavior among offenders with mental illness?" *Law and Human Behavior*, vol. 38, no. 5, 2014, pp. 439–449, http://tinyurl.com/kpblh9f.

29. Dale McNiel, *et al.*, "Prospective Study of Violence Risk Reduction by a Mental Health Court," *Psychiatric Services in Advance*, Feb. 16, 2015, pp. 1–6, http://tinyurl.com/m2x95pn. Also see "Use of Mental Health Courts Reduces Risk of Later Violence," *Psychiatric News Alert*, Feb. 18, 2015, http://tinyurl.com/pwmg8d2.

30. *Ibid.*

31. Jennifer Gonnerman, "Before the Law," *The New Yorker*, Oct. 6, 2014, http://tinyurl.com/q3x9p8j.

32. Cloud, *op. cit.*, pp. 13–14.

33. Adam Geller, "Jailed, Some Mentally Ill Inmates Land in Solitary Confinement," *The Huffington Post*, Sept. 20, 2014, http://tinyurl.com/kdaaeqt.

34. "Position Statement on Segregation of Prisoners with Mental Illness," American Psychiatric Association, December 2012, http://tinyurl.com/pt4m2u6.

35. See Terry Kupers, *Prison Madness* (1999), p. 57.

36. Ryan Devereaux, "Searching for the Truth about California's Prison Hunger Strike," *Rolling Stone*, Aug. 12, 2013, http://tinyurl.com/lujcpkn.

37. Terry Kupers, "What to do with the Survivors? Coping with Long-Term Effects of Isolated Confinement," *Criminal Justice and Behavior*, August 2008, pp. 1005–1015, http://tinyurl.com/pathorz.

38. See Peter Katel, "Solitary Confinement," *CQ Researcher*, Sept. 14, 2012, pp. 765–788.

39. See Jeffrey Metzner and Joel Dvoskin, "An Overview of Correctional Psychiatry," Psychiatric Clinics of North America, 2006, pp. 761–772, http://tinyurl.com/qjolyut. . . . Also see "Bureau of Prisons: Improvement Needed in Bureau of Prisons' Monitoring and Evaluation of Impact of Segregated Housing," Government Accountability Office, May 2013, http://tinyurl.com/q5gu53y.

40. Sisti, *et al., op. cit.*

41. Pete Earley, *Crazy* (2007), pp. 64–65.

42. E. Fuller Torrey, "Deinstitutionalization: A Psychiatric Titanic," Frontline, http://tinyurl.com/2f9osq.

43. "The Vital Role of State Psychiatric Hospitals," National Association of State Mental Health Program Directors, July 2014, pp. 1–3, http://tinyurl.com/mxtmqe9.

44. Earley, *op. cit.*, p. 65.

45. See Barbara Mantel, "Mental Health Policy," *CQ Researcher*, May 10, 2013, pp. 425–448. Also see Earley, *ibid.*, p. 69.

46. For background on how and why the mental health centers were never properly funded, see Background section in Sarah Glazer, "Treating Schizophrenia," *CQ Researcher*, Dec. 5, 2014, pp. 1009–1032.

47. Cloud, *op. cit.*, p. 8.

48. *Ibid.*, p. 9.

49. The case is *Madrid v. Gomez.* "Case Closed on Supermax Abuses at Pelican Bay," *Solitary Watch*, Feb. 15, 2011, http://tinyurl.com/lypaxn6.

50. *Madrid v. Gomez*, Jan. 10, 1995, http://tinyurl.com/q8seeyr.

51. Katel, *op. cit.*, p. 778. For text of 1995 decision in *Madrid v. Gomez*, see *ibid.*

52. *Madrid v. Gomez, op. cit.*

53. Katel, *op. cit.*, p. 780.

54. Amy C. Watson and Anjali J. Fulambarker, "The Crisis Intervention Team Model of Police Response to Mental Health Crises: A Primer for Mental Health Practitioners," Best Practices in Mental Health, December 2012, http://tinyurl.com/kdxpur3. Also see CIT International, http://tinyurl.com/n8nhtj3.

55. Bob Katzen, "Beacon Hill Roll Call Volume 40," *Somerville News Weekly*, Jan. 12, 2015, http://tinyurl.com/mpgo9xm. Also see "Governor Hickenlooper Signs Law Limiting Solitary Confinement for Mentally Ill," ABC 7, June 6, 2014, http://tinyurl.com/kaokqyh.

56. Testimony by Jack Beck, Hearing of the New York Assembly's Corrections and Mental Health Committee, The Correctional Association of New York, Nov. 13, 2014, http://tinyurl.com/mkkqru5.

57. Bill introduced by Correction Committee Chair and NY Assembly Member Daniel J. O'Donnell, http://tinyurl.com/k3szfgz.

58. New Mexico House Bill 376, introduced by Antonio "Moe" Maestas, http://tinyurl.com/lx9d3dr; Montana House Bill 490, introduced by J. Eck, http://tinyurl.com/kls9k7d.

59. "Interim Report of the Special Rapporteur of the Human Rights Council on Torture," U.N. General Assembly, Aug. 5, 2011, http://tinyurl.com/kzf4kyz.

60. New Jersey Department of Corrections testimony before the New Jersey Senate Law and Safety Committee, Feb. 12, 2015.

61. A jail guard was arrested last year in connection with the death of Jerome Murdough and the city agreed to a $2.25 million settlement with his mother. See "Rikers Guard Arrested in Connection with Homeless Veteran Who Baked to Death," The Associated Press/*The Guardian*, Dec. 8, 2014, http://tinyurl.com/loth8e5.

62. "Action Plan," Mayor's Task Force on Behavioral Health and the Criminal Justice System, 2014, http://tinyurl.com/mwlpxnr.

63. Michael Winerip and Michael Schwirtz, "New York City Plans Focus on Mental Health in Justice

System," *The New York Times*, Dec. 1, 2014, http://tinyurl.com/l2wu557.

64. Michael Winerip and Michael Schwirtz, "Even as Many Eyes Watch, Brutality at Rikers Island Persists," *The New York Times*, Feb. 21, 2015, http://tinyurl.com/k6szj9z.

65. Michael Schwirtz and Michael Winerip, "Seeking Drugs and Weapons, Rikers Locks Down Inmates for 34 Hours," *The New York Times*, March 4, 2015, p. A20, http://tinyurl.com/mclbhkf.

66. *Ibid.*

67. "President's Budget," Justice Center, Council of State Governments, Feb. 2, 2015, http://tinyurl.com/nt9q6ru.

68. Sarah Glazer, "Sentencing Reform," *op. cit.*

69. Text of the Smarter Sentencing Act of 2015, http://tinyurl.com/ny27n2s.

70. See Gregory Korte, "Bipartisan Sentencing Bill Gets White House Support," *USA Today*, Feb. 25, 2015, http://tinyurl.com/nte63oj. Also see Jacob Sullum, "The Tougher-Than-Thou Senator," *Reason*, Feb. 25, 2015, http://tinyurl.com/oxpjvg3.

71. "President's Budget," *op. cit.*

72. Funding for state mental health agencies fell $4.4 billion from FY 2010-FY2013. See "The Vital Role of State Psychiatric Hospitals," National Association of State Mental Health Program Directors, July 2014, p. 22, http://tinyurl.com/mxtmqe9.

73. Earley, *op. cit.*, p. 356.

74. Sisti, *et al.*, *op. cit.*

75. Matt A. V. Chaban, "From a Father's Anguish Comes a Plan to Help Mentally Ill Inmates," *The New York Times*, Oct. 6, 2014, http://tinyurl.com/ln9tabf.

BIBLIOGRAPHY

Selected Sources

Books

Clear, Todd R., and Natasha A. Frost, *The Punishment Imperative: The Rise and Failure of Mass Incarceration in America*, New York University Press, 2014.

A Rutgers criminal justice expert (Clear) and a Northeastern University criminologist (Frost) take a critical look at the nation's historical cycle from rehabilitation to punitive sentencing policies.

Earley, Pete, *Crazy: A Father's Search Through America's Mental Health Madness*, Berkley Books, 2007.

When the son of former *Washington Post* reporter Pete Earley broke into a neighbor's house during a manic episode, Earley decided to investigate how the mentally ill fare in jail.

Kupers, Terry, *Prison Madness: The Mental Health Crisis Behind Bars and What We Must Do About It*, Jossey-Bass Publishers, 1999.

A psychiatrist who testifies as an expert witness for plaintiffs interweaves research with his own encounters with mentally ill prisoners.

Articles

Chaban, Matt A. V., "From a Father's Anguish Comes a Plan to Help Mentally Ill Inmates," *The New York Times*, Oct. 6, 2014, http://tinyurl.com/ln9tabf.

New York City developer Francis Greenburger, whose mentally ill son was sentenced to five years for arson, plans to build a locked treatment facility for similar defendants — the first of its kind.

Devereaux, Ryan, "Searching for the Truth about California's Prison Hunger Strike," *Rolling Stone*, Aug. 13, 2013, http://tinyurl.com/lujcpkn.

When 30,000 California prisoners staged a hunger strike over solitary confinement, it spurred a debate between prison officials, who said solitary is essential for safety, and psychiatrists, who said it is psychologically damaging.

Gonnerman, Jennifer, "Before the Law," *The New Yorker*, Oct. 6, 2014, http://tinyurl.com/q3x9p8j.

After a teenager spent two out of three years in solitary confinement at New York City's Rikers Island, he emerged to suffer flashbacks and twice attempt suicide.

Winerip, Michael, and Michael Schwirtz, "Even as Many Eyes Watch, Brutality at Rikers Island Persists," *The New York Times*, Feb. 21, 2015, http://tinyurl.com/k6szj9z.

Despite city officials' vows of reform, Rikers Island guards continue to beat inmates, *The Times* reports.

Reports and Studies

"Alone and Afraid: Children Held in Solitary Confinement and Isolation in Juvenile Detention and Correctional Facilities," American Civil Liberties Union, June 2014 (revised), http://tinyurl.com/lnu7dj5.
Placing children under 18 in solitary confinement should be banned, says a civil liberties group.

Cloud, David, and Chelsea Davis, "Treatment Alternatives to Incarceration for People with Mental Health Needs in the Criminal Justice System: The Cost-Savings Implications," Vera Institute of Justice, February 2013, http://tinyurl.com/axuxsad.
A study summarizes favorable research findings on the effectiveness and cost savings of programs to keep the mentally ill out of jail.

Fellner, Jamie, "Callous and Cruel: The Use of Force Against Inmates with Mental Illness in U.S. Jails and Prisons," Human Rights Watch, forthcoming in April 2015.
The lack of mental health training for guards contributes to a needless use of force against mentally ill prisoners, a human-rights group finds.

McNiel, Dale E., et al., "Prospective Study of Violence Risk Reduction by a Mental Health Court," Psychiatric Services in Advance, Feb. 16, 2015, pp. 1–6, http://tinyurl.com/m2x95pn.
Mentally ill felony defendants who went through the San Francisco mental health court were far less likely to commit violence than similar defendants in other courts.

Peterson, Jillian K., et al., "How Often and How Consistently Do Symptoms Directly Precede Criminal Behavior Among Offenders With Mental Illness?" Law and Human Behavior, vol. 38, no. 5, 2014, pp. 439–449, http://tinyurl.com/kpblh9f.
Only 18 percent of crimes committed by mentally ill offenders could be traced directly to psychiatric symptoms, raising questions about whether psychiatric treatment alone can prevent criminal behavior.

Steadman, Henry J., et al., "Prevalence of Serious Mental Illness Among Jail Inmates," Psychiatric Services, June 2009, pp. 761–765, http://tinyurl.com/q8j9mke.
A study of five jails finds that 14.5 percent of men and 31 percent of women suffered from serious mental illness.

Subramanian, Ram, et al., "Incarceration's Front Door: The Misuse of Jails in America," Vera Institute of Justice, February 2015, http://tinyurl.com/nfm8v6d.
Jails have become "de facto mental hospitals" for the mentally ill, according to a policy group.

For More Information

American Civil Liberties Union National Prison Project, 915 15th St., N.W., 7th Floor, Washington, DC 20005; 202-393-4930; https://www.aclu.org/prisoners-rights. Advocacy program that challenges the constitutionality of placing mentally ill prisoners in solitary confinement.

Council of State Governments Justice Center, 100 Wall St., 20th Floor, New York, NY 10005; 212-482-2320; http://csgjusticecenter.org/. Advisory group that offers strategies to policymakers in reducing corrections spending and responding to people with mental illness in the criminal justice system.

National Alliance on Mental Illness, 3803 North Fairfax Dr., Suite 100, Arlington, VA 22203; 703-524-7600; www.nami.org. Grassroots organization on mental health that advocates for access to services, treatments and research.

National Center for State Courts, 300 Newport Ave., Williamsburg, VA 23185; 800-616-6164; www.ncsc.org. Independent court-improvement organization that offers extensive information on mental health courts.

National Sheriffs' Association, 1450 Duke St., Alexandria, VA 22314; 800-424-7827; www.sheriffs.org. Professional association representing thousands of sheriffs, deputies and law enforcement professionals.

Solitary Watch, P.O. Box 11374, Washington, DC 20008; solitarywatchnews@gmail.com; http://solitarywatch.com. Website sponsored by a coalition of civil rights groups critical of solitary confinement; provides breaking news and research in the field.

Treatment Advocacy Center, 200 N. Glebe Rd., Suite 801, Arlington, VA 22203; 703-294-6001; www.treatmentadvocacy center.org. Advocacy group that focuses on eliminating barriers to the effective treatment of people who are mentally ill.

Vera Institute of Justice, 233 Broadway, New York, NY 10279; 212-334-1300; www.vera.org. Research group that works with government to improve services affecting criminal justice and public safety.

13

Reforming Veterans' Health Care

Tom Price

New VA Secretary Robert A. McDonald testifies on Sept. 9, 2014, before the Senate Veterans' Affairs Committee on patient-care delays at Department of Veterans Affairs (VA) facilities. In response to the delays and other VA health-care problems, the former paratrooper and Procter & Gamble CEO announced a series of planned reforms at the beleaguered department earlier this month, including creation of a customer-service unit.

AFP/Getty Images/Mandel Ngan

From *CQ Researcher*, November 21, 2014.

Asked how his experience running Procter & Gamble prepared him to fix the scandal-marred Department of Veterans Affairs, new VA Secretary Robert A. McDonald described P&G's massive global business operations and its "laser-like focus on the customer, every single customer."

The VA — also huge, with 278,000 employees — must focus on the veteran in the same way, he said.[1] And, earlier this month, as he rolled out a series of VA reforms, McDonald announced creation of a customer-service unit led by a chief who will report directly to the secretary.[2] The message: He intends to run the VA more like a business.

When President Obama picked McDonald, 61, to head the federal government's second-largest department, the president highlighted the nominee's business and military background. Before he began his 33-year career at the world's largest manufacturer of consumer packaged goods, McDonald had graduated from West Point in the top 2 percent of his class and served five years as an Army paratrooper.

That résumé has won him support from many government officials and veterans' organizations. But others worry about his lack of experience in health care and in managing a government bureaucracy. They point to his mixed record at P&G. And they note that the VA poses massive challenges to anyone who tries to make it work.

McDonald became secretary in July, after Eric Shinseki resigned in May amid revelations of medical shortcomings and cover-ups at the VA — which may have contributed to some veterans' deaths.[3]

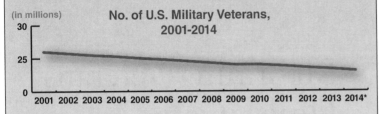

Veteran Population Shrinking

The number of U.S. military veterans fell 17 percent between 2001 and 2014, from 26 million to an estimated 21.6 million. The U.S. Department of Veterans Affairs projects the 2030 total at 16.8 million.

(in millions) — **No. of U.S. Military Veterans, 2001-2014**

2001 2002 2003 2004 2005 2006 2007 2008 2009 2010 2011 2012 2013 2014*

* Estimated

Source: Erin Bagalman, "The Number of Veterans That Use VA Health Care Services: A Fact Sheet," Congressional Research Service, June 3, 2014, p. 3, http://tinyurl.com/m6rab77; projection from "Projected Veteran Population 2013 to 2043," National Center for Veterans Analysis and Statistics, Oct. 13, 2014, http://tinyurl.com/msgwnml

The heart of the scandal was the VA's inability to make timely appointments for many of the 6.6 million patients who annually sought care in recent years — and officials' attempts to cover up the appointment delays with falsified records.

The delays were blamed on inadequate staffing, a more complex caseload, population shifts that create soaring demand at some VA facilities — mostly in the Sun Belt — and empty beds in others, antipathy to whistleblowers and what one scholar termed "perverse incentives" to meet unrealistic appointment goals.

Among McDonald's biggest challenges: He must revitalize a large bureaucracy, which he described as rigid with poor internal communications, and whose executives were willing to cheat in order to appear successful. He must recruit thousands of health care professionals at a time when the private health care system also faces severe shortages and is able to pay higher compensation. And he must "earn back the trust of the veterans," says Carolyn Clancy, who in July took over the department's medical programs as interim undersecretary for health.

McDonald, who said he needs to hire 28,000 new health care providers, declared employee recruitment "job one right now" and pledged to be "out in front and hands-on in that effort."[4] He spent much of the summer and early fall barnstorming the country to woo new

workers and meet with employees, patients, union and veterans' group leaders and important members of the hundreds of communities where the department runs some of its 150 medical centers, 819 outpatient clinics, 300 counseling centers, 135 nursing homes and 104 residential rehabilitation centers. For veterans living far from brick-and-mortar facilities, the VA maintains mobile medical clinics and veteran centers and telemedicine programs.[5]

McDonald also began to take advantage of new legislation, passed by Congress in the wake of the scheduling scandal, which enables him to fire workers more quickly than before. While disciplinary action has been initiated against about 40 employees so far, "well over a thousand" workers face actions that range from admonishment to termination, he said.

Jason Hansman, former manager of health programs at Iraq and Afghanistan Veterans of America, praises McDonald for "going around the country, doing these town halls, talking to veterans. I think that's a great first step." Similarly, American Legion Commander Michael Helm described McDonald as a hardworking reformer who deserves critics' patience as he tackles department problems.[6]

But some congressional Republicans accused the secretary of not firing enough workers quickly enough. "VA appears to be giving failing executives an opportunity to quit, retire or find new jobs without consequence," House Veterans' Affairs Committee Chairman Jeff Miller, R-Fla., charged.[7]

The VA health care system has been broken and fixed before. After repeated scandals in the 1970s, '80s and early '90s, the Clinton administration shrank the headquarters bureaucracy, modernized management practices, established a department-wide electronic record-keeping system and increased emphasis on primary and outpatient care, which tends to be cheaper and more efficient than hospitalization.[8] The result was an integrated system that won praise for offering care that was as good as or better than that delivered by private providers — and at less cost. Even today, once they get an appointment, veterans receive high quality care, according to many studies.

This year's scandal emerged in April, when Phoenix VA physician Sam Foote told government officials and the news media that hospital administrators were fraudulently claiming to be meeting a department goal of seeing patients within 14 days of their requesting an appointment. While records sent to superiors showed patients being seen within the 14 days, "in reality," Foote said, "it had been six, nine and in some cases 21 months." The inaccurate reports made hospital executives eligible for performance bonuses.[9]

Subsequent investigations by the VA's inspector general found a "systemic problem nationwide." In Phoenix, the investigators said, 1,700 veterans' names were on a secret list that tracked the real state of the appointments backlog, while the hospital's official records showed it meeting the department's two-week wait-time goal. In fact, new Phoenix patients waited an average 115 days for a first appointment.[10]

Nationwide in mid-May, 242,059 veterans were waiting between 30 and 120 days for an appointment — 4 percent of all appointments scheduled at that time. Another 57,436 were still waiting for a first appointment to be scheduled after 90 days.[11]

More disturbing, a department audit determined that 13 percent of VA schedulers were instructed to keep fraudulent records, and at least one case of fraud was uncovered at three-quarters of VA locations. Workers at 24 facilities reported being "threatened or coerced" to keep false records.[12]

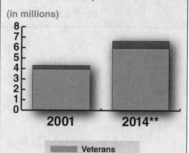

VA Patient Count Soars

The Department of Veterans Affairs (VA) treated 6.6 million patients in fiscal 2014, up 56 percent since 2001. About 710,000 patients treated in 2014 were non-veterans.*

No. of VA Hospital Patients, 2001, 2014

(in millions)

Legend:
- Veterans
- Non-Veterans

Includes some active duty or reserve military members, spouses of disabled or deceased veterans and humanitarian workers.

** Estimated

Source: Erin Bagalman, "The Number of Veterans That Use VA Health Care Services: A Fact Sheet," Congressional Research Service, June 3, 2014, pp. 2-3, http://tinyurl.com/m6rab77

"The system was overwhelmed by more patients than many hospitals could handle" and "doesn't have the capacity to serve the veterans that it is charged to serve," says Hansman, now the Iraq-Afghanistan group's director of external program relations.

The VA provides care for only 40 percent of the nation's 21.6 million veterans; the others are covered by private insurance (40 percent), Medicare, Medicaid, the Defense Department's Tricare health insurance, or are uninsured. Most active-duty military use medical facilities run by the Department of Defense, such as Walter Reed National Military Medical Center in Bethesda, Md., which itself came under fire in recent years.

As the once-vast World War II and Korean War generations die, the total number of veterans is declining. Today's population of veterans is below its peak of 29 million in 1985. The veteran population is expected to drop to 19.6 million in 2020 and to 14.5 million in 2040.[13]

But the remaining World War II and Korean War veterans are seeking more care for age-related rather than service-related problems, said Dennis Snook, a retired Congressional Research Service analyst who focused on veterans' issues.[14] And many veterans of the Korean and Vietnam wars are discovering previously undiagnosed service-related ailments — such as post-traumatic stress disorder (PTSD) or the effects of Agent Orange, a toxic defoliant sprayed widely on Vietnamese jungles, according to Rick Weidman, executive director for policy and government affairs at Vietnam Veterans of America.

Vietnam veterans also are seeking care for effects of aging "not related to military service," and post-9/11 veterans are turning to the VA at higher rates than their

Getty Images/John Moore

U.S. military veteran Lloyd Epps tests a high-tech prosthetic leg at the VA's gait and motion lab in New York City on Jan. 29, 2014. Patients are fitted with reflectors that are filmed by multiple cameras and analyzed to help the veterans improve mobility. VA facilities treat some 6.6 million patients annually.

predecessors, with more than half having filed health or disability claims. And, over the years, the department has recognized more ailments as being eligible for treatment.[15]

For more recent veterans, "battlefield health care has gotten so good that we save many lives," says Marilyn Park, the American Federation of Government Employees' legislative representative for VA issues. "But they come back catastrophically disabled and need the most complicated and lifelong care."

As the VA struggles to meet its many challenges, here are some questions that veterans, medical personnel, scholars and government executives are debating:

Should the VA budget be increased?

Four leading veterans' organizations — Veterans of Foreign Wars (VFW), Paralyzed Veterans of America (PVA), Disabled American Veterans (DAV) and American Veterans (AMVETS) — say the VA needs more money.

Specifically, they propose a $61.1 billion medical care appropriation for fiscal 2015, compared with the Obama administration's request for $59 billion. The groups also want the administration's $1.2 billion VA construction budget for 2015 more than tripled — to $3.9 billion — much of it to build medical facilities.[16]

The VA doesn't project treating more patients next year than this year, but the department expects to treat them more often: It predicts more than 95 million individual appointments this year and 100 million next, compared with 90 million in 2013. The department also faces substantial construction and maintenance backlogs of projects already approved for construction, the veterans' groups said. With the administration's current spending requests, it would take more than 67 years to complete the VA's own 10-year plan, the groups said.

"The VA budget will not begin to meet the projected needs of veterans already in the system and those coming to VA for the first time," the groups said when they released their proposals early this year.[17]

Making the case for more construction spending, VFW National Commander William Thien said, "60-year-old facilities do not get better with age."[18]

The veterans aren't alone in calling for greater VA spending. Other groups say the department needs more personnel and higher salaries for doctors and other medical professionals. Secretary McDonald has announced plans to hire an estimated 28,000 health care providers and to add between $20,000 and $35,000 to the starting salaries of physicians and dentists.

Congress this summer gave the department an emergency spending boost of $17 billion, which included $5 billion for salaries. But critics say that's not enough.[19]

Staff shortages are "the root cause of the scandals — inadequate numbers of support personnel and nurses and physicians and physicians assistants," Park, of the government employees union, says. But filling the vacancies — and adding more if necessary — will be difficult because of low VA pay rates. Private-sector doctors earn 20 percent to over two times more than VA physicians do, depending on the specialty, according to professional medical organizations.[20] VA doctors and dentists earn between $98,967 and $355,000 annually, depending on specialty and experience. Those with administrative responsibilities can earn up to $385,000.[21]

And Park warns that raising the starting pay for new hires could damage the morale of longtime employees, who haven't had a raise since 2009 due to a federal pay freeze. "We could have people with 10, 20 or 30 years' experience being paid less than new hires," she says.

McDonald, who said he is "worried about our ability to recruit and retain talent," said he will evaluate pay scales across the department.[22]

Not everyone agrees that the VA needs more money, however.

"The department has plenty of money," but "poor management is costing the department billions of dollars," Republican Sen. Tom Coburn of Oklahoma said in a 124-page "oversight report" released in June.[23] Citing reports by the Government Accountability Office (GAO) and the VA inspector general, Coburn said the department has wasted money on construction projects, vacant buildings, computer programs, unauthorized purchases and unjustified bonuses.

Construction routinely costs more than planned, he said, citing nearly $1.5 billion in cost overruns on projects in Las Vegas, Orlando, Denver and New Orleans. At the same time, he said, a 2010 GAO report showed the department was spending $175 million annually maintaining vacant property, an expense the VA said it cut to $20.2 million in 2013.[24]

Between 2006 and 2011, the department spent $5.1 million on unactivated software licenses, Coburn's report said. And the GAO found that between 2000 and 2010, the VA spent $127 million to modernize its outpatient scheduling system but didn't implement "any of the planned systems capabilities."[25]

Moreover, the report continued, employees at the VA medical center in Charleston, S.C., used government debit cards to make more than $600,000 in unauthorized and undocumented purchases between October 2011 and May 2013. The department also awarded $27.3 million in bonuses in 2013 while many federal employees were being furloughed due to budget cuts, Coburn said.[26]

Coburn is not alone in his criticism of VA spending. Anthony Principi, who was VA secretary in the George W. Bush administration, said that in a department with a 2014 budget of $153.8 billion, "no one should be falling through the cracks."[27]

"Spending more money without first properly reforming the system is unwise," said Joseph Antos, a health care scholar at the conservative-leaning American Enterprise Institute think tank. He noted that between 2003 and 2013, VA health spending increased 118 percent while enrollment of new veterans in the system increased only 25 percent.[28]

Michael Tanner, who heads health care and domestic issue research at the libertarian Cato Institute think tank, similarly argues that VA funding has increased faster than individual patient visits.

But VFW Public Affairs Director Joe Davis says critics are wrong to use gross budget figures to debate the VA's needs. "You can't use a blanket descriptor that will describe everything that's wrong with the VA or everything that's right with the VA," he says. "It depends on how it's spent."

The veterans groups' budget analysis — which runs 250 pages — concluded that Congress has underfunded the department on certain needs by about $16 billion over the last decade. Davis says the Obama administration should spend more than it plans to over the next two years to fill the gaps. "If we find, for example, that there are hundreds of unfilled positions in one particular VA hospital," then that hospital needs a bigger personnel budget, he says. "If a hospital cannot see patients because they have too few waiting rooms due to lack of major or minor construction funds," then that hospital needs more construction money.

Should veterans' health care be privatized?

Many conservatives have cited the VA scandal as proof that government is inherently incompetent and that most tasks should be left to the private sector. They suggest several possible approaches:

- Subsidizing veterans' purchase of private health insurance or Medicare coverage;
- Giving vouchers to veterans to pay health care providers directly;
- Allowing veterans to buy into the Federal Employees Health Benefit Plan; or
- Providing care to poor veterans through Medicaid.

Conservative commentator Charles Krauthammer argued for privatization because the VA health system is, he said, "a disaster" defined by rationing, wait lists, corruption and laziness.[29]

"In the business world," says University of Texas public affairs professor Howard Prince II, "it's easy to measure performance. But in a large government bureaucracy you don't have a bottom line, so you have to develop indicators that measure success." By tying promotions and bonuses to the unrealistic goal of treating patients within 14 days, the department created a "perverse incentive," Prince contends. "Managers got rewarded for meeting a standard they couldn't meet, so to get their money they instructed clerks how to keep a separate set of books."

Prince, whose research focuses on leadership and ethics, says he has found that such incentives frequently explain "why good people do bad things."

Politics prevents the VA from building and closing facilities to match changing caseloads, Cato's Tanner says. "If your district has someone sitting on the Veterans' Affairs Committee, you have a pretty good chance of getting a new hospital regardless of the occupancy of your old hospital. If you don't have the right people representing you [in Congress], you have much more difficulty."

Opponents of privatization contend that private medical facilities can't match the VA's ability to address veterans' special needs. "We have a uniquely complicated patient population," says Park, of the government employees union, "and our integrated health care system enables us to get the full picture of what combat did."

Health care scholar and journalist Suzanne Gordon said that "turning veterans over to private sector insurers and for-profit hospitals is not the solution."

"Many injured soldiers have returned from Iraq and Afghanistan with what is known as poly-trauma — PTSD plus traumatic brain injury and limb amputations," said Gordon, a visiting professor at the University of Maryland School of Nursing and an affiliated scholar with the University of Toronto Faculty of Medicine. "Few primary-care physicians — or even specialists — have much experience treating such cases in the private sector."[30]

Tanner acknowledged that the VA may need to continue treating complex battle injuries. "But most injuries and illnesses, even combat-connected ones, can be treated elsewhere," he insisted.[31]

Phillip Longman a senior research fellow at the New America Foundation — who opposes privatization — says Tanner and other critics start with a false premise: that the VA provides inferior and more costly health care. In fact, he says, the scheduling scandals obscured the fact that the quality of VA care matches or exceeds that of the private system and at less cost per patient.

A Congressional Budget Office study estimated that VA health care spending per enrollee grew 1.78 percent from 1999 to 2005, adjusted for inflation and the changing mix of patients, for instance, Longman said. During the same period Medicare spending — which pays for private care — rose 29.4 percent per capita.[32]

In addition, "from the mid-1990s through now, health care quality experts are basically unanimous in saying the VA has the highest quality of health care of any health care provider out there or is at least as high as anybody," Longman says. He attributes that to the closely integrated nature of VA care. "The typical American gets bounced around from one docpreneur to another docpreneur who treats one body part at a time and doesn't tell anybody else what he's doing, and we end up killing people," he says.

Studies by the RAND Corp., a prominent nonpartisan research organization, support Longman's contention. "By almost every measure, the VA is recognized as delivering consistently high-quality care to its patients," RAND analyst Arthur Kellermann wrote in a review of the studies on the quality of VA care. A 2004 RAND study, Kellerman wrote, found that the VA provided higher-quality care than private hospitals on almost all measures.

A 2010 review of prior research found the VA and private hospitals generally provided comparable surgical care with similar outcomes. A 2011 study determined the VA almost always did a better job of following recommended practices. A report released this year said VA mental health care outperformed private providers on seven of nine indicators.[33]

Even some privatization advocates acknowledge the quality of VA care. Prince — a wounded Vietnam veteran who retired as a brigadier general and who has a Ph.D. in psychology — describes VA care as "as good as any I've experienced anywhere." Especially praising VA's comprehensive services, he notes: "I walk around the corner to the pharmacy. I walk down the hall to radiology and they're expecting me. That's a real plus."

Studies also show that other veterans tend to like VA care as well. The 2013 American Customer Satisfaction Index, an annual independent survey of 70,000 U.S. consumers, for example, recorded almost identical opinions among outpatients at VA and private hospitals.[34] A 2013 survey by the VA found that 93 percent of patients had a favorable impression of their care.[35] When Iraq and Afghanistan Veterans of America questioned their members this year, 59 percent rated VA health care as good, 23 percent as "neither good nor bad" and 18 percent as bad.[36] Among American Legion members surveyed this year, however, 59 percent said they felt no improvement or felt worse" after VA treatment of traumatic brain injuries and post-traumatic stress disorder.[37]

Some individual VA medical facilities have shortcomings, according to Kenneth Kizer, who made major improvements when he ran the VA medical system in the 1990s. The Phoenix hospital — which he called "ground zero of the wait-time scandal" — has rates of catheter-related bloodstream infections nearly triple the national average, for instance, Kizer said.[38]

Prince complains about his dealings with nonmedical VA personnel, such as the people who man the phone lines and reception desks. "They're slow and often unresponsive," he says.

So Prince favors giving vouchers to veterans to buy private health care in order to "do away with the worst aspects of the large bureaucratic structure."

But Joyce Raezer, executive director of the National Military Family Association, says, "it doesn't make sense to give vouchers to veterans where there are no providers."[39]

Should the VA provide medical care only for service-related health problems?

Tanner, of the Cato Institute, is a veteran who believes he doesn't deserve VA health care. "I served two years in peacetime outside of Boston," he says. "Why should I be entitled to a lifetime of health care at taxpayers' expense?"

Tanner says "the idea that we owe care to the men and women who are injured in the service of their country is something that everybody agrees on across the ideological spectrum." But, he adds, "there are differences between someone who served and someone who was injured."

Although eligibility requirements are complicated, most veterans who served at least two years and were not dishonorably discharged can enroll in the VA health care system. Because the VA does not have sufficient resources

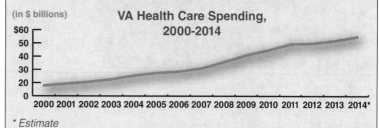

VA Health Spending Swelled in Late 2000s

Annual spending by the Department of Veterans Affairs (VA) for health care nearly tripled over the past 14 years, to an estimated $55.4 billion in 2014. Between 2007 and 2011, annual spending rose 55 percent, from $32.3 billion to $50.1 billion, due in part to rising use of services for Iraq- and Afghanistan-era veterans and expanded medical treatment options in VA hospitals.

VA Health Care Spending, 2000-2014 (in $ billions)

Estimate

Source: "Table 3.2 — Outlays by Function and Subfunction: 1962-2019," White House Office of Management and Budget, undated, http://tinyurl.com/l57s7k2

to serve all veterans, it has established a priority list.[40] Veterans with the most severe service-related disabilities are at the top, while more-affluent veterans without disabilities are at the bottom. Over time, the department has recognized more ailments as service-related — exposure to nuclear radiation and Agent Orange, for example. Access to VA care also depends on the adequacy of resources in individual communities.

Sometimes it makes sense, for a variety of reasons, for the VA to refer certain veterans to private providers. The VA paid $4.8 billion to obtain private care for more than a million patients last year, and Congress increased the amount available for that purpose this year.[41]

"It's not cost-effective to maintain VA hospitals or even clinics in many remote areas," the New America Foundation's Longman said. "And due to the declining size of the veteran population, the VA lacks a sufficient volume of patients — even in some developed areas — to justify using its own specialists."[42]

Today, the majority of VA patients are being treated for ailments unrelated to their military service, Tanner says. He and others argue that the department should treat only service-related health problems.

"The VA should focus its resources on specialized services, including treatment for combat trauma and rehabilitation that is unique to war veterans," the

The VA hospital in Phoenix has been called "ground zero" in the Department of Veterans Affairs wait-time scandal. After VA employees were found to be falsifying records to cover up lengthy appointment delays at the Phoenix facility, investigators discovered a "systemic problem nationwide" in which more than 242,000 veterans were waiting up to four months for an appointment.

American Enterprise Institute's Antos said. "As much as possible, veterans should receive their care from the broader health system, and not be kept locked up in a system that cannot handle the full caseload. The private health sector is fully equipped to deal with most of the health needs of former soldiers."[43]

That approach may have to be "part of the solution to the access issue," says Raezer of the National Military Family Association. "If there are certain kinds of care that could be provided in a more timely way, a more cost-effective way, outside the VA bricks and mortar, that could be more beneficial to the vet and free up the system to focus on the people with the war wounds," she says. The VA has the expertise and should be responsible for service-connected disabilities, "but a sinus infection is a sinus infection."

However, she notes, some war-related disabilities — PTSD and exposure to toxic substances, for instance — may not appear for decades. "We don't know the long-term effects of some of these things that our service members have experienced," Raezer says. "When does a sinus infection, or a series of sinus infections, start to indicate that they are side effects of some kind of toxic exposure a vet got while on active duty?"

The VA would need to receive copies of veterans' private-care records so department medical personnel could spot potential service-related problems that develop later, she says.

That's a key challenge highlighted by others who oppose taking the Department of Veterans Affairs out of the comprehensive-care business. "When I was in Iraq, I was around a burn pit," Hansman, of the Iraq and Afghanistan veterans' organization, says, referring to open fires in which U.S. troops burned toxic waste. "I'm a little scared that I'm going to develop a cancer or some kind of respiratory issue. A private provider might not know burn pits exist and might not be able to make the connection."

Hansman, who currently uses private insurance, says he would turn to the VA if he develops a respiratory problem "because of the experience they're going to have with burn pit issues."

Park, of the government employees union, argues that "all veterans potentially have special needs that you will miss" in private practice. "People with subtle PTSD would be missed in that system."

Longman contends that providing comprehensive — often lifelong — care is a key to the VA's success. Doctors in that system are more likely to realize that some of a patient's symptoms are related, and are less likely to miss ailments or to provide duplicative treatment, he says.

Having a patient receive both VA and private care can lead to "duplicative, uncoordinated and inefficient" treatment, according to a RAND study. Researchers uncovered "substantial duplication of services provided to veterans who obtain care from both the [VA] and the private sector via the Medicare Advantage program," which pays private contractors to cover all of an older patient's medical needs. Between 2004 and 2009, Veterans Affairs provided some $13 billion worth of care that Medicare contractors already had been paid to deliver, the RAND report said.[44]

In addition, even some VA critics concede that private care can be more expensive. The department holds down costs in many ways, including paying health care workers less than they could make in the private sector, negotiating lower prescription drug prices and avoiding unnecessary treatment.

Antos, for instance, noted the importance of limiting the amount of private care available to veterans who face long wait times. Otherwise, he said, costs would "increase sharply if veterans chose private care over VA services."[45]

Similarly, Tanner says, there "is probably going to be more cost outside the VA system than treating them in the current system. We need to limit costs in some way, and I would do it by limiting those we treat."

Tanner also acknowledges Longman's argument that "a lot of people sign up for the military because we promised them health care." As a result, he says, "we might have to phase it in," referring to proposals to restrict VA care to service-related ailments.

BACKGROUND
System Origins

Governments in America have been helping veterans since at least 1636, when the Plymouth Colony, in what later became Massachusetts, made payments to veterans disabled in the Pequot Indian wars.[46] During the American Revolution, the Continental Congress authorized financial compensation for veterans who lost a limb or suffered other serious disability.[47]

After independence, payment was left up to the newly created states, but when the Constitution took effect in 1789 Congress offered federal payments. In the early 19th century, the War Department's Pensions Bureau administered veterans' programs, which were turned over to the Navy Department in 1840, then to the Interior Department in 1849.

The federal government began providing medical care to veterans in 1834 at the Naval Asylum in Philadelphia. Later, two facilities were established in Washington, D.C. — the National Soldiers' Home in 1853 and the Government Hospital for the Insane, which opened in 1855, began treating troops during the Civil War, and was renamed St. Elizabeth's Hospital later.

As the Civil War was drawing to a close in March 1865, President Abraham Lincoln called on the nation to "care for him who shall have borne the battle and for his widow, and his orphan" — which became the motto of subsequent veterans' agencies. Congress responded by authorizing the National Asylum for Disabled Volunteer Soldiers, whose first branch opened in 1866 in a bankrupt resort at Togus Springs, Maine, five miles from Augusta. Two additional branches opened in 1867, in Dayton, Ohio, and Milwaukee. Between then and 1930, 10 more asylums — later renamed homes — opened, creating the

kernel of what is now the Veterans Health Administration within the Department of Veterans Affairs.

The early homes provided shelter and some medical care to Union veterans. Over time recreational and educational activities and facilities were added, such as libraries and theaters. African-Americans were admitted to the homes but lived in segregated quarters and ate at separate tables.[48]

In 1921, Congress created the Veterans Bureau to manage health, education and insurance programs that had been run by other agencies. The Bureau of Pensions and the National Home for Disabled Volunteer Soldiers remained separate, however.

Charles Forbes — a World War I veteran and the director of the War Risk Insurance Bureau, one of the consolidated agencies — became the first Veterans Bureau director. He quickly set the stage for future mismanagement of federal veterans' programs by taking kickbacks and selling federal property for his personal enrichment; he was convicted of bribery and conspiracy.[49] Forbes was succeeded by retired Brig. Gen. Frank Hines, who continued to direct veterans services for 22 years.

Hines launched the Veterans Bureau's hospital-based research program in 1925. By the late 1920s the National Home branches had evolved into hospitals, and in 1930 Congress created the Veterans Administration out of the previously independent Veterans Bureau, Pensions Bureau and National Home for Disabled Volunteer Soldiers. Hines became its first administrator.

The VA grew steadily, expanding from 64 to 91 hospitals and from 33,669 to 61,849 beds between 1931 and 1941. Hines retired at the end of World War II and was replaced by Omar Bradley, one of the war's most important U.S. generals.

The war had killed more than 400,000 Americans, wounded nearly 675,000 and swollen the ranks of veterans from 5 million to more than 16 million by 1946. The 97 VA hospitals with 82,241 beds hit their patient capacity, and the VA began using Army and Navy facilities as well. By 1950, there were 151 VA hospitals.

Bradley began to modernize and restructure the organization. He put Maj. Gen. Paul Hawley, chief surgeon of the European theater, in charge of VA medicine. Hawley created a Department of Medicine, began for the first time offering outpatient treatment for non-service-related disabilities, created resident and teaching fellowships at

VA hospitals and began developing affiliations with medical schools. The first affiliation linked the VA's Chicago hospital with Northwestern University and the University of Illinois.

VA researchers started investigating veterans' chronic ailments, including those associated with aging, in the late 1950s, and Congress began appropriating funds specifically for VA research.

The renaissance was short-lived, however. While VA researchers conducted ground-breaking research, Congress cut VA funding, care deteriorated at many hospitals and many Korean War veterans were denied treatment if they couldn't prove they had service-related ailments.

Vietnam-Era Problems

From early 1961 to mid-1975, the Vietnam War created another 6 million veterans, many of whom presented new problems to the VA. Because better medical care and transportation saved troops who would have died in previous conflicts, a greater portion of Vietnam veterans came home with disabilities. They also developed ailments — including substance abuse and mental illness — that led to changes in VA policies and increased caseloads.

In 1979 the VA opened special centers where Vietnam veterans could receive counseling and treatment for post-traumatic stress disorder. The centers were opened to veterans of later wars in 1991 and to World War II and Korean War veterans in 1996.

In 1978 the VA began offering special services to Vietnam veterans worried about the long-term effects of Agent Orange, and in 1981 it began caring for Vietnam veterans whose health problems had unclear causes. The VA later recognized additional illnesses linked to Agent Orange, in 1991 and in 1993, following lawsuits by veterans seeking health benefits.

In 1988 the VA recognized that some older veterans could have suffered radiation-related ailments decades earlier during nuclear weapons tests in the United States and elsewhere and during the occupation of Hiroshima and Nagasaki after those Japanese cities were leveled by U.S. atomic bombs.

Also in 1988, the Veterans Administration was elevated to Cabinet status as the Department of Veterans Affairs, with three components — the Veterans Health Administration, the Veterans Benefits Administration and the National Cemetery System.

Like their Vietnam counterparts, veterans of the 1990–91 war against Iraq complained of symptoms, dubbed the Gulf War Syndrome — such as fatigue, skin rash, headache, muscle and joint pain, memory loss, difficulty concentrating, shortness of breath, sleep problems, gastrointestinal problems and chest pain — that seemed to have no clear cause.

The VA also dealt with numerous controversies over the years. It initially disputed contentions that veterans were injured by exposures to toxic substances in the Vietnam and Iraq wars, for instance.

In 1970, *Life* magazine found rats, filth and deficient medical care at a VA hospital in the Bronx.[50] In 1974 Vietnam veteran Ron Kovic — subject of the book and film "Born on the Fourth of July" — led a 19-day hunger strike to protest poor treatment he said he received in VA hospitals, leading to the resignation of VA Administrator Donald Johnson and a federal investigation of the agency's operations.

Investigations in 1976 by the Government Accounting Office (later renamed the Government Accountability Office) found deficiencies at VA hospitals in Denver and New Orleans. Congressional investigators in 1984 accused the VA of diverting or refusing to spend $40 million that Congress had allocated for Vietnam vet readjustment assistance. A probe by the VA's inspector general in 1986 discovered that 93 VA physicians had sanctions against their medical licenses. In 1991 the department halted vascular and orthopedic surgery at its North Chicago hospital after the VA inspector general reported that improper care may have caused patient deaths in 1989 and 1990.

The VA was not implementing modern best-practices, the New America Foundation's Longman said. It "still required hospital stays for routine operations [such as] cataract surgery. A patient couldn't even receive a pair of crutches without checking in."[51]

Clinton-Era Reforms

By then, the VA had earned a reputation as a massive, dysfunctional bureaucracy. The management structure had grown, partly to help prevent the corruption that had plagued the VA earlier. When President Bill Clinton made Kenneth Kizer undersecretary for health in 1994, the new head of VA medicine found the safeguards had become absurd.[52]

CHRONOLOGY

1865-1941 *Care for veterans expands because of Civil War, World War I.*

1866 First branch of National Asylum for Disabled Volunteer Soldiers opens in Togus Springs, Maine, after Civil War creates 1.9 million Union veterans.

1867 National Asylum branches open in Dayton, Ohio, and Milwaukee.

1918 More than 200,000 U.S. soldiers are wounded in World War I, which creates 4.6 million veterans.

1921 Charles Forbes named first director of Veterans Bureau, which manages health, education and insurance programs for veterans. Bureau of Pensions and the National Home for Disabled Volunteer Soldiers remain separate.

1923 Forbes resigns over corruption allegations and is later jailed. Retired Brig. Gen. Frank Hines takes over.

1930 Veterans Bureau, Pensions Bureau and National Home for Disabled Volunteer Soldiers merge into Veterans Administration (VA). Soldiers' Home branches become hospitals.

1941 VA has 91 hospitals with 61,849 beds.

1945-Present *VA's modern medical behemoth marked by major accomplishments and failures.*

1945 More than 16 million Americans serve in military during World War II; 672,000 are wounded.

1946 Chicago VA hospital establishes first medical school affiliations, with Northwestern University and University of Illinois.

1950 VA has 151 hospitals.

1953 Nearly 6 million Americans serve in the Korean War; 103,000 are wounded.

1970 *Life* magazine exposes rats, filth and deficient medical care at VA hospital in the Bronx, N.Y.

1974 Hunger strike protesting alleged poor treatment in VA hospitals leads to federal investigation and resignation of VA administrator.

1975 Official end of "Vietnam Era" leaves VA with 6 million new veterans and new medical challenges, such as ailments caused by toxic defoliant Agent Orange, and increased incidence of substance abuse.

1976 General Accounting Office reports deficiencies at VA hospitals in Denver and New Orleans.

1977 VA scientists win first two of three Nobel Prizes, for developing a technique to measure substances in blood and for discoveries about hormone production in the brain.

1979 VA opens special centers to treat post-traumatic stress disorder.

1988 VA becomes Cabinet-level Department of Veterans Affairs; recognizes illnesses stemming from radiation exposure at nuclear weapons tests and from World War II bombs dropped on Japan.

1989 VA establishes National Center for Posttraumatic Stress Disorder.

1991 Surgery halted at North Chicago VA hospital after 1989, 1990 deaths.

1994 Kenneth Kizer becomes undersecretary for health and implements reforms, including decentralized management structure and integrated electronic records.

2003 Investigators find 236,000 veterans waiting six months or more for appointments.

2009 Improperly disinfected equipment at VA facilities puts 10,000 colonoscopy patients at risk.

2013 VA inspector general reports that 3,800 veterans were waiting for gastroenterology appointments at Dorn Hospital in South Carolina in December 2011.

2014 VA grapples with Iraq and Afghanistan veterans' severe disabilities. . . . Cover-ups for long waits for appointments lead to resignations of VA secretary and health undersecretary. . . . Former Procter & Gamble chief Robert McDonald becomes VA secretary. . . . VA reports 46,000 job vacancies. . . . FBI, Justice Department and U.S. Office of Special Counsel conduct about 100 investigations into possible VA wrongdoing.

VA Boasts Legacy of Important Medical Research

Agency scientists invented pacemaker, developed nicotine patch.

William Bauman and Ann Spungen brought some good news in late September to the beleaguered Department of Veterans Affairs. The two VA scientists received Samuel J. Heyman Service to America medals, known as "Sammies," among the most prestigious honors given to federal workers.

Bauman and Spungen, director and associate director of the VA's spinal cord research center in the Bronx, N.Y., were recognized for numerous breakthroughs in understanding and treating ailments that stem from paralysis. Among their accomplishments: establishing links between paralysis and heart and lung diseases, advancing treatments for chronic pressure ulcers, formulating new drug combinations to treat low blood pressure, improving the effectiveness of colonoscopies on paralyzed patients and overseeing development of treatments for bone loss.[1]

Prestigious as the Sammies are within the federal government, however, the awards pale beside some of the others won over the decades by scientists in the VA health service's Office of Research and Development: three Nobel prizes and seven Lasker awards for medicine, often called "America's Nobels."

Not well known by the general public, VA researchers have been seeking treatments for veterans' ailments since 1925. And their findings often are life-changing for civilians as well.

For example, VA scientists:

- Developed effective tuberculosis treatments after World War II;
- Invented the implantable cardiac pacemaker (1958);
- Performed the first successful liver transplants (1968);
- Developed the nicotine patch (1984);
- Demonstrated that aspirin therapy could reduce heart attacks (1994);
- Found that conventional diuretics treated high blood pressure more effectively than newer medications (2002);
- Showed that lutein could help prevent and reverse the symptoms of macular degeneration, an eye disease (2004);
- Determined that drugs and lifestyle changes were about as effective as surgery in treating stable coronary artery disease (2007);
- Found a process to help veterans quit smoking (2010); and
- Showed in animal studies how stem-cell therapy could help heal spinal cord injury (2012).[2]

The VA conducts research because veterans suffer many health problems not common to the general public, says Timothy O'Leary, Veterans Health Administration chief research and development officer. The department also needs to study more common problems because many VA patients suffer the same chronic and aging-related ailments as the general public, he adds.

Post-traumatic stress disorder and traumatic brain injuries are not as common among civilians as in the military, O'Leary says. As a result, he says, those illnesses don't get sufficient attention from civilian researchers, and the VA has to fill the gap. On the other hand, the VA studies hypertension because "high blood pressure affects a large amount of our population."

"I had to approve reimbursement of a secretary . . . purchasing a cable for her computer," he said. "I think it was something like $11 or $12."[53]

Kizer reduced headquarters staffing, both in Washington and in the regions. He flattened the management hierarchy and delegated day-to-day responsibilities to local and regional managers. He instituted use of statistical reports to enable higher-level executives to understand better what was happening in the individual facilities where services were delivered. He signed pay-for-performance contracts with high-ranking administrators and established streamlined procedures for dismissing incompetent doctors.[54]

Having world-class research facilities and programs helps to attract top doctors who both conduct research and treat patients, often in affiliation with medical schools, O'Leary says. One division of the research office translates the research findings into best-practices advice for VA medical facilities and other medical institutions. And, he says, the VA's large and often long-term patient population — which is tracked in a nationwide electronic medical records system — provides a unique opportunity to conduct large, long-term studies.

"Many of these vets are going to be with us for life," O'Leary says. "If it's going to take us a little longer to study a problem, we will do it." For example, he says, a 15-year VA study determined that watching and waiting is as effective as surgery in treating early prostate cancer.

Researchers currently are recruiting VA patients for what they call the Million Veteran Program. The goal is to study 1 million veterans to advance knowledge about how genes affect health.

Participants will answer questions about their health and health-related behaviors, provide a blood sample for testing and allow access to their electronic medical records. Researchers will attempt to identify genes that are associated with certain diseases and that affect how people respond to treatment. They hope the results will lead to better treatments and preventive measures.[3]

The department also has begun "point-of-care research," which uses the electronic records to make research easier, faster, less expensive and less intrusive for patients.

The first studies are comparing the effectiveness of commonly prescribed medicines. Participants agree to receive randomly prescribed medicines that are considered equally effective at treating a patient's illness. Over time, the patients' records will show if one medicine actually works better than the other. The first point-of-care study, begun in 2011, is comparing two insulin regimens.[4]

VA research has not escaped the kind of exposés that have plagued the treatment side of the health administration.

The *Austin American-Statesman* reported Sept. 7 that a $3.6 million mobile brain scanner, intended for studying combat brain injuries, has not been used in three years and has never produced a published scientific paper.

Researchers had intended to scan the brains of soldiers at Fort Hood, Texas, before and after they deployed to Iraq or Afghanistan. The scanner was to be moved by truck between the fort and VA hospitals in Temple and Waco, about 30 and 65 miles away. However, officials stopped the first and only study in 2011 when the scanner could not produce usable images and the VA did not have personnel who could fix it. That followed failure of a similar VA program five years ago at the University of Texas in Austin. Together, the programs have spent $12 million, the newspaper said.[5]

The VA recently hired a new director at the Waco Center of Excellence for Research on Returning War Veterans (which oversees the program), added employees and pledged to restart the research.[6]

— *Tom Price*

[1] "VA Scientists Honored for Groundbreaking Work," James J. Peters VA Medical Center, Sept. 24, 2014,

http://tinyurl.com/pbd39m7.

[2] "Historical Accomplishments," Office of Research and Development, Veterans Health Administration, U.S. Department of Veterans Affairs, http://tinyurl.com/y2konfq.

[3] "The Million Veteran Program Overview," Office of Research and Development, Veterans Health Administration, U.S. Department of Veterans Affairs, http://tinyurl.com/ly8ry3t.

[4] "Point of Care Research Overview," Office of Research and Development, Veterans Health Administration, U.S. Department of Veterans Affairs, http://tinyurl.com/mvo7rdu.

[5] Jeremy Schwartz, "Empty promise," *Austin American-Statesman*, Sept. 7, 2014, p. 1.

[6] Jeremy Schwartz , "VA says MRI unit provided 'lessons,' " *Austin American-Statesman*, Oct. 4, 2014, p. 1.

He established a unified system of electronic medical records that enabled more-effective and safer treatment of individual patients no matter which facility they visited. In addition, the system enabled researchers to study which treatments work best and to discover patterns in veterans' illnesses. He also increased emphasis on primary and outpatient care, which tends to be more efficient than hospitalization.[55]

The result was a system that numerous studies found is as good as or better than any other health care provider in America.

VA Tries New Approaches to Treat PTSD

Scientists cite lack of data to measure therapies' effectiveness.

Iraq combat veteran Ruben Moreno Garcia met weekly with Department of Veterans Affairs (VA) psychologist Kathryn Williams to work on his post-traumatic stress disorder, but he did it without ever leaving his living room.

Moreno Garcia sat in front of a computer in his El Centro, Calif., home while Williams did the same in her office in La Jolla more than 100 miles away. Over the Internet, they could see each other's facial expressions and hear each other speak.

Nilesh Shah, director of telemedicine at the San Diego VA hospital, says many veterans find it hard to complete the prescribed number of therapy sessions because they live too far from a treatment center or are too busy. He describes long-distance psychotherapy as "the future."[1]

A 2012 study of 207 veterans found remote and in-person therapy to be equally effective after a 12-week regimen, said San Diego psychologist Steven Thorp, who led the research.[2]

Making the therapy work is crucial to the VA because while many veterans suffer from PTSD, the effectiveness of the department's treatment of the ailment remains in question.

In a congressionally ordered report released in June, the Institute of Medicine, part of the National Academy of Sciences, credited the VA with making "a sustained commitment to PTSD management and invest[ing] substantial financial and programmatic resources to provide care." But the department doesn't collect adequate information about patients' progress, the institute said. Thus, it "can't know for sure if the treatments reduce the prevalence of PTSD or improve the patients' lives," it said.[3]

PTSD incidence among post-9/11 Iraq and Afghanistan war veterans varies year to year from 11 to 20 percent, according to the National Center for PTSD, a research and education arm of the VA. The figure is about 12 percent for veterans of the 1990-91 Persian Gulf War. Among Vietnam War veterans surveyed in the late 1980s, about 15 percent had the disorder, and about 30 percent were estimated to have had it sometime during their lives.[4] A survey released in August found 11 percent of Vietnam veterans still suffer from PTSD.[5] About 8 percent of the general population will experience the ailment at some point.[6]

PTSD develops after "something terrible and scary that you see, hear about, or that happens to you," the PTSD center said. For civilians, that could be a car crash, an earthquake or sexual abuse, for example. For veterans it's likely to be what they experienced in combat.[7]

Victims may experience nightmares, sleep problems or a state of extreme vigilance. Other symptoms include flashbacks to the traumatic event, fear, guilt, shame, depression, despair, anxiety, withdrawal, drinking or drug problems and impaired relationships.[8]

The recent Vietnam veterans survey found that those with PTSD were twice as likely to have died by age 65 as those who did not suffer the disorder, at least in part because of the unhealthy behaviors the illness encourages.[9]

Studies published in the *Journal of Traumatic Stress* reported that cognitive processing therapy reduces PTSD symptoms in veterans, and the PTSD center says the approach is one of the most effective in treating the disorder.[10] With the help of a therapist over 12 sessions, veterans learn why they are having distressing thoughts and how to overcome them.[11]

During "prolonged exposure therapy," veterans talk about the trauma they suffered until the memories no longer upset them.[12]

A more experimental therapy is called eye movement desensitization and reprocessing (EMDR). The patient discusses the traumatic events while watching the movements of the therapist's hands or fingers. As the session progresses, the therapist has the patient shift to more pleasant thoughts. Both the VA and the Defense Department endorse the therapy, but scholarly analysis is mixed. A 2008 article in the *Journal of Clinical Psychology* said the therapy reduces veterans' PTSD symptoms.[13] But a 2009 article in *Behavioral Interventions* said evidence supporting the treatment was "sparse and equivocal."[14]

Supporters of the therapy don't agree about how it works. Some theorize that following the therapist's movements diverts attention from the trauma and reduces anxiety.[15]

In biofeedback therapy, a veteran first uses instruments to monitor physiological activities such as brain waves, heartbeats and breathing. The veteran learns to control the functions with breathing techniques and positive thinking, eventually without the monitors. The technique can promote relaxation and reduce stress.[16]

Some VA facilities offer stress relief through meditation, yoga or horseback riding, and help veterans cope through readjustment and employment counseling.[17]

The Institute of Medicine report noted the VA had made a "substantial" increase in mental health staff and had expanded training of psychotherapists. And it praised the VA for funding "broad PTSD research portfolios" and collaborating with the Defense Department, National Institutes of Health and other organizations to "fill research gaps."

The staff increase does not appear to have kept up with demand, however, the report said, and quality of PTSD care is uneven across the many VA sites. As a result, the report said, just over half of Iraq and Afghanistan veterans who sought PTSD psychotherapy received the recommended number of sessions.

In addition, in 2012, only 29 percent of veterans with PTSD were treated in specialized outpatient PTSD programs and 1 percent in specialized intensive PTSD programs. The rest were seen in general mental health or primary-care clinics.

The department is responding to the criticisms. It is modifying its record-keeping system to capture more PTSD-related data, the report said. [18] And VA researchers are investigating methods — like telemedicine in California — that would make it easier for veterans to participate in a lengthy series of therapy sessions.

— *Tom Price*

Jean Somers, whose son Daniel killed himself in 2013 after his second deployment in Iraq, weeps as she testifies at a hearing of the House Veterans' Affairs Committee on July 10, 2014. The committee was examining the VA's response to high suicide rates among service members. Somers said her son, who suffered from post-traumatic stress disorder, spent nearly six years unsuccessfully trying to access the VA health and benefit systems.

[1] Tony Perry, "Remote therapy effective for vets," *Los Angeles Times*, July 5, 2013, p. 1.

[2] *Ibid.*

[3] "Treatment for Posttraumatic Stress Disorder in Military and Veteran Populations: Final Assessment," Institute of Medicine, June 20, 2014, http://tinyurl.com/o3hh7b3.

[4] "How Common is PTSD?" National Center for Posttraumatic Stress Disorder, Veterans Health Administration, U.S. Department of Veterans Affairs, http://tinyurl.com/mfwb3ru.

[5] Benedict Carey, "Combat Stress Among Veterans Is Found to Persist Since Vietnam," *The New York Times*, Aug. 8, 2014, http://tinyurl.com/nvmmese.

[6] "How Common is PTSD?" *op. cit.*

[7] "What is PTSD?" National Center for Posttraumatic Stress Disorder, Veterans Health Administration, U.S. Department of Veterans Affairs, http://tinyurl.com/o5d499s.

[8] "Symptoms of PTSD," National Center for Posttraumatic Stress Disorder, Veterans Health Administration, U.S. Department of Veterans Affairs, http://tinyurl.com/mu63sul.

[9] Carey, *op. cit.*

[10] Benjamin D. Dickstein, Kristen H. Walter, Jeremiah A. Schumm and Kathleen M. Chard, "Comparing Response to Cognitive Processing Therapy in Military Veterans With Subthreshold and Threshold Posttraumatic Stress Disorder," *Journal of Traumatic Stress*, Nov. 15, 2013, http://tinyurl.com/lnmboto; Alexandra Macdonald, Candice M. Monson, Susan Doron-Lamarca, Patricia A. Resick and Tibor P. Palfai, "Identifying patterns of symptom change during a randomized

controlled trial of cognitive processing therapy for military-related posttraumatic stress disorder," *Journal of Traumatic Stress*, May 27, 2011, http://tinyurl.com/lftv2pv; PTSD expert helps 'pick up the pieces' of shattered lives," Partnership for Public Service," *The Washington Post*, Nov. 8, 2011, p. B4.

[11] "Cognitive Processing Therapy," National Center for Posttraumatic Stress Disorder, Veterans Health Administration, U.S. Department of Veterans Affairs, http://tinyurl.com/nu9txrm.

[12] "Prolonged Exposure Therapy," National Center for Posttraumatic Stress Disorder, Veterans Health Administration, U.S. Department of Veterans Affairs, http://tinyurl.com/opek6vq.

[13] Steven M. Silver, Susan Rogers and Mark Russell, "Eye movement desensitization and reprocessing (EMDR) in the treatment of war veterans," *Journal of Clinical Psychology*, July 8, 2008, http://tinyurl.com/l2ho5qr.

[14] David L. Albright and Bruce Thyer, "Does EMDR reduce post-traumatic stress disorder symptomatology in combat veterans?" *Behavioral Interventions*, Nov. 2, 2009, http://tinyurl.com/keoju5a.

[15] "EMDR: Eye Movement Desensitization and Reprocessing," *WebMD*, http://tinyurl.com/q6mzoko.

[16] *Ibid.*

[17] "Treatment for Posttraumatic Stress Disorder in Military and Veteran Populations: Final Assessment," *op. cit.*; "TRANSCRIPT: Secretary McDonald Press Conference Outlining The Road To Veterans Day," U.S. Department of Veterans Affairs, Sept. 8, 2014, http://tinyurl.com/pzglkwm; Teresa Moss, "VA adds PTSD treatments Expanded mental-health options give veterans choices," *Arkansas Democrat-Gazette*, Sept. 8, 2014, http://tinyurl.com/4hyh4; Robert A. McDonald, "VA is critical to medicine and vets," *The Baltimore Sun*, Oct. 24, 2014, http://tinyurl.com/mjsbmxk.

[18] "Treatment for Posttraumatic Stress Disorder in Military and Veteran Populations: Final Assessment," *op. cit.*

Problems Resurface

Despite the Clinton administration reforms, problems continued to surface in the 2000s, some of them foreshadowing this year's scandal. While many facilities continued to provide good care, others fell short.

The GAO in 2000 reported "substantial problems" in research with human subjects. While investigating eight VA hospitals around the country, the GAO discovered a "disturbing pattern" of failure to follow regulations to protect the safety of human research subjects. Each hospital allowed at least one study to occur without the informed consent of subjects. At two hospitals, boards that review research proposals had members who could benefit from a study being approved.

The next year, the investigating agency said veterans often were waiting more than 60 days for medical appointments despite a 30-day goal set in 1995. Lengthy wait times — 236,000 veterans waiting six months or more in 2003 — were "a clear indication" of "lack of sufficient capacity or, at a minimum, a lack of adequate resources to provide required care," according to a commission appointed by President George W. Bush.

Sensitive personal information about 26 million veterans and military personnel was put at risk in 2006 when a laptop computer was stolen from the home of a VA worker who was not supposed to have the computer in his residence. After recovering the laptop, police said that the theft appeared to be a routine burglary and that the data hadn't been accessed. But the incident led the Bush administration to recentralize some VA management in the name of security, undoing a key Clinton reform, Longman said.[56]

In 2009, the VA admitted that 10,000 veterans were put at risk of infection during colonoscopies because equipment wasn't disinfected properly. Two years later, nine veterans contracted hepatitis because a dentist at a Dayton VA clinic failed to wash his hands or change gloves between patients.

In 2013 William Montague, former director of VA facilities in Ohio, was indicted on charges of accepting bribes and kickbacks for steering business to a VA contractor. Also that year, the VA inspector general discovered that 3,800 veterans were waiting for gastroenterology appointments at the Dorn VA Hospital in South Carolina and that the hospital had spent just $200,000 of $1 million earmarked for reducing the backlog.[57]

The VA inspector general has issued 18 reports about scheduling problems since 2005.[58]

Kizer blamed the recent problems on "an unfocused performance-measurement program, increasingly centralized control of care delivery and associated increased bureaucracy, and increasing organizational insularity."

His performance-measurement system had used about two dozen measures of quality, "all of which had substantial clinical credibility," Kizer wrote in a paper with Boston VA physician Ashish Jha in July. Now the VA employs hundreds of measures, which "not only encourages gaming but also precludes focusing on, or even knowing, what's truly important," they wrote. The VA also has shifted toward a top-down management style that has increased central-office employment from 800 in the late 1990s to almost 11,000 in 2012, they said.[59]

Calls for heads to roll began to be answered on May 16, when VA Health Undersecretary Robert Petzel resigned after admitting he knew about the appointment-delay cover-ups as early as 2010, when a top department official identified 17 schemes being used.[60] Secretary Shinseki resigned May 30 and was replaced temporarily by Deputy Secretary Sloan Gibson. The Senate voted 97–0 to confirm McDonald as secretary on July 29.[61]

In response to the scandals, Congress in July adopted emergency legislation to give the department an extra $17 billion, including $5 billion for salaries, and to require the VA to pay for private care for veterans who live more than 40 miles from a VA facility or who face delays in getting a VA appointment.[62] Congress also made it easier for the VA to fire or demote senior executives, gave a fired executive just seven days to file an appeal and required the Merit Systems Protection Board to decide the appeal within 21 days. In the past, the board's goal was to make rulings within 120 days.[63]

CURRENT SITUATION
Reforms Unveiled

The Department of Veterans Affairs is entering the first stage of a reorganization designed to avoid repeating recent scandals by focusing on and listening to the veterans it serves. Secretary McDonald unveiled the effort on Nov. 10 and said it was informed by his summer and fall travels to meet with veterans, employees and others associated with the department.

Should veterans' health care be privatized?

YES   Michael Tanner
Senior Fellow Cato Institute

Written for *CQ Researcher*, November 2014

The problems besetting our veterans' health system will not be solved by changing personnel. The problems go back at least to 1945. Nor will spending more make things better. Department of Veterans Affairs (VA) spending has been rising faster than unique patient visits since at least 2007, and last summer's legislation added $2 billion.

Rather, the VA suffers from problems intrinsic to any government-run, single-payer health care system. Like all such systems, the VA controls costs by limiting spending on care. Thus, year-to-year funding varies according to the whims of Congress.

The VA is very good, therefore, at holding down costs. But it does so largely by rationing care. For example, VA physicians are paid on a salaried basis rather than through traditional fee-for-service. As a result, they see far fewer patients per day than most doctors. Thus, while we might be shocked by how the VA covered up its waiting lists, we should not be shocked that the lists exist.

Or consider that the VA maintains a very restrictive pharmaceutical formulary that often denies veterans access to the newest and most effective drugs. Alain Enthoven and Kyna Fong of Stanford University estimated that less than one-third of the drugs available to Medicare beneficiaries are on the VA formulary. Professor Frank Lichtenberg of Columbia University found that the restricted availability of drugs has reduced the average survival of veterans under VA care by as much as two months.

The solution lies in giving veterans themselves more control over their health care. First, we should return the VA health care system to its core mission of treating combat and other service-related injuries. Nearly 56 percent of VA patients today are being treated for illnesses unrelated to their service.

Second, even veterans with service-connected illnesses should have the option of going outside the VA for care. Yes, some traumatic combat injuries require specialized treatment not widely available outside the VA. But most injuries and illnesses, even combat-connected ones, can be treated elsewhere. Recent VA reforms take positive steps in this direction but leave too much of the final decision to bureaucrats.

All veterans with service-connected injuries should be allowed to seek treatment from any doctor or facility they wish. The VA would then reimburse the provider directly. Alternatively, veterans could be provided vouchers allowing them to purchase private health insurance. Either way, the choice and, therefore, the control, should be in vets' hands.

NO   Marilyn Park
Legislative Representative for VA Issues, American Federation of Government Employees

Written for *CQ Researcher*, November 2014

All Americans deserve an integrated health care system with specialized expertise, economies of scale, effective care coordination and a mission to keep patients healthy over the long run as opposed to simply maximizing profits. Sadly, our nation's fragmented health care delivery system and chronic physician shortages leave many consumers struggling to find good providers, enduring rushed medical appointments and falling through cracks entirely.

Veterans also deserve a specialized, coordinated health care system in return for their service to this country. Fortunately, they already have one: the Department of Veterans Affairs, the nation's largest integrated health care system that is consistently rated one of the country's top customer-service organizations.

Imagine veterans with post-traumatic stress disorder (PTSD) seeking emergency room care for an emotional breakdown; female veterans suffering from military sexual trauma needing help or Vietnam-era veterans with tremors unaware of the link between Agent Orange and Parkinson's disease. Should they be sent out to this fragmented health care system to manage their own diagnoses and treatment? The American Federation of Government Employees, which proudly represents 220,000 VA employees caring for veterans every day, echoes the resounding "No" of leading veterans' groups because only the VA's veteran-centric facilities specialize in the diagnosis and treatment of signature war wounds such as spinal cord injuries, vision loss, amputations, PTSD and traumatic brain injury.

The 2014 wait-list crisis had two takeaways: VA care is top notch once veterans get through the door, and we need more providers and clinic space to ensure they're treated in a timely manner. Recent bipartisan legislation provides emergency funding for more in-house staff, tackling the wait-time issue head-on.

Proponents of VA vouchers spend millions trying to convince Congress and the public that vouchers will outperform the VA — but they can't. The provider networks cannot match the VA's expertise, care coordination or electronic medical records. Steep CEO salaries are definitely no match for the VA's low administrative costs. When the VA cannot provide the care, it already has the authority and expertise to arrange contract care on a smaller scale. In fiscal 2014 alone, veterans had more than 2 million tele-health visits through the VA's state-of the-art virtual-care program covering more than 44 clinical specialties.

The risks of massive VA vouchering are frightening, both for the viability of the VA and the rest of the nation that benefits enormously from VA best practices, training and research.

In addition to creating the post of chief customer-service officer "to drive VA culture and practices to understand and respond to the expectations of our veteran customers," McDonald announced plans to:

- Simplify the VA's structure so veterans have a single point of contact.
- Implement management reforms to improve efficiency, such as by having VA components share internal services.
- Establish "community veteran advisory councils" to coordinate with state and local organizations that also serve veterans.
- Create an online suggestion box — called My VA Idea House — by which employees can offer suggestions and vote on one another's ideas.[64]

"Please keep in mind that this is a long-term process and we are just beginning to plan how this will all unfold," McDonald said.[65] But he vowed that "we will deliver."[66]

The announcement was greeted with support and skepticism.

"We think it is a good step forward, but it is only one of a marathon of steps that are going to be required to turn this around," said Paul Rieckhoff, founder and chief executive of Iraq and Afghanistan Veterans of America. "Having a plan is easy in Washington; executing that plan is hard. We'll see over the next few years if he can make it happen."

Garry J. Augustine, Washington executive director of the Disabled American Veterans, praised McDonald's plan to simplify the department's bureaucracy. "In the old system, there were a lot of layers, and one concern was that none of the bad news got up to the secretary because of all those layers," he said.

House Veterans' Affairs Committee Chairman Miller says McDonald isn't firing people fast enough. "New plans, initiatives and organizational structures are all well and good, but they will not produce their intended results until VA rids itself of the employees who have shaken veterans' trust in the system," he said. "So far VA hasn't done that."[67]

Others complained the department has been too slow to wield the enhanced firing powers contained in the reform law passed last summer. For instance, Sen. John McCain and Rep. Jeff Flake, both Arizona Republicans, jointly charged that the new provisions are "being ignored."[68]

The department said it has proposed disciplinary action against more than 40 employees.[69] Plus, "well over 1,000" employees face investigations that could lead to sanctions that range from admonishment to termination, according to McDonald.[70] And the FBI, Justice Department and U.S. Office of Special Counsel are conducting about 100 investigations that could lead to criminal charges.[71]

The first to be fired under the new procedures was James Talton. The department announced in late October that it had ended his tenure as director of the Central Alabama Veterans Health Care System, which had been plagued by fraudulent appointment records, unread X-rays and even an employee helping a patient buy crack cocaine. Earlier, the department announced termination proceedings against Cliff Robinson, Talton's chief of staff, hailing the action as evidence of the department's "commitment to hold leaders accountable."

Besides Talton's dismissal, the department announced on Oct. 6 that it planned to fire three other executives for misconduct or failing to manage their facilities effectively.[72] But two — Susan Taylor, deputy chief of procurement for the Veterans Health Administration, and John Goldman, director of the VA medical center in Dublin, Ga., — retired before they could be fired. Taylor was accused, among other things, of improperly steering VA business to her lover. Goldman was accused of allowing employees to produce fraudulent records showing inaccurate wait times for appointments.[73]

Terry Gerigk Wolf — director of the Pittsburgh VA Health Care System, where Legionnaires' disease killed at least six patients and sickened 16 others between February 2011 and November 2012 — was fired Nov. 13 after being given extra time to argue why she should not be dismissed.[74]

VA spokeswoman Kerry Meeker pointed out that "federal employees, including VA senior executives, are entitled to a meaningful opportunity to reply to the charges and evidence supporting a proposed removal."[75]

"We are as impatient as you are," McDonald said. "But while investigations are going on, we are not allowed to take definitive action."[76]

He also defended allowing executives to retire before they're fired. "It's very common in the private sector," he said. "When I was head of Procter & Gamble, it happened all the time, and it's not a bad thing — it saves us time and rules out the possibility that these people could win an appeal and stick around."[77]

McDonald's record at P&G — a giant global business with annual sales of $83 billion, 127,000 employees and 300 brands sold in more than 180 countries — has been cited as a qualification for running the VA and as a liability.[78]

"His management skills as a former CEO make him a good fit to run the department, which has been plagued by mismanagement for years," Miller said when McDonald was appointed."

"With the big business mindset," Iraq and Afghanistan Veterans' Hansman says, "hopefully he can bring some quality and timeliness changes to the VA and operate it more like a business than a bureaucracy."

However, McDonald's lack of health care and government experience drew criticism from others. The New America Foundation's Longman, for instance, described McDonald as "a Republican soap and toothpaste salesman — a man with no experience whatsoever in running a health care or social services organization."

In addition, McDonald left P&G amid criticisms similar to those leveled recently at the VA: He moved too slowly to solve problems in a company with a "convoluted" organizational structure, said hedge fund executive William Ackman, who owned 29 million shares of P&G stock. McDonald's supporters said recalcitrant managers and a complacent corporate culture did him in — similar to what he could face within the VA bureaucracy and from members of Congress.[79]

Progress So Far

A few days before announcing its reorganization plans, the VA released a report about progress it already had made addressing the shortcomings revealed by the scandals.[80] Among other things, the VA said it had:

• Kept its clinics open longer.
• Solicited comments from veterans and the public at town hall meetings in every medical center and benefits office. The meetings will be repeated every three months.[81]
• Completed 1.2 million more appointments in July through October than in the same period in 2013.

VA employees Kristen Ruell and Ronald Robinson and fired worker Javier Soto, right, told a House hearing on July 14, 2014, about reprisals against them after they reported mismanagement at VA facilities. The VA is now moving to protect such whistleblowers, and the department has reached settlements with three, two of whom were promoted.

• Made 98 percent of appointments within 30 days of either the date the patient requested or the date a VA provider said was "clinically appropriate."

The 30-day period is a new standard adopted after an audit determined that the previous two-week goal was unrealistic. The VA will pay for private care to keep a veteran from waiting longer.

Undersecretary Clancy says what's important is that the wait meet the patient's needs and expectations, rather than the specific number of days. "If I'm worried and extremely anxious [the need] might be today or in the next day or two," she explains. "If it's just some checkup that I've got to get sometime, all I need is a predictable date."

The VA has steadily reduced wait times for new patients' first primary-care appointments — the heart of the appointment scandals — from an average of 51.23 days in mid-May to 42.08 days on Sept. 1. However, the Sept. 1 waits differed widely at individual facilities, from 82.89 days in Fayetteville, N.C., to 15.66 in Bedford, Mass. Waits for existing patients increased during that time period, but they were low to begin with — averaging 3.56 days in May and 5.83 in September.[82]

By comparison, a 15-city survey last year found average waits of 19.5 days for first appointments with private family physicians. The survey, by Merritt Hawkins, a Texas-headquartered consulting firm that recruits health care personnel, also found a wide range of wait times to see a family physician, from 66 days in Boston to five in Dallas.[83]

The department is moving to protect whistleblowers attempting to reveal VA problems. In October the U.S. Office of Special Counsel certified the VA's whistleblower protection program. And the department reached settlements with three whistleblowers, two of whom were promoted, underscoring McDonald's pledge to encourage and reward those who call attention to shortcomings.

OUTLOOK

Future Challenges

The Department of Veterans Affairs will face stiff challenges in the coming decades, many in tandem with the overall U.S. health care system.

The VA's struggle to hire enough medical personnel will be exacerbated by a nationwide shortage of doctors. Today, 30 percent of American doctors are nearing retirement age.[84] By 2020, according to the American Association of Medical Colleges, the shortage of physicians will reach 91,500, a figure that will soar to 130,600 five years later.[85]

That's due in part to the fact that physician training funded by Medicare hasn't grown since 1997, when Congress capped the number of federally subsidized residencies at 26,000.[86]

"We have a growing population and an aging population that's requiring more services, but we've been training essentially the same number of doctors since 1997," said Phillip Miller, vice president of communications for the Merritt Hawkins recruiting firm.[87] Democratic Sen. Robert Casey of Pennsylvania has introduced legislation to add 15,000 federally subsidized residencies by 2019.[88]

Some warn that the VA reform legislation passed last summer, which makes it easier to fire senior executives and shortens the appeals process, could end up making it harder to hire high-ranking executives. Some senior executives say that could lead to a return of the "spoils system," which allowed government employees to be hired and fired for partisan political reasons.

"The best current executives will retire, and excellent candidates will refrain from applying to the SES [the Senior Executive Service, which encompasses the federal government's top-ranking civil service managers]," said Carol Bonosaro, president of the Senior Executives Association, which represents senior executives. "The service may well become a place of last resort, as high-performing employees take their skills to the private sector."[89]

Others contend that the Merit Systems Protection Board, charged with protecting a nonpolitical civil service, will not be able to decide appeals of firings within 21 days, as the new law requires. "It's not physically possible," said Kristin Alden, a Washington-based lawyer who specializes in federal employment law.[90] The board's administrative law judges currently take an average of 93 days to decide an appeal.[91]

The VA also will grapple with a growing number of female patients among what traditionally was a nearly all-male clientele. Women now comprise 9 percent of America's veterans, a figure expected to reach 17 percent over the next three decades.[92]

Today, only 390,000 of the VA's 6.6 million patients are women. But that number is double the total in 2000, and the department already is struggling to meet their needs.

The VA is researching military women's experiences with sexual harassment and rape, developing prosthetics especially for women and adding women's restrooms in VA facilities.[93] But nearly a quarter of VA hospitals do not have a full-time gynecologist, and 15 percent of community clinics do not have a designated women's health provider, as required. As a result, many female veterans drive hours for care.

In addition, because of their lack of experience with women, VA health care providers make potentially life-changing mistakes. For example, VA pharmacies have given half of their female clients medicines that can cause birth defects.[94]

VA officials also must anticipate future demands without knowing how many veterans they will have to treat, what those veterans' needs will be and how much money the department will have to work with.

"Imagine what it's like to manage this institution," the New America Foundation's Longman says, "when you don't know what your budget's going to be year to year, you don't know what the U.S. military is going to be doing, you don't know whether there's going to be a war or not."

NOTES

1. Reynaldo Leal, "My name is Bob and 'I CARE,' " *Vantage Point*, U.S. Department of Veterans Affairs, Oct. 9, 2014, http://tinyurl.com/pupr6mj.

2. Robert McDonald, "Veterans Affairs Secretary McDonald Updates Employees on MyVA Reorganization Plans," Department of Veterans Affairs, Nov. 10, 2014, http://tinyurl.com/ob8qwf6.

3. Dennis Wagner, "Auditor ties VA waits to deaths," *The Arizona Republic*, Sept. 17, 2014, http://tinyurl.com/p25gu57.

4. Joe Davidson, "VA is looking for a few good doctors and nurses," *The Washington Post*, Aug. 28, 2014, http://tinyurl.com/lu6sjtl; Emily Wax-Thibodeaux, "VA secretary lays out 90-day plan for fixing troubled agency," *The Washington Post*, Sept. 8, 2014, http://tinyurl.com/q687gm5.

5. Robert A. McDonald, "VA is critical to medicine and veterans," *The Baltimore Sun*, Oct. 24, 2014, http://tinyurl.com/mjsbmxk; Leal, *op. cit.*

6. Dave Philipps, "After Hospital Scandal, V.A. Officials Jump Ship," *The New York Times*, Oct. 17, 2014, http://tinyurl.com/ogmjen4.

7. Emily Wax-Thibodeaux, "McCain to new VA Secretary: Hurry up and fire people already," *The Washington Post*, Oct. 24, 2014, http://tinyurl.com/p3zllek.

8. Phillip Longman, "The Best Care Anywhere," *The Washington Monthly*, January/February 2005, http://tinyurl.com/nzmj9t2.

9. Dennis Wagner, "The doctor who launched the VA scandal," *The Arizona Republic*, May 31, 2014, http://tinyurl.com/pr7jxeu.

10. Wesley Lowery and Josh Hicks, "'Troubling' report sparks new wave of calls for VA chief's resignation," *The Washington Post*, May 28, 2014, http://tinyurl.com/onww2sd.

11. "VA Access Audit & Wait Times Fact Sheet System-Wide Overview," U.S. Department of Veterans Affairs, June 9, 2014.

12. Greg Jaffe and Josh Hicks, "VA audit: 57,000 veterans waiting more than 90 days for appointment at medical facilities," *The Washington Post*, June 9, 2014, http://tinyurl.com/kn9fkgb.

13. Paul Giblin, "As services for vets rose, funding fell," *The Arizona Republic*, June 15, 2014, p. 1.

14. *Ibid.*; Doyle McManus, "What the VA needs next," *Los Angeles Times*, Nov. 10, 2013, p. A24.

15. *Ibid.*

16. "Annual Budget Submission," U.S. Department of Veterans Affairs, March 7, 2014, www.va.gov/budget/products.asp.

17. "The Independent Budget for the Department of Veterans Affairs Fiscal Year 2015," American Veterans, Disabled American Veterans, Paralyzed Veterans of America and Veterans of Foreign Wars, undated, http://tinyurl.com/pb3q5g4.

18. Josh Hicks, "Groups call for increased VA spending in advance of Obama's 2015 budget," *The Washington Post*, Feb. 6, 2014, http://tinyurl.com/kk8towl.

19. Emily Wax-Thibodeaux, "VA plans to offer salary boost to attract new doctors," *The Washington Post*, Sept. 17, 2014, http://tinyurl.com/k3z5jyo.

20. *Ibid.*

21. "Annual Pay Ranges for Physicians and Dentists of the Veterans Health Administration," U.S. Department of Veterans Affairs, *Federal Register*, Sept. 18, 2014.

22. *Ibid.*

23. Tom Coburn, "Friendly Fire: Death, Dismay and Delay at the VA," undated, http://tinyurl.com/jvws9gj.

24. *Ibid.*

25. *Ibid.*

26. *Ibid.*

27. McManus, *op. cit.*

28. Joseph Antos, "It's Time for Real Reform of Veterans' Health Care," *The American*, July 31, 2014, http://tinyurl.com/mtzfdvq.

29. Kristin Brown, "Krauthammer: VA scandal indicative of wider problems with government-run health care systems," Fox News, May 26, 2014, http://tinyurl.com/lqw8qnz.

30. Suzanne Gordon, "Privatization won't fix the VA," *The Boston Globe*, May 27, 2014, http://tinyurl.com/mr6loz4.

31. Michael D. Tanner, "Fixing the VA: Beyond the Usual Suspects," *The Hill*, June 13, 2014, http://tinyurl.com/l6k9d4h.

32. Phillip Longman, *Best Care Anywhere: Why VA Health Care Would Work Better for Everyone* (2012), p. 7.

33. Arthur L. Kellermann, "Socialized' or Not, We Can Learn from the VA," RAND Blog, Aug. 8, 2012, http://tinyurl.com/m3ovjad.

34. Josh Hicks, "Some key facts about VA's Veterans Health Administration," *The Washington Post*, May 30, 2014, p. A7, http://tinyurl.com/ppk3wnq.

35. Sandhya Somashekhar, "VA and its systemic health-care problems," *The Washington Post*, May 31, 2014, p. A3, http://tinyurl.com/prd9nmr.

36. Paul Giblin, "Survey looks at veterans issues," *The Arizona Republic*, July 24, 2014, p. A6, http://tinyurl.com/mvbhr4q.

37. Dennis Wagner, "VA touts progress on suicides; data tell another story," *The Arizona Republic*, Aug. 25, 2014, p. 1, http://tinyurl.com/l9hz5lv.

38. Kenneth W. Kizer and Ashish K. Jha, "Restoring Trust in VA Health Care," *The New England Journal of Medicine*, July 24, 2014, http://tinyurl.com/lm8wvlj.

39. Josh Hicks, "New details about the VA plan to allow more private care," *The Washington Post*, May 28, 2014, http://tinyurl.com/oa2a2ph; Gretel C. Kovach, "Congress passes VA reform," *San Diego Union-Tribune*, July 31, 2014, http://tinyurl.com/mfoq9su.

40. "Priority Groups Table," U.S. Department of Veterans Affairs, http://tinyurl.com/ndmbko9.

41. Michelle Andrews, "For veterans, Affordable Care Act provides more options but doesn't meet all needs," *The Washington Post*, May 7, 2013, p. E4, http://tinyurl.com/br52va9.

42. Phillip Longman, "How VA Outsourcing Hurts Veterans," *The Washington Monthly*, June 8, 2014, http://tinyurl.com/nhoonet.

43. Antos, *op. cit.*

44. David I. Auerbach, William B. Weeks and Ian Brantley, "Health Care Spending and Efficiency in the U.S. Department of Veterans Affairs," RAND Corp., 2013, http://tinyurl.com/q9u6elg.

45. Antos, *op. cit.*

46. Doug Bandow, "Firing Veterans Affairs' Eric Shinseki Was Only the Start," *Forbes*, June 2, 2014, http://tinyurl.com/mkgyvr5.

47. Unless otherwise noted, information for this historical section comes from "VA History in Brief," Department of Veterans Affairs, http://tinyurl.com/oj4kf8x; Michael Pearson, "The VA's troubled history," CNN, May 30, 2014, http://tinyurl.com/or36qr9; and Longman, 2012, *op. cit.*

48. Trevor K. Plante, "Genealogy Notes: The National Home for Disabled Volunteer Soldiers," *Prologue Magazine*, U.S. National Archives, Spring 2004, http://tinyurl.com/pmd8o4w.

49. David A. Fahrenthold, "VA successes undone by culture of cover-ups," *The Washington Post*, June 1, 2014, p. 1, http://tinyurl.com/qfln5qu.

50. For background, see Peter Katel, "Caring for Veterans," *CQ Researcher*, April 23, 2010, pp. 361–384; and Peter Katel, "Wounded Veterans," *CQ Researcher*, Aug. 31, 2007, pp. 697–720.

51. Longman, 2005, *op. cit.*

52. Fahrenthold, *op. cit.*

53. *Ibid.*

54. Kizer and Jha, *op. cit.*; Longman, 2005, *op. cit.*; Fahrenthold, *op. cit.*

55. Longman, *ibid.*

56. Larry Abramson, "Stolen Laptop with Veterans' Information Returned," NPR, June 30, 2006, http://tinyurl.com/o88kzcw; Phillip Longman, "Clueless or Craven?" *The Washington Monthly*, July 1, 2014, http://tinyurl.com/nmr9w54.

57. Katie Zezima, "Everything you need to know about the VA — and the scandals engulfing it," *The Washington Post*, May 22, 2014, http://tinyurl.com/qztd4bl.

58. Hicks, May 30, 2014, *op. cit.*

59. Kizer and Jha, *op. cit.*

60. Josh Hicks, "This memo shows that the VA knew of records manipulation in 2010," *The Washington Post*, May 20, 2014, http://tinyurl.com/q682y4b.

61. Richard A. Oppel Jr., "Senate Confirms Obama's Choice to Lead V.A.," *The New York Times*, July 29, 2014, http://tinyurl.com/nga7cmx.

62. Bob Brewin, "VA Lays Groundwork for Private Health Care," NextGov, Sept. 15, 2014, http://tinyurl.com/q6qdft7; Wax-Thibodeaux, Sept. 17, 2014, *op. cit.*

63. Josh Hicks, "The VA bill would make firings easier. Is that a good thing?" *The Washington Post*, July 29, 2014, http://tinyurl.com/ljr9t6b.

64. McDonald, Nov. 10, 2014, *op. cit.*

65. *Ibid.*

66. Dennis Wagner, "VA overhaul announced, but few details are offered," *The Arizona Republic*, Nov. 11, 2014, p.A6, http://tinyurl.com/nzd699c.

67. Richard A. Oppel Jr., "V.A. Creates Plans to Consolidate Services," *The New York Times*, Nov. 10, 2014, http://tinyurl.com/pcgdufb.

68. Wax-Thibodeaux, Oct. 24, 2014, *op. cit.*

69. "'Road to Veterans Day' Sets Conditions for Long-Term Reform at VA," *VA News*, U.S. Department of Veterans Affairs, Nov. 6, 2014, http://tinyurl.com/qbwysm2.

70. Philipps, *op. cit.*

71. Bryant Jordan, "VA Moves to Fire Already-Retired Hospital Director," *Military.com*, Sept. 26, 2014, http://tinyurl.com/oxe77qc.

72. Matthew Daly, "VA moves to ax 4 senior execs in scandal response," The Associated Press, Oct. 7, 2014, http://tinyurl.com/m96jlol.

73. Philipps, *op. cit.*

74. Mike Wereschagin, "Pittsburgh VA director gets more time to appeal firing recommendation," *Pittsburgh Tribune Review*, Oct. 18, 2014, http://tinyurl.com/pjbav7j.

75. *Ibid.*

76. Wax-Thibodeaux, Oct. 24, 2014, *op. cit.*

77. Philipps, *op. cit.*

78. "The Procter & Gamble Company," Hoovers, undated, http://tinyurl.com/pmlwyab; Greg Jaffe and Steven Mufson, "Robert McDonald, Obama's VA nominee, faced own challenges at Procter & Gamble, *The Washington Post*, July 1, 2014, http://tinyurl.com/kouykde.

79. Phillip Longman, "Clueless or Craven? The White House Gets the VA Story Exactly Backwards," *The Washington Monthly*, July 1, 2014, http://tinyurl.com/nmr9w54.

80. "Progress on the 'Road to Veterans Day' Sets Conditions for Long-Term Reform at VA," U.S. Department of Veterans Affairs, Nov. 6, 2014, http://tinyurl.com/l93c2et.

81. "'Road to Veterans Day' Sets Conditions for Long-Term Reform at VA," *op. cit.*; Wax-Thibodeaux, Oct. 24, 2014, *op. cit.*

82. "Patient Access Data," Veterans Affairs Department, http://tinyurl.com/qa457as.

83. "2014 Survey of Physician Appointment Wait Times and Medicaid and Medicare Acceptance Rates," Merritt Hawkins, http://tinyurl.com/pmx7vcb.

84. Emily Wax-Thibodeaux, "Nurse practitioners say they can help VA with staffing shortages," *The Washington Post*, Sept. 18, 2014, http://tinyurl.com/pnek6r7.

85. "Physician Shortages to Worsen Without Increases in Residency Training," American Association of Medical Colleges, Center for Workforce Studies, June 2010, http://tinyurl.com/m6rm3s8.

86. Lydia O'Neal, "Casey introduces bill to boost primary care docs," *The Philadelphia Inquirer*, June 10, 2014, p. B5, http://tinyurl.com/oxryaza.

87. Sig Christenson, "Long VA doctor waits sign of times?" *The Houston Chronicle*, June 17, 2014, p. 1, http://tinyurl.com/o9b6w9v.

88. O'Neal, *op. cit.*

89. Joe Davidson, "Senior Executive Service changes should not include mass punishment," *The Washington Post*, July 14, 2014, p. A11, http://tinyurl.com/ks8v2v2.

90. Hicks, July 29, 2014, *op. cit.*

91. Joe Davidson, "Merit board head says with new VA law 'we are absolutely in new territory,'" *The Washington Post*, Aug. 10, 2014, http://tinyurl.com/laua4mp.

92. Todd South, "Today's Veterans Have a New Look," *The Record*, Nov. 11, 2014, p. 1, http://tinyurl.com/q8zdcpk.

93. For background, see Jennifer Koons, "Sexual Assault in the Military," *CQ Researcher*, Aug. 9, 2013, pp. 693–716.

94. Garance Burke, The Associated Press, "Review finds that Veterans Affairs is falling short on female medical issues," *The Washington Post*, June 23, 2014, http://tinyurl.com/p7wh4gl.

BIBLIOGRAPHY

Selected Sources

Books

Glantz, Aaron, *The War Comes Home: Washington's Battle Against America's Veterans, University of California Press*, 2009.
A journalist who covered the Iraq War reports critically on the state of Department of Veteran's Affair (VA) services.

Longman, Phillip, *Best Care Anywhere: Why VA Health Care Would Work Better for Everyone, Barrett-Koehler Publishers*, 3rd ed., 2012.
A research fellow at the New America Foundation argues that the VA's integrated health care system is as good as or better than that of any other U.S. medical provider.

Schram, Martin, *Vets Under Siege, St. Martin's Press*, 2008.
A veteran Washington reporter examines the VA's efforts to meet the demands imposed on it by the Iraq and Afghanistan wars.

Articles

Carey, Benedict, "Combat Stress Among Veterans Is Found to Persist Since Vietnam," *The New York Times*, Aug. 8. 2014, http://tinyurl.com/nvmmese.
A new survey shows a surprisingly large number of Vietnam veterans continue to suffer from post-traumatic stress disorder.

Chandrasekaran, Rajiv, "The other wounds," *The Washington Post*, April 8, 2014, http://tinyurl.com/pafxjup.
An associate editor at *The Washington Post* who covered the Iraq and Afghanistan wars shows how bullets and bombs are not the only instruments of battlefield injury.

Jaffe, Greg, and Steven Mufson, "Robert McDonald, Obama's VA nominee, faced own challenges at Procter & Gamble," *The Washington Post*, July 1, 2014, http://tinyurl.com/kouykde.
A military writer (Jaffe) and a business writer describe new VA Secretary Robert McDonald's uneven record as CEO of Procter & Gambler.

Kellermann, Arthur L., " 'Socialized' or Not, We Can Learn from the VA," *RAND Blog*, Aug. 8, 2012, http://tinyurl.com/m3ovjad.
A think tank analyst reviews RAND's VA studies, concluding that the department delivers "consistently high-quality care."

Kizer, Kenneth W., and Ashish K. Jha, "Restoring Trust in VA Health Care," *The New England Journal of Medicine*, July 24, 2014, http://tinyurl.com/lm8wvlj.
The health undersecretary credited with turning around VA health care in the 1990s (Kizer) and a Boston VA physician say the department has slipped back into bad old habits and explain how it could recover.

McDonald, Robert A., "VA is critical to medicine and vets," *The Baltimore Sun*, Oct. 24, 2014, http://tinyurl.com/mjsbmxk.
The VA secretary argues that the department should not be privatized.

Schwartz, Jeremy, "Empty Promise," *Austin American-Statesman*, Sept. 7, 2014, p. 1.
A Texas reporter discovers that a $3.6-million mobile brain scanner, intended for studying combat brain injuries, has not been used in three years and has never produced a published scientific paper.

Wagner, Dennis, "The doctor who launched the VA scandal," *The Arizona Republic*, May 31, 2014, http://tinyurl.com/pr7jxeu.
A reporter profiles the VA doctor who told the government and the media about a scheme to cover up long waits at the Phoenix VA hospital.

Reports and Studies

"Historical Accomplishments," *Office of Research and Development, Veterans Health Administration, U.S. Department of Veterans Affairs*, http://tinyurl.com/y2konfq.

The VA research program lists its achievements, from hospital-based studies in 1925 through three Nobel Prizes to its work today on post-traumatic stress disorder and traumatic brain injury.

"How Common is PTSD?" *National Center for Posttraumatic Stress Disorder, Veterans Health Administration, U.S. Department of Veterans Affairs,* **http://tinyurl.com/mfwb3ru.**
The VA's PTSD center explains who is most likely to suffer from post-traumatic stress disorder and why.

"The Independent Budget for the Department of Veterans Affairs Fiscal Year 2015," *American Veterans, Disabled American Veterans, Paralyzed Veterans of America and Veterans of Foreign Wars,* **http://tinyurl.com/pb3q5g4.**

Four U.S. veterans' organizations present a detailed argument for why the VA needs a larger budget.

"Treatment for Posttraumatic Stress Disorder in Military and Veteran Populations: Final Assessment," *Institute of Medicine,* **June 20, 2014, http://tinyurl.com/o3hh7b3.**
A committee from the National Academy of Sciences medical component delivers a mixed verdict on the quality of VA treatment of PTSD.

"VA History in Brief," *Department of Veterans Affairs,* **http://tinyurl.com/oj4kf8x.**
The VA traces how America has cared for its veterans since the Plymouth Colony in 1636.

For More Information

American Legion, 700 N. Pennsylvania St., Indianapolis, IN 46206; 317-630-1200; www.legion.org. Largest U.S. veterans organization, with 2.4 million members in 14,000 posts; provides services to and advocates for veterans.

Disabled American Veterans, 3725 Alexandria Pike, Cold Spring, KY 41076; 877-426-2838; www.dav.org. Represents the interests of disabled veterans before the federal government and helps veterans obtain government benefits and services.

Iraq and Afghanistan Veterans of America, 292 Madison Ave., 10th Floor, New York, NY 10017; 212-982-9699; www.iava.org. Focuses primarily on the needs of those who fought in America's most recent wars.

National Center for Posttraumatic Stress Disorder, VA Medical Center, 116D 215 N. Main St., White River Junction, VT, 05009; 802-296-5132; www.ptsd.va.gov. Established in the Department of Veterans Affairs (VA) in

1989 to conduct research and disseminate information about PTSD.

National Military Family Association, 3601 Eisenhower Ave., Suite 425, Alexandria, VA 22304; 703-931-6632; www.militaryfamily.org. Advocates, conducts research and provides such services as scholarships, summer camps for children and retreats for families.

Veterans Health Administration, 810 Vermont Ave., N.W., Washington, DC 20420; 202-273-5781; www.va.gov/health. Health care arm of the VA; provides treatment to 6.6 million patients annually.

Veterans Health Administration Research and Development Office, 810 Vermont Ave., N.W., Washington, DC 20420; 202-443-5602; www.research.va.gov. Conducts research into wide range of veterans' illnesses suffered both in military service and civilian life.

14

Immigrant Detention

Reed Karaim

Honduran immigrant Maria Celeste Castro and her daughter await processing by U.S. Border Patrol officers after crossing the Rio Grande River near Mission, Texas. Severe criticism of detention conditions for immigrant families prompted the Obama administration in September to announce it would allow most women and children to be released pending asylum rulings.

From *CQ Researcher*, October 23, 2015.

Like prison inmates, the 1,550 detainees in Eloy, Ariz., wear gray uniforms and are held under guard behind high fences topped by concertina wire.

"The conditions are very depressing," says Marjorie King, a university associate at the University of Arizona in Tucson who visits the Eloy detainees on behalf of Casa Mariposa, a faith-based group that advocates for immigrants. "There's no freedom of movement. They're supervised everywhere they go. They're constantly being yelled at. It very much resembles a prison."

But the Eloy facility isn't a prison. It's a detention center operated by Corrections Corporation of America (CCA), the nation's largest private prison company, for undocumented immigrants who are awaiting deportation or a ruling on their eligibility to remain in the country.

The men and women at Eloy are part of a national immigrant detainee population that shot up from 85,000 in 1995 to 425,728 in 2014. Detainees are held for varying amounts of time, but on any given night in 2014, 33,227 immigrants, on average, were being held in federal custody. More people now pass through the immigrant detention system each year than through federal Bureau of Prisons facilities.[1] The growth has occurred despite a slowdown in illegal border crossings into the United States since 2007 and a leveling off in the nation's undocumented immigrant population, which has held steady at about 11.3 million for five years.[2]

The U.S. government's widespread use of detention of would-be immigrants is highly controversial, with defenders saying it's a way to dissuade other undocumented immigrants from coming to the

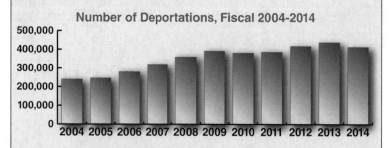

Deportations Soared in Past Decade

Federal authorities deported 414,000 undocumented immigrants in fiscal 2014, roughly 24,000 fewer than in 2013. Deportations rose by 82 percent from 2004 to 2013, when they peaked at 438,000. The share of deported immigrants with criminal backgrounds rose from 29 percent in 2008 to 45 percent in 2013. The background information on 2014 deportees was not available.

Number of Deportations, Fiscal 2004-2014

Source: 2014 data from "DHS Releases End of Year Statistics," U.S. Department of Homeland Security, Dec. 19, 2014, http://tinyurl.com/pglvoe6; data for 2004 to 2013 from Table 41, "Yearbook of Immigration Statistics: 2013 Enforcement Actions," Office of Immigration Statistics, U.S. Department of Homeland Security, January 2014, http://tinyurl.com/q8hrzgp

United States and critics saying it unnecessarily imprisons thousands of people, including women and young children and sometimes even U.S. citizens.

Many centers are run by for-profit prison companies, some of which pay detainees as little as $1 a day to do janitorial work and other menial labor at the centers.[3] The Obama administration announced in June that it was taking steps to limit the detention of women and children, many of whom have arrived over the last two years seeking asylum from violence-plagued Central America.[4] Last November, President Obama also said the government would refocus its immigration enforcement on individuals who present a threat to national security or public safety.

"Felons, not families. Criminals, not children," will be the priority, Obama said.[5]

But immigrant advocates believe the administration's effort is falling short of the president's rhetoric. "Mostly, I think it's failed," says Silky Shah, co-director of the Detention Watch Network, a national coalition working to challenge what it considers the injustices of the U.S. immigrant detention and deportation system. "We're still seeing families in detention. We still have a really high rate of detention generally."

The debate over immigrant detention centers on a complicated system in which noncitizens can end up being held through a variety of circumstances. Undocumented immigrants caught trying to cross the U.S. border often spend a short period in detention before being deported. But people who show up at border crossings requesting asylum, such as thousands of Central American families trying to escape gang violence at home, also can be detained while their claims are investigated.[6]

And immigrants who have lived legally in the United States for decades can end up in detention after serving time in the United States for certain crimes, including misdemeanors. After completing their sentences, the immigrants may be turned over to U.S. Immigration and Customs Enforcement (ICE), a federal agency within the Department of Homeland Security (DHS), for detention while the government determines whether their record merits deportation.

But those are the not the only ways in which immigrants have ended up in detention. Under an ICE program called Fugitive Operations, the agency sends teams out to find dangerous fugitive migrants. But a 2009 study by the Migration Policy Institute, a nonpartisan Washington think tank that studies the movement of people worldwide, found that three-fourths of the undocumented immigrants rounded up through the program had no criminal record.[7]

On occasion, even American citizens have been mistakenly detained and deported, without having had access to legal counsel. Jacqueline Stevens, a professor of political science at Northwestern University in Evanston, Ill., has documented more than 40 cases of U.S. citizens held in detention and believes, that on any given day, up to 1 percent of detainees could be citizens.[8]

In one case, Mark Lyttle, a North Carolinian with bipolar disease, was detained for 51 days in 2008 and deported to Mexico after an ICE official concluded his name was an alias, despite his repeated claims he was a U.S. citizen. Lyttle tried to return to the United States but was denied entrance and spent four months wandering through Mexico and Central America before a police officer in Guatemala found him sleeping on a park bench and took him to the U.S. Embassy, where officials called Lyttle's brother in the United States and quickly determined he was a U.S. citizen.[9]

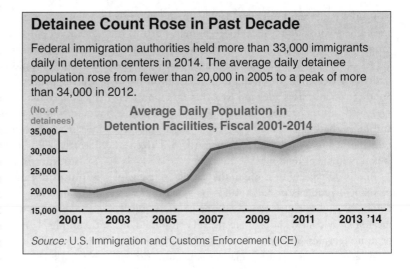

Detainee Count Rose in Past Decade

Federal immigration authorities held more than 33,000 immigrants daily in detention centers in 2014. The average daily detainee population rose from fewer than 20,000 in 2005 to a peak of more than 34,000 in 2012.

Average Daily Population in Detention Facilities, Fiscal 2001-2014

(No. of detainees)

Source: U.S. Immigration and Customs Enforcement (ICE)

Detainees do not have a right to legal counsel — the government does not provide them a lawyer — or to a speedy trial. And due to a backlog in the immigration courts, some detainees spend years in custody while their case is resolved. ICE says the average stay as of Sept. 12, 2015, was 34.6 days, but the mostly volunteer lawyers who work with detainees say many are held much longer.

"We've seen many examples of people detained for far longer periods — three, five and sometimes seven years," says Michael Tan, a staff attorney at the Immigrants' Rights Project of the American Civil Liberties Union (ACLU) in New York. "Unfortunately, there's no shortage of examples."

The system has come in for intense criticism from analysts and immigration advocates. A joint report by the U.S. Conference of Catholic Bishops and the Center for Migration Studies, a New York-based research institute that supports immigrants' rights, noted the size of the detention population and concluded, "The numbers only hint at the toll that this system exacts in despair, fractured families, human rights violations, abandoned legal claims and diminished national prestige."[10]

But advocates of stricter enforcement of immigration laws say detention is a necessary tool for controlling the influx of noncitizens and ensuring that undocumented immigrants or those who pose a threat to public safety do not disappear into the general population before U.S. officials can determine whether they should be deported.

"Detention is appropriate, and the law allows it for cases of public safety risk or a flight risk," says Jessica Vaughan, director of policy studies for the Center for Immigration Studies, a Washington think tank that supports lower immigration levels. Vaughan describes detention as "a last resort in the enforcement process" and adds, "The reality is that once people are here in the country, they are not going to comply with immigration law willingly on their own if they think they can get away with it."

The federal government's use of detention grew in the early 1980s after Cubans and Haitians showed up in unprecedented numbers along the Florida coast. But detention exploded in 1996 after Congress passed an immigration law that greatly expanded the mandatory use of detention in immigration cases.

ICE determines who gets detained, depending on circumstances. ICE says 96 percent of its detainees are "Priority 1 or Priority 2 aliens." The first category covers anyone caught crossing into the United States illegally and any immigrant, here legally or not, considered a terrorist threat, guilty of a felony or convicted of an offense tied to gang activity. Priority 2 includes immigrants convicted of repeated misdemeanors or what ICE calls "significant misdemeanors," such as most drug possession or driving under the influence convictions. It also includes visitors to the United States who, in ICE's judgment, have abused or overstayed their visa privileges.[11]

Caitlin Patler and Emily Ryo, University of California researchers, provide a fuller, more human portrait of longer-term detainees. They interviewed 562 immigrants — 88 percent of them Hispanic males — who had been detained for longer than six months in Southern California. Patler and Ryo found that, on average, the detainees had been in the United States 20 years, and more than half spoke English well. Nearly 70 percent had a spouse or child who was a U.S. citizen or lawful permanent resident.[12]

About 30 percent of those in the sample were lawful permanent residents or had a valid visa when they were detained. Eighty-six percent had one or more misdemeanor convictions, and 25 percent had committed one or more felonies. The most common convictions were for drug offenses and traffic violations, including driving under the influence.[13]

As policymakers, immigrant advocates, law enforcement officials and others debate immigrant detention policies, here are some of the questions being considered:

Does mass detention deter illegal migration?

Last year, when the Obama administration found itself facing a sudden influx of Central American families requesting asylum at U.S. border crossings, it responded by placing them in detention. The move was necessary, the administration said, to discourage other would-be Central American immigrants from making the attempt.

The families were detained even after they had passed the "credible fear" test for being granted asylum — if sent home, they feared they would face persecution. DHS Secretary Jeh Johnson said the policy was intended to send a message to other families contemplating the same journey. "If you come, it is likely you will be detained and sent back," he said.[14]

The ACLU challenged the policy in a class-action lawsuit, and early this year federal District Judge James E. Boasberg ruled the government's use of detention as deterrence violated the individual rights of those being held in custody. He issued a preliminary injunction barring the administration from detaining immigrants solely as a deterrent to future immigration.[15]

"Detention has to be justified in each individual case," explains Joanne Lin, a legislative counsel with the ACLU who works on immigration issues.

Johnson subsequently announced several changes in detention policies for women and children. Deterrence would no longer be considered a factor in detention decisions, he said, and ICE would work to expedite the hearing process to determine whether asylum seekers met the credible fear test for being allowed to stay in the country. If they did, Johnson indicated, most would be released on a reasonable monetary bond while awaiting a formal asylum hearing.[16]

Immigrant advocates hailed the court ruling and the administration's decision. "To detain somebody in order to ensure that another person thousands of miles away will not come to the U.S. — not only is it completely unjustified and inhumane, it's not working," says Shah, co-director of the Detention Watch Network.

Despite the ruling and policy change, however, anti-immigration activists say detention remains a way to make the country less attractive as a destination for those trying to enter the United States illegally. "Detention is an absolutely indispensable component of deterrence," says Dan Stein, president of the Federation for American Immigration Reform (FAIR), a citizens group that wants less immigration.

Stein says maintaining detention as a deterrent is particularly important in light of what FAIR considers the Obama administration's pro-immigrant stance. The organization believes the administration has not been aggressive enough in securing the border and has encouraged further immigration through its support of the Development, Relief and Education for Alien Minors (Dream) Act, which would allow undocumented immigrants who arrived as children to remain in the United States.

"The last remaining deterrent feature they had was the detention facilities," says Stein. "Once you have a breach in your last remaining defensive line, it's basically a free-for-all, and that's where we are now."

The question of whether the Obama administration has been lax or overly aggressive in enforcing immigration laws is bitterly contested by activists who favor more restrictive policies and those who would like to see the nation be more welcoming to immigrants. Nevertheless, policy analysts say the evidence does not support the idea that detention deters immigrants determined to escape violence in their Central American homelands.

In a declaration to the District Court in support of the ACLU's lawsuit, Cecilia Menjívar, a professor in the School of Social and Family Dynamics at Arizona State University, Mesa, said she has interviewed hundreds of migrants and potential migrants from Central America about their motives. They were driven largely by fear of the drug gangs and chaos in their home region, she said. Their fears were serious enough to overcome worries about what might happen to them during the trip north (extortion, rape and even murder are significant risks) or once they arrived in the United States.

"It is difficult to overstate the violence that has become endemic to the region," said Menjivar.[17]

She cited a conversation with a Guatemalan woman as emblematic of migrants' motivations. "We spoke of the dangers of the journey, enforcement at the border and the possibility of spending time in detention in the United States," Menjivar said. "She responded, 'I know that very well, everyone here knows that, but what's the difference between dying on the road and dying little by little here?' "[18]

But even if the detention threat factors little into the thinking of those fleeing violence, some experts say it would still weigh on other would-be immigrants. In congressional testimony, Jan C. Ting, a Temple University law professor and former Immigration and Naturalization Service official in the George H. W. Bush administration, said people inevitably measure the potential costs and benefits of trying to get into the United States.

"If we wish to deter persons immigrating to the United States illegally in violation of our legally imposed limits, we should increase the costs of illegal immigration and lower the benefits," Ting said. "People are not stupid, and will use cost-benefit analysis to act on what they believe is in their best interest."[19]

To dissuade potential immigrants, he added, efforts must extend beyond the border and include additional costs. "Deterrence is important . . . because border security alone cannot prevent large numbers of persons from illegally entering the country if they are determined to do so," Ting said. "For one thing, as many as half the illegal population of the U.S. may have entered legally on temporary visas and simply overstayed" their visas.[20]

However, many experts who track the flow of undocumented immigrants from Central America and elsewhere or have surveyed immigrants on their motives say

Donald Trump launched his campaign for the Republican presidential nomination in June by attacking immigrants as dangerous and vowing that if elected he would deport the 11.3 million undocumented immigrants living in the United States. "When Mexico sends its people, they're not sending their best," the billionaire developer declared. "They're sending people that have lots of problems. . . . They're bringing drugs. They're bringing crime. They're rapists. And some, I assume, are good people."

economic opportunity is the overwhelming consideration of most. The rise and fall of undocumented immigration "is much more consistent with labor market conditions [in the United States and immigrants' home countries] than it is in any changes in U.S. immigration enforcement regimes," says Frank Bean, a sociology professor and director of the Center for Research on International Migration at the University of California, Irvine. "That's what we've seen over and over again. Based on that, I don't think there's any likelihood that [detention] is much of a deterrent."

In fact, he says, detention paradoxically could be making immigration enforcement more difficult. "Given the threat of deportation and the reliance on the detention program, it's entirely possible that a lot of people have gone underground," Bean says. "I don't think people have stopped coming, but they've started hiding more."

Is mass detention of undocumented immigrants necessary for public safety?

On July 1, Kathryn Steinle, 32, was walking along a pier on San Francisco's waterfront with her father when police say she was shot by Juan Francisco Lopez-Sanchez, an undocumented immigrant and felon previously deported to Mexico five times.[21]

Steinle died of the wound later that day.[22] Lopez-Sanchez's attorneys contend the shooting was accidental.[23] But many Americans expressed outrage that Lopez-Sanchez wasn't in government custody or hadn't been redeported before Steinle's killing. The U.S. government had an outstanding deportation order for Lopez-Sanchez, but local authorities released him without notifying ICE.[24] San Francisco is what critics call a "sanctuary city," where city employees are prohibited from helping ICE detain or investigate immigration cases in many circumstances.[25]

The idea that undocumented immigrants, particularly from Mexico or other Latin American countries, pose a public safety risk became a central topic of the Republican presidential campaign when candidate Donald Trump, the billionaire developer and reality TV star, began his campaign by attacking immigrants as dangerous. "When Mexico sends its people, they're not sending their best," Trump declared. "They're sending people that have lots of problems, and they're bringing those problems with us. They're bringing drugs. They're bringing crime. They're rapists. And some, I assume, are good people."[26]

Trump's outspoken stance, which includes a promise to deport all 11.3 million undocumented immigrants believed to be living in the country, has been widely credited with helping to boost him to the top of Republican presidential polls.

But policy analysts say statistics show noncitizens pose less of a crime threat than citizens. Researchers who looked at cities with particularly high concentrations of legal and undocumented immigrants found those urban areas did not have higher crime rates. In fact, murder and robbery rates actually declined, according to at least two studies.[27]

Immigrants also are less likely to end up in jail or prison than citizens, according to another study that found that roughly 1.6 percent of immigrant males, ages 18–39, are incarcerated, compared with 3.3 percent of native-born males of the same age range. The researchers said the difference has existed for decades, and that native-born men were two to five times as likely to be in jail as male noncitizens.[28]

"Immigrants just don't commit crimes at as high a rate as natives do," says the University of California's Bean. "If you think about it, it makes sense. They're marginal; they're frightened; they keep a low profile."

However, other analysts say the immigrant population in detention is different from the general immigrant population. "With the exception of the families and children who came from Central America, more than 85 percent of ICE's interior caseload [cases involving detainees not apprehended at the border] are convicted criminals and people with felonies or multiple misdemeanors," says the Center for Immigration Studies' Vaughan. "Obviously, the vast majority of these people you would have to consider a public threat."

But a 2011 study by the Migration Policy Institute found that in recent years the federal efforts to detain and deport immigrants with criminal records had not been "targeted primarily or even mostly toward serious offenders."[29] Many detainees had been convicted of nonviolent drug offenses or repeated misdemeanors, says Randy Capps, the institute's director of research, U.S. programs. "The immigration enforcement priorities were so broad that a lot of people were picked up on very minor civil or criminal violations," Capps says.

The Detention Watch Network's Shah notes that convicted immigrants must serve their time in the regular U.S. penal system before they can be placed in detention while the government determines whether they should be deported. "Anybody who's in detention, if they are somebody who has been convicted of a crime, they've already paid their debt to society," she says.

Despite Obama's announcement last year that the administration was shifting its immigration enforcement focus to recent undocumented border crossers and dangerous noncitizens, the ACLU's Tan says relatively minor crimes can land even a legal immigrant in detention. "A permanent resident who has a green card could be put in deportation proceedings based on a marijuana conviction," he says.*

But FAIR's Stein says one goal of detention is to hold immigrants who could be dangerous while authorities determine whether they are a threat to the public, a process he considers essential to prevent tragedies like Steinle's killing.

---

* A green card holder is a non-U.S. citizen who has been granted authorization to live and work in the United States on a permanent basis.

"Are they criminals? The answer is maybe. . . . You want to make sure that the government has the time and the space to actually verify who the folks are [in detention]," Stein says. "If you don't, how do you explain that [decision] to an American citizen whose mother or son or daughter got murdered by someone who's in the country illegally?"

Should women and children be detained while awaiting deportation?

Perhaps nothing in immigration policy has aroused as much controversy as the Obama administration's decision in recent years to detain tens of thousands of women and children.

The situation began with last year's surge in the number of people from Central America, which included both unaccompanied children and families with children, who arrived at U.S. border stations seeking asylum. In 2014, the U.S. Border Patrol detained nearly 140,000 unaccompanied children and families traveling with children, more than double the number in 2013. That number declined in 2015, according to press reports, although women and children from the region continue to arrive at the border.[30]

Under a 1997 court order and U.S. law, most unaccompanied children are not held in long-term detention. Instead, they are placed in the care of a sponsor, often family members or close relatives already in the United States, while the government determines whether they should be deported.[31]

The administration, however, originally reacted to the surge in Central American families by detaining nearly all of them. But this June, DHS Secretary Johnson announced a new approach. "I have reached the conclusion that we must make substantial changes in our detention practices with respect to families with

Child Apprehensions Down Sharply

Border Patrol officers apprehended more than 35,000 unaccompanied children at the Southwest border in the first 11 months of fiscal 2015, down nearly 50 percent from the 2014 total. Apprehensions more than quadrupled between 2011 and 2014 because of turmoil in Central America. The nonpartisan Migration Policy Institute said the apprehensions slowed in 2015 because Mexico stepped up border patrols.

Apprehensions of Unaccompanied Children at Southwestern U.S. Border, Fiscal 2010-15

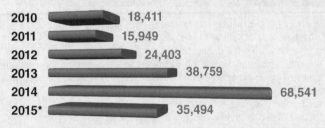

Year	Apprehensions
2010	18,411
2011	15,949
2012	24,403
2013	38,759
2014	68,541
2015*	35,494

* 2015 total is for 11 months.

Sources: 2015 data from "Southwest Border Unaccompanied Alien Children," U.S. Customs and Border Protection, undated, http://tinyurl.com/p6talth; 2010-2014 data from "U.S. Border Patrol Total Monthly UAC Apprehensions by Month, by Sector (FY 2010-FY 2014)," U.S. Customs and Border Protection, undated, http://tinyurl.com/nmt2lhn; caption information from Rodrigo Dominguez Villegas and Victoria Rietig, "Migrants Deported from the United States and Mexico to the Northern Triangle: A Statistical and Socioeconomic Profile," Migration Policy Institute, September 2015, pp. 8-9, http://tinyurl.com/pe2ccmz

children," Johnson said. "In short, once a family has established eligibility for asylum or other relief under our laws, long-term detention is an inefficient use of our resources and should be discontinued."[32] Shortly thereafter, a federal judge in California ruled the detention of the children and their mothers was illegal and said they should be released as soon as possible.[33]

But the administration has appealed the ruling, and thousands of families remain in detention awaiting hearings, which immigrant advocates say is unnecessary. "This is the category that is the least likely to flee. These are moms with babies and kids. These are people who were presenting themselves to the government voluntarily, saying, 'I'm here. I need your help,' " says the ACLU's Lin. "This population is as vulnerable, as sympathetic and as safe as you can find. In our view, there's no reason they should have been detained."

Juan Francisco Lopez-Sanchez faces murder charges following the July 1 shooting death of Kathryn Steinle, 32, a San Francisco woman who was killed while walking with her father along the city's popular Embarcadero waterfront. Sanchez is an undocumented immigrant and felon previously deported to Mexico five times. The U.S. government had an outstanding deportation order for Sanchez, but local authorities released him without notifying immigration authorities. Many Americans expressed outrage that Sanchez wasn't in custody or hadn't been redeported before Steinle's killing.

Brian Hoffman, who heads a pro-bono legal effort for detainees at the South Texas Family Detention Center in Dilley, Texas, says detention takes a toll on women and children already traumatized in their home country or on their journey to the United States. Because adult men are held separately from women and children, detention can break up families, adding to the anxiety of women and children.

"I don't think people realize how psychologically damaging detention is, especially for refugees, and for refugee children," he says. "Worse, it's completely unnecessary. None of these people are dangerous or flight risks. They're refugees."

Asylum-seekers, a specific category of refugees, are non-citizens who are unable or unwilling to return to their home country because of persecution or a well-founded fear of persecution. Under U.S. law, if asylum seekers are found to have credible cases, they are given the right to stay in the United States.[34]

But supporters of stricter immigration restrictions say the evidence indicates many of these families will likely disappear into the general population if they are not held by ICE. As an example, they cite congressional testimony last year by Juan P. Osuna, director of the Executive Office for Immigration Review at the U.S. Justice Department, who said 46 percent of unaccompanied minors released into the custody of sponsors failed to show up for their immigration court hearings.[35]

However, some of those failures appear due to a lack of understanding. Osuna said a "legal orientation" program to educate the children's caretakers about the immigration hearing process had reduced the no-show rate by 40 percent.[36]

Still, Dan Cadman, a former ICE official and current research fellow at the Center for Immigration Studies, said he expects the percentage of no-shows to grow "because many released aliens attend hearings up to the point at which they are ordered deported or directed to depart, after which they abscond rather than report for removal if they are not being held in detention."[37]

Cadman also said government statistics indicate more than 84 percent of the undocumented families who arrived at the height of the Central American surge and who were placed under some alternative to detention fled before completing the hearing process.[38]

But research by the American Immigration Council, a nonpartisan organization in Washington that supports immigrants' rights, cited two government-sponsored studies that found the opposite. The most recent, a 2014 Government Accountability Office (GAO) report, indicated 95 percent of immigrants who arrived from 2011 to 2013 who were provided supervised release instead of detention showed up for their asylum hearings.[39]

The council said research has found that applying for asylum was an "expression of faith in the legal process" and that asylum seekers released while awaiting their hearing are compelled to follow the asylum process in part to avoid the possibility of being placed in detention.[40]

BACKGROUND
The 'Golden Door'

The United States is a nation founded by immigrants. The idea that it welcomes the foreign-born who arrive hoping to build a new life is enshrined on a plaque inside the Statue of Liberty: "Give me your tired, your poor,/ Your huddled masses yearning to breathe free,/The wretched refuse of your teeming shore./Send these, the homeless, tempest-tossed to me,/I lift my lamp beside the golden door!"

But Americans' attitudes toward those huddled masses have always been more ambiguous than the statue's greeting. From the beginning, Americans have simultaneously welcomed immigrants and worried that they would change the nation. At various times, Germans, Catholics, Irish, Italians, Chinese, Mexicans and others have been villified and portrayed as threats to the national identity. Politically, periods of openness have alternated with periods of restriction.

The fear even predated U.S. independence. In 1751, Benjamin Franklin worried that an influx of German immigrants would debase his adopted city, using language that is still echoed in today's immigration debate: "Why should Pennsylvania, founded by the English, become a Colony of *Aliens*, who will shortly be so numerous as to Germanize us instead of us Anglifying them, and will never adopt our Language or Customs, any more than they can acquire our Complexion."[41]

The first mass anti-immigrant movement in the United States developed in the 1850s, when a secret Protestant fraternal organization, often called the "Know-Nothings," attracted more than a million members. The Know-Nothings took an oath to resist the "insidious policy of the Church of Rome [the Catholic Church] and all other foreign influences against the institutions of our country."[42]

The Know-Nothing movement eventually formed the American Party and ran ex-President Millard Fillmore for president in the election of 1856. The American Party would split over the question of slavery, and much of the anti-immigrant fervor dissipated during the Civil War as recent immigrants served in both the Union and Confederate armies.[43]

The detention of immigrants, usually for reasons of disease or ill health, began on a limited basis at Ellis Island in New York harbor, which served as the main port of entry for immigrants from Europe from 1892 to 1954. Most passed through in a matter of hours; only 2 percent were denied entry.[44] However, a small percentage were detained for days or weeks while their status was determined or before they were sent home.[45]

Ironically, the first mass detention in the United States of "foreign" individuals and families involved mostly U.S. citizens. During World War II, President Franklin D. Roosevelt signed Executive Order 9066, which forcibly relocated all people of Japanese ancestry, both citizens and noncitizens, to special internment camps located mostly in remote areas in the West. With the United States at war with Japan, the decision was made out of concern for national security, but two-thirds of the 117,000 people affected by Roosevelt's order were native-born American citizens.[46]

After the war, the 1952 Immigration and Nationality Act established a standard that immigrants awaiting deportation could be held no more than 90 days after the final ruling concerning their status. The law also authorized the U.S. attorney general to hold immigrants longer if he deemed it necessary.[47]

Still, the "immigration detention system had remained minimal and mostly out of public sight throughout the post-war period," according to Stephanie J. Silverman, author of a paper on the history of U.S. detention for the Centre on Migration, Policy and Society at the University of Oxford in England.[48]

This changed in 1979 and 1980, when the United States found itself dealing with hundreds of thousands of Cubans and Haitians fleeing their countries by boat for U.S. shores. When Cuban President Fidel Castro refused to take most of the Cuban migrants back, public concern grew that many were criminals or otherwise a threat to public safety.

As the U.S. government tried to determine among the flood of immigrants who should be granted asylum, it set up detention centers to hold them in Florida, Arkansas, Pennsylvania and at the Atlanta Penitentiary in Georgia.[49]

Attorney General William French Smith paroled most of the Cubans within a year in 1981, determining they were not a threat to public safety. But to discourage further Haitian immigration, President Ronald Reagan ordered the detention of all interdicted Haitians trying to enter the United States. Thousands were held at the U.S. military base at Guantanamo Bay, Cuba, and most eventually were returned to Haiti.[50]

Despite these incidents, sustained detention remained relatively infrequent until the mid-1990s.

Growth of Detention

America's most recent period of large-scale immigration began in the 1970s and included both illegal and legal entries into the country. In the mid-1980s, the number of undocumented immigrants living in the United States

CHRONOLOGY

1950-1980 *The United States establishes the foundations of today's immigration law as well as temporary large-scale detention centers to deal with a Cuban refugee crisis.*

1952 The Immigration and Nationality Act, which still underlies today's law, establishes the grounds for which an alien can be blocked from entering the United States or deported, including a criminal history or radical political views.

1965 Congress amends the 1952 law, clarifying immigrant detention by establishing that anyone clearly not allowed into the country will be detained for further investigation.

1980 A wave of Cubans arrives on U.S. shores in the "Mariel Boatlift," followed by a similar wave of Haitians. The United States resorts to mass detention while it sorts out who should be allowed to stay.

1980-1996 *Alarmed by rising illegal immigration, the United States strengthens border security and wrestles with how to treat undocumented immigrants.*

1984 President Ronald Reagan draws greater attention to illegal immigration by warning, "We've lost control of our own borders, and no nation can do that and survive."

1986 The Immigration Reform and Control Act doubles the size of the Border Patrol and creates penalties for businesses that hire undocumented immigrants; it also offers amnesty for many immigrants in the United States illegally.

1994 Operation Gatekeeper intensifies U.S. efforts to control undocumented immigration from Mexico near San Diego.

1995 The total number of immigrants held in detention over the course of the year by the federal government hits 85,000.

1996 A sweeping immigration law adds new grounds for deporting immigrants, expedites removal procedures and expands the detention of noncitizens for previous crimes.

2000-Present *The Sept. 11, 2001, terrorist attacks launch an era of heightened concern about foreign visitors and U.S. security.*

Sept. 11, 2001 Al Qaeda terrorists legally in the United States hijack four airliners and kill nearly 3,000 people.

2002 In the wake of the 9/11 attacks, Congress transfers immigration control to the newly created Department of Homeland Security (DHS), prioritizing national security in border enforcement.

2003 U.S. Immigration and Customs Enforcement (ICE), a new agency within DHS, becomes responsible for immigrant detention.

2006 Secure Fence Act calls for more than 700 miles of double-reinforced fence on U.S.-Mexico border.

2008 ICE introduces Secure Communities Program, in which police turn the fingerprints of apprehended individuals over to ICE to check whether they are immigrants who should be detained. Many communities eventually stop cooperating with the effort.

2013 The number of immigrants detained during the year tops 440,000, a fivefold increase in less than 20 years.

2014 To deter illegal immigration, ICE detains thousands of Central American women and children who have shown up at U.S. border points seeking asylum because of gang violence at home. . . . President Obama announces changes in enforcement procedures in an effort to end the targeting of longtime, law-abiding undocumented immigrants.

2015 Federal judge rules in February that the use of detention for deterrence violates the rights of detainees. . . . DHS in June revises detention policies for women and children; DHS Secretary Jeh Johnson says the changes will mean most will be held only short-term. . . . Billionaire businessman Donald Trump begins his campaign for the Republican presidential nomination in June by attacking immigrants as dangerous and vowing that if elected he will deport the nation's 11.3 million undocumented immigrants. . . . In July, a federal judge in California declares the detention of mothers and children illegal and says they should be released as soon as possible.

was estimated at 3 million to 5 million. To address the issue, President Reagan backed and Congress passed the Immigration Reform and Control Act of 1986 that established penalties for employers who knowingly hired undocumented immigrants and that greatly expanded border security.[51]

However, the act also granted legal status to undocumented immigrants who had been living in the country for five years. An estimated 2.7 million immigrants eventually took advantage of the law's "amnesty" provision, as it was commonly called.[52] The act was the last successful legislative effort to combine amnesty for longtime undocumented immigrants with stronger enforcement to keep new entrants out.

But the law failed to stanch the flow of illegal immigration, and as public frustration grew, the federal government strengthened enforcement along the border and empowered authorities to deport undocumented immigrants.[53]

In 1996 Congress passed two watershed laws, the Antiterrorism and Effective Death Penalty Act (AEDPA) and the Illegal Immigration Reform and Immigrant Responsibility Act (IIRIRA). The AEDPA required the mandatory detention of noncitizens convicted in the United States of a wide range of offenses, including minor drug crimes. The IIRIRA mandated detention for additional offenses and expanded the definition of "aggravated felonies" to include crimes considered misdemeanors under state law. This shift was significant because, under a 1990 law, noncitizens guilty of aggravated felonies could be detained indefinitely.[54]

Overall, the expansion of mandatory detention was broad enough that a noncitizen could end up in federal custody facing deportation for a crime that hadn't warranted any jail time under state law.[55] The IIRIRA was "responsible for the massive expansion of the immigration detention system in the late 1990s," wrote Silverman.[56]

In just five years, from 1995 to 2000, the average number of detainees held daily roughly tripled to just under 20,000. It continued to grow steadily, reaching 34,260 in 2012.[57]

Analysts say the creation of the Department of Homeland Security (DHS) following the terrorist attacks on the United States on Sept. 11, 2001, also played a role in the expansion of aggressive enforcement of immigration

and detention laws. As the nation expanded its national security efforts, DHS was given authority over border and immigration enforcement through ICE.

"The foundation was set in 1996, and then 9/11 happens and you have a lot more money being funneled into the system," says the Detention Watch Network's Shah.

In 2009, Congress required ICE to maintain the capacity to hold 34,000 immigrants in detention on any given night, a stipulation often referred to as "the bed mandate." The mandate has been widely criticized in the press and by many pro-immigrant activists for establishing a de facto benchmark of how many noncitizens should be in custody, regardless of whether it's legally warranted.[58]

Some analysts believe the bed mandate also helped to increase ICE's reliance on privately run detention centers.

Rise of Private Facilities

As the number of detainees grew in the last 20 years, the federal government began contracting widely with state and local jails and with private correction companies to house detainees. Today, approximately 250 detention facilities around the country hold immigrants.[59]

Capps, director of U.S. research at the Migration Policy Institute, says that although detainees are not serving time for crimes, the system is largely built on the penal model. "Almost entirely with the exception of those families in detention, they're run like regular prisons because most of the facilities are state or local prisons, or they were built to be like them," he says.

ICE has overall responsibility for the system, but "there are only a handful of detention facilities that are actually run by ICE," says Tom K. Wong, a political science professor at the University of California, San Diego, and the author of *Rights, Deportation and Detention in the Age of Immigration and Control.* "The bulk of immigration detention in the United States is contracted out to publicly traded prison firms."

Private prison companies, such as Corrections Corporation of America and The GEO Group, provide about 62 percent of the immigration detention capacity, according to an analysis by Detention Watch Network and the Center for Constitutional Rights, a New York-based legal-rights group.[60]

Critics say for-profit detention raises troubling questions. "This is where we get into the incentives to detain

Deaths in Detention Facilities Raise Alarms

"Why has the government allowed this to happen?"

Jose de Jesus Deniz-Sahagun, a Mexican national who had been apprehended trying to cross the border, died on May 20 after two days in custody at the Eloy Detention Center in Eloy, Ariz. A medical examination determined that Deniz-Sahagun killed himself by stuffing a sock down his throat, making him at least the fifth suicide at the Eloy Center in the last 10 years.[1]

Deniz-Sahagun had been on suicide watch at the center, which holds about 1,550 immigrants while they await disposition of their cases. But officers had taken him off constant watch and were instead checking on him every 15 minutes when he killed himself. His autopsy also found a plastic handle in his stomach, indicating a possible earlier suicide attempt.[2]

Deniz-Sahagun's death sparked renewed concern about the number of deaths that have occurred among immigrants held in detention by U.S. Immigration and Customs Enforcement (ICE), an agency within the Department of Homeland Security that oversees immigration detention. From 2003 to 2013, 141 people died in ICE's custody, according to the agency's records.[3] Pro-immigrant activists say the number has now topped 150.[4]

"Why has the government allowed this to happen? Immigrant lives are seen as worthless apparently," said Francisca Porchas, an activist with Puente Arizona, a grassroots group that advocates for migrants, at a protest held in Phoenix on the three-month anniversary of Deniz-Sahagan's death.[5]

ICE said about the number of deaths: "ICE takes very seriously the health, safety and welfare of those in our care. The agency is committed to ensuring that individuals in our custody receive timely and appropriate medical treatment."

The issue first came to public attention in 2008-10 through government documents obtained by *The New York Times* and the American Civil Liberties Union (ACLU) that showed a pattern of medical neglect leading to deaths and that also detailed official attempts to hide the circumstances of those deaths.[6] "Between 2007 and 2010, there were a series of truly horrifying revelations about medical care in detention," says Carl Takei, an attorney at the ACLU National Prison Project in New York City.

One of the cases involved Hiu Lui Ng, 34, a Chinese computer engineer who had lived in the United States since he was 17 and who died in detention in 2008 from cancer. He also had a broken spine. Both conditions went undiagnosed until shortly before his death. Ng, who arrived legally on a tourist visa, had a wife and two sons who were U.S. citizens, but he was detained for having missed a court date years earlier to extend his visa after the hearing notice was sent to the wrong address.[7]

Thomas K. Wong, a political science professor at the University of California San Diego, who wrote about Ng's case in a book on U.S. detention policies, says officers at a Rhode Island detention center ignored Ng's repeated pleas for medical assistance and left him lying unconscious in his cell, in pain and having defecated and urinated on himself. Guards also were caught on a security camera ridiculing Ng and insisting he could walk as they dragged him from his cell and loaded him into a van a week before his death.[8]

A year after Ng's death and others, ICE revised its policies with the intention of improving access to medical and mental health care. Since 2009, "significant reforms have been made to the immigration detention system and

people," says Wong, who says the private prison companies depend financially on a steady stream of detained immigrants.

ICE's contracts with specific facilities can include a guarantee to pay for a minimum number of immigration detention beds. "Because guaranteed minimums require payment to private contractors whether beds are filled or

not, ICE faces considerable pressure to fill them," the two groups concluded. "Local lockup quotas that serve to protect the bottom line of private companies thus incentivize the imprisonment of immigrants."[61]

In a written statement, ICE defended the practice, saying the guaranteed minimums "allow the federal government to procure beds at a reduced rate, thereby saving health care management," says Sarah Rodriguez, an ICE spokeswoman.

But Wong says the U.S. government largely ignored the treatment of detainees until they were brought to light in the press. "Unfortunately, it took something like this to get ICE to write clearer guidelines for the treatment of individuals in detention that facilities have to follow," he says.

The Eloy Detention Center, which is operated by Corrections Corporation of America (CCA) — a private contractor — has one of the worst records for immigrant deaths among ICE detention facilities. At least 14 detainees have died at Elroy since 2003, including five by suicide.

CCA did not respond to requests for an interview. In response to an inquiry about suicides at the center, ICE said that within 12 hours of being detained, "All detainees receive an initial mental health screening by a qualified health care professional or a health-trained correctional officer, who has been specially trained."

ICE denied a request by *CQ Researcher* to tour the Eloy facility. The agency said the center has posted suicide-prevention posters in English and Spanish, as well as bilingual posters highlighting the phone number to report any concerns to the Department of Homeland Security Office of Inspector General. ICE also provided a link to the agency's latest standards related to suicide prevention and intervention, which require all employees to be trained in detecting and dealing with individuals who pose a suicide risk.[9]

But Takei says ICE was slow to roll out the 2009 standards across its more than 250 detention centers, and many facilities are still following 2000 standards. "The challenge for ICE has been actually implementing those policies as opposed to having them exist only on paper," he says.

— *Reed Karaim*

Getty Images/Joe Raedle

Demonstrators in Boca Raton, Fla., protest the detention of immigrants by The Geo Group and other private corrections firms.

[1] Megan Jula and Daniel Gonzalez, "Eloy Detention Center: Why so many suicides?" *The Arizona Republic*, July 29, 2015, http://tinyurl.com/qhmyohu.

[2] *Ibid.*

[3] "List of Deaths in ICE Custody, October 2003 — December 2013," ICE Health Service Corps (formerly the Division of Immigration Health Services), undated, http://tinyurl.com/4yv3x8b

[4] Elizabeth Stuart, "Amid Faux Coffins, Protesters Demand Justice For Immigrant's Death In ICE Detention," *Phoenix New Times*, Aug. 21, 2015, http://tinyurl.com/prg7kjn.

[5] *Ibid.*

[6] Nina Bernstein, "Officials Hid Truth of Migrant Deaths in Jail," *The New York Times*, Jan. 9, 2010, http://tinyurl.com/yz8j6ku.

[7] Nina Bernstein, "Detention Center Facing Inquiry Will Get No More Immigrant Detainees," *The New York Times*, Dec. 5, 2008, http://tinyurl.com/o5t8gov.

[8] Nina Bernstein, "Documents Reveal Earlier Immigrant Deaths," *The New York Times*, Jan. 9, 2010, http://tinyurl.com/yeu7f8r.

[9] "Significant Self-Harm and Suicide Prevention and Intervention," ICE National Detention Standards 2011, U.S. Immigrations and Custom Enforcement, http://tinyurl.com/qbdjl4b.

money while giving the contractor the capability to predict the number of detainees held on a regular basis allowing for appropriate scheduling of the proper number of medical and detention personnel."

Detainees and outside observers have reported cases of abuse and neglect at both privately and publicly run facilities, with reports of medical maltreatment or neglect perhaps the most frequent.[62] "I think the government just really underestimated the need for medical services," says Hoffman, the attorney who serves immigrants at the Dilley detention center run by Corrections Corporation of America (CCA). "We've had clients with really serious conditions — infected lesions, breast cancers. We constantly have cases where

Behind the Headlines, Support for a More Humane Policy

But a sharp partisan divide persists on illegal immigration.

The 2016 presidential campaign got off to a controversial start when Republican candidate Donald Trump vaulted to the top of his party's polls after vowing to build a wall along the 1,954-mile U.S.-Mexico border and deport all 11.3 million undocumented immigrants living in the United States. Trump wasn't alone in taking a stand on illegal immigration: A majority of the GOP field promised to pursue a hard line on undocumented immigration.

But American attitudes overall are more sympathetic to undocumented immigrants than many Republican candidates. A June Gallup Poll found that 65 percent of U.S. adults favor a plan to allow immigrants living illegally in the United States to remain in the country and become citizens if they meet certain requirements over time. Gallup said that view has remained relatively stable for the past decade.[1]

Despite the media attention given to the issue, immigration ranks only third among voters' concerns, behind dissatisfaction with government and the economy, according to a September Gallup Poll.[2] A poll by the Pew Research Center taken in January, before the election cycle heated up, found that immigration ranked 12th among the public's policy priorities, just ahead of the environment.[3]

Those results could partly reflect the fact that the number of undocumented immigrants living in the United States has remained relatively constant for the past five years, at about 11.3 million, down nearly 1 million from a peak in 2007. The country actually had a net outflow of migration during the 2008 recession as jobs dried up in the United States and undocumented workers returned home.[4]

While much of the public's ire about illegal immigration has focused on Mexico, historically the largest source of undocumented immigrants, net migration from Mexico likely was zero in 2010, with just as many migrants leaving the United States as entering, according to Pew. And since then, more Mexicans have left the United States than have arrived, the research center said.[5] In fact, more non-Mexicans, including thousands of women and children from Central America seeking asylum, were apprehended along the U.S. border in 2014 than Mexicans.[6]

"The Mexican part of this population is indeed shrinking, and the general pattern is more Central Americans and more Asians," says John Skrentny, director of the Center for Comparative Immigration Studies at the University of California, San Diego.

Some analysts give Mexico credit for helping to reduce the 2014 surge in Central American immigrants. Many of those immigrants were fleeing gang violence in their home countries. "Mexico actually has taken a lot of initiative in dealing with this and stopping unaccompanied children from passing through their country," says Frank Bean, director of the Center for Research on International Migration at the University of California, Irvine.

At least one study has found that Mexico is now apprehending and returning more Central Americans than the United States.[7] That effort is occurring with U.S. assistance, which increased the funding for a long-standing collaborative security program between the two countries

we have someone say, 'My child had a fever and we waited five hours to get medical care, and then they just said he needs to drink more water and we couldn't get any medicine.' "

Some cases are more serious. In a CCA-run facility in Hutto, Texas, a guard pleaded guilty to two lesser charges after being accused of sexual assault.[63] Other investigations have found detention personnel ignored health issues that led to the death of detainees.[64]

An ICE spokesperson says the agency has issued detailed and revised guidelines, which are being implemented over time at different facilities, intended to ensure that detainees are treated humanely and that their needs are met.[65] "ICE is committed to providing all detainees in our care to include more money for stepped-up enforcement along Mexico's southern border.[8]

The changing shape of immigration, however, appears not to have resonated with at least one segment of Americans. Polls reveal a split between Democratic and Republican voters that helps to explain why Trump's position on undocumented immigration has resonated with many in his party. Over the years Republicans have been more willing than Democrats and independents to support the building of a fence along the U.S.-Mexico border and also more supportive of aggressive deportation.[9]

And the gap between the two parties is widening: A recent poll for the Chicago Council on Global Affairs shows that two-thirds of Republicans, compared with about one-third of Democrats, say "controlling and reducing illegal immigration is a very important goal for U.S. foreign policy" — the biggest partisan divide on immigration in the survey's 20-year history.[10]

While Republican attitudes may have hardened, it is uncertain whether that will remain the case. Polls show that Americans under 30 have a more positive attitude about immigrants and are more supportive of letting them stay in the country than Americans overall.[11]

— *Reed Karaim*

---

[1]Jeffrey M. Jones, "In U.S., 65% Favor Path to Citizenship for Illegal Immigrants," Gallup, Aug. 12, 2015, http://tinyurl.com/qh75yhx.

[2]Rebecca Riffkin, "Government, Economy, Immigration seen as top U.S. problems," Gallup, Sept. 17, 2015, http://tinyurl.com/qeu3nsd.

[3]"Public's Policy Priorities Reflect Changing Conditions at Home and Abroad," Pew Research Center, Jan. 15, 2015, http://tinyurl.com/kuzlpvl.

[4]Jeffrey Passel and D'Vera Cohn, "Unauthorized immigrant population stable for half a decade," Pew Research Center, July 22, 2105, http://tinyurl.com/nuvsnaw.

[5]Ana Gonzalez-Barrera and Jens Manuel Krogstad, "What we know about illegal immigration from Mexico," Pew Research Center, July 15, 2015, http://tinyurl.com/nwbxr6u.

Most Support Path to Citizenship

Nearly two-thirds of American adults say the United States should allow undocumented immigrants to remain in the country and earn their citizenship.

"What policy should the government adopt toward illegal immigrants in your state?"

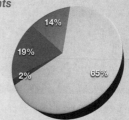

- Deport all
- Permit to remain in the U.S. in order to work
- Permit to remain in the U.S. and become citizens
- No opinion

Source: Jeff Jones and Lydia Saad, "Gallup Poll Social Series: Minority Rights & Relations — Final Topline," Gallup, June 15-July 10, 2015, p. 2, http://tinyurl.com/nev95sr.

[6]*Ibid.*

[7]Rodrigo Dominquez Villegas and Victoria Rietig, "Migrants Deported from the United States and Mexico to the Northern Triangle: A Statistical and Socioeconomic Profile," Migration Policy Institute, September 2015, http://tinyurl.com/pphwhky.

[8]Clare Ribando Seelke and Kristin Finklea, "U.S.-Mexican Security Cooperation: The Mérida Initiative and Beyond," Congressional Research Service, May 7, 2015, http://tinyurl.com/qxj7wh4.

[9]Sara Kehaulani Goo, "What Americans want to do about illegal immigration," Pew Research Center, Aug. 24, 2015, http://tinyurl.com/oa4tvuh.

[10]Craig Kafura and Sarah McElmurry, "Growing Partisan Divides on Immigration," Chicago Council on Global Affairs, Sept. 18, 2015, http://tinyurl.com/pgjysyf.

[11]"Broad Public Support for Legal Status for Undocumented Immigrants," Pew Research Center, June 4, 2015, http://tinyurl.com/owjr5zy.

---

with timely, safe, humane and appropriate treatment, which includes medical and mental health care," says Sarah Rodriguez, an ICE spokeswoman.

Corrections Corporation did not respond to requests for an interview. GEO Group responded with a written statement: "GEO's facilities provide high-quality services in safe, secure, and humane residential environments, and our company strongly refutes allegations to the contrary. Our facilities adhere to strict contractual requirements and standards set by ICE, and the agency employs several full-time, on-site contract monitors who have a physical presence at each of GEO's facilities."

The private prison company further said, "All of GEO's residential facilities are audited and inspected by [ICE]

Secretary of Homeland Security Jeh Johnson in September announced several changes in detention policies for immigrant women and children. Johnson said last year the Obama administration's detention of Central American families seeking asylum was designed to discourage other would-be asylum seekers. Early this year, however, federal District Judge James E. Boasberg issued a preliminary injunction barring the administration from detaining immigrants solely as a deterrent to future immigration.

on a routine and unannounced basis. GEO's facilities are also independently accredited by the American Correctional Association (ACA) and achieved an average score in excess of 99 percent during the most recent accreditation audits."

CURRENT SITUATION
Family-Detention Battle

The Obama administration's treatment of immigrant families held in detention continues to draw high-profile condemnation, even though the Department of Homeland Security said in September it was pressing forward with changes that would allow most women and children to be released while awaiting an asylum ruling.

On Sept. 17 the U.S. Civil Rights Commission, an independent agency, issued a critical report on conditions in family immigrant detention centers and called on the administration to promptly release detained families.[66]

Most detained families arrived from Central American countries where drug gangs and extreme poverty have left children and women particularly vulnerable,

the report noted. But the conditions in family detention centers are, in some ways, worse than those the immigrants are fleeing, the commission said.[67]

According to claims by migrants and advocacy groups, food served at one center was infested with maggots, a detainee with AIDS died after her illness was ignored by staff, transgender immigrants were mistreated and some children were sexually abused, the commission reported.[68] "No children, with or without an accompanying adult, should be forced to live in these facilities," the commission said in a letter to Obama accompanying the report.[69]

Two of the commission's eight members opposed the report, saying the allegations could not be independently confirmed. Still, the commission backed a July ruling by federal District Judge Dolly M. Gee in California ordering the release of child detainees. Dee found ICE's detention of children violated an earlier legal settlement the government had agreed to regarding the housing of children.[70]

Although the government has appealed the ruling, DHS Secretary Johnson announced detention policy changes designed to shorten the length of families' stays. "With these reforms, the detention of families is becoming short-term in most cases," Johnson said in a statement released the day after the commission's report. "We are transitioning our family residential center facilities into processing centers where individuals can be interviewed and screened rather than detained for a prolonged period of time."[71]

Families who proved initially that they face a "credible fear of persecution" in their home countries are now being released "under conditions designed to ensure they will appear in immigration court for their case," he said.[72]

Hoffman, the lawyer who heads a project to provide legal representation at the Dilley center, says he has noticed the pace picking up. "What they're going to do is try to get everybody out in 20 days," he says. He says, however, that a quicker pace will put more pressure on the pro-bono lawyers trying to make sure the women understand the legal process of applying for asylum before they are released. Without that assistance, he adds, which the government does not provide, the women can face an intimidating asylum process they don't understand.

"It's frustrating how you hear the government says there's access to counsel provided at these facilities,"

Hoffman says, "when that's only because you have volunteers who spend thousands of dollars to fly down here and rent a car on their own dime to help people."

Obama Actions Halted

Last November, Obama announced two executive actions that would have allowed an estimated 4 million undocumented immigrants to remain in the country, significantly reducing the scope of detention and deportation.[73]

However, Texas and 25 other states sued, calling the president's actions unconstitutional, and early this year a federal judge in Texas blocked the administration's plans until the issue is resolved. A federal appeals court heard arguments in July, but the case is expected to reach the Supreme Court.[74]

Obama's plan would have allowed undocumented immigrant parents of U.S. citizens and legal permanent residents who have lived in the country for at least five years to apply for relief from deportation and gain the right to work legally. The program, known as Deferred Action for Parents of Americans and Lawful Permanent Residents (DAPA), would have affected about 3.7 million undocumented immigrants, according to the Migration Policy Institute.[75]

The president's second action would have expanded an existing effort, known as Deferred Action for Childhood Arrivals (DACA), to allow more immigrant children who arrived in the United States when young and meet certain educational achievements to stay in the United States. The expansion would have brought an estimated 290,000 more young people into the program.[76]

Critics of DAPA and the DACA expansions accused the president of exceeding his executive authority in an attempt to bypass a congressional deadlock on immigration reform.[77] Legislative efforts have stalled over the question of whether undocumented immigrants who have been in the country for years should be granted a route to citizenship.[78]

The administration contends that it hasn't exceeded its authority and that the executive actions were necessary so it could focus detention and deportation on undesirable undocumented immigrants rather than those who have lived and worked in the country without serious incident for years. In announcing DAPA, Obama said the message to law-abiding, longtime immigrants was: "You can come out of the shadows."[79]

Lupillo Rivera and other immigrant-rights activists confront local citizens in Murrieta, Calif., who support the apprehension and deportation of undocumented immigrants. Two-thirds of American adults say the United States should allow undocumented immigrants to remain in the country and earn citizenship, according to public opinion polls.

However, the ongoing court battle means that any resolution over the legality of DAPA and the DACA expansion is likely to happen very late in Obama's term, leaving the administration little time to implement its proposals if they are upheld.

Shift in Priorities

In addition to the blocked DAPA and DACA initiatives, the Obama administration last year announced another change in immigration enforcement strategy that could reduce the number of detentions and deportations.

The administration ended the controversial "Secure Communities" program, in which individuals booked into a local jail had their fingerprints sent to ICE, which ran the prints through federal databases to determine whether the person was in violation of immigration laws. If so, the U.S. government could issue a "detainer," which meant states and communities were to notify ICE before releasing the person so he or she could be transferred to federal detention.[80]

Secure Communities began under President George W. Bush but was expanded by the Obama administration. The program contributed to a significant increase in detentions, along with deportations, which reached a record of more than 409,000 in 2012, leading some immigrant advocates to label Obama the "deporter-in-chief."[81]

Is U.S. immigrant-detention policy justified?

YES
Dan Cadman
Research Fellow, Center for
Immigration Studies

Written for *CQ Researcher*, October 2015

Few Americans believe in open borders. They disagree about the proper level of legal immigration and how to deal with the existing population of aliens residing illegally in the United States, but most understand the importance of immigration controls as an exercise of sovereignty, public safety and job security.

To function properly, the immigration system must have the tools needed to discourage illegal immigration.

Opponents advocate alternatives to detention such as supervised release for humanitarian and fiscal reasons. This is superficially attractive, but although release is cheaper on a daily basis, nondetained cases take longer to resolve. Backlogs are massive: It can take nearly three years to begin court hearings. So there are no long-term savings. Detention alternatives are also ineffective; in 2014 the Government Accountability Office reported that data are inadequate to determine what happens to those who leave detention.

There are significant reasons to continue detention:

- **Deterrence** — Without detention, there is no border control. Absent credible deterrence, we will face a global tsunami of the hopeful. Half the world's population lives on $2.50 daily or less. Why would they not come, if left footloose to disappear among the 11.3 million aliens already here illegally?
- **Public Safety** — Hundreds of thousands of aliens are arrested each year near land borders. They come with no identification or sometimes with forged documents. Agents often have only their word for who they are. Delving into identity is laborious when verifying foreign records of birth, nationality and criminal history, and the results are not always certain. Do we really want drug cartel members or potential terrorists walking the streets?
- **System Integrity** — Opponents say because immigration is a civil, rather than criminal, offense, detention is inappropriate. That argument holds no weight. Every legal system must have the means to enforce its rulings. Detention inhibits aliens from fleeing and protects the public. Aliens have repeatedly shown that when released on a promise to appear in court, or for removal if ordered by a judge, they break that promise. Why not? The worst that happens if absconders get caught is they will be deported — but that's what they face if they stick around. Presently, more than 900,000 undetained aliens who absconded from immigration proceedings are roaming our cities. That figure reflects the current official disinclination to use detention. It's a national disgrace no other legal system would tolerate.

NO
Mizue Aizeki
Deputy Director,
Immigrant Defense Project

Written for *CQ Researcher*, October 2015

Is it justifiable to imprison more than 400,000 people each year — including longtime green card holders, children and families, trafficking survivors and asylum seekers — for civil violations of immigration law? To lock them up for months, sometimes years, in violation of basic human rights? To hold them in harsh conditions with inadequate medical care and with only limited ability to challenge their confinement? To rip parents from children, children from parents, however deep their roots in the United States? Simple justice and fairness say "no."

The U.S. government claims mass detention deters unauthorized immigration; ensures that immigrants show up at deportation hearings; and keeps public-safety threats off the streets. But the overwhelming majority of immigrant detainees pose neither a public-safety threat nor a risk of absconding. And people who are fleeing danger or seeking to reunite with their families in the United States are not easily deterred.

But even if these justifications stood up to scrutiny, we have to weigh them against the heavy moral and human costs of policies that include locking up people in jails — 34,000 in immigrant detention on any given day, per a congressionally mandated "bed quota." These include the profound emotional, psychological and even physical toll on detainees and family members and the damage done to the rule of law when we tolerate a second-tier system of "justice" where due process rights — including the right to effective counsel and to a fair hearing — are routinely disregarded. These costs are a big part of why international human rights standards recommend nations use immigration detention as only a last resort.

We should not accept the status quo of mass detention and deportation as necessary, acceptable or normal. Since 1996, the number of immigrant detainees has increased fivefold, in an atmosphere of rising xenophobia and "law and order" hysteria.

The same punitive mindset that brought us the hyper-aggressive policing and draconian sentencing laws that put millions of people — especially people of color — behind bars is now increasingly directed toward immigrants. It has driven the increasing criminalization of immigration and the passage and aggressive implementation of harsh immigration laws, including provisions that make detention and deportation a "mandatory minimum" punishment for a growing range of offenses.

Mass incarceration is increasingly seen as a moral and public policy disaster, even by some of its original architects. Mass immigration detention and deportation are equally indefensible. Both must end.

Secure Communities also faced a growing backlash from local authorities who felt detainers were too often issued for people who had committed relatively minor crimes, such as traffic violations or nonviolent offenses. Nearly 300 cities and counties, along with the states of California, Colorado and Connecticut, stopped or limited their participation in the program.[82]

"Its very name has become a symbol for general hostility toward the enforcement of our immigration laws," Homeland Security Secretary Johnson acknowledged in announcing the decision to end the program.[83]

Replacing Secure Communities is the Priority Enforcement Program (PEP), which ICE began implementing in early 2015. Although PEP still depends on local authorities passing on information, it is intended to narrow the immigration dragnet to focus on detaining and deporting individuals with serious or repeated offenses or who have just arrived illegally. ICE spokeswoman Rodriguez says PEP has "the overarching goal of working with state and local jurisdiction to ensure dangerous criminals are transferred to ICE custody, in the interest of public safety and national security."

Deportations are expected to fall this year to slightly fewer than 230,000 — a significant drop from last year's total of 425,000.[84] Still, the administration's stated ambition of limiting detention and deportation has left both immigrant advocates and supporters of greater restrictions on immigration dissatisfied.

"The program is a disappointing rebranding of Secure Communities using somewhat narrower enforcement priorities," says Chris Rickerd, an ACLU expert on immigration enforcement. "Unconstitutional detention requests continue, as does the harmful entanglement between immigration enforcement and policing, which undermines local communities' efforts to promote immigrants' trust in police."

Conversely, Vaughan, the Center for Immigration Studies policy studies director, describes PEP as "an unnecessary and overzealous dismantling of immigration enforcement."

Conservative critics also dispute the notion that Obama has been the "deporter-in-chief," saying President George W. Bush actually sent more undocumented immigrants home. During the Bush administration, many undocumented immigrants were simply "returned" at the border, which meant nobody took their fingerprints or entered their entry attempt in their immigration records before they were put on buses and driven back to Mexico. Obama's critics say when these returns are added to more formal deportation proceedings, Bush was more aggressive in removing undocumented immigrants.[85]

However, other analysts note that the informal nature of returns — immigrants could be counted several times if they were repeatedly caught crossing the border — makes it hard to determine how many people were actually escorted out of the United States. They add that Obama's greater use of formal deportation proceedings has more serious consequences because such undocumented border crossers are identified and recorded in government databases.[86]

OUTLOOK
Stalled and Deadlocked

The future of immigration detention is inextricably tied to the country's overall policies and attitudes toward immigrants, both undocumented and those who have arrived legally. Most major polls consistently show at least a slight majority of Americans favor immigration reforms that would provide a pathway to citizenship for some undocumented immigrants. But repeated attempts to pass reform legislation have stalled in Congress.

Capps, the Migration Policy Institute research director, doesn't expect that to change anytime soon. "U.S. policy is completely deadlocked, and it has been now for a really long time," he says. "There's been no major move on legalization for 30 years, and the way politics are set up right now, it might be another 10 or 20 years before anything happens."

During this period, policy changes will be confined to executive actions or court rulings, which will limit their impact, he says, "because there's no big change through [legislative action] coming now."

The ACLU's Lin is more optimistic. "I look at the overall arc of history, and I think the proponents of legalization — a path to citizenship — are going to win . . . because the majority of the American people are with them on that and the [demographic] composition of America is changing," she says.

The growing ranks of immigrants are making their presence felt in the political process, she explains. Lin also sees a change across generations. "The younger generation is just not so concerned about this issue," she says, "so I am hopeful."

As attitudes toward immigration evolve, Shah, co-director of the Detention Watch Network, believes the use of detention will shrink. "I'm hopeful, largely because I've been working on detention for 14 years now and what I've seen of the growth of the [anti-detention] moment has been phenomenal," she says. "I hope five years down the road we have less detention beds, and given that people are actually starting to see that this idea of mass incarceration isn't working, I think there's a good chance we'll get there."

But advocates of greater restrictions on immigration see the possibility of a darker future ahead. FAIR's Stein believes the pressure on the United States and other Western nations from migrants trying to escape poorer or violent parts of the world is destined to increase dramatically in coming years. He points to the current situation in Europe, which is dealing with a flood of refugees from the Middle East as an example of what's ahead.

"The migration pressures globally are like nothing the Western democracies have ever seen, frankly, in world history," he says. "This is the beginning of a historic phase, and the U.S. has a choice. We can choose anarchy and accommodation, or we can choose sovereignty, self-determination and the rule of law."

Capps, however, says the situations facing Europe and the United States are different. "The migration situation in Europe is catastrophic right now. It reflects the situations in the Middle East and Africa, which are just as catastrophic, the worst situation since World War II probably," he says. "That is not true in our hemisphere. We are in a very different position here."

Capps says the growth of the Mexican economy and a slowing of that nation's birthrate are combining to make the United States less attractive to immigrants from Mexico, historically the biggest source of undocumented border crossers. Mexico also has been taking steps to halt the flow of Central American migrants north, he notes. "There's not a gigantic pool of migrants on our doorstep like there is in Europe," he says.

But Vaughan, of the Center for Immigration Studies, which favors lower immigration, says the recent surge in asylum seekers from Central America indicates that when people from troubled regions believe they have a chance

to be allowed into the United States, "the worldwide demand to take advantage of that is almost insatiable."

The United States is eventually going to have to adopt stricter immigration controls if it hopes to cope with the consequences of that pressure, she says. Current policy, Vaughan continues, is "really not fiscally sustainable or sustainable from a security sense."

NOTES

1. "Unlocking Human Dignity: A Plan to Transform the U.S. Immigrant Detention System," Joint Report of Migration and Refugee Services/ United States Conference of Catholic Bishops and the Center for Migration Studies, 2015, http://tinyurl.com/mzax9or.

2. Jeffrey Passel and D'Vera Cohn, "Unauthorized immigrant population stable for half a decade," Pew Research Center, July 22, 2015, http://tinyurl.com/nuvsnaw.

3. Molly Hennessy-Fiske, "Paid $1 to $3 a day, unauthorized immigrants keep family detention centers running," *Los Angeles Times*, Aug. 3, 2015, http://tinyurl.com/pgcwhle.

4. "Statement by Secretary Jeh C. Johnson on Family Residential Centers," U.S. Department of Homeland Security, June 24, 2015, http://tinyurl.com/oq22owg.

5. "Remarks by the President in Address to the Nation on Immigration," White House, Nov. 20, 2014, http://tinyurl.com/ncahyfg.

6. Daniel Gonzalez and Bob Ortega, "Surge continues but not as many Central American migrants reaching U.S.," *The Arizona Republic*, April 22, 2015, http://tinyurl.com/nodpvlw. Also see Peter Katel, "Central American Gangs," *CQ Researcher*, Jan. 30, 2015, pp. 97–120.

7. Margot Mendelson *et al.*, "Collateral Damage: An examination of ICE's Fugitive Operations Program," Migration Policy Institute, February 2009, http://tinyurl.com/ptrjch8.

8. William Finnegan, "The Deportation Machine," *The New Yorker*, April 29, 2013, http://tinyurl.com/ncpkyea.

9. *Ibid.*

10. "Unlocking Human Dignity," *op. cit.*

11. "Policies for the Apprehension, Detention and Removal of Undocumented Immigrants," Memorandum, U.S. Department of Homeland Security, Nov. 20, 2014, http://tinyurl.com/luvxvky.

12. Caitlin Patler, "The Economic Impacts of Long-Term Immigration Detention in Southern California," UCLA Institute for Research on Labor and Employment, 2015, http://tinyurl.com/nqmghxy.

13. *Ibid.*

14. Julia Preston, "Judge Orders Stops to Detention of Women and Children on Borders," *The New York Times*, Feb. 20, 2015, http://tinyurl.com/put2are.

15. *Ibid.*

16. "Statement by Secretary Jeh C. Johnson on Family Residential Centers," *op. cit.*

17. "Declaration of Cecilia Menjivar," American Civil Liberties Union, April 17, 2015, http://tinyurl.com/qexntkp.

18. *Ibid.*

19. "Examining the Adequacy and Enforcement of Our Nation's Immigration Laws," testimony of Jan C. Ting, U.S. House Committee on the Judiciary, Feb. 3, 2015, http://tinyurl.com/nsbmspx.

20. *Ibid.*

21. Matt Hamilton, "Parents of woman killed in San Francisco want tougher immigration law," *Los Angeles Times*, July 13, 2015, http://tinyurl.com/op6mbop.

22. Steve Almasy, Pamela Brown and Augie Martin, "Suspect in killing of San Francisco woman had been deported five times," CNN, July 4, 2015, http://tinyurl.com/pna3uas.

23. Hamilton, *op. cit.*

24. Emmarie Huetteman, "Republicans Look to Penalize 'Sanctuary Cities' That Shield Illegal Immigrants," *The New York Times*, July 21, 2015, http://tinyurl.com/njvyuhg.

25. "Sanctuary Ordinance," City & County of San Francisco, undated, http://tinyurl.com/m5s3b92.

26. "Full text: Donald Trump announces a presidential bid," *The Washington Post*, June 16, 2015, http://tinyurl.com/paokcpl.

27. Alex Nowrasteh, "Immigration and Crime — What the Research Says," Cato Institute, July 14, 2015, http://tinyurl.com/nmpejag. Also see Lesley Williams Reid *et al.*, "The Immigration-crime relationship: Evidence across US metropolitan areas," *Social Science Research*, Vol. 34, Issue 4, December 2005, pp. 757–780, http://tinyurl.com/qcrtq6b; and Tim Wadsworth, "Is Immigration Responsible for the Crime Drop? An Assessment of the Influence of Immigration on Changes in Violent Crime Between 1990 and 2000," *Social Science Quarterly*, 91: June 2010, pp. 531–553, http://tinyurl.com/pnoeqeb.

28. Walter Ewing, Daniel E. Martinez and Rubén G. Rumbaut, "The criminalization of Immigration in the United States," American Immigration Council, July 2015, http://tinyurl.com/nlkrt7a.

29. Randy Capps *et al.*, "Delegation and Divergence: 287(g) State and Local Immigration Enforcement," Migration Policy Institute, January 2011, http://tinyurl.com/q4xzjas.

30. Gonzalez and Ortega, *op. cit.*

31. Lazaro Zamora, "Unaccompanied Alien Children: A Primer," Bipartisan Policy Center, July 21, 2014, http://tinyurl.com/nqsn76o.

32. "Statement by Secretary Jeh C. Johnson on Family Residential Centers," *op. cit.*

33. Julia Preston, "Judge Orders Release of Immigrant Children Detained by U.S.," *The New York Times*, July 25, 2015, http://tinyurl.com/nsj2mbo.

34. "Refugees & Asylum," U.S. Citizenship and Immigration Services, updated June 16, 2015, http://tinyurl.com/keu679k.

35. "Full Committee Hearing: President's Emergency Supplemental Request," U.S. Senate Appropriations Committee, July 1, 2014, http://tinyurl.com/p6r2ptn.

36. *Ibid.*

37. Dan Cadman, "Why Alien Detention Is Necessary," Center for Immigration Studies, June 2015, http://tinyurl.com/o9szjcr.

38. *Ibid.*

39. Mark Noferi, "A Humane Approach Can Work: The Effectiveness of Alternatives to Detention for Asylum

Seekers," American Immigration Council, July 2015, http://tinyurl.com/pjhs4yb.

40. *Ibid.*

41. Roger Daniels, *Guarding the Golden Door: American Immigration Policy and Immigrants since 1882* (2004), p. 8.

42. *Ibid.*, p. 10.

43. *Ibid.*, p. 11.

44. "Ellis Island History," Statue of Liberty-Ellis Island Foundation, undated, http://tinyurl.com/ot5rouu.

45. "Ellis Island," History.com, undated, http://tinyurl.com/4t8tkqx.

46. "Teaching With Documents: Documents and Photographs Related to Japanese Relocation During World War II," National Archives, undated, http://tinyurl.com/pgsea2a.

47. Stephanie Silverman, "Immigration Detention in America: A History of its Expansion and a Study of its Significance," Centre on Migration, Policy and Society, University of Oxford, 2010, http://tinyurl.com/ppqoqte.

48. *Ibid.*

49. *Ibid.*

50. *Ibid.*

51. Faye Hipsman and Doris Meissner, "Immigration in the United States: New Economic, Social, Political Landscapes with Legislative Reform on the Horizon," Migration Policy Institute, April 16, 2013, http://tinyurl.com/n3wfe56.

52. *Ibid.*

53. "Key Immigration Laws and Policy Developments Since 1986," Migration Policy Institute, March 2013, http://tinyurl.com/ppzq6w5.

54. "Analysis of Immigration Detention Policies," American Civil Liberties Union, undated, http://tinyurl.com/nmbyqqs.

55. *Ibid.*

56. Silverman, *op. cit.*

57. "Unlocking Human Dignity," *op. cit.*

58. Nick Miroff, "Controversial quota drives immigration detention boom," *The Washington Post*, Oct. 13, 2013, http://tinyurl.com/o44jjr8.

59. "About the U.S. Detention and Deportation System," Detention Watch Network, undated, http://tinyurl.com/l6hxl4l.

60. Silky Shah, Mary Small and Carol Wu, "Banking on Detention: Local lockup quotas & the immigrant dragnet," Detention Watch Network and the Center for Constitutional Rights, 2015, http://tinyurl.com/pm3agxt.

61. *Ibid.*

62. Molly Hennessey-Fiske, "Immigrant detention centers criticized at Capitol Hill forum," *Los Angeles Times*, July 28, 2015, http://tinyurl.com/o6tl3f7; Wil S. Hylton, "The Shame of America's Family Detention Camps," *The New York Times*, Feb. 4, 2015, http://tinyurl.com/ne94q28.

63. "Hutto Sexual Abuse Case Background," American Civil Liberties Union, Oct. 19, 2011, http://tinyurl.com/67base3. Erin Green, "Dunn gets 10 months," *The Hutto News*, Dec. 2, 2011, http://tinyurl.com/pdzbfcb.

64. Nina Bernstein, "Documents Reveal Earlier Immigrant Deaths," *The New York Times*, Jan. 9, 2010, http://tinyurl.com/yeu7f8r.

65. "2011 Operations Manual ICE Performance-Based National Detention Standards," U.S. Immigration and Customs Enforcement, undated, http://tinyurl.com/ptw8xml.

66. Michael Muskal, "Detention conditions 'similar, if not worse,' than migrants' home countries, report says," *Los Angeles Times*, Sept. 18, 2015, http://tinyurl.com/osfdhkk.

67. *Ibid.*

68. *Ibid.*

69. "RE: Jenny L. Flores, et al. v. Jeh Johnson, et al. CV 85–4544 DMG (AGRx)," United States Commission on Civil Rights, Sept. 11, 2015, http://tinyurl.com/ovkoze6.

70. Preston, *op. cit.*

71. "Statement by Secretary Jeh C. Johnson on Reforms to Family Residential Centers," U.S. Department of Homeland Security, Sept. 18, 2015, http://tinyurl.com/p7a79fx.

72. *Ibid.*

73. David Nakamura, Robert Costa and David A. Fahrenthold, "Obama announces immigration overhaul shielding 4 million from deportation," *The Washington Post*, Nov. 20, 2014, http://tinyurl.com/oyrput6.

74. Molly Hennessy-Fiske, "Appeals court scrutinizes Obama immigration action as activists rally outside," *Los Angeles Times*, July 10, 2015, http://tinyurl.com/qzvaotn.

75. Muzaffar Chishtia, Faye Hipsman and Sarah Pierce, "Quick Resolution of Challenge Over Obama Administration Deportation Relief Programs Is Ever Less Likely," Migration Policy Institute, July 15, 2015, http://tinyurl.com/nhhm8wz.

76. *Ibid.*

77. Christina L. Lyons, "Presidential Power," *CQ Researcher*, March 6, 2015, pp. 217–240.

78. Joseph Tanfani, "Republicans attack Obama's action on immigration as unconstitutional," *Los Angeles Times*, Dec. 2, 2014, http://tinyurl.com/qeal7ut.

79. "Remarks by the President in Address to the Nation on Immigration," *op. cit.*

80. "Secure Communities: A Fact Sheet," American Immigration Council, Nov. 29, 2011, http://tinyurl.com/3s4chkq.

81. Jerry Markon, "Obama administration scales back deportations in policy shift," *The Washington Post*, July 2, 2015, http://tinyurl.com/psdbzhh.

82. Suzanne Gamboa, "Obama Ends Secure Communities Program That Helped Hike Deportations," NBC News, Nov. 21, 2014, http://tinyurl.com/q6u5fnx.

83. "Secure Communities," Memorandum from Homeland Security Secretary Jeh Charles Johnson, Nov. 20, 2014, Department of Homeland Security, http://tinyurl.com/pvughy2.

84. Markon, *op. cit.*

85. Nora Caplan-Bricker, "Who's the Real Deporter-In-Chief: Bush or Obama?" *The New Republic*, April 17, 2014, http://tinyurl.com/lyqqgqu.

86. *Ibid.*

BIBLIOGRAPHY
Selected Sources
Books

Golash-Boza, Tanya Maria, *Immigration Nation: Raids, Detentions, and Deportations in Post-9/11 America*, Paradigm Publishers, 2012.
An associate professor of sociology at the University of California, Merced, analyzes changes in U.S. immigration policy that followed the 9/11 terrorist attacks.

Wong, Tom K., *Rights, Deportation, and Detention in the Age of Immigration Control*, Stanford University Press, 2015.
An assistant professor of political science at the University of California, San Diego, examines how immigration policies, including the use of detention and deportation, are formulated in the United States, Europe and elsewhere.

Articles

Bernstein, Nina, "Officials Hid Truth of Immigrant Deaths in Jail," *The New York Times*, Jan. 9, 2010, http://tinyurl.com/yz8j6ku.
Documents acquired by *The New York Times* and the American Civil Liberties Union reveal that the U.S. government covered up information concerning the treatment of 107 immigrants who died in detention since October 2003.

Hennessy-Fiske, Molly, "Paid $1 to $3 a day, unauthorized immigrants keep family detention centers running," *Los Angeles Times*, Aug. 3, 2015, http://tinyurl.com/pgcwhle.
Critics say federal law allows the private companies that run many detention centers to profit unfairly from the labor of detainees, who are paid as little as $1 a day for cleaning, cooking, landscaping and other jobs at the centers.

Hylton, Wil S., "The Shame of America's Family Detention Camps," *The New York Times Magazine*, Feb. 4, 2015, http://tinyurl.com/ne94q28.
Immigrant advocates paint a grim picture of detention life for children and mothers, who can be held for months as they await eligibility hearings for asylum.

Miroff, Nick, "Controversial quota drives immigration detention boom," *The Washington Post*, Oct. 13, 2013, http://tinyurl.com/o44jjr8.
A contentious congressional "quota" that the nation hold 34,000 migrants a day, a policy informally known as the "bed mandate," has driven up the number of immigrants detained.

Preston, Julia, "Judge Orders Release of Immigrant Children Detained by U.S.," *The New York Times*, July 25, 2015, http://tinyurl.com/owlc5rg.
The Obama administration's policy of detaining women and children who arrived in the United States illegally violates a 1997 court order that set minimum housing and treatment standards for such undocumented immigrants, according to a federal judge.

Reports and Studies

"The Math of Immigrant Detention," National Immigration Forum, Aug. 22, 2013, http://tinyurl.com/o2hhuye.
An immigrant advocacy organization in Washington suggests low-cost alternatives to high-cost detention of undocumented immigrants.

"President Obama's Record of Dismantling Immigration Enforcement," Federation for American Immigration Reform (FAIR), September 2014, http://tinyurl.com/pf66h22.
A citizens group based in Washington that supports less immigration and stricter enforcement of existing laws argues President Obama has failed to make proper use of tools like detention as he supports de facto amnesty for undocumented immigrants.

"Unlocking Human Dignity: A Plan to Transform the U.S. Immigrant Detention System," Migration and Refugee Services/United States Conference of Catholic Bishops and The Center for Migration Studies, 2015, http://tinyurl.com/mzax9or.
Refugee advocacy groups argue for an alternative approach to detention that would require fewer incarcerations, especially for women and children.

Cadman, Dan, "Why Alien Detention is Necessary: A rebuttal to anti-detention advocates," Center for Immigration Studies, June 2015, http://tinyurl.com/og3kvze.
A former U.S. Immigration and Customs Enforcement official, now a research fellow with a center that supports lower immigration levels, makes the case for detention as a necessary part of the immigration enforcement process.

Passel, Jeffrey, and D'Vera Cohn, "Unauthorized immigrant population stable for half a decade," Pew Research Center, July 22, 2015, http://tinyurl.com/nuvsnaw.
Despite public concern about the rate of illegal immigration, researchers at a major demographic think tank say the number of immigrants living in the country illegally has held steady for five years.

Shah, Silky, Mary Small and Carol Wu, "Banking on Detention: local lockup quotas & the immigrant dragnet," Detention Watch Network and the Center for Constitutional Rights, 2015, http://tinyurl.com/pm3agxt.
An immigrant advocacy organization and a think tank on constitutional law examine how federal policies that guarantee payment to private contractors affects the number of immigrant detentions.

For More Information

American Civil Liberties Union (ACLU), 125 Broad St., 18th Floor, New York NY 10004; 212-549-2500; https://www.aclu.org. Advocacy group that defends constitutional rights; has represented detained immigrants in several cases.

Amnesty International, 5 Penn Plaza, 16th Floor, New York, NY 10001; 212- 807-8400; www.amnestyusa.org. U.S. branch of the international human rights or- ganization; defends the rights of detained immigrants in the United States.

Center for Immigration Studies, 1629 K St., N.W., Suite 600, Washington, DC 20006; 202-466-8185; www.cis.org. Research organization that advocates for reduced immigration into the United States.

Detention Watch Network, 1419 V St., N.W., Washington, DC 20009; 202-846-7059; www.detentionwatchnetwork. org. National coalition of organizations and individuals working to correct what it considers injustices in the U.S. immigration system.

Federation for American Immigration Reform (FAIR), 25 Massachusetts Ave., N.W., Suite 330, Washington, DC 20001; 202-328-7004; www.fairus.org. A citizens' group that seeks to stop illegal immigration and promote immigration levels con- sistent with the national interest.

Immigrant Defense Project, 28 W. 29th St., Suite 501, New York, NY 10018; 212-725-6422; http://immigrantde-fenseproject.org. A legal services and advocacy organization that seeks to minimize what it considers the harsh and dispropor- tionate consequences immigrants face in the criminal justice system.

Migration Policy Institute, 1400 16th St., N.W., #300, Washington, DC 20036; 202-266-1940; www.migrationpol-icy.org. Think tank that analyzes the movement of people worldwide and U.S. immigration policy.

Pew Research Center, 1615 L St., N.W., Suite 700, Wash-ington, DC 20036; 202- 419-4300; www.pewresearch.org. Think tank that provides demographic informa- tion on undocumented immigration and the immigrant population in the United States; conducts polling on public attitudes toward immigration and other issues.

U.S Immigration and Customs Enforcement (ICE), 500 12th St., S.W., Washing- ton, DC 20536; 888-351-4024, www.ice.gov. Department of Homeland Security agency that enforces federal laws governing border control, customs, trade and immigration; manages immigrant detention facilities for those facing possible deportation.

15

Intelligence Reform

William Wanlund

Demonstrators in Washington protest government surveillance of Americans' electronic communications on Oct. 26, 2013. A placard pictures Edward Snowden, the former National Security Agency contractor who leaked thousands of secret documents revealing the wide extent of the surveillance.

From *CQ Researcher*, May 29, 2015.

When Navy SEALs stormed Osama bin Laden's Pakistani redoubt and killed the founder of al Qaeda on May 2, 2011, American officials counted the mission among the U.S. intelligence community's finest hours.

Announcing bin Laden's demise that evening, President Obama hailed "the countless intelligence and counterterrorism professionals who've worked tirelessly to achieve this outcome. The American people do not see their work, nor know their names. But tonight, they feel the satisfaction of their work and the result of their pursuit of justice."[1]

But four years after that dramatic announcement, former intelligence officials, national security scholars and other analysts paint a mixed picture of the nation's intelligence apparatus. While applauding the fact that the United States has not suffered a catastrophic terrorist attack since 2001, they are raising serious questions about how the intelligence community was restructured in the wake of the 9/11 attacks, its approach to fighting cyberattacks and other emerging security threats and the fallout from its domestic spying and torture of suspected terrorists.

Restructuring of the nation's intelligence community is among the most contentious issues. In a massive post-9/11 overhaul, the nation's 16 intelligence agencies — ranging from the Central Intelligence Agency (CIA) to the National Security Agency (NSA) — were consolidated under the Office of the Director of National Intelligence (ODNI).*

Supporters say consolidation has helped disparate intelligence agencies do a better job of "connecting the dots" on potential security threats — a key failing in the run-up to the 9/11 attacks.[2] But critics contend that consolidation added an unnecessary and expensive

353

Intelligence Community Composed of 16 Spy Agencies

In the wake of the 9/11 attacks on the United States, the Office of the Director of National Intelligence was created by Congress in 2004 to coordinate intelligence efforts of the nation's 16 spy agencies. Each maintains its own budget and administrative structure, but all are expected to share information, coordinate activities and set national intelligence priorities with each other. The Department of Defense houses four major programs, as well as intelligence operations for each military branch. The remaining seven agencies are civilian organizations.

Structure of the U.S. Intelligence Community

Office of the Director of National Intelligence

Director: James R. Clapper

Program Managers

Central Intelligence Agency Director: John Brennan	**Defense Intelligence Agency** Director: Marine Corps Lt. Gen. Vincent Stewart	**FBI National Security Branch** Executive Assistant Director: John Giacalone	**National Geospatial-Intelligence Agency** Director: Robert Cardillo	**National Reconnaissance Office** Director: Betty J. Sapp	**National Security Agency** Director: Navy Adm. Michael S. Rogers

Departmental

Drug Enforcement Administration Office of National Security Intelligence	Department of Energy Office of Intelligence and Counter-Intelligence	Department of Homeland Security Office of Intelligence and Analysis	Coast Guard Intelligence	Department of State Bureau of Intelligence and Research	Treasury Office of Intelligence and Analysis

Services

Air Force Intelligence	Army Intelligence	Marine Corps Intelligence	Naval Intelligence

Source: "Structure," Intelligence.gov, undated, http://tinyurl.com/mgenlom

layer of bureaucracy to intelligence gathering. It remains unclear, they say, how well the agencies are sharing information and working together on common national security goals.

Paul Pillar, who retired from the CIA in 2005 after a 28-year career in senior analytical and management positions, says Congress voted to consolidate the agencies under the ODNI to placate a nervous public. The move is "best described as a response to a strong public demand after 9/11 to give the basis for politicians to say to the American public, 'We're taking corrective action,'" he says.

Robert Jervis, a professor of international politics at Columbia University in New York, says consolidation has had certain advantages. For example, he says, it allowed the 16 intelligence agencies to better manage their long-range budgeting, provide more training for intelligence agents and analysts and make sophisticated technology, such as satellite photos and communication intercepts, available across agency lines.

But, Jervis says, "there are a lot of disadvantages, too — layers of organization and paperwork, [lack of] coordination, and tremendous overlap and friction." His conclusion: "The disadvantages outweigh the advantages, and I think most informed observers feel that way."

ODNI officials defend consolidation, saying its growing pains are behind it and that intelligence collection and analysis are smoother and more productive than ever.

---

* The agencies are the Air Force Intelligence, Surveillance, and Reconnaissance Enterprise; Army Intelligence; Central Intelligence Agency; Coast Guard Intelligence; Defense Intelligence Agency; Department of Energy Office of Intelligence and Counterintelligence; Department of Homeland Security Office of Intelligence and Analysis; Department of State Bureau of Intel- ligence and Research; Department of the Treasury Office of Intelligence and Analysis; Drug En- forcement Administration Office of National Security Intelligence; Federal Bureau of Investigation's National Security Branch; Marine Corps Intelligence; National Geospatial-Intelligence Agency; National Reconnaissance Office; National Security Agency; and Office of Naval Intelligence.

Intelligence Funding Requests Rise

The Office of the Director of National Intelligence (ODNI) and Department of Defense (DOD) requested nearly $72 billion for fiscal 2016 intelligence programs, up 15 percent from fiscal 2015 requests. Combined intelligence funding grew from about $64 billion in 2007 to $80 billion in 2010 before declining for the next three years and remaining flat in 2014.

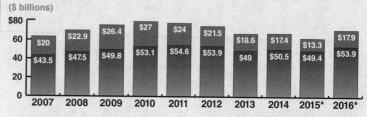

U.S. Intelligence Budget in $ billions, by program, 2007-16

($ billions)

Year	National Intelligence Programs	Military Intelligence Programs
2007	$43.5	$20
2008	$47.5	$22.9
2009	$49.8	$26.4
2010	$53.1	$27
2011	$54.6	$24
2012	$53.9	$21.5
2013	$49	$18.6
2014	$50.5	$17.4
2015*	$49.4	$13.3
2016*	$53.9	$17.9

* Requested

Source: "Intelligence Budget Data," Federation of American Scientists, updated Feb. 2, http://tinyurl.com/moa8cyy; data from Office of the Director of National Intelligence and Defense Department Budget Justifications, Fiscal Years 2007-2016

The ODNI has "successfully created a relationship of trust and understanding" among the 16 agencies, says Ted Gistaro, ODNI assistant deputy director for intelligence integration. "Our role is to be a facilitator, to bring the members of the intelligence community together to collaborate and do their individual missions. We've actually streamlined a lot of what the [intelligence community] needs to do . . . and made it easier and more effective to collaborate than they would've been able to do on their own."

Consolidation was one response to the evolving terrorist threat. So, too, was a secret order signed by President George W. Bush in February 2002 empowering the CIA to capture al Qaeda terrorists. It said the laws of war requiring humane treatment of prisoners did not apply to al Qaeda suspects.[3]

Since then, the CIA has come under intense scrutiny for its use of what it called enhanced interrogation techniques of terrorism suspects — and what critics have said was torture. The release last December of unclassified portions of a study of those interrogations by the Senate Select Committee on Intelligence set off a national debate over the value of such techniques to protect

Obama Urges Firms to Share Data on Hacks

Opponents say the plan raises privacy concerns.

Amy Pascal, co-chair of Sony Pictures Entertainment, turned on her computer on Nov. 24, 2014, and saw a startling message: "Hacked by #GOP." A group calling itself Guardians of Peace had broken into Sony's computer system and captured the production company's emails, copies of yet-to-be-released Sony films, financial records and other information.

The hackers also threatened unspecified retaliation against theaters planning to show Sony's film "The Interview," a comedy about a fictional assassination attempt against North Korean President Kim Jong-un, which was about to be released. Sony decided to let theaters wishing to show the film do so.[1] The hackers never made good on their threats, but Sony estimated that investigating and recovering from the cyber break-in cost the company some $15 million.[2]

The Obama administration wants to enlist private companies in an early-warning system, in which participants would share information about such cyberattacks with other firms and with the intelligence community in hopes of limiting the damage and scope of the attacks. Skeptics, however, worry about privacy and say the effort is unnecessary.

James Andrew Lewis, director of the Strategic Technologies Program at the Center for Strategic and International Studies, a Washington think tank, says that in 2013 the FBI notified 3,000 American companies that they had been hacked or confirmed that they had. "And those are the ones we know about — there may have been more," he says.

Cybercrime costs the United States about $100 billion annually when losses stemming from intellectual property theft, credit card fraud, recovery expenses and other costs are totaled up, Lewis says. "That's not the end of the world by any means, but it's a significant cost and a significant risk." By comparison, American students borrowed about $100 billion through the federal student loan program last year.[3]

After a computer security breach at health insurer Anthem, reported in February 2015, affected personal records of some 80 million customers and employees, the company spent at least $80 million to notify affected individuals, according to insurance industry reports.[4] A 2013 hack of Target Corp. customers' credit card information cost the company $162 million by the end of 2014.[5]

In a 2015 report to Congress, the Office of the Director of National Intelligence, which coordinates the activities of the federal intelligence agencies, ranked cyberattacks as one of the top global threats to the United States, ahead of terrorism and weapons of mass destruction. "Cyber threats to U.S. national and economic security are increasing in frequency, scale, sophistication and severity of impact," the agency told Congress in February. "We foresee an ongoing series of low-to-moderate-level cyberattacks from a variety of sources over time, which will impose cumulative costs on U.S. economic competitiveness and national security."[6]

President Obama pressed his case for information-sharing at a Feb. 13 White House summit on cybersecurity and consumer protection, encouraging companies that discover they are under attack to share information about the incident with the Department of Homeland Security's National Cybersecurity and Communications Integration Center and with others in the private sector to help them defend against similar attacks.

Obama said he wanted the private sector to set up voluntary information sharing and analysis organizations to serve as hubs for cybersecurity information-sharing and for collaboration among private organizations and with the government. Such hubs, he said, could be set up by industry sector (such as banking or health care) or by geographic region or by particular threats. Under the arrangement, companies would inform the government and one another if they detect activity on their computer systems indicating a cyberattack is occurring.[7]

Success would depend on widespread industry participation, Obama said. However, while companies would be required to protect personal information in the data they share, some fear they could still be held liable for turning over consumer information to the government. The liability protections under Obama's proposal are "far too narrow," said Matthew Eggers, senior director of national security and emergency preparedness at the U.S. Chamber of Commerce.[8]

The House of Representatives addressed those concerns in April when it passed and sent to the Senate legislation providing liability protection for companies sharing consumer data with government agencies, such as the Treasury and Commerce departments.[9] But Mark Jaycox, a legislative analyst at the Electronic Frontier Foundation, an advocacy group that supports digital privacy, dismissed the legislation as "surveillance bills in disguise [that] authorize more private-sector spying under new legal immunity provisions and use vague definitions that aren't carefully limited to protect [individuals'] privacy."[10]

"We all agree that information-sharing is one way to protect against attack," Jaycox says. But, he adds, the best approach "is streamlining and protecting the current systems, which allow information to be shared without violating privacy as long as it does not contain personal information."

Some are skeptical that the administration's plan has much to offer in the way of increased security. "Yawn. This is the 99th time I've heard of this [information-sharing] idea," said Dan Geer, chief information security officer for In-Q-Tel, a venture capital firm that invests in high-tech companies supporting the intelligence community. "The private sector in various places (such as high-end banks) is doing such a better job of information-sharing [with others in their industries] that the U.S. government has nothing to add."

Geer said a dearth of information-sharing isn't the biggest problem. "The big data breaches are so often the result of not paying attention by the victim."[11]

— *William Wanlund*

AFP/Getty Images/Jung Yeon-Je

Thor Halvorssen, president of the U.S.-based Human Rights Foundation, wears a T-shirt calling for retaliation against North Korean hacking, in Seoul, South Korea, on Jan. 20, 2015.

[3]"Federal Student Loan Default Rates," New America Foundation Federal Education Budget Report, Oct. 28, 2014, http://tinyurl.com/mvd65lc.

[4]Charlie Osborne, "Cost of Anthem's data breach likely to exceed $100 million," CNET, Feb. 12, 2015, http://tinyurl.com/qzwj2lw.

[5]"How Much did the Target, Home Depot Breaches Actually Cost?" Pymts.com, Feb. 26, 2015, http://tinyurl.com/mlx4ntb.

[6]"Worldwide Threat Assessment of the U.S. Intelligence Community," testimony of James Clapper before the Senate Armed Services Committee, Feb. 26, 2015, http://tinyurl.com/pt4l64t.

[7]"Fact Sheet: White House Summit on Cybersecurity and Consumer Protection," The White House, Feb. 13, 2015, http://tinyurl.com/oojzxfz.

[8]Matthew Eggers, statement on "Industry Perspectives of the President's Cybersecurity Information-Sharing Proposal" before the House Homeland Security Subcommittee on Cybersecurity, Infrastructure Protection, and Security Technologies, March 4, 2015, http://tinyurl.com/lyhtsex.

[9]"House Passes Cybersecurity Information Sharing Bills," *National Law Review*, April 25, 2015, http://tinyurl.com/m4b5tng.

[10]Mark Jaycox, "House of Representatives Passes Cybersecurity Bills Without Fixing Core Problems," Electronic Frontier Foundation, April 22, 2015, http://tinyurl.com/pgqzauh.

[11]Sara Sorcher, "Obama's info-sharing plan won't significantly reduce security breaches," *The Christian Science Monitor*, Feb. 25, 2015, http://tinyurl.com/mk67a6f.

[1]Mark Seal, "An Exclusive Look at Sony's Hacking Saga," *Vanity Fair*, March 2015, http://tinyurl.com/nqvdj9t.

[2]Ryan Faughnder, "Sony says studio hack cost it $15 million in fiscal third quarter," *Los Angeles Times*, Feb. 4, 2015, http://tinyurl.com/mkyhlcp.

national security. The CIA's use of such methods as waterboarding (simulated drowning), sleep deprivation and so-called rectal rehydration, the report said, was "not an effective means of acquiring intelligence or gaining cooperation from detainees."[4] The report "shows that the CIA's actions a decade ago are a stain on our values and on our history," said then-committee Chairman Dianne Feinstein, D-Calif.[5]

CIA Director John Brennan acknowledged that some techniques detailed by the panel were "abhorrent," but he did not agree that they were ineffective. "The cause-and-effect relationship between the use of [such tactics] and useful information subsequently provided by the detainee is, in my view, unknowable," Brennan said.[6]

Georgetown University law professor David Cole says the real issue is not whether a technique works but whether it is right or wrong. "Torture is prohibited regardless of its effectiveness, and it may well be impossible to determine whether the tactics were effective or not," he says. Even if the CIA's tactics thwarted planned attacks, he says, "that doesn't make the CIA's practice acceptable. We prohibit torture, like slavery and genocide, because it is wrong, not because it doesn't work."

Meanwhile, as the threat of cyberwarfare has grown, intelligence officials have taken several steps aimed at stemming attacks by both cybercriminals and terrorists.

ODNI Director James R. Clapper this year listed cybersecurity as a top threat to U.S. security. He cited potential cyberthreats from "profit-motivated criminals, ideologically motivated hackers or extremists" and "nation-states like Russia, China, North Korea and Iran."[7] James A. Lewis, who heads the cybersecurity program at the Center for Strategic and International Studies, a Washington think tank, estimates that cybercrime costs the United States about $100 billion annually.[8]

The specter of war in cyberspace intensified last November, when the computer systems of Sony Pictures Entertainment were hacked. The FBI blamed the North Korean government, though without conclusive evidence. In January Obama imposed sanctions on North Korean agencies and officials, citing the communist country's "destructive, coercive cyber-related actions."[9]

In February the White House created an office to collect and analyze intelligence about cyberthreats for distribution among intelligence community members. In addition, it has urged private companies victimized by hackers to share information about those attacks with other companies and the government. Obama also wants private technology companies to help identify and repel attacks on government and commercial computer systems and networks.[10]

Heightened attention to cybersecurity has prompted Brennan, who was confirmed as CIA chief in 2013, to reorganize the agency to better coordinate intelligence gathering and analysis. The reorganization will enable the agency to better cope with diverse national security threats, Brennan said. However, critics, including some CIA veterans, say it will weaken the agency by causing it to focus increasingly on current events and crises at the expense of its traditional strength of strategic forecasting.

"While CIA has famously failed to predict major events — most notably the rapid collapse of the Soviet Union — the unique value of [the agency] is that it generally does an extraordinary job of looking several steps ahead," said James Joyner, an associate professor of security studies at the Marine Corps Command and Staff College in Quantico, Va. "That's not a capability we can afford to lose."[11]

Meanwhile, fallout continues from another vestige of post-9/11 intelligence gathering: secret government monitoring of private electronic communications. Surveillance of American citizens' cellphone conversations and other electronic transmissions came to light in 2013 in documents leaked by former NSA contract employee Edward J. Snowden. The ensuing public outcry has led to calls to curb — or end — the NSA's mass surveillance practices. The portion of the USA Patriot Act that authorized the NSA's mass surveillance is due to expire June 1, and Congress must quickly decide whether to extend the authorization or restrict the conditions for surveillance.

In May the House of Representatives passed and sent to the Senate legislation that would extend the NSA's authority to collect communication data but would limit it to specially targeted individuals, Internet accounts or addresses.[12] However, senators are divided on whether to reform or shut down the NSA program: On May 20, with the deadline for extending the program approaching, Sen. Rand Paul, R-Ky., led a 10 1/2 hour filibuster against any effort to extend the program. Senate Majority Leader Mitch McConnell, R-Ky., prefers extending the surveillance program unchanged.

At the same time, the government is engaged in a tug-of-war with cellphone makers, urging them not to build encryption technology into their devices because it hinders intelligence agencies from intercepting the communications of suspected terrorists.

As the intelligence community adjusts to a fluid national security environment, here are some key questions being debated:

Has consolidation of oversight strengthened U.S. intelligence?

The ODNI, an umbrella organization created by the 2004 Intelligence Reform and Terrorism Prevention Act, opened on April 22, 2005, with the goal of improving communication and coordination among the 16 intelligence agencies. But the office had three directors in its first five years, with its third, Adm. Dennis Blair, lasting only 16 months.

Some attribute the rocky beginning to turf battles among Washington agencies. "Part of the problem is the continuing animosity of some individuals, organizations that hope the [director of National Intelligence] is a passing fad, can be made to fail and things will go back to the halcyon days of yore when the director of central intelligence was in charge," said Tom Fingar, former deputy director of the ODNI.[13]

Greg Treverton, chair of the ODNI's National Intelligence Council, which coordinates policy positions, acknowledges that "agency rivalries and turf battles" exist, but adds, "In the end the intelligence community's mission is to help policy."

He cites, for example, the National Intelligence Priorities Framework, a periodically updated planning document created by the ODNI with input from policymakers and the 16 spy agencies. "The agencies tell us they see the [framework] as a living document that they really build their programs around, and when priorities change, they take almost immediate action, and you see that in terms of greater analytic output and greater focus."

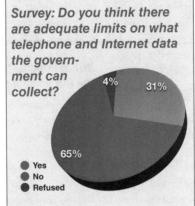

Most Want Tighter Data-Collection Limits

Sixty-five percent of Americans say limits on government collection of telephone and Internet data are inadequate, according to a recent poll.

Survey: Do you think there are adequate limits on what telephone and Internet data the government can collect?

- 4%
- 31%
- 65%

- Yes
- No
- Refused

Source: "Internet Project/GFK Privacy Panel Survey #2," Pew Research Center and GFK, May 2015, p. 45, http://tinyurl.com/mmkdoqf

Others think the problems faced by the director of National Intelligence reflect the job's built-in bureaucratic limitations. The director is in the unenviable position of having a job with great responsibility but relatively little authority, said Richard A. Best Jr., a national defense specialist at the Congressional Research Service, which advises Congress on policy issues. The office "is potentially highly influential, but it does not provide the extensive line responsibilities that Cabinet secretaries possess," Best wrote. "It requires sharing of power and close coordination and cooperation rather than decisive direction." Moreover, the director is likely to be regularly criticized "for either meddling unnecessarily or failing to exert authorities that are in fact ambiguous."[14]

The ODNI's leadership situation seems to have stabilized, however, under Clapper, whose five years on the job is equivalent to the tenure of his three predecessors combined.

Treverton credits Clapper's management style. Clapper defines where the intelligence community needs to be and then lets the agencies tell him how to get there, Treverton says. "Some of his predecessors tried to command, and that wasn't a winner."

However, Loch Johnson, regents professor of public and international affairs at the University of Georgia, worries that Clapper's management skills won't serve the intelligence community over the long term. "Jim Clapper knows everyone in the [intelligence community] and . . . can persuade them sometimes to do what he wants them to do," Johnson says. "But I don't think the next person is going to have that same kind of advantage and be able to convince agency managers to follow his will."

Notwithstanding Clapper's management, some former high-ranking intelligence officials question whether consolidation of the 16 agencies under the ODNI has improved the intelligence community's performance. "It added layers of bureaucracy, it added reviews, it made it hard to get anything done, and the large number of people involved makes it harder for analysts to call it straight," says James Woolsey, who served as CIA director from 1993–95. "With so many levels and varieties of bureaucracy involved, intelligence gets very fuzzy."

Former CIA official Pillar says, "There are a few things the ODNI can do better, for example making technological systems compatible so people can search the relevant databases within the [intelligence] community, but basically it's another layer of bureaucracy."

An ODNI fact sheet cites several instances in which consolidation has made intelligence gathering more effective. For instance, it says, two online collaborative tools — Intellipedia and A-Space — "provide [intelligence community] analysts a common platform to post information, conduct research and analysis and easily collaborate with colleagues working similar issues." When terrorists attacked hotels in Mumbai, India, in 2008, analysts used intelligence posted and discussed on A-Space to identify an al Qaeda-affiliated extremist group as the perpetrator of the attacks, the ODNI fact sheet said.

ODNI also notes that, since consolidation, the "Presidential Daily Briefing," a compendium of reports used to keep the president and other policymakers abreast of emerging intelligence concerns, now includes input from all members of the intelligence community.[15] Previously, the briefing had been solely a CIA responsibility.

But Mark Lowenthal — a former intelligence analyst who heads the Intelligence & Security Academy in Arlington, Va., a private training facility for government agencies and private-sector firms that support those agencies — says the ODNI's effectiveness suffers because the director "doesn't have budget execution authority. He can't tell the director of [the National Geospatial-Intelligence Agency] or [the National Security Agency], 'I want you to do this and not that; you have more money here and less money there.'"

Susan Gibson, the principal deputy general counsel at the ODNI, counters that "budget authority is one of [the director's] strongest authorities." However, she says, Clapper "thinks it works better when you bring everyone to the table and force them to make the hard trade-offs themselves, so you have more buy-in and greater transparency."

Despite the 2004 reforms, the intelligence community still gets things wrong, according to Mike Morell, a former CIA deputy director. In his 2015 book *The Great War of Our Time: The CIA's Fight Against Terrorism, From Al Qa'ida to ISIS*, Morell writes that intelligence experts failed to anticipate the Arab Spring of 2010–12, which saw violence and political change throughout the Middle East. Further, once it took notice, the CIA optimistically, and erroneously, predicted the Arab Spring meant the end of al Qaeda. Instead, Morell wrote, "the Arab Spring was a boon to Islamic extremists across both the Middle East and North Africa."[16]

Lowenthal says intelligence failures will always be a fact of life. "Intelligence is not a mechanical process. You're dealing with human beings and all their unknowns. We're going to miss sometimes. And even when you do have all the information, things go wrong."

Will reorganization of the CIA make it more effective?

CIA Director Brennan is shaking up his agency, creating 10 "mission centers" focusing on specific functional areas, such as economic security or weapons proliferation, and certain geographical areas — such as the Middle East or China — that present particularly complex political, strategic and economic concerns. The specific designations for the mission centers, which are expected to be operational by Sept. 30, have not been made public.

Modeled on the CIA's existing Counterterrorism Center (CTC), formed in 1986, the centers would unite the "operatives" — or spies — with the analysts who sift through information provided by the spies. Brennan said the agency's previous "stove-piping" structure, in which the spies and analysts were separated, has hampered the agency's ability to address complex issues.[17]

The director is "trying to bring the agency in line with the world as it is today," said John McLaughlin, a former CIA deputy director (2000–04) and now practitioner-in-residence at Johns Hopkins University's School for Advanced International Studies. "You can't look at any one issue in isolation."[18]

He added, "We've learned over the years that, when we put operatives and analysts together, the synergy produces a more powerful product. Typically it's the analysts who know what we know and don't know, and it's what we don't know that [the operatives] need to collect. And the sooner you close the gap, the better off you are."[19]

But Melvin A. Goodman, a former CIA and State Department analyst who now directs the National Security Project at the liberal Center for International Policy think tank in Washington, said stove-piping has had a sound basis. "A wall is needed between [the] worlds of analysis and operations to ensure independent assessments," Goodman said. "The operational world is secretive and insular." Intelligence should be neutral, he says. If policymakers tell the CIA what information it should be seeking, he says, intelligence loses its value as an objective resource.[20]

On the other hand, Goodman said, "the analytic world must be open and accessible to outside experts [such as academics and government specialists] who can offer substantive critiques." If analysts cannot take advantage of outside expertise, their work will become excessively parochial, Goodman said.

Experience with the CTC and other so-called mission centers, such as those focusing on crime and narcotics, which are the models for Brennan's reorganization, illustrate the problem with the new structure, Goodman said. They "have become more or less service centers for policymakers, answering specific questions and preparing requested briefings, but not distinguished for exploring new ideas or for sponsoring competitive analysis."[21]

Brennan's restructuring plan is "more focused on the trees than the forest," said Jane Harman, president and CEO of the Woodrow Wilson International Center for Scholars, and a former Democratic member of the House Intelligence Committee. "There's a lot more to talk about besides these new baskets and mission centers," Harman said.[22]

Noting that extremist groups such as the Islamic State (also known as ISIS) have exploited social media to deliver propaganda and recruit American and European sympathizers, Harman said the CIA's first priority should be to monitor social media to gain insights into terrorists' actions and motivational messages. "I don't see that in these new baskets," she said. "What are the messages that penetrate, what are the motivations and what are the motivations of the kids [to fight for ISIS]? I don't think the CIA is anywhere close to [knowing] that."[23]

Brennan agrees about the need to focus on social media. To do that, his reorganization will establish a Directorate of Digital Innovation to "oversee the acceleration of digital and cyber integration across all of our mission areas" as well as "the standards of our digital tradecraft," he said in a message to employees.[24]

Former CIA and NSA Director Michael Hayden, whom the CIA consulted about the reorganization, warned against implementing the reorganization too quickly. "Hybrid" organizations such as the counterterrorism center tend to be "consumed with the operational

The Central Intelligence Agency ousted Iranian Prime Minister Mohammad Mossadegh in 1953 and installed Shah Mohammad Reza Pahlavi (above, shown in 1971) as the country's leader. The agency undertook some 170 major covert actions during the Dwight D. Eisenhower administration (1953-61). The shah was overthrown in 1979 by the Islamic Revolution.

Getty Images/Keystone

challenges of the moment," Hayden said. "But you also have to pay attention to creating the basic skills, knowledge and databases" the CIA traditionally develops.[25]

Does Congress provide adequate oversight of the intelligence community?

The 1947 National Security Act said Congress must be kept "fully informed" of major intelligence activities, but successive administrations have interpreted this to mean disclosing information to only a few key members of Congress.

Depending on the degree of sensitivity of the information, intelligence officials may decide to brief only the House and Senate leadership (the so-called Gang of 4); the leadership and the chairmen and ranking members of the intelligence committees (Gang of 8); some additional committee chairmen as well; or the full intelligence committees.[26]

Some believe congressional oversight is hampered by Congress' own committee structure. Jennifer Kibbe, chair of the Government Department at Franklin and Marshall College in Lancaster, Pa., noted that the intelligence committees in Congress have exclusive budgetary jurisdiction over only a portion of the overall intelligence community — that is, only the CIA and ODNI. They share budgetary jurisdiction for the other intelligence agencies, including parts of the Justice, State, Treasury,

CHRONOLOGY

1940s-1950s *A national intelligence system takes shape.*

1942 President Franklin D. Roosevelt establishes the Office of Strategic Services (OSS), a wartime covert action arm of the military.

1947 National Security Act of 1947 creates Central Intelligence Agency (CIA) to "correlate and evaluate intelligence."

1952 National Security Agency (NSA) is established.

1953 President Dwight D. Eisenhower expands CIA's mandate to include covert action. . . . The CIA engineers the ouster of Iran's democratically elected prime minister and his replacement by Shah Mohammad Reza Pahlavi.

1960s-1970s *The scope of intelligence work broadens; overreach leads to reforms.*

1961 A CIA-led attempt to invade Cuba at the Bay of Pigs and topple communist leader Fidel Castro fails when U.S. does not send promised military support.

Early 1960s The CIA becomes involved in the Vietnam War; allegations surface of kidnap, torture and murder of Viet Cong leaders.

1977 U.S. Senate committee finds evidence of domestic spying by the CIA, NSA and Federal Bureau of Investigation (FBI), leading to creation of intelligence oversight committees in both chambers of Congress.

1978 Congress passes the Foreign Intelligence Surveillance Act, setting limits on the nature of intelligence the NSA may collect and the methods for collecting it.

1980s *Security incidents and illegal activity raise questions about the CIA's effectiveness; the end of the Cold War leads to cuts in intelligence resources.*

1981 William Casey becomes the first CIA director given Cabinet rank.

1985 Counterintelligence practices receive new scrutiny as a CIA agent defects to the Soviet Union and CIA and FBI personnel are charged with spying.

1986 Revelations of CIA and military misdeeds in the Iran-Contra affair lead to tightened restrictions on covert intelligence.

1989 Berlin Wall falls and, as the Cold War ends, intelligence budgets over the next decade are slashed.

2000s-2015 *Terrorism brings new focus, powers and controversy to the intelligence community.*

2001 Lack of communication and coordination between intelligence agencies is blamed for the failure to stop the 9/11 terrorist attacks.

2004 President George W. Bush signs legislation consolidating federal intelligence agencies under the newly created Office of the Director of National Intelligence (ODNI).

2007 Congress gives the NSA expanded latitude for warrantless monitoring of foreigners' communications.

2008 National Cyber Joint Investigative Task Force is established to confront increasing attacks on government and commercial computers.

2011 CIA-led team of Navy SEALS kills Qaeda leader Osama bin Laden.

2013 NSA contract employee Edward Snowden leaks classified information revealing global surveillance by the agency of e-mail and social media messages, including the communications of leaders of nations friendly to the United States.

2014 Senate report criticizes the CIA's use of "enhanced interrogation techniques" to obtain information from terrorism suspects. . . . U.S. blames North Korea for hacking into Sony Pictures computers.

2015 CIA Director John Brennan announces an agency reorganization to better coordinate intelligence gathering and analysis. . . . Authorization under USA Patriot Act for NSA mass surveillance of American citizens' cellphone conversations and other electronic transmissions set to expire on June 1.

Homeland Security and Defense departments, with the congressional committees responsible for overseeing those agencies, according to Kibbe.[27]

As a result, Kibbe says, "no one committee has a complete view of the intelligence community to be able to judge priorities and weigh programs against each other in times of increased need and reduced resources." In addition, she says, "individual programs can get lost, either accidentally or on purpose, in the slipstream between committees."

For example, FBI counterterrorism reform actions in the late 1990s "went unreviewed by any congressional committee, largely because the intelligence committees thought the judiciary committees would handle it, while the judiciary committees considered it an intelligence issue," Kibbe said.[28]

Handling of classified information provides another difficulty for congressional overseers. Because the executive branch decides what information should be classified and at what level, it can restrict information even from members of Congress who hold security clearances. As a result, the executive branch can "directly control what Congress can or cannot see, indirectly influencing the legislative branch's overall ability to make decisions," concluded a report by Harvard University's John F. Kennedy School of Government.[29]

For instance, some lawmakers have been particularly outspoken about how much information they received about the CIA's controversial post-9/11 interrogation techniques. Congress received "incomplete and inaccurate information" about the agency's practices, said the Senate Intelligence Committee's five-year review of CIA detention and interrogation programs, released in December. "Briefings to the full committee contained numerous inaccuracies, including inaccurate descriptions of how interrogation techniques were applied and what information was produced from the program," a committee statement said.[30]

CIA Director Brennan countered that the agency's "factual record does not support such conclusions." Nevertheless, he acknowledged that there were instances in which "representations about the program . . . were inaccurate, imprecise or fell short of Agency tradecraft standards" and "never should have happened."[31]

However, in a letter to *The Wall Street Journal*, six former CIA directors and deputy directors said, "The CIA briefed Congress approximately 30 times. Initially, at presidential direction the briefings were restricted to the so-called Gang of Eight of top congressional leaders — a limitation permitted under covert-action laws. The briefings were detailed and graphic and drew reactions that ranged from approval to no objection. . . . In September 2006 . . . the administration [briefed] full committee and staff directors on the interrogation program. . . . The committees missed a chance to help shape the program — they couldn't reach a consensus."[32]

Kibbe says the current congressional notification system is flawed. "Right now the deck is stacked in the executive branch's favor," she says. "More things should be briefed to the [full] committees. I understand you need those standards for extremely sensitive operations. But senators are expected to go to briefings at random times, usually with no warning for what it's about. They don't get to bring legal counsel or other staff. They can't take notes. They can't talk to anybody else about it. That seems like a tailor-made way to stymie oversight."

But former CIA Director Woolsey says, "I think having just a very small committee doing the oversight would probably be more effective — no more than half a dozen congressmen, half a dozen senators. Certainly there needs to be oversight, but even with fewer than a dozen people conducting oversight, we would still have more oversight of our intelligence services than any other country in the world."

Administration officials say they limit disclosures to Congress because of fear of leaks of secret information. But Rep. Devin Nunes, R-Calif., chairman of the House Permanent Select Committee on Intelligence, said in an e-mail interview with *CQ Researcher*: "Committee members swear an oath not to divulge classified information, and they take that oath seriously. The [intelligence community] is obligated to share information with the committee, and should feel confident they can do so without being concerned about leaks. The administration should look in the mirror if it is really concerned about leaks."

Jack Devine, who served for 32 years in the CIA, including in senior positions, says, "There's always a question about leaks, [but] when I look back, the leaks usually originated in the executive branch, because of petty competition or wanting to get an idea out. Congressional oversight is a very good sanity check on a secret intelligence community."

CIA's Paramilitary Activities Face Scrutiny

Critics say the agency is undercutting foreign policy.

The Central Intelligence Agency (CIA) has been conducting paramilitary activities for much of its 68-year existence. Using non-U.S. personnel, or proxy forces, it helped overthrow governments in Iran in 1953 and Chile in 1973. In the 1970s, it was accused of plotting to assassinate foreign leaders perceived as harmful to U.S. interests, prompting a 1976 congressional investigation that resulted in Congress outlawing political assassination. [1]

Today, the CIA is conducting what Jennifer Kibbe, an associate professor of government at Franklin and Marshall College, in Lancaster, Pa., calls "shadow wars," using armed drones to conduct strikes in countries with which the United States is not at war but where terrorists are active. Since 2004 the CIA has conducted at least 500 drone strikes in such places as Pakistan, Yemen and Somalia. [2] During the first six years of the Obama administration the CIA conducted nearly nine times the number of strikes as during the George W. Bush administration before him, according to the Bureau of Investigative Journalism, an independent news organization based in London. [3]

"I think we — the public, the media, the congressional oversight committees — should be paying more attention to the paramilitary role of the CIA," Kibbe says.

But former Deputy CIA Director John McLaughlin said, "I don't see paramilitary as the CIA's central focus. It's the part that's getting the public's attention, and it's arguably the most important, because it involves stopping things that pose a threat to human lives, American lives, but it's not the center" of what the CIA does. [4]

Other experts stress that the changing nature of the modern threats justifies new tactics. Loch Johnson, a professor of public and international affairs at the University of Georgia, says, "You have to ask yourself, what are we going to do about terrorist groups? And the answer probably is, you have to kill or capture the [terrorists], because you're never going to be able to bring them to the bargaining table.

"One effective way is the use of CIA drones, and I'd rather have the CIA than the Pentagon doing that," he continues. "The CIA is still small enough that you can have accountability for paramilitary operations. The Pentagon is so large that, when it comes to accountability and management, it's a joke."

Former CIA Director James Woolsey says the CIA can work fast and "has flexibility with respect to money." The agency is well equipped to carry out necessary paramilitary activities, "as long as it's done pursuant to a [presidential] finding properly submitted to certain members or committees of Congress."

Former CIA analyst Mark Lowenthal, head of the Intelligence & Security Academy, a private training institution in Arlington, Va., for government agencies and private sector firms that support them, says the CIA "becomes by default the go-to agency for things that other agencies don't want to do. The military is perfectly happy to

The University of Georgia's Johnson says congressional oversight has improved greatly in the last 40 years. "Compared to the pre-1975 era, it's like night and day," he says, referring to the period before the oversight committees were created. "There's a lot more oversight and accountability now."

However, he says, "Overall, I would say oversight is performing at quite a disappointing level right now. A lot of the committee members are 'cheerleaders,' they support the intelligence agencies — which is fine; but they support them unequivocally, and I think you need a modicum of skepticism to probe programs to make sure they're operating well. Too often, it's cheerleading without probing."

BACKGROUND
Military Intelligence

Gathering intelligence — particularly military intelligence — has been a U.S. government function since the early days of the republic. Gen. George Washington paid an agent in Boston to use "secret correspondence" to report on British troop movements. [33]

During the Civil War both sides used military spies and codebreakers. [34] Early in the 20th century, gathering domestic civilian intelligence became a Justice Department responsibility with creation of the Bureau of Investigation — later to become the FBI — mostly to handle fraud, corruption and antitrust violations. [35]

do those kinds of things in war zones, but not outside. [State Department] diplomats won't spy; it violates their official status as diplomats. And every president likes having the flexibility" that a covert paramilitary capability offers, Lowenthal says.

Jack Devine, former associate director of the CIA's Operations Directorate, which oversees covert activities, says "All covert action is approved by the president of the United States. And it's not like the president approves it with a wink and a nudge — he has to sign a document."

But drone strikes are apparently a special case. According to press reports, Obama has delegated to the CIA authority to conduct without presidential approval "signature strikes" in Pakistan against individuals whose behavior is identified with militant activity. Obama himself approves so-called "personality" strikes against specific individuals, and on all drone attacks outside Pakistan. [5]

Shoon Murray, an associate professor in the School of International Service at American University, in Washington, says the U.S. image abroad should be considered in the context of the CIA's expanding paramilitary role, particularly its drone campaigns.

"I worry that [drone attacks] do harm, both to our global image and to populations that we want to reach, not alienate," she says.

Anti-drone sentiment is particularly strong in Pakistan, where strikes targeting Islamic militants have caused civilian casualties. "The CIA has had an outsized impact on foreign policy because of the overall concern of the national security community with counterterrorism," says Cameron Munter, who was U.S. ambassador to Pakistan from 2010 to '12 and now is a professor of international relations at Pomona College in California.

In Pakistan, Munter says, "our very real needs to keep ourselves and our friends in the rest of the world safe from terrorists took up a great deal of our energy, but the long-term needs of American policy include a stable and prosperous Pakistan. You can only get to that by thinking long term. [But,] when you're working primarily on immediate tasks, the urgent overwhelms the important."

Johnson says "there's a cultural difference — the CIA's can-do, get-the-job-done spirit versus the State Department's long-range view of forging lasting relationships. The CIA is attractive to presidents because they have the delusion that there can be quick-fix solutions to tangled foreign policy issues. So, rather than relying on State Department diplomats, which sometimes involves painful, drawn-out negotiations to accomplish a foreign policy objective, or sending in the Marines, which is noisy and bloody, they hope for a quiet solution in the form of covert action. Sometimes it works, but most of the time it doesn't."

— *William Wanlund*

[1] Tim Weiner, *Legacy of Ashes: The History of the CIA* (2008), pp. 199-200.

[2] "Get the Data: Drone Wars," Bureau of Investigative Journalism, http://tinyurl.com/o2w65s9.

[3] Jack Serle, "Monthly Updates on the Covert War: Almost 2,500 now killed by covert US drone strikes since Obama inauguration six years ago," Bureau of Investigative Journalism report, Feb. 2, 2015, http://tinyurl.com/lgd89oj.

[4] "Reforming the American Intelligence System," "On Point," WBUR/National Public Radio, March 11, 2015, http://tinyurl.com/m7zqx7u.

[5] Greg Miller, "Plan for hunting terrorists signals U.S. intends to keep adding names to kill lists," *The Washington Post*, Oct. 23, 2012, http://tinyurl.com/93yhodz.

The U.S. military established a signals intelligence unit during World War I to decipher enemy codes and provide codes for its own forces. In 1919 the unit was transferred to the State Department, where it became the Cipher Bureau — also known as the "Black Chamber" — and focused on diplomatic rather than military communications. In 1929, Henry Stimson, secretary of State under newly inaugurated President Herbert Hoover, reportedly declared, "Gentlemen do not read other gentlemen's mail." Because of those ethical qualms, and for budget reasons, he disbanded the Cipher Bureau. [36]

By 1940, events in Europe were prompting U.S. leaders to believe they must prepare for possible war. In June 1942 — six months after the Japanese attack on Pearl Harbor — President Franklin D. Roosevelt created the Office of Strategic Services (OSS) under the military Joint Chiefs of Staff to "collect and analyze" strategic information [and] plan and "operate such special services as may be directed by" the Joint Chiefs. [37]

Taking lessons from British intelligence practices, OSS operatives emphasized covert action — "guerrillas, operations with resistance groups behind enemy lines, sabotage and so on," wrote Lowenthal of the Intelligence Security Academy. "These covert actions . . . had little effect on the outcome of the war [but] became the main historical legacy of the OSS [and] served as a training ground . . . for many people who helped establish the postwar intelligence community." [38]

Getty Images/Sovfoto/UIG

Captured mercenaries are held by Cuban troops after the failed Bay of Pigs invasion in 1961. The CIA-led attempt to invade the island and topple communist leader Fidel Castro collapsed when the United States failed to send promised military support. The next year, the Cuban Missile Crisis provided a crucial test for U.S. intelligence capabilities.

The Cold War

When World War II ended in 1945, President Harry S. Truman disbanded the OSS. But with the attack on Pearl Harbor still a painful national memory, and convinced that the Soviet Union was becoming a threat to the United States, Truman believed a peacetime intelligence service was needed. On July 27, 1947, he signed the National Security Act, unifying the Army, Navy and newly created Air Force under the secretary of Defense and establishing a National Security Council (NSC) to advise the president on "the objectives, commitments and risks of the United States in relation to our actual and potential military power."

The act also created the Central Intelligence Agency, "to correlate and evaluate intelligence relating to the national security" and advise the NSC. The agency would have "no police, subpoena, law-enforcement powers or internal-security functions," but would "perform such other functions and duties related to intelligence affecting the national security as the National Security Council may from time to time direct."[39]

Truman said later that he never meant for the CIA to become involved in "peacetime cloak and dagger operations." Rather, he intended to allow "the collection of all intelligence reports from every available source, and to have those reports reach me as President without . . . 'treatment' or interpretations . . . to guard against the chance of intelligence being used to influence or to lead the President into unwise decisions."[40]

In 1952, Truman created the National Security Agency (NSA) within the Defense Department. A descendant of the "Black Chamber" of the 1920s, the NSA's job was to coordinate the military's signals intelligence operations. It was highly secretive — some joked that NSA stood for "No Such Agency" — and its existence wasn't officially acknowledged until 1975.[41]

But Truman's successor, Dwight D. Eisenhower, also uneasy about a growing Soviet threat, sought broader authority for the CIA. In 1953 he ordered the agency to "train and equip underground organizations capable of launching large-scale raids or sustained warfare."[42]

During Eisenhower's administration (1953–61), the agency undertook 170 major covert actions.[43] These included ousting Prime Minister Mohammad Mossadegh of Iran and installing Shah Mohammad Reza Pahlavi in 1953, and helping to overthrow the leftist government of Guatemalan President Jacobo Arbenz Guzman in 1954. As a result, covert action became "an increasingly attractive tool for U.S. policy makers," wrote Lowenthal.[44]

Under President John F. Kennedy, the covert action program suffered a setback during the failed "Bay of Pigs" invasion of Cuba in 1961. A force of Cuban expatriates trained and armed by the CIA invaded the island, aiming to remove communist leader Fidel Castro from power. However, the CIA was unable to provide the necessary U.S. military support.[45]

The next year, Cuba also figured in the first major test of America's newest intelligence body, the Defense Intelligence Agency (DIA), created by the Pentagon in 1961 to coordinate the previously separate — and often duplicative and inefficient — intelligence-gathering operations of the Army, Navy and Air Force. In October 1962, DIA analysts concluded from high-altitude reconnaissance photos that the Soviet Union was installing nuclear missiles, aimed at the United States, in Cuba. The resulting Cuban Missile Crisis was resolved when the Soviets removed their nuclear weapons in exchange for the United States dismantling its nuclear missiles in Turkey and Italy.[46]

The Vietnam War (early 1960s-75) saw the CIA's covert workload increase. The agency "participated in every aspect of the wars in Indochina, political and military," including "secret diplomatic exchanges with enemy insurgents" and the Phoenix program, which involved kidnapping, torturing and killing communist North Vietnamese leaders, according to John Prados, senior fellow and project director of the National Security Archive at The George Washington University.[47]

Congress Steps In

From its inception the intelligence community had operated mostly autonomously, its activities generally hidden from the press and without congressional supervision. However, in December 1974, *New York Times* investigative reporter Seymour Hersh revealed that the CIA had conducted a "massive, illegal domestic intelligence operation during the Nixon administration against the antiwar movement and other dissident groups in the United States."[48]

A month later the Senate created a bipartisan committee, chaired by Frank Church, D-Idaho, to look into the allegations. The Church Committee, which investigated the FBI and NSA as well, reviewed more than 100,000 documents, interviewed 800 individuals and conducted 250 executive (closed) and 21 public hearings before issuing its final report in April 1976.[49]

The report described a "massive record of intelligence abuses over the years," and said "domestic intelligence activity has threatened and undermined the constitutional rights of Americans to free speech, association and privacy." Concluding there were "deficiencies in control and accountability" over the domestic activities of the intelligence community, the Church Committee called for ongoing congressional oversight of intelligence activities.[50] As a result, the Senate Select Committee on Intelligence was established in 1976 and the House Permanent Select Committee on Intelligence in 1977.[51]

Former intelligence analyst Lowenthal said the Church Committee and other investigations "undermined the public's faith in . . . the intelligence community, which had been largely sacrosanct. . . . [I]ntelligence has never regained the latitude it once enjoyed and has had to learn to operate with much more openness and scrutiny."[52]

The University of Georgia's Johnson, who was the first staff director of the House Intelligence Committee, says, "Before 1975, I think it's fair to say there was virtually no congressional check on intelligence activities. With the Church Committee we had a whole new era, in which we created the House and Senate intelligence committees, passed the Foreign Intelligence Surveillance Act [FISA], and put other laws and institutions in place to curb the abuse of power."

The FISA act, enacted in 1978, allowed the federal government to request judicial authority to conduct surveillance on individuals or organizations it considered dangerous. FISA also established the Foreign Intelligence Surveillance Court, made up of federal judges selected by the chief justice of the Supreme Court, to deal with those requests.

President Ronald Reagan (1981–89) took steps to revitalize the intelligence community, increasing budgets and staffing and elevating the CIA director to Cabinet rank. However, a series of security breaches and an illegal covert operation raised more controversy.

In the 1980s, federal security and counterintelligence practices were revamped after CIA agent Edward Lee Howard defected to the Soviet Union and several military, CIA, NSA and FBI personnel were arrested on espionage charges. In addition, the U.S. Embassy in Moscow was found to have been bugged by Soviet intelligence during construction.[53]

In 1986, in what became known as the Iran-Contra affair, CIA and Defense Department officials revealed that they had sold weapons to Iran in 1981 in exchange for the release of 52 American hostages held in Iran since 1979, in violation of a U.S. arms embargo against Iran. The proceeds were used to support the "Contras" (anti-communist paramilitary forces fighting the leftist Nicaraguan government) — also in violation of U.S. law. Congressional and executive branch investigations led to establishment of a CIA inspector general and a tightening of covert action reporting requirements.[54]

The fall of the Berlin Wall in 1989 and the subsequent dissolution of the Soviet Union came as almost a complete surprise to many observers, who saw the events as evidence of an intelligence failure. "We should not gloss over the enormity of [the CIA's] failure to forecast the magnitude of the Soviet crisis," wrote former CIA Director Stansfield Turner (1977–81) in 1991.[55] But former CIA Director Robert Gates (1991–93) said the agency repeatedly had warned policymakers, beginning in 1989, "of the deepening crisis and growing likelihood of a collapse of the old order."[56]

New Priorities

The Soviet Union's collapse required a new focus for the U.S. intelligence effort and brought calls for reforming and drastically down-sizing the intelligence community.

Staffing of U.S. intelligence agencies was reduced by about 23 percent at the end of the Cold War, according to ODNI DIrector Clapper. "During the mid- and late-'90s, we closed many CIA stations, reduced [human intelligence] collectors, cut analysts, allowed our overhead architecture to atrophy, neglected basic infrastructure needs such as power, space and cooling, and let our facilities decay," Clapper said.[57]

After the 9/11 terrorist attacks, many in Congress again saw "intelligence failures" at work. A staff report of the National Commission on Terrorist Attacks Upon the United States (the so-called 9–11 Commission) said terrorist threat intelligence was poorly organized and coordinated and never comprehensively reviewed. The report ended with a question: "Who is in charge of intelligence?"[58]

The full commission report, released in July 2004, called for overhauling the intelligence community.[59] Five months later Congress passed the Intelligence Reform and Terrorism Prevention Act, which created the Office of the Director of National Intelligence to manage the gathering, analysis and sharing of intelligence and oversee the agencies that contribute to the national intelligence program.[60]

Since 9/11, U.S. intelligence agencies have faced new challenges. In 2008, the federal government established a National Cyber Joint Investigative Task Force — consisting of representatives of nearly two dozen federal intelligence, military and law enforcement organizations — to address the growing incidence of cyberattacks intended to damage or destroy computer systems and conduct espionage on government or economic targets.

The intelligence community was fighting other cyber battles as well. On May 20, 2013, Snowden, the then-contract employee of the National Security Agency, flew to Hong Kong carrying a computer thumb drive with top-secret files detailing electronic mass surveillance by the NSA. In a series of leaks to newspapers and other media, Snowden revealed that the agency was monitoring email, Facebook posts and instant messages of people around the world, including foreign allies and American citizens. Subsequent revelations showed the agency has collected bulk telephone records of foreigners and U.S. citizens, along with images that can be used for facial recognition.[61]

The NSA said its bulk electronic collection programs were both legal and necessary for national security. "All three branches of government knew about these programs, approved them and helped to ensure that they complied with the law," ODNI General Counsel Robert Litt said in July 2013.[62]

NSA Director Keith Alexander said the agency's secret phone surveillance program has helped prevent "dozens of terrorist events."[63] However, a public opinion survey conducted in January 2014 showed 80 percent of U.S. adults "agree" or "strongly agree" that Americans should be concerned about the government's monitoring of phone calls and Internet communications.[64]

The same month, Obama restricted the collection of "signals intelligence" (SIGINT, or intelligence gleaned by monitoring electronic communications); defined how the intelligence community can use bulk-collected SIGINT; required an annual executive branch review of SIGINT priorities and requirements; and required each intelligence agency to safeguard personal information collected through SIGINT.[65]

CURRENT SITUATION

'Dragnet Surveillance'

Revelations of mass electronic surveillance by segments of the intelligence community continue to provoke public debate about how much surveillance the government can conduct in the name of national security without violating citizens' privacy.

On May 7 the Second U.S. Circuit Court of Appeals ruled that the NSA's mass collection of telephone records went beyond Congress' intent in passing the USA Patriot Act. The American Civil Liberties Union (ACLU) had challenged the surveillance program's constitutionality, claiming it violates the First Amendment (guaranteeing free speech) and the Fourth Amendment (protecting against illegal search).[66]

"We would expect such a momentous decision [by the NSA to surveil phone records] to be preceded by substantial debate, and expressed in unmistakable language," Judge Gerald Lynch wrote for the appeals court. "There is no evidence of such a debate."[67]

The appeals court did not halt the program, however, citing "national security interests." Lynch noted that the section of the Patriot Act that authorized the mass surveillance was up for congressional renewal and said Congress should have the chance to discuss the mass surveillance question directly. The court did not rule on the constitutionality of the practice.[68]

Should the National Intelligence director serve for a fixed term?

YES
Melvin A. Goodman
*Former CIA senior analyst; Senior Fellow,
Center for International Politics, Johns
Hopkins University; Author of The Failure of
Intelligence: The Decline and Fall of the CIA*

Written for *CQ Researcher*, May 2015

There's no solution to today's problems at the Central Intelligence Agency (CIA) and Office of the Director of National Intelligence (ODNI) unless presidents appoint stellar leaders. Too many presidents believe they must name their own CIA director, and high-ranking military officers have dominated the position of National Intelligence director. Two possible solutions: The CIA director should have a fixed term of no more than five or six years so that it will not coincide with the start of a presidential term; and the National Intelligence director should be a high-ranking civilian who understands strategic intelligence.

Turnover of CIA directors at the start of most presidential administrations for the past 40 years has led to instability and intelligence failures within the agency. A five-year term would remove the appointment of a CIA director from most election cycles and lead to directors who are less political.

Any new CIA director must reverse the agency's drift toward militarization. With his creation of "fusion centers," current director John Brennan has destroyed the bureaucratic wall between the directorates of intelligence and operations, making politicization of intelligence more likely. Brennan's management of the extensive drone program in Pakistan has contributed to the problem of militarization, although he stated at his confirmation hearing in February 2013 that the program should be in the military's hands.

The National Intelligence director needs to be a civilian to counter the Pentagon's control of most intelligence spending and personnel. Despite the Intelligence Reform Act of 2004, the Pentagon has maintained control over budgetary and personnel authority for intelligence. Military officers command most major institutions of the intelligence community, although few such officers are distinguished in strategic or long-term intelligence.

The ODNI has contributed to the problem of worst-case thinking in intelligence assessments. That has occurred at a time when military dominance of intelligence collection has contributed to neglect of nonmilitary priorities, such as arms control and disarmament as well as ethnic politics and violence.

The military's domination of the important field of satellite-imagery analysis has added to the problems caused by the CIA's paramilitary drift. Satellite imagery is particularly important for the critique of the defense budget, the likelihood of military conflict in the Third World and verification of arms control agreements. Stronger and more stable civilian leadership is needed to bolster the strategic and geopolitical context of such intelligence.

NO
Richard K. Betts
*Director, Saltzman Institute of War and Peace
Studies, Columbia University; Author of Enemies
of Intelligence*

Written for *CQ Researcher*, May 2015

A fixed term for the director of National Intelligence would have benefits and costs. The benefit of protecting the director's independence from political pressure is real but exaggerated and is outweighed by the potential cost to effectiveness in office.

To be fully effective, officials must obey the law, report honestly to Congress and advise the president without fear — actions a fixed term would promote. To have their concerns taken seriously at the highest level, however, they must also have the president's confidence. Without it, they will be ignored, circumvented or undercut as the president turns to others he or she respects and trusts. No law can force presidents to pay attention to any official or prevent them from getting others to do their dirty work.

True, a shortsighted new president could appoint a compliant political crony. A fixed term requiring the previous president's National Intelligence director to continue in office for some time would prevent that, although only for whatever time was left in the term, after which the new president could appoint whomever he or she wanted. This could easily be the new president's own crony rather than a nonpolitical professional.

Inherited National Intelligence directors might be less dependent on presidential favor but also less certain to have rapport with their president. The director's main responsibilities are managerial: to bring coherence, cooperation and efficiency to the complex of 17 agencies (including the Office of the Director of National Intelligence) in the intelligence community. The most politically sensitive activities are in the CIA and National Security Agency. A director opposed to the administration can be sidelined, leading the president's team to work directly with officials in those agencies.

The Joint Chiefs of Staff and FBI director are the other main positions with fixed terms in the national security apparatus. Membership on the Joint Chiefs is usually a terminal military assignment; the chiefs are not terribly vulnerable to retaliation for disagreeing with the administration. Moreover, even officials with fixed terms can be fired by a president for cause — as two chiefs have been over the years — and cause is whatever the president says it is.

Conceivably, the 10-year term for the director of the FBI has enabled recent FBI heads to avoid being manipulated by political leadership. J. Edgar Hoover, however, had the de facto equivalent of tenure, and the misbehavior that situation enabled highlights the drawbacks of independence.

Congress is indeed considering legislation to curb bulk collection of American citizens' phone records, after similar legislation died in the last Congress. The USA Freedom Act, which passed the House on May 13 with broad bipartisan support, would limit the NSA's collection of bulk data to when the agency is searching for specific records and has a reasonable suspicion of a terrorist connection. For example, the NSA would not be allowed to sweep up all data from a particular Internet provider or within a city or other geographical region.

The same bill has been introduced in the Senate, but its future is uncertain because senior Republicans there want to retain the monitoring program. Majority Leader McConnell has introduced legislation to prevent NSA's monitoring authority, authorized in the 2001 Patriot Act, from expiring on June 1. Sen. John Cornyn, R-Texas, the majority whip, said, "I believe if we allow these provisions to expire, our homeland security will be at a much greater risk."[69]

McConnell said he doubted the Freedom Act would pass in the Senate and raised the possibility of a compromise short-term extension.[70] In a May 20 memorandum, the Justice Department warned the NSA would have to end the program if the House and Senate do not agree on terms for extending the program by June 1, and told the NSA to "begin to take steps to wind down" the program by May 22 to "ensure that it does not engage in any unauthorized collection or use" of the data.[71]

A review of the NSA surveillance program by the Privacy and Civil Liberties Oversight Board, an independent federal body established by Congress in 2004 to balance terrorism prevention with the protection of privacy and civil liberties, concluded that the surveillance program — signed into law in 2007 — is "reasonably designed and implemented" so information acquired cannot be exploited for illegitimate purposes. However, certain aspects of the program push it "close to the line of constitutional reasonableness," the board said, including "the unknown and potentially large scope of the incidental collection of U.S. persons' communications." Overall, however, the program "has been valuable and effective in protecting the nation's security."[72]

But others, such as GOP presidential candidate Paul, have deep-seated objections to the government's surveillance program. Paul took to the Senate floor for 10–1/2 hours May 20 to argue against renewing NSA's monitoring authority. "There comes a time in the history of

nations when fear and complacency allow power to accumulate, and liberty and privacy to suffer. That time is now, and I will not let the Patriot Act, the most unpatriotic of acts, go unchallenged," Paul said.

At the very least, he said, the Senate "should debate whether or not we are going to relinquish our rights or whether or not we are going to have a full and able debate over whether or not we can live within the Constitution or whether or not we have to go around the Constitution."[73]

Encryption Debate

Meanwhile, intelligence agencies are waging a running battle with the technology industry over access to personal communications. The agencies want technology companies to guarantee government access to encrypted data on smartphones and similar devices. "Law enforcement needs to be able to access communications and information to bring people to justice," FBI Director James Comey said. Current laws that require telecommunication companies to enable law enforcement (with a court order) to wiretap landline telephones are outmoded, Comey said, and don't cover new means of communication such as cellphones.[74]

But technology companies are resisting. Apple's iPhone 6, released in September 2014, includes encryption software that only a user can unlock. Apple CEO Timothy D. Cook said the NSA "would have to cart us out in a box" before the company would allow the government access to its servers.[75]

Comey criticized Apple's decision, noting that, shortly after Apple's announcement, Google said it would follow suit with its Android operating system. "This means the companies themselves won't be able to unlock phones, laptops, and tablets . . . ," Comey said. "[Encryption] will have very serious consequences for law enforcement and national security agencies at all levels. Sophisticated criminals will come to count on these means of evading detection."[76]

But Laura Murphy, director of the ACLU's Washington legislative office, said, "We applaud tech leaders like Apple and Google that are unwilling to weaken security [in order] to allow the government yet another tool in its already vast surveillance arsenal. We hope that others in the tech industry follow their lead."[77]

Beginning in 2000, according to documents leaked by then-NSA contractor Snowden, the NSA began to work with technology companies to build "backdoors" — entry points that bypass security measures in otherwise encrypted computer systems, including cellphones — into their products to allow the agency to intercept suspect communications.[78]

Mark Jaycox, legislative analyst for the Electronic Frontier Foundation, a San Francisco-based organization that supports digital privacy, says the NSA's insistence on backdoors helped create the privacy problem. "If you mandate a backdoor in a system, that backdoor will be available, and potentially discovered and exploited by foreign adversaries," Jaycox says. "Any backdoor into our communications makes our infrastructure weaker."

Homegrown Threats

Domestic terrorists — so-called "sovereign citizens" who live in the United States but do not recognize the authority of any government — now outrank Islamic extremists on law enforcement's list of concerns, according to a 2013–14 survey on police intelligence processes conducted by a terrorism study group at the University of Maryland.[79]

Federal intelligence officials also see terrorism by the sovereign-citizen movement as a growing threat to national security. A Department of Homeland Security (DHS) intelligence assessment, reviewed by CNN but not publicly released, counted 24 violent sovereign-citizen-related attacks across the United States between 2010 and early 2014, primarily targeting law enforcement officials.[80]

The 2013 Boston Marathon bombings represent another type of homegrown threat that can emerge, particularly if federal and local law enforcement fail to share intelligence. After the bombings, which killed three people and injured 264, it was revealed the FBI had not shared intelligence with local law enforcement — or the CIA — that it had received from Russian authorities about Tamerlan Tsarnaev, one of the two brothers who perpetrated the bombings. Two years before the bombings, the Russians told the FBI that Tsarnaev was an "adherent of radical Islam" and sympathetic to violent separatist groups in Russia. The FBI investigated, but found no link, or "nexus," to terrorism.[81]

To promote information-sharing the Justice Department in 2014 reactivated its Domestic Terrorism Executive Committee, established in 1995 but largely dormant after 9/11, when attention turned to threats from international terrorists.[82] And in an effort to counter sovereign-citizen

violence, DHS established 78 state, regional and municipal "fusion centers," which collect and share intelligence from state and local law enforcement.[83]

But Michael German, a fellow with New York University's Brennan Center for Justice's Liberty and National Security Program, said the fusion centers lost their intended focus after state and local entities involved in the centers began resisting the emphasis on counterterrorism. "They wanted it to go to an all-crimes, and ultimately to an all-hazards, mission," he said. "There's been complete mission creep."[84]

OUTLOOK

Data Explosion

As technology evolves, the intelligence community will be challenged to make good, legal use of the flood of digital information coming its way.

"As we come to grips with social media, we're seeing an explosion of data," says Treverton of the ODNI's National Intelligence Council. "Selfies are our best friend," he jokes, adding, "There is so much data out there that one question is, how do we find the intelligence value that's in it in a way that's acceptable to the American people?"

Treverton says the intelligence community is developing a program, Open Source Indicators, to use social media and other "big data" to find publicly available information that could help anticipate or detect significant events, such as political or humanitarian crises or mass violence.

Technological advances also will reduce the number of successful cyberattacks but make those that occur more sophisticated and harder to combat, predicts James Andrew Lewis, director of the Strategic Technologies Program at the Center for Strategic and International Studies in Washington.

"Technology will get better, and that will squeeze out the low-end cybercriminals, eliminating maybe two-thirds of the successful attacks within 10 years," he says. That leaves the most powerful components in cyberspace — nation-states such as Russia, China, Iran and North Korea, he says. They all have the resources, determination and intelligence to succeed, he says, "and if they want to get [into a computer system] . . . they're going to succeed." Although an international agreement on cyberespionage could help reduce the problem, it wouldn't resolve it altogether, he says.

Some see the intelligence structure evolving, along with how the various agencies operate. Goodman of the Center for International Policy predicts the intelligence community will "look more and more like the Pentagon model, with greater centralization and top-down leadership. We're already seeing that trend, with [CIA Director] Brennan and his mission centers." However, he warns, "Intelligence work should foster dissent and contrariness. You need advocates for different points of view, who look at intelligence in a different way. But we've gotten away from the old [unofficial] job description: 'telling truth to power.' "

Harman, of the Woodrow Wilson Institute for Scholars, said that in 10 years the CIA's primary mission will be "covert action, an arena in which the agency can make a uniquely valuable contribution to national security." The NSA, she predicts, will move away from collecting personal data and private-sector firms will do the same task. "And traditional espionage — the use of spies to gather human intelligence — will become less valuable than open-source intelligence, especially information gleaned from social media. In each case, change will come rapidly."[85]

Gibson of the ODNI general counsel's office believes the intelligence community will become more transparent — out of necessity. "There's a feeling [among the public] that we have capabilities that we're using in an unrestrained manner," she says. "We need to be more transparent about how we constrain ourselves and how the law constrains us and how well we abide by and respect those rules.

"You can't do intelligence well in the open, so you have to find a way to do it in secret and still retain trust," Gibson says. "That's a very hard nut to crack. I think we are getting better at it, but to retain our viability into the future we're going to have to keep our eye on that."

NOTES

1. "Osama Bin Laden Dead," The White House Blog, May 2, 2011, www.whitehouse.gov/blog. In an article in *The London Review of Books* on May 21, journalist Seymour Hersh challenged the Obama administration's version of events leading up to the bin Laden raid. Hersh asserts, among other things, that the raid was conducted jointly with Pakistan's intelligence service. Administration officials deny Hersh's claims. The article is at http://tinyurl.com/o5pbvth.

2. "The 9/11 Commission Report," National Commission on Terrorist Attacks Upon the United States, July 22, 2004, http://tinyurl.com/49xkf.

3. Matt Apuzzo and James Risen, "CIA First Planned Jails Abiding by U.S. Standards," *The New York Times*, Dec. 10, 2014, http://tinyurl.com/k84ylox.

4. "Study of the Central Intelligence Agency's Detention and Interrogation Program," Senate Select Committee on Intelligence, Dec. 9, 2014, http://tinyurl.com/p2nkf98.

5. Sen. Dianne Feinstein, "Remarks on Committee Report on CIA Detention, Interrogation Program," Senate Intelligence Committee, Dec. 9, 2014, http://tinyurl.com/mbjrd2g.

6. Ellen Nakashima and Brian Murphy, "CIA chief: 'Unknowable' whether ordinary interrogation would bring same intel gains," *The Washington Post*, Dec. 11, 2014, http://tinyurl.com/kh53ef4.

7. James R. Clapper, "Opening Statement to Worldwide Threat Assessment Hearing" before the Senate Armed Services Committee, Feb. 26, 2015, http://tinyurl.com/k88z9d2.

8. Ellen Nakashima and Andrea Peterson, "Report: Cybercrime and espionage costs $445 billion annually," *The Washington Post*, June 9, 2014, http://tinyurl.com/ntu9arm.

9. "Executive Order — Imposing Additional Sanctions with Respect to North Korea," The White House, Jan. 2, 2015, http://tinyurl.com/le75bg4.

10. "Remarks by the President at the Cybersecurity and Consumer Protection Summit, Stanford University," The White House, Feb. 13, 2015, http://tinyurl.com/l8oqxxv.

11. James Joyner, "CIA Director Proposes Radical Reorganization," *Outside the Beltway*, Nov. 20, 2014, http://tinyurl.com/k8bldfm.

12. Mike DeBonis and Ellen Nakashima, "House approves measure ending NSA bulk phone data collection program," *The Washington Post*, May 13, 2015, http://tinyurl.com/lcebwwk.

13. Rachel Martin, "Is Director Of National Intelligence A Viable Post?" NPR, July 20, 2010, http://tinyurl.com/kx8kjqh.

14. Richard A. Best Jr., "Intelligence Reform After Five Years: The Role of the Director of National Intelligence (DNI)," Congressional Research Service, June 22, 2010, http://tinyurl.com/kyawnwo.

15. ODNI Fact Sheet, Office of the Director of National Intelligence, October 2011, http://tinyurl.com/mldxxk2.

16. Greg Miller, "Former CIA official cites agency's failure to see al-Qaeda's rebound," *The Washington Post*, May 3, 2015, http://tinyurl.com/nnhrf5w.

17. Mark Mazzetti, "C.I.A. to Be Overhauled to Fight Modern Threats," *The New York Times*, March 6, 2015, http://tinyurl.com/m2mc3cd.

18. "On Point" broadcast, "Reforming The American Intelligence System," WBUR/NPR, March 11, 2015, http://tinyurl.com/m7zqx7u.

19. *Ibid.*

20. Melvin A. Goodman, "Separate the C.I.A.'s Intelligence and Operations," *The New York Times*, Dec. 21, 2014, http://tinyurl.com/maec4qm.

21. Melvin A. Goodman, "A Dangerous CIA 'Reform,'" Consortiumnews.com, March 9, 2015, http://tinyurl.com/mfhbwve.

22. *Ibid.*

23. *Ibid.*

24. John Brennan, "Our Agency's Blueprint for the Future," Message to the CIA Workforce, March 6, 2015, http://tinyurl.com/lze9owx.

25. Greg Miller, "CIA Director John Brennan considering sweeping organizational changes," *The Washington Post*, Nov. 19, 2014, http://tinyurl.com/k2zo2ny.

26. Mark Lowenthal, *Intelligence: From Secrets to Policy* (2015), p. 298.

27. Jennifer Kibbe, "Congressional Oversight of Intelligence: Is the Solution Part of the Problem?" *Intelligence and National Security*, Vol. 25, No. 1, February 2010, http://tinyurl.com/l9yo8ey.

28. *Ibid.*

29. Eric Rosenbach and Aki J. Peritz, "Confrontation or Collaboration? Congress and the Intelligence Community," Belfer Center for Science and International Affairs, John F. Kennedy School of Government, Harvard University, June 2009, http://tinyurl.com/kg2vjwm.

30. "Senate Intel Committee Releases Report on CIA Detention, Interrogation Program," news release, Office of Sen. Dianne Feinstein, U.S. Senate, released Dec. 9, 2014, http://tinyurl.com/lz4flla.

31. Brennan letter to Sens. Dianne Feinstein and Saxby Chambliss, Central Intelligence Agency, June 27, 2013, released Dec. 8, 2014, http://tinyurl.com/pthaglg.

32. "Ex-CIA Directors: Interrogations Saved Lives," *The Wall Street Journal*, Dec. 10, 2014, http://tinyurl.com/kpfsswz.

33. "The Evolution of the U.S. Intelligence Community: An Historical Overview," Federation of American Scientists, http://tinyurl.com/llvfzx4.

34. *Ibid.*

35. "The Nation Calls: 1908–1923," in "A Centennial History of the FBI," Federal Bureau of Investigation, 2008, http://tinyurl.com/ltzj4ro.

36. "Pearl Harbor Review — The Black Chamber," National Security Agency, Center for Cryptologic History, Jan. 15, 2009, http://tinyurl.com/ltplzsw.

37. Franklin D. Roosevelt, "Order Establishing the Office of Strategic Services," The American Presidency Project, June 13, 1942, http://tinyurl.com/lle3ug5.

38. Lowenthal, *op. cit.*, p. 23.

39. "The National Security Act of 1947, Public Law 253, 80th Congress; Chapter 343, 1st Session; S. 758," http://tinyurl.com/kdchvpo.

40. Harry S. Truman letter to *The Washington Post*, Dec. 22, 1963, http://tinyurl.com/ycffs3x.

41. Michael X. Heiligenstein, "A Brief History of the NSA: From 1917 to 2014," *The Saturday Evening Post*, April 17, 2014, http://tinyurl.com/le6cqvw.

42. "United States Objectives and Actions to Exploit the Unrest in the Satellite States," National Security Council, June 29, 1953, http://tinyurl.com/mbvebsp.

43. "Coordination and Policy Approval of Covert Operations," Central Intelligence Agency, Feb. 23, 1967, http://tinyurl.com/n2d38k9.

44. Lowenthal, *op. cit.*, p. 25. For detailed accounts of these and other covert activities, see Tim Weiner, *Legacy of Ashes: The History of the CIA* (2007).

45. "The Evolution of the U.S. Intelligence Community: An Historical Overview," *op. cit.*

46. "DIA's role during the Cuban Missile Crisis," Defense Intelligence Agency, Oct. 20, 2014, http://tinyurl.com/mkgg6ge.

47. John Prados, "The CIA's Vietnam Histories," National Security Archive, posted Aug. 26, 2009, http://tinyurl.com/kne3pm3. Prados culled his report from secret CIA documents declassified under the Freedom of Information Act.

48. Seymour Hersh, "Huge C.I.A. Operation Reported in U.S. Against Antiwar Forces, Other Dissidents in Nixon Years," *The New York Times*, Dec. 22, 1974, http://tinyurl.com/mwtdvpm.

49. "Church Committee Created," Senate Historical Office, http://tinyurl.com/bfdzjej.

50. "Intelligence Activities and the Rights of Americans: Final Report of the Select Committee to Study Governmental Operations with Respect to Intelligence Activities," U.S. Senate, April 26, 1976, http://tinyurl.com/d8auhvq.

51. Eric Rosenbach and Aki J. Peritz, "Congressional Oversight of the Intelligence Community," Belfer Center for Science and International Affairs, John F. Kennedy School of Government, Harvard University, July 2009, http://tinyurl.com/ljnw3ko.

52. Lowenthal, *op. cit.*, p. 28.

53. "The Evolution of the U.S. Intelligence Community: An Historical Overview," *op. cit.*

54. *Ibid.*

55. Cited in Kirsten Lundberg, "CIA and the Fall of the Soviet Empire: The Politics of 'Getting it Right,' " John F. Kennedy School of Government, Harvard University, 1994, http://tinyurl.com/kar3epb.

56. Robert C. Toth, "CIA Defended on Assessing Soviets," *Los Angeles Times*, May 21, 1992, http://tinyurl.com/m4wwkjd.

57. James R. Clapper, testimony to the House Permanent Select Committee on Intelligence, April 11, 2013, http://tinyurl.com/lzquynn.

58. "The Performance of the Intelligence Community," Staff of the National Commission on Terrorist Attacks Upon the United States, http://tinyurl.com/k3jcb85.

59. "The 9/11 Commission Report," *op. cit.*

60. "Intelligence Reform and Terrorism Prevention Act of 2004," Government Publishing Office, Dec. 17, 2004, http://tinyurl.com/mzln6h3. A summary of the law's provisions is at http://tinyurl.com/kzdwot6.

61. James Risen and Laura Poitras, "N.S.A. Collecting Millions of Images From Web Images," *The New York Times*, May 31, 2014, http://tinyurl.com/ohpqzpb.

62. Robert S. Litt, "Privacy, Technology & National Security: An Overview of Intelligence Collection," speech to the Brookings Institution, July 18, 2013, http://tinyurl.com/oljf57n.

63. Tom Cohen, "NSA director: Data mining follows law, thwarts terror," CNN, June 13, 2013, http://tinyurl.com/lmrafvg.

64. Mary Madden, "Public Perceptions of Privacy and Security in the Post-Snowden Era," Pew Research Center, Nov. 12, 2014, http://tinyurl.com/p2536wh.

65. "Presidential Policy Directive — Signals Intelligence Activities," The White House, Jan. 17, 2014, http://tinyurl.com/nypwf3b.

66. Ellen Nakashima, "NSA program on phone records is illegal, court rules," *The Washington Post*, May 7, 2015, http://tinyurl.com/p9g4crh.

67. Jonathan Stempel, "NSA's phone spying program ruled illegal by appeals court," Reuters, May 7, 2015, http://tinyurl.com/lv8fb6z.

68. Nakashima, *op. cit.*

69. DeBonis and Nakashima, *op. cit.*

70. Mike DeBonis and Ellen Nakashima, "NSA may need to begin winding down surveillance program this week," *The Washington Post*, May 20, 2015, http://tinyurl.com/kh5echp.

71. Memorandum text posted online by Mike DeBonis of *The Washington Post*, http://tinyurl.com/mwgraap.

72. "Report on the Surveillance Program Operated Pursuant to Section 702 of the Foreign Intelligence

Surveillance Act," Privacy and Civil Liberties Oversight Board, July 2, 2014, http://tinyurl.com/oouh63e.

73. Jeremy Diamond, "Rand Paul wraps 10-hour 'filibuster' over NSA surveillance program," CNN, May 21, 2015, http://tinyurl.com/mbeu7py.

74. James B. Comey, "Going Dark: Are Technology, Privacy, and Public Safety on a Collision Course?" speech at Brookings Institution, Oct. 16, 2014, http://tinyurl.com/pq426z9.

75. "Exclusive: Apple's Tim Cook on NSA, What's Next as Mac Turns 30," ABC News, Jan. 24, 2014, http://tinyurl.com/qe6xrpa.

76. Comey, *op. cit.*

77. "ACLU Comment on FBI Director Comey's Encryption Speech," press release, American Civil Liberties Union, Oct. 16, 2014, http://tinyurl.com/kv6a524.

78. Nicole Perlroth, Jeff Larson and Scott Shane, "N.S.A. Able to Foil Basic Safeguards of Privacy on Web," *The New York Times*, Sept. 5, 2013, http://tinyurl.com/m9chca6.

79. "Understanding Law Enforcement Intelligence Processes," National Consortium for the Study of Terrorism and Responses to Terrorism, July 2014, http://tinyurl.com/lybl5sn. The FBI defines the sovereign citizens' movement as anti-government extremists in the United States who "believe they don't have to answer to any government authority, including courts, taxing entities, motor vehicle departments or law enforcement."

80. Evan Perez and Wes Bruer, "DHS intelligence report warns of domestic right-wing terror threat," CNN, Feb. 20, 2015, http://tinyurl.com/oa9v6y5.

81. "Unclassified Summary of Intelligence Handling and Sharing Prior to the April 15, 2013 Boston Marathon Bombings," Inspectors General of the Intelligence Community, April 10, 2014, http://tinyurl.com/n2krzqq.

82. "Statement by Attorney General Holder on Reestablishment of Committee on Domestic Terrorism," news release, Department of Justice, June 3, 2014, http://tinyurl.com/lw2qhtf.

83. "National Network of Fusion Centers Fact Sheet," Department of Homeland Security, http://tinyurl.com/acu64r6. A list of the centers is at http://tinyurl.com/9h6fmck.

84. "Fusion centers, created to fight domestic terrorism, suffering from mission creep: Critics," Homeland Security News Wire, April 21, 2015, http://tinyurl.com/lg3wr47.

85. Jane Harman, "Disrupting the Intelligence Community," *Foreign Affairs*, March-April 2015, http://tinyurl.com/k9cx3ao.

BIBLIOGRAPHY

Selected Sources
Books

Jervis, Robert, *Why Intelligence Fails: Lessons from the Iranian Revolution and the Iraq War*, Cornell University Press, 2010.
A Columbia University professor of international politics draws on his CIA-sponsored analyses of two important events characterized by consequential intelligence failures.

Lowenthal, Mark M., *Intelligence: From Secrets to Policy*, CQ Press, 2015.
A former U.S. intelligence official describes the structure of the intelligence community, the process of intelligence gathering and intelligence's role in formulating national policy.

Morrell, Michael, *The Great War of Our Time: The CIA's Fight Against Terrorism From Al Qa'ida to ISIS*, Twelve, May 12, 2015.
A former CIA deputy director discusses the agency's limited ability to predict terrorist events in the Middle East.

Sagar, Rahul, *Secrets and Leaks: The Dilemma of State Security*, Princeton University Press, 2013.
An assistant professor of politics at Princeton University examines how government secrecy in the name of "national security" can be both justified and misused.

Articles

Harman, Jane, "Disrupting the Intelligence Community: America's Spy Agencies Need an Upgrade," *Foreign Affairs*, March/April 2015, http://tinyurl.com/k9cx3ao.

The director of the Woodrow Wilson International Center for Scholars says the intelligence community needs to drastically revise how it collects and analyzes information.

Kibbe, Jennifer D., "Conducting Shadow Wars," *Journal of National Security Law and Policy*, **July 2012, http://tinyurl.com/lka2aye.**
An assistant professor of government at Franklin and Marshall College examines how Special Forces and CIA paramilitary operatives have been used to combat terrorism.

Mazzetti, Mark, "C.I.A. to Be Overhauled to Fight Modern Threats," *The New York Times*, **April 6, 2015, http://tinyurl.com/m2mc3cd.**
CIA Director John Brennan's plan for his agency's reorganization is explained.

Nakashima, Ellen, "New agency to sniff out threats in cyberspace," *The Washington Post*, **Feb. 10, 2015, http://tinyurl.com/ow7n7z7.**
The Cyber Threat Intelligence Integration Center is established to coordinate intelligence on cyberattacks.

Reports and Studies

"Committee Study of the Central Intelligence Agency's Detention and Interrogation Program," Senate Select Committee on Intelligence, released Dec. 9, 2014, http://tinyurl.com/p2nkf98.
An unclassified version of a Senate Intelligence Committee report looks at the post-9/11 detention and interrogation of suspected terrorists by the CIA.

"Executive Order 12333, United States Intelligence Activities," http://tinyurl.com/lq98y76.
Originally issued by President Ronald Reagan, the document sets out goals, expectations and responsibilities of the U.S. intelligence agencies.

Bendix, William, and Paul T. Quirk, "Secrecy and negligence: How Congress lost control of domestic surveillance," Brookings Institution, March 2015, http://tinyurl.com/kptvj6k.
Two political scientists assert that Congress neglected its oversight responsibility with respect to the intelligence community's domestic spying activities.

Brennan, John, "CIA Comments on the Senate Select Committee on Intelligence Report on the Rendition, Detention, and Interrogation Program," June 27, 2013, http://tinyurl.com/pthaglg.
In a memorandum, the CIA director responds to the Senate Intelligence Committee's report on detention and interrogation.

Clapper, James R., "Worldwide Threat Assessment of the United States Intelligence Community," statement before the Senate Armed Services Committee, Feb. 26, 2015, http://tinyurl.com/pt4l64t.
The director of National Intelligence outlines threats the United States faces.

Kean, Thomas H., *et al.*, "The 9/11 Commission Report," U.S. Government Publishing Office, July 22, 2004, http://tinyurl.com/49xkf.
A government report looks at the causes of the Sept. 11, 2001, terrorist attacks and proposes changes to the intelligence community.

Lewis, James A., "Underestimating Risk in the Surveillance Debate," Center for Strategic and International Studies, December 2014, http://tinyurl.com/kn4u8ur.
The director of the Strategic Technologies Program at the Center for Strategic and International Studies in Washington argues that communications surveillance is an essential law enforcement and intelligence tool and that it is unrealistic to think the NSA should track only known or suspected terrorists.

For More Information

Association of Former Intelligence Officers, 7700 Leesburg Pike, Suite 324, Falls Church, VA 22043; 703-790-0320; www.afio.com. Supports the objectives of the intelligence community through public education programs.

Council on Foreign Relations, The Harold Pratt House, 58 East 68th St., New York, NY 10065; 212-434-9400; www.cfr.org. International affairs think tank offering frequent publications and programs on the role of intelligence in foreign policy.

Defense and Intelligence Program, Belfer Center for Science and International Affairs, Harvard University, 79 John F. Kennedy St., Cambridge, MA 02138; 617-495-1400; http://belfercenter.ksg.harvard.edu/project/71/defense_and_intelligence.html. Conducts research and seminars on the use of intelligence in policymaking.

Intelligence Advanced Research Projects Activity, Office of the Director of National Intelligence Advanced Research Projects Activity, Washington, DC 20511; 301-851-7500; www.iarpa.gov. Conducts research and reports on new technologies for the intelligence community.

Liberty and National Security Program, Brennan Center for Law and Justice, New York University, 161 Avenue of the Americas, 12th Floor, New York, NY 10013; 646-292-8310; www.brennancenter.org/issues/liberty-national-security. Advocates policies that provide adequate national security while guaranteeing constitutional freedoms.

Office of the Director of National Intelligence, Washington, DC 20511; 703-733-8600; www.odni.gov. Federal umbrella organization overseeing and coordinating activities of the 16 members of the intelligence community.

Strategic Technologies Program, Center for Strategic and International Studies, 1616 Rhode Island Ave., N.W., Washington, DC 20036; 202-887-0200; http://csis.org/program/technology-and-public-policy. Think tank that provides research and public programs on cybersecurity and studies the relationship between public policy, technological change and innovation.

16

Police Tactics

Peter Katel

Demonstrators block Cleveland's Public Square on Nov. 25 during a protest over the fatal shooting of 12-year-old Tamir Rice, an African-American shot by a white Cleveland police officer after waving and reportedly reaching for a toy gun at a city park. A video of the shooting shows a police car driving up next to the boy, who was shot two seconds later.

From *CQ Researcher*,
December 12, 2014.

The images packed a powerful punch: men in battle dress, carrying automatic rifles, riding in armored personnel carriers and throwing noise-and-light producing "flash-bang" grenades to disperse crowds.[1]

The show of paramilitary might was happening not at a mass street demonstration in Cairo or Rio de Janeiro but the St. Louis, Mo., suburb of Ferguson. It came in response to angry, sometimes violent, protests against the death in August of Michael Brown, an unarmed 18-year-old shot to death by a city policeman.

Public and political indignation over the shooting exploded at the military appearance of the Ferguson police, helping to fuel days-long protests in the town and deepen suspicion and fear of law enforcement. "There's no question in my mind that the idea that all of this equipment . . . contributed to a mentality among the peaceful protesters that they were being treated as the enemy," Missouri Sen. Claire McClaskill, a Democrat, said in a Senate Homeland Security Committee hearing last September.[2]

The Ferguson shooting and its continuing aftermath struck a raw nerve, aggravated by a string of shootings, some fatal, arising from police-citizen encounters in several cities, including New York; Albuquerque, N.M.; Columbia, S.C., and Beavercreek, Ohio. In the Ohio case, a Walmart shopper in the Dayton suburb was seen talking on his cellphone while walking the aisles, holding a BB gun he had taken down from a shelf. Police, responding to a 911 call, shot him dead. In New York, Eric Garner died in a police choke-hold — gasping "I can't breathe" — after verbally protesting an arrest for selling single cigarettes on the street. A grand jury declined

Vehicles, Aircraft Top List of Military Supplies

The Department of Defense has supplied local police departments with more than $1.5 billion worth of surplus equipment over the past eight years. Most of the hardware was vehicles, including armored ones, aircraft and communications and detection equipment. Only $40 million worth of the equipment was for weapons.

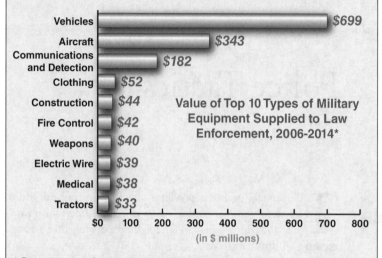

Value of Top 10 Types of Military Equipment Supplied to Law Enforcement, 2006-2014*

Vehicles	$699
Aircraft	$343
Communications and Detection	$182
Clothing	$52
Construction	$44
Fire Control	$42
Weapons	$40
Electric Wire	$39
Medical	$38
Tractors	$33

(in $ millions)

Spending data from 2006 through April 2014

Source: Analysis by David Eads and Tyler Fisher, "MRAPs And Bayonets: What We Know About The Pentagon's 1033 Program," NPR, Sept. 2, 2014, http://tinyurl.com/p3a4fqj; original data for 1033 program expenditures located at "LESO Program data," Defense Logistics Agency, http://tinyurl.com/n7koanr

to indict the officer involved, prompting widespread protests.[3]

Garner was black, and the officer who choked him was white. The Walmart shopper, John Crawford III, was black, and the two officers who shot him were white. The Ferguson shooting presented the same racial pattern — as do other, but not all — of the episodes prompting current controversies over police tactics. "Ferguson laid bare . . . a simmering distrust that exists between too many police departments and too many communities of color," President Obama said at the White House. "When any part of the American family does not feel like it is being treated fairly, that's a problem for all of us."[4]

Even some police professionals say the appearance of militarization is eroding public trust in law enforcement. "Perception is reality," said Mark Lomax, executive director of the National Tactical Officers Association — a professional organization for police special weapons and tactics (SWAT) team members. "Right now, the perception is there's a militarization of policing, which becomes a reality to a lot of people."[5]

Controversy over police tactics also intersects with intensified debate over drug laws and how they are enforced. Critics, including some former law enforcement officials, say the nation's decades-long "war on drugs" — which often involves raids by helmeted, flash-bang grenade-throwing SWAT teams — has been misguided and dangerous. The military terminology associated with U.S. anti-drug policy "evokes images of friends and foes and enemies of the police and enemies of society," says former Seattle Police Chief Norm Stamper. "If you're talking about a 16-year-old nonviolent drug offender, he's not the enemy."

In Washington much of the furor over police tactics has centered on a 23-year-old program for transferring Defense Department surplus gear to police departments, a once-informal system that expanded along with the drug war. The program is now known as "1033" after the relevant section of federal law.

Since 1990, the Pentagon has shifted more than $5.1 billion worth of surplus equipment to local and federal law enforcement entities — 96 percent of it nonlethal supplies such as office furniture, tents and forklifts, but also some 90,000 pistols and assault rifles and 600 armored vehicles. Data show big increases in equipment transfers in 2012 and 2013, when the wars in Iraq and Afghanistan were winding down.[6]

Critics say the gear encourages military-style tactics against civilians. "Cutting off the supply of military weaponry to our civilian police is the least we could do to begin the process of reining in police militarization and attempting to make clear the increasingly blurred distinction between the military and police," Peter Kraska, chair of criminal justice studies at Eastern Kentucky University in Richmond, Ky., told the Senate Homeland Security Committee in September. Kraska pioneered studies of police SWAT teams, first created in 1967 to deal with high-risk episodes such as hostage rescues.[7]

But police defenders call increased militarization a myth. Unlike the military, "SWAT teams do not engage the enemy with the purpose of destroying them; they are trained to protect life," says Chuck Canterbury, national president of the Fraternal Order of Police, the nation's largest law-enforcement union, and former operations chief of the county police department in Conway, S.C. "The majority of SWAT calls end with nobody injured; if the military had a record like that, they'd be losing the war."

And much of the Pentagon equipment, such as high-wheeled trucks and forklifts, are used in disaster-recovery missions, Alan Estevez, the Defense undersecretary in charge of the surplus equipment system, told a Senate committee in September.[8]

But during the early days of 1033, the Justice Department didn't cite disaster relief as a prime justification for the program. "The best examples of law enforcement and military participation in common missions are the 'wars' being waged against narcotics and terrorism," a 1997 Justice Department report on developing weapons and technology for military and police use stated.[9]

Among those tools were flash-bang grenades. They are part of SWAT team toolkits but have caused at least seven unintended deaths, including of a police officer, and burn injuries prompting a total of $2.1 million in settlements in two cases in 2010 and 2011.[10]

Last May, SWAT officers from Georgia's Habersham County and Cornelia city threw a flash-bang grenade

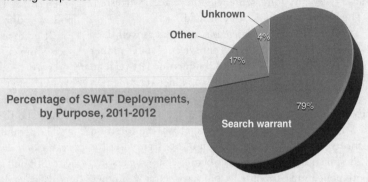

Most SWAT Deployments Are for Search Warrants

Police departments executed four out of five SWAT team deployments to serve search warrants in 2011 and 2012, according to a civil liberties organization's study of 20 law enforcement agencies. Another 17 percent of deployments were for other purposes, such as protecting visiting officials, responding to emergencies and pursuing fleeing suspects.

Source: "War Comes Home: The Excessive Militarization of American Policing," American Civil Liberties Union, June 2014, p. 31, http://tinyurl.com/myxzoju

into a house during a 3 a.m. drug raid, causing third-degree burns on a 19-month-old child and blowing a hole in his chest. The raiders were seeking a relative who wasn't home.[11]

County Sheriff Joey Terrell said authorities didn't know children were present but argued drug raids call for SWAT deployment. Drug dealers, he said, "are no better than a domestic terrorist, . . . and I think we should treat them as such."[12]

With many drug dealers today being heavily armed, drug raids can be extremely dangerous for cops. In 2012, a member of an Ogden, Utah, drug strike force was killed and five others were wounded during a raid on a house to serve a search warrant on a small-scale marijuana case suspect, who fired at police.[13]

SWAT teams are used predominantly to serve search warrants, mostly in drug cases. According to an American Civil Liberties Union (ACLU) survey, 79 percent of SWAT deployments in 2011–12 involved searches — 62 percent of them for drugs.[14]

Concern that SWAT teams are being wrongly assigned to duties that don't require a high-intensity approach runs through police circles. Inappropriate

SWAT deployments are "more prevalent in smaller agencies," says Charles "Sid" Heal, a retired Los Angeles County Sheriff's Department officer who commanded a SWAT unit. "They may get 12 callouts a year, and they have to justify their existence." Raiding a "dime-bag dealer" does not require a tactical team, but SWAT raids against high-level drug dealers are fully justified, Heal says, given the long sentences they face if arrested. "They've got nothing to lose," he adds.

Officers face other dangerous enemies as well. Last September, a sniper killed a Pennsylvania state trooper as he ended his shift. And in Albuquerque last year, an AK-47-wielding gunman with "cop killer" tattooed on his knuckles shot and gravely wounded a sheriff's deputy before being shot to death.[15]

Part of the Albuquerque gunfight was captured on officers' body-worn cameras. Support is growing for widespread use of the devices because, supporters say, both police and citizens tend to behave better when they are being recorded.

But some experts warn against placing too much faith in cameras — or in military gear. "There is a time and place for police to . . . use military weapons and tactics to end a threat to human life," former Seattle chief Stamper says, but "there are no strings attached, no training requirements or certification that the local agency is going to use that equipment under very carefully circumscribed circumstances."

As law enforcement officials, Congress and the public weigh the use of aggressive tactics and military-style equipment by police, here are some of the questions under debate:

Do SWAT teams and military tactics and weaponry have a place in policing?

Debate over militarization was well underway before recent media reports on the 1033 program and its transfers of military guns and personnel carriers to local police departments.

Much of that early debate focused on the formation of SWAT teams.

Los Angeles formed the first SWAT team, in 1967, prompted by violent events that included a sniper attack on the University of Texas at Austin campus. By the late 1990s, about 89 percent of departments in cities with 50,000 people or more had SWAT units, a rate that experts say holds true today.[16]

An upswing in the number of heavily armed criminals, mass shootings and other emergencies prompted the spread of tactical units, concluded a 2002 California commission study of the state's SWAT operations. Most countries would send a national police force to such emergencies, the study found, but U.S. law leaves most policing duties to cities, counties and states.

"It became clear that a new method of response to such complex, high-risk and often high-energy situations was needed," the study said. "Over the years, SWAT has evolved into the management of barricaded suspect situations, the service of high-risk warrants, dignitary protection and the actual rescue of hostages."[17]

The commission was formed after an 11-year-old boy was accidentally killed during a 2000 SWAT raid conducted with FBI and Drug Enforcement Administration (DEA) agents in Modesto, Calif. Then-state Attorney General Bill Lockyer was "concerned about the potential erosion of community confidence in local law enforcement agencies caused by such tragedies," the commission said.[18]

But SWAT teams are increasingly active, according to Kraska of Eastern Kentucky University, who found an increase of 57,000 SWAT deployments between 1980 and 2007.[19]

Moreover, Lomax, of the National Tactical Officers Association, told a Senate committee: "It is not uncommon for agencies to take receipt of such [military] equipment and receive little or no training on how to utilize it, when to deploy it and, equally as important, when not to deploy it."[20]

Critics including the ACLU and Radley Balko, a *Washington Post* blogger and one of the earliest critics of the expansion and growing use of SWAT teams, argues that many of them are being used to serve run-of-the-mill search and arrest warrants, unnecessarily using overwhelming force. "We see SWAT teams now in white-collar crimes, even regulatory crimes, [such as] barbering without a license" Balko, told an Albuquerque audience in November. He cited an 11th Circuit U.S. Court of Appeals decision in September that SWAT raids on Orlando, Fla., barbershops were unconstitutional.[21]

Police, as well as police critics, say many SWAT teams are misdirected to routine duties. A 2011 policy paper published by the Alexandria, Va.-based International

Association of Chiefs of Police said serving search warrants was the "most common" task of SWAT teams — with some departments sending them to every search. That policy represented "overuse of a team created to deal with high-risk interventions," the paper said.[22]

Some specialists trace what they call an overreliance on SWAT to an eagerness to acquire military equipment. "Once you get the equipment you have to develop the military mindset to use it," says sociologist Peter Moskos, a former Baltimore police officer and professor in the Law, Police Science and Criminal Justice Administration department at John Jay College of Criminal Justice in New York. "You can have the mindset without equipment, but you can do less damage."

Weapons trainers, who teach police officers that "it's a war out there, everyone is out to get you," also foster a military mentality, says Moskos. "That is not a realistic fear."

But Canterbury, of the Fraternal Order of Police, says given the fundamental difference between military and police missions, military equipment — even attention-getting mine-resistant vehicles — have effectively been demilitarized for police use. "They don't have military weapons or computer systems on them," he says. "They're nothing but an armored vehicle once law enforcement gets them."

Richard Greenleaf, director of the criminal justice major at Elmhurst College in Elmhurst, Ill., and a former sergeant in the Albuquerque Police Department, doesn't question the view that police are militarizing. But he also says police are rightly danger-conscious because of the nation's high rate of gun ownership.[23]

"America has more guns per capita than any other country in the whole world, and many of them are very powerful," Greenleaf says. "You can't not think about that when you think about the militarization of the police."

For many policing experts, an event that confirmed the need for SWAT teams as well as heavier armament for regular patrol cops was a 44-minute shootout in North Hollywood, Calif., in 1997 in which two body-armor-wearing bank robbers with several assault rifles, plus handguns, exchanged nearly 2,000 rounds with officers, including some SWAT team members. The robbers were killed, but no police died. "Patrol officers had never before been engaged in such a protracted, high-intensity firefight," Bob Parker, a former Omaha SWAT commander, wrote in *Police* magazine.[24]

Stamper, the former Seattle police chief, was in the San Diego Police Department when a gunman killed 21 people at a McDonald's restaurant there before a police sniper killed him.[25] Stamper says military capabilities are essential, but they are being overused. He largely blames politicians who constantly depicted drug enforcement in military terms. "It started with 'drug war,' " he says. "And there is a macho dimension to this that can't be denied. It's boys with toys."

Police departments that routinely use SWAT teams to serve drug-case warrants should return to standard procedures that would make most raids unnecessary, Stamper argues. "Why have 14 cops for one low-level offender?" he asks. "What about surveillance — watching for the suspect to come out? He comes out, goes into his car, and you conduct a routine traffic stop."

Heal, the former Los Angeles County Sheriff's Department commander, agrees that with low-level drug dealers, the best option is to determine "if you can do a door-knock and tell a guy to come out."

Nevertheless, he says, such determinations are subjective, with no easy formulas to apply. And in the case of higher-level traffickers, "Whether people want to believe it or not, drug dealers are inherently dangerous," Heal says. "I don't know of a single one anywhere I wouldn't consider them a threat."

Has police use of military-style tactics increased tensions with minority communities?

The community-police conflict that erupted in Ferguson after the shooting death of Brown illustrated, again, that controversies over police conduct often involve a racial dimension. Recent Justice Department investigations of police departments found discriminatory conduct toward African-Americans, and in some cases Latinos, in Maricopa County, Ariz.; East Haven, Conn.; New Orleans; Newark; Alamance County, N.C., and Portland, Ore.[26]

An analysis by the investigative news website ProPublica of fatal police shootings of teenagers ages 15–19 concluded that in 2010–2012, black teens were killed at a rate of 31.17 per million, compared to 1.47 per million among white teens.[27]

ProPublica acknowledged that the FBI data it used, which include victims' race — and which show 1,217 fatal police shootings overall, adults and minors, in those years — were "terribly incomplete." Indeed a *Wall Street*

Protesters in Los Angeles stage a sit-in on Nov. 25, one day after a grand jury decided not to indict Darren Wilson, the white Ferguson, Mo., police officer who shot and killed Michael Brown. The demonstration was one of dozens around the country since August in response to several recent cases in which unarmed African-American males have been killed by white police officers, two of whom were not indicted.

Journal investigation counted at least 1,800 deaths at police hands but found only 1,242 recorded in police department records. Some experts argued that though a racial disproportion exists, ProPublica's use of the data vastly overstated the trend. Moskos of John Jay College of Criminal Justice calculated, using the same data, that if ProPublica had analyzed 15 years of available statistics instead of three years, the results would show that black youths were nine times likelier — instead of 21 times likelier — to be killed by police than young white people — "a huge difference," Moskos wrote. The underlying data also showed 62 police shootings of all teenagers in 2010–2012 reported to the FBI. One of the ProPublica reporters said that the analysis focused on recent years because "the disparity is growing."[28]

In addition to the killings of Brown and Garner, other recent police-involved deaths of African-Americans include:

- John Crawford III, 22, shot dead by police in a Beavercreek, Ohio, Walmart, while talking on his cellphone and walking the aisles holding a BB gun he had taken down from a shelf;
- Akai Gurley, 28, a resident of a Brooklyn public housing project, who was shot while walking down a darkened stairway. Police called the shooting, by a rookie officer, unintentional; and
- Tamir Rice, a 12-year-old Cleveland boy who was shot after waving and then reportedly reaching for a toy pistol that resembled a real one.[29]

For many politicians and ordinary citizens, the deaths were only the latest illustrations of what they call police over-aggressiveness — if not hostility — when it comes to black men. President Obama is one of many to weigh in on the topic. "Too many young men of color feel targeted by law enforcement," Obama said in a speech to the Congressional Black Caucus in September. "We know that, statistically, in everything from enforcing drug policy to applying the death penalty to pulling people over, there are significant racial disparities."[30]

The deaths above did not arise from drug cases, but drug enforcement usually comes up in discussions of police and race. Police critics say drug-war tactics are one of the issues underlying the outcry over Brown's death. "The war on drugs and war on crime have been predominantly waged in racial and ethnic minority communities and too often against African-Americans," Hilary Shelton, the NAACP's senior vice president for advocacy, told the Senate Homeland Security Committee in September.[31]

A leading African-American political figure, the Rev. Al Sharpton of New York, connected the deaths of Brown and Garner to police action against minor offenses. Brown died after being stopped for walking in the street. The shooter, Officer Darren Wilson — who has resigned — said he believed Brown and a friend might have stolen cigarillos from a nearby store, although police initially said Wilson didn't know of that incident.

"Both of them were victims of this aggressive policing of alleged low-level crime," Sharpton said.[32]

Sharpton's role as a nationwide police critic is especially irritating to police who resent being portrayed as overly focused on African-Americans. "Al Sharpton is a race-baiter," says Canterbury of the FOP. He questioned why Sharpton hadn't visited Chicago, where 10 other black men were killed in crimes in the eight days before Brown was shot.[33]

In fact, Sharpton held a meeting in Chicago last year to address gun violence in the city's black neighborhoods. And in speaking at Brown's funeral, he said: "We've got to be straight up in our community, too. We have to be outraged at . . . our killing and shooting and running around gun-toting each other."[34]

Poverty, not race, is what focuses police attention on some communities, Canterbury says. "How about talking about poverty-stricken communities? Whether they're white, black, Hispanic, when you have a neighborhood that has high unemployment, high infant mortality, a high percentage of people who are on public assistance or have been on public assistance, when they don't see any chance of getting out of their circumstances, drugs are the only way they see to escape."

Some cities do deploy intensive patrols of poor neighborhoods, focusing on violations that affect quality of life. But whether that so-called "broken windows" strategy reduces crime is a long-running, unresolved debate among criminologists.[35]

Former Seattle police chief Stamper says police don't get orders to round up African-Americans. However, "You see wildly disproportionate numbers of young people, poor people, people of color apprehended, jailed — if not imprisoned — as a result of low-level, nonviolent drug offenses."

Race is an inescapable part of the picture, he argues. "We've ended up with a lot of young people of color on street corners doing hand-to-hand deals," he says. "They're low-hanging fruit. You get a lot of complaints about that behavior, and the police are called and do buy-and-busts and scoop up hundreds of thousands of offenders who fall into that demography."

Moskos, of the John Jay College of Criminal Justice, wrote about police and race in a memoir about a year he spent on the Baltimore police force patrolling poor African-American neighborhoods. He rebuts what he calls the "standard liberal line" that black people are shot because they're black.[36] "A cop is not shooting a black person," Moskos says. "A cop is shooting a person because he is afraid, justly or not."

Do body cameras prevent police misconduct?

Aside from race, another thread running through controversies over police tactics has been the explosive growth of documentary evidence in the form of digital imagery — still and video.

Some of this video evidence comes from police cameras, mounted on squad car dashboards or — more recently — worn on officers' bodies. Many police critics, and some officers, say the so-called "bodycams" offer a technological solution to problems that arise between police and citizens.

"We won't have to play this game of witnesses' memories and secret grand jury procedures," Benjamin Crump, the lawyer for Brown's family, said after the grand jury's decision not to indict Wilson for Brown's death, which was not recorded. "It would just be transparent, and we could see it ourselves, and we could hold people accountable when they have interactions with citizens."[37]

Obama embraced the growing movement calling for more bodycams, proposing spending $75 million over three years to provide up to 50,000 of the devices for local police departments. Technology, he said, can "enhance trust between communities and the police."[38]

Among the police-citizen encounters, some fatal, captured on video from body or dashboard cameras in recent years are:

Denver police commander Magen Dodge displays a body camera during a press conference on Aug. 27. Denver Police hope to equip 800 officers, including all patrol and traffic officers, with "bodycams" by 2015. Many police critics, and some officers, say the cameras can help resolve problems between citizens and police. But some law enforcement officers worry they will have limited value, and possibly limit officers' discretion.

Getty Images/Craig F. Walker/The Denver Post

Police Say 'Shoot to Wound' Is Not an Option

"If you point a gun at a police officer, you have punched your ticket."

Police veterans are of one mind when someone — a politician, a journalist, a member of the public — asks why police don't shoot to wound when they open fire, especially on an unarmed civilian.

Following the fatal shooting of Michael Brown by a Ferguson, Mo., police officer, the question came from CNN anchor Wolf Blitzer: "Why do they have to shoot to kill? . . . Why can't they shoot to injure, shall we say?"[1]

The question may seem reasonable — especially after an unarmed citizen dies in a police shooting.

In 2010, following one such death, New York state Assemblywoman Annette Robinson of Brooklyn proposed legislation that would have required a police officer to use deadly force "with the intent to stop, rather than kill." Robinson, who represents the largely African-American and low-income Bedford-Stuyvesant area, said she was responding to what she called a disproportionate number of police shootings of black men. "I do know that it happens, most often in the communities that I represent," she said, "and it happens too often."[2]

Specifically, Robinson proposed the legislation in response to the 2006 shooting death of Sean Bell, killed on his wedding day by undercover police who thought — mistakenly — that Bell and a friend, both black, were armed and about to commit a drive-by shooting.[3] But the bill died in committee amid heavy ridicule from police organizations.[4]

Police say officers in fast-moving confrontations have no time for precision shooting. "It works real well when you're shooting at a piece of paper," says Chuck Canterbury of Myrtle Beach, S.C., president of the national Fraternal Order of Police union. "We're not snipers. We're trained to point and shoot."

The objective, former police officers say, is not to kill, but to stop a threat to innocent human life. In practice, stopping a threat means shooting at the biggest target, which is the torso, what police trainers call the body's "center mass."

Former Seattle Police Chief Norm Stamper, a liberal critic of much police strategy, calls the idea that an officer can deliberately shoot to wound "a fallacy."

Police officers can be poor shots, he points out, especially in highly stressful situations. The New York Police Department reported that in 29 incidents in which officers fired their weapons, they hit at least one of their targets in only 64 percent of their shots. And in one incident, nine bystanders were injured when police fired 16 rounds at a man who had killed his ex-boss on a crowded sidewalk.[5]

Richard Greenleaf, director of the criminal justice major at Elmhurst College in Elmhurst, Ill., recalls from his days as an Albuquerque, N.M., police officer in the late 1970s and early '80s that colleagues who had been highly accurate shooters during training "in a real situation would miss 80 percent of the time."

Greenleaf says he was a bad shot on the range. But one night in 1981, he faced a man with a .22-caliber pistol who was running out of a convenience store he had just robbed. "I chased him to the back of the building," Greenleaf says. "He turned; I said, 'Oh, [no], he's going to shoot. I managed to hit him twice in three shots. He died. I do believe that if he had killed me, he would feel less remorse than I feel."

The next day, Greenleaf's girlfriend reported that a man walked into the bail bond company she ran and asked, " 'Why didn't that cop wound him?' "

Says Greenleaf: "His perception was that I should have shot the gun out of his hand."

At least one country, Israel, recognizes shooting to wound as a tactic, at least for its military (human-rights activists criticize Israeli police for shooting to kill).[6] But specially trained Israel Defense Forces (IDF) troops must go to great lengths to make such shots, which is why those tactics would be impractical for police.

"It is 10 times harder to shoot someone in the leg than to simply kill him," an ex-IDF sniper, using a pseudonym, wrote in a long account of lying in wait to wound a target at the border fence between Gaza and Israel. "The leg is narrow, easily concealed by the land and always moving."[7]

Moreover, the target must be standing. "If we shoot while he is sitting, the bullet could hit his thigh and kill him," the ex-sniper wrote. Thigh wounds can involve the femoral artery, with fatal consequences.[8]

U.S. police do have alternatives to guns, depending on the circumstances. The Taser, a device that can temporarily disable an adversary with an electric discharge, is perhaps the most widely known alternative.

But Tasers can be problematic as well. Last March, an 18-year-old Miami artist, Israel "Reefa" Hernandez, died after Miami Beach police shot him with a Taser. He had tried to run away after they saw him painting graffiti on a vacant building. The Miami-Dade medical examiner concluded that his heart failed after an "energy device discharge."[9]

In Albuquerque, a Justice Department investigation this year into improper use of force concluded that officers "frequently misused" Tasers against people who were merely ignoring orders or who posed little danger. In one case, officers fired at a man who had doused himself with gasoline. The Taser discharges set him on fire, although he survived.[10]

Donald E. Wilkes Jr., an emeritus law professor at the University of Georgia, and Athens, Ga., lawyer Lauren Farmer have compiled 618 media accounts of deaths apparently caused by police Taser discharges from 2001 through Oct. 13, 2013.[11]

Police experts are unanimous that intensive training on when to use force is essential. Former Seattle chief Stamper cited a rookie police officer's fatal shooting in November of 12-year-old Tamir Rice in Cleveland, Ohio. Rice had been waving a toy pistol. A video of the shooting — showing a police car driving up next to the boy, who was shot two seconds later — demonstrates that the shooting never had to happen, Stamper concludes, saying the officer could have taken cover behind his car and evaluated the situation more calmly.[12]

"A more mature, experienced, confident police officer would have better understood what he was facing," Stamper says.

At the same time, he says Rice's parents never should have let him outside with a replica pistol, and schools and police should ensure that children know an essential fact of life: No one seen to pose a mortal threat in the presence of police should expect to walk away, or even to survive.

"If you point a gun at a police officer, you have punched your ticket," Stamper says. "I don't care if it's a toy gun. At a minimum you are going to get two shots to the chest."

— *Peter Katel*

[1] Quoted in Ahiza Garcia, "Wolf Blitzer: Why Can't Ferguson Police Just 'Shoot To Injure?' " *Talking Points Memo*, Aug. 15, 2014, http://tinyurl.com/p8bv42l.

[2] Quoted in Brendan Scott, " 'Don't Kill' Pol in a Cop-Out — Admits: I'm No Expert," *New York Post*, May 26, 2010, http://tinyurl.com/ngaq6lx.

[3] "An act to amend the penal law, in relation to the use of deadly force by police officers," New York State Assembly, Jan. 22, 2009, http://tinyurl.com/nbclrau; Murray Weiss, "Cops furious at 'don't kill' bill," *New York Post*, May 25, 2010, http://tinyurl.com/m34xej8; Matt Flegenheimer and Al Baker, "Officer in Bell Killing Is Fired," *The New York Times*, March 23, 2012, http://tinyurl.com/oy5792m.

[4] "NY AO2952 — 2009-2010, General Assembly," http://tinyurl.com/ndc3xe5. Murray Weiss, "Cops furious at 'don't kill' bill," *New York Post*, May 25, 2010, http://tinyurl.com/m34xej8.

[5] "Annual Firearms Discharge Report," New York City Police Department, 2013, pp. 21, 27, http://tinyurl.com/mprloo3.

[6] Edo Konrad, "Intellectuals call for investigation into police shooting of Arab youth," *+972 Magazine*, Nov. 13, 2014, http://tinyurl.com/pha8ktp.

[7] Gershon Morris, "Israeli Sniper's Anguished Look Into Crosshairs," *Jewish Daily Forward*, March 21, 2014, http://tinyurl.com/mcr2vy7.

[8] *Ibid.*; Ed Nowicki, "Training for Gunshot Wound Treatment," *Law and Order*, April 2009, http://tinyurl.com/n8ashyf.

[9] Michael E. Miller, "Israel 'Reefa' Hernandez Died by Taser," *Miami New Times*, March 13, 2014, http://tinyurl.com/lz88jry; Michael E. Miller, "Teenager Israel Hernandez Dies after Miami Beach Cops Catch Him Tagging, Taser Him," *Miami New Times*, Aug. 7, 2014, http://tinyurl.com/mlwgmda.

[10] "Civil Investigation of the Albuquerque Police Department," U.S. Department of Justice, April 10, 2014, p. 3, http://tinyurl.com/n6bubpo; Patrick Lohmann, "APD guilty of Taser abuse," *Albuquerque Journal*, April 11, 2014, http://tinyurl.com/kbsgmlg.

[11] Donald E. Wilkes Jr. and Lauren Farmer, "Fatal Police Taserings, List and Annexures," December 2013, http://tinyurl.com/lnlsjh5.

[12] Emma G. Fitzsimmons, "Video Shows Cleveland Officer Shot Boy in 2 Seconds," *The New York Times*, Nov. 26, 2014, http://tinyurl.com/pajhjnl.

Blacks Rate Police Poorly for Use of Force

Seven in 10 black Americans say police do a poor job of holding other officers accountable for misconduct and treating racial and ethnic groups equally. Additionally, 57 percent of blacks say police do a poor job of using the right amount of force. By comparison, only about one-quarter of whites say police do a poor job of holding officers accountable, treating racial groups equally and using the right amount of force.

Views on Police Job Performance, by Race, 2014

How well do you think police:

Hold other officers accountable for misconduct?

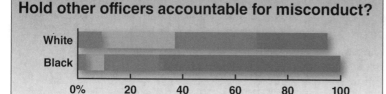

Treat racial and ethnic groups equally?

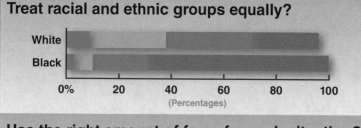

Use the right amount of force for each situation?

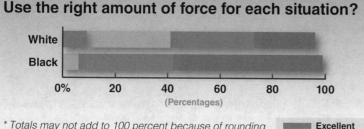

* Totals may not add to 100 percent because of rounding.

Excellent
Good
Fair
Poor

Source: "Few Say Police Forces Nationally Do Well in Treating Races Equally," Pew Research Center, Aug. 25,. 2014, http://tinyurl.com/lgh86qc

• A Hamilton, Mont., police officer in 2010 shot and killed a fleeing driver who had fired on the officer during a routine traffic stop;

• A New Mexico State Police officer in 2013 shot at a minivan containing young children, hitting no one;

• Albuquerque Police Department officers in 2014 shot dead homeless, mentally ill James Boyd, who the video showed was preparing to surrender;

• A Salt Lake City officer this year shot and killed a man reported to have a gun, who first refused to raise his hands, then lifted his shirt and reached for his waistband; he turned out to be unarmed.[39]

Body cameras — attached to an officer's belt, lapel or helmet — were introduced in Britain in 2005.[40] In Rialto, Calif., citizen complaints against officers dropped 88 percent from the previous 12 months after some officers began wearing them two years ago. "When you put a camera on a police officer, they tend to behave a little better, follow the rules a little better," Rialto's police chief told *The New York Times*. "And if a citizen knows the officer is wearing a camera, chances are the citizen will behave a little better."[41]

Cameras are spreading to departments bigger than Rialto's 54 patrol officers.

New York City began experimenting with bodycams in September, after U.S. District Judge Shira Scheindlin ruled that the city's police department was stopping and frisking a disproportionate number of black and Latino men, in violation of constitutional protections.[42]

Experts caution that good results from cameras depend on how departments use them — including specifying what kind of encounters should not be recorded, keeping a camera on until an interaction is over and obtaining consent to record crime victims.[43]

In Albuquerque, where officers began wearing lapel or belt cameras in 2010, the Justice Department found unsystematic use. "We . . . reviewed numerous reports where offices and supervisors on the scene failed to turn on their lapel cameras or belt tapes," the department said in a highly critical assessment of the department earlier this year.[44]

Indeed, shortly after the Justice Department issued its report, an Albuquerque officer shot and killed 19-year-old Mary Hawkes, claiming the suspected truck thief had pointed a pistol at him during a foot chase. The officer, Jeremy Dear, was wearing a camera, but no video of the shooting could be found.[45]

In early December, the Albuquerque department fired Dear for "insubordination," saying he had not complied with a policy to record all interactions with citizens. Officials said Dear claimed he had turned on the camera, but the camera manufacturer said it couldn't determine if the device malfunctioned, if Dear had turned it off or had never turned it on. Dear also had failed to record two previous incidents, police said. His lawyer, Thomas Grover, said Dear hadn't been told of the recording policy.[46]

Moskos at John Jay College of Criminal Justice said in an era of ubiquitous cellphone cameras, departments need to keep up with the times. "Often on these scenes, cops are the ones without cameras," Moskos says, which argues for police having their own — perhaps more complete — record of an incident.

Nevertheless, police suspicion of cameras is understandable, Moskos says "I think it's going to limit police discretion," he says. "Sometimes you just cut a guy a break. [But] what if that guy then goes out and kills someone?"

Police union president Canterbury cites research by a private firm in Mankato, Minn., that provides expert testimony in lawsuits against officers and police departments. Cameras respond better to dim light, for instance, than the human eye. But recording speed is slower than the eye.[47] "There are things an officer may see that the camera won't," Canterbury says.

He also cautions that citizens should realize that a lot of police video, including interviews with witnesses, will be public record and available to the media. "Will they make members of the public uncomfortable?" he asks. "Absolutely." And confidential witnesses could be identified.

Former Seattle police chief Stamper, who originally opposed body cameras and now supports them, warns

Looters flee with stolen shoes during widespread rioting in South-Central Los Angeles on April 30, 1992. The riots were sparked by the acquittals of three white police officers accused in the videotaped beating of black motorist Rodney King, the jury deadlocked on a fourth officer. More than 60 people died during the five days of rioting. Later that year, two of the officers were convicted of federal charges of violating King's civil rights; two were acquitted.

AP Photo/Akili-Casundria Ramsess

that they may pose serious complications for officers and, indirectly, for citizens. "Assume you're working for a hard-ass sergeant who's all about numbers, numbers, and you're a cop who's community-oriented, committed to solving landlord-tenant disputes, [and] you spend time talking with people," Stamper says. "And you've got all this on film and the sergeant says, 'You want to be social worker or a cop?' "

With greater use of cameras inevitable, citizens and police will have to adjust, experts say. "They're going to have to come to the realization that no matter how good the camera, it can't incorporate everything," Stamper says.

BACKGROUND
Troops in the Streets

Long before police militarization became a widely discussed issue, the military was used, on occasion, to enforce laws on U.S. soil.

The Posse Comitatus Act of 1878 placed limits on when the military could be used to enforce state or federal laws. It also prohibited the military from participating in emergencies, except when specifically authorized.[48] (State National Guard forces, first formally established in 1824, represented an exception, because they are under both federal and state authority; governors can deploy them to deal with natural disasters and civil disorders).[49]

CHRONOLOGY

1957-1969 *Military forces quell civil rights conflicts and urban uprisings, under exception to law barring domestic use of armed forces.*

1957 President Dwight D. Eisenhower sends Army troops to Little Rock, Ark., to enforce school desegregation.

1966 U.S. Marine veteran shoots 43 people, killing 13, from clock tower at University of Texas at Austin, prompting early fears of mass shootings.

1967 Army sent to Detroit to quell urban uprising. . . . Los Angeles forms the first police special weapons and tactics (SWAT) team.

1970-1989 *Drug war starts; military-law enforcement cooperation grows.*

1970 Congress authorizes "no-knock" searches when police suspect evidence could be destroyed if officers announce themselves.

1971 Armed forces and civil law enforcement agencies begin cooperating in drug enforcement, including small-scale loans of military equipment and personnel.

1974 Reports of abusive police searches prompt repeal of "no-knock" provision.

1981 Congress requires that the military hunt drug smugglers.

1989 Congress authorizes Defense Department to fund National Guard drug enforcement programs.

1990-1999

Military-police cooperation broadened.

1990 Congress begins formal program of providing military equipment to police departments for use in drug enforcement, later known as 1033 program.

1992 Massive, deadly riots break out in South-Central Los Angeles following acquittal of four police officers charged with brutal beating of black motorist Rodney King — a beating captured on video that was widely replayed on TV.

1996 Congress removes requirement police use surplus military equipment only in drug enforcement operations.

1999 Demonstrations against World Trade Organization meeting in Seattle met by forceful police response, including mass arrests and rubber bullets. . . . In notorious school shootings, two students attack Columbine High School in Colorado, leaving 13 dead.

2001-Present *Counter-terrorism duties assigned to police departments as a result of 9/11 attacks.*

2005 State Department calls "domestic preparedness" against terrorism a "staple of law enforcement operations."

2007 At least 80 percent of police departments have SWAT teams.

2009 Outrage follows video of transit officer shooting unarmed, prone young man in Oakland, Calif., subway station.

2011 Justice Department concludes that Maricopa County, Ariz., sheriff's department practices racial profiling and other unconstitutional actions, in one of about 20 investigations of U.S. police misconduct.

2013 Bill de Blasio elected mayor of New York City after opposing "stop-and-frisk" searches that disproportionately affect young black and Latino men.

2014 After 27 fatal shootings and other violent episodes by Albuquerque, N.M., Police Department since 2010, Justice Department reports that the department has violated constitutional limits on use of force. . . . Flash-bang grenade use in SWAT raid in Cornelia, Ga., gravely injures infant. . . . Video captures police chokehold death of Eric Garner in Staten Island, N.Y. . . . Ferguson, Mo., police officer shoots unarmed 18-year-old Michael Brown, sparking violent protests there and nationwide. . . . Military gear deployed against Ferguson demonstrators prompts congressional hearing on 1033 program and police militarization. . . . St. Louis County, Mo., grand jury declines to indict police officer Darren Wilson in death of Brown, leading to widespread protests and some violence and arson. . . . Cleveland police officer fatally shoots 12-year-old boy brandishing a toy pistol.

Nearly 80 years after Congress passed the Posse Comitatus law, President Dwight D. Eisenhower federalized the Arkansas National Guard and ordered the 101st Airborne Division to Little Rock, to enforce a high school desegregation opposed by mobs of white segregationists. He acted under a law authorizing the military to take the place of local police if they could not protect individuals or if federal law was being violated.[50]

Although the Army in that case was sent in to do a job that police wouldn't or couldn't perform, the Defense Department and local and federal law enforcement agencies, broadly speaking, already enjoyed a cooperative relationship. The agencies had received surplus military helicopters, handheld radios and other devices from World War II and the Korean War.[51]

And in the 1960s and '70s, research funded by the Justice Department developed lightweight body armor made of Kevlar, a synthetic fiber, which became widely used by both the military and police.[52] During the same period, National Guard or Army troops were sent in to quell uprisings in black urban neighborhoods: in Los Angeles in 1965; Detroit in 1967; and Baltimore, Washington and Chicago in 1968 after the assassination of the Rev. Martin Luther King Jr.[53] In the Watts section of Los Angeles (and later in Detroit), residents protesting police tactics shot at police, troops and firefighters.

Police thinking was also influenced by a 1966 massacre at the University of Texas, Austin, in which a student, a Marine veteran, shot 43 people from the campus clock tower, killing 13. The sniper episode, coupled with the urban unrest, prompted the Los Angeles Police Department in 1967 to form the country's first SWAT team.[54]

The team came to public attention during a search-warrant raid on a Black Panther Party headquarters in Los Angeles that resulted in a four-hour-shoot-out with armed occupants (no one was killed).[55]

War on Drugs

As the Los Angeles innovation drew growing interest from other police departments, the country was entering the early stages of what became known as the "war on drugs." (President Richard M. Nixon, widely credited as the author of the phrase, was more specific, declaring "war against heroin addiction.")[56]

Legislatively, the war began when Congress — pushed by the Nixon administration — passed the Comprehensive Drug Abuse Prevention and Control Act in 1970. Among other things, it authorized "no-knock" searches if police believed that evidence might be destroyed — which came to be interpreted as any drug raid on a house. The measure would prove crucial to the development in smaller cities of SWAT teams as door-battering search units.[57] Four years later Congress repealed the "no-knock" authorization after a series of drug raids led to violence and abuse by police, triggering a political scandal.[58]

Nevertheless, starting in the 1980s, police conducting raids could obtain authorization not to announce they were at the door. In the 1990s, the U.S. Supreme Court upheld no-knock searches, ruling that the Fourth Amendment's protection against "unreasonable searches and seizures" did not flatly rule out unannounced searches. And, under a 1984 Supreme Court ruling, even when a search was found to be constitutionally unjustified, evidence seized can still be used against defendants.[59]

The military and police had begun cooperating in drug enforcement cases in the 1970s, a development that would reverberate decades later. From 1971 to 1981, the Army, Air Force and Navy carried out 140 joint missions with civilian law enforcement agencies and frequently provided "minor assistance," such as training, helping to transport suspected drug smugglers and lending equipment and personnel, according to the nonpartisan Government Accountability Office (GAO), then known as the General Accounting Office.[60]

During the Reagan administration, Congress brought military and police work into closer quarters. The Military Cooperation With Law Enforcement Act of 1981 ordered the armed forces to track suspected smugglers on sea and in the air and to open military intelligence files to police departments.[61]

The pace of military aid and equipment transfers to law enforcement increased in the ensuing years. In 1989, Congress authorized the Defense Department to fund state National Guard drug enforcement programs. And law enforcement agencies at all levels, including federal, could take "counterdrug" training at National Guard schools. Defense spending on such support services totaled $30 million in 1996–98.[62]

The military established a communications network for police in Alabama, Georgia, Louisiana and Mississippi to exchange and analyze counterdrug intelligence. It also provided $96 million in technology and equipment to state and local agencies; the equipment included

Police Face Danger in Everyday Situations

Even routine traffic stops can suddenly turn deadly.

Eric Frein allegedly lay in wait outside the Pennsylvania State Police Troop R building in Blooming Grove, holding a .308 caliber rifle with a scope. At about 10:50 p.m. on Sept. 12, when Cpl. Bryon Dickson was leaving the building in uniform, his colleagues inside saw him suddenly drop to the ground.[1]

A 38-year-old Marine Corps veteran, Dickson was dead at the scene. Trooper Alex Douglass, one of the officers who tried to help him, was shot in the pelvis.[2]

The ambush prompted a 48-day manhunt for Frein, who was captured on Oct. 30.[3] Pennsylvania prosecutors said Frein confessed to killing Dickson, calling the act an "assassination," though seemingly not aimed at any officer in particular. In a message to his parents that police reported finding on his computer, Frein wrote: "The time seems right for a spark to ignite a fire in the hearts of men."[4]

Dickson never had a chance.

His killing underscores the risks police officers face daily, even in environments that seem completely safe — including their own headquarters, as the Pennsylvania case illustrated. Experts say constant danger is one reason many law enforcement officers see potential threats lurking even in the most routine encounters, a sense of constant peril that can lead to misjudgments.

"Officer safety does matter," says Peter Moskos, an associate professor in the Department of Law, Police Science and Criminal Justice Administration at the John Jay College of Criminal Justice in New York and a former one-year member of the Baltimore Police Department. "But the job does have risks. If you always wanted to be safe, you'd never leave the police station."

Statistically, officer fatalities have decreased since their post-World War II peak of 280 in 1974. By late November this year, 113 officers had been killed or died in the line of duty (42 of them in traffic accidents). That figure was up from 100 in 2013, according to the National Law Enforcement Officers Memorial Fund, a Washington-based group that keeps records on police deaths dating back to 1791.[5]

James Glennon, a former commander in the DuPage County, Ill., Major Crimes Task Force and now owner of Lifeline Training, a company that runs instructional programs for police, says seemingly ordinary police business can hold the most danger. "We're not getting shot at bank robberies, really," he said. "We're getting shot at during bike theft investigations, traffic stops, evictions."[6]

A video taken by a police officer's dashboard-mounted camera and widely circulated in police circles shows a 2010 traffic stop in Hamilton, Mont. "How's it going tonight?" Officer Ross Jessop asked as he stepped up to the window of an SUV. After the conversation with driver Raymond Davis took a less friendly turn, Jessop asked, "How much have you had to drink tonight?"

"Plenty," Davis replied. Seconds later he pointed a revolver out the window, fired and then drove away. Jessop, who wasn't hit, shot 14 rounds at the vehicle, one of which killed Davis. A six-person coroner's inquest jury later found the shooting justified.[7]

But in Columbia, S.C., former State Police Lance Cpl. Sean Groubert has been charged with aggravated assault and battery after shooting Levar Jones during a traffic stop in September. That encounter, also captured on Groubert's dashboard camera, made equally dramatic viewing.

As the two men stood outside Jones' SUV at a gas station, Groubert said, "Your license, please." Jones immediately turned and leaned far into his car. As soon as Jones straightened up, Groubert fired at least four shots in rapid succession.

Jones, on the ground, sounding stunned and in pain, yells, "I just got my license! You said get my license!"[8]

"Well, you dove head-first back into your car," Groubert said.

"I'm sorry," said Jones, who survived the gunshot in his hip.[9]

A year earlier, Groubert and his partner had been shot at by a man in an incident that also began as a routine traffic stop. The two officers, who returned the man's fire, wounding him, received commendations for valor for their actions during the confrontation.[10]

Referring to the September shooting of Jones, Chuck Canterbury, president of the Fraternal Order of Police union and a retired Conway, S.C., police officer, says, "The guy did make a quick turn and go into the car." Noting that Groubert had come under fire before, he added, "If you've not been in a situation where someone pulled a gun on you . . . I will never second-guess him."

But David Klinger, a professor of criminal justice at the University of Missouri-St. Louis, said after the shooting that it could have been avoided if Groubert had not immediately demanded the license, but asked, "Do you have a driver's license?" At that point, Jones could have said he did, and it was in his car. "Then you can say, 'OK, sure, what I want you to do is slowly reach into the vehicle. . . . And then it's not a big issue.'"[11]

As in many other police-citizen encounters that end badly, race was part of the discussion. Groubert (who was fired and charged with aggravated assault and battery) is white and Jones is black.[12]

Gloria Browne-Marshall, a constitutional law professor at John Jay College of Criminal Justice, said, "It was almost as though the officer wanted to stop the man, anyway found a reason to stop him." (Groubert had said he stopped Jones for not wearing a seatbelt, but Jones said he removed it because he was pulling into the gas station.) "Deadly force is . . . happening when there's an African-American male."[13]

Leroy Smith, director of the South Carolina Department of Public Safety, called the shooting an "isolated incident." South Carolina State Rep. Joe Neal, former chairman of the Legislative Black Caucus, said the criminal charge against Groubert would lessen African-American anger over the shooting. "This is a good exercise in how the system can work," he said.[14]

— Peter Katel

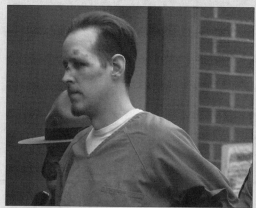

Eric Frein has been charged in the death of a Pennsylvania State Trooper last Sept. 12 in an ambush that underscored the daily risks faced by police. Frein was captured after a 48-day manhunt.

Getty Images/Kena Betancur

[1]"Affidavit of Probable Cause," Commonwealth of Pennsylvania, Pike County, Oct. 8, 2014, Docket Number CR-207-14, http://tinyurl.com/mcmmbyc.

[2]*Ibid.*

[3]"Eric Frein, Accused Killer of Pennsylvania Trooper, Arrested Using Slain Officer's Handcuffs," CNN Wire, Oct. 30, 2014, http://tinyurl.com/ltgknn2.

[4]Quoted in Pamela Lehman and Laurie Mason Schroeder, "Eric Frein in letter to mom and dad calls for 'revolution,' " *Morning Call*, Nov. 13, 2014, http://tinyurl.com/mb9n29q.

[5]"Preliminary 2014 Law Enforcement Officer Fatalities," "Officer Deaths by Year," National Law Enforcement Officers Memorial Fund, updated regularly, http://tinyurl.com/2b7co8f.

[6]Quoted in Crawford Coates, "Policing at the Level of Instinct," Calibre Press, Sept. 30, 2014, http://tinyurl.com/oa534bd.

[7]"Montana Officer Under Fire at Traffic Stop," LawOfficer, May 24, 2012, http://tinyurl.com/n5d92rn; Perry Backus, "Hamilton officer cleared in fatal shooting during January traffic stop," *Missoulian*, April 14, 2010, http://tinyurl.com/oeh75ob.

[8]John Monk, "Video Released: SC trooper charged with felony shooting at traffic stop over seat belt violation," *The Charlotte Observer*, Sept. 25, 2014, http://tinyurl.com/l5n86qd.

[9]*Ibid.*

[10]Jason Hanna, Martin Savidge and John Murgatroyd, "Video shows trooper shooting unarmed man, South Carolina police say," CNN, Sept. 26, 2014, http://tinyurl.com/k8tyvs5.

[11]"Transcript: Taking A Close Look at America's Police Force," WBUR, On Point with Tom Ashbrook, Oct. 1, 2014, http://tinyurl.com/ljmq7x7.

[12]John Monk, "Video Released: SC trooper charged with felony in shooting at traffic stop over seat belt violation," *The Charlotte Observer*, Sept. 25, 2014, http://tinyurl.com/mwberxs.

[13]"Transcript: . . .," *op. cit.*

[14]Quoted in *ibid.*; Cliff Leblanc, "Officials' silence on trooper shooting fuels anger, suspicion, demands for accounting," *The State*, Sept. 9, 2014, http://tinyurl.com/lolqp6b.

Getty Images/Stephen Lam

Getty Images/Kena Betancur

Citizen Anger

Police in Berkeley, Calif., clash with protesters on the fourth night of demonstrations sparked by recent grand jury decisions in police-involved deaths of African-American males (top). On Dec. 6, a man demands justice during the funeral service for Akai Gurley, an unarmed 28-year-old African-American man shot to death in a dark stairwell of a Brooklyn housing development by a rookie Asian-American police officer on patrol. He said his gun discharged unintentionally (bottom). Outrage spread across the political spectrum when a New York grand jury did not hand up an indictment in the death of cigarette seller Eric Garner, who was videotaped being wrestled to the ground by police officers and held in a chokehold. Calling the non-indictment "totally incomprehensible," conservative *Washington Post* columnist Charles Krauthammer said on Fox News, "The guy actually said, 'I can't breathe.'"

cryptological, night-vision and chemical analysis devices and instruments.[63]

Drawing Fire

In the 1990s, military-style law enforcement operations became more controversial, particularly after two high-

profile incidents — one in Ruby Ridge, Idaho, and one in Waco, Texas — involving federal agents.

The first incident involved a siege on the property of right-wing survivalist Randy Weaver, who was indicted in 1991 on a federal firearms charge after he refused to become an informant in a Bureau of Alcohol, Tobacco and Firearms (ATF) investigation of a white supremacist group.[64]

In 1992 federal agents were watching Weaver's property in a rural area of Idaho known as Ruby Ridge. After Weaver's dogs began barking a gunfight broke out in which a deputy marshal and Weaver's 14-year-old son were killed. FBI snipers wounded a friend of Weaver's and killed Weaver's wife, who was inside the cabin.[65] A Justice Department investigation later concluded that the rules of engagement guiding the snipers were unconstitutional.[66]

The following year, an ATF attempt to serve an arrest warrant on a compound near Waco, Texas, occupied by the Branch Davidian religious sect led to a gunfight in which four agents were killed, 16 were wounded and an unknown number of compound residents were wounded or killed. A subsequent 51-day siege ended after Attorney General Janet Reno authorized the FBI to fire tear gas into the compound. The Branch Davidians responded by setting fires within the property, which eventually killed most of the 75 people inside, according to the Justice Department and some fire consultants.[67]

Six years later the FBI revealed that it had fired explosive, "pyrotechnic" tear gas rounds, whose hot canisters can cause fires, into the compound during the final assault. But an independent follow-up report said those munitions did not start the fatal fires.[68]

That early instance of the use of military-style munitions followed a national lesson in the power of civilian technology. In 1991, a man with a videotape camera recorded the furious beating of a Los Angeles motorist who had tried to flee officers after being stopped for driving about 100 mph. Rodney King, the man who fled and was caught, was kicked, hit with batons and fired on with a Taser, in vivid footage replayed endlessly on television.[69]

Four officers were indicted in connection with the beating and their trial moved to the predominantly white town of Simi Valley. In 1992, three were acquitted, and the jury deadlocked on the fourth. That decision set off five days of riots and looting in South Los Angeles in which more than 60 people died, 10 of them shot by law enforcement officers, and the others victims of rioters and of riot-related events such as trying to put out a rioter-caused fire, or a traffic accident at an intersection whose lights had failed.[70]

Later that year, a federal grand jury indicted the four officers for violating King's civil rights. Two were acquitted; the other two were convicted at trial and sentenced to 30 months in prison. In a civil trial, a federal court awarded King $3.8 million in compensatory damages from the city of Los Angeles.[71]

The 1990s also saw cooperation between the military and the police become formalized, especially in counterdrug activities. In the 1990–91 Defense Authorization Act, later continued until 1996, Congress authorized transfers of excess military gear — including loaned pistols and rifles and ammunition and gifts of non-military equipment — to state and federal agencies for drug enforcement.[72]

Meanwhile, the Justice and Defense departments in 1994 established a technology-sharing program.[73] The National Institute of Justice cited several reasons for the deal — one was that local law enforcement agencies needed the help to keep up with criminals and drug smugglers, who themselves were increasingly getting their hands on military gear. "Narcotics traffickers and smugglers use bulletproof vests, electro-optic devices that enable them to see at night and semiautomatic and even automatic weapons," making the transfer of military equipment to local law enforcement all the more necessary, the institute concluded.[74]

In 1997 Congress reauthorized the surplus equipment transfer system — now renamed the 1033 program — and removed the requirement that the equipment be used only in drug enforcement. However, Congress said it preferred that the gear be used for counterterrorism and antidrug activities.[75]

During the same period, the Clinton administration sent American troops on peacekeeping missions in Somalia, Haiti, Bosnia and Kosovo, with orders to limit harm to civilians and property. As a result, the armed forces developed an interest in nonlethal weapons, leading to production of the flash-bang grenades that SWAT teams now use.[76]

New Tensions

The events of Sept. 11, 2001 — the first mass-casualty terrorist strike by a foreign organization in the United States — marked an entirely new development in relations between American police and citizens. In the aftermath

police departments nationwide, prompted by the federal government, added counterterrorism to their responsibilities.

"The continued threat of terrorism has thrust domestic preparedness obligations to the very top of the law enforcement agenda," a 2005 State Department report concluded. "This capacity must be considered . . . a staple of law enforcement operations."[77] The Homeland Security Department began providing grants to local police departments for antiterrorism equipment and training. By fiscal 2014, the program was totaling nearly $2 billion a year.[78]

Meanwhile, one theoretically nonlethal weapon developed under a Defense-Justice program — flash-bang grenades — was proving problematic in civilian use. Donald Wilkes Jr., a law professor emeritus at the University of Georgia, compiled — using 2003 Appellate Court decisions and media reports — a list of 39 incidents dating back to 1984 involving injuries and death from these grenades in SWAT raids.[79]

Three other developments after 9/11 have influenced the debate over police strategy and tactics:

• A large increase in the number of prison inmates since the 1980s has prompted growing criticism of mandatory sentencing laws, especially for nonviolent drug crimes.[80]
• The emergence of digital video technology, the proliferation of smartphones and security cameras and the rise of social media have led to a spate of videos posted online depicting sometimes deadly police-citizen confrontations.[81]
• A growing number of "active shooter" events in schools and public places has made police departments of all sizes aware of the need to be able to quickly respond to sudden attacks that threaten large numbers of lives.[82]

In the United States, images of police in tactical uniforms, carrying automatic rifles, became common in coverage, such as in the response to a 2012 massacre at Sandy Hook Elementary School in Newtown, Conn., and in the manhunt that followed a 2013 bombing during the Boston Marathon.

At the same time, controversy continued to grow over police conduct in minority communities. In a big-city election that received extensive coverage nationwide, liberal Bill de Blasio was elected mayor of New York, in part because he attacked the police department's

SWAT team members prepare to arrest suspects believed to be armed in a house in Wichita, Kan., on Jan. 9, 2013. Critics of SWAT teams say they are overused, mostly to serve search and arrest warrants. But supporters say heavily armed SWAT teams are necessary because of the nation's widespread gun ownership.

controversial "stop-and-frisk" tactics, which disproportionately affect black and Latino young men, according to evidence from police data used by U.S. District Judge Scheindlin in ruling that the application of the stop-and-frisk program — though not the tactic itself — was unconstitutional.

"The city's highest officials have turned a blind eye to the evidence that officers are conducting stops in a racially discriminatory manner," she wrote in her decision.[83]

By the time de Blasio took office, use of the tactic had begun to fade, *The New York Times* reported in a data analysis. Police reported 33,699 stops in the second half of 2013 — less than 10 percent of the 337,410 recorded in the first half of 2012. But the videotaped death of cigarette seller Garner in an apparent police chokehold indicated to many that questionable police conduct didn't end with de Blasio's election.[84]

Police behavior is also a major factor in other cities. The Obama administration's Justice Department has opened more than two dozen investigations into possible civil rights violations by police departments in recent years after questions arose about whether police resort to force unnecessarily.[85]

The crucial event touching off the recent national debate over police tactics occurred Aug. 9 in Ferguson, Mo., when then-Officer Wilson shot Brown during a violent street confrontation.[86] By all accounts, the conflict began inside Wilson's patrol vehicle and continued with both men outside the car. According to conflicting accounts, Brown was either charging the officer or raising his arms in surrender.[87]

The latter account gave rise to the widely adopted slogan and arm gesture of protesters in Ferguson and elsewhere: "Hands up — don't shoot."[88]

Brown's death set off weeks of street protests in Ferguson, including looting and vandalism by a minority of demonstrators, as well as tear gas and rubber bullets from police. As conflict worsened between police outfitted with military garb and equipment and increasingly bitter and angry demonstrators, Missouri Gov. Jay Nixon put Highway Patrol Capt. Ronald S. Johnson in charge of the law enforcement response in Ferguson. Johnson, an African-American, set a new tone by marching with demonstrators, dressed in his standard uniform — no combat fatigues or helmet.

"We are going to have a different approach and have the approach that we're in this together," he said.[89]

CURRENT SITUATION

Stemming the Flow

As Congress rushes to finish its year-end work before the Christmas recess, efforts in both chambers to restrict — though not end — the flow of military equipment to police departments remain on the table.

Obama entered the fray in early December, announcing that he would issue an executive order designed to ensure that the 1033 program is "transparent." The order will also be designed "to make sure that we're not building a militarized culture inside our local law enforcement."[90]

In Congress, even in a highly polarized political environment, bipartisan efforts are emerging to put more controls on the program. In the House, Democrat Hank Johnson of Georgia and Republican Raul Labrador of Idaho are pushing their Stop Militarizing Law Enforcement Act of 2014, which would limit the kinds of equipment the Pentagon can give or lend to law enforcement agencies. Labrador said the 1033 program was "introducing a military model of overwhelming force in our cities and towns."[91]

In case the legislation doesn't survive the lame-duck congressional session, Johnson asked the heads of the Armed Services committees in both chambers for a

Are U.S. police departments becoming dangerously militarized?

YES
Peter B. Kraska
Professor, School of Justice Studies,
University of Eastern Kentucky

From written testimony to the Senate Committee on Homeland Security and Governmental Affairs, Sept. 9, 2014

The research I've been conducting, since 1989, has documented quantitatively and qualitatively the steady and certain march of U.S. civilian policing down the militarization continuum — culturally, materially, operationally and organizationally. This is not to imply that all police — nearly 20,000 unique departments — are heading in this direction. But the . . . evidence demonstrates a troubling and highly consequential overall trend.

What we saw played out in Ferguson was the application of a very common mindset, style of uniform and appearance and weaponry, used every day in the homes of private residences during SWAT raids — some departments conducting as many as 500 of these a year.

Only 20 years ago, forced investigative searches of private residences, using the military special-operations model employed during hostage rescues, was almost unheard of and would have been considered an extreme and unacceptable police tactic. It is critical to recognize that these are not forced-reaction situations necessitating use-of-force specialists; instead they are the result of police departments choosing to use an extreme and highly dangerous tactic, not for terrorists or hostage-takers, but for small-time drug possessors and dealers.

Of course a militarized response is sometimes necessary and even unavoidable if done in self defense or to protect lives in imminent danger. The bulk of U.S. SWAT activity . . ., however, constitute a proactive approach. Numerous departments are choosing, based no doubt to an extent on political pressures, to generate on their own initiative high-risk events.

I also learned that the paramilitary culture associated with SWAT teams is highly appealing to a certain segment of civilian police. . . . As with special-operations soldiers . . ., these units' members saw themselves as the elite police, involved in real crime-fighting and danger. A large network of for-profit training, weapons and equipment suppliers heavily promotes paramilitary culture at police shows, in police magazine advertisements and in training programs sponsored by gun manufacturers. . . . The "military special operations" culture — characterized by a distinct techno-warrior garb, heavy weaponry, sophisticated technology, hyper-masculinity and dangerous function — was nothing less than intoxicating for its participants.

Military gear and garb changes and reinforces a war-fighting mentality among civilian police, where marginalized populations become the enemy and the police perceive of themselves as the thin blue line between order and chaos that can only be controlled through military-model power.

NO
Charles "Sid" Heal
Retired Commander, Special Enforcement
Bureau, Los Angeles Sheriff's Department;
Retired U.S. Marine Corps Chief Warrant Officer

Written for *CQ Researcher*, December 2014

The allegation of militarization of U.S. police departments ignores the extremely diversified and highly segmented nature of local law enforcement. Each of the nearly 18,000 local agencies is independent and governed only by the laws of the land and the communities they serve. Even the most widespread and notorious examples fail to reflect the attitudes of the law enforcement community at large.

How does equipment or training or appearance make our protectors dangerous? Weapons and equipment are inanimate objects. Complaints that they are too "militaristic" in appearance is like complaining a welder's helmet is ugly or atrocious. All workers are entitled to the tools and protective gear needed for the hazards they confront.

The so-called 1033 program for providing surplus equipment to law enforcement agencies is periodically reviewed, but the hyperbole and mischaracterizations used to challenge it obfuscate meaningful scrutiny. Lack of availability of essential equipment from military sources will require replacement through costly civilian manufacturers.

Many of the criticisms that drive the current controversy were first expressed by law enforcement. Corrective measures should be based on measurable attributes rather than biased perceptions to avoid the narrow-minded "baby and the bathwater" demands suggested by extremists.

The counter-terrorist mission thrust upon domestic law enforcement as a result of the 9/11 attacks was neither sought nor welcomed. Furthermore, this new responsibility was "in addition to" and not "instead of." The law enforcement and security resources required by the U.S. Department of Homeland Security specifies weapons, equipment and protective clothing that is basically identical to that required by military organizations. Failing to provide these because of their appearance or origin is both abhorrent and stupid. The tools used to fight the "war on crime" are inadequate to fight the "war on terrorism."

The use of SWAT teams to serve high-risk warrants is not based on race, culture or type of crime but rather dangerous criminal behaviors. Criminals and terrorists have increasingly equipped themselves with high-powered weapons, explosive devices and protective armor and enjoy the advantages provided by choosing the time, location and circumstances for their nefarious activities. The self-appointed carpers who oversimplify and ignore the perilous realities of underestimating adversaries have been bereft of viable alternatives.

Critics see the use of Pentagon equipment, such as this mine-resistant ambush protected vehicle in Sanford, Maine, as unnecessary, especially by small police departments. But supporters say the vehicles serve many purposes, including disaster relief. In the past eight years, the Defense Department has distributed more than $1.5 billion worth of surplus equipment to local police, mainly vehicles, aircraft and communications and detection equipment.

moratorium on transfers of some Pentagon equipment, saying Congress needs to "press pause . . . and revisit the merits of a militarized America."[92]

The bill would block transfer of what the sponsors called high-caliber weapons, grenade launchers, armed drones, armored vehicles and grenades or other explosives. Some of this material may already be blocked for police use. Current law, for instance, restricts weapons of more than 7.62 mm caliber, such as the AK-47 assault rifle.[93]

And the bill would end a requirement that police departments use Defense Department equipment within one year of receiving it. In the legislators' view, that encourages departments to use the gear inappropriately.

In the Senate, which will turn to Republican control next year, the sponsor of an identically titled bill on 1033 is Sen. Tom Coburn, an Oklahoma Republican. In a September hearing on the 1033 program he said: "Our Founders saw no role for the federal government in state and local police forces. We're on dangerous ground of undermining the very principles that built the country."[94]

Troubled Cities

A New York grand jury's decision on Dec. 3 not to indict the police officer whose chokehold led to cigarette seller Garner's death set off the second wave of autumn protests over police conduct.

"I can't breathe," marchers chanted in New York, echoing Garner's final words, captured on cellphone video. Demonstrators also took to the streets in Oakland and Los Angeles, Calif., following the grand jury's no-indictment of Officer Daniel Pantaleo.[95]

In response, Attorney General Eric Holder announced a Justice Department investigation of the Garner case. And Mayor de Blasio announced a police retraining program, including steps to de-escalate street confrontations.[96]

Patrick J. Lynch, president of the Patrolmen's Benevolent Association union said officers felt that the mayor had thrown them "under the bus." The mayor didn't say, Lynch added, "that you cannot resist arrest."[97] In the video Garner is seen loudly complaining to police about harassment, but never actively resists arrest.

However, the facts of Garner's death as shown on video brought some law-and-order conservatives to side — unlike in the Ferguson case — with police critics. Charles Krauthammer, a conservative *Washington Post* columnist, called Pantaleo's non-indictment "totally incomprehensible." Speaking on Fox News, Krauthammer said, "The guy actually said, 'I can't breathe.' "[98]

But not all conservatives agreed. Republican Rep. Peter King of New York, who represents Long Island, said that Garner died because he was obese and asthmatic. "The police had no reason to know he was in serious condition."[99]

In a reminder that growing tension over police actions isn't limited to one or two places, Holder on the day following the Garner non-indictment announced that an 18-month investigation of the Cleveland police department found a pattern of "unnecessary and excessive use of deadly force" as well as African-Americans' repeated claims that police were "verbally and physically aggressive toward them because of their race."[100]

Cleveland — the city where a policeman had shot and killed 12-year-old Rice in late November after the boy was seen in a park waving a toy replica of a gun — agreed to formulate a consent decree with Justice under which police would be supervised by an independent monitor. Albuquerque reached that kind of agreement earlier this year; and 14 other cities have signed consent decrees in recent years.[101]

> "We are going to have a different approach and have the approach that we're in this together."
> — *Missouri Highway Patrol Capt. Ronald S. Johnson, on how he would direct the law enforcement response to the protests in Ferguson, Mo.*

U.S. Attorney General Eric Holder embraces Missouri State Highway Patrol Capt. Ronald Johnson in Ferguson, Mo., on Aug. 20. Holder went to the troubled community to oversee the federal government's investigation into the shooting of 18-year-old Michael Brown by a police officer on Aug. 9. Johnson was widely credited with trying to defuse tensions through non-confrontational negotiations with protesters.

Developments in New York and Cleveland came the week after the St. Louis County grand jury's decision not to indict Wilson (now resigned from the police department) for Brown's death in Ferguson.

Immediately after county Prosecuting Attorney Robert P. McCulloch announced the decision in an evening press conference three days before Thanksgiving, protests broke out in downtown Ferguson. Although many were peaceful, violence-inclined groups torched about 12 businesses and burned some police cars, and gunfire could be heard during the disturbances.[102]

Street protests over the grand jury's decision spread beyond Ferguson and St. Louis to Oakland and San Francisco, Calif.; Chicago; New York; Washington, D.C.; and Seattle. Protesters demonstrated in shopping areas on "Black Friday," with protesters chanting, "If we don't get no justice, they don't get no profits."[103]

OUTLOOK
Re-engineering Police Culture

The debate over 21st-century police tactics should not be confused with a debate over police brutality, say critics of police adoption of military equipment, tactics and mentality.

"In the '60s and '70s cops were more brutal," says former officer Moskos of the John Jay College of Criminal Justice. "Cops are not allowed to beat people up like they used to. They may still have the attitude that 'you've got to do this or else,' but the 'else' is more limited. The rest of society has evolved; you would say it has progressed — if you're on that side — to the point where cops are not supposed to do that."

Former Seattle Police Chief Stamper characterizes old-school brutality as "punitive force" and says that today, "much of what we see as excessive force or police brutality is a perversion of officer safety tactics."

The idea that police live in constant danger reflects a drug war-spawned militarization that intensified after 9/11, Stamper says. "Many departments have treated low-level drug offenders as the enemy for so long that re-engineering the culture and structure of American policing is going to take generations."

Indeed, some police say, issues that give rise to protests and debates over police conduct are rooted in generations-old problems — not police tactics. "It's decades of racial disparity and economic disparity," Jeff Roorda, business manager of the St. Louis Police Officers Association, told CBS News. "It's not a problem with the police."[104]

Whether Justice Department investigations and police retraining programs will lead to rapid changes in interactions between police and minority group members, particularly black men, is far from clear. In angry and despairing tones that were echoed in remarks from protesters, Ta-Nehisi Coates, an influential essayist at *The Atlantic* magazine, wrote after the Ferguson non-indictment, "America does not really believe in nonviolence, so much as it believes in order. . . . The death of all our Michael Browns at the hands of people who are supposed to protect them originates in a force more powerful than any president: American society itself."[105]

Nevertheless, in Los Angeles, whose police department was once considered heavy-handed with minority com-

Getty Images/Pablo Martinez Monsivais-Pool

munities, civil rights lawyer Constance Rice, who worked with the department in a reportedly successful reform program, argues that change is possible. Like other experts, she points to fear — rather than outright racism — as the key element in many police-citizen encounters that turn violent. "I have known cops who haven't had a racist bone in their bodies," Rice told NPR. "They weren't overtly racist. They weren't consciously racist. But you know what they had in their minds that made them act out and beat a black suspect unwarrantedly? They had fear. They were afraid of black men."[106]

On Dec. 9 the National Urban League, the 103-year-old African-American civil rights organization, issued a 10-point plan it said would help ease tensions between police and citizens, which included "comprehensive retraining" of all police, appointment of special prosecutors to investigate police misconduct and "widespread use" of dashboard and body cameras.[107]

Apart from conflicts reflecting race and class divides, "active shooter" mass-killing incidents — some of the most dangerous and stressful incidents that police encounter — have been increasing in number since 2000, the FBI reported in September. And these are not likely to lessen officers' sense of ever-present peril.[108]

Former Los Angeles Sheriff's Department commander Heal notes that ordinary patrol officers may be rushed into highly dangerous "active shooter" incidents that were once reserved for SWAT teams because the new police tactical doctrine is that waiting costs too many lives. "More than 90 percent of victims are killed in the first eight minutes," Heal says.

And Fraternal Order of Police President Canterbury and other experts say military equipment, such as rifles and armored cars, are essential in dealing with mass shootings. The debate over the appropriateness of this gear for police raises the danger, Canterbury says, of "not having the equipment because of the perception that that's militarized policing."

On the nonmilitary equipment side, as a consensus forms that all police should wear body cameras, other technological approaches to policing issues are in the pipeline. In Santa Cruz, Calif., police are testing a pistol-borne sensor designed to immediately send out an alert when an officer unholsters or fires his gun.[109]

Data on how a weapon was used would help in post-incident investigations. "If we know the gun was holstered, that could resolve a critical element in the courtroom," Robert Stewart, CEO of Yardarm Technologies, a Capitola, Calif., start-up that is developing the sensor, told *PCWorld* magazine.[110]

Technology may be moving more quickly than social changes that could lessen police-citizen tensions. But, wherever the debate over militarization takes policing, experts agree the spotlight that mobile digital recording has focused on police practices is permanent and growing.

"In the age of social media," says Charles Wexler, executive director of the Police Executive Research Forum, "your actions get translated out there a thousandfold."

NOTES

1. John Eligon, "Anger, Hurt and Moments of Hope in Ferguson," *The New York Times*, Aug. 20, 2014, http://tinyurl.com/l8ps8qz.

2. "Police militarization," Google images, http://tinyurl.com/ppaqytz; "Sen. Thomas R. Carper Holds a Hearing on State and Local Law Enforcement Oversight, Panel 2," Senate Committee on Homeland Security and Governmental Affairs, Sept. 9, 2014, CQ Transcriptions LLC.

3. "Tracking the Events in the Wake of Michael Brown's Shooting," *The New York Times*, Aug. 9, 2014, http://tinyurl.com/q3rwm5j; "Beavercreek Wal-Mart police shooting: Does video tell whole story?" The Associated Press (via Cleveland.com), Sept. 30, 2014, http://tinyurl.com/pqhj2fu; J. David Goodman and Al Baker, "Wave of Protests After Grand Jury Doesn't Indict Officer in Eric Garner Chokehold Case," *The New York Times*, Dec. 3, 2014, http://tinyurl.com/nlx3dax; Dan McKay, "Video: Camper turning from officers when shot," *Albuquerque Journal*, March 22, 2014, http://tinyurl.com/ltuzozq; Coleen Heild, "Policing the police across the USA," *Albuquerque Journal*, Nov. 9, 2014, http://tinyurl.com/kp3h6h2.

4. "Remarks by the President After Meeting with Elected Officials, Community and Faith Leaders, and Law Enforcement Officials on How Communities and Law Enforcement Can Work

Together to Build Trust to Strengthen Neighborhoods Across the Country," The White House, Dec. 1, 2014, http://tinyurl.com/nj7t6yh.

5. "Sen. Thomas R. Carper . . . ," *op. cit.*

6. Written Testimony, Alan Estevez, Principal Deputy Under Secretary of Defense for Acquisition Logistics and Technology, Senate Committee on Homeland Security and Governmental Affairs, Sept. 9, 2014, http://tinyurl.com/n9flmo8; Daniel H. Else, "The '1033 Program,' Department of Defense Support to Law Enforcement," Congressional Research Service, Aug. 28, 2014, pp. 1–2, http://tinyurl.com/l79spln; Arezou Rezvani, Jessica Pupovac, David Eads and Tyler Fisher, "MRAPs and Bayonets: What We Know About the Pentagon's 1033 Program," NPR, Sept. 2, 2014, http://tinyurl.com/p3a4fqj; Alicia Parlapiano, "The Flow of Money and Equipment to Local Police," *The New York Times*, updated Dec. 1, 2014, http://tinyurl.com/oeswx3y.

7. *Ibid.*; "Sen. Thomas R. Carper . . . ," *op. cit.*

8. Written Testimony, Alan Estevez, *op. cit.*

9. "Department of Justice and Department of Defense Joint Technology Program: Second Anniversary Report," National Institute of Justice, February 1997, http://tinyurl.com/m6vgdwe.

10. Corey Mitchell, "Disquiet builds nationwide over police flash-bang use," *Minneapolis Star-Tribune*, Dec. 31, 2011, http://tinyurl.com/kpgcjax.

11. "War Comes Home: The Excessive Militarization of American Policing," American Civil Liberties Union, June 2014, p. 15, http://tinyurl.com/lakqla6.

12. Quoted in Rob Moore, "Child burned by distraction device during raid," AccessNorthGa.com, May 29, 2014, http://tinyurl.com/mc3ac4j; David Beasley, "Georgia deputies cleared after stun grenade injured toddler," Reuters, Oct. 6, 2014, http://tinyurl.com/p7padk2.

13. Nate Carlisle, *et. al.*, "Ogden officer killed in firefight 'doing exactly what he wanted to do,' " *The Salt Lake Tribune*, Jan. 6, 2012, http://tinyurl.com/mznsutg; Jessica Miller, "Police detail what went wrong in fatal shootout with Matthew David Stewart," *The Salt Lake Tribune*, July 17, 2014, http://tinyurl.com/mloq29u.

14. "War Comes Home . . . ," *op. cit.*, pp. 27, 31.

15. John Bacon, "Pa. schools close in manhunt for accused cop killer," *USA Today*, Oct. 21, 2014, http://tinyurl.com/kjmvgrv; Leslie Linthicum, "A bullet, a rescue and a long road home," *Albuquerque Journal*, Dec. 22, 2013, http://tinyurl.com/nuz9g6x; "10/26/13: Officer Luke McPeek and Others Shoot Christopher Chase," *Albuquerque Journal*, 2014, http://tinyurl.com/p5z334c.

16. Peter B. Kraska, "Militarization and Policing — Its Relevance to 21st Century Police," *Policing*, 2007, http://tinyurl.com/nc3aazu.

17. "Commission on Special Weapons and Tactics (S.W.A.T.), Final Report," Attorney General's Commission on Special Weapons and Tactics, Sept. 10, 2002, p. 3, http://tinyurl.com/pvbzm9z.

18. *Ibid.*, p. 1; Radley Balko, *Rise of the Warrior Cop: The Militarization of America's Police Forces* (2014), pp. 248–249.

19. *Ibid.*, pp. 4, 7. Michael Rubinkam, "Trooper ambush suspect caught, death penalty eyed," The Associated Press, Oct. 31, 2014, http://tinyurl.com/of3cfps; Andrew Ba Tran and Luke Knox, "Map of school shootings from 2013–14," *The Boston Globe*, June 10, 2014, http://tinyurl.com/pywyqmr; "Boston Marathon Terror Attack Fast Facts," CNN, Nov. 1, 2014, http://tinyurl.com/q7ldwbc; Kraska testimony, *op. cit.*

20. "Sen. Thomas R. Carper . . . ," *op. cit.*

21. Debra Cassens Weiss, "SWAT-like raids for barber's license checks violated Constitution, 11th Circuit says," *ABA Journal*, Sept. 22, 2014, http://tinyurl.com/mozr9nb.

22. "Special Weapons and Tactics (SWAT), Concepts and Issues Paper," International Association of Chiefs of Police, March 2011, http://tinyurl.com/njfmadw.

23. "Gun Ownership Trends and Demographics," Pew Research Center, March 12, 2013, http://tinyurl.com/q822p6y; "Gun homicides and gun ownership by country," *The Washington Post*, Dec. 17, 2012, http://tinyurl.com/c53hytw.

24. Bob Parker, "How the North Hollywood Shootout Changed Patrol Arsenals," *Police Magazine*, Feb. 28, 2012, http://tinyurl.com/mppn9w2; Rick Orlov, "North Hollywood shootout, 15 years later," *Los Angeles Daily News*, Feb. 26, 2012, http://tinyurl.com/o9f2tg7.

25. Steve Bosh, "Survivors recount San Ysidro McDonald's massacre after 30 years," KUSI News, July 18, 2014, http://tinyurl.com/produ87.

26. "Special Litigation Section Cases and Matters, Law Enforcement Agencies," U.S. Justice Department, Civil Rights Division, http://tinyurl.com/lu76yt8.

27. Ryan Gabrielson, Ryann Grochowski Jones, Eric Sagara, "Deadly Force, in Black and White," *ProPublica*, October 2014, http://tinyurl.com/qfx6qmr.

28. "Quoted in William H. Freivogel, "How Many Police Kill Black Men? Without Database, We Can't Know," St. Louis Public Radio, Dec. 10, 2014, http://tinyurl.com/k3c85bb; *Ibid.*; Rob Barry and Coulter Jones, "Hundreds of Police Killings Are Uncounted in Federal Stats," *The Wall Street Journal*, Dec. 3, 2014, http://tinyurl.com/kra7pqj.

29. "Tracking the Events in the Wake of Michael Brown's Shooting," *op. cit.*; Paddock, Parascandola and Siemaszko, *op. cit.*; J. David Goodman, "In Brooklyn, 2 Young Men, a Dark Stairwell and a Gunshot," *The New York Times*, Nov. 23, 2014, http://tinyurl.com/opw75w9; Emma G. Fitzsimmons, "12-Year-Old Boy Dies After Police in Cleveland Shoot Him," *The New York Times*, Nov. 23, 2014, http://tinyurl.com/opw75w9; "Beavercreek Wal-Mart police shooting: Does video tell whole story?" The Associated Press (via Cleveland.com), Sept. 30, 2014, http://tinyurl.com/pqhj2fu.

30. "Remarks by the President at Congressional Black Caucus Awards Dinner," The White House, Sept. 28, 2014, http://tinyurl.com/occq8f5.

31. "Sen. Thomas R. Carper . . . ," *op. cit.*

32. Quoted in Erik Badia and Corky Siemaszko, "Rev. Al Sharpton accuses Ferguson, Mo., police chief of 'smear campaign' against Michael Brown," *New York Daily News*, Aug. 16, 2014, http://

tinyurl.com/pqatdn8; Erik Eckholm, "Witness Told Grand Jury That Michael Brown Charged at Darren Wilson, Prosecutor Says," *The New York Times*, Nov. 24, 2014, http://tinyurl.com/ntyezrm; Trymaine Lee and Michele Richinick, "Police: Michael Brown stopped because he blocked traffic," MSNBC, Aug. 15, 2014, http://tinyurl.com/leltynp.

33. "Homicide Watch Chicago," *Chicago Sun-Times*, regularly updated, http://tinyurl.com/nlsfr2z; Amy Sherman, "A look at statistics on black-on-black murders," *PolitiFact Florida*, July 17, 2013, http://tinyurl.com/mhfw7f4.

34. Quoted in Steve Chapman, "Sharpton on black-on-black crime," *Chicago Tribune*, Aug. 28, 2014, http://tinyurl.com/k8sbp64; Jamelle Bouie, "Actually Blacks Do Care About Black Crime," *Slate*, Dec. 1, 2014, http://tinyurl.com/k7brpue.

35. "Broken Windows Policing," Center for Evidence-Based Crime Policy, George Mason University, undated, http://tinyurl.com/koravg6.

36. Peter Moskos, *Cop in the Hood: My Year Policing Baltimore's Eastern District* (2008).

37. Quoted in Michael B. Marois, "Body-Worn Cameras for Police Get Renewed Attention After Ferguson," Bloomberg News, Nov. 25, 2014, http://tinyurl.com/n4on8lv.

38. "Remarks by the President . . . ," *op. cit.*; Mark Landler, "Obama Offers New Standards on Police Gear," *The New York Times*, Dec. 1, 2014, http://tinyurl.com/lyde4wh.

39. Katti Gray and Dean Schabner, "UC Davis Pepper Spraying: Cops Suspended," ABC News, Nov. 20, 2011, http://tinyurl.com/7r9kk76; Matthew B. Stannard and Demian Bulwa, "BART shooting captured on video," *San Francisco Chronicle*, Jan. 7, 2009, http://tinyurl.com/bv89orh; Ryan Owens, "Cop's 'Heart Sank' on Realizing Shots Fired at Minivan Full of Kids," ABC News, Jan. 17, 2014, http://tinyurl.com/qe4wnct; Ryan Boetel, "APD detective who shot homeless camper James Boyd planning to retire," *Albuquerque Journal*, Nov. 18, 2014, http://tinyurl.com/lb9mtjn; Josh Sanburn, "Behind the Video of Eric Garner's Deadly

Confrontation With New York Police," *Time*, July 22, 2014, http://tinyurl.com/oh94f6v; Pat Reavy, "Body cam helps justify fatal South Salt Lake police shooting," KSL.com, Sept. 30, 2014, http://tinyurl.com/q8z8pqn.

40. Michael D. White, "Police Officer Body-Worn Cameras: Assessing the Evidence," Office of Justice Programs, U.S. Justice Department, 2014, p. 16, http://tinyurl.com/q87pdtu.

41. Quoted in Ian Lovett, "In California, a Champion for Police Cameras," *The New York Times*, Aug. 21, 2013, http://tinyurl.com/k5mxafg.

42. Rocco Parascandola, "60 NYPD cops set to begin wearing body cameras in pilot program," *New York Daily News*, Sept. 4, 2014, http://tinyurl.com/qgqohaf.

43. "Implementing a Body-Worn Camera Program: Recommendations and Lessons Learned," Police Executive Research Forum, U.S. Justice Department, 2014, pp. 54–56, http://tinyurl.com/lxdg7ej.

44. "Findings of civil investigation," U.S. Justice Department, April 10, 2014, http://tinyurl.com/n6bubpo; Gwyneth Doland, "Police body cameras didn't provide accountability in New Mexico," Al Jazeera America, April 16, 2014, http://tinyurl.com/l8gowe9.

45. Patrick Lohmann, "No video of Mary Hawkes shooting, APD says," *Albuquerque Journal*, May 22, 2014, http://tinyurl.com/qzlorxz.

46. Quoted in Nicole Perez, "Officer who shot Mary Hawkes fired for insubordination," *Albuquerque Journal*, Dec. 1, 2014, http://tinyurl.com/paatg2a.

47. "10 limitations of body cams you need to know for your protection," Force Science Institute Ltd., undated, http://tinyurl.com/m94y3vw.

48. *Ibid.*, pp. 5–6.

49. Maj. Gen. Timothy J. Lowenberg, "The Role of the National Guard in National Defense and Homeland Security," National Guard Association of the United States, undated, http://tinyurl.com/qbmsnbd.

50. *Ibid.*, p. 40.

51. "Department of Justice and Department of Defense Joint Technology Program: Second Anniversary Report," National Institute of Justice, Department of Justice," February 1977, p. 2, http://tinyurl.com/qyemysa.

52. *Ibid.*; Jeremy Peace, "Stephanie L. Kwolek, Inventor of Kevlar, Is Dead at 90," *The New York Times*, June 20, 2014, http://tinyurl.com/nlhzb3l.

53. Charles Doyle and Jennifer K. Elsea, "The Posse Comitatus Act and Related Matters: The Use of the Military to Execute Civilian Law," Congressional Research Service, Aug. 16, 2012, pp. 35–36, http://tinyurl.com/l29a4ea.

54. *Ibid.*, Balko, p. 62; "The UT Tower Shooting," *Texas Monthly*, undated, http://tinyurl.com/kaybz73.

55. Paul Clinton, "Daryl Gates and the origins of LAPD SWAT," *Police Magazine*, April 16, 2010, http://tinyurl.com/q2d95ql; Radley Balko, *Rise of the Warrior Cop: The Militarization of America's Police Forces* (2013), pp. 76–80; and "144 Hours in August 1965," Governor's Commission on the Los Angeles Riots, 1965, http://tinyurl.com/3zab8bg.

56. Richard Nixon, "Special Message to the Congress on Drug Abuse Prevention and Control, June 17, 1971," The American Presidency Project, University of California, Santa Barbara, http://tinyurl.com/l56dh26.

57. *Ibid.* Also see Radley Balko, *Rise of the Warrior Cop: The Militarization of America's Police Forces* (2014), pp. 81–134.

58. *Ibid.*, Balko; Clinton, *op. cit.*, p. 2.

59. Balko, *op. cit.*, pp. 116–125; "War Comes Home: The Excessive Militarization of American Policing," ACLU, June 2014, http://tinyurl.com/lx56xmg; *U.S. v. Leon*, 488 U.S. 897 (1984), http://tinyurl.com/238nbgx.

60. Ronald F. Lauve, "Statement Before the Subcommittee on Crime, House Committee on the Judiciary on Military Cooperation With Civilian Law Enforcement Agencies," General Accounting Office, July 28, 1983, http://tinyurl.com/ouckbgl.

61. Balko, *op. cit.*, pp. 96–97, 145–146.

62. "Crime Technology: Department of Defense Assistance to State and Local Law Enforcement Agencies," U.S. General Accounting Office, (now Government Accountability Office), October 1999, pp. 3–5, http://tinyurl.com/o5tfgev.

63. *Ibid.*, pp. 7–9.

64. "Department of Justice Report on Internal Review Regarding the Ruby Ridge Hostage Situation and Shootings by Law Enforcement Personnel," U.S. Justice Department, 1994, Executive Summary, http://tinyurl.com/p8q988z; Balko, *op. cit.*, pp. 200–201.

65. *Ibid.*, Balko.

66. *Ibid.*, "Department of Justice."

67. "Report to the Deputy Attorney General on the Events at Waco, Texas, February 28 to April 19, 1993, Executive Summary, http://tinyurl.com/o3yaxp7; Jim Hoft, "Author: Hillary Clinton Ordered Attack on David Koresh's Compound in Waco, Texas," *Free Republic*, March 4, 2014, http://tinyurl.com/ouqak4k.

68. "Final Report to the Deputy Attorney General Concerning the 1993 Confrontation at the Mt. Carmel Complex, Waco, Texas," Special Counsel John C. Danforth, Nov. 8, 2000, p. 29, http://tinyurl.com/nm59o2h; Matt Alsdorf, "Waco Twofer: Pyrotechnic Tear Gas and Delta Force," *Slate*, Sept. 2, 1999, http://tinyurl.com/ceduvf8.

69. Jennifer Medina, "Rodney King Dies a 47," *The New York Times*, June 17, 2012, http://tinyurl.com/8xdbzgc.

70. *Ibid.*, "Los Angeles riots: Remember the 63 people who died," *Los Angeles Times*, April 26, 2012, http://tinyurl.com/ljb86rg; Linda Deutsch, "Rodney King's Death: Reporter Remembers Trial That Sparked Riots," The Associated Press, Aug. 18, 2012, http://tinyurl.com/n7a9fhl.

71. "Los Angeles Riots Fast Facts," CNN, May 3, 2014, http://tinyurl.com/njj82eh.

72. Daniel H. Else, "The '1033 Program,' " *op. cit.*, pp. 1–2.

73. "Department of Justice and Department of Defense Joint Technology," *op. cit.*, p. 1.

74. *Ibid.*, pp. 5–6.

75. Else, *op. cit.*

76. "Department of Justice and Department of Defense Joint Technology," *op. cit.*, pp. 5, 11; "War Comes Home," *op. cit.*, pp. 2–3.

77. Lois M. Davis, *et al.*, "Long-Term Effects of Law Enforcement's Post-9/11 Focus on Counterterrorism and Homeland Security," RAND Corp., 2010, p. xv, http://tinyurl.com/k3a2tas.

78. "DHS Announces Grant Allocations for Fiscal Year 2014 Preparedness Grants," U.S. Department of Homeland Security, July 25, 2014, http://tinyurl.com/lphyxtd; Alicia Parlapiano, "The Flow of Money and Equipment to Local Police," *The New York Times*, updated Dec. 1, 2014, http://tinyurl.com/oeswx3y.

79. Donald E. Wilkes Jr., "Explosive Dynamic Entry," *Flagpole*, July 20, 2003, http://tinyurl.com/qeqzxoq.

80. Lisa D. Moore and Amy Elkavich, "Who's Using and Who's Doing Time: Incarceration, the War on Drugs, and Public Health," *American Journal of Public Health*, May, 2008, http://tinyurl.com/mnu-7awa; John Schmitt, Kris Warner, Sarika Gupta, "The High Budgetary Cost of Incarceration," Center for Economic and Policy Research, June 2010, http://tinyurl.com/27yos76.

81. "Social Media and Tactical Considerations for Law Enforcement," Community Oriented Policing Services, U.S. Justice Department and Police Executive Research Forum, 2013, http://tinyurl.com/karmhqx.

82. Tracy L. Frazzano and G. Matthew Snyder, "Hybrid Targeted Violence: Challenging Conventional 'Active Shooter' Response Strategies," Homeland Security Affairs, Naval Postgraduate School Center for Homeland Defense and Security, 2014, http://tinyurl.com/oeoj7rj.

83. Quoted in Joseph Goldstein, "Judge Rejects New York's Stop-and-Frisk Policy," *The New York Times*, Aug. 12, 2013, http://tinyurl.com/m826bvo; Michael Barbaro and David W. Chen, "De Blasio Is Elected New York City Mayor in Landslide," *The New York Times*, Nov. 5, 2013, http://tinyurl.com/ozbnwsu.

84. Mike Bostock and Ford Fessenden, "'Stop-and-Frisk' Is All but Gone From New York," *The New York Times*, Sept. 19, 2014, http://tinyurl.com/p7qma2a.

85. "Police Reform and Accountability Accomplishments Under Attorney General Eric Holder," U.S. Justice Department, Dec. 4, 2014, http://tinyurl.com/ocf4w5a.

86. Rachel Clarke and Christopher Lett, "What happened when Michael Brown met Officer Darren Wilson," CNN, Nov. 11, 2014, http://tinyurl.com/opdowzu.

87. *Ibid.*

88. Matt Pearce, "Protesters use hands-up gesture defiantly after Michael Brown shooting," *Los Angeles Times*, Aug. 12, 2014, http://tinyurl.com/ku56bs6.

89. Quoted in Elahe Izadi and Wesley Lowery, "Meet the Missouri Highway State Patrol captain who has taken over in Ferguson," *The Washington Post*, Aug. 15, 2014, http://tinyurl.com/nvscevv.

90. "Remarks by the President," *op. cit.*

91. Press release, "Reps. Johnson, Labrador introduce bill to de-militarize police," Website of Rep. Hank Johnson, Sept. 16, 2014, http://tinyurl.com/myz4s4p.

92. *Ibid.*

93. "M14 7.62mm Rifle," Federation of American Scientists, Military Analysis Network, updated Feb. 22, 2000, http://tinyurl.com/pghfqdm; Written Testimony, Alan Estevez, *op. cit.*, pp. 3–4.

94. "Sen. Thomas R. Carper Holds a Hearing," *op. cit.*

95. Vivian Yee, "'I Can't Breathe,' Is Echoed in Voices of Fury and Despair," *The New York Times*, Dec. 3, 2014, http://tinyurl.com/ndm9c3k; Bill Chapell, "Protests Spread in New York and Beyond Over Eric Garner Case," NPR, Dec. 3, 2014, http://tinyurl.com/pqj72rs.

96. Mollie Reilly, "Justice Department to Investigate Eric Garner's Death," *The Huffington Post*, Dec. 3, 2014, http://tinyurl.com/lngbeqn; Marc Santora, "Mayor de Blasio Calls for Retraining of New York Police Dept.," *The New York Times*, Dec. 4, 2014, http://tinyurl.com/o7uywau.

97. Quoted in Santora, *ibid.*

98. Quoted in Karen Tumulty, "Ferguson, Staten Island: Similar events bring very different reaction," *The Washington Post*, Dec. 4, 2014, http://tinyurl.com/mw9uykk.

99. Quoted in Nia-Malika Henderson, "Peter King blames asthma and obesity for Eric Garner's death. That's a problem for the GOP," *The Washington Post*, Dec. 4, 2014, http://tinyurl.com/mf6qcc9.

100. "Investigation of the Cleveland Division of Police," U.S. Department of Justice, Dec. 4, 2014, pp. 3, 49, http://tinyurl.com/keuaqgz.

101. Richard A. Oppel Jr., "Cleveland Police Abuse Pattern Cited by Justice Department," *The New York Times*, Dec. 4, 2014, http://tinyurl.com/mm97l4h; "Police Reform and Accountability Accomplishments Under Attorney General Eric Holder," U.S. Justice Department, Dec. 4, 2014, http://tinyurl.com/ocf4w5a.

102. Ellen Wulfhorst, Daniel Wallis and Edward McAllister, "More troops deployed in Ferguson to guard against fresh riots," Reuters, Nov. 25, 2014, http://tinyurl.com/k5drrwa.

103. Quoted in John Eligon, "Protesters United Against Ferguson Decision, but Challenged in Unity," *The New York Times*, Nov. 28, 2014, http://tinyurl.com/m7sag4f.

104. Quoted in Matt Apuzzo, "Past Remarks by Loretta Lynch, Attorney General Nominee, Offer Insight on Race Issues," *The New York Times*, Dec. 2, 2014, http://tinyurl.com/mykozju.

105. Ta-Nehisi Coates, "Barack Obama, Ferguson, and the Evidence of Things Unsaid," *The Atlantic*, Nov. 26, 2014, http://tinyurl.com/mtjyjqz.

106. Quoted in "Civil Rights Attorney On How She Built Trust With Police," NPR, Dec. 5, 2014, http://tinyurl.com/l3s86oc.

107. "10-Point Justice Plan: National urban League Police Reform and Accountability Recommendations," National Urban League, December 2014, http://tinyurl.com/m2j2k7u.

108. "FBI Releases Study on Active Shooter Incidents," FBI, Sept. 24, 2014, http://tinyurl.com/nfm5pww.

109. Zach Miners, "Startup arms cops with Internet-connected 'smart' guns," *PCWorld*, Oct. 27, 2014, http://tinyurl.com/lmwmbht.

110. Quoted in *ibid.*

BIBLIOGRAPHY

Selected Sources

Books

Balko, Radley, *Rise of the Warrior Cop: The Militarization of America's Police Forces*, PublicAffairs, 2014.
A longtime critic of police tactics traces hardening of police methods to the spread of SWAT teams.

McCoy, Candace, ed., *Holding Police Accountable*, Urban Institute Press, 2010.
A group of academics, including two former police officers, examine changes in laws and procedures guiding police conduct.

Moskos, Peter, *Cop in the Hood: My Year Policing Baltimore's Eastern District*, Princeton University Press, 2008.
A former police officer who was trained as a sociologist examines his own and colleagues' actions and attitudes in policing poor, African-American neighborhoods.

Stamper, Norm, *Breaking Ranks: A Top Cop's Exposé of the Dark Side of American Policing*, Nation Books, 2005.
A career police officer who rose to Seattle police chief criticizes drug laws and drug enforcement.

Articles

Barrett, Devlin, "Attorney General Eric Holder Urges Broad Review of Police Tactics," *The Wall Street Journal*, Oct. 8, 2014, http://tinyurl.com/nunrumb.
The outgoing Justice Department chief calls for a thorough examination of police departments' policies and actions.

Devaney, Tim, "Senators blast DOD program that 'militarized police,'" *The Hill*, Sept. 9, 2014, http://tinyurl.com/lxns2q6.
Bipartisan criticism erupted at a Senate committee hearing on transfers to police departments of military gear.

Heal, Charles "Sid," "Swarming," *The Tactical Edge*, Spring 2011, http://tinyurl.com/pke2bjb.
A former Los Angeles Sheriff's Department commander analyzes a tactic in which police in a sudden emergency rush a shooter from several directions — a method Heal calls a departure from the military approach.

Lind, Dara, "How do police departments train cops to use force?," *Vox*, Sept. 5, 2014, http://tinyurl.com/ncfnjjn.
A justice system specialist details how officers are taught when and when not to shoot.

McKay, Dan, "Video: Camper turning from officers when shot," *Albuquerque Journal*, March 22, 2014, http://tinyurl.com/ltuzozq.
A video of police shooting to death a mentally disturbed man intensified criticism of an already troubled Albuquerque, N.M., police department.

Moore, Rob, "Child burned by distraction device during raid," *Access North Georgia*, May 29, 2014, http://tinyurl.com/mc3ac4j.
A county sheriff in charge of a disastrous SWAT raid in which an infant was gravely wounded by a flash-bang grenade says his men had had no information a child was in the house but defends the operation as based on available intelligence.

Nehring, Abbie, "'Less Lethal' Flash-Bangs Used in Ferguson Leave Some Feeling the Burn," *ProPublica*, Aug. 22, 2014, http://tinyurl.com/olovoph.
A journalist reports being burned by a flash-bang grenade used against demonstrators in Ferguson, Mo., and experts debate their use as crowd-control devices.

Proctor, Jeff, "Boyd shooter: 'Welcome to ROP; mistakes now cease to exist,'" KRQE News, Oct. 7, 2014, http://tinyurl.com/pqmhewu.
An investigative reporter recounts the little-known story of a specialized Albuquerque, N.M., Police Department unit — now disbanded — whose logo was a hangman's noose.

Swaine, Jon, "Doubts cast on witness's account of black man killed by police in Walmart," *The Guardian*, Sept. 7, 2014, http://tinyurl.com/k4g3gvg.
A U.S. correspondent for a London-based newspaper probes the evidence in a police shooting that left an

unarmed man dead in a Walmart store in Beavercreek, Ohio, after picking up a BB rifle from a shelf and walking around the store with it.

Reports and Studies

Else, Daniel H., "The '1033 Program,' Department of Defense Support to Law Enforcement," Congressional Research Service, Aug. 28, 2014, http://tinyurl.com/l79spln.
A CRS specialist examines the requirements governing military equipment transfers to police.

"Police Under Attack: A Police Foundation Review of the Christopher Dorner Incident," Police Foundation, 2013, http://tinyurl.com/letwcga.

A team of career police officers working for a think tank analyzes and draws lessons from the 2013 manhunt for an ex-Los Angeles Police Department officer and U.S. Navy veteran who killed the daughter of a former superior, a police officer and a sheriff's deputy. Police shot at, but didn't kill, three civilians during the search.

"War Comes Home: The Excessive Militarization of American Policing," American Civil Liberties Union (ACLU), June 2014, http://tinyurl.com/nneqyrk.
The ACLU analyzes data from a small sample of police departments to conclude that U.S. police tactics and equipment are overly militarized.

For More Information

American Civil Liberties Union, 125 Broad St., New York, NY 10004; 212-549-2500; http://tinyurl.com/kghjobr. The rights-advocacy organization has published a series of detailed reports alleging police misconduct nationally and in several states and cities.

Law Enforcement Against Prohibition, 8730 Georgia Ave., Silver Spring, MD 20910; 301-565-0807; http://tinyurl.com/3ndoyw. The U.S.-based international organization of retired police officers, prosecutors and judges advocates legalizing and regulating drug use.

National Fraternal Order of Police, 701 Marriott Dr., Nashville, TN 37214; 615-399-0900; http://tinyurl.com/omy84xb. The nation's major police union advocates for its members on all issues affecting police safety and benefits.

National Tactical Officers Association, http://tinyurl.com/lrognsr. The main organization for SWAT team members offers training in crisis negotiation, hostage rescue, sniper shooting and other situations in which SWAT teams are mobilized.

Police Executive Research Forum, 1120 Connecticut Ave., N.W., Washington, DC 20036; 202-466-7820; http://tinyurl.com/kytrfy9. The think tank and consultancy recommends policies designed to improve police-community relations.

Police Foundation, 1201 Connecticut Ave., N.W., Washington, DC 20036; 202-833-1460; http://tinyurl.com/q85srua. Affiliated with three universities in the United States and United Kingdom, the foundation researches new developments affecting police departments and proposes strategies to deal with them.

U.S. Department of Justice, Civil Rights Division, 950 Pennsylvania Ave., N.W., Washington, DC 20530; 202-514-6255; http://tinyurl.com/lu76yt8. The division's Special Litigation Section has conducted detailed investigations and negotiated settlements — all available on the section's website — on police misconduct in numerous cities.